Also available at all good book stores

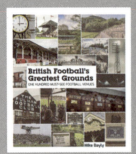

9781785316470

9781785313929

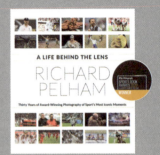

9781785315466

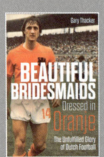

9781785318467

9781785318399

9781785317811

9781785317835

9781785317194

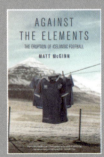

9781785317200

1960 – 2016

EURO SUMMITS

THE STORY OF THE
UEFA EUROPEAN
CHAMPIONSHIP

JONATHAN O'BRIEN

First published by Pitch Publishing, 2021

Pitch Publishing
A2 Yeoman Gate
Yeoman Way
Worthing
Sussex
BN13 3QZ
www.pitchpublishing.co.uk
info@pitchpublishing.co.uk

A CIP catalogue record is available for this book
from the British Library.

ISBN 978 1 78531 849 8

Typesetting and origination by Pitch Publishing
Printed and bound in India by Replika Press Pvt. Ltd.

CONTENTS

ACKNOWLEDGEMENTS

THANKS, FIRST and foremost, to my wonderful wife Laura, and to my family, Brigette, Seamus, John, Colm, Caomhan, Gillian, Cyjan, Caoimhe and Radha – not forgetting Diego and Tuco. Thanks, too, to Pitch Publishing's Paul and Jane Camillin, Dean Rockett, Ivan Butler, Duncan Olner and Graham Hales, all of whom were a pleasure to work with.

Paul Howard, Maeve McLoughlin, Pat Pidgeon, Eoin O'Hara, Emmanuel Kehoe, Patrick Dempsey, Dermot Crowe, George Gaskin, Gerard Crowley, Damian Corless, Garvan Grant, Donal Bradley, Johnny Mooney, Emmett O'Reilly, Julian Fleming and Vincent Gribbin all provided huge encouragement along the way. I'm indebted to Bojan Babić, Stephan Hattenhauer, Andy Hockley, David Melo, Maciej Słomiński and Rozanne Stevens for their translation assistance; to Justin Hughes for his invaluable help with the Netherlands-related material; and to Cris Freddi, whose World Cup book served as the main inspiration for me to do this.

Last but not least, special thanks to Michael Gibbons, who's written a couple of terrific books himself, and whose generosity of spirit made the difference when it came to getting this one into print.

Jonathan O'Brien
January 2021

THE BEGINNING

THE MORNING of 2 March 1955 is a cold one in Vienna. At the newly opened headquarters of Austrian football, the Haus des Österreichischen Fußballsports building on Mariahilfer Straße, the besuited top brass of the eight-month-old Union des Associations Européennes de Football are gathering to make some big decisions.

There are plenty of things on the agenda – dates of fixtures for the European football calendar, the embryonic issue of television rights – but the main order of business is the question of whether to create 'a European Cup for national teams'. One of the people in the room is a 65-year-old Frenchman named Gabriel Hanot, the editor of the French sports newspaper *L'Équipe*. Six months later, thanks chiefly to his efforts, the first edition of the European Cup itself will kick off with a fixture between Sporting Clube and Partizan Belgrade in Lisbon.

As the delegates file into the hall in Vienna and take their seats, one chair in the room is left conspicuously empty. Many miles to the west, in Paris, another Frenchman is lying in his sickbed, grappling with a grave illness that will kill him a matter of months later, and worsening his health further by fretting about what will happen in his physical absence from the meeting that he has worked for years to set up.

Some hours later, the gathering breaks up. On the substantive issue, the verdict is that there is no verdict.

═══

The morning of 21 December 2015 is an even colder one in Zürich. UEFA president Michel Platini, for so many years the arrogant and untouchable dauphin of European football, has just become its most notorious pariah.

FIFA's ethics committee has scuppered Platini's future political ambitions in devastating fashion, hitting him with an eight-year ban (later reduced to six on appeal) as punishment for pocketing a seven-figure bung from the similarly disgraced Sepp Blatter. In the aftermath, Platini blusters manfully about a 'pure masquerade' of a decision, 'rigged to tarnish my name by bodies I know well', but his once rocket-propelled career now lies in ruins.

Four weeks before Euro 2016 kicks off in Paris, Platini's final appeal to the Court of Arbitration for Sport in Lausanne succeeds only in getting his six-year ban cut further to four years. He formally quits as UEFA president later that day. 'I take note of today's decision from CAS, but I see it as a profound injustice,' he says in a statement. 'I am resigning from my duties as UEFA president to pursue my battle in front of the Swiss courts to prove my innocence in this case. Life is always full of surprises – I am henceforth available to experience more of them.'

Jacques Lambert, the head of Euro 2016's organising committee, invites Platini to as many games as he wishes to attend. But he declines, fearing that his presence will spark another conflict with FIFA. Rather than be the ghost at the feast, he stays away from the month-long tournament. 'Whenever I approach the sun, like Icarus, it burns everywhere,' he sighs in an interview with *Le Monde*. 'What annoys me the most is to be put in the same bag as the others. I find it shameful to be dragged through the mud. [Blatter] has a lot of charm, and I was somehow bewitched. Even if he wants to kill me politically, I still have a little affection for what we experienced together.'

The extraordinary things Platini achieved at the 1984 European Championship secured him a permanent place in football's highest pantheon. At one point, he was so popular in France that it was planned to name the national stadium after him. He retorted that they would regret it if he ever became an alcoholic or got arrested for a serious crime, and it was eventually named the Stade de France.

Few parallels can be drawn between Platini's life and that of Henri Delaunay, his compatriot and long-ago predecessor as ruler of UEFA. One is a household name who won three Ballons d'Or before retiring to a life of seven-star hotels, stretch limos, glitzy receptions and big dinners; the other a mild-mannered, bespectacled bureaucrat whose playing career never got out of the French amateur leagues of the 1910s, and whose time as a referee barely lasted candlelight. But without the efforts of this half-forgotten polyglot, Platini would never have had a European Championship finals to play in, a Trophée Henri Delaunay to lift, or a UEFA to take control of.

Born in June 1883 into a middle-class family in Paris, the young Delaunay would have looked on wide-eyed as football established itself as a popular pastime and spectator sport in the capital. This was part of a wider trend in which large swathes of France's middle classes, appalled by the upper-class decadence and national drift exposed by the loss of the Franco-Prussian War to Germany in 1871, gravitated towards leisure pursuits of British origin as a form of oblique protest. In Delaunay's adolescence, as he wrote years later, he idolised the early stars of French league football, 'those crazy lads having fun and jumping on each other, screaming happily'.

In 1902, the teenage Delaunay travelled to London to attend the FA Cup Final between Southampton and Sheffield United at Crystal Palace Stadium. Swept up in the noisy crowd of 77,000, he was deeply moved by what he described as a 'primal scene'. It instilled in him a lifelong Anglophilia which extended to smoking a pipe and acquiring the nickname Sir Henry. He also learned English, which helped to establish him on FIFA's Rules and Regulations Committee.

Delaunay soon became a sort of Gallic Jimmy Hill (though exuding more charm), tirelessly trebling up in the roles of player, referee and administrator. By 1907, aged 24, he was president of the Étoile des Deux Lacs club, and within a decade, he was general secretary at the Comité Français Interfederale, which later became the French Football Federation. His refereeing career, however, came to a painful end during a game between AF Garenne-Doves and ES Benevolence when the ball struck him in the face, knocked out two of his teeth and caused him to swallow his whistle.

At FIFA's congress in Rome in May 1926, he declared, 'International football can no longer be held within the confines of the Olympics, and many countries where professionalism is now recognised and organised cannot any longer be represented there by their best players.' The following February, he and Hugo Meisl, the coach of the Austrian national 'Wunderteam', proposed a pan-European international competition to run every two years, but with no governing body in existence the idea soon fell by the wayside. In 1928, at FIFA's congress in Amsterdam, Delaunay put forward the resolution for a world championship to be held among the globe's national teams; it was passed by 23 votes to five, and took place two years later in Uruguay.

But Delaunay's hopes of a European equivalent remained on ice for a decade, and then the Second World War came along. By the early 1950s, he was impatient with the lack of any unified structure in European football. He and two influential administrators, the Italian Ottorino Barassi and the Belgian José Crahay, now took matters into their own hands (Barassi had earlier hidden FIFA's Jules Rimet Trophy in a shoebox under his bed for most of the Second World War).

In 1952, the three men organised a meeting in Zürich, inviting 'only those European national associations which on the occasion of preliminary talks with Dr Barassi had in principle agreed to the project', as Crahay stiffly put it in UEFA's official 1963/64 handbook. There, Delaunay unveiled the draft statutes for the new body.

On 15 June 1954, at the Hotel Euler in Basel, UEFA formally came into being and united 28 member associations. On the advice of FIFA executive Stanley Rous, another meeting was scheduled for a week later. There, the Dane Ebbe Schwartz was named UEFA's first president, with Josef Gerö of Austria as his vice-president and Delaunay as general secretary.

But few noticed, because the World Cup finals were about to kick off 150 miles away in Geneva, where Brazil thrashed Mexico 5-0 the next day. So the birth of this new organisation effectively went unnoticed in the European press (FIFA's official bulletin for September 1954 makes no mention of it whatsoever).

Still, the work towards a continental championship could now begin. 'Delaunay believed that the idea of UEFA – a continental union of federations – and a cup competition between nations were one and the same,' said Jacques Ferran, Hanot's deputy at *France Football*. In the weeks after the Basel meeting, Delaunay published an essay, 'Is It Possible To Build A Footballing Europe?', in which he advocated the idea of a continent-wide tournament for national teams, while careful to maintain that it should not affect the business of the World Cup and that its fixture list should not interfere with any pre-existing competitions.

In March 1955, UEFA's general assembly convened its first congress in Vienna (in Delaunay's absence). FIFA's general secretary, Kurt Gassmann, expressed his opposition to the idea of a European Championship, seeing it as a threat to the World Cup. His views were echoed by many at the gathering. Only ten of the 30 member associations, almost all from eastern Europe, supported the idea. Ferran wrote years later in *L'Équipe*, 'The three-member committee responsible for this project [Delaunay, Crahay and George Graham] had spent almost six months drafting the regulations. In ten minutes in Vienna, it was swept away.'

The following September, the increasingly frail Delaunay penned an op-ed in *France Football*. 'So we now have a Union of European Football Associations,' he wrote, 'and that is all well and good; but, in my opinion, it has not yet entirely fulfilled its objective. It has become a grouping in the legal sense, but not yet in sporting terms. And yet, I'd say that this sporting aspect is as essential to it as a national competition is to an association, the South American Championship is for the South American Football Confederation or the World Cup is to FIFA.

'Our mosaic of European countries needs this outlet for sporting expression. We cannot continue living in an atmosphere of routine and obsolescence. All other sports organise European championships; will football, which has always been in the vanguard of sporting progress, remain trapped in its outdated models?'

1960

BY THE time the first ball of the European Championship was finally kicked on a September Sunday afternoon in Moscow, the man whose imagination and hard work made it possible had been dead for almost three years. Henri Delaunay passed away on 9 November 1955 from a terminal illness at the age of 72, never getting to see the culmination of his decades of assiduous work. His son Pierre took over as UEFA general secretary, first as a caretaker, then on a permanent basis.

The European Nations' Cup being stuck in development hell for more than three decades wasn't just down to the horrors of the Second World War and its aftershocks. Even after the June 1954 formation of UEFA, many of Europe's footballing powerhouses showed little interest in entering anything that wasn't the World Cup. But in the wake of Delaunay's death, his son redoubled his efforts to get the Euros off the starting blocks. The idea had already been floated at the Vienna congress the previous March. As a compromise, it was agreed that that most European of things, a commission, should be set up to examine the idea and run the rule over its workability.

At UEFA's second congress in Lisbon in July 1956, Pierre Delaunay gave it another go. His arguments were met with well-rehearsed opposition. Those against the idea pointed out that nationalistic tensions were still running high barely a decade after the end of the war; that the fixture calendar was already quite crowded; and that European football didn't need extra commercialisation. The first point was valid, the second debatable, the third laughably self-serving even then. The proposal failed to win a majority vote.

By the time of the next congress, in Copenhagen in July 1957, Pierre Delaunay had drawn up new proposals which entailed a streamlined qualifying process followed by a small four-team tournament in the summer of 1960. Still it wasn't enough; even Delaunay senior's old ally Ottorino Barassi came out against it. Accounts differ as to the breakdown of the voting. UEFA's

13

own official history says the proposal got 15 yes votes, seven no votes, four abstentions and one ballot paper left blank. Another source has it at 14 for yes, seven for no and five abstentions (including all the British associations).

But in Stockholm a year later, on the eve of the 1958 World Cup, the dam burst. After another ballot produced the same number of yes votes, president Ebbe Schwartz settled the matter after lunch by announcing that it was time to plough ahead. The draw for the qualifying round was held two days later at Stockholm's Foresta Hotel.

For a while, it looked as though there wouldn't be enough participants for the competition to be feasible. The consensus was that 16 teams were needed to make it happen, and uptake was so slow that UEFA was forced to extend the registration deadline by four months. Some arm-twisting ensued behind the scenes before a sudden torrent of late entrants ensued. Seventeen countries went into the hat, almost perfectly split between the western and eastern halves of the continent (nine to eight).

West Germany, Italy, England, Scotland, Northern Ireland, Wales, Belgium, the Netherlands and Switzerland all gave it a miss. The blazers of British football, insular to the toejam in their socks, had told UEFA in 1957 that they wanted no part of this strange new tournament, worried that it would interfere with the Home Internationals. The West Germans' reluctance had a similarly self-interested motivation behind it: their manager Sepp Herberger felt that playing in a second international tournament would take a huge physical toll on his players, and that the World Cup was enough for now. He should have been careful what he wished for. In June 1962, West Germany fell to a surprise 1-0 defeat by Yugoslavia in the World Cup quarter-final in Santiago, having played only four competitive games since 1958.

When all the horse-trading was over, the dawn of the competition was witnessed on 28 September 1958 at the Lenina Stadion in Moscow, where 100,572 people – still the third-biggest attendance in the competition's history – turned up to see the USSR beat a Hungarian team who were a sad shadow of what they'd been a few short years earlier.

The very first goal of the European Championship was tucked away after just four minutes by Anatoliy Ilyin, who robbed Hungarian sweeper Ferenc Sipos in the box and shot past goalkeeper Béla Bakó (this distinction is often wrongly credited to Ireland's Liam Tuohy, who headed the opening goal in the preliminary round against Czechoslovakia – a fixture that didn't take place until April 1959). Newspaper *Soviet Sport* reported, 'The game was very beautiful, very tense until the last second, and perfectly correct. In short, it was a meeting of true friends.' A full 364 days elapsed before the second leg in Budapest, which the USSR won 1-0 before another massive crowd.

Many of the first-round games were little more than exhibition matches. France's meeting with Greece was a 7-1 cakewalk; Spain swept Poland aside in Chorzów, Alfredo Di Stéfano and Luis Suárez both scoring twice; and Norway were hit for five in Vienna by the remnants of Austria's fine early-1950s team. The only surprise came when a Mário Coluna-inspired Portugal overcame East Germany in East Berlin. In a good sign for the event's viability, there were some huge attendances: the aforementioned 100,572 in Moscow, 78,481 in Budapest, 71,469 in Chorzów, 67,200 in Bucharest, 62,070 in Madrid. People were clearly interested in this new tournament, even if they weren't sure how seriously to take it.

The 1960 European Nations' Cup is effectively unique in footballing history for having only three quarter-finals, thanks to the full-metal-jacket paranoia of Francisco Franco, the deranged despot who other deranged despots called The Guv'nor. When Spain came out of the hat with the USSR in December 1959, the Soviets began clearing the decks for the grudge match, gathering their squad together to spend the spring of 1960 playing preparatory friendlies. One of their top officials, Andrei Starostin, was officially censured by the Kremlin for the mistake of praising the technical qualities of Spain's team in an interview (Starostin may have felt a shiver run down his spine, having spent time in the Norillag labour camp during the Second World War).

The Soviet squad was based at a sports complex owned by the Communist Party, just outside Moscow. Manager Gavriil Kachalin, having learned that his incomparable goalkeeper Lev Yashin was feeling tense, ordered the young striker Viktor Ponedelnik to take the big man out to a nearby lake for a fishing expedition to calm his nerves. 'It became a ritual,' said Ponedelnik. 'Whichever country we were playing in, we both went fishing.' In Yashin, a bona fide colossus whose force of personality matched his athletic abilities, the USSR possessed not just the greatest keeper in the world, but possibly the era's greatest player full stop.

There may have been good reasons for Yashin's anxiety. 'Even if there was an air of freedom under Khrushchev after Stalin died,' said Ponedelnik, 'we were being watched all the time. There was a spy in the team. Lev unmasked him and we warned the others. Everything went on as if nothing had happened. Do not expect me to condemn it now!'

On 18 May 1960, Real Madrid annihilated Eintracht Frankfurt 7-3 in the European Cup Final in Glasgow. The following day, Spain's selection committee of Ramón Gabilondo, José Luis Lasplazas and José Luis Costa were in Moscow to watch the USSR inflict similar punishment on Poland in a friendly, winning 7-1. The latter result concentrated minds in Madrid.

Franco was already unnerved by the propaganda implications of 'his' team losing to godless Bolsheviks (the USSR had funded the republican side during the Spanish Civil War, and the two countries had no diplomatic ties). Now he got wind of inaccurate reports that a sizeable contingent of Soviets would attend the first leg in Madrid. This, plus the thought of the USSR anthem playing and flag flying at the Bernabéu, was too much for El Caudillo. On 25 May, he instructed RFEF president Alfonso de la Fuente Chaos (sic), to tell Spain's players that they were withdrawing from the tournament. 'Orders from above,' the bureaucrat said. 'We're not going to Moscow. Franco said so.'

Even at the time, Franco's behaviour seemed risible. After all, Spain had been happy to play Poland, another communist state, in the previous round. The real reason was that while Poland were a weak opponent, the USSR were anything but.

It would emerge that Franco's handpicked successor, Luis Carrero Blanco, and another influential minister, Camilo Alonso Vega, were bending his ear. Both men were irreversibly opposed to the idea of Soviet athletes setting foot on Spanish soil at all. UEFA had no choice but to award the USSR two walkovers, home and away, so they went into the semi-finals without kicking a ball. Spain were fined by the governing body but, astonishingly, received no other punishment.

The USSR Football Federation, when they had stopped laughing, put out a statement accusing Franco of trying to please 'his US imperialist owners', while Nikita Khrushchev sneered, 'The whole world is laughing at Franco's latest trick. From his position as the right-sided defender of American prestige, he has scored an own goal.' The Soviet players saw it differently. 'It was a huge disappointment,' said Ponedelnik. 'We really wanted to compete with them. All the tickets had been sold. What a pity!'

Could Spain have won the whole thing if their dictator hadn't interfered? Hard to say. They had Alfredo Di Stéfano, the greatest outfield player of the era, and Ladislao Kubala, Luis Suárez and Paco Gento, who weren't far behind him. On the other hand, the opponents they chickened out of facing were one of the most formidable national teams in Europe; hardly any guarantees there. More to the point, Spain hadn't even managed to qualify for the recent World Cup in Sweden. And their bottom-of-the-group finish in Chile in 1962 would confirm that it was useless having wonderful players in your squad if you couldn't mould them into a cohesive team.

Years after the event, right-back Feliciano Rivilla recalled how he and his team-mates waited on tenterhooks for word to come back from El Pardo, Franco's hunting-lodge headquarters. 'We wanted to go to the USSR because we couldn't go,' he said. 'When human beings are told they can't do something, it makes them want to even more. We were left all dressed up with nowhere to go.'

And then there were seven. But while all this was going on, Pierre Delaunay's career had been blown off course. Working as general secretary on a voluntary basis from his office at 22 Rue de Londres in Paris, he was effectively sidelined in December 1959 when UEFA's general assembly voted in favour of moving its operations to Bern in Switzerland.

His work was, however, recognised with a seat on the executive committee, as well as the responsibility of overseeing the design of the new competition's trophy. A stately silver sculpture, 19in tall and weighing 6kg with engravings inspired by ancient Greek vases, it was created by Parisian silversmith Adrien Chobillon for jewellery firm Arthus-Bertrand. As Ebbe Schwartz had announced at the Stockholm congress, the trophy would bear the name of Delaunay's father.

QUARTER-FINALS
France v Austria
Portugal v Yugoslavia
Romania v Czechoslovakia
USSR v Spain (walkover awarded to USSR)

France had just fired seven goals past Greece, and their hot streak wasn't over yet. They were fragile but fearsome, their line-up full of firepower, with the two biggest guns being Just Fontaine, the 1958 World Cup's top scorer, and Raymond Kopa, winner of three consecutive European Cups with Real Madrid. The pair roomed together but barely knew each other personally, due to Kopa keeping his wristwatch on Spanish time and going to bed much later than Fontaine. They enjoyed a better understanding on the field.

Manager Albert Batteux could also call on Lucien Muller, whose languid talents had already attracted the burdensome tag of 'le petit Kopa' and would later get him an ill-fated transfer to Real Madrid. Some of France's defenders were noticeably long in the tooth, but they could outgun most opponents and they had little trouble beating Austria 5-2 at the Stade de Colombes.

Fontaine's first and second goals were both nerveless finishes into the corner when clean through on the left. He sealed his hat-trick by dribbling around Austrian goalkeeper Kurt Schmied and thumping the ball past two defenders on the line. Earlier, Jean Vincent capitalised on Karl Koller's dithering in the six-yard box to bury the third goal, and he rounded off the scoring with another tap-in when Schmied and Muller collided under the bar. Austria had briefly got it back to 3-2 with close-range goals from Walter Horak and Rudolf Pichler, the latter after Horst Nemec slalomed through midfield, but Austria's generosity had left them with too much to do.

Three and a half months went by before the second leg, by which time both teams looked very different. Austria made seven changes, France five (poor Fontaine had broken his leg while playing for Stade de Reims), but the outcome was the same: dodgy defending exposed by sharp forwards.

Nemec gave Austria an undeserved half-time lead, after which normal service was resumed. Jean-Jacques Marcel trotted up to the edge of the Austrian box without encountering a challenge, saw his shot blocked by a defender, but gobbled up the rebound and stroked it past the slow-diving Rudolf Szanwald. Then Pierre Grillet got the better of the great but ageing Gerhard Hanappi on the right wing and sent over a looping cross which Bernard Rahis headed home.

Erich Probst, one of the stars of the 1954 World Cup, equalised with the best goal of the tie, a smooth finish to round off an attractive move involving Giuseppe Koschier, Paul Kozlicek and Nemec. But Austria couldn't deal with Kopa's clever runs and sparkling passes, and he gave François Heutte a clear sight of goal which was tucked away. When Heutte then strolled past three Austrians, Erich Hasenkopf took his legs away before he could shoot; Kopa put the penalty just inside the left-hand post, more like a pass than a shot.

With France's forwards averaging more than four goals a game, their defensive shakiness didn't matter for now. In time, however, they would be exposed as multimillionaires in a discontinued currency.

It was the same story in the second quarter-final, as Yugoslavian talent swept aside limited opponents. Though not quite that limited. Portugal were blessed with two fantastic players: the supernaturally calm centre-half Germano de Figueiredo, who was about to join Benfica for £2,000 (a tiny sum even in 1960), and the Mozambican inside-left Mário Coluna, who was already there and on the way to becoming one of their greatest players. In the first leg in Lisbon, Portugal spent long periods under the cosh, undeservedly winning 2-1 with two opportunistic goals from Joaquim Santana and another Mozambican, Matateu. The fair-haired Bora Kostić's well-struck effort near the end was scant reward for all Yugoslavia's pressure.

Most people expected the natural order to be restored in Belgrade a fortnight later. They were right. Yugoslavia overran Portugal, even with Germano working overtime. Domiciano Cavém's first-half equaliser, struck hard on the run, was a false dawn: it ended 5-1, and the pick of the goals was Kostić's spectacular right-footed hammer into the top corner. Portugal's moment in the sun would come – powered by an extraordinary player who was even better than anybody Yugoslavia had – but not for another five or six years.

With ice-blue eyes and a blinding smile, Vlastimil Bubník was a visually striking man. He was also a world-class athlete, holding down a place in both Czechoslovakia's football squad and its ice hockey team. He would win a bronze medal at the 1964 Winter Olympics in Innsbruck, and was enough of a natural with the puck to be admitted into the sport's International Hall of Fame in 1997.

Against Romania in Bucharest, Bubník showed how good he was with a round ball at his feet. His running in midfield drove Czechoslovakia to an easy 2-0 victory, and he grabbed the second goal with a fine run and drive, after Josef Masopust clipped home the first from 12 yards. The likes of Masopust (who would be named European Footballer of the Year in 1962), Bubník and the stylish sweeper Ján Popluhár were too good for a Romanian team who had struggled to get past the Turks in the previous round.

A week later in Bratislava, against an inexperienced Romanian team (73 caps between the lot of them), Czechoslovakia put the game to bed inside 20 minutes. Titus Buberník scored five times for his country, and all of them came in the qualifiers of this tournament. His two goals here were easy meat, both knocked in from close range, and the irrepressible Bubník grabbed another. Czechoslovakia eased off after that, to Romania's relief.

So UEFA's new baby now had its completed line-up of semi-finalists. The quartet had a heavily Slavic flavour to it – three east European teams out of four – but the one exception had home advantage.

2.30pm, 13 December 1959
Stade Olympique de Colombes, Paris
Attendance: 43,775
Referee: Manuel Martín Asensi (Spain)

FRANCE 5 (Fontaine 7, 18, 70, Vincent 38, 82)
AUSTRIA 2 (Horak 40, Pichler 65)

FRANCE: Georges Lamia, Jean Wendling, Robert 'Bob' Jonquet, Roger Marche (c), Armand Penverne, René Ferrier, François Heutte, Lucien Muller, Just Fontaine, Raymond Kopa, Jean Vincent. **Manager:** Albert Batteux.

AUSTRIA: Kurt Schmied, Paul Halla, Karl Nickerl, Gerhard Hanappi (c), Karl Stotz, Karl Koller, Walter Horak, Helmut Senekowitsch, Horst Nemec, Rudolf Pichler, Karl Höfer. **Manager:** Karl Decker.

3pm, 27 March 1960
Praterstadion, Vienna
Attendance: 39,229
Referee: Leo Helge (Denmark)

AUSTRIA 2 (Nemec 26, Probst 64)
FRANCE 4 (Marcel 46, Rahis 59, Heutte 77, Kopa 83 pen)

AUSTRIA: Rudolf Szanwald, Johann Windisch, Erich Hasenkopf, Hanappi (c), Giuseppe, 'Giose' Koschier, Koller, Horak, Paul Kozlicek, Nemec, Wilhelm Huberts, Erich Probst.

FRANCE: Lamia, Wendling, Raymond Kaelbel, Bruno Rodzik, Jean-Jacques Marcel, Ferrier, Pierre Grillet, Muller, Heutte, Kopa (c), Bernard Rahis.

3pm, 8 May 1960
Estádio Nacional, Lisbon
Attendance: 39,978
Referee: Joseph Barbéran (France)

PORTUGAL 2 (Santana 30, Matateu 70)
YUGOSLAVIA 1 (Kostić 81)

PORTUGAL: Acúrcio Carrelo, Virgílio Mendes (c), Ângelo Martins, Fernando Mendes, Germano de Figueiredo, David Abraão Júlio, Hernâni Ferreira, Joaquim Santana, Sebastião Lucas 'Matateu', Mário Coluna, Domiciano Cavém. **Manager:** José María Antunes.

YUGOSLAVIA: Milutin Šoškić, Vladimir Durković, Fahrudin Jusufi, Ante Žanetić, Tomislav Crnković (c), Željko Perušić, Muhamed Mujić, Milan Galić, Branko Zebec, Dragoslav Šekularac, Bora Kostić. **Managers:** Ljubomir Lovrić, Aleksandar Tirnanić and Dragomir Nikolić.

4pm, 22 May 1960
JNA Stadion, Belgrade
Attendance: 43,000
Referee: Alfred Stoll (Austria)

YUGOSLAVIA 5 (Šekularac 8, Čebinac 45, Kostić 50, 88, Galić 79)
PORTUGAL 1 (Cavém 29)

YUGOSLAVIA: Šoškić, Durković, Jusufi, Žanetić, Žarko Nikolić, Perušić, Zvezdan Čebinac, Tomislav Knez, Galić, Šekularac, Kostić (c).

PORTUGAL: Acúrcio, Virgílio, Mário João Sousa, Mendes (c), Germano, David Júlio, Hernâni, Santana, Matateu, Coluna, Cavém.

3pm, 22 May 1960
Stadionul 23 August, Bucharest
Attendance: 61,306
Referee: Andor Dorogi (Hungary)

ROMANIA 0
CZECHOSLOVAKIA 2 (Masopust 8, Bubník 45)

ROMANIA: Petre Mîndru, Cornel Popa, Alexandru Apolzan (c), Valeriu Soare, Imre Jenei, Ion Nunweiller, Emanoil Haşoti, Gavril Raksi, Viorel Mateianu, Haralambie Eftimie, Nicolae Tătaru. **Manager:** Augustin Botescu.

CZECHOSLOVAKIA: Imrich Stacho, Jozef Bomba, Ján Popluhár, Ladislav Novák (c), Titus Buberník, Josef Masopust, Ladislav Pavlovič, Josef Vojta, Andrej Kvašňák, Vlastimil Bubník, Milan Dolinský. **Manager:** Rudolf Vytlačil.

4.30pm, 29 May 1960
Tehelné Pole, Bratislava
Attendance: 31,057
Referee: Leif Gulliksen (Norway)
CZECHOSLOVAKIA 3 (Buberník 1, 15, Bubník 18)
ROMANIA 0
CZECHOSLOVAKIA: Viliam Schrojf, Bomba, Popluhár, Novák (c), Buberník, Masopust, Pavlovič, Vojta, Kvašňák, Bubník, Dolinský.

ROMANIA: Mîndru, Popa, Alexandru Fronea, Soare, Vasile Alexandru, Nunweiller, Gheorghe Cacoveanu, Gheorghe Constantin, Mateianu, Constantin Dinulescu, Tătaru (c).

SEMI-FINALS
France v Yugoslavia
USSR v Czechoslovakia

At the dawn of the 1960s, foreign travel wasn't so much a rarity for most people as an exotic concept from the pages of a spy novel. Especially if you happened to come from one of the three communist countries which had qualified for the first European Nations' Cup finals.

Yugoslavia's squad spent 28 hours on a train before reaching Paris. When they pulled in at the Gare de Lyon, they found that their hosts had failed to arrange transport to their hotel, forcing them to walk another kilometre with their luggage. But the Yugoslavs wasted little time in immersing themselves in the local *joie de vivre*, *esprit de corps* and *soup du jour*, spending a happy evening at the Moulin Rouge.

France themselves were without their entire forward line from the 1958 World Cup. We've already heard about Fontaine's broken leg; Kopa too was injured; and Roger Piantoni's wrecked knee put him out for nearly a year. Moreover, there was a general lack of big-game experience in the side, with only three survivors from the World Cup. Batteux threw Roby Herbin and Michel Stievenard in at the deep end for their international debuts, and a farcical 17-1 win over provincial side Oise three days earlier was no preparation for facing a team like Yugoslavia.

Batteux had one other problem, in goal. The debonair *pied-noir* Georges Lamia, who sported a pencil moustache and an eye-catching striped jersey, was known to be a flawed keeper and the only alternative was the uncapped 22-year-old Jean Taillandier. In the event, Lamia would have the worst night of his career, bearing varying degrees of responsibility for each of Yugoslavia's five goals.

Both sides traded goals in the opening stages. After 11 minutes, Galić scored with an opportunistic curler which caught Lamia off his line. And within 60 seconds, Vincent's tantalising cross from the left went all the way in. Maryan Wisnieski strained and failed to connect with it, but tried to claim it anyway.

The Parc des Princes was barely half-full, but those present were in good voice, and France – playing in red shirts, as Yugoslavia had been named as the 'home' team – soon got on top. Just before half-time, Heutte's rising drive from the edge of the box flew past the startled Milutin Šoškić. Eight minutes after the break, another Vincent cross fed Wisnieski, whose finish was decisive for 3-1.

But Yugoslavia, with Dragan Šekularac in lambent form, pulled one back in ridiculous fashion when Lamia somehow allowed Ante Žanetić's cross from the byline to drift past him at the near post, like a preview of Amarildo's goal for Brazil in the World Cup Final two years later. Unfazed, France simply strolled upfield and scored again. Lucien Muller's pass came off Branko Zebec; Šoškić and his defenders all froze, assuming Heutte was offside, and he put away the chance after initially hesitating. 'I was so surprised to find myself alone in front of goal,' said the striker years later. 'Jean Vincent had to yell at me to knock it in.' The rotund referee Gaston Grandain, owner of a 'Hitchcockian belly' in the words of one French newspaper report, ignored Yugoslavia's protests.

Cruising at 4-2 with a quarter of an hour left, France now experienced a staggering *bouleversement*, with the roof falling in as they conceded three awful goals in four minutes. First, a long cross found Tomislav Knez unmarked at the far post: he shot straight at Lamia, who allowed it to squeeze home. Then, after a stylish Yugoslavian move down the left, Lamia dropped Kostić's shot for Dražan Jerković to knee it over the line (the French claimed handball, but Grandain said no). His nerves now in tatters, Lamia gifted Yugoslavia their winner moments later, failing to hold Knez's shot before Jerković tapped it in.

Like Albert Camus, Lamia was an Algerian-born goalkeeper, and it's probably safe to surmise that plenty of people were wishing a plague on all his houses after this horror show. 'Lamia assassine l'équipe de France,' howled the headline of a double-page photographic spread of his blunders in *Football Magazine*. In *France Football*, Jacques Ferran was no more forgiving, writing that 'on Wednesday he didn't make one mistake, or two, or three; his biggest error was simply to be there'.

A disbelieving Batteux lamented, 'At 4-2, I would have bet all my money that we'd be in the final.' More than half a century later, Lucien Muller spoke up in qualified defence of his old colleague, 'Pffff, when a keeper lets in a goal, it's always his fault. It was a collective failure. But in the last 20 minutes, he lost his mind.'

The first game in the European Championship finals is still its highest-scoring match ever. It's also the worst collapse in French footballing history, Bulgaria 1993 be damned. Šekularac's recollections of it were more rose-tinted. 'Do I remember that match? To this day, I dream about it,' he sighed. 'I took part in one of the best games in the history of football.'

⸻

The second semi-final wasn't a patch on the first. Czechoslovakia would reach the World Cup final two years later, and five of that team played here – but the USSR were just too far ahead, not only on technical ability but also the amount of work they put in. They were based in Chantilly, but there weren't many frills about this squad of strapping specimens.

The day before the game, manager Kachalin brought his squad on a trip to the island of If, just off the Mediterranean coast. The players loved it, most of them having read the Alexandre Dumas novel *The Count of Monte Cristo* (whose protagonist was imprisoned there) during their schooldays. Full-back Vladimir Kesarev was hit by appendicitis that evening, but the Georgian Givi Chokheli came in and enjoyed the smoothest international debut he could have wished for.

The opening stages at the Vélodrome were a fast-paced mess ('The ball was a frequent guest of the penalty areas of both teams,' noted one Russian account of the match), and both Viliam Schrojf and Yashin had to save well in one-on-ones from Valentin Ivanov and Bubník respectively. But once the USSR got their noses in front, it was all over. Ivanov prodded in from close range after Schrojf blocked at Ponedelnik's feet, and his second goal was quite brilliant: a twisting run through Czechoslovakia's defence, a jink inside the goalkeeper's dive, a finish belted into an open net.

For number three, the balding Valentin Bubukin's shot cannoned off a defender and Ponedelnik forced in the rebound. A minute later, the Czechoslovaks were thrown a lifeline by Slava Metreveli's handball in the box, but Josef Vojta's penalty trundled wide. Czechoslovakia had been blown away by superior firepower. 'We had Yashin,' reflected Ponedelnik. 'The credit for the win went to him. For the Czechoslovakians, it was like being up against God, and ultimately it gave them an inferiority complex.'

'[The Soviets] were better than us,' said a chastened Masopust. 'They had already adopted a kind of professionalism in their preparation, whereas in our country, everybody had other jobs.' That extra edge, already apparent, would make the difference in the final too.

8pm, 6 July 1960
Parc des Princes, Paris
Attendance: 26,370
Referee: Gaston Grandain (Belgium)

YUGOSLAVIA 5 (Galić 11, Žanetić 55, Knez 75, Jerković 78, 79)
FRANCE 4 (Vincent 12, Heutte 43, 63, Wisnieski 53)

YUGOSLAVIA: Šoškić, Durković, Jusufi, Žanetić, Zebec (c), Perušić, Knez, Dražan Jerković, Galić, Šekularac, Kostić.

FRANCE: Lamia, Wendling, Rodzik, Marcel, Ferrier, Michel Stievenard, Roby Herbin, Muller, Maryan Wisnieski, Heutte, Vincent (c).

9.30pm, 6 July 1960
Stade Vélodrome, Marseille
Attendance: 25,184
Referee: Cesare Jonni (Italy)

USSR 3 (Ivanov 34, 56, Ponedelnik 66)

CZECHOSLOVAKIA 0

USSR: Lev Yashin, Givi Chokheli, Anatoly Maslyonkin, Anatoly Krutikov, Yuri Voinov, Igor Netto (c), Slava Metreveli, Valentin Ivanov, Viktor Ponedelnik, Valentin Bubukin, Mikheil Meskhi.

Manager: Gavriil Kachalin.

CZECHOSLOVAKIA: Schrojf, František Šafránek, Popluhár, Novák (c), Buberník, Masopust, Vojta, Anton Moravčík, Kvašňák, Bubník, Dolinský.

THIRD-PLACE PLAY-OFF
France v Czechoslovakia

The disintegration against Yugoslavia knocked the stuffing out of France's fans as well as their team. Fewer than 10,000 turned up for an undistinguished third-place match at the Vélodrome, and weren't happy that Batteux picked a weakened line-up; some in the crowd vocally demanded a refund. Czechoslovakia, faced with an 'équipe fantomatique', a team of ghosts, played well within themselves to win.

Other than Schrojf catching a looping shot under his bar, little of note occurred for the first hour. Then Bubník beat the flat cap-wearing debutant keeper Jean Taillandier with a daisy-cutter from Ladislav Novák's centre, to the displeasure of the grizzled-looking chain-smokers in the crowd. The veteran Bob Jonquet, back after missing the semi-final, slipped badly as the cross came over; no way for such a good player to take his leave from international football after 58 caps. In the final minutes, Ladislav Pavlovič wrapped up the win with a soft, angled shot which passed easily through Taillandier (no improvement on Lamia) at the near post. 'My men were not good,' said Czechoslovakia's manager Rudolf Vytlačil afterwards, 'but I'm especially disappointed to have seen France play so badly.'

6pm, 9 July 1960
Stade Vélodrome, Marseille
Attendance: 9,438
Referee: Cesare Jonni (Italy)

CZECHOSLOVAKIA 2 (Bubník 58, Pavlovič 88)
FRANCE 0

CZECHOSLOVAKIA: Schrojf, Šafránek, Popluhár, Novák (c), Buberník, Masopust, Ladislav Pavlovič, Vojta, Pavol Molnár, Bubník, Dolinský.

FRANCE: Jean Taillandier, Rodzik, Jonquet (c), André Chorda, Marcel, Robert Siatka, Stievenard, Yvon Douis, Wisnieski (c), Heutte, Vincent.

FINAL
USSR v Yugoslavia

All the USSR's fixtures in the competition so far had come packaged in layers of political intrigue: the walkover against Franco's Spain, the easy wins over their unhappy satellites Hungary and Czechoslovakia. The final would be no exception.

In 1948, Yugoslavia was expelled from the Cominform, the Soviet-dominated grouping of communist parties. For the next 12 years, its leader Josip Broz Tito followed his own political path, infuriating Stalin, who might well have invaded the country had he not died in 1953. Would it be Moscow's way or Belgrade's way? Everyone was going to find out, if not in the boardroom of the Coninform, then at least on the playing fields of Paris.

Once again, the attendance was dishearteningly low, with fewer than 18,000 turning up at the Parc des Princes. 'Crowds in France wanted western European glamour, not mysterious teams from the other side of Europe,' noted Šekularac years later. Televising the match live on the day didn't help. Nor did the bad weather.

Yugoslavia's selection committee changed their goalkeeper, bringing in Blagoje Vidinić (a trained opera singer who would later manage Zaire at the 1974 World Cup) after an eye problem deprived Šoškić of sleep. They also gambled by handing an international debut to midfielder Željko Matuš. And their team made all the early running.

Before long, Yashin got down smartly to save two free kicks by Kostić. But he was a spectator when Šekularac whipped a shot just beyond the angle of post and bar, following a slick Yugoslavian move. Šekularac looked the best player on the field in the first half, at the heart of everything good his team did. With Soviet captain Igor Netto playing in a deeper role than normal to guard against the pace of Bora Kostić, the USSR looked stretched.

Yugoslavia's pressure deserved a goal. Before the break, they scored a messy one. Jerković kept the ball in play as Anatoly Maslyonkin stopped to appeal for a throw-in, then sent in a low cross which was diverted in at the near post, past a wrong-footed Yashin. The flickery old black-and-white footage doesn't prove conclusively whether it went in off Milan Galić's head, or his knee, or some other part of his anatomy – or indeed off Netto, who was marking him. But let's give the benefit of the doubt to the attacker, as we're always being told to. It was an unusual lapse by Netto, a colossus of Italian descent who was one of the best players in the world.

Half-time came at a serendipitous moment for the Soviets. Their former defender Boris Kuznetsov, who had played in the 1958 World Cup and was present with the squad, knew a little bit about shoemaking and took the opportunity to put spikes in the soles of their boots, to help them better negotiate the soggy surface. Within minutes of the restart, they were handed an undeserved equaliser. Bubukin ambled forward and struck a moderate left-footer from 25 yards, Vidinić fumbled it, and Metreveli reached the loose ball first to tap in from a narrow angle.

The goal seemed to demoralise Yugoslavia, and referee Arthur Ellis then showed remarkable leniency when Vidinić sent Ivanov flying with a professional foul. By today's footballing mores, an instant red card; in 1960, a free kick to the USSR 25 yards out and no more. Very late on, Metreveli's low cross-shot bobbled across the goalmouth, Ponedelnik slid in but missed it, and it reached Ivanov, who stabbed wide from three yards. Extra time it would be.

Playing for an additional half-hour was a novelty back then, and despite the cooling effects of the rain, tiredness saw the game become stretched. The extended period also witnessed that rarest of collector's items, a Yashin howler. Coming out for a corner that he had little hope of getting, he was relieved to see Jerković's looping header go wide.

As the second half of extra time began, Yugoslavia spurned a golden chance. Žanetić put a low cross on a plate for Galić in the goalmouth, but the striker slumped wearily to his knees as the ball skidded tantalisingly past him, just like the lager-bloated Gazza against Germany at Wembley 36 years later.

A replay seemed near-certain, but with seven minutes to go, Ponedelnik succeeded where Galić had failed. The tireless Ivanov sent a cross into the danger area, where the exhausted Yugoslav defenders left Ponedelnik unattended ('Jovan Miladinović had sucked my blood for 90 minutes, but he could do no more'). With Vidinić stranded, he rose to head it back across and into the corner.

'I didn't see how the ball went into the goal, but as soon as I headed it, a defender pushed me off my feet, and I fell down into that mud,' Ponedelnik recalled. 'Everything was wet. I couldn't see anything.' This is contradicted by the footage, which shows him toppling over with no defender near him, but never mind.

Ponedelnik's surname was also the Russian word for Monday. And while it was Sunday evening in Paris, it was almost 1am in Moscow when his goal hit the back of the net. 'Ponedelnik zabivaet v Ponedelnik' blared the newspaper headlines back home, Monday scores on Monday. 'Against the USSR, we've never had luck,' Šekularac lamented. 'The Russians, at times during the match, were totally inferior. But Ponedelnik showed no mercy.'

After the Soviets survived a goalmouth scramble at the death, Ellis blew for time to give them their first and last international trophy. In the confusion, Yashin's cap was stolen by someone who had run on to the pitch.

The Soviet players went out on the town in Paris until the sun came up. Midfielder Yuri Voinov recalled, 'We were given a bonus – something like 400 francs. But to sit in a Paris café with a glass of wine was enough. We didn't drink much. We were drunk on victory.'

Ponedelnik said, 'The bosses were concerned and very embarrassed. No one expected this win, so no one had arranged bonuses. When we got the money, it made us laugh. We took it and we moved on. We didn't have anything like that [nightlife] in Moscow. It was all dark at night. No bars, no clubs. Nobody went out. Everyone was like mice in their houses. So that night was something out of a fairytale. And they said that, back in Moscow, there wasn't one dark window. When they told us that, we literally had tears in our eyes.'

The next day, covetous Spanish eyes sized up the USSR's squad while they were feted at a reception in a restaurant near the Eiffel Tower. After receiving a tip-off, Real Madrid chairman Santiago Bernabéu walked in and offered contracts to five players on the spot. He would have had more chance of signing Dmitri Shostakovich. 'He was ready to buy half of our team, with no hesitation,' said Ponedelnik. 'Yashin, Ivanov, Netto, Metreveli and myself. We avoided the conversation. We said we had contracts with our clubs, even though there were none.'

The eventual victory parade in the Lenina Stadion drew a six-figure crowd. But in France itself, coverage was low-key: the next day's sports pages were dominated not by images of Netto lifting the Henri Delaunay Trophy, but by the appalling injuries sustained by French cyclist Roger Rivière when he plunged into a ravine during the Tour de France. *L'Équipe*, France's sporting bible, was left sufficiently cold by the new tournament to put its match report on page ten. German magazine *Das Sport* described the competition as 'a week of rain in Paris, with all the disappointments that sport usually brings', and predicted that the 'vexed issue' of fixture scheduling would remain a sticking point.

So Europe had its first champions. A handful of concrete conclusions could be drawn: that the new event had a future, that its organisers would have to promote it far more comprehensively around the continent, that those who had sat it out might want to think again and that international football wasn't exactly redefining the art form in the summer of 1960.

The four matches drew a total of 76,949 spectators: nothing special, but enough to pay the bills. The TV deal with the European Broadcasting Union pulled in some more cash, and a razor-thin profit of 24,412 francs was announced, prompting warnings that future tournaments might be staged at a loss. But you've got to start somewhere, and what we now know as the UEFA European Championship had taken its first steps.

9.30pm, 10 July 1960
Parc des Princes, Paris
Attendance: 17,966
Referee: Arthur Ellis (England)

USSR 2 (Metreveli 49, Ponedelnik 113)
YUGOSLAVIA 1 (Galić 43)
After extra time

USSR: Yashin, Chokheli, Maslyonkin, Krutikov, Voinov, Netto (c), Metreveli, Ivanov, Ponedelnik, Bubukin, Meskhi.

YUGOSLAVIA: Blagoje Vidinić, Durković, Jusufi, Žanetić, Jovan Miladinović, Perušić, Željko Matuš, Jerković, Galić, Šekularac, Kostić (c).

1964

THE MODEST maiden voyage of the European Nations' Cup was enough of a qualified success to encourage more countries to join in. The number of entrants now jumped from 17 to 29, including a couple of bigger fish in the shape of Italy and England.

But once again, West Germany remained on the outside looking in. Sepp Herberger was standing firm in his distrust of this annoying new competition that refused to just bugger off and die, so West Germany wouldn't come to the party until his time as national coach was up. Nine days after the final in Madrid, he resigned as *Bundestrainer* and slipped into retirement.

His successor, long-time assistant Helmut Schön, was initially agnostic about the European Championship, but hinted in a January 1964 interview with the magazine *Der Spiegel* that taking part in it could generate 'interesting encounters and public interest'. Within eight years, Schön had built a team good enough not only to lift the trophy in Brussels, but to be regarded as the greatest German national side of all time. But that's another story.

Scotland were another noteworthy absentee. At a time when they possessed probably the strongest national squad in their entire history, their FA short-sightedly chose to sit it out, so a team bursting at the seams with fabulous players such as Dave Mackay, Denis Law, Billy McNeill, Jim Baxter, John White, Alan Gilzean and Ian St John missed out on what was ultimately a very winnable tournament. Scotland had been good enough to thrash Spain 6-2 at the Bernabéu in June 1963; that result looked even better a year later.

England dipped their toe in, but barely lasted candlelight. Alf Ramsey, their first manager permitted to pick his own team, was also the first one to lose his debut game in charge, against an in-decline but still dangerous France. Under Walter Winterbottom, the first leg was drawn 1-1 at Wembley. To most people's surprise, Ramsey sent out an attack-minded formation for the return game in Paris, with five forwards. A farce ensued. England were 3-0 down by the break and eventually lost 5-2, with Ron Springett enduring a dreadful afternoon in goal. 'This match made one thing abundantly clear,' wrote *The Times*'s man in Paris. 'English footballers have stopped to think at the critical moment.' England's first flirtation with the European Nations' Cup was over before it had started. Ramsey would never be as adventurous again.

As a sequel to Spain's flounce in 1960, Greece withdrew when they came out of the hat with Albania, their mysterious neighbour and Stalinist foe, with whom they were still technically at war. The Albanians thus 'progressed' to the first round proper, where they were thrashed by Denmark.

Spain themselves decided to give it a proper go this time. It had belatedly dawned on Franco that he needed a new source of footballing propaganda to lend some lustre to his regime, given that Real Madrid's golden years were over. 'We barely even knew that the team had withdrawn in 1960,' admitted the Basque goalkeeper José Ángel Iribar years later. 'There had been very little coverage of it [in Spain] at the time. The censorship was dominant. Any information that was not in the government's interests did not come out.'

José Villalonga, appointed as manager in the wake of the disastrous 1962 World Cup, was determined to move away from the star system, preferring to cultivate youngsters from clubs outside Madrid and Barcelona. He still had at his disposal Luis Suárez, the Internazionale playmaker who had been named European Footballer of the Year in 1960, and class acts like Amancio Amaro and Ignacio Zoco. But Spain's qualification for the last eight was jittery. They hammered Romania 6-0 to start with, but Northern Ireland would push them all the way.

The first leg, in Bilbao in May 1963, was one of the great forgotten performances in Northern Ireland's history. Their goalkeeper, Bobby Irvine, pulled off two outlandish saves to deny Amancio, and got a standing ovation from the locals at the end. Amancio did eventually score when a fluke bounce caught out defender Alex Elder, but Willie Irvine equalised after José Vicente parried his initial shot. Unbelievably, Irvine should have won it minutes later, but knocked the ball over an open goal.

In a rain-sodden return leg at Windsor Park the following October, Spain survived some dicey moments to squeeze home 1-0. Their goal was magnificent – a long-range Paco Gento thunderbolt – but their performance was anything but, and the North were left rueing two feeble misses by Johnny Crossan.

Next up for Spain were another team in green. Ireland had just about overcome Austria in Dublin with two goals from Manchester United's iron-man defender Noel Cantwell, the second of them a very late penalty to seal a dramatic 3-2 win. Afterwards, Charlie Hurley, Ireland's captain, described it as the hardest match of his career. Amid extraordinary scenes at Dalymount Park, with the home fans repeatedly spilling out of the stands and on to the pitch, Danish referee Einar Poulsen came close to abandoning the game on several occasions. It took numerous officials and a small army of gardaí three minutes to clear the pitch before Cantwell could take the penalty. Austria's manager Karl Decker vowed to file a protest with FIFA, bypassing UEFA entirely. 'The match was by no means conducted in the proper manner,' he seethed. 'Five times there were interruptions. I have never, in my lifetime, seen anything like it.' But nothing came of it, and Ireland were in the last eight.

Hungary, now clear of their 1958 World Cup hangover, had too much firepower for Wales in the shape of Flórián Albert and Lajos Tichy. That wasn't a shock, but the exit of Czechoslovakia in the preliminary round was. The 1962 World Cup runners-up couldn't break down East Germany – who later fell to the Hungarians themselves, despite coming from behind three times to draw 3-3 in Budapest.

The 1960 runners-up, Yugoslavia, were knocked out by a modest-looking Swedish side. But things looked good for the reigning champions as they prepared to defend their title. After getting a bye in the preliminary round, the USSR made short work of Italy, winning 2-0 in Moscow before a crowd of 102,358. They also came within a minute of winning the return leg, against a team whose line-up contained real greats like Giacinto Facchetti, Gianni Rivera, Sandro Mazzola and Angelo Domenghini.

Near the end of that second leg in Rome, Lev Yashin saved a penalty by Mazzola, who sighed afterwards, 'Yashin is better at football than me.' The Black Spider stood unchallenged as the world's best goalkeeper and, by many estimates, its best player full stop. In late 1963, he was named as the European Footballer of the Year after an extraordinary season for Dynamo Moscow in which he conceded six goals in 27 games. At the ceremony, with characteristic modesty, he claimed that Yugoslavia's Vladimir Beara was instead the best around.

Like the USSR, little Luxembourg got a bye into the last 16, where they faced the Dutch. For the principality's amateurs to come away with a 1-1 draw in Amsterdam was a stunning achievement in itself. But to then win the second leg 2-1, played in Rotterdam because Luxembourg's stadium failed to meet safety regulations, defied belief. Camille Dimmer, an engineer by profession who later went into politics, scored both of Luxembourg's goals, while goalkeeper Nico Schmitt played through the pain of a dislocated shoulder. Making the result even sillier, Luxembourg had played only one international in the previous two years, a friendly against the Soviets.

The Dutch team that lost to Luxembourg contained Eddy Pieters Graafland, Sjaak Swart, Klaas Nuninga, Tonny Pronk, Coen Moulijn and Piet Keizer – all of whom went on to become bona fide legends of Dutch football, collecting eight European Cup medals between them. 'Who are we going to play against now?' wailed an editorial in *De Telegraaf.* 'San Marino? Liechtenstein? Andorra?'

QUARTER-FINALS
Denmark v Luxembourg
Spain v Ireland
France v Hungary
Sweden v USSR

Luxembourg, the story of the tournament so far, eventually got their humble Stade Municipal tidied up to UEFA's satisfaction. But they were up against it even before a ball was kicked in the last eight: Dimmer, who had turned the lights out on the Dutch, was out injured.

And Denmark had a talisman of their own: striker Ole Madsen, who would score 42 times in an eventual 50 caps. His most famous goal, against Sweden in a 1965 friendly, saw him pounce on a defender's mistake with a wonderful improvised back-heel that Zlatan Ibrahimović would have been proud of. A contemporaneous match report claimed that he 'tackles like a steamroller, spinning like a top [with] a ballet dancer's balance, [and] is as quick as a hound', while a modern-day Danish account of this game called him 'a one-man army'.

Quite an advance billing. But first, Luxembourg made a statement of their own. In the opening minute, their excellent captain Louis Pilot scored with a sudden shot from the edge of the box. Madsen didn't take long to cancel it out, dribbling past three opponents and shooting left-footed past Nico Schmitt.

Again Luxembourg impertinently went in front, through Henri Klein, and again Madsen forced his way through singlehandedly to bring Denmark level. He got his hat-trick right at the start of the second half, left unmarked in the box after good midfield play by Ole Sørensen, but he and Kjeld Thorst were snared 'at least 20 times' by Luxembourg's offside trap, and another Klein shot soon made it 3-3 on 51 minutes. Thorst and Carl Bertelsen wasted good chances late on, but Denmark now knew Luxembourg were no mugs.

In Copenhagen six days later, on a rock-hard and rutted pitch ('a lunar landscape', as one Danish correspondent put it), they got another fright. More first-half goals were exchanged in quick-fire fashion. Johny Leonard tapped into an empty net following a mix-up between goalkeeper Erik Lykke

Sørensen and Kai Johansen, but within minutes that man Madsen equalised by heading in Henning Enoksen's centre.

Madsen's second goal, 20 minutes from the end, was controversial. Schmitt, hit moments earlier by a bottle thrown from the crowd, immediately dropped the ball at the feet of Bertelsen, who put it on a plate for his hungry striker. Schmitt's furious protests were in vain – but with just six minutes to go, his near-namesake Adolphe Schmit took advantage of confusion in the Danish defence and converted a loose ball.

So to a play-off in neutral Amsterdam, where fog in the first half and a blizzard in the second made it a long afternoon for everybody. The inevitable Madsen settled it when, four minutes before the interval, he trapped John Danielsen's centre with his knee and shot home. Denmark survived a deluge of high balls in the second half to progress to their first ever international tournament; Luxembourg wouldn't win another European Championship qualifier until June 1995.

———

Even England had ditched the selection committee pantomime by now, but Ireland were still clinging to it, and would do so until 1969. Johnny Carey was a figurehead manager, with the FAI picking the line-ups, so Ireland didn't stand a chance against Spain.

Before the first leg in Seville, another spanner was hurled into the works when Manchester United and Sunderland's FA Cup tie went to a second replay. United refused to release Noel Cantwell and Tony Dunne, and while Sunderland allowed Charlie Hurley to make the trip, the big man would be playing his third match in five days.

With Hurley having a nightmare and Amancio a stormer, Spain wiped the floor with Ireland in the rain at the Sánchez Pizjuán, scoring four times in a one-sided first half. 'Even the elements are with us,' said one of the Irish selectors before kick-off, displaying the prescience for which the FAI's name has long been a byword. After 12 minutes, Hurley hit a terrible pass intended for Tommy Traynor; Amancio intercepted it, ran through on the right and rolled his shot in off a post. Soon afterwards, Josep María Fusté made it 2-0 with a savagely struck 25-yarder as nobody closed him down.

A month or so after this match, Andy McEvoy finished the season as the second-highest scorer in the English top flight with Blackburn, behind only Jimmy Greaves, but was back in the League of Ireland before he was 30. Had he scored those goals 50 years later, he would have been a worldwide star and wealthier than Croesus. Here, he pulled one back from a narrow angle after brushing aside a challenge, but Spain simply went up another gear and struck again when Marcelino set up Amancio with a low cross.

Provider and poacher swapped roles for the fourth goal, which was forced in from close range.

With McEvoy's injury reducing Ireland to ten men, Spain toyed with them in the second half, settling for 5-1. Marcelino's shot nicked off the hapless Hurley, and though goalkeeper Alan Kelly got a hand to it, the ball squirmed in. The *Irish Times*'s man in Seville, Seamus Devlin, tried and failed to channel his inner W.B. Yeats by calling it 'one of the worst performances ever by any gaggle of wild geese from the Emerald Isle'.

Cantwell and Dunne were back for the second leg at Dalymount Park, far too late. In desperation, the FAI's wise monkeys now shoved Cantwell up front. The move had some logic to it, given that he was among the best headers of a ball in English football, and he should have had a penalty when Ferran Olivella took him down. But Spain's hogging of the ball meant that he got hardly any service. Kelly made a string of excellent saves, and Pedro Zaballa, playing superbly on the right, headed in Carlos Lapetra's cross for the first goal then scored from ten yards for the second. A dream debut for the Barcelona striker – who never played for Spain again.

Villalonga's rebuilding process, replacing the big names with hungry tyros who had something to prove, was gathering momentum. Suárez, the only superstar he trusted, was the squad's oldest player at 29. The positive effects of La Liga's ban on foreign imports were now starting to make themselves felt.

===

France had been beguiling but brittle in 1960, and the intervening years weren't kind. Raymond Kopa's artistry and Just Fontaine's finishing wouldn't cover up a multitude of sins this time: both men were gone, and what remained was fluttery but insubstantial.

Hungary were well placed to capitalise. Even without the highly rated teenager Ferenc Bene, who was injured, the line-up they fielded here would form the nucleus of their third great side, after the squad that reached the 1938 World Cup Final and the eternally celebrated *Aranycsapat* of the 1950s. Flórián Albert was a wonderfully gifted number ten (though he wore nine here), Lajos Tichy a prolific scorer with a mighty right foot, Sándor Matrai an unflappable sweeper.

In Paris, French fallibility was summed up by the sight of Néstor Combin cheaply giving the ball away in midfield to Ferenc Sipos. One simple pass to Lajos Tichy later, France were split down the middle. Tichy squared it to the unattended Albert, who belted it over the diving goalkeeper Pierre Bernard.

Within seconds of restarting, France again lost the ball unnecessarily, and you couldn't do such things against a team this good. Tichy gobbled it up, played a one-two with Albert and drilled the shot low into the corner.

France now finally began playing. Combin almost got one back with an acrobatic bicycle-kick early in the second half, and when Georges Lech's fierce drive came back off the bar, Lucien Cossou's follow-up header was saved on the line by Antal Szentmihályi. Hungary gritted their teeth and wrapped it up when Tichy fired home after Gyula Rákosi had pulled the ball back from the byline. Cossou glanced in a near-post header from Joseph Bonnel's corner, but the game and the tie were over by then.

A month later in Budapest, Hungary remained unruffled after Combin pounced to give France an early lead, and Sipos equalised with a 25-yard free kick that Bernard should have saved. The goalkeeper did slightly better on the winning goal, saving well in a scramble before Bene buried the loose ball. Once again, France had been too shaky at the back to get the better of the big boys, a recurring theme in their footballing history.

==

The USSR weren't European champions for nothing. From top to bottom, their team had no obvious weaknesses. There was substantial scoring power in the forward line; the lantern-jawed midfielder Valery Voronin had supernatural positional sense in midfield, thinking several passes ahead of everyone else; Albert Shesternyov was as good as any defender in Europe; and Yashin, of course, was in a class of his own.

In Stockholm, they swarmed all over a limited Swedish team, and Valentin Ivanov made the breakthrough with a fine shot – but the USSR wasted numerous opportunities, allowing Sweden's solitary top-class player to rescue a draw near the end. Six years earlier, in the 1958 World Cup quarter-final, the Fiorentina winger Kurt Hamrin had destroyed the Soviets, scoring one of Sweden's two goals and creating the other. Now he delivered the goods again with a clean finish past Yashin. This time, though, the reprieve was temporary.

A fortnight later in Moscow, the Swedes looked overawed in the presence of another huge crowd at the Lenina, who acclaimed Yashin as he was presented with the 1963 Ballon d'Or award on the pitch by Max Urbini, editor of *France Football*. Before long, the USSR went ahead with a simple goal. Viktor Ponedelnik ran through on the left, kept his cool and prodded the ball through the legs of the advancing Arne Arvidsson.

Now 27, Ponedelnik was still the Soviets' main threat, packing a powerful shot and blessed with superb close control. When Galimzyan Khusainov fed him 25 yards out, there seemed no immediate danger – until he simply looked up and planted a magnificent right-footed drive beyond Arvidsson.

Hamrin, an equally great attacker in a much weaker team, briefly gave Sweden hope with an effort that was a rerun of Ponedelnik's first, making Yashin look a little foolish in the process. But Voronin soon put the game and the tie to bed with another shot through Arvidsson's legs, after Ponedelnik's simple pass caught the Swedish defence square. As in 1960, the Soviets' blend of athleticism and talent looked a match for anyone.

'In terms of physical fitness, there was no team in the world which could compare with us,' said Ponedelnik. Urbini, enthralled by what he had seen, wrote, 'Perfect physical endurance, courage, determination, clarity of tactical thinking – these are the qualities that the hosts had over the guests. Thanks to the Russians [sic], we saw what we might call big football.'

7.30pm, 4 December 1963
Stade Municipal, Luxembourg
Attendance: 6,921
Referee: Pierre Schwinte (France)

LUXEMBOURG 3 (Pilot 1, H. Klein 23, 51)
DENMARK 3 (O. Madsen 9, 31, 46)

LUXEMBOURG: Nico Schmitt, Erny Brenner, Jean-Pierre 'Jim' Hoffstetter, François Konter, Fernand Brosius, Ady Schmit, Jean Klein, Paul May, Johny Leonard, Louis Pilot (c), Henri Klein. **Manager:** Robert Heinz.

DENMARK: Erik Lykke Sørensen, Kai Johansen, Jens Jørgen Hansen, Bent Hansen, John Madsen (c), Jens Petersen, Carl Bertelsen, Kjeld Thorst, Ole Madsen, Ole Sørensen, John Danielsen. **Manager:** Poul Petersen.

8pm, 10 December 1963
Idrætsparken, Copenhagen
Attendance: 36,294
Referee: Joseph Barbéran (France)

DENMARK 2 (O. Madsen 16, 70)
LUXEMBOURG 2 (Leonard 13, Schmit 84)

DENMARK: E.L. Sørensen, Johansen, J.J. Hansen, B. Hansen, J. Madsen (c), Petersen, Bertelsen, Danielsen, O. Madsen, O. Sørensen, Henning Enoksen.

LUXEMBOURG: Schmitt, Brenner, Hoffstetter, Konter (c), Brosius, Schmit, J. Klein, May, Leonard, Pilot, H. Klein.

PLAY-OFF

8.30pm, 18 December 1963
Olympisch Stadion, Amsterdam
Attendance: 5,700
Referee: Piet Roomer (Netherlands)

DENMARK 1 (O. Madsen 41)
LUXEMBOURG 0

DENMARK: E.L. Sørensen, Johansen, J.J. Hansen, B. Hansen, J. Madsen (c), Petersen, Bertelsen, Thorst, O. Madsen, Enoksen, Danielsen.

LUXEMBOURG: Schmitt, Brenner, Hoffstetter, Konter, Brosius, Schmit (c), J. Klein, May, Leonard, Pilot, H. Klein.

8.30pm, 10 March 1964
Estadio Ramón Sánchez Pizjuán, Seville
Attendance: 27,137
Referee: Lucien Van Nuffel (Belgium)

SPAIN 5 (Amancio 12, 29, Fusté 15, Marcelino 33, 89)
IRELAND 1 (McEvoy 22)

SPAIN: José Ángel Iribar, Feliciano Rivilla, Ferran Olivella (c), Isacio Calleja, Ignacio Zoco, Josep María Fusté, Amancio Amaro, Chus Pereda, Marcelino Martínez, Juan Manuel Villa, Carlos Lapetra. **Manager:** José Villalonga.

IRELAND: Alan Kelly, Theo Foley, Tommy Traynor, Ray Brady, Charlie Hurley (c), Mick Meagan, Johnny Giles, Andy McEvoy, Alfie Hale, Amby Fogarty, Joe Haverty. **Manager:** Johnny Carey and FAI selection committee.

3pm, 8 April 1964
Dalymount Park, Dublin
Attendance: 38,027
Referee: Gérard Versyp (Belgium)

IRELAND 0
SPAIN 2 (Zaballa 25, 88)

IRELAND: Kelly, Tony Dunne, Willie Browne, Brady, Hurley (c), Johnny Fullam, Giles, McEvoy, Noel Cantwell, Paddy Turner, Hale.

SPAIN: Iribar, Rivilla, Olivella (c), Calleja, Zoco, Fusté, Pedro Zaballa, Pereda, Marcelino, Villa, Lapetra.

3pm, 25 April 1964
Stade Olympique de Colombes, Paris
Attendance: 35,274
Referee: Cesare Jonni (Italy)

FRANCE 1 (Cossou 73)
HUNGARY 3 (Albert 15, Tichy 16, 70)

FRANCE: Pierre Bernard (c), Georges Casolari, Pierre Michelin, Marcel Artelesa, André Chorda, Joseph Bonnel, Lucien Muller, Georges Lech, Néstor Combin, Roby Herbin, Lucien Cossou. **Manager:** Henri Guérin.

HUNGARY: Antal Szentmihályi, Sándor Mátrai, Kálmán Mészöly, László Sárosi, István Nagy, Ferenc Sipos, János Göröcs, Gyula Rákosi, Lajos Tichy (c), Flórián Albert, Máté Fenyvesi. **Manager:** Lajos Baróti.

5.30pm, 23 May 1964
Népstadion, Budapest
Attendance: 70,120
Referee: Concetto Lo Bello (Italy)

HUNGARY 2 (Sipos 24, Bene 55)
FRANCE 1 (Combin 2)

HUNGARY: Szentmihályi, Mátrai, Mészöly, Sárosi, Nagy, Sipos, Károly Sándor (c), Rákosi, Tichy, Ferenc Bene, Fenyvesi.

FRANCE: Bernard (c), Casolari, Daniel Charles-Alfred, Artelesa, Chorda, Bonnel, Édouard Stako, Lech, Fleury Di Nallo, Combin, Ángel Rambert.

4pm, 13 May 1964
Råsunda Stadion, Solna
Attendance: 36,937
Referee: Jim Finney (England)

SWEDEN 1 (Hamrin 88)
USSR 1 (Ivanov 62)

SWEDEN: Arne Arvidsson, Hans Rosander, Lennart Wing, Orvar Bergmark (c), Åke Johansson, Hans Mild, Kurt Hamrin, Harry Bild, Agne Simonsson, Örjan Martinsson, Örjan Persson. **Manager:** Lennart Nyman.

USSR: Lev Yashin, Eduard Mudrik, Albert Shesternyov, Vladimir Glotov, Valery Voronin, Aleksei Korneev, Igor Chislenko, Valentin Ivanov (c), Eduard Malofeev, Gennady Gusarov, Valery Korolenkov. **Manager:** Konstantin Beskov.

7pm, 27 May 1964
Tsentralnyi Lenina Stadion, Moscow
Attendance: 99,609
Referee: Arthur Holland (England)

USSR 3 (Ponedelnik 32, 56, Voronin 83)
SWEDEN 1 (Hamrin 78)

USSR: Yashin, Mudrik, Shesternyov, Glotov, Voronin, Korneev, Chislenko, Ivanov (c), Viktor Ponedelnik, Gusarov, Galimzyan Khusainov.

SWEDEN: Arvidsson, Rosander, Wing, Bergmark (c), Mild, Anders Svensson, Hamrin, Bild, Simonsson, Martinsson, Persson.

SEMI-FINALS
Spain v Hungary
USSR v Denmark

Just as things got serious for Spain, their main man returned, bringing with him the best right foot in the world. Luis Suárez had been named European Footballer of the Year in 1960, and a year later Internazionale broke the world transfer record for him, paying £142,000 to Barcelona. Apart from his obvious gifts as a player, his slicked-back hair and deep-set eyes made him an immediately recognisable figure.

Like his Uruguayan namesake of 50 years later, Suárez could also be a nasty piece of work. Six weeks before this tournament, in the European Cup semi-final, he savagely kicked Borussia Dortmund's Dieter Kurrat in the groin, in full view of referee Branko Tešanić, yet stayed on the field. Not long afterwards, Tešanić was spotted sunning himself at an Adriatic resort, immediately confessed that his holiday was on Internazionale's tab, and was banned for life. Inter themselves remained in the competition and won the final 3-1 against Real Madrid in Vienna, with Suárez playing superbly. A tainted triumph in an era full of brown-suited shysters handing expensive wristwatches to referees in hotel rooms.

Against Hungary, Suárez excelled for half the match, and the Bernabéu crowd chanted his name for much of the evening, even though he had spent six seasons at Barcelona. Composed and ingenious, he was one of those players who seemed to make opponents instinctively back off as soon as he took possession. In its match report, Seville newspaper *ABC* admiringly called him a 'Toscanini del fútbol'. He was the only artist in a side of tradesmen: Juventus refused to allow left-winger Luis Del Sol to participate, deciding the Coppa Italia was more important, while Paco Gento had been frozen out after quarrelling with Villalonga.

Hungary, too, were without key men Gyula Rákosi (appendicitis), János Göröcs (ankle), and Károly Sándor (muscle strain). And after 35 minutes, Kálmán Mészöly gave Suárez too much space to get in a cross which another Hungarian defender nearly handled in the box. It dropped perfectly for Chus Pereda, who nodded it into the top corner as goalkeeper Szentmihályi stood still. But in the second half, Suárez took a knock and his influence waned. Hungary kept pressing for an equaliser in the 30°C heat; and with six minutes left, a bad mistake by José Angel Iribar threw them a lifeline.

The parallels between the goalkeeper and one of his successors, Luis Arconada, were striking. Both were natives of the Basque province of Gipuzkoa, both were agile and brave, and both had a regrettable tendency to make avoidable gaffes. A year after this match, against Ireland in Dublin, Iribar almost cost Spain qualification for the 1966 World Cup when he dropped a cross into his own net, his concentration broken by Noel Cantwell shouting at him.

His error here was less humiliating, but still one to forget. As he spilled István Nagy's shot, Bene beat him to the loose ball and shrugged off Olivella's lunge to force it over the line. Minutes later, Bene almost won it for Hungary, but this time Iribar came out well to save.

Hungary's stamina had been a talking point before the game, so Spain were probably dreading extra time: they doused themselves with bottles of water before the restart. But Szentmihályi's save from Amancio with his legs was the only other highlight until the winner arrived eight minutes from the end. Marcelino jumped unopposed to head Lapetra's corner downwards (most reports say it was Fusté, but it's number nine on the footage, not six), and as the ball hit the ground, Amancio stuck out his left foot to divert it past Szentmihályi. Hungary appealed for a flag, but there was another defender playing Amancio onside. Spain were in 'their' final, to the relief of Franco and his toadies.

'It was only from six yards out, but it still had great merit,' Amancio remarked years later. 'There have been better and more beautiful goals, but in the end it's the bottom line that counts. That semi-final was even more difficult than the final. Hungary were a great power back then. I've no idea why they declined so much. They had it all.'

The other semi-final, in Barcelona, wasn't a fair fight: half of Denmark's first-choice team had dropped out since beating Luxembourg. Goalkeeper Erik Lykke Sørensen and defender Kai Johansen turned professional with Greenock Morton in Scotland, breaching the DBU's amateurs-only rule; striker Harald Nielsen did the same with Bologna in Italy; wing-half Jens Petersen was sitting a commerce exam; and defender John Madsen dropped out for family reasons.

Beating Malta, Iceland and Luxembourg was inadequate preparation for facing a team like the USSR. Both sides were technically amateurs but, in truth, the battle-hardened Soviets were more professional than all but the very best club sides in western Europe.

Most of the Catalan crowd were vocally pro-Soviet, risky behaviour in Spain back then. Overrunning Denmark in midfield, the USSR had the match settled by half-time. Voronin scored the first, hitting a rising drive after a corner wasn't cleared properly. Then Ponedelnik took a pass by Igor Chislenko and beat debutant goalkeeper Leif Nielsen with a rasping shot.

Ivanov's late effort was easily the best, a stylish finish after jinking past three opponents. The well-behaved Danes committed hardly a single foul, not that resorting to strong-arm stuff would have got them anywhere.

Like an alarming number of other Soviet footballers from the 1960s and 1970s, several of this USSR team lived tragically short lives. Viktor Anichkin died from heart disease aged just 34, while liver cancer claimed the great Shesternyov at 53.

The story of Voronin, a multilingual bookworm and jazz fan, was the saddest of all. Never recovering psychologically from a car crash in the late 1960s which left him disfigured and ended his career, he sank into alcoholism and was only 44 when he was murdered in May 1984. 'When you finished playing, nobody needed you,' said Ponedelnik. 'You were thrown on to the street. Many of the top lads died. They started to drink. Clubs didn't reach out to them. Nobody helped them.'

8pm, 17 June 1964
Estadio Santiago Bernabéu, Madrid
Attendance: 75,000
Referee: Arthur Blavier (Belgium)

SPAIN 2 (Pereda 35, Amancio 112)
HUNGARY 1 (Bene 84)
After extra time

SPAIN: Iribar, Rivilla, Olivella (c), Calleja, Zoco, Fusté, Amancio, Pereda, Marcelino, Luis Suárez, Lapetra.

HUNGARY: Szentmihályi, Mátrai, Mészöly, Sárosi, Nagy, Sipos, Bene, Imre Komora, Albert, Tichy (c), Fenyvesi.

10.30pm, 17 June 1964
Camp Nou, Barcelona
Attendance: 38,556
Referee: Concetto Lo Bello (Italy)

USSR 3 (Voronin 19, Ponedelnik 40, Ivanov 87)
DENMARK 0

USSR: Yashin, Viktor Shustikov, Shesternyov, Mudrik, Voronin, Viktor Anichkin, Chislenko, Ivanov (c), Ponedelnik, Gusarov, Khusainov.

DENMARK: Leif Nielsen, J.J. Hansen, Kaj Hansen, B. Hansen, Birger Larsen, Erling Nielsen, Bertelsen, Sørensen, O. Madsen (c), Thorst, Danielsen.

THIRD-PLACE PLAY-OFF
Hungary v Denmark

The disappointed Hungarians took a long time to finish off this brave Denmark team before a tiny crowd at the vast Camp Nou. Manager Lajos Baróti picked five reserves, but Flórián Albert – so good in the two World Cups either side of this tournament – retained his place. He played a prominent part in the slick move that created Hungary's opening goal, with Bene applying the decisive touch.

Denmark survived several Hungarian near-misses (and a handball in their own box) before grabbing a surprise equaliser near the end. Kálmán Ihász failed to cut out Sørensen's pass, and a grateful Bertelsen knocked it past Szentmihályi. By extra time, though, the part-timers were weary. Birger Larsen took down Albert for a penalty which Dezső Novák converted, before making it 3-1 with a thumping free kick following another handball.

The Danes went home with dignity intact, but 20 years ticked by before they qualified for anything again. An even longer period of cold turkey awaited Hungary: for more than 50 years, this was their only win in the European Championship finals until they defeated Austria in Bordeaux in

2016. 'It was typical of the strength of our football in those days that the bronze medal was not met rapturously by domestic public opinion,' wrote Tamás Hegyi in *Nemzeti Sport* in 2013.

8pm, 20 June 1964
Camp Nou, Barcelona
Attendance: 3,869
Referee: Daniel Mellet (Switzerland)
HUNGARY 3 (Bene 11, Novák 107 pen, 110)
DENMARK 1 (Bertelsen 82)
After extra time
HUNGARY: Szentmihályi, Dezső Novák, Mészöly, Kálmán Ihász, Ernő Solymosi, Sipos (c), János Farkas, Zoltán Varga, Albert, Bene, Fenyvesi.
DENMARK: L. Nielsen, Bent Wolmar, K. Hansen, B. Hansen, Larsen, E Nielsen, Bertelsen, O. Sørensen, O. Madsen (c), Thorst, Danielsen.

FINAL
Spain v USSR

On the day before the final, at Spain's base in Berzosa del Lozoya in the hills outside Madrid, José Villalonga held a sandbox in his hands. Using it to construct a makeshift model of a pitch, he dotted it with pebbles (representing his own men) and pine cones (the Soviets). Stones, he reminded his players, were harder and stronger.

His coaching repertoire was full of simple but effective tricks like this, designed to trigger positive thoughts in players' minds. 'Villalonga was a great physical trainer,' said left-back Isacio Calleja. 'He wasn't an extraordinary strategist, he was simply fundamental. And he did it with a smile that won everybody over.'

Iribar recalled, 'Everything was much simpler than today. There were sessions and drills, like now, but not so much about tactics, opponents, studies, analysis. When we talked about other teams, there was no equipment to view their games. I remember we hadn't even seen the other semi-final. We only had some verbal information [on the USSR], but Villalonga had watched them play. There was more improvisation back then. The players had more freedom to confer on the pitch than today.'

The game was watched by the largest crowd in European Championship finals history (79,115). 'The atmosphere was extraordinary,' said Iribar. 'We knew we had a great responsibility. It was more than a football match. There were two ideologies face to face: communism versus a right-wing dictatorship. The Soviets were represented as real devils, red with horns, but we saw them on the pitch and of course they were quite normal men.'

Franco milked every last drop from the occasion, leading the 26-year-old future king Juan Carlos on to the Bernabéu pitch to wave to the great unwashed. Meanwhile, a delighted Yashin met his childhood hero Ricardo Zamora, Spain's legendary 1920s keeper, in the tunnel before kick-off.

The first ten minutes were enjoyably open, with Spain sweeping forward in their dark blue away jerseys (the USSR had won the toss to play in red and white). Suárez was at the eye of the storm from the start. Early on, he thumped a free kick just over the bar. Then his probing pass forced Yashin to come out smartly before Marcelino could score. And in the sixth minute, he robbed Ivanov on the right, danced past Eduard Mudrik, exchanged passes with Lapetra and sent over a dangerous cross. The normally rock-solid Shesternyov missed his header completely, and Pereda belted it in.

The USSR's equaliser, two minutes later, was equally slapdash. Anichkin's pass down the left gave the slim little Tatar winger Galimzyan Khusainov an opening to shoot, but he managed only a tame little toe-poke – which Iribar inexplicably allowed to bobble under his grasp. Another clanger to add to the one in Dublin.

No other European Championship final has ever got off to such a cracker of a start. But it was a false dawn. The rest of the first half was full of congested midfield play, misplaced final balls and continuous fouling. Yashin saved from Pereda and Iribar made a meal of spooning Chislenko's shot around the post, but that was all. In the meantime, referee Arthur Holland let Olivella away with two unpleasant challenges on Chislenko, who took revenge by punching his assailant in the kidneys.

Early in the second half, with rain pouring down, Holland made his worst decision of the evening, turning a blind eye to Zoco's foul on Chislenko in the box after the right-winger had beaten three Spaniards with a burst of pace. Incidents like this are why it's generally difficult to work up much enthusiasm for tournaments won by the hosts.

The consensus has it that Suárez's influence on the match waned sharply after Voronin kicked him (accidentally) just after the hour. It's true that he did little in the time remaining, but he had already begun dropping deep to escape Voronin's clutches. This freed Voronin himself to come forward, and he almost scored with a low shot which Iribar pushed behind.

It took a good goal to separate the two teams near the end. Like Spain's first, it originated on the right wing (a detail that Franco might have enjoyed if he had known anything about football). Pereda turned Anichkin inside out before crossing towards the penalty spot, Viktor Shustikov failed to clear, and Marcelino leaned back sharply to direct a great header just inside the near post. Yashin, for once, might have done better.

Few television cameras were present in the stadium, and the exact moment of Pereda's contribution accidentally went unrecorded by host broadcaster TVE. For newsreel purposes, it plugged the gap with a brief clip of Amancio putting the ball into the box, as if he, and not Pereda, had created the goal. The fiction was perpetuated for decades, but in 1992, Pereda finally got to see a BBC archive recording of the entire move from start to finish, whereupon he broke down weeping.

Olivella lifted the trophy while surrounded by photographers, hacks and local worthies, yet none of his team-mates could be seen. They were all standing some distance away, alongside the despondent Soviets. Then, as the USSR's players trudged towards the tunnel, vociferous jeering broke out in the stands. Perhaps it's best not to dwell on what might have happened had they, and not Spain, scored a late winner.

Upon returning to Moscow, manager Konstantin Beskov was fired after a personal scalding from Nikita Khrushchev, who screamed at him, 'You have disgraced the Red Banner! You have let down the honour of the Soviet state!' Beskov himself reflected in 2005, 'The loss to the Francoists in the presence of the dictator was, in the opinion of the country's leadership, not sporting but political. They couldn't forgive us for losing in front of him. They carpeted me, saying I wasn't up to the task. It was hard to endure all this.'

Spain's own relief was overwhelming. Iribar recalled, 'When we won, we were full of joy, we were so into it. Then a few days passed and we realised that if we'd lost, the situation would have been so different. It was a game we had to win at all costs, otherwise there would have been a hunt for culprits. Some players would never have been picked again. We would've gone from heroes to zeroes. Football is like that.'

The Spanish media made sure the punters got the message that this had been a triumph for Iberian strength, bravery and authoritarian politics. 'Never has there been displayed a greater popular enthusiasm for the state, born from the victory over communism,' gurgled one Madrid paper. A week later, TVE reran the entire match, though the viewership figures in Euskadi and Catalunya have sadly not survived for posterity.

But in terms of technical prowess and entertainment, 1964 had been an undeniable step down from its already ordinary predecessor. 'The standard of play was not particularly high,' wrote Roger Macdonald in *World Soccer*, 'and the Spanish team is only promising and far from being a major force in European football.' Suárez himself conceded decades later, 'We were a good team, but possibly not one of the best Spain has had. Other Spain sides I played in were much better than the 1964 one, yet never managed to achieve anything.'

The day after the match, the squad were received at the Royal Palace of El Pardo by Franco, for whom all this was manna from heaven. Before the dictator took his leave, José Villalonga laid it on thick: 'Because it has been a fair triumph, it is even more pleasant for us to offer the victory to His Excellency the Head of the State, who has been an exceptional witness of how these boys have fought for it.' He went on to link the win to Spain's football silver medal at the Olympics 44 years earlier.

'To date, we've always heard the epic story of Antwerp,' he said. 'I believe that what our boys have done now could set an example for the next 44 years.' But no golden age ensued, no decade or even half-decade of dominance. Villalonga himself was sacked two years later, after West Germany and Argentina dumped his team out of the World Cup at Villa Park. And Spain wouldn't win another international trophy for 44 years.

6.30pm, 21 June 1964
Estadio Santiago Bernabéu, Madrid
Attendance: 79,115
Referee: Arthur Holland (England)

SPAIN 2 (Pereda 6, Marcelino 84)
USSR 1 (Khusainov 8)

SPAIN: Iribar, Rivilla, Olivella (c), Calleja, Zoco, Fusté, Amancio, Pereda, Marcelino, Suárez, Lapetra.

USSR: Yashin, Shustikov, Shesternyov, Mudrik, Anichkin, Korneev, Voronin, Chislenko, Ponedelnik, Ivanov (c), Khusainov.

1968

THE MENTION of 1968 fills the mind's eye with images of a troubled world tottering on its axis: the Prague Spring, the Tet Offensive, the bloody demises of MLK and RFK, the beach under the Paris pavements, the first sparks of Northern Ireland's Troubles, black fists raised on the Olympic podium in Mexico City.

You could, were you so minded, draw facile parallels between the waves of global upheaval and the somewhat less momentous changes in the air at UEFA's headquarters in Bern. But if you did, you would be wasting your time: the governing body's big alterations to its continental showpiece were pencilled in long before 1968. Ten qualifying groups replaced the two-leg knockout ties in the early rounds, to placate member associations who wanted more fixtures. The finals themselves were rebranded from the European Nations' Cup to the equally snappy European Football Championship.

Yet again, West Germany failed to show up, this time against their will. When Helmut Schön stepped into Sepp Herberger's shoes in November 1964, he made clear his willingness to go where his predecessor had feared to tread. But West Germany's maiden campaign quickly veered off the autobahn.

It came down to winning away to Albania, whom the Germans had already routed 6-0. But Schön, deprived of several injured stars, overcompensated wildly by picking four strikers, two of whom – Hans Küppers of 1860 Munich and Peter Meyer of Borussia Mönchengladbach – were novices. Albania wasn't an ideal place to throw people in at the deep end. Going through customs at Tirana airport, Schön's players had to wash their hands in soapy water. 'For fear that we would pollute Albania with bacteria,' said Wolfgang Weber. Günter Netzer recalled, 'There were no cars at the stadium, only bicycles. We just didn't take Albania seriously.'

On the day, West Germany were frustrated by the Qemal Stafa's pockmarked pitch, which made passing football an impossibility (Hannes Löhr angrily called it 'a potato field'). A dismal 0-0 draw put them out, to widespread astonishment around Europe. Meyer complained afterwards that nobody had passed to him, to which playmaker Wolfgang Overath responded, 'I had no idea what Meyer would do if I did pass to him.'

Schön called it 'my worst day as a coach', and the tabloid *Bild* mounted an unsuccessful campaign to replace him with 1954 World Cup winner Max Merkel. To date, it's the only time that Germany – in any form – have failed to qualify for a major tournament: Germans refer to it as *Die Schmach von Tirana*, the shame of Tirana. In April 1968, when the tournament's quarter-finals were being played, most German newspapers gave it fourth billing behind the Bundesliga, the European Cup and the semi-professional Regionalliga West.

For the third European Championship in a row, Spain's campaign was marred by political trouble. As their players lined up in Prague in October 1967, the Czechoslovakian military band began playing the pro-republican Himno de Riego, instead of the Marcha Real, which Franco had restored as Spain's anthem after the Civil War. Cock-up or conspiracy? When the match finally got under way, Spain lost 1-0, though Franco demanded and got an official apology from the Czechoslovakian FA. But Czechoslovakia's subsequent home defeat by Ireland, thanks to a late winner from Turlough O'Connor, saw Spain top the group and face a quarter-final against the world champions.

For logistical reasons, Group 8 of the qualifiers doubled as the 1966/67 and 1967/68 British Home Championships. The local derby factor made England's passage to the last eight a bumpy one. Along the way, Alf Ramsey's team suffered one of the most memorable home defeats in their history, against the one opponent they dared not lose to.

Scotland's 3-2 win at Wembley on 15 April 1967 before a crowd of 99,063 occupies a special place in the Caledonian psyche, not so much for the actual performance, but for a moment in the second half which didn't produce a goal. After two languid back-heels by Jim McCalliog and Denis Law, the wayward playmaker Jim Baxter engaged in five keepy-uppies while sauntering down the left wing. Manager Bobby Brown berated him afterwards, but the juggling has survived longer in the collective Scottish memory than their three goals put together.

The result was achieved with only four of the Celtic players who lifted the European Cup in Lisbon weeks later, an indication of Scottish football's extraordinary strength in depth at the time. But when Scotland then lost 1-0 in Belfast, England mopped up the mess by winning 3-0 in Cardiff.

Their eventual rematch took place in Glasgow in February 1968. When a bystander in Prestwick Airport's arrivals hall cried out, 'Welcome to Scotland, Sir Alf!', in reply, Ramsey growled, 'You must be fucking joking.' Before an astonishing crowd at Hampden Park (134,461, still a European Championship record by a mile), Yogi Hughes's only international goal cancelled out Martin Peters's close-range finish. But, at the death, Hughes also missed from one yard out – so one of the most talented groups of footballers Scotland has ever produced wouldn't come to the party.

England's biggest threats seemed to be the USSR and Italy. The Soviets had scored freely in their group, and while Lev Yashin and most of the other heroes of 1960 were gone, good players like the brawny Georgian defender Murtaz Khurtsilava and the flame-haired striker Anatoliy Banishevskiy had replaced them. And some veterans – the cool-headed defender Albert Shesternyov, the clever midfielders Igor Chislenko and Valery Voronin – had stuck around.

Italy were still healing from the trauma of their most humiliating result. After North Korea sensationally knocked them out of the 1966 World Cup at Ayresome Park, the FIGC replaced Edmondo Fabbri with his chain-smoking assistant Ferruccio Valcareggi, whose mien of old-school decency veiled a sharp tactical brain.

Valcareggi's favoured gameplan was hard-boiled *catenaccio*, with a couple of stars entrusted to make the difference at the other end. Apart from Gigi Riva, Cagliari's lethal finisher, he could call upon Gianni Rivera and Sandro Mazzola, two of the best midfielders in the world. But this luxury came with a price. Rivera and Mazzola were footballing identical twins, unable to be accommodated in the same line-up.

Within two years, Valcareggi would be gripped by paralysis over them at the 1970 World Cup; they could not 'co-exist', he publicly lamented. Ultimately, he opted for the compromise of *la staffetta*, the relay, with one of them (generally Mazzola) starting the game and the other coming on later. This unwieldy arrangement led to Rivera, one of Italy's greatest ever footballers, getting just six minutes in the final against Brazil.

But for now, Valcareggi felt able to use both. His efforts to solve this puzzle were fascinating to behold, but his side's defensive steel would prove even more important to their chances of winning what turned out to be the grimmest European Championship ever staged.

QUARTER-FINALS
England v Spain
Bulgaria v Italy
France v Yugoslavia
Hungary v USSR

The 1966 World Cup, the crowning moment of English football, had also seen all Spain's weaknesses laid bare. José Villalonga duly paid the price, as did most of his team: Amancio Amaro and Ignacio Zoco were the last men left standing from 1964's European champions.

At Wembley, Spain showed little inclination to attack – hardly a surprise, given that Villalonga's successor Domènec Balmanya had coached Atlético Madrid to the 1965/66 Spanish title with a team built around a defence of bouncers. They sat back and frustrated England until the 84th minute, when they fell asleep at a free kick. Roger Hunt touched it short to Bobby Charlton, who sidestepped an onrushing defender and planted a low drive beyond Salvador Sadurní's right hand.

Spain were more ambitious in the Bernabéu five weeks later, but the return of the great Paco Gento wasn't enough. Centre-back Francisco Gallego got injured in a challenge with the fearsome Norman Hunter in the first half and had to struggle on for the entire match, effectively leaving Spain with ten men. Gallego did, however, have enough strength left to create a chance for Amancio on 48 minutes, which hit a defender's legs and looped over the helpless Peter Bonetti (the Spaniards call it 'the goal of the lame').

But England's physical superiority soon told. First, Martin Peters was left unmarked to head in Bobby Charlton's corner. Then Hunt pulled the ball back for Hunter to shoot, and again the ball went in off a defender, this time Juan Manuel Canós. Ramsey exuded smugness afterwards, saying, 'This [nine-match unbeaten run] must end some time, but where? And who is good enough to do it?' Poor Balmanya, meanwhile, was savaged in the Spanish press for his conservatism, then fired by the RFEF.

====

Few teams were more predictable than Bulgaria in the 1960s and 1970s: always good enough to qualify for a World Cup, never good enough to win a game once they got there. Their formidable home record spoke for itself, so the sight of them putting three past Italy in Sofia wasn't a shock. They opened the scoring when Nikola Kotkov, tripped in the act of shooting, got up to fire the penalty past Ricky Albertosi.

Italy were generally useless, not helped by losing Armando Picchi early on to a pelvic injury after he collided with Dimitar Yakimov. Valcareggi unwisely let the semi-delirious player go back on, whereupon he stood on the wing like a statue. But they equalised on the hour with some good luck. After Stancho Bonchev saved Gianni Rivera's shot, Dimitar Penev beat Pierino Prati to the rebound but knocked it into his own net.

Another rebound restored Bulgaria's lead, as Italy lost another player to a painful clash. When Albertosi rose to claim a corner, he and a Bulgarian smashed into each other, and the ball fell kindly for Dinko Dermendzhiev to score. The goalkeeper had to go off, and his replacement Lido Vieri almost immediately cost Italy a third goal under a cross before Tarcisio Burgnich saved the day.

Bulgaria soon went 3-1 up anyway, Petar Zhekov capitalising on Italian ball-watching to clip the ball over Vieri. But the debutant Prati pulled back an important goal late on when he was allowed ample time to shoot, with the Bulgarians stopping for an offside flag that never came. The 3-2 scoreline was a let-off for Italy, second best throughout despite the presence of both Rivera and Mazzola.

For the second leg in Naples, Valcareggi again picked both men, and Italy prevailed easily against tentative opponents. First, Prati raced in behind Aleksandar Shalamanov to score with an opportunistic diving header, with a horde of photographers sprinting on to the pitch to compete for the best shot of his celebration. Early in the second half, Angelo Domenghini's free kick flew in off the foot of a post, and Bulgaria gave up after that. Italy were named as tournament hosts a few days later.

———

France were expected to have it tough against Yugoslavia, even though the east Europeans had seen nearly half their team (Milutin Šoškić, Fahrudin Jusufi, Velibor Vasović, Vladica Kovačević and Milan Galić) move to western European clubs, ending their international careers at a stroke. In Marseille, their young replacements looked good, but it was France who went closest in the first half, when Fleury Di Nallo spectacularly hit the bar.

Yugoslavia's fabulous winger Dragan Džajić, switching between flanks, was clattered by Jean Baeza as he flew down the left midway through the second half. He dusted himself off, then swung a free kick to the back post, where Vahidin Musemić rose highest to head home. But with nine minutes remaining, Di Nallo rushed through a big gap in Yugoslavia's defence, lifting the ball over Ilija Pantelić for a cheeky equaliser. Relief for France, but they were dreading the away leg with good reason.

Louis Dugauguez's team were duly blown away in an exhilarating first half in Belgrade. Džajić again dazzled, to the extent that his marker, debutant Vincent Estève, never played for France again. Still only 21, Džajić was already established as one of the most brilliant attackers in the European game. A smitten Pelé described him as 'the Balkan miracle, a real wizard. I'm just sorry he's not Brazilian, because I've never seen such a natural footballer.'

After only three minutes, his sculpted cross from the left eluded Musemić, but young Ilija Petković dived headlong to force it home. Musemić then scored with a cross-shot that took a deflection on its way in. Džajić got the third himself, moving inside a defender to score with his underrated right foot.

Petković, having a more enjoyable international debut than poor Estève, dribbled past two defenders and the keeper for number four: the Yugoslavian TV commentator compared his 'slalom' to Jean-Claude Killy, who had just dominated the Winter Olympics in Chamrousse. Džajić wasn't finished yet, outpacing Jean Djorkaeff and crossing for Musemić to tap in. Di Nallo's goal at 4-0, rolled into the corner when clean through, was the emptiest of consolations. Rajko Mitić's new-look Yugoslavia suddenly looked like a team to be avoided.

====

The fourth quarter-final pairing was heavy with political resonance, in this of all years. When the USSR sank to a 2-0 defeat in Budapest, the locals weren't the only ones who enjoyed the scoreline.

The Soviets' craggy manager, Mikhail Yakushin, gambled untypically impulsively by picking the talented Torpedo Moscow striker Eduard Streltsov up front. Streltsov had already spent the peak years of his career in the gulag archipelago, after being forced to confess to a politically motivated rape allegation. Now, out of form and struggling to meet the demands of Yakushin's fitness regime, he told the coach, 'It's better not to pick me. I'll end up letting you down.' He hardly touched the ball, and this was his final cap.

Hungary owed both their goals to criminal errors by Soviet keeper Anzor Kavazashvili. Under no pressure, he fumbled János Farkas's tame shot into the net, then dived over Gyula Rákosi's low cross before János Göröcs slammed it into an open goal. Yuri Istomin hit the bar at 0-0 and Károly Fáter made a courageous save from Banishevskiy, but the USSR were otherwise dire.

Like Streltsov, Kavazashvili was dumped for the return leg. His replacement Yuri Pshenichnikov had little to do as the USSR turned everything around in Moscow. Banishevskiy created the opening goal by going around goalkeeper Gyula Támas and pulling the ball back into the goalmouth, where it went in off Ernő Solymosi's legs. Támas, unsighted, then allowed Murtaz Khurtsilava's chipped free kick to bounce in as two Soviets ran in front of him.

Hungary simply couldn't get the ball to Flórián Albert, who had been named European Footballer of the Year months earlier. And the USSR saved the best for last, Anatoliy Byshovets hammering in Gennady Yevryuzhikhin's slide-rule pass from a sharp angle. A sickener for Hungary, which would be dwarfed by what befell them in Irapuato 18 years later.

7.45pm, 3 April 1968
Wembley Stadium, London
Attendance: 95,000
Referee: Gilbert Droz (Switzerland)

ENGLAND 1 (B. Charlton 84)
SPAIN 0

ENGLAND: Gordon Banks, Cyril Knowles, Ray Wilson, Alan Mullery, Jack Charlton, Bobby Moore (c), Alan Ball, Roger Hunt, Mike Summerbee, Bobby Charlton, Martin Peters. **Manager:** Alf Ramsey.

SPAIN: Salvador Sadurní, Iñaki Sáez, Juan Manuel Canós, José Martínez 'Pirri', Francisco Gallego, Ignacio Zoco (c), Manuel Polinario 'Poli', Amancio Amaro, Fernando Ansola, Ramón Grosso, José Claramunt. **Manager:** Domènec Balmanya.

8.30pm, 8 May 1968
Estadio Santiago Bernabéu, Madrid
Attendance: 90,000
Referee: Josef Krnávek (Czechoslovakia)

SPAIN 1 (Amancio 48)
ENGLAND 2 (Peters 55, Hunter 81)

SPAIN: Sadurní, Sáez, Canós, Pirri, Gallego, Zoco, Joaquím Rifé, Amancio, Grosso, Manuel Velázquez, Paco Gento (c).

ENGLAND: Peter Bonetti, Keith Newton, Wilson, Mullery, Brian Labone, Moore (c), Ball, Peters, Hunt, B. Charlton, Hunter.

5pm, 6 April 1968
Stadion Vasil Levski, Sofia
Attendance: 68,000
Referee: Gerhard Schulenburg (West Germany)

BULGARIA 3 (Kotkov 12 pen, Dermendzhiev 66, Zhekov 73)
ITALY 2 (Penev 60 og, Prati 83)

BULGARIA: Stancho Bonchev, Aleksandar Shalamanov, Boris Gaganelov (c), Dimitar Penev, Dobromir Zhechev, Dimitar Yakimov, Georgi Popov, Petar Zhekov, Georgi Asparuhov, Nikola Kotkov, Dinko Dermendzhiev. **Manager:** Stefan Bozhkov.

ITALY: Enrico Albertosi (Lido Vieri 66), Tarcisio Burgnich, Giacinto Facchetti (c), Mario Bertini, Giancarlo Bercellino, Armando Picchi, Angelo Domenghini, Antonio Juliano, Sandro Mazzola, Gianni Rivera, Pierino Prati. **Manager:** Ferruccio Valcareggi.

4pm, 20 April 1968
Stadio San Paolo, Naples
Attendance: 95,000
Referee: Gottfried Dienst (Switzerland)

ITALY 2 (Prati 14, Domenghini 55)
BULGARIA 0

ITALY: Dino Zoff, Burgnich, Facchetti (c), Giorgio Ferrini, Aristide Guarneri, Ernesto Castano, Domenghini, Juliano, Mazzola, Rivera, Prati.

BULGARIA: Simeon Simeonov, Shalamanov, Ivan Dimitrov, Gaganelov (c), Penev, Zhechev, Popov, Hristo Bonev, Asparuhov, Yakimov, Dermendzhiev.

4pm, 6 April 1968
Stade Vélodrome, Marseille
Attendance: 35,423
Referee: Erwin Vetter (East Germany)

FRANCE 1 (Di Nallo 78)
YUGOSLAVIA 1 (Musemić 66)

FRANCE: Marcel Aubour, Jean Djorkaeff, Claude Quittet, Bernard Bosquier (c), Jean Baeza, Roby Herbin, Jacky Simon, Charly Loubet, Néstor Combin, Fleury Di Nallo, Georges Bereta. **Manager:** Louis Dugauguez.

YUGOSLAVIA: Ilija Pantelić, Mirsad Fazlagić (c), Dragan Holcer, Borivoje Đorđević, Blagoje Paunović, Ljubomir Mihajlović, Džemaludin Mušović, Ivica Osim, Vahidin Musemić, Dobrivoje Trivić, Dragan Džajić. **Manager:** Rajko Mitić.

4.30pm, 24 April 1968

Stadion Crvena Zvezda 'Marakana', Belgrade
Attendance: 47,747
Referee: Paul Schiller (Austria)

YUGOSLAVIA 5 (Petković 3, 33, Musemić 12, 80, Džajić 24)
FRANCE 1 (Di Nallo 34)

YUGOSLAVIA: Pantelić, Fazlagić (c), Holcer, Rudolf Belin, Mladen Ramljak, Mihajlović, Ilija Petković, Osim, Musemić, Trivić, Džajić.

FRANCE: Aubour, Djorkaeff, Quittet, Bosquier (c), Baeza, Yves Herbet, Vincent Estève, Robert Szczepaniak, Loubet, Di Nallo, André Guy.

5pm, 4 May 1968
Népstadion, Budapest
Attendance: 71,556
Referee: Laurens van Ravens (Netherlands)

HUNGARY 2 (Farkas 22, Göröcs 85)
USSR 0

HUNGARY: Károly Fáter, Dezső Novák, Kálmán Ihász, Kálmán Mészöly (c), Ernő Solymosi, Lajos Szücs, László Fazekas, János Göröcs, Zoltán Varga, János Farkas, Gyula Rákosi. **Manager:** Károly Sós.

USSR: Anzor Kavazashvili, Viktor Anichkin, Albert Shesternyov (c), Murtaz Khurtsilava, Yuri Istomin, Valery Voronin, Igor Chislenko, Volodymyr Kaplychnyi, Anatoliy Banishevskiy, Eduard Streltsov, Eduard Malofeev. **Manager:** Mikhail Yakushin.

7.30pm, 11 May 1968
Tsentralnyi Lenina Stadion, Moscow
Attendance: 91,129
Referee: Kurt Tschenscher (West Germany)

USSR 3 (Solymosi 22 og, Khurtsilava 59, Byshovets 72)
HUNGARY 0

USSR: Yuri Pshenichnikov, Valentin Afonin, Shesternyov (c), Khurtsilava, Anichkin, Voronin, Chislenko, Kaplychnyi, Banishevskiy, Anatoliy Byshovets, Gennady Yevryuzhikhin.

HUNGARY: Gyula Támas, Novák, Ihász, Mészöly, Solymosi, Szücs, Imre Komora, Varga, Flórián Albert (c), Farkas, Rákosi.

SEMI-FINALS
Italy v USSR
Yugoslavia v England

The first semi-final was always likely to be tight and taut. In an eventual seven competitive internationals against the USSR, Italy would score just once: a last-minute equaliser by Rivera in a Euro qualifier in 1963. The Soviets themselves managed just five goals in those seven matches.

Heavy rain sheeted down in Naples, making the prospect of sexy football remoter still. In the opening seconds, Rivera collided painfully with Valentin Afonin, and was effectively out of the match after that. And both sides made chances, but not many.

The Soviets might have had a soft penalty when the ball bounced up on to Antonio Juliano's hand; Prati's fine shot cleared the angle of post and bar; and Shesternyov's even better effort drew a good save from Dino Zoff. The goalkeeper – winning only his second cap – was visibly nervous before the match, prompting his opposite number to approach him. 'I gave him a pat on the back and told him, "Don't worry. Everything will be fine",' recalled Pshenichnikov.

Early in the second half, Byshovets left Giacinto Facchetti for dead (no mean feat), only to see Banishevskiy side-foot his low centre across the face of the goal. And though Mazzola should have had a penalty when Volodymyr Kaplychnyi barged him over, the USSR looked the better side over the 90 minutes. Near the end, Aleksandr Lenyov brought a good save from Zoff at his near post.

Both teams were tiring in the downpour, but only one had home advantage. 'The crowd were extraordinary,' said Zoff, 'and it gave us a massive boost in terms of confidence. Their support kept us going in a big way. Every time the Soviets got the ball, they jeered.'

Extra time brought another headache for Valcareggi: defender Giancarlo Bercellino's knee gave way, reducing Italy to nine fit men. After a long period on the back foot, Italy shook themselves like a big dog and rumbled forward. Pshenichnikov clutched Facchetti's header under the bar, before beating away Prati's angled shot; and with two minutes left, Domenghini unleashed a right-foot rocket which clipped the inside of the post.

Finally, referee Kurt Tschenscher called time. Like substitutions, penalty shoot-outs weren't yet with us, so everything now rested on the dimensions of a one-lira coin. The captains, Facchetti and Shesternyov, went to Tschenscher's dressing room, along with Lenyov ('I've no idea how I ended up in there'), manager Yakushin ('I did everything I could to get into that room') and UEFA observer Agustín Pujol.

The Italians were led by a lucky general. Mazzola said, 'We were not relaxed, but confident. Because we considered [Facchetti] a lucky person.' Tschenscher asked, 'Heads or tails?' Shesternyov, who didn't understand English, stayed silent. Facchetti, who did, said, 'Tails.' Sixty-eight thousand Neapolitans, waiting in the stands with hearts in mouths, let out a colossal roar when they saw him emerge from the tunnel with his arms raised. What might have happened from a crowd control perspective if the coin had landed the other way up?

And so, after playing a combined 26 hours of football, Italy marched on and the USSR went home because a small piece of metal landed one way up rather than the other. 'We were very down,' said Pshenichnikov. 'If it had been penalties, at least we could've done something.' Not Italy's problem, but still a ludicrous and unsatisfying way to settle a semi-final.

'Once, we used to find footballers by whistling at the top of coal mines. The Slavs, it seems, entice them out of the mountains,' Geoffrey Green of *The Times* wrote from his Florentine perch before the second semi-final between England and Yugoslavia. 'Looking into the mirror of the Arno river, as it flows treacherously by, I see only a desperate struggle ahead for [Bobby] Moore and his men.'

Despite its setting, there was nothing ornate or cultured about this encounter, which made the Italy-USSR game look like a sparkling kaleidoscope of footballing delights. It was the first really nasty European Championship match, between two aggressive teams who detested each other on sight. No one ever calls it the Battle of Florence, but they should. Referee José María Ortíz de Mendíbil awarded 49 free kicks, yet never seemed in control.

Afterwards, Dobrivoje Trivić would be cast as the villain of the piece by the English press. The defender certainly acted unpleasantly all night. Alf Ramsey claimed afterwards that he kicked Bobby Charlton and Alan Mullery in the first two minutes; he may well have done so, but it's not apparent on the footage.

But some other things did get captured on film. In the fifth minute, Norman Hunter viciously stamped on Ivica Osim's leg, leaving him a passenger for the rest of the game. 'He dragged himself through the match,'

Džajić recalled. 'He stayed near the sideline. It was as if we had ten men.' Osim himself diplomatically reflected in 2012, 'The calmness of the way [England] played was the most impressive thing about them. They were fully focused on their plan, and that was something we didn't have. For them everything happens with the head, everything else is not so important.' Up to a point!

Soon afterwards, Trivić himself was clattered painfully from behind by Mullery, who had already chopped Džajić. By today's rules, Mullery would have been sent off a lot earlier but, this being 1968, had to wait a while longer.

For long stretches of the game, what sounded like an air-raid siren but was probably a police car could clearly be heard from outside the Stadio Comunale, providing an apposite soundtrack to this orgy of true crime. Off camera, with the ball miles away, Petković was scythed down by an Englishman and required lengthy treatment. And the hits kept on coming: Ray Wilson on Musemić, Mirsad Fazlagić on Alan Ball, Ball on Milan Damjanović, Peters on Trivić. After Miroslav Pavlović hit Brian Labone with another bad challenge, Trivić ran to get involved, whereupon the exasperated Ortiz de Mendíbil physically shoved him away.

More than half an hour passed before a chance was created, and Ball booted it over the bar. Just before the break, Charlton did the same with a speculative volley. But after half-time, some actual football broke out. Osim – who could hardly even walk – managed to scoop a pass through to Džajić, and the winger's low drive passed dangerously across the face of Gordon Banks's goal. A minute later, Džajić charged into the box before crumpling under Keith Newton's challenge. It had the whiff of a penalty, but the referee waved play on.

In the second half, England created nothing while continuing to misbehave. Labone clobbered Džajić, and Trivić was flattened by the saintly Moore. All these heavy English challenges made a mockery of Mullery's claim years later that 'every Yugoslavian player that day spent the whole game kicking us': the match recording strongly suggests that England were less sinned against than sinning. Still, there was always Trivić. His umpteenth foul, again on Ball, ignited a shoving match which saw a linesman run on to the field to break it up.

Yugoslavia continued to look the better team, and with two minutes left, Džajić grabbed what little glory there was. On the left, our old friend Trivić curled a long cross towards the English goalmouth. With Moore caught in two minds – head it away, or let Banks come out for it? – Džajić nipped in behind him, chested it down and lifted it over the keeper from close range.

'I could have handled it, but that's not my way,' Moore said, perhaps stuck for excuses.

With the game winding down, Trivić sneakily kicked Mullery yet again, drawing blood from his calf. Maddened by the pain, Mullery took instant revenge. 'I turned around and kicked him in the how's your fathers,' he said years later, though it looks more like a hack at Trivić's legs on the footage. Ortíz de Mendíbil sent him off: the first England player to meet such a fate, in their 424th international. It was also the first expulsion in a European Championship finals game.

Ramsey sympathised with Mullery afterwards, 'He came in, looked at me with a stern face and said, "I'm glad somebody retaliated against those bastards." He even paid the £50 that I got fined by the FA.' Instead, the manager saved his spleen for Ortiz de Mendíbil and the Yugoslavs. But it was hard to see this one as a miscarriage of justice. The majority of the bad tackles were English, and Banks was the busier of two underworked goalkeepers.

'If you pick a player of Hunter's disposition, who fells Osim in the opening minutes and renders him ineffective for the rest of the match, you lose your right to strike the moral attitudes adopted by Alf Ramsey after the game,' wrote Brian Glanville in *World Soccer*. In *The Times*, Green was equally unimpressed: 'The only difference between the warring parties was that the English tackling was more open to view; the Slavs applied with a subtle concealment which was just as damaging.'

In a UEFA documentary more than 40 years later, Yugoslav defender Blagoje Paunović accused England of arrogance. Bobby Charlton retorted, 'I can't accept that. We were confident, yes. Not arrogant.' But while England could still call themselves world champions for two more years, this result showed what happened when they didn't play all their games at home.

6pm, 5 June 1968
Stadio San Paolo, Naples
Attendance: 68,582
Referee: Kurt Tschenscher (West Germany)

ITALY 0
USSR 0
Italy won on a coin toss after extra time

ITALY: Zoff, Burgnich, Facchetti (c), Ferrini, Bercellino, Castano, Domenghini, Juliano, Mazzola, Rivera, Prati.

USSR: Pshenichnikov, Afonin, Shesternyov (c), Aleksandr Lenyov, Gennady Logofet, Istomin, Malofeev, Kaplychnyi, Banishevskiy, Byshovets, Yevryuzhikhin.

9.15pm, 5 June 1968
Stadio Comunale, Florence
Attendance: 21,834
Referee: José María Ortíz de Mendíbil (Spain)

YUGOSLAVIA 1 (Džajić 86)
ENGLAND 0

YUGOSLAVIA: Pantelić, Fazlagić (c), Holcer, Milan Damjanović, Trivić, Paunović, Petković, Osim, Miroslav Pavlović, Musemić, Džajić.

ENGLAND: Banks, Newton, Wilson, Mullery, Labone, Moore (c), Ball, Peters, Hunt, B. Charlton, Hunter.

Sent off: Mullery (90).

THIRD-PLACE PLAY-OFF
England v USSR

Nobby Stiles was fit at last (as was Geoff Hurst), but his velvety skills were wasted on a fixture that lacked competitive white heat. The crowd at Rome's Stadio Olimpico were only there for the final, which took place immediately afterwards. Eduard Malofeev headed straight at Banks in the opening minutes, but after that, it was mostly England: Pshenichnikov showed good reactions to save at close range from Charlton, and Roger Hunt smacked a fine chance over the bar.

Both of England's goals were made in the East End. For the first, Moore sortied upfield, Peters crossed from the left, and Hurst held it up before Charlton arrived to smash it past Pshenichnikov. The second one had West Ham stamped all over it too. Gennady Logofet dallied in midfield and was robbed by Peters, who tried his luck from the edge of the box. The weak effort ran kindly for Hurst, who almost lost the ball to the brave Pshenichnikov but managed to stab it in.

Ramsey, wrote one Fleet Street critic, 'mistrusts skill unless it comes dripping in sweat'. England had brought little except aggression to an already stony tournament, but third place was impressive for a first attempt. It was also as good as they would manage in any European Championship to date. In fact, this result is the only time they have won a knockout game in the finals without needing penalties – if a third-place play-off can be described as such.

6.45pm, 8 June 1968
Stadio Olimpico, Rome
Attendance: 68,817
Referee: István Zsolt (Hungary)

ENGLAND 2 (B. Charlton 39, Hurst 63)
USSR 0

ENGLAND: Banks, Tommy Wright, Wilson, Nobby Stiles, Labone, Moore (c), Peters, Hunter, Hurst, B. Charlton, Hunt.

USSR: Pshenichnikov, Afonin, Shesternyov (c), Lenyov, Logofet, Istomin, Malofeev, Kaplychnyi, Banishevskiy, Byshovets, Evryuzhikin.

FINAL
Italy v Yugoslavia

A terrible tournament got a passable final, which wasn't enough to save it. Yugoslavia toned down the physicality, and Italy were more daring than against the USSR – but these were two cautious teams and positive play was never on the cards. Italy badly missed the recuperating Rivera – and Mazzola, whom Valcareggi surprisingly rested.

Yugoslavia's line-up had an average age of 23, the youngest in any European Championship final. In the Roman lion's den, they bared their teeth more than once. Paunović, Jovan Aćimović and the dreaded Trivić left marks on Prati, Domenghini and Antonio Juliano respectively in the opening stages.

Yugoslavian goalkeeper Ilija Pantelić looked riddled with tension from the start. When Giorgio Ferrini's optimistic long shot bobbled in front of him, he spilled it and was grateful to see a defender hack clear. Later, under pressure from Lodetti, he dropped a cross before recovering to make a point-blank save from Facchetti.

Prati then broke through on the left before wellying a shot high and wide. Hardly champagne football, but there was more to enjoy in the first 15 minutes than in the entirety of Yugoslavia-England.

It was reported in later years that referee Gottfried Dienst was nobbled for this showpiece occasion by Italo Allodi, the crooked Internazionale general manager who enjoyed a lucrative sideline as a match-fixer. The allegations centre on an incident early on, when Ferrini appeared to flatten Musemić in the box and Dienst waved play on. 'The referee was for Italy,' Džajić claimed years later. 'It showed throughout the match. And I'm not alone in this opinion. Even today, I don't understand how a final could unfold that way. It still hurts to talk about it.'

Italy drew encouragement from Pantelić's apparent terror of high balls. When he completely missed another cross, the ball landed on the thigh of Domenghini, who was off balance and could only force it wide as the net yawned. But now Yugoslavia, who had offered nothing, suddenly went ahead with a strange goal. Trivić, taking a brief break from injuring people, ran down the right and crossed to Džajić. Though the winger's first touch was poor, his second saw the ball bounce gently into the net.

While the second half was played at a fast pace by 1968's standards, Italy made little headway and looked vulnerable to Džajić's trickery on the break. With 50 minutes gone, he slipped away from a defender and stabbed an angled shot which Zoff clutched at the near post. At the other end, when Juliano headed down Lodetti's corner, the ball got stuck under the feet of Anastasi before Fazlagić thumped it away.

Even though there was still a lot of the game left, Italy's attacks already smelled of well-founded panic. When the irrepressible Džajić left Facchetti in his wake, Zoff pushed away his low cross – but only to Musemić. The sight of an empty goal seemed to unnerve the striker, who absently passed it to Ernesto Castano instead of burying it. Hindsight allows us to note that in this moment, Yugoslavia lost the cup and Italy won it.

Still, it was looking good for Mitić's team until, with ten minutes left, Paunović flattened Lodetti on the edge of the D. Angelo Domenghini's powerful right foot saved his country, rifling the free kick through the wall and past the stationary Pantelić. The Yugoslavians complained that Dienst had allowed it to be taken while he was still overseeing the retreat of their wall; the footage doesn't confirm it either way.

Extra time began with Milan Damjanović inflicting an outrageous foul on Domenghini, yet another example of how the Yugoslavs' talent was tinged with a streak of real nastiness. And hardly anything happened after that. 'To be honest, we didn't deserve to draw,' admitted Zoff years later. Now came the first (and last?) replay in the history of the finals.

It was Monday evening in the Eternal City, and fewer than half of the original crowd came back for seconds. But two hard games had sapped the energy from Yugoslavia's youngsters, as well as ruling out two of their best players: Petković, developing an ulcer before kick-off, joined Osim on the sidelines. Mitić, aware his reserves weren't good enough, didn't have the strength in depth to make any other changes.

Italy were playing poker with a stronger hand, and plugged their gaps with quality replacements. The unsung Juventus centre-back Sandro Salvadore replaced Ferrini; Roberto Rosato and the inventive Picchio De Sisti strengthened the midfield; and Mazzola was at last picked. Most crucially of all, Valcareggi's lethal weapon was back from a long absence with a broken leg.

Nicknamed *Rombo di Tuono*, the Thunderclap, Gigi Riva was the deadliest finisher Italian football has ever produced: some accolade. His 35 goals for the national team remain a record to this day, a staggering achievement after so many years – but at this stage of his career, aged 23, he only had six. His greatest moments still lay ahead of him. Starting here.

In the 12th minute, Riva pounced on a loose ball to hit a low left-footer which Pantelić pushed around the post. Yugoslavia cleared the corner unconvincingly, and when Domenghini's shot bobbled through to bounce against Riva's legs, he stayed cool to score on the turn with that priceless left foot as the Yugoslavs forlornly appealed for offside.

Yugoslavia's best chance now came and went. Again Musemić was the guilty man. After Rosato stupidly fouled the balding Idriz Hošić near the corner flag, Džajić curled a nasty inswinger into the goalmouth for Musemić to head wastefully wide. The bounce of the ball made it a harder chance than it looked, but he still should have scored.

With Mazzola and Domenghini getting the room Italy hadn't enjoyed in the first game, a second goal now arrived. Domenghini, in a meadow of open space, fed De Sisti, who in turn picked out Anastasi. Flipping the ball up with his right instep, the youngster used the same foot to send a terrific volley hurtling into the corner, a goal fit to win any major tournament.

Yugoslavia's tired legs and young minds found that throwing men forward simply handed Italy's clever midfielders gaps to exploit. 'Our morale was at zero,' Džajić reflected. 'We were devastated after the first final. We'd had the title there in our hands, and it escaped from us.' Džajić himself looked shattered, allowing Burgnich to sleepwalk through the evening. Meanwhile, the incomparable Giacinto Facchetti strutted up the left flank and played as a winger for the rest of the match.

Fireworks and flares lit up the Roman night sky as the teams walked off at half-time. And only some untypically bad finishing by Riva saved Yugoslavia from an embarrassment. He headed wide from six yards, even worse than Musemić's miss, and later had a point-blank shot blocked after poor Pantelić couldn't catch Mazzola's cross; Anastasi banged in the rebound, but both he and Riva were offside. The goalkeeper later dropped yet another Mazzola ball, only for Riva to blaze over an open goal.

By the end, the Stadio Olimpico was a fiery panorama of *tricolori* and flaming torches. Skipper Facchetti, holding the trophy, was chaired around the pitch by delirious fans before security personnel escorted him to safety. 'It was a marvellous night,' Riva reminisced. 'The morning after, I found myself at Fiumicino Airport, with no idea how I got there.'

But if you weren't Italian, 1968 was impossible to look back on with fondness, and not just because a host team had come out on top again. Not only had the competition been desperately boring overall, it was by far the filthiest of the three European Championships so far.

Džajić was clearly a star – and, crucially, knew how to look after himself – but he had shone only in small doses. Still, that was more than anyone else managed in this rotten competition. David Miller of *World Soccer*, criticising both Italy and England, wrote, 'If it now requires eight or nine defenders to win championships, they are not worth winning.' Leslie Vernon, in the same publication, went further: 'These goalless, clueless football "marathons" were nothing more than a nightmare of destruction, anti-propaganda, for the countless millions suffering in front of their television sets all over Europe.'

The only real redeeming feature of 1968 was that at least world-class players like Mazzola, Facchetti, Rivera and Riva had something to show for their long international careers, though it was purely symbolic in Rivera's case. The 20-year-old Anastasi became the youngest player to win the competition (a record not broken until 2016, by Portugal's Renato Sanches). The attendances, too, were magnificent: 59,847 per game, still a record.

And yet, a decade since the very first ball was kicked, we still hadn't seen a memorable tournament. The European Nations' Cup had put down strong roots in the football calendar by now, but it was crying out for something transcendent to elevate it to greatness.

9.15pm, 8 June 1968
Stadio Olimpico, Rome
Attendance: 68,817
Referee: Gottfried Dienst (Switzerland)

ITALY 1 (Domenghini 80)
YUGOSLAVIA 1 (Džajić 39)
After extra time

ITALY: Zoff, Burgnich, Facchetti (c), Ferrini, Guarneri, Castano, Giovanni Lodetti, Domenghini, Pietro Anastasi, Juliano, Prati.

YUGOSLAVIA: Pantelić, Fazlagić (c), Holcer, Damjanović, Paunović, Petković, Jovan Aćimović, Pavlović, Musemić, Trivić, Džajić.

REPLAY

9.15pm, 10 June 1968
Stadio Olimpico, Rome
Attendance: 32,866
Referee: José María Ortíz de Mendíbil (Spain)

ITALY 2 (Riva 13, Anastasi 31)
YUGOSLAVIA 0

ITALY: Zoff, Burgnich, Facchetti (c), Sandro Salvadore, Guarneri, Roberto Rosato, Giancarlo 'Picchio' De Sisti, Domenghini, Anastasi, Luigi 'Gigi' Riva, Mazzola.

YUGOSLAVIA: Pantelić, Fazlagić (c), Holcer, Damjanović, Paunović, Idriz Hošić, Aćimović, Pavlović, Musemić, Trivić, Džajić.

1972

COLOUR WAS the enduring theme of Euro 72, and not just because of the effervescence of its winners. Yellow and red cards were introduced for the first time, and it was the first European Championship to be televised at least partly in colour. There were even some yellow-and-black Telstar balls bouncing around in the final stages. Substitutions, too, were introduced: two per team per game.

Having shaken off their shame of Tirana, West Germany were the team to beat. They laid down a marker by beating Poland 3-1 in Warsaw, in front of a crowd swelled by the presence of 50,000 citizens of the GDR, giving it the feel of a home qualifier for them.

Helmut Schön had so many great players to pick from that his reserve XI would have made the quarter-finals with ease. Franz Beckenbauer's transition from midfielder to attacking libero was complete; Gerd Müller, the world's best striker, seemed uncontainable; Sepp Maier, Berti Vogts, Jürgen Grabowski and Sigi Held were all still around. And there were two intriguing young newcomers from Bayern Munich, left-back Paul Breitner and attacker Uli Hoeneß. Both were just 20, but looked and played like men far older.

The big question was whether Schön would name Günter Netzer or Wolfgang Overath as his playmaker. He initially compromised by picking both, but the combination never gelled. The matter was settled when Overath had groin surgery in early 1972, clearing the decks for one of world football's most magnetic personalities to take centre stage.

It feels trite to call the lustrous-haired Netzer one of football's first rock stars, but that was exactly what he was. 'I really was a bit spoiled,' he mused years later. 'Many things had come too easily to me. My self-confidence was astonishingly great.' After amassing a collection of Ferraris, he opened Lovers' Lane, a nightclub which became a hangout for Mönchengladbach's beautiful people. Even the septuagenarian Sepp Herberger dropped in one evening.

Hennes Weisweiler, Netzer's coach at Borussia Mönchengladbach, growled, 'He's gone completely mad.'

Netzer claimed he opened the nightclub due to 'financial necessity' rather than sybaritic habits. 'I said to Weisweiler, "Give me the opportunity to earn my own money,"' he recalled. 'And so I found myself, for instance, managing the club's newspaper. I had a playboy image: the long hair, the sports cars. This image was completely false. But it never bothered me. I was amused by all the fuss. Those Ferraris meant nothing, I just wanted a nice car.'

West Germany's quarter-final opponents would be the team they had dumped out of the World Cup in León two years earlier. England's qualifying group hadn't been testing, but neither the omens nor the form book looked good. Of the two golden Bobbys, Charlton was gone and Moore was showing his age.

Dutch clubs were dominating the European Cup after decades of irrelevance, but the Netherlands couldn't convert Feyenoord's and Ajax's triumphs into good international form for now. Their Yugoslavian conquerors would face the USSR, who'd qualified by grinding out a goalless draw in Seville.

Belgium and Italy would face each other in a forbidding test of mutual steeliness. The Belgians' rugged defence was topped off by Wilfried Van Moer's midfield skills and the lethal forward Paul Van Himst. But they started as underdogs against the holders, a formidable outfit who had reached the final of that World Cup in Mexico City (where, admittedly, Brazil obliterated them). Ferruccio Valcareggi's praetorian guard were fancied to prevail, but either way it would be tight.

In all regards, 1972 proved to be a huge turning point for the European Championship. Had the competition served up another moribund edition, it might never have recovered. Instead, it now strode out of the darkness and into the light, led by a Westphalian nightclub impresario with fabulous hair.

QUARTER-FINALS
England v West Germany
Italy v Belgium
Hungary v Romania
Yugoslavia v USSR

Extraordinarily given the eventual outcome, West Germany's preparation for their match of matches at Wembley was shrouded in gloom. 'Leave the fear at home!' begged a headline in *Kicker* magazine's preview. 'If we don't lose by five, we'll have achieved a good result,' Netzer said to Beckenbauer, half-joking, during the flight to London. Beckenbauer laughed off the comment.

But he and Bayern Munich, who supplied the core of the team, were in disarray after bad defeats by Köln (5-1), Duisburg (3-0) and Rangers (2-0).

Helmut Schön was without some familiar faces. Wolfgang Overath and Berti Vogts were injured, the Schalke 04 match-fixing scandal ended the international careers of Reinhard Libuda and Klaus Fichtel, and fitness issues ruled out the veteran Karl-Heinz Schnellinger. In came Breitner (20), Hoeneß (20) and Georg Schwarzenbeck (22), all from beleaguered Bayern.

On the morning of the match, goalkeeper Sepp Maier awoke with an inflamed elbow, and understudy Wolfgang Kleff was put on standby. Maier would play, but his ailment was kept secret (even from Schön) until after the game. The manager himself was green around the gills from a stomach bug.

And green was the colour as West Germany walked out at a packed Wembley in their Ireland-like change strip. It was a rainy Saturday evening, but Netzer later described the conditions as 'perfect … these unique lawns [were] like a pool table, with an incredible atmosphere. The ground was perfectly smooth. It had just rained, it was perfect for our technique.'

English nostrils flared early on. Paul Madeley crunched Netzer from behind, and Alan Ball stood on him as he tried to get to his feet. Shortly afterwards, Francis Lee spitefully tried to kick Herbert Wimmer as they tussled near the touchline. But roughing up these Germans was never going to be enough.

The usual home-and-away dynamics were swiftly inverted as England massed nearly their entire team in their own half and West Germany streamed forward. With nobody getting tight on Netzer – a tactic almost unheard of in 1972 – it was all too easy for Schön's team. The opening goal wasn't long in coming. Moore tried to dribble past two opponents in his own box but gave the ball away, and Müller cushioned it to Grabowski, who laid it off to Hoeneß. The shot was weak, but its dipping trajectory made a fool of Banks, who seemed to slip as it drifted between him and his right-hand post.

Soon, another bout of German inter-passing forced Moore to deflect Netzer's shot behind for a corner. As the English centre-halves stood around like the showroom dummies Kraftwerk would later sing about, Wimmer's glancing header forced Banks into a good save.

Though Emlyn Hughes's volley clipped the bar in the second half, West Germany stayed in command – and England's equaliser felt unearned when it came. Beckenbauer's lazy ball was intercepted by Bell, who exchanged passes with Madeley and hit a strong shot which Maier couldn't hold. Lee followed up to tap in from almost under the bar.

Although 1-1 would still have been a great result for West Germany, they now promptly broke England over their knee. With five minutes to go, Held streaked up the left. Moore made sure to trip him outside the box – but referee Robert Héliès, well behind the play, gave a penalty. Although Banks got both hands to Nezter's kick, it squeezed over the line via the post.

West Germany's masterfully economical third goal epitomised the chasm between the teams. Held robbed the hapless Hughes and found Hoeneß, who beat two men and played a lovely reverse pass for Müller to rattle a shot on the turn inside the post. Müller would later win the 1974 World Cup Final with a very similar effort.

The sight of England having their eye wiped at Wembley by foreign interlopers would become a familiar one in later years. But in 1972, an experience like this was nothing short of an acid bath for English football. Other than the Hungarian humiliation of 1953, long enough ago to be dismissed as an aberration, teams simply did not walk all over England in their own backyard. The match had been close in some respects – the outcome wasn't settled until the final minutes, and England never gave up – but exhibition-like in others.

In truth, Alf Ramsey had signed his team's death warrant by letting Netzer have the freedom of Wembley. Ulfert Schröder, the German sportswriter, noted, 'There has hardly been a Bundesliga game in which Netzer has had as much leeway as he enjoyed here.' Today, the German footballing public regard it as the greatest match ever played by any of their national sides, to the point of calling the line-up *Der Wembley-Elf.*

An awestruck *L'Équipe* described the German performance as 'football from the year 2000', while *Gazzetta dello Sport* called it 'picture-book football that shocked the English'. At home, *Bild* went for 'Ramba-Zamba Fußball', fairground football. In England, the headlines were bleak: 'Oh, what a black day for England' (*Sunday Express*); 'Funeral in Berlin is all we can expect' (*Sunday People*). But Ian Wooldridge of the *Daily Mail* noted, 'These 11 German players have buried more hatchets in 90 minutes than all the diplomats in the last 27 years … this was a German team to make a nonsense of the pulp magazine conception of the German character, and to make a few million adults realise that their prejudices are as obsolete as Bismarck's spiked helmet.'

It was one man's day above all others. In his 1978 autobiography, *Fußball*, Schön wrote, 'I will never forget this image all my life: as he stormed through the midfield under the floodlights with his long, flowing blond hair, the ball on his foot – that was just a glorious sight.' No prizes for guessing who the manager was on about. 'Netzer twirled his baton, and everyone danced to his tune,' Ludger Schulze purred in *Die Mannschaft*, a 1986 history of the German national team.

Netzer himself, decades later, put it even more simply. 'I don't like these inter-generational cross-comparisons – but at Wembley, we were very close to perfection. There was harmony among all of us. I don't remember ever playing in a team that exuded such joy. But that doesn't mean you're going to win. You can play a great game and still lose. In this particular case, that would have been tragic.'

With admirable optimism, Moore, Rodney Marsh, Martin Peters and Martin Chivers posed in Avengers-style bowler hats for a *Daily Mirror* photoshoot before flying out to Berlin for the second leg a fortnight later. But there the jocularity ended, as Ramsey had Netzer terminated with extreme prejudice. 'The whole England team have autographed my leg!' he groaned at the end of a grim, violent match in which Norman Hunter and Peter Storey repeatedly brutalised him while referee Milivoje Gugulović looked the other way.

England had effectively swapped one type of humiliation for another: Ramsey's crude containment strategy extinguished whatever chance they had of turning the tie around. It was the baldest of admissions that his team lagged light years behind their opponents.

Early on, Marsh glanced a corner goalwards and Chivers lunged for it, but Horst-Dieter Höttges blocked on the line. Netzer hit a dipping free kick just over, and Held went closer when his shot on the run grazed the top of the bar. In the second half, Schwarzenbeck cleared under pressure from Marsh in West Germany's goalmouth. And that was your lot, from both teams.

West Germany reacted caustically to Ramsey's caveman tactics. Schön described the worst challenges as 'brutal tackling aimed at the bones', while Beckenbauer said England had 'confused the football pitch with a jungle'. In response, Alan Ball pig-headedly called the Germans 'cry-babies' and accused them of trying to 'make villains of us', in another example of unwillingness to face footballing reality. The 1970s weren't going to get any better for England after this.

=====

Italy's stalemate against Belgium in Milan was far less nasty, but equally uneventful. Valcareggi picked a line-up containing most of the 1968 side; but here, the biters were bit, as they would be in Rome eight years later. In front of an angry home crowd, Belgium executed an expert stifling job on their opponents.

At one point in the second half, with Belgium's full-back Maurice Martens lying injured on the grass, referee Petar Nikolov let play continue. This was too much for Belgian manager Raymond Goethals, who walked on to the pitch gesticulating, forcing Nikolov to blow up. Goethals was then taken below decks by the carabinieri, but the tantrum had done its job: in the confusion, Léon Dolmans got subbed on for Martens.

'What a memory!' Goethals laughingly recalled in 1994. 'The referee didn't want to stop the match. So I threw Dolmans on. But I was in such a hurry that he didn't have time to tie his laces, and he went on to the field with only one boot! The carabinieri then locked me in the dressing room. But I gave them all the trinkets of the Belgian FA that I had on me, so they let me see the end of the game. In Italy, you really do buy everything!'

This stuff was par for the course with 'Raymond-la-Science', a football man as wily as any other. Luigi Riva, getting little service, went close with a header in the opening stages and an agile volley near the end, both of which Christian Piot tipped adroitly over the bar. 'The best match of my career? Undoubtedly yes!' the goalkeeper recalled in 2016. 'There are days like that where you feel that nothing can happen to you. But the main reason for this result was the extraordinary defensive organisation set up by Goethals.'

Paul Van Himst was starved of the ball, but Goethals wouldn't have lost much sleep over that. In an exciting climax, Ricky Albertosi saved well from Jean Dockx, and young Franco Causio rattled the Belgian bar at close range on his international debut.

A fortnight later, in Brussels, Italy relinquished their crown on a bad night for the great Giacinto Facchetti, their pillar for so many years. After he needlessly bodychecked Semmeling near the corner flag, the winger curved the free kick to the back post, where the 5ft 6in Wilfried Van Moer rose above numerous taller men and bulleted a header into the top corner. On Belgian TV, the commentator's scream of ecstasy caused him to lose his breath and endure a coughing fit.

But Van Moer was a hunted man and Mario Bertini's appalling lunge broke his leg before the interval (Bertini didn't reappear for the second half either, and was never capped again). Belgium, unfazed and phlegmatic, stuck to the task. When Sandro Mazzola lost possession, a swift counter-attack saw Van Himst get ahead of Facchetti and nudge Lambert's cross past Albertosi with his thigh for 2-0.

Fabio Capello won a penalty near the end when Georges Heylens tripped him, and Riva smashed it past Piot, but Italy had left it too late. Belgian joy was heightened afterwards when UEFA selected them to host the final tournament – though tempered by the knowledge that they would have to do without poor Van Moer.

In middle Europe, two old foes fought it out over three legs. Hungary were favourites against Romania, but badly missed the injured Flórián Albert and didn't risk Ferenc Bene until an hour had passed in Budapest. But Romanian complacency gifted them an early goal. László Branikovits robbed a dozing defender, and his clipped low shot hit goalkeeper Răducanu Necula in the chest before looping in under the bar.

Romania almost found a quick equaliser when, after goalkeeper István Géczi misjudged a corner, Flavius Domide's shot was acrobatically blocked on the line by László Bálint. But Hungary should have been out of sight by half-time. Antal Dunai shot straight at Necula, Sándor Zámbó volleyed against the bar and Branikovits hit the post of an open goal. With finishing like that, the Hungarians were asking for it, and Lajos Sătmăreanu headed a simple equaliser after Géczi flapped at another corner.

In the second leg in Bucharest, Hungary opened the scoring after Zámbó's long shot crashed off the bar, István Szöke stabbing the ball in so quickly that the TV camera missed it. Romania's equaliser, too, came from a rebound, the talented midfielder Nicolae Dobrin chipping Géczi and three defenders after Emerich Dembrovschi hit the post. Dobrin, who had missed all of Mexico 70 with sunstroke, was Romania's best player of the era by a mile. To his eternal anguish, his transfer from Argeş Pitesti to Real Madrid was scuppered by dictator Nicolae Ceauşescu on the grounds that he was a 'national asset' who, for reasons of optics, couldn't be allowed to leave Romania and grow rich on a foreign payroll.

Necula made a great point-blank stop from Lajos Szücs before Lajos Kocsis restored Hungary's lead, taking his time after good work by Bene at the byline. But Angelo Niculescu's substitutions turned the tide for Romania, with Mircea Lucescu's cross putting the second equaliser on a plate for Alexandru Neagu. Meanwhile, the giant Necula saved Kocsis's penalty after one of Hungary's bigger names allegedly ducked out of taking it.

The 2-2 result meant a play-off in neutral Belgrade three days later. Kocsis opened the scoring for Hungary with a good goal, storming through from midfield and prodding his shot high into the net. Soon, though, the uncontainable Dobrin teed up Dembrovschi, whose shot was blocked by a defender before Neagu, lurking nearby, scooped it in.

With a minute to go, however, the ball broke off a Romanian defender in the box, and Szöke's shot whistled across Necula into the corner. Beating Romania always felt especially sweet to Hungary, for obvious reasons, but it was hard to see them doing much in the finals.

=====

In Belgrade, the USSR packed their midfield and used only one striker against Yugoslavia. They were up against it for long periods, especially on their right, where Revaz Dzodzuashvili was given the runaround by Dragan

Džajić. 'I was told beforehand that he wasn't in shape, so I didn't prepare well,' the Georgian defender admitted. 'I played very badly. He was better than [George] Best.'

Eduard Kozynkevych's muscular drive shook the crossbar in the first half, but after the interval the USSR were fortunate that their opponents' finishing was frequently wild, and that goalkeeper Yevhen Rudakov was on top of his game to help them secure a 0-0 draw. Afterwards, their manager Nikolai Gulyaev alleged that some players had arrived 'insufficiently prepared', singling out the flame-haired Azerbaijani striker Anatoliy Banishevsky.

The second leg in Moscow drew another vast crowd on a warm, sunny day. Yugoslavia should have opened the scoring when Mladen Ramljak's cross skittered tantalisingly into the goalmouth, only for three of his team-mates to duck the responsibility, passing it to each other in turn like a primitive prototype of late-period Wengerian Arsenal.

The USSR then missed a slew of chances. Banishevsky screwed up a one-on-one with Enver Marić, Gennady Yevryuzhikhin shot wide from close range and Yuri Istomin chipped over an open goal. Yugoslavia couldn't hold out forever, and early in the second half, Kolotov outpaced two defenders before poking his shot under Marić.

With Yugoslavia tiring, Banishevsky scored the second with a ripping drive near the penalty spot. And some terrible goalkeeping by Marić in the dying seconds, charging off his line without cause, allowed Kozynkevych to head an easy third goal.

Two weeks later, the Soviets were thrashed 4-1 by West Germany in a friendly in Munich, ending Gulyaev's four-game reign as manager. He would stay on for the finals as assistant coach, in another example of the impenetrable vagaries of sporting politics in Brezhnev's USSR. Aleksandr Ponomaryov, manager of the Olympic team, replaced him.

7.45pm, 29 April 1972
Wembley Stadium, London
Attendance: 96,800
Referee: Robert Héliès (France)

ENGLAND 1 (Lee 77)
WEST GERMANY 3 (Hoeneß 26, Netzer 85 pen, Müller 89)

ENGLAND: Gordon Banks, Paul Madeley, Emlyn Hughes, Colin Bell, Bobby Moore (c), Norman Hunter, Francis Lee, Alan Ball, Martin Chivers, Geoff Hurst (Rodney Marsh 60), Martin Peters. **Manager:** Alf Ramsey.

WEST GERMANY: Sepp Maier, Horst-Dieter Höttges, Paul Breitner, Georg Schwarzenbeck, Franz Beckenbauer (c), Herbert Wimmer, Jürgen Grabowski, Uli Hoeneß, Gerd Müller, Günter Netzer, Sigi Held. **Manager:** Helmut Schön.

4pm, 13 May 1972
Olympiastadion, West Berlin
Attendance: 76,122
Referee: Milivoje Gugulović (Yugoslavia)

WEST GERMANY 0
ENGLAND 0

WEST GERMANY: Maier, Höttges, Breitner, Schwarzenbeck, Beckenbauer (c), Wimmer, Heinz Flohe, Hoeneß (Jupp Heynckes 71), Müller, Netzer, Held.

ENGLAND: Banks, Madeley, Hughes, Peter Storey, Moore (c), Roy McFarland, Hunter (Peters 73), Ball, Bell, Chivers, Marsh (Mike Summerbee 58).

3.30pm, 29 April 1972
Stadio Giuseppe Meazza 'San Siro', Milan
Attendance: 26,561
Referee: Petar Nikolov (Bulgaria)

ITALY 0
BELGIUM 0

ITALY: Enrico Albertosi, Tarcisio Burgnich, Giacinto Facchetti (c), Gianfranco Bedin, Roberto Rosato, Pierluigi Cera, Angelo Domenghini (Franco Causio 46), Sandro Mazzola, Pietro Anastasi, Armando 'Picchio' De Sisti, Luigi Riva. **Manager:** Ferruccio Valcareggi.

BELGIUM: Christian Piot, Georges Heylens, Maurice Martens (Léon Dolmans 53), Jean Thissen, Erwin Vandendaele, Jean Dockx, Léon Semmeling, Wilfried Van Moer, Raoul Lambert, Paul Van Himst (c), Jan Verheyen. **Manager:** Raymond Goethals.

Booked: Van Moer (64).

8pm, 13 May 1972
Stade Émile Versé, Brussels
Attendance: 63,549
Referee: Paul Schiller (Austria)

BELGIUM 2 (Van Moer 23, Van Himst 71)
ITALY 1 (Riva 86 pen)

BELGIUM: Piot, Heylens, Dolmans, Thissen, Vandendaele, Dockx, Semmeling, Van Moer (Odilon Polleunis 46), Lambert, Van Himst (c), Verheyen.

ITALY: Albertosi, Burgnich, Facchetti (c), Mario Bertini (Fabio Capello 46), Luciano Spinosi, Cera, Romeo Benetti, Mazzola, Roberto Boninsegna, De Sisti, Riva.

Booked: Piot (71), Boninsegna (71).

5pm, 29 April 1972
Népstadion, Budapest
Attendance: 68,585
Referee: David Smith (England)

HUNGARY 1 (Branikovits 11)
ROMANIA 1 (Sătmăreanu 56)

HUNGARY: István Géczi, Tibor Fábián, Miklós Páncsics (c), Péter Vepi, Lajos Szűcs, László Bálint, László Fazekas, László Branikovits, Lajos Kocsis (Ferenc Bene 59), Antal Dunai, Sándor Zámbó. **Manager:** Rudolf Illovszky.

ROMANIA: Răducanu Necula, Lajos Sătmăreanu, Nicolae Lupescu, Augustin Deleanu, Cornel Dinu, Ion Dumitru, Mircea Lucescu (c), Emerich Dembrovschi, Flavius Domide, Anghel Iordănescu, Radu Nunweiller. **Manager:** Angelo Niculescu.

Booked: Szűcs (59), Dumitru (17), Dinu (45),, Nunweiller (74).

5pm, 14 May 1972
Stadionul 23 August, Bucharest
Attendance: 60,300
Referee: Kurt Tschenscher (West Germany)
ROMANIA 2 (Dobrin 14, Neagu 81)
HUNGARY 2 (Szöke 5, Kocsis 36)

ROMANIA: Necula, Sătmăreanu, Lupescu, Deleanu, Dinu (c), Dumitru, Dembrovschi (Lucescu 74), Nicolae Dobrin, Domide, Iordănescu (Alexandru Neagu 66), Nunweiller.

HUNGARY: Géczi, Fábián, Páncsics, Bálint, Péter Juhász, István Juhász, Szücs, Kocsis (Lajos Kű 61), Bene (c), István Szöke (Dunai 66), Zámbó.

Booked: Necula (24), Deleanu (84), Szöke (7), Fábián (81).

PLAY-OFF

8pm, 17 May 1972
JNA Stadion, Belgrade
Attendance: 32,130
Referee: Christos Michas (Greece)
HUNGARY 2 (Kocsis 27, Szöke 89)
ROMANIA 1 (Neagu 34)

HUNGARY: Ádám Rothermel, Fábián, Páncsics, Bálint, P. Juhász, I. Juhász, Kocsis, Kű, Bene (c), Szöke, Zámbó.

ROMANIA: Necula, Sătmăreanu, Lupescu, Deleanu (Bujor Hălmăgeanu 65), Dinu (c), Dumitru, Lucescu, Neagu, Dobrin, Domide, Nunweiller.

Booked: Páncsics (25), Dobrin (76).

4pm, 20 April 1972
Stadion Crvena Zvezda 'Marakana'
Attendance: 99,000
Referee: Rudi Scheurer (Switzerland)
YUGOSLAVIA 0
USSR 0

YUGOSLAVIA: Enver Marić, Mladen Ramljak, Dragoslav Stepanović, Miroslav Pavlović, Blagoje Paunović, Dragan Holcer, Božo Janković, Branko Oblak, Josip Bukal (Dušan Bajević 85), Jovan Aćimović, Dragan Džajić (c). **Manager:** Vujadin Boškov.

USSR: Yevhen Rudakov, Revaz Dzodzuashvili, Murtaz Khurtsilava (c), Volodymyr Kaplychnyi, Yuri Istomin, Aleksandr Makhovikov (Volodymyr Troshkin 62), Oleg Dolmatov, Anatoliy Baidachnyi, Anatoliy Banishevsky, Anatoliy Konkov, Eduard Kozynkevych (Gennady Yevryuzhikhin 77). **Manager:** Nikolai Gulyaev.

Booked: Makhovikov 29.

5pm, 13 May 1972
Tsentralnyi Lenina Stadion, Moscow
Attendance: 103,000
Referee: Aurelio Angonese (Italy)

USSR 3 (Kolotov 53, Banishevsky 74, Kozynkevych 90)
YUGOSLAVIA 0

USSR: Rudakov, Dzodzuashvili, Khurtsilava (c), Nikolai Abramov, Istomin, Viktor Kolotov, Troshkin, Baidachnyi (Boris Kopeikin 66), Banishevsky, Konkov, Yevryuzhikhin (Kozynkevych 46).

YUGOSLAVIA: Marić, Ramljak, Stepanović, Pavlović, Paunović, Holcer (Ilija Petković 57), Janković, Oblak (Jure Jerković 72), Zoran Antonijević, Aćimović, Džajić (c).

SEMI-FINALS
USSR v Hungary
West Germany v Belgium

The finals got off to the most low-key start imaginable at an almost deserted Stade Émile Versé in Brussels, where the USSR elbowed their unhappy satellite state out of the European Championship for the third time in 13 years.

Because Belgium v West Germany kicked off simultaneously, the match was watched by just 1,659 people, the tiniest crowd in the history of the finals. Leslie Vernon, writing in *World Soccer* magazine, estimated the crowd as 'about 32 Belgians at the start, 1,000 Hungarians, and the members of an obviously overstaffed Soviet embassy'. Had the match taken place in Moscow or Budapest, it would have drawn one of the largest crowds for any sporting event in 1972. Instead, it attracted fewer people than a Scottish third-division fixture. 'The band, blowing out their cheeks and their hearts, almost outnumbered those of us in the stands,' wrote *Times* correspondent Geoffrey Green.

Interviewed years later, Hungary's striker Lajos Kű remarked of the USSR, 'They seemed invincible. We thought, "If we beat them, we'll end up in Siberia – so we really mustn't beat them!"' The comment, even in half-jest, said much about Hungary's mindset. And a bad game was made worse by the heavy, rain-soaked pitch.

Though Albert was still unfit, Hungary edged a woeful first half, with Rudakov punching away Sándor Zámbó's shot and clutching István Kocsis's free kick. At the other end, Géczi saved at Volodymyr Onyshchenko's feet. But the standard of play was summed up by the sight of Kocsis taking a free kick and playing a clever reverse pass, only to find that no team-mate had made a run.

After 53 long minutes, the USSR scored the goal that their risk-free play didn't deserve. The stocky Anatoliy Baidachnyi won a corner, then took it himself. Miklós Páncsics headed it out only as far as Anatoliy Konkov, whose half-volley clipped Péter Juhász on its way in.

Though Hungary's response was strangely and disappointingly docile, they could have rescued themselves near the end, when Dzodzuashvili took Dunai's legs in the box for a clear penalty (Troshkin, reaching for an old stereotype, described the challenge as 'typical Georgian fervour', and another Georgian, captain Murtaz Khurtsilava, was booked for dissent in the aftermath). But Zámbó's kick was at an ideal height for Rudakov, who plunged left to keep it out. Szöke, following up, belted the rebound into the side-netting.

In the last minute, after the Soviets made a mess of clearing a corner, Páncsics fired the loose ball too high when, with more composure, he would have scored. The USSR had reached yet another European Championship final, their third out of four, with fewer frills than ever. Afterwards, said Kű, 'People were pouring into the changing room, accusing us of selling the game.' Budapest newspaper *Népsport* noted sadly that Hungary 'only had enough strength to get up to the edge of the Soviet box'. Defeatism or realism? Maybe both.

===

Thirty-five miles away, in Antwerp, there wasn't enough room on the terraces to swing a cat. West Germany's lean, mean, green machine stuck with their newly fabled away jersey, whose mystical properties delivered the goods again. Schön afterwards derided the Bosuilstadion's pitch as 'an unplayable stone desert', but his team had little trouble on it.

With Van Moer still in plaster, Belgium stood little chance. Even their home advantage felt hollow, with referee Bill Mullan jeered by half the crowd whenever he penalised West Germany. 'There were so many Germans at that game,' Belgian defender Georges Heylens recalled. 'It didn't annoy us, but it unsettled us. You could feel that whenever the Germans had the ball, there was a huge swathe of people behind them.'

Things might have turned out different had Belgium put away the game's first chance. Semmeling lost Breitner and prodded a clever pass to Lambert, who turned past Schwarzenbeck and saw his shot whizz across the face of the goal.

When West Germany did score on 24 minutes, their fair-haired conjurer was inevitably behind it. Netzer was allowed a ludicrous amount of time to survey the scene from his position on the right – foolish enough against a decent player, and suicidal against him. He floated a centre into the box, and Gerd Müller reacted quickest, heading it over the stranded Piot, who had come out trying to punch. Piot and his manager Goethals both blamed the wind afterwards.

Many years later, the goalkeeper changed his tune. 'It's my fault!' he said. 'After the best game of my career against Italy, I played my worst against the Germans. I went too late to find myself between Thissen and Müller. As soon as I got back to the dressing room, I told my friends this one was on me.' Heylens saw it differently: 'We cannot blame Christian, after all he'd done for us. It happens to everyone to have a bad day. We were all responsible because it was the team as a whole that lacked rigour, and we fought back too late. I maintain that these Germans were not invincible.'

Belgium tried hard in the second half, Maier saving from Semmeling's shot and Heylens's half-volley. But West Germany continued to own the ball. Netzer might as well have been playing in a pair of old Asics: like Ramsey, Goethals didn't put a man on him, and he enjoyed the freedom of Antwerp to spray his platinum passes around.

Netzer was often accused of taking it easy during games: at Gladbach, Hennes Weisweiler once sneered that 'the law of offside is when the big blond asshole passes the ball too late'. Not that he cared. 'Some people said I was lazy on the pitch, but I always said we had to use the resources optimally,' he said. 'I preferred to save my strength for ideas. "Hacki" Wimmer, who was a very good player, had great lungs and loved to run. So he took advantage of me, and I took advantage of him!'

The goal that clinched West Germany's place in the final showed the insanity of failing to close down a world-class player. Netzer picked out Müller behind the Belgian defence with a stunning long pass, where the striker controlled it and poked it beyond the onrushing Piot.

Belgium's consolation goal was a gem, at least. When Dockx's pass was blocked by Beckenbauer, he got lucky second time round and picked out Polleunis, who held off Wimmer before walloping a right-footer into the roof of the net. And West Germany almost threw it away near the end, when Erwin Vandendaele rose above Beckenbauer to head Lambert's corner wide. But a draw would have been absurd. 'We should've been able to beat them,' lamented Van Himst, but he was kidding himself.

8pm, 14 June 1972
Stade Émile Versé, Brussels
Attendance: 1,659
Referee: Rudi Glöckner (East Germany)

USSR 1 (Konkov 53)
HUNGARY 0

USSR: Rudakov, Dzodzuashvili, Khurtsilava (c), Kaplychnyi, Konkov, Istomin, Kolotov, Troshkin, Baidachnyi, Banishevsky (Givi Nodia 69), Volodymyr Onyshchenko. **Manager:** Aleksandr Ponomaryov.

HUNGARY: Géczi, Fábián, Páncsics, Bálint, P. Juhász, I. Juhász, Kocsis (Flórián Albert 61), Kű, Bene (c) (Dunai 61), Szöke, Zámbó.

Booked: Khurtsilava (83), Bálint (65).

8pm, 14 June 1972
Bosuilstadion, Antwerp
Attendance: 55,669
Referee: Bill Mullan (Scotland)
WEST GERMANY 2 (Müller 24, 72)
BELGIUM 1 (Polleunis 83)

WEST GERMANY: Maier, Höttges, Breitner, Schwarzenbeck, Beckenbauer (c), Wimmer, Hoeneß (Grabowski 59), Heynckes, Müller, Netzer, Erwin Kremers.

BELGIUM: Piot, Heylens, Dolmans, Thissen, Vandendaele, Dockx, Semmeling, Martens (Polleunis 70), Lambert, Van Himst (c), Verheyen.

Booked: Vandendaele (17).

THIRD-PLACE PLAY-OFF
Belgium v Hungary

Thanks to high ticket prices, the game nobody wanted to play in was also the game nobody wanted to watch. In Liège, another small crowd saw Belgium spend most of their time fouling Hungary's talented forwards. They also scored two goals; one was sublime, the other ridiculous.

First, Raoul Lambert controlled a long ball, stepped neatly inside Páncsics and István Juhász, then blasted a wonderful left-footed drive into the top corner. Minutes later, Lambert intercepted Tibor Fábián's slack pass, charged up the left and sent a low cross into the goalmouth. Páncsics stepped over it for Géczi to collect, but the goalkeeper had anticipated his captain clearing it instead – and it trickled past both of them for Van Himst to tap it in. It was his 30th international goal, and he never scored an easier one. 'That was my last goal for the national team? Really?' he exclaimed in 2016. 'Frankly, I don't remember it.'

The half-time entertainment was a West German supporter scuttling on to the field waving his country's flag, only to be clouted by the truncheon of an angry Belgian policeman. After Lambert threw away a wonderful opportunity to make it 3-0, taking the ball around Géczi before shooting wide, Hungary got back into the game. Mihály Kozma swung a long cross over to Kű, who was pushed over by Semmeling, then put the penalty in the corner. But Van Himst and Lambert missed good chances before the end, so it could have been worse for Hungary, who wouldn't be seen at the Euros again until 2016.

Not for the last time, Belgium had extracted the utmost from their resources. 'Our strength, besides the talent of our few great players, was a great team spirit,' said Heylens. 'The team had four Standard [Liège] players, four from Anderlecht, two from Brugge and one from Sint-Truiden. They didn't come from everywhere, like today. My bronze medal, I still take it out and look at it often.'

8pm, 17 June 1972
Stade Maurice Dufrasne, Liège
Attendance: 6,184
Referee: Johan Einar Boström (Sweden)

BELGIUM 2 (Lambert 24, Van Himst 28)
HUNGARY 1 (Kű 53 pen)

BELGIUM: Piot, Heylens, Dolmans, Thissen, Vandendaele, Dockx, Semmeling, Polleunis, Lambert, Van Himst (c), Verheyen.

HUNGARY: Géczi, Fábián, Páncsics (c), Bálint, P. Juhász, I. Juhász, Mihály Kozma, Kű, Dunai, Albert, Zámbó (Szűcs 46).

Booked: Dolmans (63), P. Juhász (60).

FINAL
West Germany v USSR

In the shadow of the Atomium, which loomed over the Heysel Stadium like a vast metallic spacecraft from another galaxy, West Germany delivered their second signature performance of 1972. It set the benchmark for the rest of the decade: Brazil's destruction of Italy in Mexico City two years earlier had been an explosion of artistry, but this felt more rounded, more complete.

The Soviets just didn't have enough attacking firepower to trouble West Germany. Anatoliy Byshovets was laid up with the knee injury that ended his career a year later, and the teenager Oleh Blokhin wasn't yet trusted. For West Germany, right-back Berti Vogts nursed faint hopes of making an 11th-hour recovery from his injury, but burst into tears when he realised he wouldn't play. Schön dragged him into the bathroom and shouted, 'This isn't a good example for the others to see before a European Championship final!' Höttges was a quality replacement, but Schön could have picked Klaus Kinski or Willy Brandt for all the difference it made on the day.

The first of Netzer's many dazzling contributions saw him weight a perfect through ball to Müller; goalkeeper Rudakov, alert to the danger, sprinted out to clear. Netzer then fed Jupp Heynckes, whose feint left Troshkin on the deck. The striker's shot was blocked by a forest of Soviet legs, but it fell kindly for Müller, whose instant blast was kept out by Rudakov's reflex save. Immediately, another sculpted Netzer pass saw Heynckes get in a cross-shot which Rudakov leaped to save. All this in the first seven minutes.

With the mostly German crowd blaring klaxons and hunting horns whenever Netzer took possession, West Germany's speedy attacks seemed even more exhilarating in the din. Most of their moves were down the left, where a decision had clearly been taken to target Dzodzuashvili. Breitner played a one-two with Hoeneß before shooting across the face of the goal; Rudakov acrobatically clutched Kremers' shot via a wicked deflection off Müller; Hoeneß headed Kremers' cross against the bar; Wimmer slashed a long shot too high; and Kremers should have had a penalty when Dzodzuashvili tripped him. An absolute onslaught.

It was only a question of when. The answer was the 27th minute. Beckenbauer glided forward from halfway, not so much eluding two Soviets as ignoring them. He found Müller, who teed it up for Netzer to have a crack. The shot dipped viciously, clanging off the bar. Istomin headed the ball away, but only as far as Heynckes, who sent a fierce half-volley back into the danger area. Rudakov sprang to keep it out, but Müller instinctively buried the rebound.

Although Maier had to tip Dzodzuashvili's 30-yard piledriver over the bar, the torture soon resumed. Rudakov saved Heynckes' downward header with his knees, then parried Netzer's free kick before it crept into the top corner. West Germany were so comfortable that Maier got away with dribbling around Konkov near his own corner flag. Meanwhile, when Volodymyr Kaplychnyi clothes-lined Netzer, both were booked: Kaplychnyi for the violence, Netzer for the apoplectic reaction.

At the interval, the USSR's one crumb of comfort was that there was still only a goal in it. Not for long. Murtaz Khurtsilava surrendered possession to Wimmer who, 12 German passes later, burst into the Soviet box and clipped a neat left-footed shot across Rudakov. Wimmer, an inestimable lieutenant to the bigger names, truly deserved that moment.

The third goal hardly mattered. Schwarzenbeck exchanged passes with Müller and Heynckes before forcing his way into the box. Khurtsilava closed down and he lost control, but the ball broke kindly for Müller, who joyfully scooped it home.

West Germany now eased off, stringing together 30 uninterrupted passes at one point. 'They are a pleasure to watch,' wrote Geoffrey Green in *The Times*. 'Elegant and imaginative, they have an infinite variety to their game as they stroke the ball around in a flood of angles on the ground and in the air. It is like light being fed through a prism. By comparison, these Russians [sic], though they fought to their last breath, were staid, pedestrian and coarse-grained. It was like watching the academician, the courtier, face the honest peasant labourer.'

The barrel-chested Khurtsilava came up from defence to strike a stupendous 30-yard shot against the bar, but it was a fleabite on the hide of a very big beast. And now the delirious German fans could contain themselves no longer. Running down from the terraces and streaming on to the Heysel's athletic track, they began invading the pitch faster than the Belgian police could remove them. Referee Ferdinand Marschall halted the game for a while, and Maier threw two of them off the field himself. 'They were very understanding,' he said in 2012.

At the final whistle, they charged back on to the field in a human wave of black, red and yellow. Minutes later, Franz Beckenbauer lifted the trophy with only some flimsy barriers and a thin blue line of Brussels's finest separating him from the jubilant mob.

It was the most one-sided final in the tournament's history, hewn from top-quality materials. 'I believe we showed today that there is more to football than massed defence,' Schön said pointedly. 'I hope our win here will be a lesson for football around the world. Defensive football must be abandoned at all costs. The game must flow.'

For the second time in two months, the European media rained hosannas on West Germany's heads. *Gazzetta dello Sport* claimed that one would 'need a machine gun' to stop them, and *La Libre Belgique* called them the modern-day heirs to Austria's 1930s Wunderteam. 'One can hardly imagine that a more cohesive performance is possible,' mused *L'Équipe*. 'This team has no equals in Europe.' At home, they were christened the *Jahrhundertelf*, the team of the century. There have been better European Championships, but hardly a better side to win one.

Let's give the last word to Heide Rosendahl, the West German pentathlete, who earlier in 1972 vented her displeasure after finishing second to Müller in a sports personality poll. 'All he does is hang around the penalty area and score goals,' she sniped. And?

4pm, 18 June 1972
Stade du Heysel, Brussels
Attendance: 43,437
Referee: Ferdinand Marschall (Austria)

WEST GERMANY 3 (Müller 27, 58, Wimmer 52)
USSR 0

WEST GERMANY: Maier, Höttges, Breitner, Schwarzenbeck, Beckenbauer (c), Wimmer, Hoeneß, Heynckes, Müller, Netzer, Kremers.

USSR: Rudakov, Dzodzuashvili, Khurtsilava (c), Kaplychnyi, Istomin, Kolotov, Troshkin, Baidachnyi, Banishevsky (Kozynkevych 66), Konkov (Dolmatov 46), Onyshchenko.

Booked: Netzer (44), Kaplychnyi (44), Khurtsilava (66).

1976

THE DECADE had begun with Brazil making an example of Italy in Mexico City, but by the mid-1970s, the greatest show on earth wore white and black. After seeing off the Netherlands in Munich on 7 July 1974, West Germany held the world and European titles simultaneously, standing unchallenged as the best team on the planet.

It was hard to see how they could be stopped, despite a sleepy qualification campaign and the loss of several of their old guard. Gerd Müller had retired from international football, while Paul Breitner and Günter Netzer were ostracised by DFB president Hermann Neuberger after they joined Real Madrid without consulting him in advance. Helmut Schön became frustrated at having to beg Madrid to release the pair for each international, and effectively froze Netzer out of the 1974 World Cup (ironically, in 1981, Breitner would return in the creative role that had once been Netzer's personal property).

Some of the qualifying groups were extraordinarily competitive. Group 5 contained two of the three best teams at the 1974 World Cup, plus another of the continent's traditional superpowers. At the climax, Poland lost 3-0 in Amsterdam, then couldn't break down Italy in Warsaw. So the Netherlands topped the group by a point.

Their manager George Knobel had coached Ajax during 1973/74, when he fell out with the club's stars after criticising their fondness for partying. At the start of that season, Johan Cruyff left for Barcelona after a dressing-room ballot was held to decide the team captaincy, something he saw as an outrageous challenge to his authority. But economic realities meant that Cruyff would have been Barcelona-bound no matter what.

Although Ajax sacked him in April 1974, the KNVB picked Knobel to replace Rinus Michels after the World Cup. He came armed with a tough-guy assistant in Jan Zwartkruis, but the good cop and the bad cop couldn't prevent the Netherlands squad being pulled in opposing directions by the Randstad-Brabant divide (Amsterdam's city slickers against the lads from the provinces).

When Cruyff and Johan Neeskens flew in very late from Barcelona for the Poland game, the PSV Eindhoven striker Willy van der Kuijlen sneered, 'I see the kings of Spain have arrived.' A fist-fight ensued. Cruyff then issued an ultimatum: he, Neeskens and Wim van Hanegem would quit the national team unless Van der Kuijlen and goalkeeper Jan van Beveren, another PSV man, were moved aside. 'Either these whingers are out, or I go,' he told Knobel, who acquiesced.

Van Beveren had fallen out with Cruyff after refusing to hire Cruyff's father-in-law, businessman Cor Coster, as a financial adviser. He also endured unpleasant bullying at international get-togethers: one night, he found his hotel room bed drenched in cold water. When he died in June 2011, Cruyff wrote, 'The conflict that we once had as players, I consider a momentary thing. Sometimes things happen at certain moments, but that's all it is.' Easy for him to say.

The Netherlands' neighbours, Belgium, made the last eight after a tense goalless draw in Paris. The French won only one qualifier, at a time when many of their players were doing great things for Saint-Étienne in Europe. Romanian guru Ştefan Kovács, expensively appointed after winning back-to-back European Cups with Ajax, proved a colossal let-down. 'We felt he didn't care,' said midfielder Jean-Michel Larqué. 'I remember one absolutely surreal pre-match talk: he gathered us in a hallway, where waiters and staff were constantly passing between him and us.' Striker Hervé Revelli agreed: 'Kovács had the Ajax halo over his head, but he didn't have the same players any more.'

To universal surprise, Wales were the only British team in the quarter-finals. After losing in Vienna, they reeled off five straight wins, the biggest a 2-1 victory in Budapest. In the quarter-finals, they would face an unpredictable Yugoslavian team who'd seen off Northern Ireland and Sweden.

Where Wales succeeded, Scotland floundered. After coming home unbeaten from the 1974 World Cup, their campaign never recovered from a 2-1 defeat by Spain at Hampden Park. Meanwhile, as in 1964, Ireland briefly glinted before falling away. At the outset, they battered the USSR at Dalymount Park with QPR's Don Givens scoring all three goals, giving easily the best performance in their history. Their invariably awful away form, however, hobbled them and the Soviets won the group easily.

The USSR would meet their old foes Czechoslovakia, who had begun disastrously by losing 3-0 at Wembley. But England then slipped to a costly goalless draw at home to Portugal, abruptly ending the technocrat Don

Revie's managerial honeymoon. By the time they drew again in Lisbon, the group was already in Czechoslovakian hands.

Exactly a year after losing at Wembley, the east Europeans got their own back in Bratislava, winning a match that had been abandoned after 17 minutes the previous day due to fog. Mick Channon put England ahead by lobbing Ivo Viktor, but two headers either side of half-time won the day for Czechoslovakia, one from Zdeněk Nehoda, the other from Dušan Galis.

Revie bemoaned Czechoslovakian 'provocation', which was rich coming from someone who had built Leeds's midfield around Billy Bremner and John Giles. Still, he had a point. Czechoslovakia repeatedly engaged in ale-house tactics, with referee Alberto Michelotti eventually sending off substitute goalkeeper Alexander Vencel for invading the pitch and shoving him. 'What the artistic Bohemians of old would have thought of some of their heirs is beyond contemplation. Manners went downhill,' Geoffrey Green disgustedly wrote in *The Times*.

Needing a heavy win in Lisbon, England instead drew 1-1, and were lucky not to lose as Toni Oliveira and Nené missed good chances for Portugal. With Czechoslovakia's final fixture a gimme against Cyprus, Revie's team were done for.

Czechoslovakia were, at the very least, known unknowns: in December 1975, *France Football* had named them team of the year. But in an age when saturation TV coverage of global leagues and online stats databases were unborn concepts, Revie's famous dossiers on the opposition were as close to modern-day micro-coaching as anybody got, and much good they had done him in Bratislava. Other teams failed to pay similar attention to detail. Dutch winger René van de Kerkhof recalled decades later, 'Our attitude was, "Who the hell are Czechoslovakia?"'

QUARTER-FINALS
Yugoslavia v Wales
Spain v West Germany
Czechoslovakia v USSR
Netherlands v Belgium

Yugoslavian football in the 1970s was a maddening mix of skill and passivity. When they were bad (or couldn't be bothered) they were capable of losing to almost anybody. But when they were good, they were unplayable.

In Zagreb, even without the wonderful Dragan Džajić (adjudged unfit by manager Ante Mladinić after a long journey from his club in Corsica, to his fury), they quickly sprang for Welsh throats. After 30 seconds, Terry

Yorath's slip allowed Danilo Popivoda to shoot against Momčilo Vukotić's legs as Malcolm Page played everyone onside. Vukotić reacted quicker than everyone else, slipping the loose ball past goalkeeper Dai Davies.

The Yugoslavians, streetwise and clever, scored again early in the second half. Branko Oblak's feint put Rod Thomas on the ground, the tall Ivica Šurjak headed his centre back across goal, and Popivoda slid in to score at close range. One of Wales's many, many bad days in eastern Europe.

The second leg at Ninian Park a month later was one of the great dust-ups of the decade. Viewed through today's eyes, it's the footballing equivalent of *The Sweeney*. Wanton thuggery, pitch invasions, beleaguered coppers, a porridgey playing surface, a seething sea of sideburns and bell-bottoms on the terraces – it's all here. Seventies football in the raw.

Rudi Glöckner was an experienced referee who had handled the 1970 World Cup Final, but he came with a reputation for eccentricity and would have a bad afternoon here. First, Leighton Phillips stamped on Dražen Mužinić, who had clattered him behind Glöckner's back; the referee booked Phillips, but not Mužinić. Shortly afterwards, Popivoda fell theatrically in the box under Page's challenge. Glöckner, miles behind the play, gave a penalty; Josip Katalinski converted amid much Welsh protest.

Within moments, little Brian Flynn thumped Džemal Hadžiabdić (later of Swansea) after being kicked from behind. Hadžiabdić went down like a sack of Rhondda coal; Flynn escaped with a booking. From the Welsh free kick, he hooked John Toshack's knock-down against the post.

Needing three goals to force a play-off in Milan, Wales roused themselves for an equaliser, Ian Evans slamming the ball home after Enver Marić saved from Arfon Griffiths. In the second half, they thought they had gone ahead when John Mahoney miscued a bicycle-kick and Toshack smashed the rebound past Marić. But Glöckner disallowed the goal for Mahoney's high foot. Although the whistle was audible before Toshack scored, it was a whimsical decision at best.

The crowd, already angry, now chanted 'Sieg heil!' as Glöckner remonstrated with Wales's assistant manager Cyril Lea, who had walked on to the field. Evans and Flynn ejected a pitch invader, as more fans tried to scale the perimeter fencing 'like animals escaping a zoo', as *The Times* put it. For a time, it seemed the match would be abandoned.

The volatile Yorath, who had crippled Bayern Munich's Björn Andersson in the 1975 European Cup Final, somehow avoided being sent off despite stamping on Hadžiabdić and almost breaking Slaviša Žungul's leg. Near the end, he sealed Wales's woeful afternoon, hitting a feeble penalty too close to Marić after the goalkeeper tripped Toshack.

At the final whistle, with some inevitability, hundreds of Welshmen invaded the pitch. Sixteen policemen were needed to escort Glöckner to the dressing room; a corner flag was hurled at him, but instead speared one of the police in the neck. Meanwhile, Jurica Jerković punched a Wales fan who verbally abused him in the tunnel.

UEFA initially banned Wales from the 1980 finals but, on appeal, the punishment was reduced to a closure of Ninian Park for the qualifiers. Yugoslavia, in contrast, were awarded the four-team finals, so eastern Europe would be hosting its first international tournament.

In Madrid, West Germany got the draw they had come for. Sepp Maier had been at the centre of controversy while playing for Bayern in this city weeks earlier, breaking the nose of Real Madrid's Roberto Juan Martínez before a Madrid fan invaded the pitch to attack him. Here, he made a rare error to give Spain the lead.

The 5ft 9in Santillana was freakishly good in the air, using his spring heels to hang up there for outlandish amounts of time. He outjumped Georg Schwarzenbeck and killed Gregorio Benito's cross before prodding home as Maier reacted slowly. If that was saveable, West Germany's equaliser wasn't. The veteran José Ángel Iribar got a finger to Erich Beer's spectacular 25-yarder, but couldn't stop it.

In Munich two weeks later, West Germany enjoyed a let-off at 0-0, when Maier's kamikaze charge allowed Santillana to give Quini an open goal. Off balance and facing the wrong way, Quini knocked it against the underside of the bar from close range.

Spain were otherwise never in the game, and fell behind to a beautiful goal when Uli Hoeneß acrobatically volleyed Beer's cross over his own shoulder. Hoeneß, very much in the mood, then bustled José Antonio Camacho off the ball, charged downfield, held off another defender and shot against the post: not bad for someone just back from meniscus surgery. And when Iribar's replacement Miguel Ángel couldn't hold Beckenbauer's shot, Klaus Toppmöller gobbled up an unmissable tap-in.

Muhammad Ali, attending his first and possibly last football match, left at the interval with a one-word verdict: 'Boring.' He missed a second-half thunderstorm, Toppmöller nearly blasting a sitter out of the stadium, Juan Manuel Asensi squandering a one-on-one with Maier, and Maier himself slipping painfully on the wet running track while taking a goal kick.

Another comfortable West German win and another disappointing Spanish defeat, in a decade that witnessed many of both. Spain's manager

Ladislao Kubala tried to blame the Olympiastadion pitch, but few were listening. 'Spanish football is becoming more historical and less actual,' lamented columnist Julián García Candau.

═══

After their shellacking in Dublin, the USSR sacked Konstantin Beskov and brought in Valeriy Lobanovskiy, who turned them into a club side – that club being his own Dynamo Kiev. The idea was that innate familiarity with each other's play would let the team run itself like a powerful supercomputer.

For the first leg away to Czechoslovakia, Lobanovskiy picked eight men from his alma mater. But if the chemistry failed to spark, the Soviets could look robotic and workmanlike. And here, three-quarters of their midfield (Volodymyr Muntiyan, Leonid Buryak and Anatoliy Konkov) were out injured.

The ČSAF knew what it was doing by holding the match in Bratislava: eight of Václav Ježek's line-up were Slovaks, an inversion of the national team's usual demographics. In wet conditions, they scored their first goal in controversial circumstances. When Jaroslav Pollák was brought down, the Soviet defenders stopped, thinking referee Hilmi Ok had given a free kick. Instead, he waved play on, and Jozef Móder's shot passed through goalkeeper Aleksandr Prokhorov too easily.

Czechoslovakia doubled their lead after half-time, when Antonín Panenka's free kick skidded under a badly organised Soviet wall and into the bottom corner. And young Oleh Blokhin's bad miss near the end, when clean through, made an already tricky second leg even harder for the USSR.

In the lion's den in Kiev a fortnight later, Viktor's reflexes kept out Blokhin, Veremeev and Konkov in the first half, before Móder deflated the huge crowd by rifling a free kick into the top corner. The USSR equalised when Buryak fired another powerful drive through a crowded goalmouth – but Karol Dobiaš's quick breakaway and Móder's cool finish for 2-1 put everything to bed.

Blokhin didn't live up to his billing, not for the last time. But his otherwise meaningless late equaliser, a chip over Viktor, deprived Czechoslovakia of the bragging rights of a famous win on the soil of their communist owners: this was the closest the USSR ever came to losing a competitive game at home, in 55 qualifiers.

It's difficult to understate how much gloom this result heaped upon Soviet football's collective psyche. The decision to rely on Dynamo Kiev had blown up in the USSR's faces, with many players suffering from 'great physical and psychological stress', according to one Soviet report. Years later, defender Volodymyr Troshkin said the players 'wrote a letter of resignation' after this match, having spent nine of the previous 12 months in a training camp: 'We were very tired. There was a treadmill, and loads of barriers – jump over this, crawl under that, and so on to infinity.' Lobanovskiy was fired, and the only country to qualify for the first four Euros would sit out the next three.

Think of the Netherlands at the 1974 World Cup, and all the old clichés come flooding into the mind's eye: free-flowing Total Football, even more free-flowing haircuts, Cruyff's turn, marvellous goals, iron tackling, luminous *Oranje* shirts, mellow vibes of peace and love and player power. Yet we would never have seen any of it but for a linesman's blunder seven months earlier.

In November 1973, the Dutch needed a point from their final qualifier against Belgium in Amsterdam. On 89 minutes, the Belgians landed the mother of all knockout punches when Jan Verheyen headed home the goal that seemingly sent them to the finals in West Germany. But not so fast: up went Soviet linesman Rudusov's flag, despite three Dutch defenders playing Verheyen onside. Belgium went out without conceding a single goal – still a record.

No danger of Dutch complacency ahead of this first leg in Rotterdam, then, and they duly drowned Belgium in De Kuip (The Tub). First, Cruyff took out the entire Belgian wall by rolling a free kick to Wim Rijsbergen on the edge of the box, and the full-back thumped it in. After that, it was the Rob Rensenbrink show: the Anderlecht attacker scored with a near-post header from Cruyff's corner, then burst between three defenders to dribble around Piot and tap into an empty net, and rounded things off by heading in Johnny Rep's cross. Meanwhile, Neeskens converted a typically ruthless penalty after Georges Leekens punched Willy van de Kerkhof's chip over the bar. One of the great Dutch performances of the era, on a par with their destructions of the three South American giants in 1974.

Raymond Goethals quit as Belgium's manager before the second leg in Brussels. His successor Guy Thys handed international debuts to six newcomers, including goalkeeper Jean-Marie Pfaff, who saved another Neeskens penalty in the second half.

Roger Van Gool restored some Belgian pride by scoring with a low free kick, but with the recalled Wim van Hanegem pulling the strings, the Netherlands scored a good goal and a great one after half-time. Rep rounded Piot to score after nice work by Ruud Krol and Cruyff, and a fluid move ended with Cruyff brilliantly lofting Krol's pass into the top corner. Belgium had to suck it up, but Thys soon polished so many young diamonds that they were far superior to the Dutch by 1980.

5.30pm, 24 April 1976
Stadion Maksimir, Zagreb
Attendance: 36,917
Referee: Paul Schiller (Austria)

YUGOSLAVIA 2 (Vukotić 1, Popivoda 55)
WALES 0

YUGOSLAVIA: Ognjen Petrović, Ivan Buljan (c), Džemal Hadžiabdić, Dražen Mužinić, Ivica Šurjak, Josip Katalinski, Branko Oblak, Danilo Popivoda, Jovan Aćimović, Momčilo Vukotić (Jurica Jerković 60), Drago Vabec. **Manager:** Ante Mladinić.

WALES: Dai Davies, Rod Thomas, Malcolm Page, John Mahoney, Leighton Phillips, Ian Evans, Leighton James (Alan Curtis 83), Brian Flynn, John Toshack, Terry Yorath (c), Arfon Griffiths. **Manager:** Mike Smith.

Booked: Mužinić (57).

3pm, 22 May 1976

Ninian Park, Cardiff
Attendance: 30,346
Referee: Rudi Glöckner (East Germany)

WALES 1 (Evans 38)
YUGOSLAVIA 1 (Katalinski 19 pen)

WALES: Davies, Phillips, Page, Mahoney, David Roberts, Evans, James, Flynn, Toshack, Yorath (c), Griffiths (Curtis 46).

YUGOSLAVIA: Enver Marić, Mužinić, Buljan (c), Hadžiabdić, Šurjak, Katalinski, Popivoda, Borislav Đorđević, Jerković, Oblak, Slaviša Žungul (Franjo Vladić 61).

Booked: Phillips (16), Flynn (21), Yorath (47), Jerković (17).

9pm, 24 April 1976
Estadio Vicente Calderón, Madrid
Attendance: 51,171
Referee: Jack Taylor (England)

SPAIN 1 (Santillana 21)
WEST GERMANY 1 (Beer 60)

SPAIN: José Ángel Iribar, Juan Cruz Sol (c), Gregorio Benito, José Luis Capón, Migueli Bernardo (Sebastián Alabanda 70), José Antonio Camacho, Ángel María Villar, Vicente Del Bosque, Carlos Alonso 'Santillana', Enrique Castro 'Quini' (Jesús Satrústegui 81), José Ignacio Churruca. **Manager:** László 'Ladislao' Kubala.

WEST GERMANY: Sepp Maier, Berti Vogts, Bernard Dietz (Peter Reichel 81), Georg Schwarzenbeck (Bernd Cullmann 46), Franz Beckenbauer (c), Rainer Bonhof, Bernd Hölzenbein, Herbert Wimmer, Erich Beer, Dietmar Danner, Ronnie Worm. **Manager:** Helmut Schōn.

Booked: Benito (83), Dietz (35).

4pm, 22 May 1976
Olympiastadion, Munich
Attendance: 77,673
Referee: Robert Wurtz (France)

WEST GERMANY 2 (Hoeneß 17, Toppmöller 43)
SPAIN 0

WEST GERMANY: Maier, Vogts, Dietz, Schwarzenbeck, Beckenbauer (c), Bonhof, Hölzenbein, Wimmer, Beer, Uli Hoeneß, Klaus Toppmöller.

SPAIN: Miguel Ángel González, Sol (Ignacio Kortabarría 18), José Martínez 'Pirri', Capón, Juan Manuel Asensi, Camacho, Quini, Villar (José Antonio Ramos 46), Santillana, Del Bosque, Churruca.

Booked: Pirri 44, Camacho 51.

6pm, 24 April 1976
Tehelné Pole, Bratislava
Attendance: 47,621
Referee: Hilmi Ok (Turkey)

CZECHOSLOVAKIA 2 (Móder 34, Panenka 47)
USSR 0

CZECHOSLOVAKIA: Ivo Viktor, Karol Dobiaš, Jozef Čapkovič, Anton Ondruš (c), Koloman Gögh, Jozef Móder (Lubomír Knapp 81), Antonín Panenka, Marián Masný, Jaroslav Pollák, Ladislav Petráš (Karel Kroupa 18), Zdeněk Nehoda. **Manager:** Václav Ježek.

USSR: Aleksandr Prokhorov, Volodymyr Troshkin, Anatoliy Konkov, Viktor Matyivenko, Mykhaylo Fomenko, Stefan Reshko, Viktor Zvyagintsev, Volodymyr Onyshchenko (Leonid Nazarenko 68), Viktor Kolotov (c), Evgeni Lovchev (Volodymyr Veremeev 57), Oleh Blokhin. **Manager:** Valeriy Lobanovskiy.

7pm, 22 May 1976
Tsentralnyi Stadion, Kiev
Attendance: 76,495
Referee: Alastair Mackenzie (Scotland)

USSR 2 (Buryak 53, Blokhin 87)
CZECHOSLOVAKIA 2 (Móder 45 pen, 82)

USSR: Yevhen Rudakov, Troshkin, Konkov (Aleksandr Minaev 56), Lovchev, Fomenko (c), Zvyagintsev, Volodymyr Muntiyan, Onyshchenko, Leonid Buryak, Veremeev, Blokhin.

CZECHOSLOVAKIA: Viktor, Dobiaš, Čapkovič (Ladislav Jurkemik 80), Ondruš (c), Gögh, Móder, Ján Pivarník, Masný, Pollák, Dušan Galis (Jan Švehlík 86), Nehoda.

Booked: Troshkin (37), Móder (60).

2.30pm, 25 April 1976
De Kuip, Rotterdam
Attendance: 48,706
Referee: Jean Dubach (Switzerland)

NETHERLANDS 5 (Rijsbergen 18, Rensenbrink 28, 58, 85, Neeskens 80 pen)
BELGIUM 0

NETHERLANDS: Piet Schrijvers, Wim Suurbier, Wim Rijsbergen, Adri van Kraay, Ruud Krol, Johan Neeskens (Jan Peters 84), Wim Jansen, Johnny Rep, Rob Rensenbrink, Johan Cruyff (c), Willy van de Kerkhof. **Manager:** George Knobel.

BELGIUM: Christian Piot (c), Eric Gerets, Gilbert Van Binst, Maurice Martens, Georges Leekens, Julien Cools (François Van der Elst 46), René Vandereycken, Roger Van Gool, Raoul Lambert (Jacques Teugels 83), Ludo Coeck, Jan Verheyen. **Manager:** Raymond Goethals.

Booked: Rijsbergen (65), Verheyen (29), Van der Elst (56).

8pm, 22 May 1976
Stade du Heysel, Brussels
Attendance: 19,050
Referee: Alberto Michelotti (Italy)

BELGIUM 1 (Van Gool 27)
NETHERLANDS 2 (Rep 61, Cruyff 77)

BELGIUM: Jean-Marie Pfaff, Van Binst, Michel Renquin, Martens (c), Bob Dalving, Cools, Van der Elst, Van Gool (Hervé Delesie 65), Willy Wellens, Vandereycken, René Verheyen. **Manager:** Guy Thys.

NETHERLANDS: Schrijvers, Suurbier, Rijsbergen, Van Kraay, Krol, Neeskens, W. van de Kerkhof, Rep, Rensenbrink, Cruyff (c), Wim van Hanegem (Peters 87).

Booked: Martens (49), Delesie (83).

SEMI-FINALS
Czechoslovakia v Netherlands
Yugoslavia v West Germany

The Dutch entered the tournament in disarray. George Knobel offered his resignation to KNVB chairman Jacques Hogewoning, who first rejected it, then said he would accept it after the tournament. The story broke in the Dutch press on the day of the semi-final against Czechoslovakia in Zagreb.

Knobel's relations with his stars had been deteriorating badly. He would say decades later that the players had viewed Czechoslovakia merely as an administrative hurdle to be cleared before the final: 'They were thinking only of revenge for 1974.' Ivo Viktor felt the same way: 'They didn't respect us. They saw themselves as already in the final against the Germans. And we handled the weather better than they did.'

The match was one of the stormiest of the decade in all senses, as rain lashed the Croatian city all evening. Referee Clive Thomas held an umbrella over the two captains as they shook hands before kick-off, and after only a few minutes of play the pitch markings were barely visible.

With the ball sliding around treacherously, there was an electric pace to the game right away. Czechoslovakia were much the better side in the first half, radiating the confidence that comes from 17 games unbeaten. Their blond right-back Ján Pivarník was a revelation, but rarely stayed in that position for long, overlapping relentlessly and forcing Rensenbrink to retreat and stick closely to him. And when the giant Anton Ondruš's powerful header from Panenka's set-piece looped into the far corner soon afterwards, the goal was no more than Czechoslovakia deserved.

The Dutch looked rudderless as Czechoslovakia came at them. Piet Schrijvers saved in one-on-ones with Marián Masný and Móder, and desperate lunges by Rijsbergen and Adri van Kraay stopped Móder and Nehoda from scoring. Before half-time, a fast break-out gave Czechoslovakia a three-on-one situation which Nehoda messed up.

It would have been a tricky game for any referee, but the notoriously pedantic Thomas made things far worse. Beforehand, he told both teams that 'we weren't to question his decisions', in the words of Ruud Geels. Here, inexplicably, he abandoned his usual outlook and let many obvious fouls go.

But his patience had limits, as Pollák found out on the hour. The balding midfielder, perversely refusing to retreat at free kicks, was eventually booked. Soon afterwards, he hacked Neeskens (whose scream of pain was audible on the footage) and was sent off.

An attritional, if entertaining, game now became a bloody scrap. Out of nothing, the Dutch equalised when Ondruš wildly sliced into his own net while trying to put Geels's cross out for a corner. But, almost immediately, the Netherlands tossed away their momentum as Neeskens was red-carded for brutally fouling Nehoda. Still, Czechoslovakia wobbled, with Viktor making three decent saves from Rensenbrink in the final stages, but hung on to reach extra time.

At this point, the rain finally stopped. And against the odds, Czechoslovakia found a second wind, with substitute František Veselý injecting some zest into their forward line. It was his dipping cross in the 114th minute that found the unmarked Nehoda, who headed home. As the Dutch prepared to restart the match, they lost another player – Van Hanegem – in circumstances that have never fully been explained.

To Van Hanegem's anger, Cruyff had been crunched by Panenka in the build-up to Nehoda's goal. According to Thomas's own account, it went something like this. Van Hanegem told him, 'No goal – very bad decision.' Thomas told him not to say it again, but he did. Thomas then said, 'If you step one foot over that [halfway] line, I'll show you the red card.' Van Hanegem did so, and was sent off, but supposedly refused to go at first (the footage is inconclusive). With Thomas set to abandon the game, the midfielder finally walked off.

Years afterwards, Thomas described the game as 'the hardest of my career', and called the Dutch team 'prima donnas'. He went on, 'Cruyff was one of the worst, but then he always had been. You had to nail him right at the very beginning, because if he knew he had control of you, then you'd had it. I saw too many matches where Cruyff had control of referees.' Van Hanegem, in a 2008 documentary, derided him as 'incredibly vain, an annoying little fellow'.

Dispirited and disgusted, the Netherlands left themselves wide open for the third goal. Panenka's clever first-time pass caught out a tired defence and Veselý, finding himself in acres of space, swerved past the onrushing Schrijvers and booted it in, capping one of the great European Championship slugfests.

So the 1974 rematch everyone had wanted went down the drain – and, just as in that World Cup final, Cruyff had failed to deliver in a huge game (his booking would have put him out of the final anyway). 'You could tell from Cruyff's body language that he didn't really feel like playing,' said Willy van de Kerkhof.

Cruyff left the KNVB with three preconditions for his return: more money for the national team, gentler training sessions, and less time spent training in general (ultimately, he would play only five more times for his country). Watching the game at the gargantuan Metropol hotel in Belgrade, the West Germans had little sympathy. 'It's high time that Meneer Cruyff realised the football field is not there just for his vanity,' sniped Uli Hoeneß, whose own ego was in no danger of falling into the missing persons file.

———

In Belgrade the following night, West Germany and Yugoslavia fought out a splendid contest that would be remembered for Dieter Müller, the 22-year-old Köln striker, making the most spectacular debut in international football history.

By the time he arrived, Yugoslavia should have been out of sight. Džajić later described their exhilarating first 45 minutes as 'maybe the best half the Yugoslav national team have ever played: if we'd gone 4-0 up, the Germans couldn't really have complained'.

They took the lead with an unusual goal. Oblak's huge high ball sailed through the air and landed right on the boot of Popivoda, who controlled it superbly, outpaced Beckenbauer and stabbed it under Maier. Soon afterwards, Ivan Buljan's cross deflected evilly off Schwarzenbeck and was tipped over by the goalkeeper.

Bubbling with effervescence, Yugoslavia hardly let West Germany out of their own half. Maier saved Katalinski's hard free kick, kept out another powerful effort from Buljan, and was finally undone by Žungul's cross, which he fumbled before Džajić kneed it over the line.

West Germany looked irretrievably inferior, yet almost pulled one back before the break when Katalinski kicked Hoeneß's shot off the line. In the second half, Yugoslavia's momentum continued to propel them forward. Džajić slalomed down the left wing, Maier was again poor for the cross, and the ball fell to Jerković, who had the goal at his mercy but shot disastrously wide.

The match turned on that moment, and the goal that threw West Germany a lifeline was a fluke: substitute Heinz Flohe's speculative drive took a massive deflection off Wimmer to leave goalkeeper Ognjen Petrović helpless. And suddenly Yugoslavia's passes were more imprecise, their runs less cavalier, their fans quieter.

With 11 minutes left, young Müller was introduced. 'I don't think Schön made the decision,' he recalled. 'I think Jupp Derwall said to him, "Put Dieter Müller on."' Tall and beefy, he had one job: get on the end of crosses. Within minutes, he scored the simplest of goals. Šurjak left him unmarked, and he headed in Bonhof's corner with his first touch in international football.

The whip had changed hands. Hoeneß just missed with a well-struck drive, and Petrović flipped Beer's hard shot over the bar. In the first half of extra time, Yugoslavia briefly rediscovered their first-half groove – but a Katalinski free kick, a dangerous header by the same player, another near-fatal header by Žungul and a Franjo Vladić piledriver were all repelled by Maier. With no third goal to show for all this, reflected Oblak, 'the whole team folded; usually, it's just two or three guys to blame'.

Now West Germany turned the screw. Petrović saved well from Bonhof and Beer, and finally Flohe set up the killing blow. He beat Jerković twice on the left and fired a low centre across to Bernd Hölzenbein, who unselfishly pulled it back to Müller (again unmarked) to slam it into the roof of the net.

With that, Yugoslavia were gone. After Bonhof ran at their weary defence and shot against the post, Müller tucked away the rebound at his leisure. He wouldn't even have made the squad but for Klaus Toppmöller's drunken car crash weeks earlier. 'I once got six goals in one match in the Bundesliga, but to score that hat-trick, in a game of such importance, was incredible,' he recalled. 'Suddenly, overnight, I became a superstar.' He wasn't finished yet.

8.15pm, 16 June 1976
Stadion Maksimir, Zagreb
Attendance: 17,969
Referee: Clive Thomas (Wales)

CZECHOSLOVAKIA 3 (Ondruš 19, Nehoda 114, Veselý 118)
NETHERLANDS 1 (Ondruš 73 og)
After extra time

CZECHOSLOVAKIA: Viktor, Dobiaš, Čapkovič (Jurkemik 106), Ondruš (c), Gögh, Móder (František Veselý 91), Panenka, Pollák, Masný, Nehoda, Pivarník.

NETHERLANDS: Schrijvers, Suurbier, Rijsbergen (Van Hanegem 37), Van Kraay, Krol, Neeskens, Jansen, Rep (Ruud Geels 65), Rensenbrink, Cruyff (c), W. van de Kerkhof.

Booked: Pollák (51, 60), Dobiaš (102), W. van de Kerkhof (57), Cruyff (78).
Sent off: Pollák (60), Neeskens (76), Van Hanegem (115).

8.15pm, 17 June 1976
Stadion Crvena Zvezda 'Marakana', Belgrade
Attendance: 50,562
Referee: Alfred Delcourt (Belgium)

WEST GERMANY 4 (Flohe 64, Müller 82, 115, 119)
YUGOSLAVIA 2 (Popivoda 19, Džajić 30)
After extra time

WEST GERMANY: Maier, Vogts, Dietz, Schwarzenbeck, Beckenbauer (c), Bonhof, Hölzenbein, Wimmer (Dieter Müller 79), Beer, Hoeneß, Danner (Heinz Flohe 46).

YUGOSLAVIA: Petrović, Buljan, Šurjak, Katalinski, Mužinić, Popivoda, Jerković, Oblak (Vladić 106), Žungul, Aćimović (c) (Luka Peruzović 106), Džajić.

THIRD-PLACE PLAY-OFF
Yugoslavia v Netherlands

Euro 76 was such a terrific tournament that even the third-place play-off was a delight. In Zagreb, Yugoslavia and the Netherlands put on a super show instead of feeling sorry for themselves.

With Neeskens and Van Hanegem suspended, Rijsbergen injured and Cruyff back in Barcelona, the Dutch called up four players from home – Kees Kist, Wim Meutstege, Henk van Rijnsoever and Jan van Deinsen – in order to have enough outfield substitutes. But they began positively, with the livewire Ruud Geels seemingly determined to embarrass Knobel for not starting him against Czechoslovakia: Rensenbrink's pass allowed him to outpace Mužinić and slide the ball under Petrović.

The Netherlands, exuding a much better attitude this time, soon scored again. Willy van de Kerkhof ran on to Jan Peters's floated pass and scored with an angled shot which crept inside the near post, making Petrović look bad.

Yugoslavia got back into it when Katalinski lashed in a loose ball after the Dutch failed to clear their lines. Early in the second half, debutant substitute Vahid Halilhodžić nearly pulled a Müller and scored with his first touch in international football, but Schrijvers managed to save.

In a pulsating final half-hour, Rensenbrink spurned a close-range opportunity, Willy van de Kerkhof scooped a shot on to the bar, Popivoda wasted a one-on-one against Schrijvers, Geels and Kees Kist failed to finish off counter-attacks, and Halilhodžić's header just missed the far post. A marvellous spectacle, and Džajić's curled free kick equaliser ensured 30 more minutes of it.

If the players didn't fancy extra time, they never let on. Kist's 30-yard thunderbolt rattled the bar, Suurbier nodded Katalinski's header off the line, and Krol dribbled around two defenders before stabbing wide. Geels finally settled things, running on to Kist's pass and scoring with another low drive which Petrović should have kept out. Yugoslavia went home (or, rather, stayed at home) with the wooden spoon: nothing to be ashamed of in a tournament this good.

8.15pm, 19 June 1976
Stadion Maksimir, Zagreb
Attendance: 6,766
Referee: Walter Hungerbühler (Switzerland)

NETHERLANDS 3 (Geels 27, 107, W. van de Kerkhof 39)
YUGOSLAVIA 2 (Katalinski 43, Džajić 82)
After extra time

NETHERLANDS: Schrijvers, Suurbier, Van Kraay, Peter Arntz (Kees Kist 70), Krol (c), Jansen (Wim Meutstege 46), W. van de Kerkhof, René van de Kerkhof, Geels, Peters, Rensenbrink.

YUGOSLAVIA: Petrović, Buljan, Šurjak, Katalinski, Mužinić, Jerković, Oblak, Žungul (Vahid Halilhodžić 46), Popivoda, Aćimović (c) (Vladić 46), Džajić.

FINAL
Czechoslovakia v West Germany

At a one-third-full Marakana, surely it was asking too much to expect a fourth classic in five days? Seemingly not. And the deadlock was broken early on. Masný's cut-back found Ján Švehlík near the edge of the area. His shot was well saved by Maier, and the ball broke to Nehoda, who rolled it across the goalmouth. Ondruš missed it but, at the far post, Švehlík didn't.

On the bench, Helmut Schön sorrowfully shook his head. Soon afterwards, Schwarzenbeck's elbow left Švehlík bloodied and requiring treatment. Sergio Gonella, whose craven refereeing would compromise the World Cup Final in Buenos Aires two years later, took no action.

Before long, Ivo Viktor was stirred into the first of his many saves. Müller's pass gave Beer a shooting chance on the right, but the goalkeeper swiftly charged it down. A minute later, he punched Bonhof's piledriver into the air. Bonhof then flashed a free kick just past the post and, capping a stirring spell for West Germany, Viktor pulled off his best stop yet, pushing Hölzenbein's curler over the bar.

It was plain that Czechoslovakia couldn't sit on their lead forever. So they promptly scored again. When Schwarzenbeck painfully took out Koloman Gögh near the corner flag, Masný's inswinging free kick was headed out by

Beckenbauer to Dobiaš, who let it bounce, then struck a well-aimed half-volley inside Maier's far post.

But the Germans hit back quickly. When Gonella played advantage after Móder roughly fouled Wimmer, Bonhof sent over a good cross and Müller scored with a hooked volley into the ground, for his fourth goal in 80 minutes of international football.

The second half began with a near miss, Švehlík's shot on the turn whistling just wide after Flohe cheaply coughed up possession. But it was increasingly becoming Ivo Viktor's match. First, he blocked Müller's shot, clutched the rebound at Beer's feet, then showed amazing reaction speed to keep out Beer again. On the hour, Hoeneß blasted the ball against a defender, Viktor saved brilliantly from Beer on the rebound, Hoeneß could only run it against the face of the post, and the goalkeeper dived on the loose ball with relief. In his final competitive international, Viktor was picking a good time to give the performance of his life.

The excitement never relented. Schwarzenbeck booted Ondruš's shot off the line, Viktor saved hard shots from Bonhof and Beckenbauer, and when Schwarzenbeck misjudged Masný's cross, Nehoda headed against the post. As time ticked away, Bonhof's free kick brushed Nehoda and was looping under the bar before Viktor palmed it over. Later still, Pivarník's storming run ended with Beckenbauer cushioning the ball into Maier's hands when an own goal seemed likely.

Time was almost up when Bonhof swung a corner into Czechoslovakia's crowded box. West Germany had plenty of tall men, but now a player who stood 5ft 6.5in saved them. Ondruš, strangely vulnerable in this match, allowed little Hölzenbein to get there a split-second before Viktor to head home at the near post. 'It was my fault,' Viktor recalled. 'I wasn't aggressive enough going for the ball. I was tired and lost my concentration.'

So to extra time, with Viktor making more good saves from Flohe and Müller, and Gonella looking the other way when Schwarzenbeck flattened Nehoda. Now European football would witness something never before witnessed in a final: a penalty shoot-out, which UEFA had only agreed to hours before the game.

A German football yearbook from the era records some exchanges between Schön's players before the shoot-out.

Dietz, 'No, I'll drop [if I take one]. I'm broken.'

Beckenbauer, 'I don't know if I can shoot, with this injured shoulder.'

Hoeneß, 'I can't. I'm completely exhausted.'

Schwarzenbeck, 'I've not taken a penalty in nine years. Why now?'

Maier, 'I'll take one.'

Beckenbauer, 'Out of the question.'

To Masný went the honour of scoring the first penalty in a major shoot-out. Bonhof's kick, a tired effort by a great player, went in off a post; Nehoda's flew down the middle. Maier illegally jumped off his line at each penalty, but Gonella was asleep. Eventually, with Czechoslovakia 4-3 up, it was Hoeneß's turn.

Viktor, who hadn't touched the previous three German penalties, didn't get near this either. It didn't just go over the bar, it nearly hit the moon. Hoeneß said afterwards, 'I usually pay attention to the goalkeeper and push it into the corner. However, because I was so exhausted, I was taking no chances, and I hit it with full force. I saw the ball climb higher and higher, like a rocket. It whizzed towards the clouds. At that moment, everything around me went grey.'

Hoeneß, who would go on to become one of the most powerful men in European football at his beloved Bayern Munich, joked about it through gritted teeth decades later, 'I think they found the ball a year ago. They had a war and the stadium was destroyed, and they found the ball.'

Antonín Panenka sauntered up. 'His pulse was under 60,' said Pivarník, 'but mine was past 200.' Everyone knows what happened next. The stuttery little run-up, the scuffed stab of the boot, the gentle parabola that saw the ball hang in the air before landing gently in the net while Maier, on his knees, gaped at it. The European press dubbed it 'the falling leaf', but in Czechoslovakia, it would be known as the *vršovický dloubák*, the dwarf of Vršovice, after the district of Prague where Panenka's club Bohemians were based.

'I don't think Maier took it very well,' said Panenka years later. 'I suspect he probably doesn't like the sound of my name. I never wished to make him look ridiculous, though.' Czechoslovakian bureaucrats informed him after the match that, had he screwed up his party piece, Gustáv Husák's regime would have made an example of him: 'Thirty years working down the mines.'

And so, just six years after their whitewash at Mexico 70, Czechoslovakia were the kings of Europe. Dazed and drained, they went up to collect the trophy without realising they were wearing the swapped white shirts of West Germany; only Viktor and Panenka still had their own jerseys on. But who cared?

Of all the managers to win the European Championship, Václav Ježek is perhaps the least heralded. A heavy smoker and poetry buff who liked to unwind by driving vintage cars in the countryside, he routinely knocked back a glass of rum before matches. Later in life, he built a massive (and, at the time, illegal in Czechoslovakia) constellation of satellite dishes on the roof of his Prague home in order to watch Serie A and the Bundesliga. 'Ježek was impulsive and able to rouse us. [Jozef] Vengloš, his assistant, was more of a calming influence, cultivated and educated. Together, this combination worked great,' said Panenka.

So much incident was crammed into Euro 76 that, per capita, it has no rivals as the most exciting international tournament ever. 'The general level of the four games seemed to me quite astonishing,' marvelled Brian Glanville in *World Soccer*. The magazine's editorial described the event as 'a week, we feel, in which footballers and football rediscovered what the game is all about … Czechoslovakia, West Germany, the Netherlands and Yugoslavia played without fear, and football lived again'.

In January 2016, Prague newspaper *Idnes* interviewed three senior citizens who, as far as anyone could prove, were the only Czechoslovakian fans to attend the final. They had journeyed 1,000km south to Belgrade from the Bohemian town of Semily. One of them, Zdeněk Strnad, recalled how he saw locals contemptuously dropping their match tickets on the ground in front of the Marakana before kick-off. Their loss.

8.15pm, 20 June 1976
Stadion Crvena Zvezda 'Marakana', Belgrade
Attendance: 30,790
Referee: Sergio Gonella (Italy)

CZECHOSLOVAKIA 2 (Švehlík 8, Dobiaš 25)
WEST GERMANY 2 (Müller 29, Hölzenbein 90)
Czechoslovakia won 5-3 on penalties after extra time

Shoot-out: Masný 1-0, Bonhof 1-1, Nehoda 2-1, Flohe 2-2, Ondruš 3-2, Bongartz 3-3, Jurkemik 4-3, Hoeneß shot over, Panenka 5-3.

CZECHOSLOVAKIA: Viktor, Dobiaš (Veselý 94), Čapkovič, Ondruš (c), Pivarník, Gögh, Panenka, Móder, Masný, Nehoda, Švehlík (Jurkemik 80).

WEST GERMANY: Maier, Vogts, Dietz, Schwarzenbeck, Beckenbauer (c), Bonhof, Hölzenbein, Wimmer (Flohe 46), Müller, Beer (Hannes Bongartz 80), Hoeneß.

Booked: Dobiaš (55), Móder (59).

1980

ON 12 November 1977, Italy were awarded their second European Championship finals in 12 years. UEFA president Artemio Franchi had hinted a
month earlier that the 1980 tournament would be hosted by 'a great footballing
nation', an unsubtle way of conveying that his homeland had got the nod
ahead of Switzerland. When it was confirmed, Franchi predicted the event
would reap 'sparkling revenues' and predicted crowds of 50,000 per game.

But the expansion to eight teams, a logical step after the brilliance of
1976, came at exactly the wrong moment. The interregnum between the
Argentinian and Spanish World Cups was a period when low-risk defensive
football held sway, hackers could injure forwards without risk of a red card,
and classy European national teams were thin on the ground.

Making things far worse, UEFA abolished the semi-finals. The two group
winners would go straight into the final, with the runners-up contesting the
third-place match. Aware that defeat at any point would mean near-certain
elimination, almost all the teams donned defensive chainmail. The format
was also financially suicidal, depriving UEFA of two semis' worth of extra
revenue.

In another change, the hosts now qualified automatically, and duly spent
1978/79 and 1979/80 warming up with a succession of friendlies. Then, just
three months before the tournament, Italian football reeled from one of the
juddering body blows it inflicts upon itself every few years.

In March 1980, restaurateur Alvaro Trinca and fruit wholesaler Massimo
Cruciani approached the Italian authorities with allegations that they had
been lured into a Serie A betting ring by bookies in their social circle, then
lost huge sums when the pre-agreed results failed to materialise. They also
alleged that numerous Serie A clubs and players were implicated.

This was the tipping point, because a month earlier Lazio's Maurizio
Montesi had spilled his guts to the authorities days after breaking his leg

against Cagliari. The much-maligned Italian judiciary, to give them their due, took swift action, resulting in surreal scenes at stadia up and down the country, with players being arrested by carabinieri while walking off the pitch after matches had finished.

The press dubbed the scandal *Totonero*, black Toto, a reference to the popular *Totocalcio* football betting game. Franchi resigned from his other job as head of the Italian FA. And, for once, actual punishments were handed out. Milan and Lazio were relegated to Serie B, and three more top-flight clubs were deducted points. Most of the players involved were obscure journeymen, but Ricky Albertosi, Italy's goalkeeper at Euro 68 and Mexico 70, was caught in the sting and received a two-season ban.

The affair claimed one other big scalp. Lanerossi Vicenza striker Paolo Rossi, who had starred for Italy at the 1978 World Cup, got hit with a three-year ban that was cut to two years on appeal. This deprived Italy's manager Enzo Bearzot of his sharpest forward just weeks before the tournament. Fiorentina playmaker Giancarlo Antognoni was acquitted, and the rest of Italy's squad had no involvement – but the damage to morale was incalculable.

All this was great news for West Germany, who were adjusting to life after Helmut Schön. His long-time assistant Jupp Derwall, whose metallic hairstyle had earned him the nickname Häuptling Silberlocke (Chief Silver-Curl), now held the reins. Derwall was far less of a tortured artist than the brooding Schön, and other than an embarrassing 0-0 draw in Malta, the qualifiers were straightforward.

In a strong squad, just one player survived from 1976, sweeper Bernard Dietz, whom Derwall made captain. Karl-Heinz Rummenigge was about to pick up the first of two European Footballer of the Year awards, the 20-year-old Köln playmaker Bernd Schuster added glamour to the midfield, and there was a new goalkeeper in the burly figure of another Köln man, Toni Schumacher. The Bundesliga was so strong at the time that, weeks earlier, it had supplied all four semi-finalists in the UEFA Cup.

Who in Group 1 could stop West Germany? Not Czechoslovakia, who turned up with a squad full of ageing veterans. And surely not Greece, making their debut at a major tournament. Scoring four against Hungary in Salonika hinted that the Greeks had something going for them, but they had failed to win any of their five warm-up games.

It seemed doubtful, too, whether the Netherlands had the right stuff any more. Jan Zwartkruis, their assistant manager in 1976, was now in charge and ruling with a rod of iron (even his surname translated as 'black cross'). His team left it late to qualify on a dramatic night in Leipzig, coming back from two down to beat East Germany 3-2 before a stunned crowd of 92,000.

The squad contained some ageing class acts – Ruud Krol, Arie Haan, Johnny Rep, the Van de Kerkhof twins – but Rob Rensenbrink, Wim Jansen and Wim Suurbier had all left the stage. Most sorely missed was Johan Neeskens, still only 28, who had skipped the defeat by Poland in the qualifiers at short notice, much to Zwartkruis's anger. Neeskens, who left Barcelona under a cloud in the summer of 1979, was now in the NASL with New York Cosmos, making a fistful of dollars but also struggling with a cocaine habit, a drink problem and a gambling addiction.

There were concerns about Zwartkruis's ability to get the best out of his players. A serial disciplinarian who had been a captain in the Royal Netherlands Air Force, he was regarded by many as the real power behind Ernst Happel's throne during the 1978 World Cup in Argentina. His energy-sapping training sessions prompted complaints, at which point he relaxed his grip. 'He gave me my first cap, so he must have been a good coach!' quipped defender Hugo Hovenkamp when Zwartkruis died in March 2013. 'Joking aside, he was a very amiable man. Too decent for football, actually. But he trained us so incredibly hard. Sometimes too hard. That was the contradiction – he was such a terribly nice man, with two faces.'

In the other group, Italy would kick off in Milan against opponents of whom little was expected. Things had gone stale for Spain under Barcelona legend Ladislao Kubala, who had been in charge since 1969. Kubala claimed to have numerous enemies at the RFEF, darkly hinting at irreconcilable differences with its general secretary Agustín Domínguez. Just before the finals, his players presented him with a watch pre-set to count down the number of hours remaining before he returned to Catalonia. The gesture could be interpreted in a number of ways.

England, now managed by West Ham old boy Ron Greenwood, qualified for their first tournament since 1970 without evoking many superlatives. Their clubs were in the middle of a long spell of dominance of the European Cup, which hadn't translated into similar paydirt at international level.

The consensus was that if you could stop the brilliant Kevin Keegan (once described by Günter Netzer as 'the most perfect footballer I have ever seen'), which was easier said than done, you were halfway to beating England. Like Bearzot, Greenwood would be without his best finisher. Trevor Francis had torn his achilles tendon, causing him to miss not only this tournament, but also Nottingham Forest's European Cup Final win over Hamburg in Madrid.

England's build-up left much to be desired. Wales hammered them 4-1 at the Racecourse Ground in Wrexham three weeks before the competition, with winger Leighton James tearing holes in their square defence. The

Nottingham Forest stopper Larry Lloyd had been regarded as certain to make Greenwood's squad – but he was destroyed by the fleet-footed James, ending up on his knees for one of the goals, and never played for England again.

As it turned out, Belgium would be the surprise. Other than Wilfried Van Moer, lured out of international retirement at 35, nobody remained from Raymond Goethals's 1970s side. But Guy Thys had spent the past few years assembling a good if workmanlike team, packed with rugged defenders and hard-running midfielders. Agile goalkeeper Jean-Marie Pfaff was a colourful loudmouth ('un peu kamikaze, un peu fou', as *L'Équipe* described him), the bearded full-back Eric Gerets was unflappable, and Jan Ceulemans had become one of the best right-sided attackers in Europe.

After drawing their first four qualifiers, Belgium won the other four to pip Austria to qualification by a point. They clinched things with an impressive 3-1 win in Glasgow, scoring all their goals in a ten-minute spell in the first half. 'You would be very silly to underrate us,' Thys said. 'People talk as if Italy and England are the only teams in our group.' He went on to lie that 'there is no way we'll sit back in defence'.

Days before the finals kicked off, the fate of the tournament's international television broadcast hung in the balance when workers at Italian state channel RAI threatened to strike. Ultimately, the TV bosses stumped up the money at the last minute and the live coverage went ahead uninterrupted. Had they known in advance how Euro 80 was going to turn out, they might well have told the technicians to shove it up their zoom lenses.

GROUP 1
West Germany, Czechoslovakia, Netherlands, Greece

The Italian public are rightly regarded as fervent, obsessive aficionados of football. But most of them took the summer of 1980 off. With UEFA signally failing to promote its flagship event properly, depressingly minuscule crowds were a recurring feature of the tournament. Just 11,059 people turned up at Rome's Stadio Olimpico for the opener between West Germany and Czechoslovakia, in an atmosphere so flat that the sound of players chesting the ball down was occasionally audible on the TV broadcast. Not kicking it – chesting it.

On the morning of the match, West Germany's utility man Herbert Zimmermann stood up too quickly and damaged his sciatic nerve, putting him out of the competition. So Derwall picked no fewer than seven players who could be classed as defenders, while leaving out the extravagant Schuster. His risk-averse outlook was rewarded as his team ground down a Czechoslovakian side who, as expected, were shadows of their 1976 selves.

With the West Germans playing like Eintracht Frankfurt reserves on a bad night and Czechoslovakia repeatedly passing back to goalkeeper Jaroslav Netolička at the slightest sign of danger, the first half was the footballing equivalent of a late bus. Uli Stielike, popping up unexpectedly on the left, turned inside Ladislav Vízek and curled a shot just over the crossbar. Shortly afterwards, the skilful Vízek himself took the long way around two Germans, but his low cross rolled tantalisingly wide of the far post.

The sense of ennui enveloping the afternoon peaked (or cratered) when, after Nehoda's speculative shot flew miles over, Toni Schumacher trudged some 30 yards to retrieve the ball from behind his goal in front of a deserted terrace, with nobody there to fetch it for him. At half-time, in the press box, Argentina's manager César Luis Menotti closed his notebook and lit a cigarillo, telling a German journalist, 'When nothing's going on, I smoke like a chimney. I've only become a chain-smoker in the last few years because of bad football.'

The game's one moment of class took nearly an hour to arrive. Near the corner flag, Hansi Müller flicked the ball backwards over Jozef Barmoš's head, then used the outside of his left foot to clip a cross to the far post, where Rummenigge rose above Netolička's pathetic half-jump to head home. Slim and cultured, looking more Iberian than Teutonic, Müller was a *soi-disant* artist who never got his hands dirty. Early in his career, one of his coaches at Stuttgart said of him, 'A ball hit his shin, otherwise his socks would have remained spotless, like the rest of his kit.'

The game died painfully slowly, although Netolička saved well at close range from the giant Hans-Peter Briegel following a corner. In the last minute, Müller and Rummenigge again combined well, but Müller miscued wide. West Germany had their revenge for Belgrade, but in the least inspiring manner imaginable.

Derwall ascribed his team's lame performance to the hot conditions, as well as complaining mysteriously that 'the Czechoslovakians played much too scientifically'. Meanwhile, Dietz blamed the Olimpico pitch: 'The grass is so dull that every ball immediately slows down and stops in a place where none of us are.' Speaking in 2008, Vízek described it as 'not a nice match: the Germans and us were afraid of each other'. The tournament could only get better – but it wouldn't.

═══

In Naples that evening, the Netherlands made a meal of tediously scraping past Greece. In the most football-mad city in this football-mad country, fewer than 15,000 souls filed through the San Paolo turnstiles. Already Euro 80 was looking like a dead duck.

Initially, nothing went right for the Dutch. Goalkeeper Piet Schrijvers retired early with a head injury after colliding with Thomas Mavros, international debutant Martien Vreijsen was so ineffectual on the wing that Zwartkruis hooked him at half-time, and Ruud Krol indulged himself with complacent flicks in his own box.

Their unfancied opponents were prepared to mix it. 'The Greeks have been learning how to be physical,' the former West German World Cup winner Max Merkel observed in his *Der Spiegel* column. 'They now hit ribs and kidneys harder than the ball.'

Confounding the expectations of them, Greece were calm and competent. Early on, the lively Mavros's header found Georgios Kostikos, who almost forced it in from point-blank range. Mavros came close again early in the second half when, after he had wasted another close-range chance, mutual dithering between Michel van de Korput and substitute keeper Pim Doesburg gave him a second bite.

The second half saw some dangerous tackles, all let go by the permissive referee Adolf Prokop. And an act of idiocy by their own goalkeeper ultimately cost Greece the draw. Vasilis Konstantinou had earlier made a good stop from Hovenkamp at his near post. Now he dived full-length to save a Dick Nanninga header that was going wide, but inexplicably kicked the striker's leg while a defender was clearing the danger. Konstantinou pig-headedly lay down feigning injury after the penalty was awarded; Kees Kist, unperturbed by a delay of more than two minutes, hit the spot-kick hard and low into the corner. 'In Greece, a penalty like that would cost you a lot of money,' Mavros muttered. But Konstantinou had clearly been at fault.

With two minutes left, the Dutch nearly paid for their lazy performance when the tall Anthimos Kapsis, who had stuck to Johan Cruyff like a leech in the 1971 European Cup Final, saw a header pushed on to the bar by Doesburg. Zwartkruis may have simply over-trained his team, something Hovenkamp later alluded to: 'In the build-up to Italy, we worked so hard that I was 4kg under my usual playing weight. It was too much of a good thing.'

It seemed certain that West Germany would teach these drippy Dutch a lesson three days later, and they did. By some distance the most enjoyable game of an anaemic tournament, it was a show of swaggering German firepower rather than an absorbing contest in the hot Neapolitan sun. Klaus Allofs grabbed a hat-trick, but the day belonged to somebody else.

Bernd Schuster had just six international caps going into this match, but was already convinced of his own greatness, with some justification. Franz Beckenbauer had to talk him out of a lucrative but ill-advised move to New

York Cosmos, and he would eventually sign for Barcelona after the finals. Here, making light of the 'new Netzer' baggage, he drifted between the right wing and the middle, his technical gifts lighting up the match.

Piet Schrijvers had recovered from his facial wounds, but looked hesitant and punched everything that came his way. He could do nothing about West Germany's first goal, the product of great work by Schuster, who twisted away from two defenders to crack a hard shot against the post. Allofs, following up, stuck away the rebound.

West Germany now took full control. Schuster seemed to be playing in three positions simultaneously, and the not-fully-fit Müller was running through his own repertoire too. Schrijvers and Hovenkamp between them cleared Horst Hrubesch's header off the line, while Rummenigge should have had a penalty when Van de Korput bundled him over. With Johnny Rep snuffed out by Manni Kaltz, the Netherlands looked as insipid as they had been against Greece.

As always with this fixture, needle was ever-present. Numerous dirty challenges went in, mostly from the Dutch, and Rummenigge complained of 'roughness, sometimes going beyond what's permissible'. The bad feeling boiled over as the first half ended. René van de Kerkhof elbowed Schuster in the head, and Haan and Schumacher nearly came to blows when they collided. Following that corner, Huub Stevens and Schumacher became embroiled in more handbags as Rep got involved too. Derwall, noticing Schumacher's temper boiling over, sent a substitute to stand behind his goal and calm him down.

On the hour, 1-0 became 2-0. Schuster dispossessed Haan too easily and fed Müller, who casually set up Allofs for an outside-of-the-foot drive that nestled in the corner. Within minutes, West Germany were out of sight: the irrepressible Schuster darted to the byline, and Allofs knocked in the cross with his knee. The little Fortuna Düsseldorf striker hadn't caught the eye at all, apart from the small matter of scoring a hat-trick. Derwall had decided to drop him after his lame performance against Czechoslovakia, but reconsidered. 'Things sometimes look different after a night's sleep,' said the manager. 'If you believe in a player one day, you must believe in him the next.'

Zwartkruis's team mounted a fightback in the closing stages, probably out of sheer embarrassment. Nanninga headed wide, Haan shot straight at Schumacher, and a dreadful decision by referee Robert Wurtz gifted them a penalty. Bennie Wijnstekers was tripped well outside the box by 19-year-old Lothar Matthäus, but made sure to fall inside it. Rep's kick into the top corner was unstoppable.

With five minutes left, Willy van de Kerkhof applied more orange gloss to the scoreline when he banged a magnificent shot low to Schumacher's left, but a draw would have been a nonsense. The game ended with Schuster and Rep seeming to headbutt each other in front of Wurtz, who indulgently separated them before giving Rep a talking-to for dissent.

Gerald Sinstadt, double-jobbing as an ITV commentator and a journalist, wrote in *The Times* the next morning, 'West Germany's road to Rome is as broad and inviting as the sunniest autostrada.' Zwartkruis agreed: 'I'm sure the Germans will reach the final.' This was a fresh-faced German squad, the youngest they ever took to a major tournament: discounting Dietz and Cullmann, the average age was 23 years and four months.

Years later, Rummenigge fondly recalled how Derwall created a 'great atmosphere' by booking into a Holiday Inn in central Rome and allowing visits from the wives and girlfriends. The teenage Matthäus caused a media stir by striking racy poses with his other half for the press's cameras. 'He was positively mad,' chuckled Rummenigge.

As mentioned, Euro 80 was plagued by extremely low attendances, in contrast to the only other time that Italy hosted the tournament. Czechoslovakia's unconvincing win over Greece in Rome witnessed the smallest of all, with just 4,726 souls rattling around inside a stadium which held 86,500 at the time.

In the subsequent twilight of his career at Rapid Vienna, Antonín Panenka would win a reputation for doing nothing whatsoever except scoring every free kick he took. Here, his curler over the Greek wall was well-aimed but hardly moving at the speed of light, and a better goalkeeper than Konstantinou wouldn't have fumbled it in at the foot of the post.

Greece, again unfazed, equalised when Nikos Anastopoulos outjumped Ladislav Jurkemik to head Mavros's centre past Czechoslovakia's new goalkeeper Stanislav Seman. The scorer then narrowly failed to connect with another cross three yards out, so the Czechoslovakians were relieved when they went 2-1 up against the run of play. Ján Kozák stole the ball from Mavros to set in motion a move which ended with Vízek neatly chipping Panenka's through ball over Konstantinou.

This pedestrian Czechoslovak side took more than an hour to finish the job. When Kozák's cross from the right sowed confusion in the Greek box, Nehoda pounced to belt it in from close range. Konstantinos Iosifidis almost scored a spectacular own goal near the end, diverting Verner Lička's cross past his own post, but 3-1 flattered Czechoslovakia. Though the reigning champions were still on life support, the competition's useless format meant that neither they nor the Netherlands could now reach the final, unless Greece somehow pulled the rug out from under West Germany.

=====

First, however, they had to play each other in a near-deserted and dilapidated San Siro whose multi-towered refurbishment was still some years away. Both teams had declined badly but with the rain pouring down, as it had in Zagreb in 1976, the Dutch got on top early. First, Frans Thijssen barrelled his way through three challenges to side-foot against the post. Moments later, Anton Ondruš almost scored another own goal as he had in 1976, bringing a quick reaction out of Netolička.

But first blood went to Czechoslovakia. With the Netherlands temporarily down to ten men (René van de Kerkhof had been lamed by Rostislav Vojáček's bad challenge), Jurkemik ran deep into Dutch territory and found Masný, who held up the ball until Vízek arrived. The striker showed great footwork to pick his way past three Dutchmen – one of a tiny handful of good moments in this tournament not involving Bernd Schuster – and squared it to give Nehoda a tap-in.

On the hour, the Netherlands found a bizarre equaliser. When Krol rolled a free kick to Kist on the edge of the box, he slipped on the wet grass as he shot, but it still squeezed into the bottom corner. Van de Korput had a late headed goal disallowed for offside, seemingly wrongly, but both sides knew they realistically couldn't make the final no matter what they did.

Afterwards, Zwartkruis dourly claimed that the presence of the Dutch squad's other halves were a fatal distraction. If it sounded like an exercise in deflection, so did the players' complaints that he had flogged them to death. Neither he nor they had done their stuff, and the Dutch didn't qualify for another tournament until 1988. Which, admittedly, would be worth the wait.

=====

That evening in Turin, it was back to the grindstone for West Germany. Derwall already knew the Netherlands-Czechoslovakia result by the time his team kicked off against Greece, but he sent out another defensive line-up anyway, resting Schuster, Dietz and Allofs (all on yellow cards). Meanwhile, Greek manager Alketas Panagoulias picked five reserves.

The match wasn't a complete waste of time, and West Germany created a handful of chances, mostly aerially. Rummenigge's header from Horst Hrubesch's centre brought an over-dramatic save out of Eleftherios Poupakis, and Hrubesch himself nodded one of Kaltz's trademark *Bananenflanken* (curling crosses from the right) too high. Rummenigge then missed with yet another header after Briegel's tireless running set him up.

Briegel himself, yet to adopt his trademark socks-around-ankles look, was living up to his nickname of *Die Walz von der Pfalz*, the steamroller from Rhineland-Palatinate. He strode past four Greeks on the right before shooting straight at Poupakis, whose jersey featured the strangest-looking shirt number in the history of football; the supposed 21 appeared more like 91, with the 9 crudely scrawled in blue marker.

In the second half, Rummenigge lobbed the onrushing Poupakis from long range but saw it bounce wide, and substitute Kalle Del'Haye's cameo was summed up when he thrillingly beat two men on the right before hitting an awful cross behind the goal. With ten minutes left, Christos Ardizoglou's 25-yarder clanged against the post: this was as close as Greece ever came to putting one over on the Germans, who remained undefeated against them as of early 2021.

The previous day, Derwall's squad had received an audience with Pope John Paul II. 'Twice, they didn't let us in because we were wearing unsuitable clothes,' Hrubesch recalled. When they eventually got inside, Il Papa made a V-sign in their general direction. Gerhard Krall, sports editor of the *Hamburger Morgenpost*, fancifully interpreted this as a sign that Hrubesch would either score two or create two. After this match, he sadly told the striker, 'You can't even trust the Pope any more.'

5.45pm, 11 June 1980
Stadio Olimpico, Rome
Attendance: 11,059
Referee: Alberto Michelotti (Italy)

WEST GERMANY 1 (Rummenigge 56)
CZECHOSLOVAKIA 0

WEST GERMANY: Harald Schumacher, Manni Kaltz, Bernard Dietz (c), Karlheinz Förster, Bernd Förster (Felix Magath 60), Uli Stielike, Bernd Cullmann, Hans-Peter Briegel, Karl-Heinz Rummenigge, Hansi Müller, Klaus Allofs. **Manager:** Jupp Derwall.

CZECHOSLOVAKIA: Jaroslav Netolička, Jozef Barmoš, Ladislav Jurkemik, Anton Ondruš (c), Koloman Gögh, František Štambachr, Ján Kozák, Antonín Panenka, Miroslav Gajdůšek (Marián Masný 68), Zdeněk Nehoda, Ladislav Vízek. **Manager:** Jozef Vengloš.

Booked: Dietz (71), Allofs (79).

8.30pm, 11 June 1980
Stadio San Paolo, Naples
Attendance: 14,990
Referee: Adolf Prokop (East Germany)

NETHERLANDS 1 (Kist 65 pen)
GREECE 0

NETHERLANDS: Piet Schrijvers (Pim Doesburg 16), Bennie Wijnstekers, Michel van de Korput, Hugo Hovenkamp, Ruud Krol (c), Huub Stevens, Arie Haan, Willy van de Kerkhof, René van de Kerkhof, Kees Kist, Martien Vreijsen (Dick Nanninga 46). **Manager:** Jan Zwartkruis.

GREECE: Vasilis Konstantinou, Ioannis Kyrastas, Konstantinos Iosifidis, Anthimos Kapsis (c), Georgios Foiros, Christos Terzanidis, Dinos Kouis, Spiros Livathinos, Thomas Mavros, Georgios Kostikos (Maik Galakos 78), Christos Ardizoglou (Nikos Anastopoulos 69). **Manager:** Alketas Panagoulias.

Booked: W. van de Kerkhof (62), Mavros (44).

5.45pm, 14 June 1980
Stadio San Paolo, Naples
Attendance: 26,546
Referee: Robert Wurtz (France)

WEST GERMANY 3 (Allofs 20, 60, 66)
NETHERLANDS 2 (Rep 80 pen, W. van de Kerkhof 85)

WEST GERMANY: Schumacher, Kaltz, Dietz (c) (Lothar Matthäus 73), K. Förster, Stielike, Briegel, Müller (Magath 65), Bernd Schuster, Horst Hrubesch, Rummenigge, Allofs.

NETHERLANDS: Schrijvers, Wijnstekers, Van de Korput, Hovenkamp (Nanninga 46), Krol (c), Stevens, Haan, W. van de Kerkhof, R. van de Kerkhof, Kist (Frans Thijssen 69), Johnny Rep.

Booked: Schuster (55), Stevens (44).

8.30pm, 14 June 1980
Stadio Olimpico, Rome
Attendance: 4,726
Referee: Pat Partridge (England)

CZECHOSLOVAKIA 3 (Panenka 6, Vízek 26, Nehoda 63)
GREECE 1 (Anastopoulos 14)

CZECHOSLOVAKIA: Stanislav Seman, Barmoš, Jurkemik, Ondruš (c), Gögh, Jan Berger (Verner Lička 23), Kozák, Panenka, Masný, Nehoda (Gajdůšek 74), Vízek.

GREECE: Konstantinou, Kyrastas, Iosifidis, Kapsis (c), Foiros, Terzanidis (Galakos 46), Kouis, Livathinos, Mavros, Kostikos (Charalambos Xanthopoulos 57), Anastopoulos.

5.45pm, 17 June 1980
Stadio Giuseppe Meazza 'San Siro', Milan
Attendance: 11,889
Referee: Hilmi Ok (Turkey)

CZECHOSLOVAKIA 1 (Nehoda 16)
NETHERLANDS 1 (Kist 59)

CZECHOSLOVAKIA: Netolička, Barmoš, Jurkemik, Ondruš (c), Gögh, Rostislav Vojáček, Kozák, Panenka (Štambachr 90), Masný (Lička 67), Nehoda, Vízek.

NETHERLANDS: Schrijvers, Wijnstekers, Van de Korput, Hovenkamp, Krol (c), Jan Poortvliet, Thijssen, W. van de Kerkhof, R. van de Kerkhof (Kist 15), Nanninga (Haan 46), Rep.

Booked: Rep (71), Haan (79).

8.30pm, 17 June 1980
Stadio Comunale, Turin
Attendance: 13,901
Referee: Brian McGinlay (Scotland)

GREECE 0
WEST GERMANY 0

GREECE: Eleftherios Poupakis, Ioannis Gounaris, Xanthopoulos, Petros Ravousis, Lakis Nikolaou, Takis Nikoloudis (c) (Georgios Koudas 65), Livathinos, Kouis, Mavros (Kostikos 80), Galakos, Ardizoglou.

WEST GERMANY: Schumacher, Kaltz, Briegel, K. Förster, B. Förster (Mirko Votava 46), Stielike, Cullmann (c), Müller, Hrubesch, Rummenigge (Kalle Del'Haye 66), Caspar Memering.

Booked: Gounaris (71).

GROUP 1	P	W	D	L	F	A	GD	Pts
WEST GERMANY	3	2	1	0	4	2	+2	5
CZECHOSLOVAKIA	3	1	1	1	4	3	+1	3
NETHERLANDS	3	1	1	1	4	4	0	3
GREECE	3	0	1	2	1	4	– 3	1

West Germany qualified for the final, Czechoslovakia qualified for the third-place play-off.

GROUP 2
Italy, Spain, Belgium, England

Ten years on from their heatmare in León, England dipped their toe back into the waters of tournament football. Dismayingly, however, their meeting with Belgium in Turin wouldn't be remembered for the football – even if it featured one of the nicest goals they ever scored in a major competition.

Guy Thys, who claimed England were favourites to win the tournament, deployed an offside trap which drove them to distraction on the day. 'The foreign press were astonished at the exceptional way we played offside, believing we were working overtime on it in training,' said defender Michel Renquin. 'But we never practised it. It was just a matter of game intelligence. I would look to my right, see Eric Gerets, and push back up.'

Ray Clemence parried René Vandereycken's free kick early on, but England soon took command. Tony Woodcock had already squandered a free header by the time they went ahead in stylish fashion. When Walter Meeuws headed away Trevor Brooking's cross, it fell for Ray Wilkins, who lifted it cleverly over two Belgians while nipping between them. The ball seemed to take an age to come down, but when it did, Wilkins cushioned another lovely lob over Pfaff. It took Belgium little time to equalise. Wilfried Van Moer's corner from the right wasn't cleared properly, a scramble ensued, and Jan Ceulemans stormed through a thicket of defenders to bang the ball home. As it went in, a large group of locals who had gained access to the England end of the Comunale erupted noisily, either in support of Belgium (a country with a sizeable Italian immigrant community) or in a spirit of anti-Englishness.

'The Italian public had taken up our cause, and that was really surprising,' said Ceulemans. And fighting soon broke out behind Clemence's goal. Earlier that afternoon, in central Turin, some England fans had fought a running battle on the streets with roughly 100 Italians, resulting in 36 arrests. The Turinese carabinieri were on a hair-trigger, and their baton-charge on the terraces was backed by tear gas.

The game was stopped by referee Heinz Aldinger for five minutes, not least because Clemence had been badly affected by the gas ('All of a sudden, my eyes went all glassy, and I started crying – I remember going over to the bench and they poured water over my face'). He would have fared even worse had there not been a running track separating the stands from the pitch. Within moments, Kenny Sansom joined the goalkeeper in the dugout, his own eyes streaming.

The lengthy delay killed England's momentum. In the second half, Woodcock scored with a neat finish, but up went the flag, supposedly for an offside by Sansom. Neither team created much otherwise, despite the patient probings of Van Moer. 'The little feller must have one of the best football brains in the world,' said Wilkins, who swapped shirts with him at the end. 'He never flagged.'

In a non-footballing sense, English embarrassment was near-total. 'While I was shedding tears outwardly, inwardly we were all sobbing,' Clemence wrote in his column for *Match* magazine. There was talk of an immediate ban from international competitions, but UEFA let England off with an £8,000 fine instead, one pound for every English fan estimated to be in Italy for the finals.

'We are ashamed of people like this,' Greenwood said. 'We have done everything to create the right impression here, then these bastards let you down. I wish they would all be put on a boat and dropped in the ocean.' From a manager who was hardly a rent-a-gob, this was strong stuff. In *The Observer*, Hugh McIlvanney noted, 'We ship [hooligans] abroad by the plane-load, and continental Europe in particular has come to regard them as only marginally more welcome than consignments of the Black Death. At this European Championship, it is not difficult to find people who would have been happier if England had competed by post.'

Meeuws and Vandereycken, selected for drug tests afterwards, were so dehydrated that they had to drink 15 beers between them to produce urine samples. They arrived back at the team hotel visibly the worse for wear, to the delight of the Belgian press. Not that the camp had been an alcohol-free zone to begin with. 'The Czechoslovakians were staying in the same hotel as us,' recalled skipper Julien Cools, 'and they couldn't understand how we could get results when they saw us sitting around tables with impressive trays of beer in front of us. Thys understood it was useless to impose iron discipline on us. He'd made up his mind to encourage us to feel at home.'

——

At San Siro, Italy-Spain pulled a decent crowd, but many of the locals were only there to voice their disgust at the *Totonero* affair. Some took it too far, and out came the riot police's batons again. Dino Zoff later spoke of the 'terrible tension' on the bus to the stadium and, sure enough, Italy played like a team with other things on their mind.

The angular-boned Francesco Graziani struggled to fill Paolo Rossi's boots, and was kept quiet by the terrifying Migueli, who had once put four stitches in Joe Jordan's face during the 1975 European Cup semi-final between Barcelona and Leeds. Nonetheless, Graziani ought to have had a penalty after 42 minutes, blatantly being pulled back by Quini after taking the ball around goalkeeper Luis Arconada. The performative nature of his fall dissuaded referee Károly Palotai, and he was cautioned for whingeing about it. Earlier, he had shot too high on the turn after Franco Causio had juggled the ball six times on the edge of the box. Causio, otherwise poor, was the main target of the crowd's derision.

Giancarlo Antognoni, the best player on the field, went closer with another long-range drive, and set up Claudio Gentile for a diving header well saved by Arconada. Jesús Zamora gave Antognoni a run for his money, embarking on numerous clever runs from midfield. But when Kubala introduced the sparky winger Juanito, Bearzot instantly and depressingly responded by bringing on the gnarled hatchet-man Romeo Benetti.

With 20 minutes left, after another fine Zamora run was ended with brutal finality by Fulvio Collovati. Juanito curved the free kick over the wall and off the underside of the woodwork, the ball landing right on Zoff's line. So, as disappointing as 0-0 was for Italy, it could have been worse. 'Bearzot has always been a lucky man: we must give him credit,' sighed *Corriere della Sera*. Spain's teenage stopper Miguel Tendillo, who coolly sat on Roberto Bettega throughout, flew back to Madrid under protest days later to do his months of national service.

——

Belgium now started to show what they were made of, overcoming the technically superior Spanish 2-1 in Milan. 'We had no stars or divas in the team,' said Meeuws, 'just 11 players emptying their guts to get the result.'

An agile and brave goalkeeper, Arconada now conceded a goal almost as cheap as the dreadful blunders he committed in the 1982 World Cup and Euro 84. After Erwin Vandenbergh dummied beautifully, Gerets exchanged passes with Meeuws before seeing his weak shot trundle past the goalkeeper's flapping hand. There was something very Belgian about two hard-bitten defenders coming up from the back to score.

François Van der Elst had already missed two chances by then, and Vandenbergh went closer with a shot that whizzed wide. So Spain were relieved to equalise before the break. Referee Charles Corver pushed away the permanently petulant Juanito when he upbraided a Belgian after being fouled; but as the dust settled, he floated a free kick to the far side of the box, where Quini got in behind Renquin and scored with a header that Pfaff might have saved.

But within a minute, Spain's captain Juan Manuel Asensi, who hadn't recovered fully from Roberto Bettega's brutal challenge three days earlier, hobbled off. With him gone, Belgium got the upper hand, and another vicious Vandereycken free kick brought a spectacular save out of Arconada before the break.

Van Moer, meanwhile, was unhurried and unerring in possession. His injury against Italy in 1972 had been the first of four leg breaks in as many years, keeping him sidelined for most of the 1970s. He was running a café in Limburg when Thys tempted him back into the fold. 'It was a poker player's gamble that came off,' said the manager. 'He's a great player with exceptional class and vision.' Van Moer himself admitted, 'I shared the fears of the press. I was afraid of not being up to the task.'

Early in the second half, Satrústegui and Quini wasted good chances. The streetwise Belgians soon made Spain pay. Jan Ceulemans – known as Sterke Jan (Jan the Strong) for his hard running – charged down the right, and his cross looped off Vicente del Bosque to fall nicely for the composed Cools, who lifted the finish over Arconada.

In the last minute, substitute René Verheyen spurned a golden chance to make it 3-1, shooting against Arconada's legs after Vandenbergh set him up. The miss meant that if Italy beat England by two goals that evening, they would need only a draw against Belgium to make the final.

Afterwards, the RFEF's president Pablo Porta publicly tried to hang Arconada. 'He has not justified his billing in goal,' sniped the bureaucrat, before referring to the rest of the Spanish squad as 'the infantry'. Upon returning home from Italy, Arconada diplomatically informed the press at Barajas airport, 'Porta has told me he didn't say that.'

Meanwhile, Cools revealed that his team's post-match unwinding had gone on until '4am or 5am', raising worrying questions about the condition of Meeuws's and Vandereycken's livers by now. Belgium were on their way.

Italy's showdown with England in Turin was seen as likely to confirm the destiny of Group 2. But would it go ahead at all? Nauseated by the hooliganism of three days earlier, mayor Diego Novelli threatened to have the match cancelled entirely. Eventually, he settled for banning the sale of alcohol at the stadium.

'We were made to feel as welcome as lepers,' remarked Clemence. A bus hired by travel agents Thomas Cook – mercifully empty at the time – was set ablaze in the city centre, and the tour operator said 250 of its customers simply remained in their hotels and watched the game on TV. 'Punters are leaving Turin in droves,' said a spokesman.

With safety in numbers, about 900 English fans gathered at Turin's railway station and walked down to the Comunale with a police escort, before having to charge into the stadium under a rain of missiles. But the authorities' ring of steel saw the game pass off without trouble, though a firecracker hit Emlyn Hughes on the neck as he warmed up. 'We came out in our Admiral tracksuits,' recalled Kenny Sansom, 'and then the Italians, fantastically suntanned, appeared in these incredible ice-blue silk tracksuits and Ray-Bans. We felt like we were 1-0 down already.'

Ron Greenwood's team selection seemed counter-intuitive. Clemence, blameless against Belgium, was replaced by Peter Shilton due to the perverse policy of rotating the goalkeepers regardless of form. Garry Birtles, who had 13 minutes of international football under his belt, was picked up front, and Ray Kennedy replaced Trevor Brooking.

In a tight game, watched by the biggest crowd of the tournament, England couldn't break out of Italy's shackles. 'I had Marco Tardelli on me the whole game,' Keegan lamented. 'He didn't get it all his own way, but I didn't score.'

The Italians should have broken the deadlock inside 30 seconds: Bettega headed Gabriele Oriali's cross wide after Phil Neal was caught napping at right-back, a sign of things to come. Soon afterwards, another centre from the left, this time by Antognoni, found both Graziani and Bettega unmarked in front of goal. Graziani miscontrolled, and Shilton smothered the ball before Bettega could score.

Italy kept up the pressure in the second half, getting plenty of joy on their left, where Neal was struggling. Although Kennedy did volley against the post with Zoff beaten, Graziani shot straight at Shilton after squeezing past Dave Watson, and another left-wing raid saw Graziani head Causio's cross over the bar. Neal ended up as Liverpool's most decorated footballer ever, but his weaknesses were obvious on nights like this.

Sure enough, the winning goal came down his side. Graziani charged past his feeble tackle and squared the ball for Tardelli, who materialised between two defenders in the goalmouth to score on his home ground. Belgium had Gerets in that position, Italy had Gentile, West Germany had Kaltz, but England had Neal. That was the difference.

There was no trouble in Turin afterwards, but it was a different story in Rome where celebrating locals looted upmarket shops and boutiques. 'It's always nice to beat England,' said Bearzot, 'but we aren't in the final yet.' For England, it was another failure to go the extra mile, with a squad who had 19 European Cup medals between them. 'When you play Italy in Turin, it's never going to be a garden party, but I wasn't over-impressed by the Italians,' Wilkins sniped. 'All that skill and they play eight in defence. At home, too!'

Keegan was engulfed in a media storm the following day, when a reporter from Turinese newspaper *Tuttosport* misquoted him as saying that referee Nicolae Rainea had been bribed. The actual quote was, 'On their own ground, well, they always seem to get a bit of help from referees. But I'm not saying they are bought or anything, just that the 50-50 decisions always went to Italy.' Keegan said later, 'It's pretty obvious that I was misunderstood, and frankly I'm sick of the whole business.' The journalist subsequently apologised.

======

And so to Naples, where the English and Spanish campaigns expired of natural causes. With nothing to play for except the booby prize of the third-place match, Greenwood turned to 22-year-old Tottenham starlet Glenn Hoddle, whom he had infamously dropped after an exciting debut and goal against Bulgaria with the immortal words, 'Disappointment is part of football.'

In the event, Hoddle failed to take his opportunity. But there was no shortage of entertainment, as the match was error-strewn to the point of farce. One of those cock-ups gave England the lead. When Antonio Olmo made a hash of clearing Wilkins's header, Brooking fired home at the far post.

Spain should have equalised straight away, but Santillana lashed a shot wide after out-jumping Watson. Meanwhile, Zamora was once again excelling. Playing a one-two with Julio Cardeñosa, he broke through to force a save from Clemence, and Mick Mills cleared the rebound off the line. England didn't heed the warnings. After half-time, another of Zamora's surging sorties from deep ended with Clemence pulling him down in the box. Dani put the penalty in off a post.

Dani could have doubled his money when Watson double-fouled Enrique Saura for another penalty. He again sent Clemence the wrong way – but referee Erich Linemayr ordered a retake because he had stopped for a split-second during his run-up. Second time round, his kick was feeble and Clemence saved it easily.

England's eventual winner came when the baseball-capped Arconada kept out Terry McDermott's stunning volley with a great reaction save, only for Tony Woodcock to stick away the loose ball. Near the end, Rafael Gordillo headed Dani's centre on to the bar, but England could have won by more than 2-1: Arconada pulled off a terrific double stop from McDermott and Keegan, and twice denied substitute Paul Mariner. At the death, another mad scramble in the Spanish box somehow failed to yield a third English goal.

'We came here with a reputation that we didn't live up to,' Keegan said. 'You can go on all day looking for reasons why. If we haven't learned anything from our games, we're never going to get any better. We have to go in one direction or the other – total football or defensive football. I hope it will be total football.'

Some felt the problems lay elsewhere. Jupp Derwall told Hugh McIlvanney in *The Observer* that the root cause was the harum-scarum nature of English league football. 'It's all ding-dong, from one end to the other, like a tennis match. Too many players are playing at a speed that their technique cannot cope with. When I saw England attack [against Italy] by having defenders send high balls into the goalmouth, I said, "This is not Greenwood's way."'

That evening, an appalled Roman crowd witnessed a rerun of the 1972 quarter-final as Belgium made the hosts drink their own rancid medicine. Universally written off before the tournament as 'numero quattro' in the four-team group, their massed defence and midfield grimly suffocated the life out of Italy, securing the 0-0 draw that put them into the final.

Bearzot's arrogant pre-match dismissal of the Belgian offside trap – 'Such a relic of football, applied only by bunglers, cannot stop a modern attacking team like Italy' – was made to look foolish. 'The tactical rigour had been applied against England; spontaneity and genius had prevailed against Spain; and implacable realism was going to prevail against Italy,' wrote Belgian journalist Christian Hubert in his history of the national team.

'Even I didn't expect us to get this far,' Thys said, but that was just kidology. He now dropped Erwin Vandenbergh, of whom perhaps too much had been expected. 'All of Europe presents him as a star,' Thys said of the

21-year-old striker, 'but for me, he's too soft and young. He still has a lot to learn. I expect much more from Ceulemans than him.'

Belgium committed countless fouls – mostly petty, occasionally horrible – to break up the play, and repeatedly refused to retreat ten yards at free kicks, to the hypocritical disgust of the locals. They were happy to soak up whatever Italy could offer. Which, with Antognoni being roughed up in midfield, wasn't much. The Fiorentina virtuoso was gone before half-time, a victim of Vandereycken's nasty foul near the touchline.

Decades later, the Belgian enforcer was still in denial: 'He injured himself by trying to avoid one of my tackles. He jumped, and fell brutally on the athletics track that surrounded the pitch. In fact, I didn't even touch him. If I wanted to frighten Antognoni, it was because, a few moments earlier, Van Moer had been literally assaulted by Benetti. We had to show we were not prepared to let that be done to us.' Within minutes, a mass brawl was narrowly averted after Luc Millecamps spotted Tardelli sneakily moving the ball forward at a free kick behind referee António Garrido's back.

Italy's best opportunity slipped away before the interval, when Pfaff made a brave and outstanding double save from Graziani. The keeper displayed similar courage when diving at Alessandro Altobelli's feet in the second half. He later spilled a Causio free kick, but recovered to clasp the ball in time.

Italy howled for a penalty when Meeuws seemed to handle just inside the box, but Garrido instead gave a free kick on the edge. 'He failed to spot a clear penalty for us,' moaned Bearzot. 'This is a case for the highest football court.'

Late on, after Pfaff yet again risked life and limb, Bettega shot into the side-netting. Then, when Causio had a clear run on goal, the goalkeeper flew off his line to save at the Juventus man's feet. Ceulemans might even have won it in the final seconds, but shot wearily wide.

No matter. Belgium were in their first ever international final by the thinnest margin possible, goals scored. 'We've defeated the Italians by Italian means,' Thys crowed. Renquin said years later, 'Thys was the ideal mastermind: a bridge between the [Flemish and Walloon] communities, a very intelligent man who knew the right things to say. He was perfect for our generation, who included some big mouths.'

For Italy, the end of the road was the end of the world. A furious Bearzot refused to praise Belgium after the game, calling them 'a dirty team [who] spent the whole match beating us; it was a manhunt'. Thys would later say, 'Bearzot, who is a friend, had tears in his eyes at the press conference afterwards. He reproached us for our wait-and-see attitude. I was amazed at his reaction: I'd been expecting congratulations. After all, we'd beaten the Italians at their own game! I had learned well from him!'

The witchfinders general of the Italian press gave Bearzot less of a scalding than might have been anticipated. 'The dream vanished: now we aim for third place,' sighed *Gazzetta dello Sport* in one of the typical responses. The manager survived, and would ultimately have his day in the sun. Spanish sun, to be precise.

5.45pm, 12 June 1980
Stadio Comunale, Turin
Attendance: 15,186
Referee: Heinz Aldinger (West Germany)

BELGIUM 1 (Ceulemans 30)

ENGLAND 1 (Wilkins 27)

BELGIUM: Jean-Marie Pfaff, Eric Gerets, Luc Millecamps, Walter Meeuws, Michel Renquin, Julien Cools (c), René Vandereycken, Wilfried Van Moer (Raymond Mommens 87), François Van der Elst, Erwin Vandenbergh, Jan Ceulemans. **Manager:** Guy Thys.

ENGLAND: Ray Clemence, Phil Neal, Kenny Sansom, Phil Thompson, Dave Watson, Ray Wilkins, Kevin Keegan (c), Steve Coppell (Terry McDermott 78), David Johnson (Ray Kennedy 69), Trevor Brooking, Tony Woodcock. **Manager:** Ron Greenwood.

8.30pm, 12 June 1980
Stadio Giuseppe Meazza 'San Siro', Milan
Attendance: 46,816
Referee: Károly Palotai (Hungary)

ITALY 0
SPAIN 0

ITALY: Dino Zoff (c), Claudio Gentile, Antonio Cabrini (Romeo Benetti 57), Gabriele Oriali, Fulvio Collovati, Gaetano Scirea, Marco Tardelli, Franco Causio, Roberto Bettega, Giancarlo Antognoni, Francesco Graziani. **Manager:** Enzo Bearzot.

SPAIN: Luis Arconada, José Ramón Alexanko, Miguel Bernardo 'Migueli', Miguel Tendillo, Rafael Gordillo, Juan Manuel Asensi (c), Enrique Saura, Jesús Zamora, Enrique Castro 'Quini', Daniel Ruíz-Bazán 'Dani' (Juan Gómez 'Juanito' 54), Jesús Satrústegui. **Manager:** László 'Ladislao' Kubala.

Booked: Graziani (44), Satrústegui (12).

5.45pm, 15 June 1980
Stadio Giuseppe Meazza 'San Siro', Milan
Attendance: 11,430
Referee: Charles Corver (Netherlands)

BELGIUM 2 (Gerets 17, Cools 65)
SPAIN 1 (Quini 36)

BELGIUM: Pfaff, Gerets, Millecamps, Meeuws, Renquin, Cools (c), Vandereycken, Van Moer (Mommens 73), Van der Elst, Vandenbergh (René Verheyen 82), Ceulemans.

SPAIN: Arconada, Alexanko, Migueli, Tendillo (Francisco José Carrasco 79), Gordillo, Asensi (c) (Vicente Del Bosque 37), Saura, Zamora, Quini, Juanito, Satrústegui.

Booked: Meeuws (22), Migueli (30).

8.30pm, 15 June 1980
Stadio Comunale, Turin
Attendance: 59,646
Referee: Nicolae Rainea (Romania)

ITALY 1 (Tardelli 79)
ENGLAND 0

ITALY: Zoff (c), Gentile, Benetti, Oriali, Collovati, Scirea, Tardelli, Causio (Giuseppe Baresi 89), Bettega, Antognoni, Graziani.

ENGLAND: Peter Shilton, Neal, Sansom, Thompson, Watson, Wilkins, Keegan (c), Coppell, Garry Birtles (Paul Mariner 76), Woodcock, Kennedy.

Booked: Benetti (10), Tardelli (19).

5.45pm, 18 June 1980
Stadio San Paolo, Naples
Attendance: 14,440
Referee: Erich Linemayr (Austria)

ENGLAND 2 (Brooking 19, Woodcock 61)
SPAIN 1 (Dani 48 pen)

ENGLAND: Clemence, Viv Anderson (Trevor Cherry 85), Mick Mills, Thompson, Watson, Wilkins, Keegan (c), Glenn Hoddle (Mariner 77), Woodcock, Brooking, McDermott.

SPAIN: Arconada, Alexanko, Secundino Suárez 'Cundi', Antonio Olmo, Gordillo, Francisco Javier Uría, Saura, Zamora, Carlos Alonso 'Santillana' (c), Juanito (Carrasco 46), Julio Cardeñosa (Dani 46).

Booked: McDermott (72), Carrasco (72).

8.30pm, 18 June 1980
Stadio Olimpico, Rome
Attendance: 42,318
Referee: António Garrido (Portugal)

ITALY 0
BELGIUM 0

ITALY: Zoff (c), Gentile, Benetti, Oriali (Alessandro Altobelli 46), Collovati, Scirea, Tardelli, Causio, Bettega, Antognoni (Baresi 35), Graziani.

BELGIUM: Pfaff, Gerets, Millecamps, Meeuws, Renquin, Cools (c), Mommens (Vandenbergh 78), Vandereycken, Van der Elst, Van Moer (Verheyen 49), Ceulemans.

Booked: Oriali (28), Causio (63), Vandereycken (33), Meeuws (51),, Van der Elst (70).

GROUP 2	P	W	D	L	F	A	GD	Pts
BELGIUM	3	1	2	0	3	2	+1	4
ITALY	3	1	2	0	1	0	+1	4
ENGLAND	3	1	1	1	3	3	0	3
SPAIN	3	0	1	3	2	4	− 2	1

Belgium qualified for the final, Italy qualified for the third-place play-off.

THIRD-PLACE PLAY-OFF
Italy v Czechoslovakia

Against Czechoslovakia in Naples, playing for a worthless consolation prize, Italy remained horribly blunt for a team with so many good players. Netolička showed great agility in dealing with a header from Alessandro Altobelli, who later unwittingly deflected Claudio Gentile's fantastic volley over the bar – but it was barren stuff, enlivened only by the best shot of the competition.

Early in the second half, Panenka caught Italy unawares by rolling a corner long to Ladislav Jurkemik, who was loitering 25 yards out. The defender never struck a football more sweetly in his life, sending an absolute slasher streaking into the top corner. Zoff had a recurring habit of being beaten from long range, but neither he nor anyone else could have stopped this.

With 17 minutes left, when Causio scooped a free kick into the goalmouth, Graziani leaped above Ondruš to head the equaliser. Zoff prevented Czechoslovakia winning it near the end, using both fists to beat away Nehoda's shot after Miroslav Gajdůšek had played the striker in.

The match went straight to penalties without any extra time, possibly due to the demands of Italian TV schedules rather than any desire to spare the punters 30 more minutes of rotten football. Spookily, Czechoslovakia's first five penalty takers were the same men who had taken their kicks in the 1976 final – in the same order.

After 16 successful efforts, Collovati's penalty squirmed out of the hands of Netolička, who grabbed the ball just before it fully crossed the line. Barmoš then claimed the wafer-thin sliver of glory on offer, thumping his kick into the top corner. UEFA took the hint and abolished the third-place play-off for good, to the anguish of millions.

8.30pm, 21 June 1980
Stadio San Paolo, Naples
Attendance: 24,652
Referee: Erich Linemayr (Austria)

CZECHOSLOVAKIA 1 (Jurkemik 54)
ITALY 1 (Graziani 73)
Czechoslovakia won 9-8 on penalties after 90 minutes
Shoot-out: Causio 0-1, Masný 1-1, Altobelli 1-2, Nehoda 2-2, Baresi 2-3, Ondruš 3-3, Cabrini 3-4, Jurkemik 4-4, Benetti 4-5, Panenka 5-5, Graziani 5-6, Gögh 6-6, Scirea 6-7, Gajdůšek 7-7, Tardelli 7-8, Kozák 8-8, Collovati saved, Barmoš 9-8.

CZECHOSLOVAKIA: Netolička, Barmoš, Jurkemik, Ondruš (c), Gögh, Vojáček, Kozák, Panenka, Masný, Nehoda, Vízek (Gajdůšek 64).

ITALY: Zoff (c), Gentile, Cabrini, Baresi, Collovati, Scirea, Tardelli, Causio, Bettega (Benetti 83), Altobelli, Graziani.

Booked: Jurkemik (41).

FINAL
West Germany v Belgium

Appropriately for a man who resembled Klaus Kinski after many hard months in the gym, Horst Hrubesch's nickname was *Das Kopfballungeheuer*, the Header-Monster. 'I always tried to play in a way that was as simple as possible,' he once remarked. Eighty-one of his 136 Bundesliga goals were scored in the air. His career had taken its time to get going, and he hadn't turned professional until 1975, aged 24.

The final was only Hrubesch's fifth international cap. 'Everything really happened so fast in the end,' he reminisced. 'Müller and Schuster, the two playmakers, were both geniuses, so it was quite simple for me.' He had yet to score in the competition, but picked a good time to show the world that there was more to his game than being 6ft 2in tall.

The Belgians were already in dreamland. So unexpected was their progression to the final that the KBVB failed to plan ahead, resulting in some frantic late-night phone calls before they secured a hotel in Rome at very short notice. Meanwhile, a number of the squad had to cancel pre-booked family holidays.

'Most of us still had regular day jobs and played football too,' Pfaff recalled. 'When we left for Italy, we saw it as sort of a holiday. But our efforts did not suffer from that, not one bit.' They also made light of a pay dispute with their FA, although Cools growled, 'Our officials argue that the KBVB is not as rich as that of Italy, West Germany or England. But that does not prevent them from being here in Italy, eating and drinking like the best. They're dancing with delight because we are in the final. We feel we should get something out of it too.'

In stark contrast to his treatment of Algeria two years later, Derwall wasn't taking Belgium lightly, describing their offside trap as 'a Maginot Line on wheels'. If his team were to finish the job, they could count on the neutral vote: most of the crowd at a half-full Stadio Olimpico were still angry with Belgium for strangling their heroes out of the competition.

When the Germans went ahead, it was no surprise that Schuster created the goal. He played a one-two with Allofs and chipped the return pass over Gerets. It landed on the barrel chest of Hrubesch, lurking on the edge of the box. The big striker let it bounce, then half-volleyed magnificently into the far corner for his first international goal.

But Schuster, perhaps still drunk on the potency of his own gifts, immediately gave the ball away in his own half to Ceulemans, whose instant pass put Van der Elst clean through. The striker blazed high and wide as Schumacher charged out of his goal.

His mistake notwithstanding, Schuster was at the heart of everything, picking team-mates out with raking passes. When he had a go from 25 yards, Pfaff moved quickly to save. Then Klaus Allofs tried his luck, bringing another good stop from the goalkeeper. It was starting to look like a West German cakewalk.

But ten minutes into the second half, big Briegel limped off after coming off worst in a painful clash with Vandereycken, and Belgium found a measure of control. Gerets and Meeuws both shot wide, and Vandereycken's piledriver forced Schumacher into a brilliant stop, the first save he'd had to make.

By now, Schuster's influence had waned. On 75 minutes, he made his first meaningful contribution in some time – a bad one. When he lost the ball 40 yards out, Kaltz accidentally poked it to Van der Elst, who headed straight for goal. Uli Stielike took his legs at least a yard outside the box, but he landed inside it. Referee Nicolae Rainea, well behind the play, gave a penalty. Vandereycken sent Schumacher the wrong way.

Alarmed, West Germany stepped up a gear. As Müller shaped to pull the trigger from Rummenigge's cross, Renquin's magnificent block frustrated him. Then another Rummenigge surge ended with Gerets, the coolest of customers, saving the day. And when Dietz's shot deflected off two Belgians to give Schuster a chance, Pfaff got down smartly again.

UEFA had decreed that extra time could be used here, unlike the third-place match. 'I remain convinced that Belgium would have won during extra time,' Hrubesch said in 2000. 'We were cooked.' But with 90 seconds left, tired Belgian minds and legs presented West Germany with their winner.

Rummenigge, preparing to take a corner on the left, spotted a photographer he knew sitting nearby. He reportedly told the lensman to focus on Hrubesch in the goalmouth (though, in truth, the footage suggests it was a nanosecond-brief exchange if it even happened). The ball sailed across, no one picked up Hrubesch as he arrived late, and with Pfaff caught in two minds, he nodded it in from almost under the bar.

'That goal had been worked on a hundred times,' Hrubesch revealed. 'Not just in the national team's training sessions, but at Hamburg. Manni Kaltz would take corners from the right, Felix Magath from the left, and I knew exactly where to place myself.' Pfaff's response: 'I made a mistake? Maybe. After all, I'm not God!' As the celebrations began, Krall of the *Hamburger Morgenpost* gleefully reminded Hrubesch, 'You see, the Pope was right! He meant this match!'

The best team had won, without doubt, but there wasn't much else positive to say about Euro 80. The official West German book of the event was moved to call it 'a hideous disfigurement of football'. Everything about it reeked of fear and cynicism. The low standard of play, the paucity of goals (the lowest since 1968), the pitiful crowds, the endless fouling and the hooliganism all conspired to produce a tournament best forgotten. Even the official mascot, a Pinocchio-like wooden cartoon, looked cruddy and cheap.

Artemio Franchi, desperately battling to save face, conceded that ticket prices had been too high. UEFA's own official history noted years later with bland understatement that 'the format did not meet with great success'. Nobody except Nehoda and Kist managed to score in more than one game, and the final, West Germany-Netherlands and England-Spain were the only genuinely watchable matches. Only a handful of individuals enhanced their reputations: Schuster, Rummenigge, Vízek, Scirea, Antognoni, Zamora and several Belgians.

El País called the competition 'the downfall of the gods', noting that 'the absence of high-level players has been the most striking feature of the tournament'. Norman Fox wrote in *The Times* that 'the tournarnent has not furthered the abused cause of attractive football'. Jacques Ferran, the editor of *France Football*, remarked that many of the players had acted more like boxers than footballers, showing a noticeable lack of respect towards the officials. This last point was backed up by the West German referee Heinz Aldinger, who noted that as soon as a decision went against somebody, 'The otherwise smiling young men of all the eight nations playing here became furies.'

And speaking of the Pope, which we were, his remark at the outset that 'these football games are too much competition for me' had shown him to be less than infallible. The tournament in 1984 was going to have to be a good one.

8.30pm, 22 June 1980
Stadio Olimpico, Rome
Attendance: 47,864
Referee: Nicolae Rainea (Romania)

WEST GERMANY 2 (Hrubesch 10, 89)
BELGIUM 1 (Vandereycken 72 pen)

WEST GERMANY: Schumacher, Kaltz, Dietz (c), K. Förster, Stielike, Briegel (Cullmann 55), Müller, Schuster, Hrubesch, Rummenigge, Allofs.

BELGIUM: Pfaff, Gerets, Millecamps, Meeuws, Renquin, Cools (c), Mommens, Vandereycken, Van der Elst, Van Moer, Ceulemans.

Booked: K. Förster (58), Millecamps (36), Vandereycken (55), Van der Elst (90+1).

1984

ABSURD THOUGH the idea seems today, 1984 was make or break for the European Championship. After the pitiful crowds and bleak football of 1980, UEFA moved quickly to shore up its showpiece, reintroducing the semi-finals and scrapping the unloved third-place play-off.

Awarding the finals to France, never a hotbed of football fever, was a huge gamble. Knowing that another sparsely attended tournament couldn't be countenanced, UEFA president Artemio Franchi ploughed millions of Swiss francs into a massive promotional campaign around the continent. He tragically didn't live to see the end result himself, dying in a car crash in Tuscany in August 1983.

Franchi's native Italy, fresh from winning the 1982 World Cup, essentially took a four-year break from competitive football. Failing to score in five of their eight qualifiers, they hit rock bottom by losing 5-0 over two games to the mediocre Swedes. Not until their final fixture, against little Cyprus in Perugia, did they manage a win.

Romania exploited Italy's decline, grinding out a stalemate in Florence, beating them at home, and finally securing qualification on a tense night in Bratislava. A methodical, workmanlike team who looked to the blond creator László Bölöni to make things happen, they would kick off in Saint-Étienne against Spain, who had qualified in bizarre fashion.

After their 1982 World Cup debacle, the Spanish appointed the wily Miguel Muñoz as manager and soon found themselves in a straight fight with the Netherlands for qualification. As the group drew to a close, the Dutch beat Malta 5-0 in Rotterdam, which meant Spain had to beat the Maltese by 11 goals four nights later.

Seville's Estadio Benito Villamarín was less than half-full to see Juan Señor miss an early penalty. When Santillana did open the scoring, Malta instantly equalised via a huge deflection. Spain led only 3-1 at the break, yet somehow scored nine more times in a madcap second half, with most of the goals hammered in from close range. Señor himself grabbed the 12th in the final minutes. Netherlands manager Kees Rijvers, who had spent the evening playing cards with his neighbours rather than watch the game, was fired.

Yugoslavia's qualification was even more topsy-turvy, with their eccentric manager Todor Veselinović making huge line-up changes in every match. A surreal 4-4 draw at home to Wales, in which they threw away a pair of two-goal leads, set the tone for their campaign.

The goals dried up for the Welsh after that game: just three more in five matches. Defeat in Sofia left them needing to beat Yugoslavia at Ninian Park to qualify, but Robbie James's solo effort was cancelled out when the usually immaculate Neville Southall let Mehmed Baždarević's tame shot creep past him. Wales now needed the Yugoslavia-Bulgaria match a week later to end all square, which would put them through on goal difference. Either of the two east European sides would qualify if they won.

At 2-2, with a minute left in Split, Wales were heading for the promised land – whereupon Bulgaria's Radoslav Zdravkov somehow messed up a situation where he and two colleagues had only Yugoslavian goalkeeper Zoran Simović to beat, with no defenders around. Moments later, at the other end, Ljubomir Radanović headed home Zlatko Vujović's cross, and Yugoslavia were through in outlandish circumstances. Wales's best ever crop of players – Southall, Ian Rush, Kevin Ratcliffe, Joey Jones, Brian Flynn, Mickey Thomas, Mark Hughes – would never play in a major tournament. 'I feel like death,' said their manager Mike England.

In Group 2, Portugal recovered from a 5-0 crushing in Moscow by surprisingly winning 1-0 in Poland (the scorer, Carlos Manuel, had a habit of grabbing vital goals for his country), meaning a final-day win over the Soviets in Lisbon would be enough. When Sergei Borovsky fouled Fernando Chalana outside the box, referee Georges Konrath wrongly awarded a penalty, which Rui Jordão converted. The pedestrian Soviets made just one good chance, missed by Khoren Oganesian – so Portugal were in their first European Championship.

They looked unlikely to be the life and soul of the party in France. Manager Fernando Cabrita used Porto's strong defence as his foundation stone and left out the electric young winger Paulo Futre. He had room for only one individualist: Chalana, whose left foot was so educated it could have delivered lectures at the Sorbonne. Or was it his right? 'Everyone thought I was left-footed, because I used it for penalties,' he said. 'I played with both feet interchangeably.'

Cabrita, not fully trusted by the FPF, worked with a 'technical commission' of António Morais, António Oliveira and José Augusto Torres, each man representing one of Portuguese football's Big Three. This resulted in an amicably divided squad who ate at tables segregated along club lines. 'During the training sessions, we could be found in three separate groups. Unbelievable, right?' said Chalana.

Belgium qualified ahead of a disappointing Scotland, but looked much diminished since 1980. A domestic match-fixing scandal saw seven Standard Liège players receive long bans, so Guy Thys lost his two best defenders – right-back Eric Gerets and stopper Walter Meeuws – as well as Gerard Plessers and Jos Daerden. 'My defence was beheaded,' he sighed.

Denmark, who Belgium would meet in Group A, had made astonishing strides under German coach Sepp Piontek, qualifying well ahead of Bobby Robson's lacklustre England. After scraping a 2-2 draw in Copenhagen, England were handed a rare defeat at Wembley by Allan Simonsen's penalty. Little Simonsen, for years Danish football's only ray of light, would finally get to play in a major tournament at 31 – and with plenty of back-up.

Only six of Denmark's 20-man squad played at home, a reflection of their warp-speed improvement. Their main striker, Preben Elkjær, was an all-action rampager who terrorised defences with physicality and pace. The wild card was teenager Michael Laudrup, already shining in Serie A with Lazio. Søren Lerby's aggression and Frank Arnesen's dangerous runs powered the midfield, while veteran sweeper Morten Olsen was showing no wear and tear. Denmark would take some stopping.

The opening game pitched them into the lion's den, against France in Paris. Still managed by the urbane Michel Hidalgo, the hosts were favourites to win the competition – not least because, after Jean-Luc Ettori and Jean Castaneda's howlers at España 82, they had finally found a good goalkeeper in Joël Bats. There was also a fearsome new ball-winner, the Basque Luis Fernandez. He happily played second fiddle to Michel Platini, who'd just claimed the second of three consecutive European Footballer of the Year awards.

Approaching 29, Platini was at the apex of his powers. Effectively two great players in one, a world-class playmaker and a nerveless striker, he preferred the latter role. '*Platoche* didn't want to make passes,' said Fernandez. 'He wanted to finish the job.'

At France's training camp in Font-Romeu in the Pyrenees, Platini chafed at team doctor Marc Bichon's altitude training tests. 'Your methods never scored a goal against anybody! I'm not a cyclist!' he yelled, after getting cramp on a bike. Bichon threatened to declare him unfit, but said years later, 'I didn't have the means to tell Platini that. Nobody could say that.'

Could the West Germans, who had stopped France by foul means on that shattering night in Seville in 1982, derail them again? They would have to do it without Bernd Schuster, who skipped a qualifier in Albania to attend his daughter's birth. The DFB was unamused and, with some inevitability, Schuster retired from international football in February 1984 (though he broke his foot before the finals anyway).

The qualifiers were an ordeal for Jupp Derwall's team. After twice losing 1-0 to Northern Ireland, they finally stumbled over the line when Gerd Strack's late header saved them against Albania's ten men in Saarbrücken. The midfield was a flair-free zone: Schuster, Paul Breitner, Hansi Müller and Felix Magath were all absent for varying reasons, and Derwall replaced them with grinders like Wolfgang Rolff and Rudi Bommer. Some optimistic German journalists peddled the idea that this was a 'tournament team' which would click when the serious business started. But would it?

GROUP A
France, Denmark, Belgium, Yugoslavia

'L'Europe en habit bleu,' Europe is dressed in blue, blared *L'Équipe*'s front page on the morning of the opening match. But at the Parc des Princes, the grim fate that befell Allan Simonsen overshadowed all else on the night.

Euro 84 should have served as the climax of the little magician's long international career. 'It's going to be the game of my life,' he said beforehand. But as the first half wound down, he and Yvon Le Roux both went for a 50-50 ball. His left leg snapped in the challenge like a wishbone and he was stretchered off, his face ashen with shock.

Even before that awful moment marred the match, the hosts had struggled for fluency, with Klaus Berggreen strangling Platini. 'They were hyper-disciplined,' Fernandez said of Denmark. 'They played like they were starved.' For long periods, France simply didn't feed Platini, who wrote in his *Gazzetta dello Sport* column, 'Maybe I'm wrong, but I got the impression that our Bordeaux contingent [Giresse, Tigana, Lacombe and Battiston] tended to pass to themselves, probably for reasons of automation, pure reflex. I didn't find myself at the heart of the action too often.'

Danish goalkeeper Ole Qvist, whose side parting and moustache made him a dead ringer for Mr Pringles of crisps-in-a-tube fame, did well to keep out two Platini headers. But in the end, good luck made the difference. Ivan Nielsen, trying to intercept Giresse's pass to Lacombe, inadvertently teed up Platini just outside the box. His shot grazed the falling Busk's head, leaving Qvist stranded.

Enough time remained for Manuel Amoros to disgrace himself. After John Lauridsen and then Jesper Olsen hacked him, he hurled the ball at

Olsen's head (it missed), then headbutted him full in the face. Referee Volker Roth instantly sent Amoros off as angry Danes surrounded him. 'I was a young Spanish hothead,' he admitted years later. 'The Danes pissed me off. And when I missed Olsen with the ball, it pissed me off even more!'

=====

The following evening, a new star was born as Guy Thys set Enzo Scifo loose on Yugoslavia in Lens. The 18-year-old, winning only his second cap, was the youngest player in the history of the finals to date. Slim and sharp, playing like someone ten years older, he found plentiful gaps in Yugoslavia's exposed midfield. He said decades later, 'I spotted the Italian coach [Enzo Bearzot] in the stands. That blew me away. I wanted to show him what I could do.' Bearzot praised him for playing 'an extraordinary match with a very cool head'.

Yugoslavia began brightly, with Sulejman Halilović missing three half-chances in the opening stages. But Belgium – wearing quirky Argyle-patterned white shirts – took the lead when Walter De Greef's long pass found Erwin Vandenbergh 25 yards out. The striker's shot cannoned off Srečko Katanec's knee to float high over Zoran Simović, as unstoppable as Platini's goal the previous night.

The Belgians went 2-0 up in first-half stoppage time with a goal from their other new boy, debutant centre-back Georges Grün. Simović came out for Scifo's corner but clawed at thin air, allowing Grün to score with a looping header. 'Defensively, I delivered an average performance,' he wrote in his 1986 autobiography. 'But that goal saved my match.'

Despite bringing on a Scifo of their own, 19-year-old Dragan Stojković, Yugoslavia might have lost by more. Simović atoned for his earlier error with an impressive double stop from Nico Claesen, and Nenad Stojković blocked Vandenbergh's goal-bound shot. 'After this victory, we sailed on an ocean of euphoria, with the help of the press,' recalled Scifo. 'We already saw ourselves in the final. However, one could ask the question: were we too strong, or were the Yugoslavs very weak?'

=====

Scifo's fears were prescient. On a sweltering afternoon at the new Stade de la Beaujoire in Nantes, France ate him and his team without salt. Grün headed off the line in the opening seconds after Didier Six caused mayhem on the right; and, minutes later, Giresse rolled an indirect free kick to Patrick Battiston, who nearly broke the bar from 30 yards. Platini instinctively trapped the rebound, sidestepped a defender and smashed an equally powerful left-footer into the corner.

Soon afterwards, Pfaff prevented Six making it 2-0 after the white-haired Walter De Greef passed the ball straight to the winger. De Greef, Grün and Paul Lambrichts had just eight caps between them: playing behind this defence of greenhorns, Pfaff needed to be at his best. Soon he was diving at the feet of Platini, who vaulted acrobatically over him in a tableau so spectacular that Adidas used it in an ad campaign.

Belgium were already overwhelmed. Scifo, who had picked up an early knock when Platini tackled him, was soon bypassed by Giresse and Tigana in midfield. 'Everything went too fast,' he lamented. 'There were no solutions for the runs [France] were making, we were unable to string together three consecutive passes, and we lacked strength of character. At times, Platini even had the luxury of directing the play while walking.' The hard-bitten René Vandereycken was swamped in his holding role, dropping too deep as he tried to protect his inexperienced defenders.

Briefly, Belgium fought back. Fernandez kicked Jan Ceulemans's header off the line, Michel De Wolf came up from left-back to shoot against the bar, and Vandenbergh missed badly with a far-post header. France promptly finished them off before half-time. First, Giresse exchanged passes with Tigana and chipped Pfaff for the afternoon's best goal. Then Six flew down the right, rounded Pfaff and crossed to Giresse, who lifted it back into the goalmouth for Fernandez to head in.

The second half brought more bejewelled passes and extravagant flourishes. After another long spell of pressure, Bernard Genghini released Six, who was knocked over by Pfaff. The goalkeeper was the penalty king of the Bundesliga, saving an astonishing 64 per cent of kicks he faced, but he wasn't getting this one: Platini thrashed it down the middle, sending holy white smoke rising up from the spot. Near the end, the French captain rounded off an exhilarating afternoon, heading Giresse's free kick in off the post for 5-0.

This match was the coming-out party for Le Carré Magique, the magic square, Michel Hidalgo's midfield of all the talents. Putting it crudely, Fernandez tackled, Tigana ran, Giresse created and Platini scored, but each did a little bit of everything – though Platini getting his hands dirty in his own half was a rare sight, while Tigana scored once in 57 caps. 'Platini was our playmaker, he made the decisions,' Giresse said. 'I tried to read the game and plug gaps. Tigana had tremendous mental strength and a very precise way of playing. Fernandez contributed aggression, commitment and adaptability.'

=====

Like France, Denmark scored at will against Yugoslavia in Lyon that evening. Unlike France, they could easily have leaked five themselves. Their attacks resembled an animated cartoon on fast-forward, with players swarming up the pitch and making clever runs into the box – but they left plenty of grass behind them too.

Early on, Frank Arnesen skinned Radanović on the right and crossed into the goalmouth. Yugoslavia's new goalkeeper Tomislav Ivković left too much room at his near post, and his gloves diverted the ball into his own net.

Yugoslavia almost hit back instantly, but when Mehmed Baždarević played in Safet Sušić, the cultured playmaker clubbed the chance wide. Denmark swiftly doubled their lead. Elkjær curled a teasing ball into the goalmouth, Laudrup and Ivković converged on it, and Laudrup won the race. It was going in, but Berggreen poked it home under the bar anyway.

Having seen enough, Todor Veselinović took off the visibly disgusted Baždarević. But Yugoslavia would have been ahead at half-time if they had kept their heads in front of goal. Qvist saved at Boro Cvetković's feet, made a superb reflex stop from the same player, and clutched Ivan Gudelj's header. Not that Denmark were idling. Lerby scuffed wide after another thrilling move, before his back-heel put in Elkjær to shoot straight at Ivković.

The pace never let up after the interval. Ivković kept Yugoslavia in the game with a reflex save from Arnesen; Berggreen was denied by Nenad Stojković's block; Ivković, in credit by now, made another brilliant stop from Laudrup; and Qvist foiled Vujović twice in a minute.

Late on, Yugoslavia caved in. Gudelj pushed Elkjær over in the box, and Arnesen scored from the spot to seal it. The fourth and fifth goals were harsh on Yugoslavia, but easy on the eye. Elkjær blasted home following great work by Berggreen and Laudrup, and substitute John Lauridsen bent a stylish shot into the far corner.

Afterwards, Veselinović fainted from stress and was hospitalised overnight. His counterpart Piontek allowed Denmark's players a 2.30am curfew, and an entire boulevard of bars in central Lyon was drained dry of beer by Danish fans – who simply switched to wine. Lighting up a tournament was thirsty work.

====

With little at stake, France and Yugoslavia could take things easy in Saint-Étienne. The party mood permeated the crowd, too. Early on, the game was halted when a cockerel strutted on to the field, while another one hopped around in the Yugoslavian goalmouth.

'The Yugoslavs had more depth and skill than Belgium: they could hurt you,' said Fernandez. They carved France open with a tremendous goal. Miloš Šestić dribbled past Tigana and Giresse, played a one-two with Sušić, and lashed an arrowing drive into the top corner. Giresse immediately hit the bar with a volley, but France were booed off at half-time. In the dressing room, Hidalgo furiously kicked a water bottle. 'I was angry with myself,' he said. 'It was my fault. The players had enjoyed the 3-5-2 [against Belgium].'

He reshuffled his team, and the goals flowed in the second half. Young Jean-Marc Ferreri created the first instalment of Platini's treble, robbing Radanović and threading a lovely pass to Platini, who ran behind a defender to guide the ball under Simović with his left foot.

Next, an intricate move down the right involving Domergue, Ferreri, Tigana and Giresse ended with Battiston crossing for Platini to guide home a superb diving header. He called it 'the most beautiful' of his nine Euro 84 goals, adding caustically, 'It was a poor cross from Patrick. If it had been good, I wouldn't have had to dive to the ground like that!' (Battiston's reply, 'Michel is very demanding.')

Yugoslavia kept at it, Bats saving with his legs from Baždarević, but they could do nothing about Platini's third. 'We had a free kick,' Lacombe recalled. 'Michel shifted the ball two feet. Sušić looked at him and said, "What are you doing?" Michel replied, "Here, I'm at home. I do what I want!"' Taking almost no run-up, he stroked a sumptuous shot over the wall and into the top corner.

Near the end, Max Bossis tripped substitute Stjepan Deverić in the box. Bats moved slightly on his line before saving Radanović's limp penalty, so referee André Daina ordered a retake. Radanović left it to young Dragan Stojković, who thumped it into the top corner. Deverić almost salvaged a point after beating three Frenchmen and shooting just wide, but Yugoslavia went home whitewashed. 'It was a real shame in 1984,' said Zlatko Vujović. 'We weren't well prepared with "Tose" Veselinović, nor did he know us well.'

A fine match had a tragic footnote. Yugoslavia's team doctor, 65-year-old Božidar Milenović, suffered a heart attack while running on to the pitch to treat an injured player in the second half, and died in hospital the following day.

===

In Strasbourg, Belgium and Denmark went at each other like alley cats for a place in the semis. From the start, it was a match for those who liked their meat raw: in the opening minutes, Elkjær elbowed Vandereycken in the face, and Vandereycken himself hit Lerby and Laudrup with late tackles.

But before long, a great game unfolded. Claesen's overhead kick looped spectacularly over the bar, Elkjær's bustling run was ended by Pfaff taking man and ball extremely illegally, and Morten Olsen almost knocked Vandenbergh's cross into his own net. Soon, Belgium – who needed to win – went ahead. Vandereycken floated a free kick into the box, and Olsen's header went straight to Grün. He cushioned it for Ceulemans to miscue badly, but the shot's feebleness surprised Qvist and it crept in off the post.

Before half-time, the industrious Franky Vercauteren doubled Belgium's lead with the goal of the tournament. Collecting a throw from Claesen on the left, he nodded the ball over Bertelsen's head and, from the far edge of the Danish box, crashed a wonderful shot over Qvist and into the top corner. Denmark were stunned – but, crucially, hit back within a minute. Elkjær tumbled theatrically under De Greef's challenge for the second time in the match, referee Adolf Prokop bought it this time, and Arnesen buried the penalty.

At half-time, Belgium were still going through. In the pivotal incident of the evening, a minute into the second half, Ceulemans's first-time pass sent Vandenbergh running through on goal – but the striker shot against Qvist's legs. He later reflected, 'After my miss, we collapsed. My international career was never really the same after that.'

Piontek soon threw on Kenneth Brylie, bringing the quotient of Anderlecht players on the field to nine. The switch paid off quicker than Piontek could have dreamed of. Within four minutes, Arnesen put an unmissable cross on to the substitute's head for 2-2.

Both teams now lost their minds. De Greef elbowed Elkjær, De Wolf's shin was raked by Arnesen, Elkjær kicked out at Scifo, De Greef took revenge on him, and De Wolf chopped down Laudrup. The match boiled over when Vandereycken kicked Arnesen hard on the knee: Morten Olsen booted the ball at him, then shoved him to the ground. 'If I'd had a gun, I would have shot him,' Olsen remarked. Prokop booked Vandereycken, but didn't even speak to Olsen. Minutes later, Ludo Coeck committed the worst foul of the night, on Berggreen.

Belgium never looked like getting the third goal they needed, and Denmark killed them on the counter-attack as Elkjær stretched those long legs one last time. Lei Clijsters's clearance hit De Greef and fell kindly for him, but there was nothing lucky about how he evaded De Wolf, pushed the ball beyond De Greef and lifted the ball over Pfaff (who spitefully kicked him on his way past).

A delighted Piontek now extended his squad's curfew to 5am. 'There's no point in sending them to bed at 1am after such a big game,' he said. 'It's also okay if they drink five, ten, 15 beers and smoke some cigarettes. They just have to keep their agreements. If that means breakfast at 11am, then they have to show up. And they did.'

Belgium's rawness in key positions had proved fatal. 'With Gerets and Meeuws present, the defeat against France would never have happened,' mused Vandenbergh. 'And their presence would certainly have helped the team to keep their cool against Denmark.' Ceulemans agreed: 'Euro 84 should have been the pinnacle of our generation. But we had to go to the tournament with some guys who had neither the experience, nor – with all the respect I can pay them – the international class.'

One of them, De Greef, was scapegoated for the result and never played international football again. 'I paid in cash for Belgium's failure at Euro 84,' he said in 2020. 'A victim was needed, and that was me.'

8.30pm, 12 June 1984
Parc des Princes, Paris
Attendance: 47,570
Referee: Volker Roth (West Germany)

FRANCE 1 (Platini 78)
DENMARK 0

FRANCE: Joël Bats, Patrick Battiston, Manuel Amoros, Max Bossis, Yvon Le Roux (Jean-François Domergue 61), Luis Fernandez, Jean Tigana, Alain Giresse, Bernard Lacombe, Michel Platini (c), Bruno Bellone. **Manager:** Michel Hidalgo.

DENMARK: Ole Qvist, Søren Busk, Søren Lerby, Morten Olsen (c), Ivan Nielsen, Klaus Berggreen, Jens Jørn Bertelsen, Allan Simonsen (John Lauridsen 46), Preben Elkjær, Michael Laudrup, Frank Arnesen (Jesper Olsen 80). **Manager:** Sepp Piontek.

Booked: J. Olsen (88).
Sent off: Amoros (87).

8.30pm, 13 June 1984
Stade Félix Bollaert, Lens
Attendance: 41,774
Referee: Erik Fredriksson (Sweden)

BELGIUM 2 (Vandenbergh 28, Grün 45+1)

YUGOSLAVIA 0

BELGIUM: Jean-Marie Pfaff, Georges Grün, Leo Clijsters (Paul Lambrichts 35), Walter De Greef, Michel De Wolf, René Vandereycken, Franky Vercauteren, Enzo Scifo, Erwin Vandenbergh, Nico Claesen, Jan Ceulemans (c). **Manager:** Guy Thys.

YUGOSLAVIA: Zoran Simović, Nenad Stojković, Ivan Gudelj, Velimir Zajec (c), Faruk Hadžibegić, Srečko Katanec, Mehmed Baždarević (Dragan Stojković 61), Miloš Šestić, Sulejman Halilović, Safet Sušić, Zlatko Vujović (Boro Cvetković 79). **Manager:** Todor Veselinović.

Booked: Hadžibegić (54).

5.15pm, 16 June 1984
Stade de la Beaujoire, Nantes
Attendance: 51,359
Referee: Bob Valentine (Scotland)

FRANCE 5 (Platini 4, 75 pen, 89, Giresse 33, Fernandez 44)
BELGIUM 0

FRANCE: Bats, Battiston, Domergue, Bossis, Fernandez, Tigana, Giresse, Bernard Genghini (Thierry Tusseau 80), Lacombe (Dominique Rocheteau 66), Platini (c), Didier Six.

BELGIUM: Pfaff, Grün, Lambrichts, De Greef, De Wolf, Vandereycken (Ludo Coeck 46), Vercauteren, Scifo (René Verheyen 53), Vandenbergh, Claesen, Ceulemans (c).

Booked: Tigana (40), Claesen (17).

8.30pm, 16 June 1984
Stade de Gerland, Lyon
Attendance: 34,745
Referee: Augusto Lamo Castillo (Spain)

DENMARK 5 (Ivković 8 og, Berggreen 16, Arnesen 69 pen, Elkjær 82, Lauridsen 84)
YUGOSLAVIA 0

DENMARK: Qvist, Ole Rasmussen (John Sivebæk 61), Busk, M. Olsen (c), Nielsen, Lerby, Berggreen, Bertelsen, Elkjær, Laudrup, Arnesen (Lauridsen 79).

YUGOSLAVIA: Tomislav Ivković, Branko Miljuš, N. Stojković, Zajec (c), Katanec (Halilović 58), Ljubomir Radanović, Baždarević (D. Stojković 23), Gudelj, Cvetković, Sušić, Vujović.

Booked: Zajec 14.

8.30pm, 19 June 1984
Stade Geoffroy-Guichard, Saint-Étienne
Attendance: 47,589
Referee: André Daina (Switzerland)

FRANCE 3 (Platini 59, 62, 77)
YUGOSLAVIA 2 (Šestić 32, D. Stojković 82 pen)

FRANCE: Bats, Battiston, Domergue, Bossis, Fernandez, Tigana, Giresse, Jean-Marc Ferreri (Daniel Bravo 77), Rocheteau (Tusseau 46), Platini (c), Six.

YUGOSLAVIA: Simović, Miljuš, N. Stojković, Zajec (c), Radanović, Baždarević (Katanec 85), Gudelj, D. Stojković, Vujović (Stjepan Deverić 60), Sušić, Šestić.

8.30pm, 19 June 1984
Stade de la Meinau, Strasbourg
Attendance: 36,911
Referee: Adolf Prokop (East Germany)

DENMARK 3 (Arnesen 41 pen, Brylle 60, Elkjær 84)
BELGIUM 2 (Ceulemans 26, Vercauteren 39)

DENMARK: Qvist, Rasmussen (Kenneth Brylle 57), Busk, M. Olsen (c), Nielsen, Lerby, Berggreen, Bertelsen, Elkjær, Laudrup, Arnesen (Sivebæk 79).

BELGIUM: Pfaff, Grün, Clijsters, De Greef, De Wolf, Vandereycken, Vercauteren (Eddy Voordeckers 62), Scifo, Vandenbergh, Claesen (Coeck 46), Ceulemans (c).

Booked: De Greef (62), Vandereycken (65).

GROUP A	P	W	D	L	F	A	GD	Pts
FRANCE	3	3	0	0	9	2	+7	6
DENMARK	3	2	0	1	8	3	+5	4
BELGIUM	3	1	0	2	4	8	− 4	2
YUGOSLAVIA	3	0	0	3	2	10	− 8	0

France and Denmark qualified.

GROUP B
West Germany, Portugal, Romania, Spain

'We just don't know where we stand,' Uli Stielike moaned before West Germany kicked off against Portugal in Strasbourg. The sweeper was talking in general terms, but knew his goalkeeper Toni Schumacher was agitating for him to be dropped to accommodate Gerd Strack, Schumacher's Köln team-mate. Stielike appealed to DFB president Hermann Neuberger to intervene with 'a strong word'; Neuberger replied that while Schumacher was entitled to criticise team-mates, he shouldn't do so publicly.

If West Germany's line-up lacked skill, it had no shortage of brawn. 'We got a little scared when we walked out on to the field with all these big players,' Fernando Chalana recalled, 'and us, the little Portuguese, physical weaklings. And yet we were very good.'

The Germans' best chance came in the seventh minute, when Bento's casual throw-out and Álvaro Magalhães's equally loose back-pass presented Rudi Völler with the ball in Portugal's goalmouth. Disaster was narrowly averted by Bento parrying Völler's shot behind for a corner.

Memories of España 82 were fresh, so Schumacher was relentlessly jeered by the locals, especially when saving Jaime Pacheco's long-range rocket. Meanwhile, the frail Chalana showed some beautiful touches. 'I would rather watch Chalana for five minutes, with his gypsy locks and flapping shirt-tail and bewitching feet, than I would West Germany for a whole match,' wrote David Miller in *The Times*. But most of the play was West Germany's. Klaus Allofs ballooned miles over when Bento failed to come for a cross, and shaved a post with a free kick in the second half. At the death, they went close twice more. First, Bento turned Allofs' shot around the post; and when the otherwise impeccable António Lima Pereira missed a header, the ball wouldn't come down for Völler, who bludgeoned it wide.

'We played very nervously,' Derwall growled, before bemoaning the quality of his midfield. *Kicker* magazine described the performance as 'a relapse into the worst times' and, years later, in their German-language history of the Euros, Dietrich Schulze-Marmeling and Hubert Dahlkamp called it 'catastrophic football'. It wasn't that bad, but the dropped point would cost West Germany dearly.

======

The Romanian FA were taking the possibility of defections to the West so seriously that they disconnected the TVs in their players' hotel rooms, to reduce the chances of spiritual contamination by bourgeois propaganda. The squad themselves were forbidden to talk to the media, with all phone calls to their rooms re-routed to the delegation's security officer.

'We weren't given much money per day, $5 or something,' recalled striker Rodion Cămătaru. 'We bought jeans. I was impressed that many Romanians living in France turned up to watch us train. They brought us stuff because they knew we were miserable.'

Manager Mircea Lucescu seemed to think he was trapped in an Alan J. Pakula conspiracy thriller. In March, his opposite number Miguel Muñoz had travelled to Craiova to see Romania beat Greece in a friendly. Afterwards, Muñoz asked Lucescu for a video tape of the match. Lucescu initially claimed it hadn't been filmed, then promised to send Muñoz a copy, which of course never arrived. His paranoia was such that Romania trained in a secret location (a field beside an oil refinery) three days before meeting Spain.

But in Saint-Étienne, before the tournament's smallest crowd, the east Europeans were the more adventurous of two ordinary teams. Spain undeservedly went in front when Nicolae Ungureanu lost possession to Juan Señor, who quickly played Ricardo Gallego through on goal. As the midfielder accelerated past goalkeeper Silviu Lung, he was pulled down. Francisco Carrasco hit the penalty down the middle, but Lung had already gone the wrong way.

Romania's equaliser was a really well-worked goal. Holding off two defenders, Marcel Coraş dribbled across the Spanish box, then neatly laid the ball off to László Bölöni, whose left foot powered the ball into the near corner. As Romania briefly seized the initiative, Michael Klein set up Mircea Rednic to blaze wide from seven yards.

But in the second half, there was hardly any action at all, other than José Antonio Camacho's magnificent block diverting Coraş's shot over the bar. Both teams settled for a draw well before the end, and got booed off. 'Tonight, we burned the boots. We played nondescript football, with very few ideas,' said Muñoz.

═══

It was touch and go that West Germany showed up to face Romania in Lens at all. Despite having a police escort, their team bus took the wrong exit off a motorway. One hour of white-knuckle driving along country roads later, they arrived at the Félix-Bollaert so late that even the DFB's bigwigs helped to unload the luggage.

They had an early fright when Cămătaru nodded a free header into Schumacher's hands, but they were soon dictating the game. On 25 minutes, Norbert Meier sent over a delicate cross, Lung missed it, and Rudi Völler scored with a firm header. Straight from the kick-off, Michael Klein ran deep into German territory (so quickly that the main TV camera missed it completely) and was flattened by Stielike, earning the sweeper a deserved booking.

West Germany's grip on the game seemed tight, but 20 seconds into the second half Romania drew level. Like their goal against Spain, it was an elegant move involving Bölöni, whose pass down the middle was beautifully dummied by Klein. A distracted Matthäus lost Coraş, who ran on to the pass and finished low into the corner. Romania were clearly capable of quality football, yet hardly ever engaged in it.

West Germany's winner owed much to Allofs' persistence. He kept a sputtering move alive on the left, found Rummenigge, and the captain flicked it on for Völler to score again with a finish that hit Ioan Andone on its way in. But Romania had one shot left in their locker. In the last minute, Bölöni's 30-yard screamer was hurtling into the top corner until Schumacher threw himself across to save superbly. Derwall's team could breathe again.

===

'We'll dance to the music after this,' Fernando Cabrita had quipped after the West Germany game, a way of saying that Portugal needed to be more expansive. But there was little evidence of it as they played out a 1-1 draw with Spain in Marseille.

Manuel Bento had a busy opening period, pulling off a superb reflex stop from Santillana's volley, then saving with his legs from Gallego. In the second half, he showed his jittery side, spilling Santillana's shot and then recovering before Rafael Gordillo could pounce.

Again it was Chalana's match. He began the move for Portugal's goal, hitting an ambitious pass out to the left. Álvaro squared it for António de Sousa, who looked up and lifted a splendid chip over Luis Arconada. 'We'd watched a few videos of Spain, and noticed that Arconada used to come off his line. It was an excellent goal, spectacular, within the reach of great geniuses,' said Sousa in 2016, accurately if immodestly.

Spain almost went 2-0 down when Chalana dodged Gallego and cracked a shot off the bar, but made the most of their let-off. Portugal didn't clear Carrasco's corner, Andoni Goikoetxea headed it into the goalmouth, João Pinto missed his clearance, and substitute Manuel Sarabia swung at thin air too before Santillana smacked the loose ball home.

Spain could have won late on, but Bento saved well from Carrasco with his legs. Portugal had survived again, but if they were going to make the semis, they would have to overcome the personal beefs plaguing their camp behind the scenes.

'There were a lot of problems,' striker Diamantino said in 2016, 'starting with the big divide between the Benfica and Porto cliques. And you had one manager [Cabrita] pulling in one direction, another one [Morais] pulling in another direction, and another [Torres] who didn't get involved. Everything was done on the hoof. The results concealed the problems.'

Lucescu seemed unaware that beating Portugal in Nantes would save Romania (if Spain didn't beat West Germany). His team had the players to thrive – Bölöni was a passer of tremendous vision, Coraş lively in attack, Hagi already a real talent – but his craven tactics sterilised them. Emphasising the point, he left Hagi on the bench again.

Portugal, meanwhile, knew a 0-0 draw would put them out unless West Germany beat Spain. In a dreadful first half, the closest Romania came to scoring was when Nicolae Negrilă's shot deflected randomly into the side-netting: Bento, wrong-footed, grinned knowingly as the ball rolled back on to the pitch. Meanwhile, Chalana was a marked man, taking three heavy hits in the first 15 minutes. He was then stretchered off after a terrible foul by Mircea Irimescu, who had earlier elbowed Jordão in the head.

Before half-time, Diamantino's half-volley caught Romanian goalkeeper Dumitru Moraru having a nap. Falling backwards, he managed to chest it against the inside of the post and catch it. But that was an isolated incident, and things were no better in the second half. One Spanish newspaper summed it up: 'It was chilling to think that either of these two teams could reach the semi-finals and thus proclaim themselves one of the best sides in Europe. Both sides attacked, but so poorly that the fiercest *catenaccio* was preferable to this dance of nonsense. At times, the crowd ended up asking for the bull to be returned to the pens.'

Both teams were looking stumped for ideas until Portugal's veteran substitute intervened with nine minutes left. The 34-year-old Nené's 22nd and last goal for Portugal wouldn't have won any beauty contests, but it was the most important of his career. Left unmarked, he clumsily volleyed António Frasco's cross into the turf, thus giving Moraru no chance of saving it.

Decades later, Lucescu's assistant Mircea Rădulescu blamed Romania's lethargy on a long domestic season. 'The players were a shambles in training,' he said. 'They were tired and had no appetite. And Hagi was just 19, and had a certain timidity compared to the rest.' Cămătaru added, 'We had too much respect for our opponents. We were coming from the communist bloc and had an inferiority complex, though Lucescu tried to clear it out of our heads. We had no experience of tournaments. We were all novices.'

For most of the night in Paris, as the West Germans played easily their best football of the competition, Spain looked to be going down without a fight.

'The Germans had speed, quality, strength,' said defender Antonio Maceda. 'They were awesome.'

The onslaught began when Briegel outjumped Maceda to head Allofs' corner on to the bar. 'What a beast!' the sweeper marvelled. 'He had calves as big as my quadriceps. Marking him was like trying to push a huge boulder.' Spain were being overrun. Völler saw Camacho clear his cross off the line, Arconada turned his angled shot around the post after he ran half the length of the field, Briegel crashed another header against the underside of the bar, and Andy Brehme's shot came back off the upright. Meanwhile, the sinister Andoni Goikoetxea lamed himself while crunching Völler from behind.

West Germany should have been out of sight, yet almost trailed at half-time. Salva García ran on to Carrasco's clever back-heel, and Stielike tripped him in the box. But Salva stayed down for a while, so Carrasco waited almost two minutes to take the penalty. Just before he did, a firecracker landed in the area. Whether it affected Carrasco's concentration or not, Schumacher saved his weak kick easily.

Reprieved, West Germany blew two more opportunities early in the second half. Allofs was put clean through by Völler, then Meier – but both times he shot straight at Arconada. Spain now began to gain a foothold, with Schumacher racing out to block Carrasco's shot and Stielike clearing Maceda's header off the line.

Then came one of the most important saves in any European Championship. Allofs neatly found Rummenigge, who swerved away from Camacho to leave the goal at his mercy – but Arconada reacted with superhuman speed to parry the hard shot. The goalkeeper, laying the ghosts of his miserable World Cup to rest, then made another superb save from Matthäus's dipping half-volley.

In Nantes, Nené's goal sank Romania. Portugal moved on to the same points, goal difference and goals scored as West Germany. If nothing changed, lots would be drawn to separate them – eliminating Spain, who were now minutes away from the trapdoor and looking tired.

In the final moments, the substitute Pierre Littbarski took a useless shot instead of heading for the corner to eat up time. He would live to regret it. Arconada retrieved the ball and his team embarked on what one Spanish paper called 'a suicide attack: no defenders nor midfielders, everyone became forwards'.

With 89 minutes and 15 seconds on the clock, Matthäus fouled Francisco, who knocked the free kick over to Señor on the right. The midfielder floated a diagonal cross into the box, the ball hanging in the Parisian night sky for a long time. The Germans didn't pick up Maceda, Schumacher was caught between coming out and staying on his line, and Carrasco's near-post run fatally distracted Briegel and Stielike. Maceda's stooping header went straight at Schumacher, but had enough power to squeeze over the line after coming off his gloves. 'In the last minute, the last hope, and Maceda has scored!' screamed Spanish state broadcaster TVE's commentator.

As play restarted, a shellshocked Schumacher crouched in the back of his net, staring into the distance. Seconds later, referee Vojtech Christov blew up. In the blink of an eye, the defending champions were out.

'Although I'm a non-smoker, Derwall and I shared a cigarette on the pitch afterwards. We were all destroyed,' Schumacher recalled. Miguel Muñoz wept, having dodged the hangman's noose again. 'This man was born with a flower up his arse,' said RFEF president Pablo Porta, invoking the traditional Spanish idiom for unearned luck.

In its own way, this was one of the best ever European Championship matches, though it's never perceived as such. 'It was the biggest disappointment of my career,' mused Karlheinz Förster. 'I'm convinced we would have made it through the semi-final, because we'd always pulled ourselves together on the pitch despite the team spirit not being so strong. But there was a real lack of luck against Spain, which we honestly hadn't budgeted for.'

It was beyond dispute that West Germany had been unfortunate, and that the better team had gone. But sympathy was in short supply. They weren't an easy bunch to warm to: a gang of big names bristling with self-regard and peddling functional football. Too many fresh memories of Battiston, and Algeria; too many insufferable alpha males shouting the odds.

The French press loved it, of course. 'German football, this brute animal, deserves to be drowned in its own urine,' wrote one columnist in *Libération*, while *Le Soir* declared that 'the German monster has survived too long'. In Spain itself, *El País* went into overdrive: 'Ecstasy, madness, a real binge: last night, Spanish football rediscovered its soul.'

When a journalist asked Derwall if he had been sacked, he replied, 'Do you want me to punch you in the mouth?' The next day, he was greeted by chants of 'Derwall, Derwall, ha ha ha' in the arrivals hall of Frankfurt airport. He responded angrily, calling them 'primitives'. A week later, he was gone. Hermann Neuberger couldn't get hold of Helmut Benthaus in the following days – Stuttgart's manager, who had just won the Bundesliga, was on holiday in Canada and unreachable – but somewhere in Munich, a 38-year-old Bild columnist named Franz Beckenbauer was waiting for the phone to ring.

5.15pm, 14 June 1984
Stade de la Meinau, Strasbourg
Attendance: 44,707
Referee: Romualdas Juška (USSR)

WEST GERMANY 0
PORTUGAL 0

WEST GERMANY: Harald Schumacher, Uli Stielike, Andy Brehme, Karlheinz Förster, Bernd Förster, Guido Buchwald (Lothar Matthäus 67), Hans-Peter Briegel, Wolfgang Rolff (Rudi Bommer 67), Rudi Völler, Karl-Heinz Rummenigge (c), Klaus Allofs. **Manager:** Jupp Derwall.

PORTUGAL: Manuel Bento (c), João Domingos Pinto, António Lima Pereira, Eurico Gomes, Álvaro Magalhães, António Frasco (António Veloso 79), Carlos Manuel Correa, António de Sousa, Rui Jordão (Fernando Gomes 85), Fernando Chalana, Jaime Pacheco. **Manager:** Fernando Cabrita.

Booked: Álvaro 40.

8.30pm, 14 June 1984
Stade Geoffroy-Guichard, Saint-Étienne
Attendance: 16,972
Referee: Alexis Ponnet (Belgium)

ROMANIA 1 (Bölöni 35)
SPAIN 1 (Carrasco 22 pen)

ROMANIA: Silviu Lung, Mircea Rednic, Costică Ştefănescu (c), Gino Iorgulescu, Michael Klein, Nicolae Ungureanu, Marin Dragnea (Aurel Ţicleanu 57), László Bölöni, Rodion Cămătaru, Marcel Coraş, Romulus Gabor (Gheorghe Hagi 76). **Manager:** Mircea Lucescu.

SPAIN: Luis Arconada (c), Santiago Urquiaga, José Antonio Camacho, Antonio Maceda, Andoni Goikoetxea, Rafael Gordillo, Juan Antonio Señor, Víctor Muñoz, Carlos Alonso 'Santillana', Ricardo Gallego (Julio Alberto Moreno 73), Francisco José Carrasco. **Manager:** Miguel Muñoz.

Booked: Iorgulescu 71.

5.15pm, 17 June 1984
Stade Félix Bollaert, Lens
Attendance: 31,803
Referee: Jan Keizer (Netherlands)

WEST GERMANY 2 (Völler 25, 66)
ROMANIA 1 (Coraş 46)

WEST GERMANY: Schumacher, Stielike, Brehme, K. Förster (Buchwald 80), B. Förster, Matthäus, Briegel, Norbert Meier (Pierre Littbarski 65), Völler, Rummenigge (c), Allofs.

ROMANIA: Lung, Rednic, Ştefănescu (c), Ioan Andone, Klein, Ungureanu, Dragnea (Ţicleanu 62), Bölöni, Cămătaru, Hagi (Ioan Zare 46), Coraş.

Booked: Stielike (26), Ştefănescu (48).

8.30pm, 17 June 1984
Stade Vélodrome, Marseille
Attendance: 24,364
Referee: Michel Vautrot (France)

PORTUGAL 1 (Sousa 52)
SPAIN 1 (Santi llana 73)

PORTUGAL: Bento (c), João Pinto, Lima Pereira, Eurico, Álvaro, Frasco (Diamantino Miranda 78), Carlos Manuel, Sousa, Jordão, Chalana, Pacheco.

SPAIN: Arconada (c), Urquiaga (Señor 79), Camacho, Maceda, Goikoetxea, Julio Alberto (Manuel Sarabia 71), Gordillo, Víctor, Santillana, Gallego, Carrasco.

Booked: Eurico (45+1), Carrasco (25).

8.30pm, 20 June 1984
Stade de la Beaujoire, Nantes
Attendance: 24,464
Referee: Heinz Fahnler (Austria)

PORTUGAL 1 (Nené 81)
ROMANIA 0

PORTUGAL: Bento (c), João Pinto, Lima Pereira, Eurico, Álvaro, Frasco, Carlos Manuel (Tamagnini Gomes 'Nené' 67), Sousa, Jordão, Chalana (Diamantino 18), Gomes.

ROMANIA: Dumitru Moraru, Rednic, Ştefănescu (c), Iorgulescu, Klein, Nicolae Negrilă, Ungureanu, Mircea Irimescu (Gabor 59), Cămătaru (Ionel Augustin 35), Bölöni, Coraş.

Booked: Diamantino (77), Irimescu (15), Iorgulescu (27).

8.30pm, 20 June 1984
Parc des Princes, Paris
Attendance: 47,691
Referee: Vojtech Christov (Czechoslovakia)

SPAIN 1 (Maceda 90)
WEST GERMANY 0

SPAIN: Arconada (c), Señor, Camacho, Maceda, Goikoetxea (Salvador García 'Salva' 26), Julio Alberto (Francisco López 78), Gordillo, Víctor, Santillana, Gallego, Carrasco.

WEST GERMANY: Schumacher, Stielike, Brehme (Rolff 76), K. Förster, B. Förster, Matthäus, Briegel, Meier (Littbarski 61), Völler, Rummenigge (c), Allofs.

Booked: Goikoetxea (25), Meier (59).

GROUP B	P	W	D	L	F	A	GD	Pts
SPAIN	3	1	2	0	3	2	+1	4
PORTUGAL	3	1	2	0	2	1	+1	4
WEST GERMANY	3	1	1	1	2	2	0	3
ROMANIA	3	0	1	2	2	4	− 2	1

Spain and Portugal qualified.

SEMI-FINALS
France v Portugal
Denmark v Spain

On its way to the Vélodrome, the French team bus collided badly with another vehicle, leaving Jean Tigana with a cut forehead and cheek. When the vehicle eventually arrived at the stadium, he told his team-mates, 'We cannot lose tonight.' He would personally see to it that they didn't.

In the evening sun, the first 20 minutes of one of the most unforgettable internationals of all time were dismayingly poor. Passes went astray every few seconds, stoppages abounded, France kept humping long balls up to the 5ft 7.5in Lacombe, and at one point Manuel Bento's goal kick sailed all the way downfield to his opposite number Bats. Meanwhile, Didier Six was relentlessly jeered by the locals, who hadn't forgotten his involvement in Olympique Marseille's 1980 relegation.

Jaime Pacheco then felled Platini 25 yards from goal. Though the free kick opportunity looked ideal for him, he left it to Jean-François Domergue. The floppy-haired left-back speared it just beyond João Pinto's head on the end of the wall, past a stationary Bento and into the top corner.

Turgid during the first half, France began the second explosively. Less than 45 seconds had elapsed when Platini caressed a pass into the path of Fernandez, who lashed his shot into Bento's midriff before volleying the rebound wide. In a frenzied five-minute spell, Giresse came close to scoring three times: a rasping drive which Bento fisted over the bar, another shot against the goalkeeper's legs, and a volley from Six's cross that whizzed narrowly wide. Meanwhile, António Frasco should have been sent off for violently fouling Platini.

But Chalana wasn't somebody you could leave to his own devices. He dinked a neat ball into the box as Battiston stood off, and it fell to Jordão, unmarked ten yards out. The Angolan-born striker scored with a dipping header which gave Bats no chance.

Back came the hosts. Giresse's inch-perfect ball sent Platini racing in, and when Bento saved from him and Six in quick succession, the ball looped high into the night, came down and bounced off the bar for a corner. But Portugal's will to survive was summed up by the sight of Eurico chipping the ball away from Álvaro (who was about to take a free kick) and over the perimeter fencing, eating up more time and earning him a booking.

Extra time began with more unorthodox goalkeeping by Bento: when Platini scooped Battiston's low cross into the air, he jumped up like a jack-in-the-box to punch the dropping ball clear. At the other end, the less colourful but more reliable Bats pushed Nené's powerful header over the bar.

Portugal had hardly ventured forward all night, but now they exploited French fatigue to the fullest. Again the inimitable Chalana, who had switched wings, was involved. Making a fool of Domergue, he sent over a cross which dropped perfectly for Jordão. The striker miskicked his volley into the ground, it bounced up at a crazy angle, and Bats could only look on in horror as it floated into the top corner.

On the bench, Hidalgo was gripped by pessimism. 'I said to myself, "Yet again, no luck, we will lose,"' the manager recalled. Seville flashbacks flooded through French minds. 'There was a small shudder, a little doubt, some sighs,' said Giresse. 'Then we relaunched the machine.'

But not before looking down the barrel. After France messed up a corner, Nené sprinted into their near-empty half, then sent Chalana down the right. The return ball was on a silver platter for Nené, who met it cleanly – but Bats calmly came off his line, blocked the shot and fell on the rebound. 'I've relived this nightmare from back to front and back again, dozens and dozens of times,' Nené lamented in 2016. Before this tournament, Bats had never played a competitive international; you wouldn't have known it.

By now, Portugal had pulled everyone behind the castle walls, even Chalana and Jordão. Platini appealed for a penalty when he fell across Eurico, but referee Paolo Bergamo ignored him. France were looking more ragged by the minute, their desperation epitomised by two awful crosses from Bruno Bellone that almost ended up in the Mediterranean.

Portugal were six minutes away from the final when Giresse's hard shot was blocked by a defender's leg before Domergue sent it back into the box. Le Roux, up from the back, whacked it against another defender. It squirted through to Platini who, shaping to shoot, crumpled under João Pinto's challenge. Penalty or dive? Before Bergamo could decide, birthday boy Domergue scuttled in from the left and side-footed the loose ball over Bento. It was 2-2, with all four goals scored by players wearing the number three.

A shoot-out seemed certain. But this unforgettable match had one more spasm left. With 90 seconds remaining, just as Hidalgo's assistants Henri Guérin and Marc Bourrier were deciding France's penalty-takers, Tigana – whose birthday it also was – rose to the occasion.

If Platini was the glamorous film star of this French team, the Mali-born Tigana was its low-key heartbeat. Technically immaculate and a tireless worker, he was strangely overlooked by Europe's glamour outfits during his career. He would try hard throughout the summer of 1984 to get a move to Italy but, amazingly, nobody showed interest. After the tournament, he handed out his phone number to Italian journalists but, again, no Serie A clubs called. For some reason, he said ruefully, French players weren't wanted there – Platini being the exception that proved the rule.

Now Tigana showed why Bordeaux's gain was *calcio*'s loss. 'I had legs, I was a diesel,' said Fernandez. 'I finished matches very strongly. But Jean was a Mercedes, a Ferrari. We really wanted to get to that final. We had a tough mind collectively.'

Driving forward, Tigana sought out Platini, but Lima Pereira, who had been outstanding all night, intercepted his pass. Refusing to give up, Tigana pounced on the ball and burst past Eurico, charging like a spindly stallion with the last of his strength. He held off João Pinto and cut the ball back for Platini, who was waiting on the six-yard line. Showing extraordinary coolness in the heat of the moment, Platini stopped the ball dead, turned and fired it into the roof of the net as Bento and his defenders threw themselves at it too late. He began his celebratory run past a rapturous ocean of *tricolores* fluttering madly behind the goal. Lacombe recalled, 'I thought the Vélodrome would collapse. It was moving everywhere.'

The devastated Portuguese made no attempt to restart quickly, and Bergamo added on just ten seconds of stoppage time anyway. 'Eusébio was there, and he consoled us in the dressing room,' Chalana recalled. 'Sometimes I watch the video of the game, and I still wonder how we lost.'

But this was indisputably the right result for the tournament, and for football. An official from Juventus, entering France's dressing room, bristled at the sight of his prize asset smoking a cigarette. 'Michel, we've booked a hotel in Sardinia for your family holiday,' he said. Platini, crushing the cigarette butt under his heel, replied, 'I'm going to Los Angeles.' But first to Paris.

=====

Lyon's Stade de Gerland wasn't quite packed out for the second semi-final, but it witnessed another magnificent match: not on the same level as France-Portugal for artistry, but its equal for incident. Pity about the outcome.

The vaguely supernatural nature of Spain's win over West Germany had sent confidence flooding through their previously parched veins. 'We'll beat Denmark,' declared Santillana, 'and we'll win because this team is lucky, with the luck that favours the winners.' Sure enough, Spain started the stronger, Ole Qvist keeping out Carrasco's header with a fantastic reflex save.

Denmark shrugged off that close shave and went ahead minutes later. When Arnesen crossed from the right, Maceda gave the mighty Elkjær enough room to soar high for a header which Arconada palmed on to the crossbar. Søren Lerby was on to the loose ball like a flash, rifling it into the net from two yards out. His upraised-arms celebration, racing away joyfully with a forest of Danish flags fluttering behind him, was one of the images of the tournament.

The Danes had the smell of blood in their nostrils, and Arnesen had a good case for a penalty when Julio Alberto felled him. Spain were again grateful for George Courtney's remarkably generous refereeing when Víctor nearly crippled Jens Jørn Bertelsen with an outrageous lunge, easily the worst foul of Euro 84. Bertelsen, fortunate not to have suffered the same fate as Allan Simonsen, hopped in agony before collapsing – but Courtney merely played a useless advantage.

Within moments, Víctor assaulted Busk from behind, then gave him a sneaky kick in the head as he fell. Courtney's response was a belated yellow card. Spain were a decent team – and a nasty one, red in shirt, tooth and claw.

In the second half, Arnesen went the long way around two defenders before his shot came back off the post. And after Elkjær dodged Víctor's latest murderous challenge, his pass released Lerby, who shot feebly at Arconada. Inside 60 seconds, as Denmark's defence pushed up, Señor scuttled past them and found himself clean through (with three other Spaniards offside, though linesman Keith Miller's flag stayed down); Qvist ran bravely off his line to make his latest good stop. Back came Denmark. Laudrup's cavalry charge down the left caused a goalmouth scramble which saw Elkjær's shot kept out by Arconada's knee; in the chaos, Arnesen found Lerby, who blazed wildly across the goal.

With such wasteful finishing, Denmark were asking for it. Just after Manuel Sarabia burst past four men and hit the post, Carrasco's header was bouncing out for a goal kick before the tireless Gordillo kept it in. When his cross was nicked off Carrasco's toe by Busk, Maceda smashed the loose ball into the bottom corner. Poor Qvist lay spread-eagled in his goalmouth like a piece of flattened roadkill.

Denmark now suffered two more setbacks in quick succession: the exhausted Arnesen went off, and Berggreen was booked for bodychecking Gordillo. Given the things Courtney had let go in the first half, the yellow card seemed astonishing. When Berggreen later hauled Gordillo down in identical fashion, Courtney did nothing. Roulette-wheel refereeing.

The Danes fought hard to finish it in injury time. Arconada beat away Laudrup's ferocious shot, and the corner produced another goalmouth stramash. But Spain survived – again.

In extra time, Nielsen horribly miscontrolled the ball outside his own box, but when Santillana stole it from him, Qvist rode to the rescue. Even then, Santillana almost managed to head in the rebound, but Morten Olsen crowded him out. Denmark were buckling. With Nielsen exposed again,

Sarabia's low cross was on a plate for Carrasco – but Lerby's telescopic right leg got there first.

As extra time's second half began, Berggreen pulled Camacho's shirt in midfield. Unbelievably, Courtney showed him a second yellow. A barely defensible decision according to the laws of the game, but amazingly petty in the context of a hard-fought game where vicious fouls had gone unpunished. 'If a pull-back deserves this, I'd have been sent off 100 times in my career,' said Berggreen. But even this wasn't enough for Muñoz. 'The referee gave me the impression of acting with premeditation,' he said, referring to the bookings which would see Maceda and Gordillo miss the final. There's no pleasing some people.

After Arconada made an outstanding double save from Elkjær's whipped free kick and Nielsen's close-range follow-up, it was on to penalties. Laudrup's kick was saved, but he retook it because Arconada had twitched (the keeper got a yellow card for protesting). Lerby's penalty was the best, struck with unnerving power into the top corner.

Elkjær later said he felt 'an enormous pressure on my chest' as he prepared to take his kick at 4-4. Perhaps that was why he leaned fatally backwards to blast it over the bar, a terrible fate for the best striker in the tournament. Sarabia, the last Spanish taker, was so nervous that he walked up to the penalty spot wearing his tracksuit top before being told to remove it. But he kept his nerve, and Spain were in the final. Surely Muñoz's dead-eyed hackers weren't actually going to win the entire thing. Were they?

8pm, 23 June 1984
Stade Vélodrome, Marseille
Attendance: 54,848
Referee: Paolo Bergamo (Italy)

FRANCE 3 (Domergue 25, 114, Platini 119)
PORTUGAL 2 (Jordão 74, 98)
After extra time

FRANCE: Bats, Battiston, Domergue, Bossis, Le Roux, Fernandez, Tigana, Giresse, Lacombe (Ferreri 67), Platini (c), Six (Bellone 102).

PORTUGAL: Bento (c), João Pinto, Lima Pereira, Eurico, Álvaro, Frasco, Sousa (Nené 63), Pacheco, Jordão, Diamantino (Gomes 46), Chalana.

Booked: Lima Pereira (26), Eurico (90), Gomes (105).

8pm, 24 June 1984
Stade de Gerland, Lyon
Attendance: 47,843
Referee: George Courtney (England)

SPAIN 1 (Maceda 67)
DENMARK 1 (Lerby 7)

Spain won 5-4 on penalties after extra time

Shoot-out: Brylle 0-1, Santillana 1-1, J. Olsen 1-2, Señor 2-2, Laudrup 2-3, Urquiaga 3-3, Lerby 3-4, Víctor 4-4, Elkjær shot over, Sarabia 5-4.

SPAIN: Arconada (c), Salva (Urquiaga 102), Camacho, Maceda, Gordillo, Julio Alberto (Sarabia 61), Señor, Víctor, Santillana, Gallego, Carrasco.

DENMARK: Qvist, Sivebæk, Busk, M. Olsen (c) (Brylle 113), Nielsen, Lerby, Berggreen, Bertelsen, Elkjær, Laudrup, Arnesen (J. Olsen 69).

Booked: Gordillo (20), Salva (21), Víctor (29), Maceda (86), Arconada (during penalty shoot-out), Berggreen (70, 106), J. Olsen (74), Elkjær (120+1).

Sent off: Berggreen (106).

FINAL
France v Spain

'The Spanish national team have never been renowned for the quality of their football,' wrote Keir Radnedge in *World Soccer* during the tournament. In 1984, this was an inarguable fact: Spain had spent decades underperforming dreadfully at international level. In the same issue, Brian Glanville dismissed their club football as 'squalid and brutal', writing in the context of Barcelona's excesses in the 1981/82 European Cup Winners' Cup and the kidney transplants that routinely passed for tackling in La Liga. But here Spain were in the final, having played little good football while dishing out some disgraceful challenges. Any outcome other than a French victory in Paris seemed unthinkable – in both senses.

Before France walked out on to the pitch at the Parc des Princes, Platini told them, 'Guys, after the anthems, just do one thing: look at the cup. Look at it and it will come to us.' In the event, they froze horribly. Their nerves seemed to be transmitted to the French military band, which raced through Spain's anthem as though the conductor had an urgent root canal appointment.

In a cagey first half, Platini dropped deeper and deeper to escape Camacho's attentions. Slowly, Spain gained the upper hand. When the jack-in-the-box Santillana climbed above Le Roux to head across goal, France were lucky that Víctor was too short to put away the chance.

Referee Vojtech Christov, a huge improvement on Courtney, nonetheless let Julio Alberto and the inevitable Víctor away with assaults on Tigana and Fernandez. When Gallego got booked for rugby-tackling Bellone, Fernandez joined him for dissent, another sign of French tension. Not long afterwards, Carrasco chopped down Fernandez; Julio Alberto stupidly kicked the ball against the prone player, who rolled around embarrassingly. 'They targeted me to make me crack,' said the Andalucían-born Fernandez. 'They called me *renegado* [traitor].'

France should have been losing by half-time. Battiston nodded Santillana's header off the line, and Carrasco set up the same player to shoot badly wide. The hosts looked to be throwing away the chance of a lifetime.

At the interval, Hidalgo urged his players to remember their days in Font-Romeu, where mountain walks and gentle kick-abouts healed their tired limbs. 'We had 50 games in our legs, and we were just knackered,' recalled Lacombe. 'There, we became a team. It was like a secret society. During the finals, we received thousands of postcards. Hidalgo told us to look at them before matches. I remember one which said, "Think of the people who have woven your jersey".'

Just before the hour, France got the sort of luck that even the greatest teams sometimes need. Outside the Spanish box, Lacombe went down with Salva close by. Though a replay suggested he had slipped, Christov gave a free kick. The angle gave Platini little to aim at, but his right foot bent it low around the wall. Luis Arconada dived on the ball – but let it squirm catastrophically out of his grasp. Inadvertently nudging it over the line with his arm and hip, he jack-knifed to claw it back, but it was too late.

Now, at last, France began to play. Giresse burst through on the left, forcing Salva to live up to his name with a last-ditch clearance. Soon afterwards, Arconada got behind Lacombe's volley. And after Tigana darted past three Spaniards, Giresse dragged a shot inches wide.

As tiredness began to bite, Spain failed to trouble Bats in the remaining half-hour. But with five minutes left, Yvon Le Roux – earlier cautioned for clattering Santillana – tripped the onrushing Sarabia and earned himself a second booking, making him the first man ever sent off in a European Championship final. 'It's still stuck in my craw,' he said in 2016.

All that remained was for the puppyish Bellone to seal the win. As the match entered stoppage time, Hidalgo clenched both fists in his dugout, screaming at his team to see things out. Within seconds, Tigana's pass split Spain's defence like a hatchet on balsa wood. Bellone ran on, then chipped a lovely little finish over Arconada as the goalkeeper raced off his line.

On the sidelines, Hidalgo dissolved into tears. 'We didn't play a great game, but that's nothing if we win,' he said. 'We just won the first title of French football. We are proud and happy, above all.' As *L'Équipe* noted the next morning, 'The bard of the beautiful game had been converted to realism.' Hidalgo was immediately offered the position of sports minister in Laurent Fabius's new government, but said no (to his later regret).

But the glory was primarily Platini's: photogenic, charismatic and second only to Diego Maradona as a footballer over the whole decade. It's fair to say that 1984 was his *belle année*. 'He had such confidence!' Lacombe exclaimed. 'He'd just won the Italian league, he was top scorer there, he'd won the European Cup Winners' Cup. So when he arrived in Font-Romeu, he said to us, "We'll be champions of Europe. Everything that I touch, I win." And it was true. One day, we went to the casino, he put a coin in the slot and he hit the jackpot!'

Platini himself recalled, 'It was the only tournament where I wasn't injured. In 1982, I had a groin problem. In 1986, I had a nerve problem. In 1984, I wasn't injured, and I was able to perform to my peak.' His nine goals in five games were a high-water mark in the history of the event. 'There are 100,000 people in France who run as quickly and jump as high as me,' he said. 'But there aren't even 50 who see as fast as me. My secret: I have the vision.'

He was modestly rewarded by contemporary standards, earning 400 million lire a year at Juventus (roughly €300,000 today). In 2013, French magazine *So Foot* noted, 'When Alain Boghossian, a decent player, signed for Parma in 1998, he earned as much in a month as the great Michel Platini earned in a year at Juve. That says it all.' Which might help to explain certain decisions Platini took later in life.

It felt totally right that this sublime French team had claimed a trophy. 'We'd never won anything,' said Hidalgo in 2016. 'It's tiring to hear it repeated, it takes some juice out of you. It means you're not good enough and people don't believe in you. And after Seville, it wasn't easy to believe in ourselves. Platini was the only one who'd won things. The others hadn't.'

They were suitably dashing winners of a sparkling competition packed with drama and artistry. The *Frankfurter Allgemeine Zeitung*, comparing the tournament extremely favourably to 1980, put it best: 'The art of playing football has finally caught up with the addiction to winning at all costs.' There were a few dissenters.

One Italian journalist wrote, 'The French have a mediocre defence, a fine midfield and a Serie C attack.' You wondered what words he had left for his own countrymen, who at the time were plumbing fresh depths with every match.

Tournaments won by host nations are sometimes seen as devalued currency. Not this one. France ended the calendar year of 1984 with 12 wins out of 12, standing tall as the finest international team in the world, and Euro 84 was their crowning glory. It was the best of times, it was the best of times.

8pm, 27 June 1984
Parc des Princes, Paris
Attendance: 47,368
Referee: Vojtech Christov (Czechoslovakia)

FRANCE 2 (Platini 57, Bellone 90+1)
SPAIN 0

FRANCE: Bats, Battiston (Amoros 73), Domergue, Bossis, Le Roux, Luis Fernandez, Tigana, Giresse, Lacombe (Genghini 80), Platini (c), Bellone.

SPAIN: Arconada (c), Urquiaga, Salva (Roberto Fernández 86), Gallego, Camacho, Julio Alberto (Sarabia 77), Señor, Víctor, Santillana, Carrasco, Francisco.

Booked: Luis Fernandez (30), Le Roux (54, 85), Gallego (26), Carrasco (30).
Sent off: Le Roux 85.

1988

THE BRILLIANCE of 1984 was a hard act to follow. But if anyone could, West Germany could. On 15 March 1985, at one of UEFA's big dinners, they and their state-of-the-art stadia carried the day 5-1, with a joint Scandinavian bid getting the remaining vote and England's bid being wholly ignored.

There was just one problem: Moscow and its satellites didn't want to see West Berlin hosting glitzy sporting spectaculars. The three Warsaw Pact countries on UEFA's executive committee (Czechoslovakia, Bulgaria and the USSR) insisted that the city be regarded as part of the GDR for bidding purposes. A veiled threat was made that the east European nations might pull out of the competition. So, to Chancellor Helmut Kohl's displeasure, the Deutscher Fußball-Bund's president Hermann Neuberger scrubbed the decaying but grandiose Olympiastadion from the list of venues.

Fourteen years after hosting and winning the World Cup, West Germany nursed realistic hopes of doing the business again. Their squad had undergone a huge rebuild in the wake of Mexico 86, overseen by Franz Beckenbauer, who had gone back on the words he uttered after the 1982 World Cup in Spain: 'One of the things I realised [while watching the tournament] was that I would never make a good coach.'

Although Karl-Heinz Rummenigge, Hans-Peter Briegel, Harald Schumacher, Klaus Allofs, Felix Magath and the Förster brothers were all gone, replacements such as the energetic blond striker Jürgen Klinsmann, the tiny playmaker Olaf Thon and the tough stopper Jürgen Kohler all looked good. But there were doubts about sweeper Matthias Herget, who had won more than 30 caps since 1983 without looking the part. The German media were on Beckenbauer's back too. Paul Breitner, his former Bayern colleague, was his sternest critic, accusing him of using 'truly insane' tactics which sowed 'panic and horror' among the team. Just 13,000 turned up to watch the Germans draw 1-1 with Yugoslavia in Bremen on 4 June, and *Kicker* magazine accused Beckenbauer of being 'on shaky legs, just 100 hours before the start'.

West Germany's main threat in Group A had been similarly overhauled: Italy's team was pulsing with fresh blood after years of decay. Azeglio Vicini's line-up overflowed with exciting young talents like Milan's teenage left-back Paolo Maldini, Roma playmaker Giuseppe Giannini and Sampdoria striker Roberto Mancini. First among equals was another Sampdoria youngster, Gianluca Vialli, hyped as the best forward Italian football had produced since Gigi Riva. 'Vialli is as effervescent as Asti Spumante,' marvelled Vicini.

The Italians and Germans looked likely to make short work of an ageing Denmark. The Danes' shocking collapse against Spain in the second round of Mexico 86 had inflicted terminal damage: in a qualifying section containing Czechoslovakia and Wales, they scored only four goals in six matches, the kind of number they might have managed as minnows in the 1970s. Nothing was expected from them in a group completed by their least favourite opponent.

Spain, still managed by Miguel Muñoz, were a fresher-faced outfit than the gang of hackers who had nearly won Euro 84. They needed some help to qualify, however, and were grateful to Austrian goalkeeper Klaus Lindenberger for acrobatically saving Gheorghe Hagi's 92nd-minute piledriver on the final qualifying night in Vienna. Had it gone in, Romania would have qualified. Spain lived to swashbuckle another day.

Their team was built around the glamorous young pin-ups of Real Madrid, who were in the middle of a run of five consecutive Primera Liga titles. Talents like Emilio Butragueño, Míchel, Manuel Sanchís and Rafael Martín Vázquez looked a match for most, even if they had yet to make a serious impression on the European Cup with their club.

England qualified without problems, capping an easy campaign with a ruthless destruction of Yugoslavia in Belgrade. Bobby Robson had plenty of scoring power at his disposal, with Gary Lineker being fed by Liverpool's John Barnes and Peter Beardsley, and Bryan Robson still formidable at 31. The big question was how much the post-Heysel ban on English clubs in Europe, about to enter its fourth season, would hamper England's ability to handle continental opposition. And centre-back Terry Butcher's injury put the onus on two youngsters, Mark Wright (24) and Tony Adams (21). Their opponents in Group B were an intriguing trio.

As in 1976, Valeriy Lobanovskyi's USSR line-up was dominated by players from his alma mater Dynamo Kiev. 'His lads formed the backbone, but he never favoured anyone,' said goalkeeper Rinat Dasaev. They had sizzled all too briefly at the 1986 World Cup before losing to an inferior Belgium. Four months later, they went to Paris and destroyed an over-the-hill France while playing beautiful football. Stocked with quality in every position, they looked formidable and fascinating.

England's opening fixture looked the most intriguing tie of the first round. Regarded as the only-here-for-the-beer runts of Group B, Ireland had scraped in with almost the last kick of the qualifiers – a kick in a game that didn't involve them. Bulgaria needed only a point against Scotland in Sofia to qualify, and were getting it until substitute Gary Mackay suddenly popped up to shoot past Borislav Mihaylov, sending Ireland to an international tournament for the first time. Jack Charlton, suddenly a national hero after barely 18 months as Irish manager, sent his Scottish opposite number Andy Roxburgh champagne, while Mackay himself was deluged in gifts, letters and invitations to visit Ireland.

In a curious way, Charlton was years ahead of his time: no other side of the era chased and pressed as diligently as Ireland did. 'We're not going to have any nice stuff here,' he told his squad early in his reign. 'It's going to be very straight. We're going to get the ball, put it over the full-back's head and have runners in behind. We're going to close everything up and we're going to turn the whole backline; as soon as they're turned, we're on our way.' But there was more to them than long balls and endless chasing.

Group B was completed by the Netherlands, with the redoubtable Rinus Michels back for his third stint in charge. It was said of Michels, in slightly bad taste, that his time as a gym teacher for deaf children in the 1960s had exacerbated his habit of barking out lengthy, uninterrupted monologues. The West German winger Pierre Littbarski, who had played under him at Köln, called his training methods 'inhuman'. Michels retorted that he would buy Littbarski an extra ball 'so you can dribble at home'. Other Köln players said, off the record, that they thought Michels was punishing them for the sins of the Nazis!

But the Dutch were lucky to be in the finals at all. During their penultimate fixture against Cyprus in Rotterdam, a smoke bomb exploded in the goalmouth and Cypriot goalkeeper Andreas Charitou passed out from nausea. The Netherlands won 8-0, but Cyprus looked likely to get a 3-0 walkover – tossing the group into the hands of Greece, who were in second place and still to play the Dutch at home. Instead, however, to Greek outrage, UEFA cravenly ordered the game to be replayed behind closed doors in Amsterdam, knowing the Dutch would win easily (4-0) and bring a huge, free-spending, hard-drinking support base across the border to West Germany. This wasn't the last rub of the green the Netherlands would enjoy in Euro 88.

Dutch ability wasn't in doubt: Marco van Basten, Ruud Gullit, Frank Rijkaard and Ronald Koeman were among the best emerging talents in the world. But lack of big-game experience was a concern: none of the squad had played in a tournament before. Johan Cruyff, not for the first or last time, stuck his oar in, advising Michels to play with three strikers and criticising the non-selection of Rob Witschge, one of his pets at Ajax.

You wouldn't have expected Michels, a hardened martinet who reputedly sang Italian opera arias in the shower, to put up with that. Nor did he. 'Cruyff is merely a coach starting off,' he retorted. 'Successes with Ajax in the Eredivisie? What does that mean? It's a boy scouts' competition. What we need today are football soldiers. Players who can suffer and battle. Every game we play is a battle. I'm not talking about Cruyff, but players like Van Hanegem! Neeskens!' No one could do internecine infighting like the Dutch.

With the Netherlands and England both likely to bring large hooligan firms, the German authorities mounted a massive and costly security operation. 'When the thugs arrive, the big stick has to come out,' said Hermann Neuberger. 'It's the only language they understand.' Undercover officers infiltrated the big gangs, and the screening process for England fans was so vigorous that the FA failed to sell its allocation of 8,500 tickets per game.

The *polizei* used the 1988 European Cup Final between PSV Eindhoven and Benfica in Stuttgart as a dress rehearsal. Günther Rathgeb, the city's head of police, told the media that while one could not 'prevent every little fight', there would be 'no big bang' at Euro 88. In the event, there were plenty of middling-sized ones.

GROUP A
West Germany, Italy, Denmark, Spain

As the *Deutschlandlied* rang out before the opening match at the Rheinstadion in Düsseldorf, an enterprising photographer captured Franz Beckenbauer standing stiffly to attention beside Berni, Euro 88's goofy rabbit mascot, who towered over him. Der Kaiser wasn't smiling by the end of the game either. His team looked self-conscious in the spotlight, while Italy took their cue from the headline in the Roman daily *La Repubblica* that morning: 'Primo, non rischiare', first, no risks.

Matthias Herget, as many had feared, was a big weakness for the Germans, gifting Giuseppe Giannini a shooting opportunity after just 20 seconds. He soon got caught out again by Vialli's pace, forcing Immel to sprint out and block at close range.

Early in the second half, just after Lothar Matthäus smashed an audacious long-range volley inches wide from Andy Brehme's corner, Italy went ahead. After West Germany twice failed to clear near their own corner flag, Herget weakly kicked the ball against Roberto Donadoni, who slipped it across to the unmarked Roberto Mancini. The striker's angled finish passed through Immel's hand and into the far corner. The famously headstrong Mancini, whose failure to score in his first 13 internationals had provoked much domestic ridicule, now charged off to howl abuse at his enemies in the press box. 'Scoring this goal was, for me, a liberation. But I didn't make any gestures,' he lied.

Referee Keith Hackett played a big role in West Germany's equaliser minutes later. Penalising Italy's goalkeeper Walter Zenga for taking too many steps with the ball, he awarded an indirect free kick inside the box. Whether he was right is anyone's guess: at the crucial moment, the TV coverage cut away to West Germany's subs warming up. Irritated, the Italians assembled a wall with a hole (and two Germans) in it. Littbarski touched the ball short to Brehme, who saw a gap between Donadoni and Mancini: his low shot slithered into the bottom corner.

Herget, booed by his own fans, had his lack of pace exposed again near the end when he brought down Mancini on the edge of the box, but Hackett waved play on. Not the most auspicious of games for the referee, or for West Germany, who spent too much time rolling the ball around in midfield. Beckenbauer was philosophical afterwards: 'For 25 minutes, we controlled the game. Then we lost the thread, found it, then lost it again, and so on for the whole match.'

In rainy Hanover the following day, Spain had it easy against the over-the-hill Danes. Sepp Piontek's team sorely missed the injured Frank Arnesen, and Preben Elkjær was pushed too far forward to race in from deeper positions as he had at Euro 84.

The dashing Míchel ran the game, and gave Spain an early lead after exchanging passes with Ricardo Gallego and prodding a neat finish under goalkeeper Troels Rasmussen. But Denmark didn't buckle immediately. After Søren Lerby robbed Gallego, the elegant Michael Laudrup evaded two defenders before scoring with a left-footer that flew past Andoni Zubizarreta.

Piontek entrusted little Jan Heintze to man-mark Míchel, a tactic which had worked for PSV Eindhoven in the European Cup two months earlier. But Heintze couldn't contain his quarry, and another cavalry charge by Míchel ended with John Sivebæk taking his legs in the box. He went for pure power with the penalty, but Rasmussen kept it out. Justice of sorts had been done: three other Spaniards were encroaching at the crucial moment.

At half-time, Spain lost their veteran captain José Antonio Camacho to a shoulder injury sustained while rugby-tackling Elkjær. But they regained the lead with the worst officiating decision of the tournament. José Mari Bakero played a pass across the box to Emilio Butragueño, who was a full yard offside: even in real time, it looked a shocker. Butragueño stayed cool and slotted the ball through Rasmussen's legs.

The *coup de grâce* came midway through the second half. Morten Olsen was substituted, suffering from blurred vision, while Spain stood over a free kick 30 yards out. When it was eventually taken, Rasmussen allowed Rafael Gordillo's looping shot to drift in off the underside of the bar, misjudging its flight and getting his feet tangled up in the net.

Late on, Flemming Povlsen applied a flattering gloss to the scoreline when he headed Heintze's long cross in off the far post. Denmark almost stole an improbable equaliser in the last minute when Míchel charged down Elkjær's shot, but they wouldn't have deserved it.

At the final whistle, Lerby angrily berated referee Bep Thomas, then snarled at a ballboy who had optimistically asked for his shirt. 'So far in my career, I've never believed in the concept of a nemesis,' sighed Piontek. 'But now I say: please let me be happy in the future against the Spaniards.' His opposite number Muñoz coyly dodged questions about the Butragueño incident, though two huge TV screens behind him were replaying it over and over: 'I have seen the goal and nothing else. That's a question you have to ask another man.'

======

This dying Danish team already stood little chance against the hosts in Gelsenkirchen, but Piontek's panicky reaction to the Spain defeat sealed their fate. The 24-year-old Peter Schmeichel replaced Rasmussen and performed well, but Morten Olsen's move to central midfield was an unmitigated disaster: up against the strong-running Matthäus, the 38-year-old was taken to the cleaners. And with big Wolfgang Rolff sitting on Laudrup all afternoon, Eike Immel had so little to do in goal that the *Kölner Express* gave him a rating of 0/10 for 'non-participation'.

Like Olsen, Lerby had a nightmare in midfield, epitomised by an early club-footed touch in the centre circle that set up a German counter-attack. Minutes later, his terrible defensive header fell kindly for Rudi Völler: Schmeichel did brilliantly to save the flicked shot, but Klinsmann devoured the rebound in front of an open goal. Somewhere in Hanover, a young ballboy was smirking.

Denmark's feebleness lulled West Germany into lethargic wastefulness. Völler clipped Matthäus's cross over the bar, Sivebæk almost turned Thon's cross into his own net, and Frank Mill's diving header hit the post. But before the end, a local boy gave the Gelsenkirchen crowd something to savour. The impressive Olaf Thon was playing his last 'home' game in the Parkstadion, weeks ahead of his big move from Schalke to Bayern Munich. Now, four minutes from time, he got the jump on Ivan Nielsen to head home Littbarski's corner. A moment to forget for Nielsen, who was nine inches taller.

Meanwhile, the once-awesome Elkjær had ruptured his achilles, so this was his final cap at just 30. 'The good years are over,' sighed Lerby, whose own international career wasn't long for this world either.

=====

Míchel's stylish performance against Denmark and his new seven-year, £10,000-a-week contract at Real Madrid had made him a subject of fascination for the media ahead of Spain's clash with Italy in Frankfurt. But on the night, the 19-year-old Paolo Maldini ate his lunch by overlapping relentlessly down the left. 'Míchel was completely annihilated by Maldini, who followed him like a faithful dog,' enthused the veteran Italian football columnist Gianni Brera.

The opening stages were dotted with fouls, with the aggressive Víctor kicking Italians as if it were going out of fashion; Vialli soon took revenge with such force that Víctor's left boot came off. Later, as Riccardo Ferri and Míchel tussled, the centre-back punched Míchel on the side of the head and was lucky to escape with a booking.

Strip away the machismo, though, and this was a good match: not packed with goalmouth incident, but with plenty of fine play to enjoy. Without creating many chances, Italy called the tune. Vialli fired wide after Carlo Ancelotti set him up, and Donadoni floated a corner on to the crossbar. Early in the second half, Mancini stabbed the ball tamely at Zubizarreta; and on the hour, Giuseppe Giannini spectacularly volleyed inches wide. Then Butragueño made his first and last contribution, slicing embarrassingly in front of an open goal. Not to be outdone, Mancini headed Vialli's cross straight at Zubizarreta, an equally bad miss.

Vialli, a blueblood who had grown up in a 60-room Renaissance castle in Lombardy, showed on 73 minutes why he had been hyped to hell in the run-up to the finals. The veteran Alessandro Altobelli, who'd only come on two minutes earlier, cleverly stepped over Ferri's pass to turn it into a defence-splitter. Vialli was on to it like a shot, twisting past Tomás on the left before guiding a low shot across Zubizarreta and inside the far post.

Spain hardly responded at all – their strikers, *El País* noted, were 'more isolated than an ugly girl at a school disco' – and Manuel Sanchís should have been sent off for elbowing Altobelli in the face. Muñoz's bizarre post-match remarks that it wasn't his place to tell Zubizarreta to stop hitting the goal kicks long (a tactic which forced little Bakero and Butragueño to contest futile aerial duels with Italy's tall defenders) suggested that he was mentally somewhere else already.

———

As expected, the clapped-out Danes waved Italy through in Cologne. Vialli missed three good chances in the first half: the best one, in only the second minute, saw him fire over the bar after Schmeichel flapped at a cross. Mancini's volley also brought a reaction save out of the goalkeeper, who later stopped him in a one-on-one. Italy were fortunate that Ferri and Ancelotti got away with, respectively, kicking John Eriksen in the face and clattering Laudrup: bookings for either would have seen them miss the semi-final.

Deep into the second half, Vicini's good luck with his bench continued. Less than half a minute after coming on, Altobelli collected Vialli's cross and held off Nielsen before ramming the ball in. And Italy's other substitute scored within two minutes of his own arrival. Another cross, by the overlapping Bergomi, rolled all the way across the goalmouth to Luigi De Agostini, who slipped it under Schmeichel.

It had been a tournament too far for Denmark. The elder statesmen were past it, the youngsters were of variable quality, and Laudrup had sagged under the burden of expectation. 'It was beautiful while it lasted,' said Klaus Berggreen. 'But you need to have the courage to say, "That's enough." I'm going to make room for the younger generation.' Elkjær, Lerby and Søren Busk left the stage too. Piontek gave it one more campaign, but quit after a heartbreaking defeat in Bucharest in November 1989 saw his team miss Italia 90.

———

A relocation to the lakeside resort of Rottach Egern gave the West Germans' morale a lift as they prepared to face Spain in Munich. The brooding Rudi Völler was the exception to their ebullient mood. He hadn't scored for his country since September 1987, and had played poorly against Denmark. Although Beckenbauer continued to back him ('If Rudi wants to play, he plays'), he was plainly on borrowed time.

But after half an hour at the Olympiastadion, Völler finally got the lucky break he had craved. Littbarski's pass deflected off Rafael Martín Vázquez's heel and came to Klinsmann, who instantly pushed the ball into the path of his strike partner. Völler was equally swift to react, shaking off Genar Andrinúa and guiding a great finish into the far corner.

Spain, who had to win, never looked like coming back from behind. Martín Vázquez did shoot narrowly wide at 0-0, but Zubizarreta was lucky not to be sent off for handling outside the area. Míchel, meanwhile, was an irrelevance, completely outshone by another man wearing number eight.

Lothar Matthäus, at this stage of his career, was regarded as an effective workhorse rather than a world-class midfielder. Days before Bayern lost the 1987 European Cup Final to Porto in Vienna, Ulrich Kuhne-Hellmessen of *Kicker* wrote of him, 'The accusation still hangs in the air: strong games against weak opponents, weak games against strong opponents.' Displays like this one changed people's minds, including that of Kuhne-Hellmessen, who later wrote a biography of him. Time and again, Matthäus set off on decisive, dashing bursts through midfield with the ball at his feet, drawing opponents towards him and creating space for his strikers. One such run, early in the second half, saw him charge past three defenders, accelerate into the box and back-heel the ball to the on-running Völler, who stroked another neat finish home.

The Spanish took their frustrations out on Rolff and Klinsmann, who were hacked down by Víctor and Sanchís in quick succession. Late on, Bakero made Immel work twice with an acrobatic volley and a near-post drive, but his team's race was run by then. Völler should have claimed a hat-trick when he nodded substitute Wolfram Wuttke's cross too high, an easier chance than the two he had scored. Afterwards, he fought back tears, defending his record as 'an absolute match-winner' who had come through 'the hard times'.

Spain, though, faced yet another journey back to the drawing board. 'Spanish football is hopeless,' wrote Alex Martínez Roig in *El País*. 'Euro 88 has been an example of how not to do things.' Muñoz now stepped down after six years as manager. 'Why should I feel guilty?' he asked the Spanish media. 'Am I a criminal?'

8.15pm, 10 June 1988
Rheinstadion, Düsseldorf
Attendance: 62,552
Referee: Keith Hackett (England)

WEST GERMANY 1 (Brehme 56)
ITALY 1 (Mancini 52)

WEST GERMANY: Eike Immel, Thomas Berthold, Andy Brehme (Uli Borowka 76), Jürgen Kohler, Guido Buchwald, Matthias Herget, Pierre Littbarski, Lothar Matthäus (c), Rudi Völler (Dieter Eckstein 82), Jürgen Klinsmann, Olaf Thon. **Manager:** Franz Beckenbauer.

ITALY: Walter Zenga, Giuseppe Bergomi (c), Paolo Maldini, Riccardo Ferri, Fernando De Napoli (Luigi De Agostini 86), Franco Baresi, Carlo Ancelotti, Giuseppe Giannini, Roberto Mancini, Gianluca Vialli (Alessandro Altobelli 90), Roberto Donadoni. **Manager:** Azeglio Vicini.

Booked: Maldini (6), Ancelotti (57).

3.30pm, 11 June 1988
Niedersachenstadion, Hanover
Attendance: 55,707
Referee: Bep Thomas (Netherlands)
SPAIN 3 (Míchel 5, Butragueño 53, Gordillo 67)
DENMARK 2 (Laudrup 24, Povlsen 82)

SPAIN: Andoni Zubizarreta, Tomás Reñones, José Antonio Camacho (c) (Miquel Soler 46), Genar Andrinúa, Manuel Sanchís, Víctor Muñoz, Rafael Gordillo (Rafael Martín Vázquez 77), Ricardo Gallego, Emilio Butragueño, Miguel González 'Míchel', José Mari Bakero. **Manager:** Miguel Muñoz.

DENMARK: Troels Rasmussen, John Sivebæk, Søren Busk, Morten Olsen (c) (Lars Olsen 66), Ivan Nielsen, Søren Lerby, John Helt (John Jensen 46), Jan Heintze, Preben Elkjær, Michael Laudrup, Flemming Povlsen. **Manager:** Sepp Piontek.

Booked: Camacho (45+3), Víctor Muñoz (48), Tomás Reñones (69).

5.15pm, 14 June 1988
Parkstadion, Gelsenkirchen
Attendance: 64,812
Referee: Bob Valentine (Scotland)
WEST GERMANY 2 (Klinsmann 10, Thon 87)
DENMARK 0

WEST GERMANY: Immel, Buchwald (Borowka 33), Brehme, Kohler, Wolfgang Rolff, Herget, Littbarski, Matthäus (c), Völler (Frank Mill 75), Klinsmann, Thon.

DENMARK: Peter Schmeichel, Sivebæk, Heintze, L. Olsen, Nielsen, M. Olsen (c), Lerby, Kim Vilfort (Klaus Berggreen 73), Elkjær, Laudrup (John Eriksen 63), Povlsen.

Booked: Rolff (81), Elkjær (37), Povlsen (84).

8.15pm, 14 June 1988
Waldstadion, Frankfurt
Attendance: 47,506
Referee: Erik Fredriksson (Sweden)
ITALY 1 (Vialli 73)
SPAIN 0

ITALY: Zenga, Bergomi (c), Maldini, Ferri, De Napoli, Baresi, Ancelotti, Giannini, Mancini (Altobelli 70), Vialli (De Agostini 90+1), Donadoni.

SPAIN: Zubizarreta, Tomás, Soler, Andrinúa, Sanchís, Víctor, Gordillo (c), Gallego (Martín Vázquez 68), Butragueño, Míchel (Aitor 'Txiki' Begiristain 72), Bakero.

Booked: Ferri 34.

8.15pm, 17 June 1988
Müngersdorferstadion, Cologne
Attendance: 53,951
Referee: Bruno Galler (Switzerland)

ITALY 2 (Altobelli 67, De Agostini 87)
DENMARK 0

ITALY: Zenga, Bergomi (c), Maldini, Ferri, De Napoli, Baresi, Ancelotti, Giannini, Mancini (Altobelli 67), Vialli, Donadoni (De Agostini 85).

DENMARK: Schmeichel, Bjørn Kristensen, L. Olsen, M. Olsen (c) (Berggreen 68), Nielsen, Jensen, Heintze, Per Frimann (Vilfort 58), Eriksen, Laudrup, Povlsen.

Booked: Laudrup (22), Kristensen (71).

8.15pm, 17 June 1988
Olympiastadion, Munich
Attendance: 72,308
Referee: Michel Vautrot (France)

WEST GERMANY 2 (Völler 30, 52)
SPAIN 0

WEST GERMANY: Immel, Borowka, Brehme, Kohler, Rolff, Herget, Littbarski (Wolfram Wuttke 63), Matthäus (c), Völler, Klinsmann (Mill 85), Thon.

SPAIN: Zubizarreta, Tomás, Camacho (c), Andrinúa, Sanchís, Víctor, Gordillo, Martín Vázquez, Butragueño (Julio Salinas 51), Míchel, Bakero.

Booked: Thon (47), Herget (69), Martín Vázquez (34), Gordillo (77), Sanchís (80).

GROUP A	P	W	D	L	F	A	GD	Pts
WEST GERMANY	3	2	1	0	5	1	+4	5
ITALY	3	2	1	0	4	1	+3	5
SPAIN	3	1	0	2	3	5	− 2	2
DENMARK	3	0	0	3	2	7	− 5	0

West Germany and Italy qualified.

GROUP B
England, Ireland, Netherlands, USSR

At the draw for the finals in Düsseldorf the previous January, chuckles and low whistles echoed through the hall as Uli Stielike's son pulled the balls marked Ireland and England out of the punchbowl. The weight of a shared history, the Jack Charlton factor, the presence of almost Ireland's entire squad in the English First Division – it was almost too perfect.

At face value, even Ireland's own public barely rated them: only 12,000 turned up at Lansdowne Road for a friendly against Yugoslavia seven weeks before the finals. In the event, almost 20,000 of their fans would travel to West Germany for the tournament, many of them Irish people working all over Europe. One group, travelling in a battered Renault 4, were taken off the autobahn by a police escort for going too slowly.

Many observers made the mistake of assuming that because Ireland's supporters were only there for a good time, so was their team. In sunny Stuttgart, however, they put England on the canvas after seven minutes. Kevin Moran's hoofed free kick was going out for a goal kick until Mark Wright unwisely headed it back. Winger Tony Galvin hooked the dropping ball into the box, where Kenny Sansom miscued it upwards. Out-jumping the taller Tony Adams, John Aldridge nodded it across to Ray Houghton, who rose spring-heeled to head past Peter Shilton into the far corner. On the bench, Jack Charlton jumped up and cracked his head painfully off the dugout roof.

Ireland had surely scored too early. But England had one of those afternoons where nothing would fall kindly for them or break their way. All season, Beardsley and Barnes had been uncontainable, banging in 35 goals between them for Liverpool. Here, with Houghton on the other team, they couldn't rekindle the magic. Beardsley blew the best chance of the game, ballooning over a gaping goal after Packie Bonner saved from Gary Lineker.

Sluggish and supposedly suffering from hepatitis, which begs the question as to why he was even playing, Lineker saw one effort kept out by Bonner's knee and another clip the bar. But Ireland had chances of their own in the second half. Shilton tipped Ronnie Whelan's volley on to the bar, and young substitute Niall Quinn failed by millimetres to get his head on Houghton's teasing cross.

In the final minute of a draining afternoon, Glenn Hoddle's free kick was met powerfully by substitute Mark Hateley, but Bonner hurled himself across to claw the header away. 'Sometimes you think somebody up there likes you,' said Charlton. Moran described it as 'the hardest 90 minutes' he had ever played, which was something coming from one of the toughest defenders in the English league. Second-favourites to win the tournament on the morning of the match, England now had one foot and most of their suitcases in the departure lounge.

====

Along with Denmark, the USSR had played the sexiest football of Mexico 86. But against the Netherlands in Cologne, they packed away their so-called 'football from the year 2000' and performed a tactical volte-face, winning 1-0 with a distinctly Italian shut-out. 'We've learned our lesson from Mexico that it's not wise to attack at all costs,' Valeriy Lobanovskyi said beforehand. 'It's more important to win.'

Playing in fishscale-patterned orange shirts, the Dutch were swallowed up. Rinus Michels selected Johnny Bosman over Marco van Basten (who had picked up three separate injuries in an alleged friendly between Milan and

Real Madrid), but the tall Ajax striker made no impression. Ruud Gullit, hyped to the point of irritation before the finals, fared no better: when he moved over to the right to escape Oleksiy Mykhaylychenko, he was tracked by the relentless Anatoliy Demyanenko. John van 't Schip languished like a lost dog on the other side, and little Oleksandr Zavarov moved around so much that the bow-legged enforcer Jan Wouters had nobody to mark.

Still, the Netherlands had enough chances to win. Rinat Dasaev punched two Koeman thunderbolts over the bar, parried Gullit's shot, turned Van 't Schip's awkward bouncer around the post, kept out Bosman's header and Wouters's volley, and calmly prevented Volodymyr Bezsonov heading an own goal. One of very few Muslims to play for the USSR, the tall, gaunt Dasaev always kept a copy of the Koran inside his goalkeeping bag. 'I had it there as a presence,' he said. 'You couldn't exactly open it during a game and read a surah.'

Early in the second half, the Soviets sounded a warning when Ihor Belanov darted past the flat-footed Adri van Tiggelen and forced Hans van Breukelen to save well. Moments later, Vasyl Rats's fantastic long pass picked out Belanov on the right, again facing van Tiggelen. This time he waited, then threaded the ball across the edge of the box where Rats, in full stride, struck a super left-footer across Van Breukelen. A strong candidate for best one-two of all time.

Van Basten now came on, but the Netherlands hit too many long balls up to him and Gullit, forcing him to drop deep. Vagiz Khidiyatullin later deflected Gullit's header on to his own bar, but the USSR held out, with another Rats effort grazing a post near the end. The saturnine Lobanovskyi's face was blank at the final whistle, but this was a win to savour.

'My strikers were only at 50 per cent of their normal level,' reflected Michels. 'Maybe the pressure was too great. We are merely an outsider – the expectations are set much too high.' But he then stuck the knife into his underperforming captain. 'Gullit missed the boat. He had a free role in this game, and he couldn't support the team when they needed him. And as a team, we are too soft. Not winners. We were losing the game, and in the second half we only had four fouls. That's highly unprofessional.'

Michels now had a big decision to make on his strikers. 'After the first game, I thought, "I'm going to go home, because he's not going to use me",' said Van Basten in 2012. 'But then Michels said, "I can't promise anything – but I'll need you".'

═════

The England-Netherlands match was now effectively an elimination play-off. In blazing sunshine, a capacity crowd at the Rheinstadion saw the best match of the tournament. England battled hard but their young central defenders simply couldn't handle Michels's not-so-secret weapon. Restored to the line-up, Van Basten channelled his anger into a performance of virtual perfection.

England made the brighter start, however. Bryan Robson's clever chip caught out Ronald Koeman, who turned away from it as it bounced off his head. Lineker latched on to it and ran around Van Breukelen, but pushed it on to the post of an open goal from a sharp angle. Not quite a sitter, but he would have buried it against Poland or Paraguay in 1986.

Six minutes before half-time, England struck Dutch timber again. Hoddle curled a free kick around the wall, and it came off the inside of the same upright Lineker had hit.

Lucky not to be two down, the Netherlands broke the deadlock after their third let-off of the afternoon. Frank Rijkaard crunched Lineker, but referee Paolo Casarin waved play on and Gullit galloped down the left. His low centre found Van Basten, who turned Adams inside out, twisting like a whirlwind before jabbing a sharp shot beyond Shilton. Adams had done nothing wrong: van Basten was just too good. In first-half stoppage time, he almost struck again. Gerald Vanenburg's excellent pass put him clean through to take the ball around Shilton, but Gary Stevens cleared his shot off the line.

England's equaliser, early in the second half, was an awesome show of force of will. Playing a one-two with Lineker, Robson shook off two Dutchmen, stormed into the box, jabbed the ball against Van Breukelen's arm, and saw it bobble in as Van Tiggelen tangled himself up in the net. It wouldn't have won any beauty contests, but it kept England alive.

The Netherlands defended deep and often desperately, but with 18 minutes left, their cobra sprang again. Gullit slipped a neat pass to Van Basten on the edge of the box, and he took one touch before drilling another superb finish across Shilton. Within minutes, England were dead and buried. Wim Kieft flicked on Erwin Koeman's corner to the far post, and you-know-who smashed it into the roof of the net for his hat-trick.

It was the greatest game of Van Basten's sadly curtailed career, which is saying something: four chances, three goals, one clearance off the line. Michels's change of heart had paid off handsomely. 'I freely admit I was wrong,' he said.

After Van Basten's third goal, crowd trouble flared in the England end. Earlier, there had been running battles between English and German fans in Düsseldorf city centre. In all, some 500 England fans were arrested, along with 400 Germans. Earlier, a group of Dutch fans rampaged through a car park reserved for England supporters.

Hans Lisken, Düsseldorf's police chief, said, 'The German fans wanted to show who's in command in the Rhineland. The English fans didn't start the trouble.' Margaret Thatcher's sports minister Colin Moynihan, however, described the supporters involved as 'worse than animals, because I know of no animals which would behave in this manner'. *The Sun*, Thatcher's loudest cheerleader, displayed its usual restraint in calling for England to be thrown out of Euro 88.

＝＝＝

You didn't get this sort of thing with Ireland, whose cheerful fans now moved on to Lower Saxony for the next chapter of their fairytale. Everyone expected another rearguard action from the tournament's Cinderella outfit against the USSR in Hanover – but, perverse to the last, they came out and attacked, dominating the match and playing slick football.

The majority of Ireland's players had technical ability in abundance, but Charlton's brutalist tactics had kept it in check for years. They looked a different team here, walking all over one of the best sides in the world. 'With the Irish, it was very hard,' Belanov said. 'They didn't let you play. Also, they were very well prepared physically. And psychologically, too, they had 11 brave fighters on the field.'

The USSR sorely missed the class of the suspended Hennadiy Lytovchenko, hardly winning a tackle during a one-sided first half. With Paul McGrath's swollen knee ruling him out, Kevin Sheedy stepped into the Irish midfield and instantly looked the part. Alongside him, Ronnie Whelan was even better.

Houghton, a shining light in Liverpool's title win, had brought his domestic form with him and ran Demyanenko ragged, no mean feat. Early on, he pounced on Mick McCarthy's misdirected shot to force an amazing reflex save from Dasaev, only to be given offside. Then he glided past three Soviets and hit a slashing shot which the goalkeeper was at full stretch to save.

Soviet discomfort was summed up by Mykhaylychenko's 40-yard volleyed back-pass to Dasaev under no pressure. Ireland then went ahead with an unforgettable goal. McCarthy's monumental long throw sailed over everybody except Whelan, who somehow jumped four or five feet in the air and volleyed it into the top corner from the edge of the box. Dasaev got a hand to it but couldn't keep it out. TV replays revealed that Whelan's shin, not his boot, had made the decisive contact. But who cared?

In the second half, Ireland were denied a clear penalty and a man advantage. Sheedy's chip put Tony Galvin through, and Dasaev flew off his line to lunge two-footed at the winger, sending him flying – and injuring himself in the process, which probably spared him a red card. He spent the next few minutes hobbling around, holding his hip in obvious pain. Soon, he collided with Galvin again – innocently this time – and he was a stricken bystander seconds later as Aldridge ineptly side-footed Galvin's cross over the bar at close range. Lobanovskyi instantly took him off.

The USSR's equaliser on 75 minutes was unexpected and undeserved. After Belanov hacked Demyanenko's long ball over Moran, Oleh Protasov nipped in to slot the ball through Bonner's legs. A draw was meagre return for Ireland's best ever performance, but it could have been worse: late on, Chris Hughton's hesitancy almost let Belanov in before Bonner rescued the situation.

Afterwards, Lobanovskyi refused to talk to the Soviet press, who complained that he and his team were ignoring them while barricaded into an 'hermetically sealed fortress' (in the words of Soviet paper *Izvestiya*) outside Stuttgart. News agency TASS's match report noted in dry Kremlinspeak, 'The USSR team realised no more than 60 per cent of their potentialities in Hanover. The uncoordinated efforts of the Soviet players were stopped in a simple but resolute manner by the Irish defence.'

The USSR looked much better in Frankfurt three days later, bundling England out of the tournament without trouble. Bobby Robson's name was booed when it was read out over the PA before kick-off; and, as they had done against Ireland, his team coughed up a soft early goal. Glenn Hoddle, very disappointing in what turned out to be his final international, was robbed with ease by Sergei Aleinikov, who accelerated into the box, turned past Dave Watson and placed his shot beyond goalkeeper Chris Woods. 'We made the most miserable of starts, which made us very edgy,' lamented Robson.

In hot conditions, the red-shirted Soviets kept the pressure on. Protasov twice outpaced Adams and hit a pair of hard shots, the first inches wide, the second off the post. In between, Lytovchenko's long pass found Belanov all alone, but he miscued badly. All this, plus the goal, in the first 15 minutes.

England were being overrun, yet suddenly found an equaliser from nowhere. Even on his worst days, Hoddle's dead-ball deliveries were usually good, and Adams rose high to glance home his free kick. Shortly afterwards, Trevor Steven headed into the turf and up on to the bar. But when Hoddle again suicidally surrendered possession in his own half, Rats curled over a centre for Mykhaylychenko to bury a simple header from five yards.

In the second half, Protasov wastefully shot straight at Woods, and the chain was finally pulled when substitute Viktor Pasulko knocked in another Rats cross at close range for 3-1. Some argued that English clubs' years of exile from European competitions had finally told on the national team – but the same weaknesses had been obvious in Italy in 1980, at a time when those clubs were not just competing in Europe but ruling it.

—————

With Ireland one point away from the semi-finals, their fans streamed up the autobahns to Gelsenkirchen in their thousands, many living off emergency credit-union loans from home. The Dutch arrived in even greater numbers, and on yet another sweltering day, the packed Parkstadion was a bubbling ocean of green and orange.

Without creating many clear openings, the Netherlands got on top. Bonner punched Van Tiggelen's piledriver over the bar, Erwin Koeman stole in behind Gullit to head wide, Van Basten was stopped by McCarthy's magnificent challenge, and Ronald Koeman swung at fresh air with the goal at his mercy. But Ireland came closest of all in the 16th minute. Their only corner of the day was met by Paul McGrath, whose header thumped off a post, hit Vanenburg on the back and ricocheted on to the post again. Aldridge lunged to poke it in, but his leg was a few millimetres too short and Van Breukelen gratefully dived on the ball.

After the interval, Ireland wearily retreated towards their own goal as they tried to see out time. The guard dog Wouters, of all people, was the Netherlands' main threat. He ambled forward to rattle the bar from out on the right, then floated a chip on to the roof of the net.

Michels's substitutions saw the Dutch end up with four strikers on the pitch (a precursor of Louis van Gaal's meltdown at Lansdowne Road in September 2001). 'They were really panicking,' said Houghton. 'They didn't know how to break us down.' But with seven minutes left, McGrath headed Wouters's cross out only as far as Ronald Koeman, 25 yards distant. The blond sweeper crashed his shot downwards into the grass, the ball bounced up at a crazy angle, and one of those Dutch substitutes reacted quickest.

The 6ft 3in Wim Kieft, ungainly but effective (Van Basten called him 'that big tree'), now pulled off the ugliest, most important header of his life. Turning 360 degrees instantly, he got enough of his forehead on to the spinning ball to divert its course and deceive the stranded Bonner, who watched aghast as it bounced softly inside the post. Van Basten was two yards beyond the last defender, but linesman Heinz Holzmann kept his flag down, and the Netherlands were home free.

'I thought it was going wide,' Kieft said in 2020. 'Ronald Koeman didn't hit the shot that well, and it had an enormous spin on it. I was just hitting it on a reflex. I thought it was going wide, then it spun back. I watched it all the way. It was such a strange feeling. I guess sometimes you need a bit of luck, eh? Van Basten was offside. Definitely offside.'

A 'Vorsprung durch Jack' banner greeted Ireland at Dublin Airport, while the Napoleonic prime minister Charles Haughey compared Kieft's goal to the slaying of Brian Ború. The team's open-top bus parade through Dublin drew an adoring crowd of 300,000, almost ten per cent of the country's population. Charlton said disbelievingly, 'It makes me wonder what the reception would be like if we actually won something.'

Back in Gelsenkirchen, the Dutch wore the dazed smiles of men who knew they had got away with it. Celebrating in the dressing room, they threw radio reporter Kees Jansma into the bath. 'Ik zit nog bij te komen,' Michels told Dutch TV in barely translatable Amsterdammer dialect; 'I've yet to come round.'

3.30pm, 12 June 1988
Neckarstadion, Stuttgart
Attendance: 51,573
Referee: Siegfried Kirschen (East Germany)

IRELAND 1 (Houghton 7)
ENGLAND 0

IRELAND: Packie Bonner, Chris Morris, Chris Hughton, Mick McCarthy, Kevin Moran, Ronnie Whelan, Paul McGrath, Ray Houghton, John Aldridge, Frank Stapleton (c) (Niall Quinn 64), Tony Galvin (Kevin Sheedy 77). **Manager:** Jack Charlton.

ENGLAND: Peter Shilton, Gary Stevens, Kenny Sansom, Mark Wright, Tony Adams, Neil Webb (Glenn Hoddle 60), Bryan Robson (c), Chris Waddle, Gary Lineker, Peter Beardsley (Mark Hateley 83), John Barnes. **Manager:** Bobby Robson.

8.15pm, 12 June 1988
Müngersdorferstadion, Cologne
Attendance: 54,336
Referee: Dieter Pauly (West Germany)

USSR 1 (Rats 54)
NETHERLANDS 0

USSR: Rinat Dasaev (c), Volodymyr Bezsonov, Vagiz Khidiyatullin, Oleh Kuznetsov, Anatoliy Demyanenko, Vasyl Rats, Hennadiy Lytovchenko, Oleksiy Mykhaylychenko, Oleh Protasov, Oleksandr Zavarov (Tengiz Sulakvelidze 90), Ihor Belanov (Sergei Aleinikov 81). **Manager:** Valeriy Lobanovskyi.

NETHERLANDS: Hans van Breukelen, Berry van Aerle, Adri van Tiggelen, Ronald Koeman, Frank Rijkaard, Jan Wouters, Gerald Vanenburg (Marco van Basten 58), Arnold Mühren, Johnny Bosman, Ruud Gullit (c), John van 't Schip. **Manager:** Rinus Michels.

Booked: Lytovchenko (21), Khidiyatullin (40).

5.15pm, 15 June 1988
Rheinstadion, Düsseldorf
Attendance: 63,940
Referee: Paolo Casarin (Italy)

NETHERLANDS 3 (Van Basten 44, 73, 76)
ENGLAND 1 (Robson 54)

NETHERLANDS: Van Breukelen, Van Aerle, van Tiggelen, R. Koeman, Rijkaard, Wouters, Vanenburg (Wim Kieft 60), Mühren, Van Basten (Wilbert Suvrijn 87), Gullit (c), Erwin Koeman.

ENGLAND: Shilton, Stevens, Sansom, Wright, Adams, Hoddle, Robson (c), Trevor Steven (Waddle 69), Lineker, Beardsley (Hateley 72), Barnes.

8.15pm, 15 June 1988
Niedersachsenstadion, Hanover
Attendance: 38,308
Referee: Emilio Soriano Aladrén (Spain)

IRELAND 1 (Whelan 39)
USSR 1 (Protasov 75)

IRELAND: Bonner, Morris, Hughton, Moran, McCarthy, Whelan, Sheedy, Houghton, Aldridge, Stapleton (c) (Tony Cascarino 81), Galvin.

USSR: Dasaev (c) (Viktor Chanov 69), Sulakvelidze (Sergei Gotsmanov 46), Khidiyatullin, Kuznetsov, Demyanenko, Rats, Aleinikov, Mykhaylychenko, Protasov, Zavarov, Belanov.

3.30pm, 18 June 1988
Waldstadion, Frankfurt
Attendance: 48,335
Referee: José Rosa dos Santos (Portugal)

USSR 3 (Aleinikov 3, Mykhaylychenko 28, Pasulko 73)
ENGLAND 1 (Adams 16)

USSR: Dasaev (c), Bezsonov, Khidiyatullin, Kuznetsov, Rats, Aleinikov, Lytovchenko, Mykhaylychenko, Protasov, Zavarov (Gotsmanov 86), Belanov (Viktor Pasulko 44).

ENGLAND: Chris Woods, Stevens, Sansom, Dave Watson, Adams, Steve McMahon (Webb 54), Robson (c), Steven, Lineker (Hateley 69), Hoddle, Barnes.

Booked: Protasov (42).

3.30pm, 18 June 1988
Parkstadion, Gelsenkirchen
Attendance: 64,731
Referee: Horst Brummeier (Austria)

NETHERLANDS 1 (Kieft 83)
IRELAND 0

NETHERLANDS: Van Breukelen, Van Aerle, van Tiggelen, R. Koeman, Rijkaard, Wouters, Vanenburg, Mühren (Bosman 79), Van Basten, Gullit (c), E. Koeman (Kieft 51).

IRELAND: Bonner, Morris (Sheedy 46), Hughton, Moran, McCarthy, Whelan, McGrath, Houghton, Aldridge, Stapleton (c) (Cascarino 83), Galvin.

Booked: Wouters (60).

GROUP B	P	W	D	L	F	A	GD	Pts
USSR	3	2	1	0	5	2	+3	5
NETHERLANDS	3	2	0	1	4	2	+2	4
IRELAND	3	1	1	1	2	2	0	3
ENGLAND	3	0	0	3	2	7	−5	0

The USSR and the Netherlands qualified.

SEMI-FINALS
West Germany v Netherlands
Italy v USSR

Franz Beckenbauer freely admitted he would rather have faced Ireland, and not just because the Netherlands had better players. Officially, the Dutch were allocated 15,000 of the 56,000 tickets; the visual evidence in Hamburg suggested otherwise. 'It would've been nice to have played the match in Germany,' Frank Mill said sarcastically. It was a mighty occasion, but weight of history counted against it being a classic football match, and tension filled the air all night.

Beforehand, intrigue swirled around Beckenbauer's line-up. Pierre Littbarski's name appeared on the official team sheets but the manager, deciding to save him for extra time, falsely put it around that he had a stomach bug and picked Frank Mill instead. 'Beckenbauer forced me to say that I felt bad,' Littbarski said. 'It directly affected my professional dignity.'

The occasion seemed to get to Mill, who contributed hardly anything. At one point, Ronald Koeman's soft back-pass nearly let him in, but Van Breukelen got there first, jumping into him with an upraised knee, then roaring at him, 'Ich hoffe das du fokking stirbst!' – 'I hope you fucking die!'

Coming out of the tunnel for the second half, Michels was resoundingly jeered by the home fans and responded with a middle finger. On 55 minutes, a debatable decision gave West Germany the lead. Klinsmann, setting off on a burrowing run, lost Van Tiggelen and Erwin Koeman before bursting into the box. He came together with Rijkaard, then collapsed exaggeratedly as he so often did. Referee Ioan Igna pointed to the spot, prompting an enraged Van Tiggelen to blast the ball against his back from several yards away.

Dutch TV commentator Evert ten Napel, thinking back 14 years to Bernd Hölzenbein's dive, groaned, 'Oh no! We've fallen for it again. It happens again!' But Rijkaard had been foolish to throw out a leg which Klinsmann was always going to tumble over. Van Breukelen got both hands to Matthäus's penalty, but couldn't stop it.

There followed a strange and unsavoury incident when Völler, who had just been kicked by Wouters, tried to get up but was shoved to the ground by Ronald Koeman and had his hair pulled for good measure. A stronger referee would have sent Koeman off.

The Netherlands were looking short of ideas when, on 75 minutes, Igna awarded a much dodgier penalty. Van Basten ran into the box, then stumbled over Kohler's tackle but got straight back up. To everyone's amazement, the referee's whistle cut sharply through the din. Van Basten's face betrayed his own surprise. If nothing else, Igna was no homer. As Koeman waited to take the penalty, Brehme told Immel to dive left. Koeman then put it in the other corner.

Littbarski now came on, offering more in 11 minutes than Mill had in 79. He almost claimed an improbable late winner for West Germany when Gerald Vanenburg headed his wickedly inswinging corner off the line.

How vital that clearance was. With 90 seconds left, the Dutch landed the killing blow, the most cherished moment in their footballing history. Wouters's pass gave Van Basten the chance to run at Kohler, who didn't dive in this time. That allowed Van Basten to outpace him, stretch out that long right leg and reach the ball with an opportunistic little toe-poke. His aim was so perfect that it made Immel's sprawling dive look bad. The ball nestled softly in the far corner. 'Het Volksparkstadion is van Oranje!' roared Ten Napel.

At the final whistle, Koeman swapped shirts with Thon before walking down to the Dutch end and pretending to wipe his backside with the German jersey. The mayor of Aachen later wrote a private letter to Koeman, telling him his behaviour had stirred up tensions in the border town and inviting him to pay a conciliatory visit. Koeman never responded. 'It wasn't good what Ronald did,' Thon said in 2013. 'But we shouldn't exaggerate. He didn't break anybody's leg; he didn't tear anyone's achilles to shreds. So I forgive him.'

To celebrate, the Dutch team and their partners headed off to a Hamburg nightclub (Gullit booked a private room to prevent any hassle on the dance floor). Michels confessed to harbouring 'an extra feeling of satisfaction, for reasons that I don't want to go into now'. Back in the Netherlands, millions poured on to the streets to celebrate, in the country's biggest public gathering since Liberation Day in May 1945. There were also outbreaks of violence in towns along the border – including Aachen.

For Beckenbauer, the aftermath was a prolonged ordeal. When he called it 'our most unfortunate defeat in decades' and 'the best game we played in the tournament', Jürgen Leidemann of *Der Spiegel* shot back, 'In four years in charge, he has not significantly improved the quality of German football. Individuality is embodied by the *Teamchef* alone: the players are reduced to functions, like workpieces in a machine, on whose perfection Beckenbauer constantly relies.' Like Enzo Bearzot in 1980, Beckenbauer clung to his job. And, like Bearzot, within two years all was forgiven.

====

The day before the second semi-final in Stuttgart, Giuseppe Giannini told Italian journalists, 'I feel too much euphoria around. We must try to remain calm.' But composure wouldn't decide the match: the Soviets were simply more streetwise. Italian national teams are usually packed with old hands, but the line-up Vicini picked had an average age of 24.

Eleven of the 22 on the pitch were on a yellow card. In the second minute, Oleh Kuznetsov was first to pick up another, ploughing through Vialli to put himself out of the final. Volodymyr Bezsonov had done the same to Mancini moments earlier, but escaped.

Unfazed by a noisy and mostly Italian crowd, the USSR made the early running. Aleinikov and Lytovchenko both drilled shots into Zenga's hands, while Protasov curled another one just over. But Vialli came closer when, after prolonged head-tennis outside the Soviet box, his shot barely cleared the angle of post and bar. Shortly before half-time, Italy made and spurned the two best opportunities yet. First, Vialli got above Khidiyatullin but headed Donadoni's cross downwards and badly wide, his hangdog expression saying it all. A minute later, Giannini met Mancini's set-piece with a much better header – but Dasaev was in the right place to push it over the bar with a stunning reflex save.

When the teams came out for the second half, the weather had turned foul, another advantage for the USSR. 'The rain made the surface very heavy,' Vicini said. 'We were technical and fast, but they were more powerful. On that pitch, it made all the difference.'

Just after the hour, the USSR suddenly cut Italy open. A mix-up between Mancini and De Napoli allowed Kuznetsov to feed Mykhaylychenko, who spotted Lytovchenko's run into the box. Giuseppe Bergomi missed the tackle, and though Franco Baresi blocked Lytovchenko's shot, he smartly stabbed the rebound into the corner. Lobanovskyi leapt out of his dugout, though his face was as impassive as ever.

Italy were still seeing stars when the Soviets floored them a second time. Again the move came down the left. Aleinikov threaded a lovely ball to Zavarov, who outpaced Bergomi, saw Protasov sprinting into the box, and picked the striker out with a square ball. Protasov, in full stride, leaned back to scoop his finish in a delicate arc over Zenga.

The USSR should have won by more than 2-0, with both Mykhaylychenko and Aleinikov going close near the end. The chastened Italians, taken to school by their elders, went home to lick their wounds and prepare for their own World Cup. Their conquerors were confined to barracks in luxury hotels for almost the entire duration of the tournament, and were on the equivalent of £19 per day in pocket money. Their reward for this coolly minimalist win was a shopping trip in central Stuttgart.

8.15pm, 21 June 1988
Volksparkstadion, Hamburg
Attendance: 56,116
Referee: Ioan Igna (Romania)

NETHERLANDS 2 (R. Koeman 74 pen, Van Basten 89)
WEST GERMANY 1 (Matthäus 55 pen)

NETHERLANDS: Van Breukelen, van Aerle, van Tiggelen, R. Koeman, Rijkaard, Wouters, Vanenburg, Mühren (Kieft 58), Van Basten, Gullit (c), E. Koeman (Suvrijn 89).

WEST GERMANY: Immel, Brehme, Borowka, Kohler, Rolff, Herget (Hans Pflügler 44), Mill (Littbarski 79), Matthäus (c), Völler, Klinsmann, Thon.

Booked: Van Breukelen 60.

8.15pm, 22 June 1988
Neckarstadion, Stuttgart
Attendance: 61,606
Referee: Alexis Ponnet (Belgium)

USSR 2 (Lytovchenko 61, Protasov 64)
ITALY 0

USSR: Dasaev (c), Bezsonov (Demyanenko 37), Khidiyatullin, Kuznetsov, Rats, Aleinikov, Lytovchenko, Mykhaylychenko, Protasov, Zavarov, Gotsmanov.

ITALY: Zenga, Bergomi (c), Maldini (De Agostini 65), Ferri, De Napoli, Baresi, Ancelotti, Giannini, Mancini (Altobelli 46), Vialli, Donadoni.

Booked: Kuznetsov (2), Bezsonov (32), Gotsmanov (45), Baresi (33), De Napoli (78), Ferri (85).

FINAL
Netherlands v USSR

Before the final in Munich, the Dutch players presented Rinus Michels with a watch inscribed 'Thanks from the team, Euro 88'. Moved to tears, he said that if they won, they would do Dutch football a great service by dispelling the idea that everything was better in the past – and if they lost, he would hand back the timepiece.

At the Olympiastadion, the first two opportunities fell to the cultured Hennadiy Lytovchenko. In the second minute, he shot wide. On the half-hour, he blew a much better chance. When Zavarov found Belanov 50 yards downfield with a wonderful pass, the striker twisted away from Adri van Tiggelen and Berry van Aerle to open up space for himself. He then laid the ball off to Lytovchenko, who stepped past Rijkaard – but shot straight at the grateful Van Breukelen. A glaring miss, it was punished three minutes later.

After Dasaev punched Gullit's free kick over the bar, Erwin Koeman's corner was headed away. But Koeman gobbled up the loose ball and hoisted it into the box. Van Basten nodded it back into a goalmouth that was now empty, all the Soviets having run out to play offside, and Gullit sprinted in to head home.

But the USSR should have equalised before half-time. After high crosses by Rats and Demyanenko created confusion, the ball got stuck under Mykhaylychenko's legs and broke to Belanov who, leaning back, shot over.

Eight minutes into the second half, the Netherlands doubled their lead with a genuinely iconic goal. Van Tiggelen robbed Lytovchenko in midfield before spotting Arnold Mühren's overlap on the left. Mühren's high cross floated all the way over to the far side of the box, in the general direction of Van Basten, who was well out from goal at a no-hoper angle.

Now came the crowning moment of Euro 88. Van Basten drew back that peerless right foot, its ankle heavily taped. As the cross fell to earth, he was two feet off the ground when he made perfect contact with it on the volley. The ball whistled past Rats's shoulder, flew over Dasaev's outstretched glove, and dipped under the crossbar like a heatseeking missile. On the sidelines, Michels stood up and clutched his face, unable to believe what he had just seen. Afterwards, he called it 'a goal more beautiful than the most ambitious script'.

Three decades on, Dasaev was still smarting. 'It was a stroke of luck, even Marco himself has said it. Give him another hundred opportunities to try it and he won't do it that way. A keeper can't be infallible.' Belanov was more realistic: 'No one would have got that shot. If Dasaev was five metres tall, then maybe.'

But this match was far from over. When Demyanenko hoisted a free kick into the box, the Dutch defenders nervously flubbed two clearances before Belanov hooked the loose ball against the post. Seconds later, another awful clearance – by Erwin Koeman – went up in the air. Protasov headed it on, and when Sergei Gotsmanov kept it in play, Van Breukelen rashly flattened him from behind. Penalty.

In the days before PSV Eindhoven's European Cup Final against Benfica in Stuttgart a month earlier, Van Breukelen phoned an Eredivisie coach named Jan Reker, who had kept a card database on thousands of different players since the 1970s. It included details of where some of them placed their penalties. Reker happily shared his archive with Van Breukelen, who used the data to save António Veloso's spot-kick on the night and make PSV champions of Europe. The database also included a card about Belanov.

The Ukrainian was done no favours by a delay of two minutes before he could take the penalty, during which Van Breukelen and Rijkaard both got in his face. His kick, when it came, was powerful – but Van Breukelen dived right and it cannoned off his knee.

Why the unfit striker had taken the penalty at all was a question for Lobanovskyi to answer. 'I was very upset, because I knew the whole country had been watching and hoping,' Belanov reflected. 'For a week afterwards, I hardly slept. And when I did fall asleep, oh, the nightmares.'

And that was that. '[Belanov's] failure broke us,' said Rats. 'The guys were on their hands and knees. They gave up, surrendered. If the West Germans had been in our place, they would have fought to the end. Mentality!'

At the final whistle, Lobanovskyi stood still, a man alone, not making eye contact with his players. He later blamed his forwards ('We created three pure chances and took none of them: you don't win anything on averages like that'), UEFA's scheduling ('The Netherlands had 24 hours extra to recover from their semi, and it showed – it gave them an unfair advantage') and the absurd rule of carrying yellow cards from the qualifiers into the finals ('There is no second Kuznetsov'). No one knew it at the time, but this would be the USSR's last match in the European Championship finals.

Just two and a half years after failing to qualify for Mexico 86, the Netherlands had won their first international trophy. Their achievement was built not around beautiful football (although having two ball-players as central defenders was a high-risk tactic which Michels got away with), but on rock-hard resolve, excellent technique and considerable good fortune. Michels himself acknowledged as much: 'We were lucky in the decisive moments.'

Van Basten, Gullit, Koeman and Rijkaard now became global stars, but it was also a triumph for less heralded types like full-back Van Aerle. When the squad went on a victory cruise of Amsterdam's canals the next day, watched by more than a million onlookers, it was the first time he had ever visited the city for anything other than Eredivisie games. As the cruise wound its way along, drunken revellers clambered on to dozens of houseboats, sinking several of them.

Of course, the real climax had happened four days earlier. 'We all know the semi-final was the real final,' Michels said. On the Dutch-German border, a motorway bridge was spray-painted on the German-facing side with the words 'Und jetzt fahren sie in das land des Europa-meister': 'You are now driving in the land of the European champions'.

Before the finals, Johan Cruyff had dismissed Michels's team as 'de patat-generatie', the chip shop generation: immature, flighty, no use when the (ahem) chips were down. Two years later, in his new job at the KNVB, Michels took revenge by ensuring that Cruyff wouldn't manage the Netherlands at Italia 90. Though that wasn't a bad one for Cruyff to miss out on.

In terms of tactical sophistication and fitness levels, 1988 was a big step up from 1984: no round-bellied, bandy-legged wingers here. But the defining characteristic of Euro 88 was its uniformity of standard. There were no bad games, but no classics either. The teams were evenly matched, with only Denmark looking out of place, and nobody won a game by more than two goals.

Michels could now retire in peace (temporarily, it turned out), after laying his German demons to rest with the help of his thoroughbred. Van Basten, only 23, seemed more like 28 or 29, already the finished article. No one knew it, but he had little time left. His last meaningful football match would be the 1993 Champions League Final on this same Olympiastadion pitch. Two years later, the ankle injury that just wouldn't go away ended his career. 'I thought I would play until I was 36 or 38,' he told *L'Équipe* decades later. 'It just didn't work out.' But for now, he was the young king of European football.

3.30pm, 25 June 1988
Olympiastadion, Munich
Attendance: 72,308
Referee: Michel Vautrot (France)

NETHERLANDS 2 (Gullit 33, Van Basten 54)
USSR 0

NETHERLANDS: Van Breukelen, van Aerle, Van Tiggelen, R. Koeman, Rijkaard, Wouters, Vanenburg, Mühren, Van Basten, Gullit (c), E. Koeman.

USSR: Dasaev (c), Demyanenko, Khidiyatullin, Aleinikov, Rats, Gotsmanov (Serhiy Baltacha 68), Lytovchenko, Mykhaylychenko, Protasov (Pasulko 71), Zavarov, Belanov.

Booked: Wouters (37), Van Aerle (50), Demyanenko (32), Lytovchenko (34), Khidiyatullin 42.

1992

A COUNTRY like Sweden couldn't stage the European Championship today. Not with 16 teams, let alone 24, and certainly not without a co-host to help shoulder the burden. But in the late 1980s, when the bidding got under way for the ninth edition of the finals, such a thing was still eminently possible. So a bloodhound-faced Stockholmer who sat on UEFA's executive committee began working the phones and suites in the corridors of power.

Lennart Johansson was helped by the fact that Spain, Sweden's only rival, had already bagged Expo 92 and the Barcelona Olympics. On 17 December 1988, Sweden secured the tournament. Eighteen months later, Johansson himself defeated Freddy Rumo to win the UEFA presidency. Heady days for Swedish blazers all round.

Only four venues were used, all in the south of the country, making Euro 92 a tournament of short distances. One stadium, Norrköping's Idrottsparken, held just 19,414 spectators. 'I'm convinced that the idea of small stadia was the right one,' said Swedish FA president Lars-Åke Lagrell, adding helpfully, 'The big money is made nowadays from the sale of TV broadcasting rights.' Meanwhile, ABBA's Benny Andersson was hired to write a theme tune for the event. What he came up with was, sadly, no 'Summer Night City'.

Sweden's footballing prospects looked unclear after losing all three games 2-1 at Italia 90. New manager Tommy Svensson reshaped the side around young forwards Tomas Brolin, Martin Dahlin and Kennet Andersson. Goals had flowed in the friendlies: six against Austria, five against Poland, four against Denmark and Yugoslavia. The consensus was that making the last four would constitute success.

Scotland had accompanied Sweden out the door in that World Cup group. Manager Andy Roxburgh survived some scalding criticism and steered his team to their first European Championship finals, edging out Switzerland, Romania and Bulgaria. Little, however, was expected of them in a murderous group containing the Netherlands, a unified Germany, and the newest international side in the world.

The USSR didn't last long enough as a national entity to take part in their sixth European Championship. As the qualifiers progressed, the vast country slid onwards to political oblivion, eventually collapsing in November 1991. The Soviet team would participate under the banner of the hastily assembled Commonwealth of Independent States, which didn't include Georgia or the Baltic republics.

On 13 January 1992, the two-day-old CIS Football Federation was awarded the USSR's place at the finals. The team would be wound up as soon as their involvement in Euro 92 ceased. 'For all of us, it's the last chance,' sweeper Oleh Kuznetsov said.

The USSR's campaign was livened up by three draws: an entertaining 2-2 ding-dong at home to Hungary, and two absorbing 0-0s with Italy. The first, in Rome, was littered with promising dead-ball situations and from one, Roberto Baggio scored a spectacular free kick, realising too late that it was indirect. Later, Franco Baresi's mistake put Oleh Protasov clean through to shoot over a gaping goal. A year later in Moscow, weeks before the USSR ceased to exist, the margins remained fine. Walter Zenga denied Andrei Chernyshov at close range, and Ruggiero Rizzitelli rattled a post.

Italy paid a high price for those draws, and for a rotten 2-1 defeat in Oslo. For the second time in three Euros, they would be watching on television at home – at a time when Serie A's native produce was top-drawer, with players as good as Alessandro Orlando and Alessandro Melli going uncapped. Manager Azeglio Vicini walked the plank after the Norway debacle; Arrigo Sacchi, fresh from winning back-to-back European Cups with Milan, arrived too late to turn things around.

Like Italy, Spain underperformed desperately. Luis Suárez had already been sacked as manager by the time they lost 2-0 in Iceland. Reykjavik was the most humiliating introduction imaginable for his successor Vicente Miera, who soon moved sideways to take over the 1992 Olympic football squad. Ángel María Villar, the RFEF's formidable president, burst into tears afterwards; an underling quickly led him into another room so that the locals wouldn't see him weeping. '*La selección* requires surgical intervention, under general anaesthesia,' growled *El País* the next day.

In the same group, France set a new record by winning all eight qualifiers, including a 3-1 and 2-1 double over Spain. Their manager, golden boy Michel Platini, had reversed their ailing fortunes and strung together a 19-match unbeaten run that only ended at Wembley in February 1992. Failure to win any of their five preparatory friendlies prompted Platini to mutter, 'I'm pleased we've not peaked too early.' But his team looked good, defensively strong and well-drilled in midfield – and the once-profligate Jean-Pierre Papin was now Marco van Basten's only rival as the best striker in Europe.

France's clean sweep included a 5-0 home win over Albania, many of whose squad defected at Charles de Gaulle Airport. Food shortages and political unrest were gripping the impoverished Balkan nation, and in November 1991 Spain pleaded with UEFA to spare them a pointless trip to Tirana, where they felt their safety couldn't be guaranteed. On 13 December, after numerous unsuccessful attempts to contact the Albanian FA, UEFA cancelled the fixture just as Spain's squad were boarding their flight in Madrid.

England stumbled into the finals ahead of Ireland, who would have deservedly won at Wembley but for Ray Houghton's shocking late miss. The Irish then tossed away a 3-1 lead in Poznań after bad errors by David O'Leary and Packie Bonner, so England needed only a point in the same city a month later. Graham Taylor's team, trailing 1-0 near the end, got away with murder again when goalkeeper Chris Woods sent Poland's Jan Furtok flying into the air for an indisputable penalty. Referee Hubert Forstinger gave a corner instead; two minutes later, Gary Lineker's far-post volley sent England to Sweden.

Taylor already wore the pained expression of a man who knows that, whatever way he turns, he's screwed. The manager had lost his best centre-half, Tony Adams, and his only real playmaker, Paul Gascoigne, to injury (self-inflicted in the case of Gascoigne, who had lamed himself trying to dismember Nottingham Forest's Gary Charles in the 1991 FA Cup Final). Taylor had only himself to blame, though, for leaving out Chris Waddle of Olympique Marseille while bringing along the likes of Tony Daley. He had a weird fondness for ordinary players, possibly a hangover from his days at Watford, where he had worked wonders on a shoestring.

The Berlin Wall came down before the qualifying draw but, almost inevitably, East Germany and West Germany went into the same group. In late 1990, German political unification occurred and the GDR's national team duly ceased to exist. By then, however, West Germany were world champions, and unification seemed certain to strengthen their hand. 'I'm sorry for the rest of the world,' Franz Beckenbauer hubristically crowed after the dismal 1990 World Cup Final against Argentina in Rome, 'but we won't be defeatable in the coming years.'

It took only three months for Luxembourg, of all teams, to make Beckenbauer look silly and his successor Berti Vogts look bad. Three up at the break, West Germany leaked two quick goals in the second half and, by the end, they were hanging on grimly against one of Europe's smallest countries.

Goalkeeper Bodo Illgner spared their blushes, parrying Marc Birsens's shot around the post. On an embarrassing day all round, German hooligans rioted outside Luxembourg's tiny stadium, hurling bottles at bystanders in the absence of a local firm to fight with. 'We were lucky that Luxembourg were happy with the scoreline and didn't throw everything forward in the final stages,' Rudi Völler remarked. The Germans then lost to Wales, and qualification was secured only with a sweaty victory in Brussels.

Group 4 was where the real action was. It got off to a surreal start when the Faroe Islands, playing their first competitive international, sensationally beat Austria 1-0. The glory fell to midfielder Torkil Nielsen, a timber merchant by trade, who saw his powderpuff shot creep past goalkeeper Michael Konsel. Viennese newspaper Kurier howled that 'our professionals were disgraced by a bunch of hobby-kickers', and manager Josef Hickersberger was soon out on his ear. The Faroes subsequently drew in Belfast and, like Austria, finished on three points.

The brave islanders were ultimately a sideshow in this group. Yugoslavia, built around a superb Red Star team that would soon lift the European Cup, took Denmark apart in Copenhagen in November 1990, winning more easily than the 2-0 scoreline suggested. Danish manager Richard Møller Nielsen had only succeeded Sepp Piontek because the DBU's preferred candidate, Horst Wohlers, was still under contract at Bayer Uerdingen. His team's subsequent 2-1 win in Belgrade seemed immaterial as Yugoslavia walked away with the group.

But the Balkans' political weather had already turned foul. On 25 June 1991, Slovenia seceded from Yugoslavia, sparking a ten-day conflict that killed 63. The same day, Croatia announced its independence, after a referendum returned a 93 per cent Yes vote. In March 1992, another plebiscite in Bosnia-Herzegovina produced a second Yes. The Yugoslav army then retreated from Bosnia, bequeathing its hardware to local Bosnian Serb militias. As the fighting spiralled into war, and the death toll skyrocketed (an eventual 140,000 would perish), the UN imposed sanctions that included a sporting boycott.

By now, 'Yugoslavia' was effectively a Red Star and Partizan selection. In May 1991, the Croatian contingent – talents like Robert Prosinečki, Zvonimir Boban, Robert Jarni and Davor Šuker – left the squad for their physical safety. Srečko Katanec, the Slovenian midfielder, had already gone. Macedonian striker Darko Pančev, whose penalty won that European Cup for Red Star in Bari, dropped out too. And when Bosnia's March 1992 referendum was passed, Faruk Hadžibegić, Fahrudin Omerović, Refik Šabanadžović and Mehmed Baždarević got out before it was too late.

Manager Ivica Osim, himself of Slovenian-Bosnian descent, resigned on 23 May 1992 as his home city of Sarajevo was being shelled. 'On the scale of human suffering, I cannot reconcile events at home with my position as national team manager,' he said. Eight days later, UEFA expelled Yugoslavia from Euro 92. 'We can no longer pretend that nothing has happened,' said Lennart Johansson. 'We need to look the political reality in the eye.' By then, a 17-strong Yugoslavian squad was already in Sweden, under Osim's assistant Ivan Čabrinović. They now flew home, inadvertently leaving an unpaid bill for a five-day training camp behind them.

UEFA gave Yugoslavia's place to Denmark, who had been aware for some time that this was a live possibility – but when the final decision came, they had just nine days to fully prepare. Captain Lars Olsen recalled in 2016, 'There was a debate in Denmark on the question of going to Sweden or not. Fortunately, the DBU said okay. Flemming Povlsen, our striker, was asked if the team were only prepared well enough to play 90 minutes. He said, "Yes, 30 against England, 30 against Sweden and 30 against France!"'

Denmark looked like prospective tournament whipping-boys, not least because their shining star Michael Laudrup had fallen out with Møller Nielsen in late 1990 and quit international football. Even this bolt from the blue couldn't tempt him back. The consensus was that the Danes would turn up and 'play three games' (in the words of Laudrup's brother Brian), then enjoy their holidays.

They were acutely aware of the appalling human cost that had put them into the competition and, far less importantly, that they had stepped into the shoes of a better team. 'I took something away from players who'd played well and deserved to be there,' said midfielder John Jensen. But he and Denmark would take away something else from Euro 92 too.

GROUP 1
Sweden, France, Denmark, England

The opening match, played in beautiful summer evening sunlight in Stockholm, provided the first clue that something had gone haywire with France's team of all the talents. Platini picked seven Olympique Marseille players, but against Sweden they showed little mutual understanding. Eric Cantona made no impact, and the Tahiti-born Pascal Vahirua was a passenger on the left wing.

Before the tournament, Platini revealed that he had spent only 40 days with his squad since late 1988: 'In that time, you cannot work much and you don't change much.' Sweden, by contrast, had been billeted for weeks at an old stately home in a forest outside Stockholm, and looked like more of a team. With Jonas Thern directing traffic, they played confidently and deserved their half-time lead. The beanpole Kennet Andersson won a corner, Anders Limpar swung it over, and centre-back Jan Eriksson (a semi-pro studying biology and chemistry at night school) made a late run into the box, untracked by France's defenders. Rising high at the right moment, he sent a strong header past goalkeeper Bruno Martini.

Disjointed though they were, France should have had a penalty when Eriksson pulled down Jean-Pierre Papin, but referee Aleksei Spirin waved play on. Papin received hardly any service – but he got the solitary chance he needed in the second half, showing why Milan had just spent £10m on him to break the world transfer record. The lively substitute Christian Perez sent a pass over the top for him to chase beyond the last defender and control with his head as he ran. His finish was a sublime right-foot rocket low across goalkeeper Thomas Ravelli into the far corner, one of the goals of the tournament.

But the hosts finished the stronger, and Martini rescued France by keeping out Klas Ingesson's header at his near post. 'I thought the crowd were fantastic,' Swedish striker Martin Dahlin said afterwards. 'Normally, they look down at their hands and say, "That is good."'

'Let me do the worrying. That's what I'm paid for,' Graham Taylor told the folks back home before England faced Denmark in Malmö. 'Get your feet up in front of the telly, get a few beers in and have a good time.'

The bonhomie was for show only. When ITV's Elton Welsby, interviewing Taylor via satellite link, asked him about his line-up, he barked, 'That's none of your business.' A surprised Welsby replied, 'It may be none of my business, but I'm sure the fans watching back home will be interested to know.' In the studio, Ron Atkinson observed that if Taylor didn't cool it, his obvious agitation would filter through to his players.

A decent man who was in over his head, Taylor could have been forgiven some tetchiness. As well as all his other absences, injuries to Paul Parker, Lee Dixon, Gary Stevens and Rob Jones left him without a recognised right-back, forcing him to turn to Manchester City's centre-half Keith Curle. Peter Schmeichel recalled, 'When we saw England's team sheet, we said, "Hey, guys, we have a shot here."'

Denmark, hardly tournament-tuned themselves, appeared to be playing off the cuff from memory: not so much Danish dynamite as fireworks at lunchtime. England, attacking an end festooned in Union Jacks, created some chances in the first half. David Platt's close-range shot was clutched by Schmeichel, who later turned Alan Smith's scuff around the post. Meanwhile, Paul Merson dribbled past three Danes before his appalling effort went out for a throw.

But before the interval, Curle should have got a second yellow for pulling back the speedy Henrik Andersen. In the second half, Denmark gradually got the upper hand, and on the hour, Bent Christensen's lay-off fell for the on-running Jensen, whose low shot beat the sprawling Woods before hitting the inside of the post and bouncing back out into the keeper's arms.

The game then petered out, though Kim Christofte's late cross narrowly missed Kim Vilfort's head while drifting past the post. In the BBC studio, Des Lynam was unimpressed, asking Jimmy Hill and Terry Venables, 'Well, gentlemen, that was supposed to be the easy one, wasn't it?'

====

Hooliganism marred the build-up to England's meeting with France in Malmö three days later, kicking off when two fans refused to come down from the roof of a beer tent. Another ten were arrested after incidents on a train. The rioting went on for two nights, resulting in 22 injuries, eight deportations, a ransacked petrol station and an ITN camera crew nursing bruises.

Appositely, the match itself was the poorest of the competition. 'Both countries were too mindful of defence,' Italy's manager, Arrigo Sacchi, told the BBC's Barry Davies afterwards. Coming from an Italian manager, that said something.

Taylor made Andy Sinton his latest right-back, and put Carlton Palmer at sweeper. Leeds wrecking-ball David Batty was brought into the midfield, and the 21-year-old Alan Shearer got his chance up front. For France, Platini's recall of his 1984 comrade Luis Fernandez signalled his continued intention to play the percentages.

Papin's toe-poke, which brought a fine save from Woods, provided the only excitement in a wretched first half. Fernandez's horrible challenge on Batty got only a yellow instead of the red it deserved; Batty waited until the second half to take revenge, clattering Fernandez equally nastily. The veteran was targeted with several heavy challenges in the course of the afternoon, and eventually limped off. Papin, too, was hurt by Des Walker's dreadful foul.

After the interval, Jocelyn Angloma's downward header was kept out by Sinton's boot and Woods's glove on the line. Nothing else happened until, eight minutes from time, Boli abruptly headbutted Pearce in retaliation for an earlier foul on Angloma, leaving a gaping cut on his face. 'I'm sure it was an accident,' Pearce deadpanned afterwards. He came back on bandaged up, then almost broke the underside of the crossbar with an unnervingly powerful free kick. The shaken French spent the final few minutes endlessly passing the ball back to Martini.

'This is a tournament,' Platini said. 'Our first duty is not to concede goals. It doesn't look good. The fans don't like it. I understand. But this is how it is.' France already seemed a different team from the one that had waltzed through the qualifiers, managed by somebody with a very different pedigree.

Meanwhile, more cracks were appearing in Taylor's jovial façade. 'I get criticised for whatever I say and do,' he said. 'There's no respect or dignity. No status to the job. I get crucified.' That evening, during another interview on the BBC, he angrily accused Lynam of asking Gary Lineker loaded questions.

=====

In Stockholm, Sweden capitalised by going top of Group 1 with an entertaining 1-0 win over Denmark in the Öresund derby. The half-Venezuelan Dahlin, seizing his chance, was a handful throughout and went close midway through the first half, bursting through on goal before shooting over.

Denmark had a decent spell before half-time, with Christofte's powerful free kick well saved by Ravelli, but Sweden were on the front foot for most of the night. Just before the hour, they found a deserved winner. Thern's vision allowed Dahlin to elude Andersen, and when the striker's low cross was diverted away from Stefan Schwarz by Olsen, it landed on the toe of the on-running Tomas Brolin, who didn't have to break stride.

Danish substitute Torben Frank missed the equaliser when he hesitated to throw himself at Kim Vilfort's header in front of goal. The cherubic Brolin, who looked closer to 12 than 22, should have doubled his money near the end, but dithered over a sitter after Dahlin set him up: when he eventually shot, Olsen scrambled it off the line. But Sweden's unexpected guests had surely outstayed their welcome. 'Denmark are out of the championship, that looks like a fact. Goodbye to Denmark, and goodbye from us,' said one of their TV commentators, signing off from Stockholm.

=====

So it was win or bust for Denmark in Malmö, against a French side who surely had to click into gear now. In 2016, Peter Schmeichel told *L'Équipe* that an unnamed France player 'asked one of our guys in the tunnel if we could take it easy against them, because they would have a semi-final to play'. Lars Olsen named the Danish player as John Sivebæk, and one German source claims the Frenchman was Sivebæk's Monaco team-mate Emmanuel Petit, an unused sub on the night. Olsen described France's players as 'joking, very casual', and they were once again insipid, against spirited opponents who had nothing to lose.

Kim Vilfort had left the Danish camp in sad circumstances, flying home to be with his terminally ill daughter. In came the blond Henrik Larsen, whose impact was instant. He gave Denmark a surprise early lead, half-volleying ferociously into the roof of the net after Povlsen headed Andersen's long free kick into his path. As France prepared to restart, Boli shook a fearsome fist *pour encourager les autres*.

Andersen was rampant on the left, torturing the veteran Manuel Amoros. Martini grabbed his teasing cross at the feet of Frank, and another of his dangerous set-pieces ricocheted off several Frenchmen before Povlsen shot wide. When yet another Andersen free kick caused confusion, Sivebæk hacked the ball back into the danger area, but it wouldn't come down properly for Frank, who was crowded out.

After half-time, Deschamps and Cantona put half-chances straight at Schmeichel, who then saved well from Fernandez's 25-yarder. Their equaliser was another jewel from the most lethal right foot in the tournament. When the otherwise invisible Cantona crossed from the right, Jean-Philippe Durand's back-heel took out Sivebæk and Christofte to give Papin a tiny sight of goal. That was all he needed, curling a superb finish around Schmeichel's left hand and into the corner.

Minutes later, Papin should have put France ahead. But when Cantona pulled the ball back, Deschamps took the chance off his toe and poked it wide, prompting an apoplectic reaction. And now the guillotine came down on Platini's superstars. When Sivebæk's pass set Povlsen free on the right, he looked just offside – but Austrian linesman Alois Pemmer didn't flag, Boli failed to cut out the cross, and substitute Lars Elstrup (whose goals had kept Luton Town in the top flight in 1990/91) tapped it in.

France had thrown it all away, stinking out the tournament like a footballing Pepé Le Pew. Blame was ascribed to various factors: the Marseille-PSG rivalry within the squad, Platini being too close to the senior players because he had retired relatively recently, and the spotless qualification making a rod for the team's back. Platini himself resigned.

'We respected him, we knew what he'd brought to the French team, we knew the player he was,' said Papin years later. 'I think he was the right man. We were perhaps too confident. But when you win all your qualifiers, can't you have a bit of confidence? It was a hard lesson to digest, but unfortunately that's sport, you can't always win everything.'

France's dazed conquerors could barely comprehend it. 'I was going to take 14 days' holiday in Greece,' said Larsen afterwards. 'Then it came that we were going to play in the European Championship, so I changed my plans. I was going to take a trip, only to Crete, after our third game. Now I'm not going to Greece.'

═══

In Stockholm, a similar story played itself out as a 'big' team crashed out at the hands of unfashionable opponents. But at first, it looked as though England would eject Sweden from their own party. David Platt's knack of extracting the most from his abilities would earn him a £6.5m move to Juventus after this tournament. Always a good bet for a goal in a big match, after just three minutes he mishit Lineker's cross into the ground and saw the huge bounce deceive Ravelli.

England could have wrapped the game up before half-time. The quick but inconsistent winger Tony Daley dragged a shot so badly wide that it almost turned into a perfect cross for Lineker, and when Pearce's cross found him free in front of goal, he headed well over. At the other end, Sweden were denied a clear penalty when Batty chopped down Brolin.

Exhausted by the interval, England wouldn't manage a shot on target in the second half. Soon, Ingesson turned Taylor's latest right-back, Batty, to force a corner – and Eriksson came up to score a carbon copy of his goal against France, outjumping Palmer for another strong header. A minute later, Walker nearly scored a spectacular own goal under pressure from Dahlin.

Needing only a draw, Sweden smelled blood. Pearce hacked clear after Ingesson's cross caused mayhem, substitute Johnny Ekström shot savagely into the side-netting, Pearce blocked Thern's powerful effort with his increasingly battered face, Martin Keown's tackle prevented a certain goal for Ekström, and Joachim Björklund escaped a red card for an outrageous foul on Sinton.

Taylor rolled the dice, replacing Lineker with Alan Smith, a substitution which would haunt him forever. Lineker had vanished after setting up Platt's goal, but Smith would contribute nothing at all. 'We needed to hold the ball up because Sweden were coming at us. That's why I got Alan Smith on,' Taylor rationalised years later. But seven minutes from the end, Brolin won it with an unforgettable piece of magic. Playing one-twos with Ingesson, then Dahlin, he looked up, spotted Woods off his line and chipped the goalkeeper with a sublime stroke into the top corner.

'The first thing that went wrong was half-time. We could have done without that,' Taylor said afterwards, making a brave bid for quote of the tournament. Though he hardly deserved his subsequent turnipping by *The Sun*, it was obvious he wasn't the right man. He kept his job and, soon enough, England would regret that too.

The post-match violence (36 English arrests, 28 Swedish) was almost overlooked. Since becoming UEFA president in 1990, Lennart Johansson had campaigned for English clubs to be readmitted to Europe. Now, embarrassed by their fans in his homeland, he threatened them with expulsion from future tournaments. But even worse trouble would break out the following evening in Gothenburg, with not an Englishman in sight.

8.15pm, 10 June 1992
Råsunda Stadion, Solna
Attendance: 29,860
Referee: Aleksei Spirin (CIS)

SWEDEN 1 (Eriksson 25)
FRANCE 1 (Papin 58)

SWEDEN: Thomas Ravelli, Roland Nilsson, Jan Eriksson, Patrik Andersson, Joachim Björklund, Klas Ingesson, Stefan Schwarz, Jonas Thern (c), Kennet Andersson (Martin Dahlin 74), Tomas Brolin, Anders Limpar. **Manager:** Tommy Svensson.

FRANCE: Bruno Martini, Jocelyn Angloma (Luis Fernandez 66), Manuel Amoros (c), Basile Boli, Bernard Casoni, Laurent Blanc, Didier Deschamps, Franck Sauzée, Jean-Pierre Papin, Eric Cantona, Pascal Vahirua (Christian Perez 46). **Manager:** Michel Platini.

Booked: Schwarz (39), Thern (87), Angloma (35), Cantona (53).

8.15pm, 11 June 1992
Malmö Stadion, Malmö
Attendance: 26,385
Referee: John Blankenstein (Netherlands)

DENMARK 0
ENGLAND 0

DENMARK: Peter Schmeichel, John Sivebæk, Kent Nielsen, Lars Olsen (c), Henrik Andersen, Kim Christofte, John Jensen, Kim Vilfort, Flemming Povlsen, Bent Christensen, Brian Laudrup. **Manager:** Richard Møller Nielsen.

ENGLAND: Chris Woods, Keith Curle (Tony Daley 62), Stuart Pearce, Martin Keown, Des Walker, Carlton Palmer, Trevor Steven, David Platt, Alan Smith, Gary Lineker (c), Paul Merson (Neil Webb 71). **Manager:** Graham Taylor.

Booked: Sivebæk (84), Keown (9), Curle (11), Daley (68).

5.15pm, 14 June 1992
Malmö Stadion, Malmö
Attendance: 26,535
Referee: Sándor Puhl (Hungary)

ENGLAND 0
FRANCE 0

ENGLAND: Woods, Andy Sinton, Pearce, Keown, Walker, Palmer, Steven, David Batty, Alan Shearer, Lineker (c), Platt.

FRANCE: Martini, Amoros (c), Boli, Casoni, Blanc, Fernandez (Perez 75), Deschamps, Sauzée (Angloma 46), Papin, Cantona, Jean-Philippe Durand.

Booked: Batty (70), Fernandez (31).

8.15pm, 14 June 1992
Råsunda Stadion, Solna
Attendance: 29,902
Referee: Aron Schmidhuber (Germany)

SWEDEN 1 (Brolin 59)
DENMARK 0

SWEDEN: Ravelli, R. Nilsson, Eriksson, P. Andersson, Björklund, Ingesson, Schwarz, Thern (c), Dahlin (Johnny Ekström 77), Brolin, Limpar (Magnus Erlingmark 90).

DENMARK: Schmeichel, Sivebæk, Nielsen, Olsen (c), Andersen, Christofte, Jensen (Henrik Larsen 63), Vilfort, Povlsen, Christensen (Torben Frank 52), Laudrup.

Booked: P. Andersson (41), Andersen (14).

8.15pm, 17 June 1992
Malmö Stadion, Malmö
Attendance: 25,673
Referee: Hubert Forstinger (Austria)

DENMARK 2 (Larsen 8, Elstrup 78)
FRANCE 1 (Papin 61)

DENMARK: Schmeichel, Sivebæk, Nielsen (Torben Piechnik 63), Olsen (c), Andersen, Christofte, Jensen, Larsen, Povlsen, Frank (Lars Elstrup 68), Laudrup.

FRANCE: Martini, Amoros (c), Boli, Casoni, Blanc, Durand, Deschamps, Perez (Christophe Cocard 81), Papin, Cantona, Vahirua (Fernandez 46).

Booked: Povlsen (14), Frank (45+2), Casoni (15), Perez (32), Boli (38), Deschamps (74).

8.15pm, 17 June 1992
Råsunda Stadion, Solna
Attendance: 30,126
Referee: José Rosa dos Santos (Portugal)

SWEDEN 2 (Eriksson 52, Brolin 83)
ENGLAND 1 (Platt 4)

SWEDEN: Ravelli, R. Nilsson, Eriksson, P. Andersson, Björklund, Ingesson, Schwarz, Thern (c), Dahlin, Brolin, Limpar (Ekström 46).

ENGLAND: Woods, Batty, Pearce, Keown, Walker, Palmer, Webb, Sinton (Merson 76), Lineker (c) (Smith 62), Platt, Daley.

Booked: P. Andersson (43), Schwarz (69), Björklund (71), Daley (10) Webb (81).

GROUP 1	P	W	D	L	F	A	GD	Pts
SWEDEN	3	2	1	0	4	2	+2	5
DENMARK	3	1	1	1	2	2	0	3
FRANCE	3	0	2	1	2	3	−1	2
ENGLAND	3	0	2	1	1	2	−1	2

Sweden and Denmark qualified.

GROUP 2
Netherlands, Scotland, CIS, Germany

After the euphoria of 1988, the Netherlands soon reverted to type and their Italia 90 campaign was a best-forgotten fiasco marred by small-minded infighting and apathetic performances. Yet again, the KNVB sent for the grand old man of Dutch football. Rinus 'De Generaal' Michels put out the fires, reached for his old reliables and guided them through a weak qualifying group.

The team he sent out against Scotland in Gothenburg contained eight of the 11 men who had started the Euro 88 final. One of the three newcomers, the blond 23-year-old Dennis Bergkamp, was a revelation here, elusive and dangerous. His speed of thought produced the only goal 15 minutes from the end, latching on to a couple of aerial flicks by Marco van Basten and Frank Rijkaard before hooking the loose ball under Andy Goram.

For Scotland, Paul McStay showed poise in midfield and Richard Gough was brave at the back, but the whip hand always lay with the Dutch. Ruud Gullit, electric on the right wing, on one occasion bamboozled Dave McPherson with three successive drag-backs. Later, he shot too high after a fantastic flowing move, and saw another effort go wide following a goalmouth scramble. Meanwhile, Goram beat away Rijkaard's angled cross-shot.

The spirited Scots missed Gordon Strachan, absent through injury. Their only good chance fell to the bubble-permed McPherson, who shot horribly wide after Ronald Koeman sluggishly played him onside. In the second half, when Gough headed Gullit's sliced clearance just wide, it was very much an isolated incident. But hardly anything had been expected of Scotland to begin with.

———

That evening in Norrköping, to most people's surprise, Germany almost came unstuck against the ultra-defensive CIS.

The presence of the mediocre Manfred Binz at sweeper showed how strongly Germany were wedded to their formation: they simply had to use a libero even if he wasn't up to the job. Lothar Matthäus, Berti Vogts's first choice, was injured, but it still seemed extraordinary that there wasn't anybody else better in the whole country than Binz – who, like Matthias Herget in 1988, just wasn't international-class.

The CIS camp was in disarray, hardly a surprise given the social and economic chaos back home. At a shambolic training base in Novogorsk before the finals, their players bridled at ramshackle accommodation and rutted pitches. 'Our preparation is a disaster,' sighed manager Anatoliy Byshovets, 'Our sport reflects what's going on in politics and the economy.'

In Norrköping, his team lined up to the strains of Beethoven's 'Ode to Joy' instead of the old USSR anthem, then fanned out into a 4-6-0 formation that Vogts took an age to suss out. The furthest player forward was Igor Dobrovolsky on the right, leaving Germany's defenders with nobody to mark, while winger Andrei Kanchelskis played as a second right-back. It worked so well that only a piece of genius saved Germany from a devastating defeat.

Vogts's team lived on crumbs for an hour: a curving Guido Buchwald drive, a header over the bar by Rudi Völler (who had earlier broken his arm, ending his tournament at half-time), and an angled shot over the bar from Thomas Häßler. 'The CIS are proving surprisingly organised for a country that is the epitome of disorganisation,' said Barry Davies on the BBC.

For the first hour, the CIS's only 'shot' was a Dobrovolsky cross which fell out of the sky and bounced off Bodo Illgner's crossbar. Then, suddenly, Stefan Reuter's foolhardiness handed them a penalty. The right-back inexplicably charged at Dobrovolsky, flattening him like a big kid knocking over a smaller one in a school kick-about. Referee Gérard Biguet pointed to the spot as cigarette lighters rained down from behind the goal. Dobrovolsky sent Illgner the wrong way, while more than one commentator sniggered that Reuter should go back to his news agency.

Vogts immediately subbed the defender for Jürgen Klinsmann, who should have replaced Völler. As time ran out, Germany began humping desperate balls into the box. Häßler curled a free kick inches wide, then saw his low cross cause panic in the goalmouth before Akhrik Tsveiba hacked it away. Karl-Heinz Riedle's header dropped on to the bar and, with one minute to go, big Buchwald's volley whizzed wide.

Just as all seemed lost for Germany, young Viktor Onopko lost the ball and Dmitri Kuznetsov pushed Thomas Doll over on the edge of the box for a free kick. Up came little Häßler ('Small for a German,' noted Bobby Charlton on the BBC) to take the last shot of the evening.

The angle and positioning made it seemingly impossible for Häßler to get the ball back down under the bar after lifting it over the wall, but, somehow, his splendid right foot whipped it past goalkeeper Dmitri Kharin into the top corner with mind-blowing precision, helped by Klinsmann ducking on the end of the wall at the last second. Germany were alive again.

Igor Shalimov, who knew Häßler well from Serie A, had gone off injured minutes beforehand. 'I'd seen him do it for Roma, putting it in that corner. But I couldn't tell Kharin from the bench. No matter how loud I screamed, he wouldn't have heard. It's a pity I wasn't on the field at that moment.'

A wonderful instance of great skill under extreme pressure, it may have been written in the stars. Vogts had told Häßler beforehand, 'You're going to have a great year. Today you'll score, and soon you'll be a father.' Vindicated, the manager described the goal as 'a wink from God'. Byshovets said, 'It's always maddening to see a victory taken in the final seconds, but I've got to be satisfied with my players, because it's not easy to prepare under the current conditions in the republics.'

=====

Needing a point against Germany to survive, Scotland confounded expectations by having a real go. Illgner tipped Gough's header over the bar, then raced off his line to save at the feet of Brian McClair; from the resulting corner, Gary McAllister volleyed inches wide. It typified Scottish luck that their best chance again fell to McPherson, who got on the end of McAllister's floated free kick but thrashed his effort too high.

After all these warnings, Germany came alive, Klinsmann heading a corner against Goram's shins. Against the run of play, they then went ahead with a strike the goalkeeper could do nothing about. Klinsmann held the ball up under pressure from Gough, and Riedle fired a low shot through his strike partner's legs with Goram unsighted.

Barely a minute into the second half, Scotland coughed up the sort of ridiculous goal they always seemed to concede in big games. Stefan Effenberg's cross took a huge deflection off Maurice Malpas's leg to loop up in an insanely high arc, and it dropped just inside the far post for 2-0.

On the hour, Andy Möller nearly made it three, whacking a shot against the post. With nothing to lose, Scotland now had their best spell. Illgner moved fast to stop Ally McCoist's header, before McStay's follow-up flew into his ribs. A goalmouth scramble then saw Illgner save from McCoist and Pat Nevin; later, he got down at McStay's feet.

Straight away, Häßler cracked another hard shot against Goram's other post. Still Scotland didn't give up. Stewart McKimmie came up from right-back to volley just over, McClair went close twice, and substitute Kevin Gallacher botched a header in front of the posts. As usual, Scotland's lack of a lethal striker had killed them.

They were out after two games, but they and their cheerful fans had been a credit to the tournament. 'We gave everything we had, but the Germans did what we didn't do – they finished,' manager Andy Roxburgh lamented. In the record books, it looks like just another routine win for a superpower over a minnow – but it was much more than that.

———

Losing a point so sickeningly against Germany hadn't diminished Anatoliy Byshovets's determination to keep everything locked down. In Gothenburg, his team erected another huge wall which the Netherlands failed to scale.

Oleksiy Mykhaylychenko's farcical 60-yard back-pass to Kharin in the second half summed up the CIS's outlook: they were so negative that, afterwards, Byshovets berated them for their reluctance to shoot from long range. 'What is happening to you?' he shouted. 'Many of you have scored from distance. What are you afraid of?'

But he could hardly talk: he wasted Kanchelskis, his best attacker, as a man-marker on Bryan Roy. Kanchelskis ran so hard that he damaged his achilles near the end, only for team doctor Zurab Ordzhonikidze to tell him he had to stay on, as the CIS had already used two subs. Meanwhile, young Onopko played a blinder on the left, pocketing Gullit, who went off long before the end.

The CIS didn't hide in their own half for the entire match – just the vast majority of it. Hans van Breukelen got behind Dobrovolsky's volley, then came out smartly to save from Igor Kolyvanov. But otherwise, it was effectively the Netherlands against Kharin. In the same stadium, 34 years earlier to the day, Lev Yashin had given the performance of his life to save the USSR from an annihilation by Brazil in the 1958 World Cup. Kharin's display brought back some of those old black-and-white newsreel memories.

'In this game, our goalkeeper became a real discovery for all football fans,' the Russian journalist Oleg Kucherenko wrote admiringly. Kharin saved well at Bergkamp's feet after Sergei Aleinikov underhit a back-pass, turned Rijkaard's header around the post, kept out a hard shot by the same player, and acrobatically punched Van Basten's looping header over the bar. 'I don't think his play today demands any commentary at all,' Byshovets said with pride.

Van Basten pushed Kharin hard for man of the match, working maniacally to set up chances for Rijkaard (twice) and Roy. Near the end, he sneaked into a gap to meet Johnny van 't Schip's cross with a wonderful diving header into the far corner – but linesman Arne Paltoft's flag shot up, even though Tsveiba had played everybody onside. Infuriated, Van Basten went in hard on Oleh Kuznetsov, for which he wasn't even cautioned.

Hilariously, the CIS could have won it at the end when Sergei Kiriakov hared after Jan Wouters's dozy back-pass, before Van Breukelen dived at his feet. Their armadillo routine had now put them in a strong position to progress.

═══

After two rounds of fixtures, Euro 92 was crying out to the football gods for a few glasses of the hard stuff. Now, in the nick of time, the Netherlands and Germany served up a magnificent match, going at each other hammer and tongs at the Nya Ullevi.

Even allowing for Völler, Reuter and Buchwald's injuries, Berti Vogts's tombola team selection was inexplicable. He kept Binz at sweeper instead of the far superior Matthias Sammer, put stopper Thomas Helmer in midfield, and brought in journeyman Michael Frontzeck for a first competitive cap since November 1985, playing him out of position at left-back for good measure. Rinus Michels must have licked his lips.

On another balmy evening, the *Deutschlandlied* was whistled so vociferously that their players broke ranks well before it ended. There was similar intensity on display from the kick-off. Some of the Netherlands' interplay on the counter-attack was irresistible, pulling Germany's makeshift rearguard asunder.

Jürgen Kohler, whose pocket Van Basten had picked in Euro 88, took revenge by suffocating him at Italia 90. Tonight, he marked the striker for the 11th time in their careers (they regularly met in Serie A), and clobbered him in the third minute, 30 yards out. That reducer came at a price. When Koeman floated the free kick into the box, Frank Rijkaard outjumped Effenberg and his header sailed unstoppably high, dipping under the bar and in. Illgner, rooted to the spot, seemed to think it was going miles over.

Häßler almost hit back instantly by turning Koeman inside out, forcing Van Breukelen to save with his knees. The Netherlands responded by doubling their lead with another odd goal. Germany gave away another long-range free kick, and clearly expected Koeman to blast it. But he touched it short to Rob Witschge, who hit a subterranean shot along the grass. Riedle stepped out of place in the wall, and the ball trundled inside Illgner's right-hand post. Nowhere near as skilful as his brother Richard, Witschge was ultimately a lot more use.

In a thrilling first half, the Netherlands could easily have been five or six up at the break, lording it over the Germans the way they had wanted to in the 1974 World Cup Final. Brehme, at right-back for once, cleared Van Basten's powerful shot; Gullit blazed over from Rijkaard's knock-down; Van Basten volleyed venomously off the bar at the end of a brilliant team move; Roy shot wide after leaving Helmer for dead; the besieged Illgner saved good efforts from Gullit (twice) and Rijkaard – and these were only the most significant incidents.

Dutch hunger was epitomised by Van Basten sprinting 50 yards to foul Möller deep in the Dutch half. But Häßler was magnificently defiant as his team were swamped, always inventive, always picking out great passes. Early in the second half, his shot deflected off Witschge and forced Van Breukelen into an agile save.

At the break, Sammer replaced Binz, and Germany finally dragged themselves back into the match. Häßler's corner was met by the redoubtable Klinsmann, who soared spring-heeled above Frank de Boer to score with a downward header. Minutes later, Rijkaard headed Brehme's cross against his own bar, an unwitting imitation of his earlier goal, and Häßler rasped a shot just wide.

The Dutch were in danger of throwing it away. But Michels acted, taking off young De Boer, who had been pushed around by Klinsmann. Rijkaard went back to defence, and Aron Winter replaced him in midfield. It was

Winter who started the move that put Germany to sleep. Evading Sammer on the right, he looked up to see Van Basten unselfishly pointing out Bergkamp, who stooped to bury the swirling cross with a diving header.

The Dutch always enjoy putting one over on Germany, but this payback for the spittle-flecked *sturm und drang* clash at San Siro in Italia 90 tasted particularly sweet. Vogts sweated on the Scotland-CIS result before knowing whether his team were safe, but early developments in that game ensured he could relax.

Sadly, some German fans couldn't take their beating. Hours before the match, there were disturbances in Gothenburg involving neo-Nazis. Now several hundred more rampaged through the city centre, vandalising shops, attacking Dutch fans with tear gas and crowbars, and forcing Swedish police to cordon off numerous streets.

Back home, it was 1988 all over again as anarchy reigned on the Dutch-German border. One report claimed that a company of Dutch soldiers, based at a NATO compound in the German town of Seedorf, trashed every German-plated vehicle they saw. Hundreds of Dutch people needed a police escort to return to their homes in Enschede after watching the match in the German village of Gronau, while a nightclub in Kerkrade was blasted by homemade bombs which injured three people. You wondered what would have happened if the result had knocked Germany out – but, thanks to Scotland, it hadn't.

Decades on, Anatoliy Byshovets was forced to deny lurid accusations in the Russian media that some CIS players were inebriated while playing Scotland in Norrköping. 'This is nonsense,' he said. 'What happened was that we underestimated them. We thought there would be no problems. It was just one of those games.'

Andy Roxburgh, speaking in 2016, agreed: 'I think they might just have got caught with a wee bit of complacency.' In his autobiography, Andrei Kanchelskis wrote, 'When the game kicked off, we weren't mentally ready. Two of our squad, Oleksiy Mykhaylychenko and Oleh Kuznetsov, played for Rangers and our management seemed to think that because of this, the Scotland players wouldn't try too hard. We were deluded. There was no way footballers like Brian McClair and Ally McCoist were just going to let us win.'

If not literally drunk, the CIS were soon punch-drunk as two useless pieces of good fortune fell into Scotland's lap at last. First, Paul McStay had a go from 25 yards. The ball struck the base of the post, rebounding into the net off Kharin's arm.

Andy Goram moved fast to stop Onopko's quickly taken free kick from floating in, but soon Scotland were two up via another big deflection. McClair's drive from the edge of the box, via Kakhaber Tskhadadze's elbow, was his first goal for his country after 26 caps. and nobody was taking it off him.

Byshovets had subjected his players to intensive shooting drills after the Netherlands game, but most of their efforts here drifted into the stands. Serhiy Yuran wasted their best opportunity of the first half, blasting too high after Mykhaylychenko created the opening.

After the interval came 'a long and tedious siege by toothless wonders', as one Russian journalist wrote. Not until the 82nd minute did the CIS make another chance. Dobrovolsky dribbled around Goram, but when he shot, Jim McInally knocked it off the line; the rebound fell to Igor Korneev, but Goram threw himself in the way. A minute later, Pat Nevin was tripped by Tskhadadze at the other end, and Gary McAllister's penalty sealed one of Scotland's greatest ever wins.

'We had to at least win that last match, to say, "Well, this was a team that was worth being there",' reflected Roxburgh. The 5,000 Tartan Army foot-soldiers who got to Sweden made the best of impressions. One grateful Norrköping publican reaped the equivalent of £17,000 in a single night, a gargantuan sum in 1992, while the photo of a Scotland fan kissing a blonde Swedish policewoman was one of the images of the tournament.

Meanwhile, the CIS went gently into that geopolitical night, splitting up into a dozen independent republics. After seven World Cups and six European Championships, this was a sad way to sign off.

5.15pm, 12 June 1992
Nya Ullevi, Gothenburg
Attendance: 35,720
Referee: Bo Karlsson (Sweden)

NETHERLANDS 1 (Bergkamp 77)
SCOTLAND 0

NETHERLANDS: Hans van Breukelen, Berry van Aerle, Adri van Tiggelen, Ronald Koeman, Frank Rijkaard, Jan Wouters (Wim Jonk 55), Rob Witschge, Bryan Roy, Marco van Basten, Ruud Gullit (c), Dennis Bergkamp (Aron Winter 86). **Manager:** Rinus Michels.

SCOTLAND: Andy Goram, Stewart McKimmie, Maurice Malpas, Richard Gough (c), Dave McPherson, Stuart McCall, Gary McAllister, Paul McStay, Ally McCoist (Kevin Gallacher 74), Brian McClair (Duncan Ferguson 80), Gordon Durie. **Manager:** Andy Roxburgh.

Booked: Witschge (25).

8.15pm, 12 June 1992
Idrottsparken, Norrköping
Attendance: 17,410
Referee: Gérard Biguet (France)

CIS 1 (Dobrovolsky 63 pen)
GERMANY 1 (Häßler 90+1)

CIS: Dmitri Kharin, Andrei Chernyshov, Oleh Kuznetsov, Akhrik Tsveiba, Volodymyr Lyutyi (Viktor Onopko 46), Igor Shalimov (Andrei Ivanov 83), Dmitri Kuznetsov, Andrei Kanchelskis, Igor Dobrovolsky, Oleksiy Mykhaylychenko (c), Igor Kolyvanov. **Manager:** Anatoliy Byshovets.

GERMANY: Bodo Illgner, Stefan Reuter (Jürgen Klinsmann 64), Andy Brehme, Jürgen Kohler, Guido Buchwald, Manfred Binz, Stefan Effenberg, Thomas Häßler, Rudi Völler (c) (Andy Möller 46), Karl-Heinz Riedle, Thomas Doll. **Manager:** Berti Vogts.

Booked: Dobrovolsky (68), Kharin (74), Tsveiba (87).

5.15pm, 15 June 1992
Idrottsparken, Norrköping
Attendance: 17,638
Referee: Guy Goethals (Belgium)

GERMANY 2 (Riedle 30, Malpas 47 og)
SCOTLAND 0

GERMANY: Illgner, Buchwald, Brehme (c), Kohler, Matthias Sammer, Binz, Effenberg, Häßler, Riedle (Reuter 69, Michael Schulz 76), Klinsmann, Möller.

SCOTLAND: Goram, McKimmie, Malpas, Gough (c), McPherson, McCall, McAllister, McStay, McCoist (Gallacher 70), McClair, Durie (Pat Nevin 55).

Booked: Häßler (87), McCall (90).

8.15pm, 15 June 1992
Nya Ullevi, Gothenburg
Attendance: 34,400
Referee: Peter Mikkelsen (Denmark)

CIS 0
NETHERLANDS 0

CIS: Kharin, Chernyshov, O. Kuznetsov, Tsveiba, Onopko, Sergei Aleinikov (D. Kuznetsov 57), Mykhaylychenko (c), Kanchelskis, Serhiy Yuran (Sergei Kiriakov 65), Dobrovolsky, Kolyvanov.

NETHERLANDS: Van Breukelen, Van Aerle, van Tiggelen, Koeman, Rijkaard, Wouters, Witschge, Roy, Van Basten, Gullit (c) (Johnny van 't Schip 72), Bergkamp (Eric Viscaal 80).

Booked: Tsveiba (22), Koeman (26), Wouters (68).

8.15pm, 18 June 1992
Nya Ullevi, Gothenburg
Attendance: 37,725
Referee: Pierluigi Pairetto (Italy)

NETHERLANDS 3 (Rijkaard 4, Witschge 15, Bergkamp 72)
GERMANY 1 (Klinsmann 53)

NETHERLANDS: Van Breukelen, van Tiggelen, Frank de Boer (Winter 61), Koeman, Rijkaard, Wouters, Witschge, Roy, Van Basten, Gullit (c), Bergkamp (Peter Bosz 87).

GERMANY: Illgner, Brehme (c), Michael Frontzeck, Kohler, Binz (Sammer 46), Thomas Helmer, Effenberg, Häßler, Riedle (Doll 77), Klinsmann, Möller.

Booked: Kohler 50.

8.15pm, 18 June 1992
Idrottsparken, Norrköping
Attendance: 17,638
Referee: Kurt Röthlisberger (Switzerland)

SCOTLAND 3 (Kharin 7 og, McClair 17, McAllister 84 pen)
CIS 0

SCOTLAND: Goram, McKimmie, Tom Boyd, Gough (c), McPherson, McCall, McAllister, McStay, McCoist, McClair (Jim McInally 68), Gallacher (Nevin 79).

CIS: Kharin, Chernyshov, Kakhaber Tskhadadze, O. Kuznetsov, Onopko, Aleinikov (D. Kuznetsov 46), Mykhaylychenko (c), Kanchelskis, Yuran, Dobrovolsky, Kiriakov (Igor Korneev 46).

Booked: McCall (71), Chernyshov (52), D. Kuznetsov (83), Mykhaylychenko (84).

GROUP 2	P	W	D	L	F	A	GD	Pts
NETHERLANDS	3	2	1	0	4	1	+3	5
GERMANY	3	1	1	1	4	4	0	3
SCOTLAND	3	1	0	2	3	3	0	2
CIS	3	0	2	1	1	4	− 3	2

The Netherlands and Germany qualified.

SEMI-FINALS
Sweden v Germany
Netherlands v Denmark

Kept alive by other people's hard work, Germany made the most of their let-off, strolling into their fourth European Championship final in six tournaments with a smooth win over Sweden. Again, however, disorder raged afterwards. Some 200 people, mostly locals, were arrested in the capital for smashing up cars, pubs and cafés, and a teenage Swedish girl was stabbed non-fatally by a German who then evaded arrest.

But back to the football. Andy Brehme, restored to his usual berth on the left, was outstanding all evening. His phenomenal energy levels and footballing brain made him one of the most daunting individuals in world football to play against. Lothar Matthäus reflected, 'Brehme was one of my best partners in the team, because he had good eyes. He was a very smart player. You couldn't tell if he was left-footed or right-footed, because he had both legs and could shoot to the highest level.' For the record, Brehme was right-footed.

Thomas Häßler was irresistible all evening, staking a strong claim to be the player of the tournament. Stefan Schwarz might just have done a job on him, but Schwarz wasn't there after two bookings in the first round. In the sixth minute, Häßler played a sparkling one-two with Klinsmann, who did the same with Karl-Heinz Riedle before Ravelli saved his fierce shot. Shortly afterwards, Eriksson took down Riedle, and Häßler – who else? – stepped up to take the free kick. Ravelli, expecting another curler into the far corner, positioned himself and his wall accordingly. Häßler simply put it the other side, leaving the goalkeeper nailed to the spot.

Sweden, unable to stop giving away free kicks in dangerous positions, might have been punished twice more by Brehme before half-time. When Häßler touched one indirect to him, he hit such a strong shot that the crossbar vibrated for several moments, and Ravelli then scrambled to save from him at the foot of a post. In between, Effenberg sublimely put Sammer through to shoot straight at the keeper. It couldn't last. Just before the hour, Häßler's trickery released Sammer on the left, and the unmarked Riedle swept the low cross into the far corner for 2-0.

The match temporarily threatened to become a contest when Helmer brought down Ingesson and Brolin stroked the penalty home. But Germany wouldn't let this slip. Their third goal was cleverly created by a man with the initials T.H. – although not that one. Helmer evaded Limpar on the right, then played an excellent pass for Riedle to sneak between two Swedes and guide a cool finish across Ravelli. This wasn't the last time that Helmer would pop up to create a goal in a Euros semi-final.

Before the end, Sweden gave their fans one last thrill. Ingesson humped a long ball into the box, and big Kennet Andersson rose above Illgner to head into the empty net. Too little, too late, and perhaps Sweden had subconsciously been happy just to get this far. Afterwards, Vogts praised Häßler to the heavens, claiming that only Van Basten rivalled him as player of the tournament. Euro 92's shortest player (5ft 5.5in) was also its best.

===

Denmark were so relaxed that, the day before they faced the Netherlands in Gothenburg, Møller Nielsen let them pig out on fast food on their way back from training. 'The players were saying, "We're sick of this pasta at every meal,"' said Lars Olsen years later. 'The policemen escorting us came into the McDonald's with us. A great moment.'

No one gave them much chance against a team that had just wiped the floor with Germany. They had other ideas. 'It was, in my opinion, the best match a Danish team has ever played,' said Olsen. 'Many people refer to the

1984–1986 side. Not me. Preben Elkjær has a big mouth, but I know he would have given anything to be on our team.'

De Boer, who had looked ropey against Germany, had another bad game here at left-back. Early on, he was robbed by Brian Laudrup, whom the sluggish Koeman allowed to reach the byline and send over a fine cross. Van Breukelen punched thin air and Henrik Larsen, waiting at the back post, scored with a downward header. The Netherlands didn't panic. Bergkamp skipped through four tackles before Schmeichel saved at his feet, but referee Emilio Soriano Aladrén had already given a free kick for one of those challenges, which Koeman thumped over the bar. The equaliser duly arrived on 23 minutes. Rijkaard headed Rob Witschge's cross down for Bergkamp, whose shot deceived Schmeichel, bouncing in front of his gloves as he dived.

Back came the indefatigable Danes. Kim Vilfort, returned from home, nodded Povlsen's cross into the goalmouth, where Laudrup's close-range header was blocked by Koeman, but Larsen came steaming in to smash the loose ball home. The goal made him Euro 92's joint top scorer.

In the second half, Denmark continued to show no regard for Dutch reputations. The lively Povlsen turned Van Tiggelen inside out before shooting narrowly wide, Larsen headed Vilfort's cross off target, and a poor defensive header gave Jensen a sight of goal, but – are you sitting down, Arsenal fans? – his shot was useless.

Denmark then lost one of their best men as Henrik Andersen, already out of the final after being booked for tripping Gullit, collided with Van Basten. His screams of pain were audible on the TV coverage as he sat on the grass staring at his crushed kneecap, which resembled a moon crater.

The Dutch became increasingly frantic. Gullit broke through to force a decent save from Schmeichel, and Wim Kieft's hopeful cross almost found its way into the net off a defender. Finally, they broke the door down. Witschge's corner wasn't cleared properly and fell to Rijkaard, who banged the ball in before celebrating with visible sheepishness, as he had against Germany.

But Denmark managed to survive extra time. Schmeichel beat away Roy's shot on the turn, Gullit headed wide, and the biggest scare of all came when Van Basten, who had been superb all evening, curved a brilliant cross into the area. Gullit and Schmeichel both went for it, and it was bouncing into the net until substitute Claus Christiansen booted it away.

As the penalties got under way, the advantage surely lay with the Dutch. But Van Basten now experienced the lowest moment of a tournament in which nothing went right for him, despite superhuman performance levels.

His penalty was at the right height for Schmeichel, who didn't need to stretch to save it. 'We are human beings,' Van Basten said. 'I'm not disturbed because I missed. Someone has to miss. We couldn't come down from the euphoria of that [Germany] match.'

Van Breukelen, repeatedly trying to unsettle the Danish takers by getting in their faces, got a hand to three of their five penalties, but couldn't stop any. Vilfort got the loudest cheer of the night from a crowd who knew what he had gone through. Finally, up came Kim Christofte, who took a one-step run-up, rolled it into the corner, then did a 360-degree jig before his colleagues mobbed him.

The Big Mac Gang (as the local press dubbed them) were in the final, even if no one quite knew how. Three weeks earlier, Danish voters had rejected the Maastricht Treaty, throwing the EU into disarray. But Møller Nielsen's team didn't want to go home from their Euro party just yet.

8.15pm, 21 June 1992
Råsunda Stadion, Solna
Attendance: 28,827
Referee: Tullio Lanese (Italy)

GERMANY 3 (Häßler 11, Riedle 59, 89)
SWEDEN 2 (Brolin 64 pen, K. Andersson 90)

GERMANY: Illgner, Reuter, Brehme (c), Kohler, Buchwald, Helmer, Sammer, Effenberg, Riedle, Klinsmann (Doll 89), Häßler.

SWEDEN: Ravelli, R. Nilsson, Eriksson, Roger Ljung, Björklund, Ingesson, Joakim Nilsson (Limpar 58), Thern (c), Dahlin (Ekström 72), Brolin, K. Andersson.

Booked: Riedle (29), Buchwald (36), Reuter (43), Effenberg (3), Ljung (14), Dahlin (72).

8.15pm, 22 June 1992
Nya Ullevi, Gothenburg
Attendance: 37,450
Referee: Emilio Soriano Aladrén (Spain)

DENMARK 2 (Larsen 6, 33)
NETHERLANDS 2 (Bergkamp 24, Rijkaard 86)
Denmark won 5-4 on penalties after extra time
Shoot-out: Koeman 0-1, Larsen 1-1, Van Basten saved, Povlsen 1-2, Bergkamp 2-2, Elstrup 2-3, Rijkaard 3-3, Vilfort 4-3, Witschge 4-4, Christofte 5-4.

DENMARK: Schmeichel, Sivebæk, Piechnik, Olsen (c), Andersen (Claus Christiansen 70), Christofte, Jensen, Vilfort, Larsen, Povlsen, Laudrup (Elstrup 57).

NETHERLANDS: van Breukelen, van Tiggelen, De Boer (Wim Kieft 46), Koeman, Rijkaard, Wouters, Witschge, Roy (Van 't Schip 115), Van Basten, Gullit (c), Bergkamp.

Booked: Andersen (15), Rijkaard (42).

FINAL
Denmark v Germany

Before Euro 92, *Kicker* magazine asked the Bundesliga's 18 coaches who would win the tournament. Everyone went for Germany. And while all 18 answers would probably have been hastily amended after the Dutch defeat, the natural order of the universe had since restored itself. The Netherlands were gone. Germany had survived. And now was the moment for the heartwarming Danish bubble to be ruthlessly pricked by cold Ruhr Valley steel.

The final was a meeting between the best-prepared team and the one that turned up on the hoof. The 52-strong German party included four coaches, two medical professors and four masseurs; immense resources by the standards of 1992. Even a fully ready Denmark couldn't have competed with that.

On the last sunlit evening of a tournament full of them, the Danes began with visible hesitancy, as if they felt they didn't belong there. After four minutes, Schmeichel plucked a cross off Klinsmann's head. After six, Sammer stormed through from midfield and played in Reuter, whose dinked finish was kept out by the goalkeeper's huge hands. After ten, Buchwald had a go following more good play by Sammer.

'If Germany had scored, there was no way that we could have won that game,' said Olsen. 'We were on our last legs, and all our lack of preparation [was] really starting to show.' Instead, Denmark landed the opening blow with their first attack.

Out on the right wing, Vilfort took man and ball to rob Andy Brehme. Referee Bruno Galler seemed about to blow, but didn't. The ball rolled to Povlsen, whose best option looked like Larsen a few yards away. Instead, he pulled the ball back to the edge of the box, where someone else was waiting.

Nicknamed Faxe (the name of a frankly foul-tasting Danish beer) after his Brøndby youth team-mates drenched him with it as a prank one day, John Jensen could run all day and win the ball with some regularity. But he was renowned for his erratic shooting, usually leaning back at the moment of connection. Not here, though. As Effenberg threw himself horizontally in the way like a ski-jumper, Jensen got his body over the ball for once and unleashed the shot of his life, a beauty that hurtled just under Illgner's crossbar.

'We were all tired and nervous,' Jensen said. 'Then, with this goal, we were awake.' He now had the taste for it, hitting a half-volley which Illgner fumbled behind for a corner. The Germans immediately decided that here lurked an unexpected source of terror, and began fouling him in rotation, seven times in all.

Deep into the second half, a crazy spell of play almost yielded three goals. First, Laudrup's run drew the German defenders towards him before he played in Vilfort, who shot wastefully wide. Germany responded by almost scoring twice in a minute. Klinsmann's cross was on a plate for Riedle a yard out, but Kent Nielsen's spectacular bicycle kick under the crossbar hooked it away. From a corner moments later, Schmeichel did well to keep out Klinsmann's header.

As so often happens, the team under the cosh came up with something out of nothing. With 12 minutes left, Denmark scored one of the most flagrantly illegal goals ever witnessed in a European Championship, let alone in a final.

Povlsen thumped a free kick into the German wall and Claus Christiansen headed it back towards their box, where it came to Vilfort 25 yards out. Even in real time, without the aid of replays, it was plain to see that he had used his hand to bring the ball under control. He stepped inside Helmer to hit an unremarkable shot along the ground, which carried just enough power to elude Illgner and go in off the post.

'There was no way we could have survived extra time. Every time the Germans went forward, they looked like they were going to score,' said Laudrup. 'And then we managed to break away, and Kim finished them off.' Handball or no handball, nobody with a heart could begrudge Vilfort his moment. Weeks later, his daughter Line passed away from leukaemia.

Germany were vanquished. 'The last 15 minutes were easy,' said Olsen. 'We knew we were home and dry.' Some German fans holding an inflatable Henri Delaunay Trophy asked to be let out of their enclosure, then walked down to the Danish end and handed over their silver prize.

The European Championship had witnessed the most sensational story in its history – until 2004, anyway. A possibly apocryphal quote had Buchwald describing Denmark's loose play in stereotypically German terms: 'The Danes were all over the place. There was no order.' But Vogts found the right words, 'Look, anyone who beats France, the Netherlands and Germany is a worthy champion.'

Euro 92 is often dismissed as low-grade and unserious, as if a competition won by such a badly prepared team couldn't have been much cop. In truth, it was a tournament of two halves. The opening two rounds of fixtures were uninspired, yielding only a goal per game – but the second act was carefree and dramatic.

Adding another layer of surrealism, Denmark had pulled it off without their greatest ever talent. 'Michael Laudrup stopped playing for us because he wanted to concentrate on Barcelona,' said Lars Olsen. 'He'd just won the European Cup with them. The best player in the history of Denmark! Maybe if he'd been there, we wouldn't have won – we might have played differently with a playmaker like him. But I certainly did miss him.'

Of Denmark's squad, only Schmeichel went on to enjoy a truly top-class career, winning a mountain of silverware with Manchester United. The others all either flopped at decent-sized clubs (or, in Laudrup's case, spent their peak years in Scotland) or retired early for one reason or another, or went back to the sleepy pastures of Danish club football. Denmark would ultimately miss USA 94 on goals scored, losing to Spain's ten men on a tense night in Seville.

But for now, it was time to party. The day after the final, almost a million people greeted the squad at a parade in Copenhagen. 'It really sank in when we were in the town hall for the celebrations with the rest of Denmark,' said Schmeichel. 'That was truly unbelievable, "Christ, we actually did this, it's not a dream."'

Meanwhile, roughly a thousand miles to the south-east, ethnic cleansing continued to spread across the Balkans like a virus. 'We won it for Denmark, of course,' Schmeichel said. 'But we won it for Yugoslavia as well.'

8.15pm, 26 June 1992
Nya Ullevi, Gothenburg
Attendance: 37,800
Referee: Bruno Galler (Switzerland)

DENMARK 2 (Jensen 19, Vilfort 78)
GERMANY 0

DENMARK: Schmeichel, Sivebæk (Christiansen 66), Nielsen, Olsen (c), Piechnik, Christofte, Jensen, Vilfort, Larsen, Povlsen, Laudrup.

GERMANY: Illgner, Reuter, Brehme (c), Kohler, Buchwald, Helmer, Sammer (Doll 46), Häßler, Riedle, Klinsmann, Effenberg (Andreas Thom 80).

Booked: Piechnik (32), Effenberg (35), Häßler (39), Reuter (55), Doll (83), Klinsmann (88).

1996

AFTER 30 years, football came home. With some help from the Germans, who got behind their bid, England were awarded the finals on 6 May 1992 in Lisbon, seeing off Austria, Greece, Portugal and the Netherlands. Some interpreted it as UEFA bringing them back in from the cold after the horrors of Heysel.

Euro 96 witnessed several new departures. Three points were now on offer for a win, and if two teams finished level on points, their head-to-head result would override goal difference. Most significantly, the tournament doubled in size to 16 teams (a decision made six months after England received hosting responsibilities). Greed was the obvious motive – more games, more TV money – but there was pragmatism behind it too.

Between March 1991 and January 1993, Europe witnessed an epochal geopolitical shift. The USSR disintegrated, Yugoslavia descended into war, and Czechoslovakia underwent a peaceful Velvet Divorce. By early 1994, UEFA's membership had jumped from 35 to 49, and 16 new countries now made their European Championship debuts.

Some exploited the element of surprise. Slovenia drew with 1994 World Cup runners-up Italy, Latvia shocked Austria 3-2, Georgia crushed Wales 5-0 in Tbilisi, Macedonia came with minutes of beating European champions Denmark and, most impressively, Belarus sensationally beat a Netherlands team of young superstars. But none of these sides came close to qualifying. The biggest disappointment was Ukraine: expected to do great things after providing the USSR's backbone for decades, they never recovered from a shocking start at home to Lithuania and Slovenia.

Another new face, the Alpine principality of Liechtenstein, surpassed all expectations by drawing 0-0 with Ireland in a surreal match played on a mountainside. The arthritic Irish then lost 3-1 twice to Austria (who still didn't qualify, due to a crazy 5-3 defeat in Belfast). Jack Charlton's long reign ended with a play-off at Anfield which the Netherlands could have won by far more than 2-0. Most of the Dutch team came from Ajax, whom Louis van Gaal had moulded into the best club side in Europe. Despite that bad day in Minsk and another in Prague, manager Guus Hiddink had talent to burn.

Italy were a puzzle. They had come within a penalty of winning USA 94 without ever looking convincing, then trailed in behind Croatia in their Euro qualifying group. Overthinking everything, manager Arrigo Sacchi ostracised Roberto Baggio, who had saved his bacon three times in that World Cup. Gianfranco Zola got the nod instead: a marvellous player, but no Baggio. Young Alessandro Del Piero wasn't fit, and Sacchi was reduced to pleading in vain with 36-year-old Franco Baresi to come out of international retirement. Italy looked equally capable of winning the whole thing or losing all three first-round matches.

Romania and Bulgaria, the surprise packets of that World Cup, both qualified but were past their peak. Bulgaria did, however, feature in the most exciting game of the qualifiers, coming back from 2-0 down to beat Germany 3-2 in Sofia. Despite the scoreline, it was Germany's best performance since Italia 90, and they looked strong in both senses of the word, bristling with big lads who could play.

After their catastrophic failure to qualify for USA 94, France were regrouping under a new manager, Aimé Jacquet. They looked no great shakes in the qualifiers, drawing four of their first five games 0-0, but they had a good defence and a new playmaker in the burly, balding 23-year-old Zinedine Zidane. However, Jacquet left out Jean-Pierre Papin, David Ginola and his captain Eric Cantona, who had served a ban in England for kicking a racist fan. The decision would have looked better had Cantona not just inspired Manchester United to a domestic Double.

Spain looked unlikely to end their long streak of underachievement, with manager Javier Clemente's decision to leave out brilliant teenage forward Raúl baffling many. Portugal's midfield glistened with talent but, as ever, they lacked a good striker. And the Czech Republic found themselves in the Group of Death with Italy, Germany and Russia, their prospects seemingly stillborn. But at least they were there: after losing catastrophically to Luxembourg, Jan Suchopárek's late equaliser in Oslo kept them on life support, and they won their final three games to pip Norway, who had looked home and dry weeks earlier.

The hipsters' choice were newly independent Croatia, who had looked slick in the qualifiers and featured many of Yugoslavia's youthful stars from the late 1980s. In their second game, they would meet Denmark, of whom nothing was expected: everyone knew 1992 had been a one-shot deal.

Like two late buses, Scotland's first European Championship appearance in 1992 was followed by their second as Craig Brown squeezed all the juice out of a mediocre squad. Years later, he said the SFA had told him that if he didn't qualify for a tournament held in England, then 'you know the consequences'. Inevitably, the draw pitted them against the hosts, whose build-up was the usual mix of hope and neurosis.

England expected – and the job of meeting those expectations had fallen to Terry Venables. Affable, clubbable and quotable, Venables had an infinitely better rapport with the press than his beleaguered predecessor Graham Taylor, but his team struggled to convince during an endless run of friendlies. Discounting the Lansdowne Road riot in Dublin in February 1995, England lost only once in 19 warm-up games, a 3-1 lesson at the hands of Brazil – but also played out grim stalemates with Norway (twice), Uruguay, Romania, Colombia and Croatia. Alan Shearer, Venables's preferred striker, couldn't buy an international goal, and doubts surrounded the fitness of the untameable Paul Gascoigne, who was now enjoying himself up in Scotland with Rangers.

Questions had swirled around Venables's business affairs for years, and in January 1996 he announced he would step down after Euro 96 even if England won it. A fortnight before the tournament, during a bizarrely unnecessary trip to Hong Kong, his players were the subject of tabloid headlines after drinking in a bar. Flying home, they reached for the hard stuff again, causing damage worth thousands of pounds to the aircraft. At least a Swiss side who England had beaten 3-1 seven months earlier would provide obligingly meek opposition in the opening game. Wouldn't they?

GROUP A
England, Switzerland, Scotland, Netherlands

As the ball opened on a sunny Saturday at Wembley, John Major was a surprise no-show in the VIP box. But the embattled Conservative prime minister had made the right call, sparing himself an afternoon of lumpen football and a nasty surprise near the end.

For roughly 40 minutes, England played respectably. Gascoigne indulged himself with a rabona, and Swiss keeper Marco Pascolo fisted Gary Neville's long-range volley over the bar. The breakthrough came when Paul Ince's pass through three defenders saw Shearer let the ball roll on to his hammerhead right foot before smacking a murderous shot in off the bar for his first international goal since August 1994.

Switzerland looked desperately ordinary – but before the break, they suddenly gave England a huge fright. Kubilay Türkyilmaz left Stuart Pearce for dead on the right, and Marco Grassi scooped his low cross up on to the underside of the bar from close range.

As the sun beat down in the second half, England fell apart. The ineffectual Steve McManaman and Teddy Sheringham went off, followed by the exhausted, purple-faced Gascoigne. The substitutions made no difference and, to the horror of the home crowd, Switzerland equalised near the end. Tony Adams headed a high ball straight to Grassi, whose shot was blocked by Pearce's arm. Türkyilmaz sealed his fine performance by slotting the penalty into the corner.

With England now in total disarray, Grassi's last-minute shot almost crept inside the near post before David Seaman turned it behind. 'The manager [Artur Jorge] told us England would storm at us because of the home crowd and the pressure on them,' said Swiss captain Alain Geiger. 'We had to let them rage out. England cannot play like that for 90 minutes.'

———

At Villa Park two days later, Kevin Gallacher, Scott Booth and John Collins were the only under-30s in Scotland's team, while the Netherlands line-up's average age was just under 25. But Hiddink's youthful Ajax jewels ran out of ideas long before the end.

Early on, the rotund Andy Goram saved superbly from Clarence Seedorf, and Stuart McCall deflected Gaston Taument's follow-up over the bar. From the corner, Ronald de Boer's shot hit Stewart McKimmie before Collins clearly handled it on the line. Scotland were grateful for referee Leif Sundell being unsighted. 'The referee was standing in a very bad position,' said Hiddink. 'At international level, you have to see things like that.'

Although Edwin van der Sar kept out Gary McAllister's free kick, the traffic was one-way. McCall's terrific tackle stopped Johan de Kock from scoring, and Goram kept out a Dennis Bergkamp shot that came at him through half a dozen bodies. Then Bergkamp, escaping Colin Calderwood for once, was put through by Edgar Davids but couldn't walk the ball around the goalkeeper.

In the second half, Seedorf's header flew down into the turf and up over the bar, and the impressive Colin Hendry cleared another by Aron Winter off the line. But for once in their lives, Scotland clung on and got the job done.

———

Hiddink made Davids the scapegoat, benching him against Switzerland – a decision with far-reaching repercussions. Dutch TV footage showed him complaining to Seedorf on the sideline during the first half and, after getting only ten minutes as a sub, he growled afterwards that Hiddink 'needs to get his head out of some players' asses so he can see better'. Seedorf himself was so indisciplined in the first half that Hiddink withdrew him after 26 minutes.

Jordi Cruyff weathered so many unfavourable comparisons to his father that he put 'Jordi' on the back of his shirt rather than his surname, but he was a decent player with an eye for goal. After seeing Stéphane Henchoz bicycle-kick his header off the line, he gave the Dutch an undeserved lead with a near-post drive when Pascolo failed to punch away a corner.

The second goal came from a quick breakaway. Van der Sar's up-and-under was chased downfield by Bergkamp, who saw his shot parried by Pascolo but banged in the rebound. The Netherlands were home and dry, albeit unimpressively, but the match ended up being an afterthought.

Whenever talk turns to the Dutch implosion of Euro 96, the race factor usually gets mentioned. Photographer Guus Dubbelman of Amsterdam newspaper *De Volkskrant* managed to get into the grounds of Sopwell House, the squad's Hertfordshire base, and took a picture that showed the black players sitting at one table, the white players at two others, and Hiddink yelling at Dubbelman to leave. The sight of the apparent segregation planted the idea in the Dutch public's head that an ethnically divided team was pulling in different directions.

This was far from the full story. Reserve striker Youri Mulder said years later that the seating arrangements were because the squad's chef cooked some Surinamese food which only the black players wanted. 'In order not to give it to all tables, the black players sat together,' he said. And if one looks carefully, the extremely white Richard Witschge is at the same table as Seedorf, Kluivert et al.

There was certainly bad odour in the Dutch camp. But the main bone of contention was money: Ajax's pay gap. While the likes of Danny Blind and the De Boers were on 700,000 guilders a year, Kluivert and Davids were earning fractions of that. The indignant wonderboys were then told by Ajax to be grateful just to wear the shirt. Blind, the squad's elder statesman, sided with the board, creating bad feeling which now spilled over into Euro 96. An unedifying scene.

——

Enraged by tabloid stories that Teddy Sheringham, Jamie Redknapp and Sol Campbell had gone clubbing after the opening match, Terry Venables angrily upbraided the 'traitors' of the press. Gascoigne was picked again, but looked so portly that some wondered whether he had actually gained weight since the Swiss game. And for half the match against Scotland, England were again dreadful.

Beneath blazing sunshine, in front of a crowd which reportedly included 14,000 corporate guests, they spent the first half playing impotent keep-ball as Scotland contentedly looked on. Sheringham later said Venables had told them to play in 'a controlled fashion – no good getting too fired-up and getting sent off'. Had they been any more 'controlled' than this, they would have had no pulse.

At half-time, Venables threw on Jamie Redknapp. The midfielder would be overpraised by the English media for his cameo, but he did make a difference, allowing McManaman to move on to the right. And it was Redknapp who began the move for England's first goal. He found McManaman, who set Neville free down the flank to fire over a good cross. Shearer arrived at the back post like a shark smelling blood in the water, thumping his header home.

Scotland responded well. Gordon Durie, bandaged up after a clash of heads, saw Seaman claw away his dangerous header and, on 78 minutes, he reached McCall's low cross ahead of Adams, who felled him. Penalty. But Gary McAllister – distracted by the wind moving the ball slightly on the spot – hit it centrally at the right height for Seaman, whose elbow deflected it over. 'Only a sadist could fail to sympathise with McAllister as he nurses a pain that will never leave him,' wrote Hugh McIlvanney in the *Sunday Times*.

As Scotland winced, Gascoigne seized the moment to score the goal of his life. Improvising magnificently, he collected Darren Anderton's pass, flicked the ball over Hendry's head, ran around the centre-back, then stunningly whacked his shot low to Goram's right. His celebration, spreadeagled on the turf as his team-mates squirted an energy drink down his throat in homage to the 'dentist's chair' of those boozy Hong Kong nights, was one of the images of the tournament. 'Where's Hendry?' he asked. 'Has he gone to get me a pie?' Again abysmal for nearly the whole match, he now bathed in the fountain of national adulation. That's showbiz.

=====

So Scotland had to beat Switzerland, then pray that England thrashed the Netherlands or vice versa. Their main hope of goals, Ally McCoist, was a lethal hitman in the SPL but invariably came up short in Europe when it mattered. Early on at Villa Park, he missed two chances easier than the one he would later score: Pascolo scooped his close-range shot out from under the bar, then kicked away a similar effort.

But McCoist's 19th and final international goal was a peach. Exchanging passes with McAllister, he belted the return ball into the top corner for Scotland's first goal in almost six and a half hours.

As Switzerland slid out of the competition with a whimper, Ramon Vega nearly headed an own goal, and Johann Vogel's endless hacking should have earned him three yellows. Before the end, though, Scotland got caught on the break and Goram made a marvellous save from Türkyilmaz's header. Meanwhile, something extraordinary was happening down in London.

———

The Dutch camp was now a snake pit of mutual distrust. Davids was gone, sent home after a blazing row with Hiddink, who almost did the same to Seedorf following another confrontation. *Voetbal International* reported that Danny Blind's demeanour following Davids's departure was 'jubilant, as if he's holding a trophy'. Seedorf told the magazine, 'It's not three or four players. The problem is much bigger. You don't understand.'

England were an infinitely happier group, and the heights they scaled in this match owed everything to new-found conviction and self-belief. In the opening minutes, Richard Witschge blocked Shearer's half-volley from a corner on the line. From another corner, England had the lead. McManaman fed Ince, who back-heeled the ball behind himself, and Blind took the bait by tripping him. Shearer rarely missed penalties, and this one was no exception.

For now, the Dutch stayed calm. Bergkamp, the lone striker, worked hard and pounced on Gareth Southgate's feeble back-header to bring a decent save from Seaman. At the interval, it felt like any other closely contested international.

But now came the deluge. England went two up with the simplest of goals, Sheringham heading Gascoigne's corner past the frozen Van der Sar. Suddenly rampant, they made it 3-0 with one of the best goals in their history. Gascoigne exchanged passes with Anderton and McManaman, before finding the turn of pace everyone had thought he had lost. Accelerating past Winter, he played a lethal sideways pass to Sheringham. As de Kock slipped, Sheringham pivoted to side-foot the ball to Shearer, whose ferocious finish into the roof of the net felt like a moment of English catharsis.

The stunned Dutch instantly coughed up a fourth goal. Van der Sar, in bits by now, couldn't hold Anderton's shot after it deflected off Blind, and Sheringham poked in the rebound. Up in the press box, one English journalist was overheard saying, 'Well, it can only go downhill from here.'

As things stood, the Netherlands were out on goal difference – but England saved them by slackening off. With 12 minutes left, Kluivert took Bergkamp's lay-off and placed a cool finish through Seaman's legs, putting them through on goals scored. They had survived – just – but their media's response was equal parts horror and bewilderment. *NRC Handelsblad*'s Erik Oudshoorn wrote, 'Tactics are irrelevant when players are so tame that they lose their personal duels one by one. There was an incomprehensible mood about the Dutch team last night.' Years later, Hiddink was still stinging. 'Don't open old wounds,' he said. 'It was a big defeat. I felt isolated.'

The English press stampeded to hail Venables as a tactical godhead. *The Guardian*'s Richard Williams wrote, 'So much worked well for England that it is hard to envisage their performances sliding back into the old mediocrity.' It took four days for that prediction to go arse about face. Over in tabloid land, the *Daily Mail*'s Jeff Powell and *The Sun*'s John Sadler, who had both written England off after the opening game, immediately executed reverse-ferrets. Powell called their performance 'the best since 1966', while Sadler declared that 'they DO have the players to win this tournament'. There'll always be an England.

3pm, 8 June 1996
Wembley Stadium, London
Attendance: 76,567
Referee: Manuel Díaz Vega (Spain)

ENGLAND 1 (Shearer 23)
SWITZERLAND 1 (Türkyilmaz 83 pen)

ENGLAND: David Seaman, Gary Neville, Stuart Pearce, Paul Ince, Tony Adams (c), Gareth Southgate, Steve McManaman (Steve Stone 69), Paul Gascoigne (David Platt 77), Alan Shearer, Teddy Sheringham (Nick Barmby 69), Darren Anderton. **Manager:** Terry Venables.

SWITZERLAND: Marco Pascolo, Sébastien Jeanneret, Yvan Quentin, Alain Geiger (c) (Marcel Koller 69), Ramon Vega, Stéphane Henchoz, Johann Vogel, Ciriaco Sforza, Marco Grassi, Kubilay Türkyilmaz, Christophe Bonvin (Stéphane Chapuisat 67). **Manager:** Artur Jorge.

Booked: Neville (26), Adams (80), Vogel (28), Quentin (43), Grassi (84), Vega (89).

4.30pm, 10 June 1996
Villa Park, Birmingham
Attendance: 34,363
Referee: Leif Sundell (Sweden)

NETHERLANDS 0
SCOTLAND 0

NETHERLANDS: Edwin van der Sar, Michael Reiziger, Winston Bogarde, Johan de Kock, Richard Witschge (Phillip Cocu 78), Clarence Seedorf, Edgar Davids, Ronald de Boer (c) (Aron Winter 68), Dennis Bergkamp, Jordi Cruyff, Gaston Taument (Patrick Kluivert 63). **Manager:** Guus Hiddink.

SCOTLAND: Andy Goram, Stewart McKimmie (Craig Burley 85), Tom Boyd, Colin Calderwood, Colin Hendry, Stuart McCall, Gary McAllister (c), John Collins, Gordon Durie, Kevin Gallacher (Billy McKinlay 56), Scott Booth (John Spencer 46). **Manager:** Craig Brown.

Booked: Witschge (26), Taument (28), Boyd (4), Gallacher (31).

7.30pm, 13 June 1996
Villa Park, Birmingham
Attendance: 36,800
Referee: Atanas Uzunov (Bulgaria)

NETHERLANDS 2 (Cruyff 66, Bergkamp 79)
SWITZERLAND 0

NETHERLANDS: Van der Sar, Reiziger, Danny Blind (c), Bogarde, Winter, Seedorf (De Kock 26), Witschge, R. de Boer (Davids 80), Bergkamp, Cruyff (Kluivert 84), Peter Hoekstra.

SWITZERLAND: Pascolo, Marc Hottiger, Quentin, Jeanneret (Alexandre Comisetti 69), Vega, Henchoz, Vogel, Sforza (c), Türkyilmaz, Grassi, Chapuisat.

Booked: Seedorf (14), Jeanneret (32), Chapuisat (40), Türkyilmaz (62), Grassi (72).

3pm, 15 June 1996
Wembley Stadium, London
Attendance: 76,864
Referee: Pierluigi Pairetto (Italy)

ENGLAND 2 (Shearer 53, Gascoigne 79)
SCOTLAND 0

ENGLAND: Seaman, Neville, Pearce (Jamie Redknapp 46, Sol Campbell 85), Ince (Stone 80), Adams (c), Southgate, McManaman, Gascoigne, Shearer, Sheringham, Anderton.

SCOTLAND: Goram, McKimmie, Boyd, Calderwood, Hendry, Tosh McKinlay (Burley 82), McCall, McAllister (c), Durie (Eoin Jess 87), Collins, Spencer (Ally McCoist 67).

Booked: Ince (68), Shearer (75), Collins (29), Spencer (38), Hendry (70).

7.30pm, 18 June 1996
Villa Park, Birmingham
Attendance: 34,946
Referee: Václav Krondl (Czech Republic)

SCOTLAND 1 (McCoist 37)
SWITZERLAND 0

SCOTLAND: Goram, McKinlay (Booth 60), Boyd, Calderwood, Hendry, Burley, McCall, McAllister (c), McCoist (Spencer 84), Collins, Durie.

SWITZERLAND: Pascolo, Hottiger, Quentin (Comisetti 81), Vega, Henchoz, Koller (Raphaël Wicky 46), Vogel, Sforza (c), Türkyilmaz, Bonvin, Chapuisat (Sébastien Fournier 46).

Booked: Calderwood (23), McCall (28), Collins (42), Vega (23), Vogel (53), Wicky (55), Fournier (65).

7.30pm, 18 June 1996
Wembley Stadium, London
Attendance: 76,798
Referee: Gerd Grabher (Austria)

ENGLAND 4 (Shearer 23 pen, 57, Sheringham 51, 62)
NETHERLANDS 1 (Kluivert 78)

ENGLAND: Seaman, Neville, Pearce, Ince (Platt 68), Adams (c), Southgate, McManaman, Gascoigne, Shearer (Barmby 76), Sheringham (Robbie Fowler 77), Anderton.

NETHERLANDS: Van der Sar, Reiziger, Blind (c), Bogarde, Winter, Seedorf, Witschge (De Kock 46), R. de Boer (Cocu 73), Bergkamp, Cruyff, Hoekstra (Kluivert 72).

Booked: Sheringham (41), Ince (43), Southgate (90), Winter (18), Blind (23), Bergkamp (67).

GROUP A	P	W	D	L	F	A	GD	Pts
ENGLAND	3	2	1	0	7	2	+5	7
NETHERLANDS	3	1	1	1	3	4	− 1	4
SCOTLAND	3	1	1	1	1	2	− 1	4
SWITZERLAND	3	0	1	2	1	4	− 3	1

England and the Netherlands qualified.

GROUP B
Spain, Bulgaria, France, Romania

Bulgaria were finding north-east England less agreeable than their various sun-drenched bases at USA 94. Abruptly leaving their hotel in Scarborough, where they complained of having nothing to do, they decamped instead to the bright lights of Doncaster.

At a half-empty Elland Road, they and Spain opened Group B with a 1-1 draw. In a sleepy first half, Hristo Stoichkov volleyed over the bar for Bulgaria, and Spain's anorexically thin golden boy Julen Guerrero side-footed a sitter too high after the balding Yordan Lechkov botched a header.

Like Lechkov, Trifon Ivanov's distinctive appearance had seen him stand out at USA 94, and here, a fresh shiner made the defender look even more caveman-like than usual. In the first half, he tried two ludicrous 40-yard shots. One caught goalkeeper Andoni Zubizarreta out, bouncing just outside the post. The other nearly decapitated Stoichkov.

Despite a poor season at Parma, the glowering Stoichkov remained a terrifying opponent. Early in the second half, he scored a magnificent goal, letting Iliyan Kiriakov's floated pass drop over his shoulder then volleying it into the top corner. But linesman Enrico Preziosi's flag wrongly went up, wiping out one of the greatest strikes in any European Championship and prompting howls of abuse from the irascible Stoichkov.

Soon, he opened Spain up again, hitting a fabulous cross-field ball to Emil Kostadinov, who got bundled over by Sergi Barjuán just before he could shoot. Zubizarreta, who rarely saved penalties, didn't get near this one as Stoichkov drilled it in off the post.

Bulgarian joy was short-lived, as the gaunt Petar Hubchev hauled down José Luis Caminero outside the box and was sent off. A spate of substitutions

– two Bulgarian, one Spanish – held up the free kick for nearly three minutes. Eventually, Fernando Hierro drove it into the wall, but the rebound fell to Sergi, whose cross-shot was diverted in at close range by one of the newly arrived subs, Alfonso Pérez.

Barely a minute later, Juan Antonio Pizzi's moronic hack on Radostin Kishishev saw referee Piero Ceccarini produce another red card and at ten-a-side the game petered out. Afterwards, Spain's manager Javier Clemente moaned about Stoichkov's behaviour ('Even when he could play fair, he doesn't want to'), but he had been the best player on show by miles.

===

France's meeting with Romania in Newcastle promised plenty – including Gheorghe Hagi and a young Zinedine Zidane on the same pitch – but delivered little. The teams, who had met twice in the qualifiers, knew each other too well.

There were unkind whispers that Christophe Dugarry owed his place in the French squad to his status as Zidane's friend. A real curate's egg of a striker, ungainly and erratic, he scored a strange goal after 22 minutes. Youri Djorkaeff floated a ball into the box, Romania's burly goalkeeper Bogdan Stelea came out too late, and Dugarry outjumped him and Gheorghe Mihali to send a backward header looping gently into the unguarded net.

The Romania of 1994 would have responded with scintillating, multi-pronged attacks. But the closest this lot came were when Bernard Lama clutched Hagi's curving free kick and, later, when substitute Viorel Moldovan dodged two defenders before shooting into the Leazes Stand. Zidane was very disappointing, contributing only a free kick which Stelea punched away, but France saw out time in comfort.

===

Romania and Bulgaria, it was clear, had left their USA 94 magic behind under the American sun. Like two ageing Hollywood stars teaming up for one last buddy-buddy blockbuster, their meeting at a near-deserted St James' Park confirmed that their moment had passed.

But Stoichkov's instincts remained as sharp as ever. Early on, when Krasimir Balakov fed him the ball 40 yards out, he arrowed into the heart of Romania's defence. Miodrag Belodedici fatally slipped and lost him as he darted into the box, feinted to his left, then neatly prodded the ball past Stelea.

Hagi, Stoichkov's mirror-image in so many ways, saw his excellent free kick saved by Borislav Mihaylov, and soon Romania equalised with a wonderful strike – but the officials failed to notice. Dorinel Munteanu, teed up by Hagi's short corner, crashed an angled shot off the underside of the bar which landed at least a foot behind the line. But referee Peter Mikkelsen and linesman Henning Knudsen blinked at the wrong moment.

'I didn't feel angry straight away,' Munteanu recalled. 'I was thinking that there was plenty of time to score again. It was only afterwards that I got pissed off, especially when I saw how far it was over the line.' It was an afternoon to forget for Mikkelsen, who later wrongly booked Tsanko Tsvetanov for Daniel Borimirov's brutal foul on Costel Gâlcă.

Romania, a decent but luckless team, dominated the second half. Mihaylov acrobatically flipped away Hagi's cross-shot, and Daniel Prodan should have scored twice, sending a diving header past the far post and later shooting wide with Bulgaria's defence at sixes and sevens. Unable to break through, they were now out after two games. Manager Anghel Iordănescu was stoic about the Munteanu incident: 'I refuse to make any comment about that. Defeat is defeat.'

‗‗‗

By now, it was clear France wouldn't be the great entertainers of Euro 96 as they played out a boring draw with Spain in Leeds. 'The game was as dry as a stone,' *El País* noted. 'The disregard for the basics turned the ball into an annoying artefact.' Again, Jacquet's team squatted on a 1-0 lead but didn't get away with it this time.

The highlight of a dire first half came when Vincent Guérin's 25-yarder bounced dangerously in front of Zubizarreta, who pushed it away. Just after half-time, Djorkaeff injected some quality, latching on to Christian Karembeu's pass and prodding a low shot into the corner for France's one really good moment of the tournament.

With ten minutes left, Dugarry almost settled it when his header brushed the post. But Spain's late equaliser came about through sheer desperation more than anything else. On the left, Kiko held off Lilian Thuram and crossed; Bixente Lizarazu screamed for Didier Deschamps to leave it, but the captain didn't hear him and his header came out to Javier Manjarín, who pulled it back for Caminero to scuff it untidily past Lama's unimpressive dive. 'You're vigilant for 85 minutes, and then an uncontrollable factor upsets everything,' grumbled Lizarazu.

‗‗‗

Regardless, a point against Bulgaria in Newcastle would see France through. Recent history notwithstanding, this was an over-the-hill Bulgarian team and the French had little to fear. Even their nemesis, Emil Kostadinov, was absent with hamstring trouble.

Despite the unstinting efforts of Lechkov, who never stopped trying to create openings, Bulgaria were flaccid throughout. Meanwhile, Stoichkov disgraced himself by racially abusing Marcel Desailly ('Shitty blacks, shitty country, shitty skin'). Later, he laughably claimed that 'it's normal, it happens all over the pitch'. UEFA did its see-no-evil routine, and he escaped punishment.

But France had Bulgaria's number this time. After Mihaylov jack-knifed to turn Djorkaeff's free kick around the post, Blanc outjumped Lubo Penev at a corner to score with a fine header. With Bulgaria floundering, Dugarry charged down Hubchev's clearance and tried to chip Mihaylov, but the bewigged goalkeeper pushed it behind. He made it a hat-trick of good stops by beating away Djorkaeff's shot.

Although Zidane still looked subdued, France were untroubled and went 2-0 up when Penev headed Djorkaeff's free kick into his own net under pressure from Blanc. A lumbering target man in a team without wingers, this was the one clear header he had in the tournament.

Stoichkov, a world-class footballer despite his repugnant behaviour, threw Bulgaria a lifeline by curling a marvellous free kick into the top corner, the only goal of its kind in the tournament. Like Jean-Pierre Papin in 1992, he had performed amazingly well in a pedestrian team. But France weren't finished: in the last minute, Karembeu sent Patrice Loko through to round Mihaylov and shoot past Ivaylo Yordanov on the line. Bulgaria now had to sweat on the Spain-Romania result.

═══

Needing a win to survive, the Spanish were initially given the runaround at Elland Road. Adrian Ilie shot badly over when Hagi sent him through, and Gică Popescu's drive was deflected just wide by Rafael Alkorta after a free-kick routine involving a dummy and a back-heel.

It typified Romania's fortunes in this tournament that they fell behind via a freakish double deflection. When José Emilio Amavisca's shot hit Pizzi's leg and then Anton Doboș's knee, little Manjarín tucked away the loose ball. But the equaliser, Romania's only goal of the tournament, was beautifully worked. Ovidiu Stângă played a one-two with Hagi before setting Florin Răducioiu free to run on and slide the ball under Zubizarreta.

In the second half, aware that Bulgaria were losing, Spain got their act together. Florian Prunea palmed Manjarín's half-volley over the bar and saved from Amavisca, while Petrescu cleared off the line from Hierro. Finally, with a minute to go, they saved themselves. As Prodan lay injured in the box, playing everybody onside, Sergi crossed to the far post. Alfonso nodded it back, and substitute Guillermo Amor stooped to head in at close range.

'Romania played some excellent football,' Clemente said. 'They didn't deserve to go out. They're better technically than some in this group.' He didn't specify whether that included Spain. The win had done nothing for his mood: he manhandled radio reporter Jesús Gallego for interviewing Amor without authorisation, forcing Elland Road security to bundle him away.

2.30pm, 9 June 1996
Elland Road, Leeds
Attendance: 24,006
Referee: Piero Ceccarini (Italy)

SPAIN 1 (Alfonso 74)
BULGARIA 1 (Stoichkov 65 pen)

SPAIN: Andoni Zubizarreta (c), Alberto Belsué, Sergi Barjuán, Rafael Alkorta, Abelardo Fernández, Fernando Hierro, José Luis Caminero (Donato Gama da Silva 82), Julen Guerrero (José Emilio Amavisca 51), Juan Antonio Pizzi, Luis Enrique Martínez, Guillermo Amor (Alfonso Pérez 73). **Manager:** Javier Clemente.

BULGARIA: Borislav Mihaylov (c), Radostin Kishishev, Trifon Ivanov, Iliyan Kiriakov (Tsanko Tsvetanov 72), Petar Hubchev, Zlatko Yankov, Yordan Lechkov, Krasimir Balakov, Lubo Penev (Daniel Borimirov 78), Hristo Stoichkov, Emil Kostadinov (Ivaylo Yordanov 73). **Manager:** Dimitar Penev.

Booked: Caminero (27), Sergi (39), Amor (42), Abelardo (89), Stoichkov (29), Kishishev (55), Yankov (77).

Sent off: Pizzi (75), Hubchev (71).

7.30pm, 10 June 1996
St James' Park, Newcastle
Attendance: 26,303
Referee: Hellmut Krug (Germany)

FRANCE 1 (Dugarry 25)
ROMANIA 0

FRANCE: Bernard Lama, Lilian Thuram, Éric Di Meco (Bixente Lizarazu 68), Vincent Guérin, Laurent Blanc, Marcel Desailly, Didier Deschamps (c), Christian Karembeu, Christophe Dugarry (Patrice Loko 68), Zinedine Zidane (Alain Roche 80), Youri Djorkaeff. **Manager:** Aimé Jacquet.

ROMANIA: Bogdan Stelea, Dan Petrescu (Iulian Filipescu 78), Tibor Selymes, Gheorghe Mihali, Miodrag Belodedici, Gheorghe 'Gica' Popescu, Ionuţ Lupescu, Dorinel Munteanu, Florin Răducioiu (Viorel Moldovan 46), Gheorghe Hagi (c), Marius Lăcătuş (Adrian Ilie 56). **Manager:** Anghel Iordănescu.

Booked: Di Meco (20), Mihali (49), Selymes (71), Ilie (90).

4.30pm, 13 June 1996
St James' Park, Newcastle
Attendance: 10,000
Referee: Peter Mikkelsen (Denmark)

BULGARIA 1 (Stoichkov 3)
ROMANIA 0

BULGARIA: Mihaylov (c), Kishishev, Ivanov, Tsvetanov, Yordanov, Yankov, Lechkov (Boncho Genchev 90+3), Balakov, Penev (Nasko Sirakov 72), Stoichkov, Kostadinov (Borimirov 32).

ROMANIA: Stelea, Petrescu, Selymes, Belodedici, Daniel Prodan, Popescu (Ilie 78), Lupescu (Costel Gâlcă 46), Munteanu, Răducioiu, Hagi (c), Lăcătuş (Moldovan 29).

Booked: Kishishev (48), Tsvetanov (64, retrospectively awarded to Borimirov).

6pm, 15 June 1996
Elland Road, Leeds
Attendance: 35,626
Referee: Vadim Zhuk (Belarus)

SPAIN 1 (Caminero 85)
FRANCE 1 (Djorkaeff 48)

SPAIN: Zubizarreta (c), Jorge Otero (Francisco Narváez 'Kiko' 59), Juan Manuel López, Alkorta, Abelardo, Hierro, Sergi, Caminero, Alfonso (Julio Salinas 83), Luis Enrique (Javier Manjarín 55), Amavisca.

FRANCE: Lama, Jocelyn Angloma (Roche 65), Lizarazu, Guérin (Thuram 81), Blanc, Desailly, Deschamps (c), Karembeu, Loko (Dugarry 74), Zidane, Djorkaeff.

Booked: Luis Enrique (12), Amavisca (53), Otero (56), Blanc (43), Karembeu (60), Djorkaeff (63).

4.30pm, 18 June 1996
St James' Park, Newcastle
Attendance: 26,976
Referee: Dermot Gallagher (England), replaced by Paul Durkin (England) in the 28th minute

FRANCE 3 (Blanc 21, Penev 63 og, Loko 90)
BULGARIA 1 (Stoichkov 69)

FRANCE: Lama, Thuram, Lizarazu, Guérin, Blanc, Desailly, Deschamps (c), Karembeu, Dugarry (Loko 70), Zidane (Reynald Pedros 62), Djorkaeff.

BULGARIA: Mihaylov (c), Emil Kremenliev, Ivanov, Tsvetanov, Hubchev, Yankov (Borimirov 79), Lechkov, Yordanov, Penev, Stoichkov, Balakov (Georgi Donkov 82).

Booked: Desailly (3), Dugarry (36), Ivanov (8), Kremenliev (13).

4.30pm, 18 June 1996
Elland Road, Leeds
Attendance: 32,719
Referee: Ahmet Çakar (Turkey)

SPAIN 2 (Manjarín 11, Amor 84)
ROMANIA 1 (Răducioiu 29)

SPAIN: Zubizarreta (c), López, Sergi, Alkorta, Abelardo (Amor 64), Hierro, Miguel Ángel Nadal, Manjarín, Pizzi (Alfonso 57), Kiko, Amavisca (Guerrero 72).

ROMANIA: Florian Prunea, Petrescu, Selymes, Anton Doboş, Prodan (Lupescu 86), Popescu, Ovidiu Stângă, Gâlcă, Răducioiu (Ion Vlădoiu 77), Hagi (c), Ilie (Munteanu 66).

Booked: Kiko (35), Nadal (59), Hagi (21), Ilie (47), Gâlcă (77).

GROUP B	P	W	D	L	F	A	GD	Pts
FRANCE	3	2	1	0	5	2	+3	7
SPAIN	3	1	2	0	4	3	+1	5
BULGARIA	3	1	1	1	3	4	−1	4
ROMANIA	3	0	0	3	1	4	−3	0

France and Spain qualified.

GROUP C
Germany, Czech Republic, Russia, Italy

The Group of Death's opening pages unfurled very quietly in front of thousands of empty seats at Old Trafford. Germany broke little sweat in beating the Czech Republic, scoring two carbon-copy goals within minutes of each other in the first half. Christian Ziege and Andy Möller both strode purposefully down the left, swerved inside Miroslav Kadlec, and rattled low right-footers into the bottom corner.

The 23-year-old Pavel Nedvěd would go on to become one of the great midfielders of European football. But although he lifted Karel Poborský's cross over a gaping goal just after Möller scored, he and his compatriots looked terrified throughout. 'Our players were just overawed,' said Czech manager Dušan Uhrin. 'The Germans, this huge stadium: everything.' Goalkeeper Petr Kouba kept out Fredi Bobic's volley, Möller and Thomas Häßler wasted good chances, Thomas Helmer nodded a sitter wide, and Ziege had another header cleared off the line by Nedvěd.

Referee David Elleray, notorious in the Premier League as a pettifogging pedant, handed out an absurd ten bookings in a match that never felt remotely nasty, while ignoring the worst tackle of all, by Germany's guard dog Dieter Eilts on Jiří Němec. 'I would've expected an English referee to be more understanding of the physical game,' German manager Berti Vogts complained. 'The only person he didn't book was me.' The other cloud on Vogts's vista was the early loss of skipper and defensive pillar Jürgen Kohler, to a knee injury that ended his tournament.

Arrigo Sacchi knew the score. 'I'll either have kisses landing on my bald head, or tomatoes,' he quipped good-naturedly. And Russia looked like a stiff opening test for Italy. They had won 14 of their previous 15 internationals, and most of the rebels who missed USA 94 had returned.

But at Anfield, they began disastrously. Goalkeeper Stanislav Cherchesov scuffed a clearance straight to Angelo Di Livio, who cushioned it first-time to Pierluigi Casiraghi, lurking near the edge of the box. Cherchesov barely moved as Casiraghi rattled the chance into the bottom corner, before running to the near-empty Anfield Road Stand to celebrate in front of about ten Italian fans.

Knocking the ball around tidily, Russia soon deservedly equalised. A move down the left saw Valeriy Karpin's shot rebound to little Ilya Tsymbalar, who dodged two defenders and beat Angelo Peruzzi at the near post with an angled shot, eerily similar to Stan Collymore's winner for Liverpool against Newcastle on the same patch of grass two months earlier.

Otherwise, Russia couldn't shoot straight to save their lives: Igor Kolyvanov (twice), Andrei Kanchelskis and Aleksandr Mostovoi all put terrible efforts into the Kop. Meanwhile, the 5ft 5in Zola – the last player you would want to convert a free header – nodded a great opportunity wide.

Paolo Maldini struggled so badly to cope with Kanchelskis's pace that, at the interval, Sacchi introduced Roberto Donadoni to help him. But Russia's lack of ruthlessness was punished early in the second half. Zola slipped a nice reverse pass through to Casiraghi, who slammed a first-time finish between Cherchesov and the near post.

Leaving gaps as they chased the game, Russia might have lost by more. Viktor Onopko's mistake forced Cherchesov to race off his line to thwart Zola and the clearly unfit substitute Fabrizio Ravanelli tapped a feeble finish into the goalkeeper's hands.

Another sub, Igor Dobrovolsky, squandered Russia's last chance with a wild shot that almost landed in Stanley Park. All Italy now needed to make the last eight, probably with Germany for company, was a result against the seemingly insipid Czechs. After one round of fixtures, the Group of Death already seemed done and dusted.

====

But that reckoned without Sacchi's madness. Four and a half years into the job, he had already called up a staggering 87 players. Now, fatally underestimating the Czechs, he dropped five of his front six. 'Revolution is not the right word,' he said. 'You can't play in the European Championship with only 11, 12 or 13 players, and I have great faith in all my 22.' Performing open-heart surgery when only nips and tucks were needed, he saw his team flatline on the operating table in a marvellous match.

Maldini, wobbly against Russia, was atrocious here and played a role in the Czechs' early opening goal. When Poborský dodged his weak challenge and curled a delicious centre into the box, Nedvěd stole in behind Roberto Mussi, chested it down and tapped it past Peruzzi.

After Maldini was exposed again, Alessandro Costacurta handled Poborský's cross in the box. But referee Antonio López Nieto didn't spot it, and Diego Fuser robbed Suchopárek before breaking upfield. The midfielder's cross was turned in by Enrico Chiesa, who had scored 22 of Sampdoria's 59 Serie A goals in 1995/96 to force himself into Sacchi's squad.

Italy looked likely to win, but Luigi Apolloni had other ideas. Already on a booking, the flame-haired defender hurled himself through the back of Kuka – in the Czech half of the field. López Nieto played advantage, but when play eventually halted, he hadn't forgotten about Apolloni and gave him a second booking.

Suddenly, ten-man Italy were in a hole. Poborský's pass handed Nedvěd a clear chance, but he tripped before pulling the trigger. And when Kuka found space near the corner flag, Maldini was again at fault, extending only a lazy leg before Kuka's cross was volleyed into the far corner by Radek Bejbl, arriving late with nobody tracking his run. So much for Italian defending's eternal verities.

With so many new faces, Italy struggled for fluency in the second half and the Czechs wasted chances to kill them off. Vladimír Šmicer burst through but shot at Peruzzi, Suchopárek thumped a close-range chance over the bar (Maldini, next to him, was asleep), and when Bejbl teed up Šmicer, Peruzzi again came to the rescue.

Yet Italy could still have survived. In stoppage time, substitute Zola superbly picked out Casiraghi, who chested the ball past Kadlec to give himself a sitter, only to fire the ball into a Kop full of disbelieving Italians.

Back home, the rotten tomatoes were being picked and bagged. Totò Riina, the Sicilian Mafia *capo di tutti capi* on trial in Florence for countless murders, ominously told his lawyer, 'Sacchi uses suicide tactics and suicide choices.' A less worrying but equally damning verdict came from the great Gianni Rivera: 'You simply don't change a winning team. I get the impression Sacchi wanted to prove that he's more important than the players.'

The next day, an IRA bomb exploded in central Manchester, injuring 212 people and causing vast damage. The meeting of Germany and Russia, initially in doubt, went ahead after Old Trafford was guarded overnight and swept for suspect devices.

Russia shaded an exciting first half, with the lively Tsymbalar and Mostovoi again shining, but were again unfortunate. First, Tsymbalar's shot bounced into the turf before hitting the post, and Kolyvanov headed the rebound straight at goalkeeper Andy Köpke. And before half-time, when Mostovoi was brought down by Köpke in the box, referee Kim Milton Nielsen missed it and Kolyvanov ineptly wafted the loose ball over the bar.

Germany's superb sweeper made the breakthrough for them early in the second half. In 1995, Adidas had used Matthias Sammer in an ad campaign entitled 'Firehead', a nod to his red hair. His playing style incorporated ice as well as fire: a ferocious competitive spirit allied to a clinical appreciation of spaces and angles. Now he came up from the back as Möller picked him out. His first-time shot was well saved by Dmitri Kharin, but he shovelled in the rebound from close range.

Russia lost heart after Yuri Kovtun was sent off for a brain-dead foul on Eilts. Jürgen Klinsmann, back after missing the Czech game through suspension, finished them off. His first goal was sublime: turning suddenly and pushing the ball past Yuri Nikiforov in one fluid movement, he ran on to stroke a shot into the top corner with the outside of his right boot. 'King Klin, ein Beckenbauer-Tor!' exclaimed one German TV commentator. A Beckenbauer goal indeed.

It made 'Klinsi' the first man to score in three European Championships, and with seconds left, he made it 3-0 after Stefan Kuntz's hard work handed him a simple chance. Russia were now all but out, despite playing well. 'Some of our players were bad, and others were very bad,' said their fearsome manager Oleg Romantsev, ridiculously harshly. 'When you're talking about moral qualities, our team is the worst equipped in the whole tournament.'

Italy, now up against it, would need a better result against Germany at Old Trafford than the Czech Republic got against Russia. And if the Czechs won, Italy had to beat the seemingly invincible Germans by three. Belatedly, Sacchi recalled Zola, Casiraghi and Roberto Di Matteo, though you still felt that this team was what his all-conquering Milan team of 1988–1991 might have been like without its three Dutch superstars.

Reaching for the kitchen sink was hardly in Italy's DNA, but they began brightly. Early on, Köpke beat away Fuser's volley. Minutes later, Sammer's clearance was charged down by Casiraghi. The striker tried to go around Köpke, who professionally fouled him – but referee Guy Goethals didn't even book the keeper. Köpke compounded the insult, easily saving Zola's weak penalty.

The miss weighed heavily on Italy and, for all their possession, they carved out few chances. Köpke, punching everything that came at him, kept out two good efforts by Donadoni and one by Fuser. With half an hour left, Thomas Strunz walked the plank after scything down Donadoni for a second yellow card, getting pelted with missiles by Italian fans on the Stretford End as he trudged towards the tunnel.

The final stages of the match were punctuated by roars of ecstasy and then screams of despair from those Italian fans in possession of radios, as the score in the other game see-sawed this way and that. 'I saw people cheering,' Maldini said afterwards. 'I was hopeful. Then I looked at the faces on our bench, and I understood.'

At a half-empty Anfield, Russia began listlessly, giving the Czechs two cheap headed goals in the first 20 minutes. After Luboš Kubík's curling free kick was turned around the post by Cherchesov, Russia's defenders failed to pick up Suchopárek as he nodded home the corner. Then, for the second goal, Kuka headed Němec's long ball high into the air, and seemingly wide – only for the ball to drop randomly inside Cherchesov's far post. Kuka had the self-awareness to smile sheepishly.

The Czechs could have been 5-0 up by half-time. Michal Horňák and Poborský hit the bar with a volley and a long cross respectively, and Cherchesov tipped Patrik Berger's free kick on to a post. But Russia, perhaps succumbing to what Norman Mailer called the strange sense of calm that descends when everything has turned to shit, were a different team after half-time.

They pulled one back with yet another header, Mostovoi sneaking into the Czech box to glance home Khokhlov's cross. Then they equalised with a goal that seemed to fool the eye on initial viewing. Omari Tetradze exchanged one-twos with Vladislav Radimov as they both burst into the box, before Němec took Radimov's legs. The ball broke to Tetradze, whose close-range shot hit Kouba before softly floating into the net.

The Czechs were still just about safe, as long as Italy didn't score against Germany. For the fourth time, they hit the woodwork, Poborský's piledriver shaking the upright. Soon came another blast from distance, and this one went in. Russia's substitute Vladimir Beschastnykh, left to his own devices by tired defenders, was given a ludicrous amount of time to shoot powerfully into the top corner for 3-2.

Russia almost put the Czechs to bed with a three-against-two break, but Mostovoi dithered and got crowded out. And this deeply odd match had one more late twist. Kubík picked out Šmicer with a lofted pass, and as Nikiforov arrived too late, his shot trundled just inside the far post, past the static Cherchesov. The unfashionable outsiders were through – and Italy's superstars were gone.

'If I could somehow replay the tournament, I'd change only minimal things,' Sacchi blustered. He sneaked out through a side entrance at Milan's Linate airport the following day, while pressure mounted for him to quit. In *La Repubblica*, under the headline 'Sacchi, resigning is a duty', columnist Gianni Mura wrote, 'At least 15 million Italians watch each Azzurri match: you can't sell them fireflies for lanterns. Sacchi's unpopularity cannot depend only on bad journalists.' He survived, only to quit months later and return to Silvio Berlusconi's sleazy embrace at San Siro. But that didn't work out either.

5pm, 9 June 1996
Old Trafford, Manchester
Attendance: 37,300
Referee: David Elleray (England)

GERMANY 2 (Ziege 26, Möller 32)
CZECH REPUBLIC 0

GERMANY: Andy Köpke, Stefan Reuter, Christian Ziege, Jürgen Kohler (c) (Markus Babbel 14), Thomas Helmer, Matthias Sammer, Dieter Eilts, Andy Möller, Fredi Bobic (Thomas Strunz 65), Thomas Häßler, Stefan Kuntz (Oliver Bierhoff 83). **Manager:** Berti Vogts.

CZECH REPUBLIC: Petr Kouba, Radek Látal, Jan Suchopárek, Miroslav Kadlec (c), Michal Horňák, Radek Bejbl, Jiří Němec, Pavel Nedvěd, Pavel Kuka, Karel Poborský (Patrik Berger 46), Martin Frýdek (Radek Drulák 46). **Manager:** Dušan Uhrin.

Booked: Ziege (28), Möller (58), Babbel (59), Reuter (70), Häßler (77), Bejbl (20), Nedvěd (45+2), Kadlec (67), Drulák (67).

4.30pm, 11 June 1996
Anfield, Liverpool
Attendance: 35,120
Referee: Les Mottram (Scotland)

ITALY 2 (Casiraghi 5, 52)
RUSSIA 1 (Tsymbalar 21)

ITALY: Angelo Peruzzi, Roberto Mussi, Paolo Maldini (c), Luigi Apolloni, Alessandro Costacurta, Demetrio Albertini, Angelo Di Livio (Diego Fuser 62), Roberto Di Matteo, Pierluigi Casiraghi (Fabrizio Ravanelli 80), Alessandro Del Piero (Roberto Donadoni 46), Gianfranco Zola. **Manager:** Arrigo Sacchi.

RUSSIA: Stanislav Cherchesov, Omari Tetradze, Yuri Kovtun, Viktor Onopko (c), Yevgeni Bushmanov (Igor Yanovsky 46), Vladislav Radimov, Andrei Kanchelskis, Valeriy Karpin (Sergei Kiriakov 63), Igor Kolyvanov, Aleksandr Mostovoi, Ilya Tsymbalar (Igor Dobrovolsky 71). **Manager:** Oleg Romantsev.

Booked: Albertini (14), Donadoni (83), Onopko (8), Kolyvanov (31), Kovtun (82).

7.30pm, 14 June 1996
Anfield, Liverpool
Attendance: 37,320
Referee: Antonio López Nieto (Spain)

CZECH REPUBLIC 2 (Nedvěd 4, Bejbl 35)
ITALY 1 (Chiesa 18)

CZECH REPUBLIC: Kouba, Látal (Václav Němeček 88), Suchopárek, Kadlec (c), Horňák, Bejbl, Němec, Nedvěd, Kuka, Berger (Vladimír Šmicer 64), Poborský.

ITALY: Peruzzi, Mussi, Maldini (c), Apolloni, Costacurta, Albertini, Fuser, Dino Baggio (Amedeo Carboni 39), Ravanelli (Casiraghi 58), Enrico Chiesa (Zola 78), Donadoni.

Booked: Suchopárek (20), Látal (50), Kuka (59), Kadlec (90), Apolloni (7), Fuser (90+1). Sent off: Apolloni (29).

Chus Pereda of Spain (far left) shoots past USSR goalkeeper Lev Yashin in the 1964 final in Madrid, watched by the biggest ever attendance at any European Championship finals match

Football of the spheres: Jupp Heynckes of West Germany accelerates past Yuri Istomin of the USSR in the 1972 final in Brussels

Rob Rensenbrink of the Netherlands is shadowed by Czechoslovakia's Ján Pivarník during the stormy 1976 semi-final in Zagreb

West Germany's Bernd Schuster, the shining light of the 1980 finals, races away from the Netherlands' Willy van de Kerkhof in Naples

Danish dynamite: Søren Lerby in the thick of things against Spain in the classic 1984 semi-final in Lyon

Luis Arconada's fatal fumbling of Michel Platini's free kick costs Spain the big prize against France in the 1984 Final in Paris

Franz Beckenbauer surveys the Parkstadion panorama as West Germany sweep Denmark aside in Gelsenkirchen in 1988

The complete striker: Marco van Basten's predatory finishing buried England in Düsseldorf in 1988

Jean-Pierre Papin tucked away the only two chances that came his way at the 1992 finals, yet France still went home early

'The Danes were all over the place. There was no order': Denmark are euphoric after ambushing Germany in the 1992 final in Gothenburg

The dentist will see you now: Paul Gascoigne is deluged after his wonder-goal for England against Scotland at Wembley in 1996

Slaven Bilić's kick at Christian Ziege was one of many violent incidents that went unpunished as Germany overcame Croatia at Old Trafford in 1996

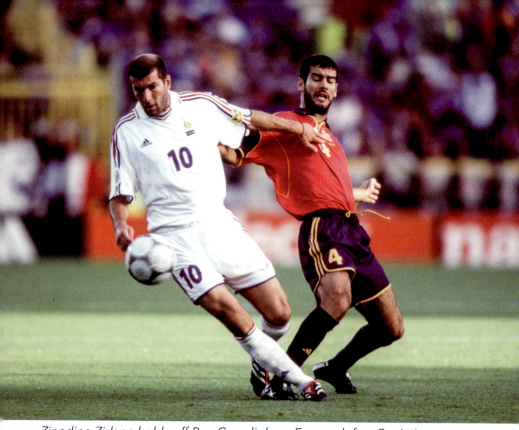

Zinedine Zidane holds off Pep Guardiola as France defeat Spain in a magnificent match in Brugge in 2000

Spot prize: Francesco Toldo saves Paul Bosvelt's penalty in Amsterdam to break Dutch hearts and send Italy into the final of Euro 2000

Euro 2004 ended as it began: with Greece humbling hosts Portugal. In the opening match in Porto, 19-year-old Cristiano Ronaldo flattens Giourkas Seitaridis for a penalty

The inspirational Pavel Nedvěd gives the performance of his life as the Czech Republic come back from 2-0 down to beat the Netherlands in Aveiro in 2004

Two-hit wonder: Andrei Arshavin of Russia all too briefly looked like the continent's best player at the 2008 finals

Fernando Torres of Spain is too quick for Germany's Philipp Lahm and Jens Lehmann in the 2008 final in Vienna

Handle with care: half the Italian team encircle Spanish playmaker Andrés Iniesta in Gdańsk in 2012

A distraught Cristiano Ronaldo weeps after being taken out early by France's Dimitri Payet in the 2016 final in Paris – but Portugal have the last laugh

3pm, 16 June 1996
Old Trafford, Manchester
Attendance: 50,760
Referee: Kim Milton Nielsen (Denmark)

GERMANY 3 (Sammer 56, Klinsmann 77, 90+1)
RUSSIA 0

GERMANY: Köpke, Reuter, Ziege, Babbel, Helmer, Sammer, Eilts, Möller (Strunz 87), Jürgen Klinsmann (c), Häßler (Steffen Freund 67), Bierhoff (Kuntz 85).

RUSSIA: Dmitri Kharin, Tetradze, Kovtun, Yuri Nikiforov, Onopko (c), Radimov (Karpin 46), Dmitri Khokhlov (Igor Simutenkov 66), Kanchelskis, Kolyvanov, Mostovoi, Tsymbalar.

Booked: Babbel (16), Bierhoff (32), Kanchelskis (13), Onopko (30).
Sent off: Kovtun (71).

7.30pm, 19 June 1996
Old Trafford, Manchester
Attendance: 53,740
Referee: Guy Goethals (Belgium)

GERMANY 0
ITALY 0

GERMANY: Köpke, Strunz, Ziege, Freund, Helmer, Sammer, Eilts, Möller (Marco Bode 89), Klinsmann (c), Häßler, Bobic.

ITALY: Peruzzi, Mussi, Carboni (Moreno Torricelli 76), Maldini (c), Costacurta, Albertini, Fuser (Di Livio 81), Di Matteo (Chiesa 67), Casiraghi, Zola, Donadoni.

Booked: Strunz (11), Casiraghi (18).
Sent off: Strunz (59).

7.30pm, 19 June 1996
Anfield, Liverpool
Attendance: 21,128
Referee: Anders Frisk (Sweden)

RUSSIA 3 (Mostovoi 49, Tetradze 54, Beschastnykh 85)
CZECH REPUBLIC 3 (Suchopárek 6, Kuka 19, Šmicer 88)

RUSSIA: Cherchesov, Tetradze, Sergei Gorlukovich, Nikiforov, Yanovsky, Karpin (c), Khokhlov, Radimov, Kolyvanov (Mostovoi 46), Simutenkov (Vladimir Beschastnykh 46), Tsymbalar (Igor Shalimov 67).

CZECH REPUBLIC: Kouba, Látal, Suchopárek, Luboš Kubík (c), Horňák, Bejbl, Němec, Nedvěd, Kuka (Šmicer 69), Berger (Němeček 90), Poborský.

Booked: Nikiforov (5), Radimov (26), Tsymbalar (28), Yanovsky (61), Nedvěd (60), Němec (77).

GROUP C	P	W	D	L	F	A	GD	Pts
GERMANY	3	2	1	0	5	0	+5	7
CZECH REPUBLIC	3	1	1	1	5	6	− 1	4
ITALY	3	1	1	1	3	3	0	4
RUSSIA	3	0	1	2	4	8	− 4	1

Germany and the Czech Republic qualified.

GROUP D
Denmark, Portugal, Croatia, Turkey

The weakest of the four groups witnessed a sprinkling of delightful football at the outset. Portugal were a joy to watch as they ran rings around Denmark at Hillsborough, with their mastery of midfield often making it seem as if they were playing with 13 or 14 men. 'This is the football everyone in Europe wants to watch,' said manager António Oliveira. 'We want to play in a way that people will applaud.'

But a moment of laziness gave the Danes a surprise lead in the first half. When Portuguese goalkeeper Vítor Baía's clearance hit the otherwise useless Mikkel Beck in the face and rebounded out to the left, Brian Laudrup hared after it, cut inside Paulinho Santos and thrashed home a wonderful shot for one of the best goals of the tournament.

Portugal resumed their silky onslaught. Luís Figo created space for himself in the box, but lifted his shot over the bar, while Peter Schmeichel saved impressively from Rui Costa's low free kick and made two even better stops from João Pinto, one in each half.

Portugal eventually equalised when António Folha's cross bounced in the Danish box and Ricardo Sá Pinto headed it in. But it was clear their tippy-tappy self-indulgence wouldn't be tolerated by better teams than Denmark, and they got two warnings near the end, when Brian Laudrup shot against Baía's legs and Claus Thomsen headed over.

Still, Portugal should have won. Near the end, Schmeichel suicidally charged off his line and collided with Marc Rieper, but Domingos spooned wide of an open goal. 'Desperdício,' sighed Lisbon newspaper *Record*, what a waste.

———

The much-touted Croatians suffered first-night nerves against Turkey in Nottingham, with all their stars failing to convince. The anonymous Zvonimir Boban was hooked before the hour, Robert Prosinečki was at his indolent worst, Davor Šuker spent the game diving, and Alen Bokšić faded after clashing heads with Vedat İnceefe.

This was Turkey's first taste of a tournament since 1954, and their 20,000 noisy supporters wanted to savour every second. 'It's like Istanbul in the town centre,' said one English Turk outside the City Ground. Those excellent fans had little to cheer in the rain; their team had no cutting edge up front, and there was some inevitability about Croatia's late winner.

Goran Vlaović was lucky to be alive, let alone playing: the previous September, he'd had a blood clot removed from his brain. Early on, Turkish keeper Rüştü Reçber thwarted him after Tolunay Kafkas's awful back-pass let him in. Now, Aljoša Asanović fed him and he nicked it past Rahim Zafer's lunge to give himself a clear run on goal. As Alpay Özalan resisted the temptation to take his legs, he ran around Rüştü and scored from a tight angle.

UEFA gave Alpay a Fair Play award for his sportsmanship, although he was later labelled a 'traitor' by less idealistic folk back home. Croatia were up and running, but only just.

======

Three days later, Turkey slumped to another defeat at the City Ground, against opponents who again looked emasculated in attack. Rui Costa mused beforehand that if Portugal could pick his Fiorentina team-mate Gabriel Batistuta, they would win Euro 96. Oliveira replied sharply that if he wasn't happy with his team-mates, he could get an Argentinian passport. But given Portugal's wastefulness here, you could see what he meant.

Turkey might have had two penalties when Saffet Sancaklı got sandwiched by two defenders and Manuel Dimas tripped Hakan Şükür. But for most of the day, they looked on as their opponents called the tune. In an incident that summed up all Portugal's strengths and weaknesses, Sá Pinto missed from six yards after Rui Costa danced past four Turks. Later, from Sá Pinto's flick-on, Hélder Cristóvão sliced shockingly wide.

Ultimately, it fell to Portugal's shaggy-haired stopper to make the difference: when a corner came out to Fernando Couto, he planted a low volley past Rüştü. The result eliminated Turkey, no surprise given their inability to trouble opposition goalkeepers.

======

Denmark looked there to be taken, but again Croatia were slow to move through the gears at Hillsborough. Indulged by referee Marc Batta, they committed several spiteful fouls in the first half. Mario Stanić went in high on Michael Schjønberg and stamped on Jes Høgh, while Boban booted Michael Laudrup in the family jewels.

Throughout, Denmark's fans knowingly sang Queen's 'We Are the Champions', but their strikerless team carried little threat. Henrik Larsen, the hero of 1992, blew their best opportunity when he headed tamely against Asanović's midriff.

After the interval, Šuker took over. Bony and pinched-looking, he was a referee's nightmare, continually trying to con them with simulation and exaggeration. He was also a world-class finisher. His penalty opened the scoring after Schmeichel bundled over Stanić, but it was the final ten minutes that made him a star.

First, after Igor Štimac and Brian Laudrup had both hit the woodwork, Boban slid in to convert Šuker's cross to make it 2-0. Then, from just inside the Danish half, Šuker hit a huge, booming shot that was dipping under the bar until Schmeichel got back to clutch it on the line. In the last minute, though, Šuker made Schmeichel pay: the goalkeeper had gone up for a corner before racing back to his goal, only to be left stranded as Šuker lifted an exquisite chip over him. At last everyone was getting to see the Croatia that had been hyped to hell for months.

======

Denmark could only survive if they beat Turkey by three and Croatia defeated Portugal. They fulfilled their part of the bargain at a sleepy Hillsborough, where the first 45 minutes passed off without incident.

After the break, Rüştü saved Rieper's header superbly, but was soon overwhelmed. Brian Laudrup took the ball around him after capitalising on Ogün's slip; Allan Nielsen stabbed in Michael Laudrup's pass following more Turkish hesitancy; and Alpay's outstretched leg diverted home another shot by Brian Laudrup after a fluid move. Rüştü should have been sent off late on when he handled outside his own box, but referee Nikolai Levnikov, knowing there was only a minute left, showed mercy.

Turkey's entire squad was home-based, and it showed, with Orhan Çıkırıkçı's stinging shot the only effort that tested Schmeichel. 'At least we've justified our place here. We weren't like Greece in the last World Cup,' said midfielder Abdullah Ercan, somewhat parochially.

======

'Germany would suit me fine next, because they play proper football,' Croatia's manager Miroslav Blažević blustered before resting seven players against Portugal. 'They'd be the best-suited team for us to play next.' At half-time, he hastily threw on three big guns, but by then Portugal were out of sight.

After four minutes, Sá Pinto missed Carlos Secretário's cross completely, but Figo chested it down and poked it under goalkeeper Marijan Mrmić. With Croatia looking totally uninterested, João Pinto side-footed home Portugal's second goal after Sá Pinto bicycle-kicked Couto's header into the goalmouth.

Even after their triple-bypass surgery at the break, Croatia remained useless. Boban, one of the reinforcements, complacently lost the ball in a dangerous position, leading to Domingos wasting a header. The third goal was a farce: Dubravko Pavličić's clearance hit Slaven Bilić in the back, Domingos ran on to the loose ball, and shot in off the far post. The two best teams had gone through, but Blažević would get his idiotic wish of playing the strongest side in the competition.

7.30pm, 9 June 1996
Hillsborough, Sheffield
Attendance: 34,993
Referee: Mario van der Ende (Netherlands)

DENMARK 1 (B. Laudrup 22)
PORTUGAL 1 (Sá Pinto 53)

DENMARK: Peter Schmeichel, Thomas Helveg, Jens Risager, Jes Høgh, Marc Rieper, Brian Steen Nielsen, Claus Thomsen (Torben Piechnik 83), Henrik Larsen (Kim Vilfort 90+1), Mikkel Beck, Michael Laudrup (c), Brian Laudrup. **Manager:** Richard Møller Nielsen.

PORTUGAL: Vítor Baía (c), Paulinho Maio dos Santos, Hélder Cristóvão, Fernando Couto, Manuel Dimas, Oceano Cruz (António Folha 37), Luís Figo (Domingos Paciência 62), Paulo Sousa (José Tavares 79), Ricardo Sá Pinto, Manuel Rui Costa, João Vieira Pinto. **Manager:** António Oliveira.

Booked: Risager (14), Helveg (30), Paulinho Santos (9), Oceano (24), Sá Pinto (41), Sousa (58), João Pinto (73).

7.30pm, 11 June 1996
City Ground, Nottingham
Attendance: 22,406
Referee: Serge Muhmenthaler (Switzerland)

CROATIA 1 (Vlaović 86)
TURKEY 0

CROATIA: Dražen Ladić, Mario Stanić, Robert Jarni, Igor Štimac, Slaven Bilić, Nikola Jerkan, Aljoša Asanović, Robert Prosinečki, Davor Šuker (Dubravko Pavličić 90), Zvonimir Boban (c) (Zvonimir Soldo 57), Alen Bokšić (Goran Vlaović 73). **Manager:** Miroslav Blažević.

TURKEY: Rüştü Reçber, Vedat İnceefe, Ogün Temizkanoğlu (c), Rahim Zafer, Alpay Özalan, Tolunay Kafkas (Saffet Sancaklı 89), Tugay Kerimoğlu, Abdullah Ercan, Hakan Şükür, Arif Erdem (Hami Mandirali 82), Sergen Yalcın. **Manager:** Fatih Terim.

Booked: Asanović (40), Boban (55), Soldo (90), Tolunay (31).

4.30pm, 14 June 1996
City Ground, Nottingham
Attendance: 22,670
Referee: Sándor Puhl (Hungary)

PORTUGAL 1 (Couto 66)
TURKEY 0

PORTUGAL: Baía (c), Paulinho Santos, Hélder, Couto, Dimas, Sousa, Figo, Folha (Tavares 46), Sá Pinto (Jorge Cadete 65), Rui Costa, João Pinto (Hugo Porfírio 77).

TURKEY: Rüştü, Vedat, Ogün (Rahim 46), Recep Çetin, Alpay, Oğuz Çetin (c) (Arif 69), Tugay, Abdullah, Hakan, Sergen, Saffet (Tolunay 63).

Booked: Paulinho Santos (45+1), Figo (58), Tavares (72), Abdullah (43), Vedat (65), Rahim (73), Tolunay (76).

6pm, 16 June 1996
Hillsborough, Sheffield
Attendance: 33,671
Referee: Marc Batta (France)

CROATIA 3 (Šuker 53 pen, 90, Boban 81)
DENMARK 0

CROATIA: Ladić, Stanić, Jarni, Štimac, Bilić, Jerkan, Asanović, Prosinečki (Mladen Mladenović 88), Šuker, Boban (c) (Soldo 82), Vlaović (Nikola Jurčević 82).

DENMARK: Schmeichel, Helveg (Jacob Laursen 46), Michael Schjønberg, Høgh, Rieper, B.S. Nielsen, Thomsen, Larsen (Stig Tøfting 69), Vilfort (Beck 59), M. Laudrup (c), B. Laudrup.

Booked: Stanić (20), Prosinečki (23), Vlaović (39).

4.30pm, 19 June 1996
Hillsborough, Sheffield
Attendance: 28,671
Referee: Nikolai Levnikov (Russia)

DENMARK 3 (B. Laudrup 50, A. Nielsen 69, Alpay 84 og)
TURKEY 0

DENMARK: Schmeichel, Helveg, Schjønberg (Larsen 46), Høgh, Rieper, B.S. Nielsen, Allan Nielsen, Thomsen, Erik Bo Andersen (Søren Andersen 88), M. Laudrup (c), B. Laudrup.

TURKEY: Rüştü, Vedat, Ogün, Recep (c) (Bülent Korkmaz 68), Alpay, Tugay, Tayfun Korkut, Abdullah, Hakan (Arif 46), Orhan Çıkırıkçı (Saffet 68), Hami.

Booked: Helveg (57), Larsen (81), Tugay (44), Tayfun (61), Rüştü (89).

4.30pm, 19 June 1996
City Ground, Nottingham
Attendance: 20,484
Referee: Bernd Heynemann (Germany)

PORTUGAL 3 (Figo 4, João Pinto 33, Domingos 82)
CROATIA 0

PORTUGAL: Baía (c), Carlos Secretário, Hélder, Couto, Dimas, Oceano, Figo, Sousa (Tavares 70), Sá Pinto (Domingos 46), Rui Costa (Pedro Barbosa 61), João Pinto.

CROATIA: Marijan Mrmić, Pavličić, Jarni (c), Dario Šimić, Bilić, Soldo, Mladenović (Asanović 46), Jurčević, Igor Pamić (Šuker 46), Prosinečki (Boban 46), Vlaović.

Booked: Pamić (10), Jarni (30), Pavličić (36).

GROUP D	P	W	D	L	F	A	GD	Pts
PORTUGAL	3	2	1	0	5	1	+4	7
CROATIA	3	2	0	1	4	3	+1	6
DENMARK	3	1	1	1	4	4	0	4
TURKEY	3	0	0	3	0	5	− 5	0

Portugal and Croatia qualified.

QUARTER-FINALS
England v Spain
France v Netherlands
Germany v Croatia
Portugal v Czech Republic

In Madrid, sports paper *Marca* let rip with a front-page screamer for the first quarter-final at Wembley: 'Los toros bravos contra las vacas locas!' England didn't quite play like mad cows, but in the three lions' den, Javier Clemente's bulls were superior throughout.

England survived three close calls in a one-sided first half. Manjarín put Kiko in to finish calmly under Seaman but the goal was ruled out for a tight offside, Julio Salinas shot home after some slick Spanish passing but got flagged despite Adams playing him onside, and when Manjarín himself raced through, his woeful second touch allowed Seaman to save.

Early in the second half, England got a fourth let-off when Alfonso wriggled past Gascoigne, who tripped him for a blatant penalty. Instead, absurdly, referee Marc Batta booked Alfonso for diving. For good measure, Gascoigne screamed abuse at him.

Eventually, England woke up. First, McManaman's header wouldn't come down for Sheringham, who poked it into Zubizarreta's hands. Then, after Adams's magnificent tackle stopped Caminero scoring, a quick English break saw Gascoigne present Shearer with a sitter which he booted into the stands at close range. Forgotten now, it was one of the worst misses of the competition.

In extra time, Spain still owned the ball, and Alfonso's shot was deflected inches wide by the colossus Adams – though Steve Stone might have had a penalty when Juanma López kicked him. England were dreading the shoot-out, but all four of their kicks were good, with Pearce celebrating his successful conversion by screaming so loudly that he seemed in danger of a stroke. Hierro almost broke the bar, and Seaman clinched it by saving Miguel Ángel Nadal's tame effort. The hosts were through without remotely deserving it.

Afterwards, Clemente lambasted Gascoigne, who had been stretching and jumping during the Spanish anthem. Gazza's crassness was echoed in the behaviour of some English fans afterwards, who taunted Spanish supporters outside Wembley. 'What fuels this ugly and xenophobic triumphalism – apart from alcohol? Crawl forward sections of the tabloid press,' wrote Glenn Moore in *The Independent*. The climate around England's exploits was now one of national hysteria.

That evening, at Anfield, more unearned luck sent France into the semi-finals at the Netherlands' expense. The 83rd minute of a tedious game was pivotal: when Marcel Desailly blatantly handled in the box, referee Antonio López Nieto gave a free kick instead. Phillip Cocu struck it hard, but Laurent Blanc's long leg deflected it on to the post.

The disappointing Bergkamp was hauled off after an hour, but with France as poor as they had been against Spain, the few chances in normal time all fell to the Dutch. Ronald de Boer headed Witschge's corner wide, Cocu blazed over when Bergkamp teed him up, and at the death Seedorf burst through to shoot straight at Lama.

In extra time, Zidane's clever reverse pass fell perfectly for Djorkaeff, whom Van der Sar foiled with one of the best saves of the competition. But there was something oddly inevitable about Seedorf being the only man to fail in the shoot-out, hitting his penalty much too close to Lama. France trudged on, boring everybody and impressing nobody.

=====

It was reported before the tournament that Croatia saw themselves as ambassadors for their newborn country. But their behaviour against Germany at Old Trafford made a mockery of that. Beforehand, Blažević declared, 'We'll fight against the German Stukas and Messerschmitts with kamikaze pilots,' and his team seemed childishly desperate to kick the Germans black and blue.

Germany weren't blameless – Klinsmann angrily hacked Vlaović after Robert Jarni stamped on his foot – but the filth flowed mostly in one direction. Referee Leif Sundell let the following incidents go without showing any card: Vlaović steaming into Reuter from behind; Štimac raking Möller's knee; Mehmet Scholl being flattened by Stanić; Eilts, Reuter and Boban clobbering Šuker, Asanović and Kuntz respectively; Boban's elbow gashing Steffen Freund's forehead; Štimac touching a linesman's face while protesting a throw-in award; and, worst of all, Bilić savagely kicking Ziege in the chest a few feet away from Sundell, who couldn't have missed it.

Klinsmann had clearly been targeted. Stanić barged him painfully in the back, and Štimac's two-footed lunge lamed him before half-time. But he stayed on long enough to put Germany in front. Sammer stormed upfield again, Nikola Jerkan inexplicably handled the bouncing ball in the box, and Klinsmann (gritting his teeth in pain) swept the penalty home before hobbling off.

That rarest of phenomena, German complacency, handed Croatia their equaliser early in the second half. Freund, played into trouble by Sammer's sloppy pass, saw Nikola Jurčević block his clearance; it fell kindly for the predator Šuker, who cleverly used the sole of his boot to drag the ball around Köpke before scoring. But Croatia's momentum was instantly destroyed when Štimac finally got his marching orders for another horrible tackle, on Scholl. Within a minute, Germany had their winner. Sammer and Bilić both lunged at Scholl's cross, and the German libero pounced to score with a ruthlessness Šuker would have admired.

Scholl should have made it 3-1 near the end, but kneed wide after Kuntz set him up. So Germany staggered on, counting their cuts and bruises as they faced a titanic semi-final against England without their inspirational captain.

At Villa Park that evening, a dire quarter-final between the Czechs and Portugal was adorned by one of the most astonishing goals ever witnessed in a major tournament. When Karel Poborský got the ball on the left early in the second half, inspiration seized him in the unlikeliest of ways.

Setting off on a seemingly doomed run, the winger burst between four Portuguese, somehow emerged from the red-and-green thicket with the ball still at his feet, and suddenly scooped an outlandish lob over the advancing Vítor Baía. The ball sailed maybe six yards in the air before dropping back to earth and landing in the back of the net, like a psychedelic remix of Šuker's goal against Denmark. Poborský was visibly as startled as anyone. 'I almost did it too well,' he reflected.

Portugal had been mugged, but could hardly complain. In the first half, Ricardo Sá Pinto put their best opportunity straight at Kouba. Not until the closing moments did they create another chance, which substitute Jorge Cadete headed wide – hindered by Domingos running into his path, much to his anger.

The goal aside, it was a sorry excuse for a match. Suchopárek set the tone, getting booked after 44 seconds for chopping João Pinto, and there were many more bad fouls in an unpleasant second half which the experienced referee Hellmut Krug just about kept control of. Late on, Látal was sent off for chopping Dimas; and Kuka, Bejbl and Suchopárek would miss the semi-final too. But that was the last thing on Czech minds.

3pm, 22 June 1996
Wembley Stadium, London
Attendance: 75,440
Referee: Marc Batta (France)

ENGLAND 0
SPAIN 0
England won 4-2 on penalties after extra time
Shoot-out: Shearer 1-0, Hierro hit bar, Platt 2-0, Amor 2-1, Pearce 3-1, Belsué 3-2, Gascoigne 4-2, Nadal saved.

ENGLAND: Seaman, Neville, Pearce, Platt, Adams (c), Southgate, McManaman (Barmby 109), Gascoigne, Shearer, Sheringham (Fowler 109), Anderton (Stone 109).

SPAIN: Zubizarreta (c), Belsué, Sergi, Alkorta (López 72), Abelardo, Hierro, Nadal, Amor, Kiko, Manjarín (Caminero 46), Salinas (Alfonso 46).

Booked: Neville (47), Abelardo (1), Belsué (40), Alfonso (50).

6.30pm, 22 June 1996
Anfield, Liverpool
Attendance: 37,465
Referee: Antonio López Nieto (Spain)

FRANCE 0
NETHERLANDS 0
France won 5-4 on penalties after extra time
Shoot-out: De Kock 0-1, Zidane 1-1, R. de Boer 1-2, Djorkaeff 2-2, Kluivert 2-3, Lizarazu 3-3, Seedorf saved, Guérin 4-3, Blind 4-4, Blanc 5-4.

FRANCE: Lama, Thuram, Lizarazu, Guérin, Blanc, Desailly, Deschamps (c), Karembeu, Loko (Dugarry 61, Pedros 80), Zidane, Djorkaeff.

NETHERLANDS: Van der Sar, Reiziger, Blind (c), Bogarde, De Kock, Cocu, Witschge (Youri Mulder 80), R. de Boer, Kluivert, Bergkamp (Seedorf 60), Cruyff (Winter 69).

Booked: Deschamps (7), Karembeu (48), De Kock (68), Kluivert (89), Bogarde (90).

3pm, 23 June 1996
Old Trafford, Manchester
Attendance: 43,412
Referee: Leif Sundell (Sweden)

GERMANY 2 (Klinsmann 21 pen, Sammer 59)
CROATIA 1 (Šuker 51)

GERMANY: Köpke, Reuter, Ziege, Babbel, Helmer, Sammer, Eilts, Möller, Bobic (Kuntz 46), Klinsmann (c) (Freund 39), Mehmet Scholl (Häßler 88).

CROATIA: Ladić, Stanić, Jarni, Štimac, Jerkan, Bilić, Asanović, Jurčević (Mladenović 78), Šuker, Boban (c), Vlaović.

Booked: Sammer (5), Klinsmann (7), Štimac (18).
Sent off: Štimac (57).

6.30pm, 23 June 1996
Villa Park, Birmingham
Attendance: 26,832
Referee: Hellmut Krug (Germany)

CZECH REPUBLIC 1 (Poborský 53)
PORTUGAL 0

CZECH REPUBLIC: Kouba, Látal, Suchopárek, Kadlec, Horňák, Němeček (c) (Berger 90), Bejbl, Němec, Kuka, Šmicer (Kubík 85), Poborský.

PORTUGAL: Baía (c), Secretário, Hélder, Couto, Dimas, Oceano (Folha 65), Figo (Cadete 82), Sousa, Sá Pinto (Domingos 46), Rui Costa, João Pinto.

Booked: Suchopárek (1), Šmicer (23), Látal (43), Bejbl (55), Kuka (69), Hélder (11), Sá Pinto (40), Secretário (59), João Pinto (90+1).

Sent off: Látal (82).

SEMI-FINALS
France v Czech Republic
England v Germany

Another day, another half-empty stadium, as France and the Czechs snoozed away the afternoon in the first semi-final in Manchester. The 43,877 attendance was a work of fiction (Old Trafford's Scoreboard End was empty), and the missing spectators showed prescience in staying away. At half-time on the BBC, Des Lynam sighed, 'We are un-thrilled.'

The Czechs had barely half their usual line-up available due to injuries and suspensions. Uhrin threw in five benchwarmers and greenhorns, giving defender Pavel Novotný an international debut, and just about got away with it against a French team who yet again played like zombies.

Nothing worth mentioning took place in the first hour. Thereafter, things briefly came alive as Djorkaeff first struck the bar with a dipping shot, then volleyed Zidane's cross too high. Otherwise, France yawned themselves to death, rolling the ball around in the sun as the Czechs stood off. Hugh McIlvanney, in the *Sunday Times*, called it 'a seemingly endless exercise in negativity calculated to make the sparse audience crave the thrills of watching car bumpers rust'.

Near the end of extra time, Blanc almost won it, but sliced Djorkaeff's cross wide. And so to penalties. Substitute Reynald Pedros, who had tried hard to breathe life into France's moribund attack, missed in sudden death by shooting against Kouba's legs. 'Of course I feel guilty,' he said. 'The rest of the team didn't have a go at me; I'm suffering my bad luck alone.' He was scapegoated for the result, much to Aimé Jacquet's relief.

The Czechs were a penalty away from the final. After some confusion around who would take it (Luboš Kubík, who had already scored, thought it was his turn again), captain Miroslav Kadlec reluctantly came forward. 'It was the longest walk I've ever made,' he recalled. 'It came into my head that I mightn't be able to watch TV for ten years.' He resisted the temptation to try a Panenka: 'I put it down the centre. It turned out well.'

France's tournament had died with a whimper. 'Les Bleus perdent sans jouer,' lamented *Libération*'s headline; the Blues lose without playing. Zidane, billed in advance as box-office gold, looked worn out from his marathon season with Bordeaux, including a 22-game, ten-month UEFA Cup run. Interviewed by *L'Équipe* later in 1996, he sounded jaded: 'I really needed to put all that [Euro 96] behind me. I was not saturated with football, I love it too much to be saturated, but I was so tired! And my morale was also low, because the Euros hadn't panned out for me as I wanted.'

The absent Eric Cantona had said that kids watching France's games would have headed for the gym rather than play football. 'Well, "Canto" says what he thinks,' replied Zidane, 'and he may be right.'

======

That evening, at a sold-out, pulsating Wembley, at last there was some real football as England and Germany fought each other like huge dinosaurs. And the hosts, lining up in denim-like grey/blue, got off to the start of their dreams. Köpke punched Ince's volley over the bar, Adams flicked Gascoigne's corner on, and the unmarked Shearer hurled himself at it to head his fifth goal of the tournament. But this German team didn't do panic attacks.

With Klinsmann crocked, Vogts had turned to 33-year-old Stefan Kuntz. He had scored only nine times in the Turkish league in 1995/96, but he was big, tough, technically reasonable and hard-working – and he had never finished on the losing side for Germany. In the 16th minute, he had his moment. Thomas Helmer, coming up from the back, played a one-two with Möller before sliding the ball across into the goalmouth, where Kuntz got in front of Stuart Pearce to side-foot home.

Andy Möller, captain for the night, was easily Germany's best player, tirelessly chasing and harrying like a demon. Eilts, too, did the work of two men as usual. But England were edging it. Shearer headed two good chances off target, berating himself for his wastefulness, and Reuter's thigh blocked the same shot-from-a-corner routine that England had used against the Dutch.

In the second half, Germany remained dangerous. Ziege and Scholl combined to set Eilts free on the left, and Helmer arrived late to lift the cross just over the bar. Ten minutes from the end of normal time, Pearce fouled Möller, then tried to 'help' him up (i.e. invade his personal space to rile him). Möller's angry reaction was met with a booking by referee Sándor Puhl, putting him out of the final. Later, David Platt should have been sent off for raking Sammer's knee, but Puhl didn't even show a yellow.

Extra time brought the potential horrors of the golden goal. With both teams now tiring – extraordinarily, Venables made no substitutions – chances began coming again. When Platt's pass freed McManaman to get to the byline, Köpke dived to cut out the cross, but Anderton beat him to it, hooking a shot against the post which rebounded into Köpke's arms.

Then it was time for English hearts to miss a beat. After Seaman palmed Möller's powerful shot over the bar, Kuntz soared to head the corner splendidly into the net – but Puhl disallowed it for shirt-pulling. The replays were inconclusive and, at any rate, a golden goal would have been cruel on either team.

Now came the pivotal moment of the tournament, and of one man's career. Shearer sent a cross skittering across the goalmouth; Köpke dived low, but it eluded him and came to Gascoigne, charging towards an open goal at the far post. Germany were sunk.

But the agony was Gazza's. He was fatally slow to draw back his left leg, his toecap missed the ball by millimetres, and it rolled out for a throw. All those late nights, those thousands of pints and kebabs, had come home to roost in one nanosecond. Had he made contact, England were in the final on home soil against the gutsy but unexceptional Czechs. Köpke, realising what had just happened, consoled him with a hug.

In the final seconds, Adams's header created confusion in the German box, but Eilts's hip deftly guided the ball to safety. 'Natürlich Eilts!' exclaimed ZDF's commentator, before comparing him to Nobby Stiles. But he recused himself from the penalties, telling Vogts, 'If I take one, it's no guarantee of anything.' Just before the end, Vogts had thrown on Thomas Strunz specifically to take one. Sammer realised the penalty would be Strunz's first touch of the night, so the defender did some ball-juggling before the shoot-out. In the event, he slammed his kick into the top corner.

Seaman got nowhere near any of Germany's other penalties either. Köpke was powerless for five of England's, but Gareth Southgate's soft, frightened little kick was at the ideal height for the goalkeeper. 'When he hit it, it was all wrong,' Venables wrote in his memoir. 'But at least he had the guts to take it.'

'And then,' recalled Helmer, 'Andy Möller put himself forward and said, "My turn now, hey?"' Up strode the midfielder to crown his magnificent display. He walloped his kick past Seaman, then strutted off, hands on hips, towards the 7,000 German fans occupying one corner of Wembley.

Venables said goodbye to the adoring media the next day at Bisham Abbey, patting away countless softballs. *The Independent*'s headline, 'Legacy of a modernist', was typical. Most papers glossed over the uncomfortable fact that England had only looked the part in two home fixtures out of five.

The Telegraph's Henry Winter enthused, 'Tactically, England have become far more sophisticated. Gone, surely, are the days of that dinosaur, the English stopper reared on red steak. Centre-halves must now control a ball and move it on accurately. Glenn Hoddle will doubtless build on such strong foundations. England's new coach will find himself with a group of players for whom fear has become an alien concept.' But England didn't even make the quarter-finals of France 98, and Hoddle was gone eight months later.

At least the result infuriated Piers Morgan. The *Mirror* editor, who had been publishing jingoistic drivel throughout the tournament, had previewed the Germany game with a front-page headline of 'Achtung! Surrender! For you, Fritz, ze Euro 96 championship is over!', photoshopping the Second World War helmets on to Gascoigne and Pearce. He bore considerable responsibility for the post-match violence. A massive riot broke out in Trafalgar Square, German-made cars were set ablaze all over London, and in Brighton, a Russian teenager almost died after being mistaken as German and getting stabbed five times. *Private Eye* didn't call the man 'Piers Moron' for nothing.

4pm, 26 June 1996
Old Trafford, Manchester
Attendance: 43,877
Referee: Les Mottram (Scotland)

CZECH REPUBLIC 0
FRANCE 0
Czech Republic won 6-5 on penalties after extra time
Shoot-out: Zidane 0-1, Kubík 1-1, Djorkaeff 1-2, Nedvěd 2-2, Lizarazu 2-3, Berger 3-3, Guérin 3-4, Poborský 4-4, Blanc 4-5, Rada 5-5, Pedros saved, Kadlec 6-5.

CZECH REPUBLIC: Kouba, Horňák, Kadlec, Karel Rada, Němeček (c), Němec (Kubík 84), Pavel Novotný, Nedvěd, Šmicer (Berger 46), Poborský, Drulák (Martin Kotůlek 70).

FRANCE: Lama, Thuram (Angloma 83), Lizarazu, Roche, Blanc (c), Guérin, Desailly, Sabri Lamouchi (Pedros 62), Loko, Zidane, Djorkaeff.

Booked: Nedvěd (77), Němeček (83), Kubík (97), Thuram (43), Roche (50), Lizarazu (64).

7.30pm, 26 June 1996
Wembley Stadium, London
Attendance: 75,862
Referee: Sándor Puhl (Hungary)

GERMANY 1 (Kuntz 16)
ENGLAND 1 (Shearer 3)
Germany won 6-5 on penalties after extra time
Shoot-out: Shearer 0-1, Häßler 1-1, Platt 1-2, Strunz 2-2, Pearce 2-3, Reuter 3-3, Gascoigne 3-4, Ziege 4-4, Sheringham 4-5, Kuntz 5-5, Southgate saved, Möller 6-5.

GERMANY: Köpke, Reuter, Babbel, Freund (Strunz 118), Helmer (Bode 110), Sammer, Eilts, Möller (c), Kuntz, Scholl (Häßler 77), Ziege.

ENGLAND: Seaman, Pearce, Adams (c), Southgate, Ince, Platt, McManaman, Gascoigne, Shearer, Sheringham, Anderton.

Booked: Reuter (46), Möller (80), Gascoigne (73).

FINAL
Germany v Czech Republic

England's party was over, and so was their interest. On his chat show *TFI Friday*, Chris Evans summed up the national mood when he childishly tore up two tickets for the final. At a non-packed Wembley, those locals who did turn up lent their support to the Czechs; and for a brief time, they looked likely to get what they wanted.

Germany's tired, torn squad was carrying two suspensions (Möller and Reuter), four long-term injuries (Kohler, Bobic, Mario Basler and René Schneider) and four starters who were manifestly unfit (Klinsmann, Eilts, Helmer and Ziege). Reserve goalkeepers Oliver Kahn and Oliver Reck were given outfield jerseys in case they had to be called upon. UEFA, shamefully, also allowed Berti Vogts to call up two new players: he picked one, midfielder Jens Todt. Dušan Uhrin was given the same option, but tactfully declined.

Germany shaded an uneventful first half, with Kuntz twice going close. First, his point-blank shot was half-saved by Kouba; as the ball dropped into the goal, Karel Rada hooked it off the line. Then, when Ziege's clever pass released Kuntz on the left, Kouba came out to save well.

Eilts, unable to run after colliding with Němec, retired at the interval. And on the hour came the final refereeing blunder of a tournament full of them. As Poborský sped along the right flank, Sammer nailed him just outside the box – but he landed in a heap inside the area, and referee Pierluigi Pairetto pointed to the spot. Instead of a free kick and a red card, a penalty and no card.

Patrik Berger, Sammer's Dortmund team-mate, stepped up. His powerful kick flew under Köpke's elbow. The Czechs were now half an hour away from being crowned champions of Europe. Vogts decided to roll the dice one last time, bringing on a striker who hadn't kicked a ball in the tournament since the first-round win over Russia.

Like Horst Hrubesch in 1980, Oliver Bierhoff was an international novice and known for being an aerial danger without getting credit for much else. 'I couldn't dribble, but I had other qualities,' he said. 'Some players can play anywhere; I had a smaller registry. At Euro 96, Mehmet Scholl sarcastically nicknamed me Speedy. I could live with that. I knew my limits.' But his first goal hardly changed the popular perception of him. When Ziege curled a free kick over from the right, he steamed in at the far post to equalise with a strong downward header.

Both teams almost won it in normal time. The unheralded Rada again intervened crucially, blocking Klinsmann's shot with his legs; at the death, Šmicer's drive saw Köpke go full-length to save. But now it was golden goal time again. Vogts had criticised it after the group stage: 'Imagine a player making a mistake in the 92nd minute, it's a goal for the opponents and the match is off. Very unfair. If UEFA want to be the standard-bearers of fair play, they should think how that poor guy would feel.'

After four more minutes of cagey sparring, that scenario came to pass. On the edge of the Czech box, with his back to goal and Kadlec harassing him, Bierhoff worked the ball on to his left foot before shooting on the turn. It went straight at Kouba, who let it squirm through his gloves and in, handing Germany the trophy in an instant. Not as bad as Luis Arconada in 1984, but not great. Kuntz, following up, didn't touch it ('I would've been offside'). History does not record how empathetically Vogts consoled Kouba afterwards.

Vogts's managerial reputation would take a battering in later years, but at Euro 96 he had the right stuff. Faced with a tough draw and countless injuries, he kept his head, maximised his resources and dragged Germany over the line. 'He managed to form a team that stuck together through thick and thin,' Jürgen Kohler recalled. 'Mentally, we were beasts.'

To Vogts went the glory. To his opposite number, the obscurity. No place on the big-ticket management carousel awaited the ruddy-faced Uhrin, whose next three jobs were in Saudi Arabia, Israel and Kuwait. At least his players lined their pockets, earning lucrative moves to Manchester United, Liverpool, Atlético Madrid and Lazio. One Czech newspaper captured the moment with a headline of 'Golden boys get silver'.

But if football had come home, it hadn't been worth the wait. The abiding memories of a disappointing tournament were of athleticism trumping talent in half-deserted stadia. England's five matches accounted for almost 30 per cent of the competition's total attendance of 1.27 million, and the standard of play vindicated the apathy. The entire knockout phase witnessed just seven goals from open play, the competition was stained with officiating howlers, and only a few individuals (Stoichkov, Shearer, Nedvěd, Poborský, Šuker, Sammer, the indefatigable Eilts) shone. Paolo Maldini somehow ended up in UEFA's team of the tournament despite giving the poorest performance of his career against the Czechs.

Still, the bottom line was the bottom line. At the end, UEFA's profits totalled £91.2m, five times the amount reaped from Euro 92. Never mind the quality, feel the wad.

7pm, 30 June 1996
Wembley Stadium, London
Attendance: 73,611
Referee: Pierluigi Pairetto (Italy)

GERMANY 2 (Bierhoff 73, 95)
CZECH REPUBLIC 1 (Berger 59 pen)
Germany won on the golden goal in extra time

GERMANY: Köpke, Babbel, Ziege, Eilts (Bode 46), Helmer, Sammer, Strunz, Scholl (Bierhoff 69), Kuntz, Klinsmann (c), Häßler.

CZECH REPUBLIC: Kouba, Suchopárek, Rada, Horňák, Kadlec (c), Bejbl, Němec, Nedvěd, Kuka, Berger, Poborský (Šmicer 88).

Booked: Helmer (63), Sammer (69), Ziege (91), Horňák (47).

2000

IF YOU can't outbid them, join them. On 14 July 1995, UEFA's executive committee took a leap into the unknown, awarding the tournament to two countries for the first time. Under the slogan of 'Football Without Frontiers', the Netherlands and Belgium were determined to get along. 'Ours was a marriage of love,' said Michel D'Hooghe, the KBVB president, comparing it to Japan and South Korea's chillier relationship at the 2002 World Cup.

To many observers' surprise, including senior UEFA officials, the final would take place not in Amsterdam but at Rotterdam's Feyenoord Stadion, known to locals as De Kuip (The Tub) for its atmospheric structure. Eyebrows were also raised at the selection of Charleroi's rickety Stade du Pays to host the most explosive fixture of the first round, England v Germany. 'If something happens there, that's a problem for my Dutch colleagues,' said D'Hooghe, before walking off whistling.

Reigning champions Germany were hardly in any state to keep it respectable, let alone retain their crown. Berti Vogts had gone, and his successor was picked after a pass-the-parcel recruitment process that saw the job offered to Roy Hodgson, Paul Breitner, Uli Stielike and, finally, to a long-forgotten figure from two decades earlier.

Erich Ribbeck, Jupp Derwall's assistant at Euro 80 and España 82, had spent the past ten years playing golf in Tenerife, earning him the sobriquet 'Robinson Crusoe' from the German press. His ageing, creaking team staggered over the qualification line with a nervy 0-0 draw in Munich against Turkey, who missed three chances in the first eight minutes alone. Germany survived, but the portents looked desperate.

England's passage to the finals was similarly underwhelming. Glenn Hoddle resigned as manager in February 1999 after making indefensible remarks about disabled people, but he had been under pressure anyway after losing in Stockholm and drawing at home to Bulgaria. The ebullient

Kevin Keegan took over and steered England into a play-off against Scotland. They seemed to sew it up in the first leg in Glasgow, Paul Scholes scoring twice, but the return at Wembley was another matter. Scotland swamped England's midfield and should have won by more goals than Don Hutchison's header. David Seaman's splendid save from Christian Dailly saw England through, but Keegan's boundless bonhomie wasn't covering up a multitude of sins.

England would be the only home nation at the finals. Northern Ireland were an also-ran in Germany's group, while Wales won in Copenhagen but did little else. Ireland, evolving into a good side under Mick McCarthy, saw qualification heartbreakingly snatched away after failing to clear a 94th-minute corner in Skopje, and then lost an ill-tempered play-off to Turkey on away goals.

After winning the World Cup at home, France got a severe cold shower in a group that went down to the wire. On the final night, expected to demolish Iceland at the Stade de France, they blew a 2-0 lead before winning 3-2. Russia were top of the group thanks to Valery Karpin's free kick against Ukraine – but with two minutes left in Moscow, Russian goalkeeper Aleksandr Filimonov gruesomely fumbled Andriy Shevchenko's set-piece into his own net, eliminating his team entirely and sending France through as group winners.

The jubilant Ukrainians, assuming they had done the hard part, promptly lost their play-off against Slovenia to Milenko Ačimovič's extraordinary 50-yard lob. Managed by Sampdoria legend Srečko Katanec, Slovenia had finished well behind Norway in a weak group and were perceived as a novelty outfit. Their neighbours Italy crept into the finals unimpressively: Dino Zoff, their 1982 hero, looked a cautious and uninspiring manager, but there was general acceptance that he wasn't working with quality materials, with Serie A clubs suffering numerous humiliating defeats in the 1999/2000 Champions League.

The Netherlands were in the mix simply by being at home, but they looked a flawed team. In two seasons as manager, Frank Rijkaard had won four friendlies out of 17. An 11-match winless run spanned all of 1999, including a home defeat by Morocco and a violent 5-5 draw with Belgium. 'You wouldn't judge Pavarotti by the way he sings in the shower,' Rijkaard protested. Still, the Dutch looked in better shape than their co-hosts. 'Nobody's giving us a chance,' sighed Belgium's cigar-chomping, whisky-savouring manager Robert Waseige. 'Sometimes, when I listen to the fans, it's as though we are not even involved.' But he and his team would play their part in a memorable, unforgettable tournament.

GROUP A
Germany, Romania, England, Portugal

Group A's opener between Germany and Romania witnessed one of the saddest sights in football history: 39-year-old Lothar Matthäus being left in the dust by 35-year-old Gheorghe Hagi as they slowly chased a loose ball. Matthäus had warmed up for Euro 2000 with three months at NY/NJ MetroStars in Major League Soccer. After this match, the *Frankfurter Allgemeine Zeitung* described him as 'ein sicherheitsrisiko', a security risk.

Under Erich Ribbeck, discipline had slipped so badly that corners were only practised in training if Germany's senior players felt like it. Before this match, the Bayern quartet of Jens Jeremies, Christian Ziege, Markus Babbel and Dietmar Hamann plotted to overthrow Ribbeck and install Matthäus, who, to his credit, told them he wanted no part of it.

In Liège, Germany's performance was almost unprecedentedly catastrophic, seeming to unfold in dreamlike slow motion. They didn't so much give Romania an easy ride as a chaise longue and a foot massage. Early on, Dorinel Munteanu released Adrian Ilie, who sprinted past the stumbling Thomas Linke. His low cross was gleefully thumped into the roof of the net by Viorel Moldovan at the back post.

With Germany's offside trap malfunctioning comically, Moldovan (twice) and Dan Petrescu missed more chances. At one point, Kahn had to race out of his goal and head to safety while his sweeper Matthäus was walking around in the centre circle. Rather than weathering the storm, Germany looked on helplessly as Romania failed to pocket the free gifts – and then abruptly equalised when Mehmet Scholl drove a fine shot into the top corner, its curve deceiving goalkeeper Bogdan Stelea.

But Romania continued to dominate. When Jens Nowotny's trip on Ilie in the box went unpunished, Ilie and Hagi protested so apoplectically that referee Kim Milton Nielsen booked them both. In the second half, Hagi was almost sent off for trying to get a German cautioned before Nielsen belatedly realised he was on a yellow. At the death, Kahn's save from Ilie put the goal at Moldovan's mercy – but he shot against Matthäus's legs before clubbing the rebound wide. Two points tossed down the drain for Romania, who seemed unprepared for Germany's awfulness.

═══

For all England's shortcomings, it was undeniable that Kevin Keegan's sunny-side-up enthusiasm had lifted spirits. After one of his press conferences, a German journalist exclaimed, 'I'm not used to this with our managers. This is more like *The Muppet Show*.'

His team got off to a flier against Portugal in Eindhoven. Jorge Costa lazily allowed David Beckham to retrieve a loose ball, stop it dead and sling in a cross to an unmarked Scholes, whose fine header flew in off the underside of the bar. Portugal responded brightly, with Seaman pushing Rui Costa's drive around the post, but England promptly sucker-punched them. Beckham, for once in his career, beat a man (Manuel Dimas) before dinking over another good cross for Steve McManaman to side-foot into the roof of the net for 2-0.

In these situations, responding quickly is crucial to survival. Portugal did so with a spectacular but strange goal. Luís Figo ran some 40 yards into England's half, then suddenly belted a long-range shot that flashed into the top corner as Seaman stood still. It was hailed as one of the goals of the tournament, but replays showed its trajectory was altered by Tony Adams's leg.

Self-belief flooded through Portuguese veins and soon they were level. A long sequence of passes heavily involving Abel Xavier and Paulo Bento ended with João Pinto glancing Rui Costa's centre in off the far post, for arguably the best team goal of the tournament.

Portugal's winner, midway through a second half they dominated, was a masterpiece of simplicity. Substitute Dennis Wise lost possession with his first touch, and Rui Costa slipped another lethal pass through to Nuno Gomes as Adams reacted too slowly. The striker's first touch wasn't good, but he had enough time to lift the ball over Seaman with his second. A bad night all round for Adams: a back injury ended his tournament minutes later.

Spanish newspaper *AS* memorably derided Seaman as 'a piece of meat with eyes' for being stationary on the first goal and slow off his line for the third. But the real story was the poise shown by Portugal in a predicament where most teams would have wet the bed.

=====

Expected to be a free-flowing feast, the meeting of Portugal and Romania in Arnhem was one long snooze. Romanian manager Imre Jenei changed his formation to smother Portugal's cultured midfield and Figo, so good against England, was kept quiet by young Cristian Chivu. Switching wings, he got nowhere against Cosmin Contra either.

But he still made the difference late on. The fourth official's board indicated three added minutes, but not until the fifth did Figo float a free kick on to the head of unmarked substitute Costinha, who nodded home. Jenei was stoical: 'We won't protest. A match isn't over until the referee says so.'

A caution for fouling João Pinto put the ageing Hagi out of the England game, but that wasn't necessarily the mortal wound to Romania that it once would have been. He did, however, manage one murderous drive in the 86th minute which Baía tipped over. The goalkeeper otherwise cut an inadequate figure, flapping at nearly everything, but his team could now take it easy against Germany. 'Normally, at this stage, we'd be on the beach or watching it on television,' said manager Humberto Coelho.

======

If Portugal-Romania had been a bore, England-Germany was the battle of the brontosauruses, the resistible force meeting the movable object. Heightening the sense that the match represented Euro 2000's nadir, violence flared in Charleroi before the game. Riot police used water cannon and tear gas on both sets of fans, with hundreds arrested.

England were the better of two poor teams, with Kahn pushing Michael Owen's header on to a post and punching away Scholes's half-volley. Beckham should have been sent off before half-time for elbowing Ulf Kirsten in the chest, but the indulgent Pierluigi Collina merely booked him. A pivotal decision, as it transpired. Early in the second half, he swept a set-piece into Germany's goalmouth. Nowotny and Jeremies let it bounce over to Alan Shearer, who stooped to head it back across Kahn and in.

Germany now squandered three big chances. Carsten Jancker shot over after holding off Sol Campbell, Scholl showed great close control before blazing across the face of the goal, and Kirsten met Sebastian Deisler's corner with a downward header which hit Seaman's leg before the huge Jancker, toppling like a chainsawed tree in a forest, stabbed wide.

The 20-year-old Steven Gerrard fouled Hamann nastily near the end, bragging afterwards that his Liverpool colleague had 'screamed like a girl'. Neither team had any business hanging around in this top-drawer tournament, and stumbled on to their final showdowns reeking of decay and disarray.

======

Euro 2000 is invariably cited as German football's Year Zero, the moment when it finally faced up to savage root-and-branch reform. When they say Euro 2000, however, what they're really referring to is what happened against Portugal B in Rotterdam, as a football giant hit rock bottom with unimaginable force.

Lumpen in attack and leaden in defence, Germany managed one good move all night, with Marco Bode hitting the post at the end of it. Within minutes, they were behind. Pauleta's deflected cross looped over Kahn, and Sérgio Conceição scuttled in to head home under the bar. He collapsed in a heap alongside Kahn in the back of the net, rubbing his eyes in apparent disbelief at German generosity.

Conceição's second was equally kindly gift-wrapped. He cut inside Linke and bypassed Hamann before shooting weakly at Kahn, but the goalkeeper made one of the worst errors of his long career, unaccountably letting it slip through his gloves.

In the very last meaningful act of a 150-cap international career, Matthäus lost the ball to set up Portugal's third. Capucho played Conceição in, and he hoovered up his hat-trick with a fine low shot. Paulo Rink took cheap revenge in stoppage time, forearm-smashing him in the mouth.

Ribbeck resigned immediately, returning to his Spanish bolthole. It was Germany's biggest European Championship defeat, and their worst showing in any tournament since the 1938 World Cup. Since then, every other German manager had won the World Cup or the European Championship, or both; Ribbeck couldn't even get out of a first-round group. Ruhr Valley steel had never buckled so softly.

Rudi Völler later defied the odds by dragging most of the same players to the 2002 World Cup Final. For the moment, however, they were the laughing stock of Europe. 'All of Europe is laughing at our "heroes": thank God the suffering is over,' lamented Cologne paper *Express*. In a 17-page analysis, *Kicker* concluded that 14 of the squad shouldn't play international football again. *Der Spiegel* lamented, 'One got a sense that most of these wealthy drips didn't understand what had happened. They didn't comprehend the emotional embarrassment. They never took the national team seriously. Germany was just another club to them, one which paid badly and had a laughable coach. The crash of Rotterdam was a shock for which there were no excuses. No referee was guilty, no bad weather, no hostile crowd: only German football itself.'

Bild upped the ante, running a front page of Zinedine Zidane alongside a giant bratwurst in a Germany strip. 'This is a footballer,' said the headline, 'and this is a German footballer.' Weeks later, in circumstances that might politely be described as murky, FIFA awarded Germany the 2006 World Cup. 'We can no longer play,' wrote columnist Matthias Geyer, 'but in organisation we're still world-class.'

———

'We've always done well against England,' observed Viorel Dinu Moldovan, who had scored in his country's win over them in Toulouse two years earlier. 'They don't have special gifts. They're dangerous from free kicks and Beckham crosses well, but they play predictable football.' And Romania looked better without the suspended Hagi, freed from their apparent contractual obligation to funnel every move through his ageing limbs.

When Seaman got injured in the warm-up, Nigel Martyn stepped into England's goal at a few minutes' notice. He had already saved from Ilie and Moldovan before Chivu's high ball ballooned over him, thudded against the far post and rebounded in. Chivu had clearly been targeting Moldovan, but this would do.

But Romania, brittle as well as skilful, lost their concentration before the interval. Paul Ince burst into the box, Chivu hacked him down, and Shearer rifled home the penalty for his 30th and final international goal. In first-half stoppage time, things looked even better for England. Scholes's wonderful pass sent Owen skipping through a flimsy offside trap to beat Stelea to the ball and slot it in from an angle, like a budget remake of his 1998 wonder-strike against Argentina.

'At half-time, I asked the team to attack more,' Jenei recalled. 'I'd noticed England had big problems in goal and central defence.' So it proved. Shortly after half-time, Martyn punched Petrescu's cross out to Munteanu, loitering outside the box. The veteran midfielder chested it, took aim and volleyed it home precisely; a golden moment for an excellent and underrated player.

Gritting their teeth, Keegan's team tried to grind out the draw they needed. Romania ran out of ideas and could only create two more half-chances, both spurned by Adrian Mutu. But then, for the second tournament running, they cut the legs from under England in the dying moments. Or, rather, a Romanian had his legs cut from under him, when Moldovan accelerated into the box and was clumsily felled by Phil Neville. Penalty.

'Our usual taker was Hagi, who was suspended,' Jenei said. 'Second choice was Munteanu. But Ioan Ganea, a special character, so to speak, grabbed the ball. I said to myself, "Well, if you take on such a responsibility, it's all yours." He was very sure of himself. He couldn't miss.' And he didn't.

There was no hooliganism from England's fans this time – but no wit, steadiness or basic *savoir faire* from their players. 'Can we pass it better? Can we control a game? No,' sighed Keegan. Richard Williams observed in *The Guardian*, 'Like the Portuguese, the Romanians were on speaking terms with the ball, while the English – like the Germans – just tried to kick it from A to B.'

In *The Independent*, James Lawton predicted, 'Sooner or later, Kevin Keegan takes the fall. We can be sure about this. It is the easiest option. The team boss comes and goes – and the whole wretched caravan lurches on ever more deeply into the desert.' Four months later, after Germany sank England in the last match at the old Wembley, Keegan resigned while conferring with FA chief David Davies in a toilet cubicle: a busted flush in more ways than one.

6pm, 12 June 2000
Stade Maurice Dufrasne, Liège
Attendance: 28,500
Referee: Kim Milton Nielsen (Denmark)

GERMANY 1 (Scholl 28)
ROMANIA 1 (Moldovan 5)

GERMANY: Oliver Kahn, Markus Babbel, Christian Ziege, Thomas Linke (Marko Rehmer 46), Jens Nowotny, Lothar Matthäus (Sebastian Deisler 78), Jens Jeremies, Thomas Häßler (Dietmar Hamann 73), Paulo Rink, Oliver Bierhoff (c), Mehmet Scholl. **Manager:** Erich Ribbeck.

ROMANIA: Bogdan Stelea, Dan Petrescu (Cosmin Contra 69), Liviu Ciobotariu, Iulian Filipescu, Cristian Chivu, Gheorghe Popescu, Constantin Gâlcă, Dorinel Munteanu, Viorel Moldovan (Ionuț Lupescu 85), Gheorghe Hagi (c) (Adrian Mutu 73), Adrian Ilie. **Manager:** Imre Jenei.

Booked: Ilie (41), Hagi (41).

8.45pm, 12 June 2000
Philips Stadion, Eindhoven
Attendance: 31,500
Referee: Anders Frisk (Sweden)

PORTUGAL 3 (Figo 22, João Pinto 37, Gomes 59)
ENGLAND 2 (Scholes 3, McManaman 18)

PORTUGAL: Vítor Baía (c), Abel Xavier da Silva, Jorge Costa Almeida, Fernando Couto, Manuel Dimas, Paulo Bento, José Luís Vidigal, Luís Figo, Nuno Soares 'Gomes' (Nuno Gonçalves 'Capucho' 89), Rui Manuel Costa (Roberto Deus Severo 'Beto' 85), João Vieira Pinto (Sérgio Conceição 75). **Manager:** Humberto Coelho.

ENGLAND: David Seaman, Gary Neville, Phil Neville, Sol Campbell, Tony Adams (Martin Keown 82), Paul Ince, David Beckham, Paul Scholes, Alan Shearer (c), Michael Owen (Emile Heskey 46), Steve McManaman (Dennis Wise 58). **Manager:** Kevin Keegan.

Booked: Baía (89), Ince (44).

6pm, 17 June 2000
GelreDome, Arnhem
Attendance: 18,200
Referee: Gilles Veissière (France)

PORTUGAL 1 (Costinha 90+5)
ROMANIA 0

PORTUGAL: Baía (c), Carlos Secretário, Jorge Costa, Couto, Dimas, Bento, Vidigal, Figo, Gomes (Ricardo Sá Pinto 56), Rui Costa (Francisco da Costa 'Costinha' 87), João Pinto (Conceição 56).

ROMANIA: Stelea, Contra, Chivu, Filipescu, Popescu, Gâlcă, Petrescu (Florentin Petre 64), Munteanu, Moldovan (Ionel Ganea 69), Hagi (c), Ilie (Laurențiu Roşu 78).

Booked: Figo (30), Hagi (16), Petrescu (22), Contra (27).

8.45pm, 17 June 2000
Stade du Pays de Charleroi, Charleroi
Attendance: 27,700
Referee: Pierluigi Collina (Italy)

ENGLAND 1 (Shearer 53)
GERMANY 0

ENGLAND: Seaman, G. Neville, P. Neville, Campbell, Keown, Ince, Beckham, Scholes (Nick Barmby 71), Shearer (c), Owen (Steven Gerrard 61), Wise.

GERMANY: Kahn (c), Babbel, Ziege, Deisler (Michael Ballack 72), Nowotny, Matthäus, Jeremies (Marco Bode 78), Hamann, Carsten Jancker, Scholl, Ulf Kirsten (Rink 70).

Booked: Beckham (41), Jeremies (43).

8.45pm, 20 June 2000
De Kuip, Rotterdam
Attendance: 45,000
Referee: Dick Jol (Netherlands)

PORTUGAL 3 (Conceição 35, 54, 71)
GERMANY 0

PORTUGAL: Pedro Espinha (Joaquim da Silva 'Quim' 90), Beto, Jorge Costa, Couto (c), Rui Jorge Dias, Paulo Sousa (Vidigal 72), Costinha, Capucho, Sá Pinto, Pedro Resendes 'Pauleta' (Gomes 67), Conceição.

GERMANY: Kahn (c), Rehmer, Linke, Nowotny, Hamann, Matthäus, Ballack (Rink 46), Scholl (Häßler 60), Jancker (Kirsten 69), Deisler, Bode.

Booked: Beto (26), Ballack (25), Jancker (26), Deisler (87), Rink (90+1).

8.45pm, 20 June 2000
Stade du Pays de Charleroi, Charleroi
Attendance: 27,000
Referee: Urs Meier (Switzerland)

ROMANIA 3 (Chivu 22, Munteanu 48, Ganea 89 pen)
ENGLAND 2 (Shearer 41 pen, Owen 45+4)

ROMANIA: Stelea, Contra, Chivu, Filipescu, Gâlcă (Roşu 68), Popescu (c) (Miodrag Belodedici 32), Petrescu, Munteanu, Moldovan, Mutu, Ilie (Ganea 74).

ENGLAND: Nigel Martyn, G. Neville, P. Neville, Campbell, Keown, Ince, Beckham, Scholes (Gareth Southgate 81), Shearer (c), Owen (Heskey 66), Wise (Barmby 75).

Booked: Chivu (18), Petrescu (40), Contra (44), Ilie (45+1), Filipescu (71), Shearer (64).

GROUP A	P	W	D	L	F	A	GD	Pts
PORTUGAL	3	3	0	0	7	2	+5	9
ROMANIA	3	1	1	1	4	4	0	4
ENGLAND	3	1	0	2	5	6	− 1	3
GERMANY	3	0	1	2	1	5	− 4	1

Portugal and Romania qualified.

GROUP B
Belgium, Sweden, Italy, Turkey

This being Belgium, the opening ceremony in Brussels came with a touch of the surreal. Rather than glasses of water perched atop umbrellas or giant bags of mayonnaise-coated chips, we got Michelin men on stilts and the world's largest mannequin booting a massive football around. After that, Belgium-Sweden looked an unappetising contest on paper, but it wasn't bad on grass.

The Belgians, attacking vibrantly in front of a noisy home crowd, got a lucky break before half-time when Sweden's veteran right-back Roland Nilsson shipped a blow to the head. Within moments, Bart Goor robbed him, charged into the box and drilled a low shot under Magnus Hedman. Nilsson retired at half-time, his tournament over.

The second half began with another Belgian bang: Branko Strupar fed Émile Mpenza, who handled to bring the ball under control, then almost broke the net with a right-foot ripper. 'I don't think it was a handball, I know it was,' said Hedman. 'My eyes don't lie.' But it happened quickly enough for referee Markus Merk to be forgiven.

With unsung anchorman Yves Vanderhaeghe giving the performance of his life (Brussels paper *Le Soir* dubbed him 'l'aspirateur mouscronnois', the hoover from Mouscron), it was all going too well for Belgium. Their goalkeeper soon brought them back to earth with an astonishing gaffe. Receiving Philippe Léonard's back-pass, Filip De Wilde stood on the ball in his own goalmouth, presenting Johan Mjällby with an empty net. 'It was like the whole world collapsed,' he babbled.

But he made up for it by saving impressively from Freddie Ljungberg in a one-on-one. Late on, the outcome was sealed when Patrik Andersson, booked in the first half after whacking Mpenza, was shown a straight red for an even worse foul on Goor. The Belgian press went temporarily mad, with headlines of 'Europhoria' and 'Belgium goes into orbit'; they were wise to milk it while it lasted.

===

Gianluigi Buffon's hand injury, a headache for Dino Zoff, also opened the door for Francesco Toldo. The Fiorentina goalkeeper would have a tournament to remember, but got off to a nervy start against Turkey in Arnhem. In only the second minute, he looked on aghast as Ogün Temizkanoğlu's hopeful 60-yard punt almost bounced all the way in.

For Italy, Antonio Conte was a constant menace and far more of a threat than the sunken-cheeked Filippo Inzaghi, who spurned a headed sitter. When another wayward Inzaghi effort came off Alpay Özalan's legs, Conte improvised brilliantly to score with a close-range overhead kick.

But Turkey were a different animal from the hesitant debutants of 1996, and their equaliser owed everything to Toldo's jitters. As he tried to punch away Sergen's free kick, Okan Buruk (5ft 6.5in) embarrassingly beat him (6ft 5in) to it with a downward header.

Inzaghi, enduring a nightmare, then squandered a one-on-one with Rüştü Reçber – but had the last laugh after hitting the deck when Ogün shouldered him legally. Hugh Dallas, a referee known for unexpected decisions in Scottish football, gave a penalty which Inzaghi converted before running off howling like a madman, as if he had somehow silenced his critics.

Substitute Alessandro Del Piero could have scored two more, hitting the underside of the bar from a free kick and seeing Alpay deflect his shot on to the post. Italy deserved the win, but their defending was 'often so generous it betrays a glorious tradition', noted *The Guardian*. Watch this space.

Three nights later, they instantly blitzed the co-hosts in Brussels. In the second minute, Conte missed with a volley. In the fifth, De Wilde saved superbly from Paolo Maldini and Inzaghi at close range. In the sixth, Belgium buckled: Albertini chipped a free kick into the box, and the hair-banded playboy Francesco Totti eluded Nico Van Kerckhoven to head home.

But, as was their wont, Italy sat back, allowing Belgium to pepper their goal. Goor hit the bar, while Toldo repelled Mpenza's low drive, Wilmots's point-blank shot, Lorenzo Staelens's half-volley and Nilis's swerving free kick. Italy were looking shaky until, on 66 minutes, Stefano Fiore popped up with one of the best goals of the competition, playing a neat one-two with Inzaghi (otherwise useless again) and curving an exquisite shot beyond De Wilde.

As Belgium lost heart, Italy could have won by 3-0 (Joos Valgaeren headed into his own net, but Marco Delvecchio had fouled him), or even 4-0 (Del Piero almost caught De Wilde out with a lobbed free kick). Without looking entirely convincing, they were already through.

More like an arm-wrestle than a football match, Turkey and Sweden's hideous goalless stalemate in Eindhoven was notable only for the worst foul of Euro 2000, by Johan Mjällby on Muzzy Izzet in the second half, which referee Dick Jol bizarrely let go. Jol later booked Mjällby for kicking the ball away.

Turkey took 71 minutes to trouble Hedman, who beat away Sergen's drive before Okan, following up, shot over. Sweden were better, just about. Kennet Andersson's free kick and angled shot tested Rüştü, who also saved well at Ljungberg's feet. Henrik Larsson, making his first start since his October 1999 leg break, was understandably quiet. Both teams were booed off at the end. 'We're making progress, but at the speed of a turtle,' observed one Istanbul paper.

=====

Against Italy, Sweden finally went for it. Mjällby's header was cleared off the line by Angelo Di Livio before Larsson sent Ljungberg through to shoot wastefully wide, his third one-on-one miss in three games. Then, against the run of play, the shaven-headed Luigi Di Biagio headed in Del Piero's near-post corner.

Sweden kept trying, with Larsson their driving force. Getting 90 minutes under his belt against Turkey had been a tonic for him, and he played superbly here, bringing Sweden level with a great goal. Kennet Andersson's slide-rule pass saw him stay onside, dance past Toldo and roll the ball in.

But Sweden weren't quarter-final material, and Italy saw them off late on. After Daniel Andersson lost the ball cheaply in his own half, Vincenzo Montella fed Del Piero, who tricked Olof Mellberg with a drag-back before shooting past Hedman. Rough on Larsson, but not on the rest.

=====

Belgium would curse their failure to bury Turkey in a one-sided opening spell in Brussels. Mpenza blazed wide twice in the first three minutes before later having a goal chalked off for offside, Rüştü blocked Nilis's angled drive, and Goor's shot flicked off Fatih Akyel and missed by inches.

But Turkey survived, and punished Belgium in stoppage time at the end of the half (added on because of referee Kim Milton Nielsen's thigh injury). Alpay's high ball soared into the evening sky, bounced in the Belgian box and went up in the air again. De Wilde mistimed his jump against the 6ft 3in Hakan Şükür, and was in no-man's-land as the striker headed into the empty net. Afterwards, Waseige pointedly refused to blame his goalkeeper: 'The ball came down very slowly.' Isaac Newton was unavailable for comment.

In the second half, Mpenza squandered the two chances that would have seen Belgium home, aiming a flying header too close to Rüştü, then putting another wide. And when Belgium's defence pushed up in a suicidally high line, Tayfur unlocked the door by finding the tiny Suat Kaya, whose low cross from the right was on a plate for Hakan.

De Wilde, whose tournament was nothing if not eventful, flattened Arif Erdem with a WWE-style clothesline near the end and was sent off, forcing defender Éric Deflandre to go in goal because Waseige had used all his subs. 'Euro 2000 was a real fiasco for me,' De Wilde reflected in 2020. 'Whiskey didn't help me forget my schoolboy errors.'

8.45pm, 10 June 2000
Stade Roi Baudouin, Brussels
Attendance: 46,700
Referee: Markus Merk (Germany)

BELGIUM 2 (Goor 43, É. Mpenza 46)
SWEDEN 1 (Mjällby 53)

BELGIUM: Filip De Wilde, Eric Deflandre, Philippe Léonard (Nico Van Kerckhoven 72), Lorenzo Staelens (c), Joos Valgaeren, Yves Vanderhaeghe, Bart Goor, Gert Verheyen (Jacky Peeters 88), Lokonda 'Émile' Mpenza, Marc Wilmots, Branko Strupar (Luc Nilis 69). **Manager:** Robert Waseige.

SWEDEN: Magnus Hedman, Roland Nilsson (Teddy Lučić 46), Patrik Andersson (c), Joachim Björklund, Olof Mellberg, Johan Mjällby, Niclas Alexandersson, Daniel Andersson (Yksel Osmanovski 70), Kennet Andersson, Jörgen Petterson (Henrik Larsson 50), Freddie Ljungberg. **Managers:** Lars Lagerbäck and Tommy Söderberg.

Booked: Verheyen (65), Nilis (77), Van Kerckhoven (90), P. Andersson (45).
Sent off: P. Andersson (81).

2.30pm, 11 June 2000
GelreDome, Arnhem
Attendance: 22,500
Referee: Hugh Dallas (Scotland)

ITALY 2 (Conte 52, Inzaghi 70 pen)
TURKEY 1 (Okan 61)

ITALY: Francesco Toldo, Gianluca Zambrotta, Paolo Maldini (c), Alessandro Nesta, Fabio Cannavaro, Gianluca Pessotto (Mark Iuliano 62), Demetrio Albertini, Antonio Conte, Filippo Inzaghi, Francesco Totti (Angelo Di Livio 83), Stefano Fiore (Alessandro Del Piero 75). **Manager:** Dino Zoff.

TURKEY: Rüştü Reçber, Tayfur Havutçu, Ogün Temizkanoğlu (c), Fatih Akyel, Alpay Özalan, Ümit Davala (Tugay Kerimoğlu 76), Okan Buruk (Ergün Penbe 88), Tayfun Korkut, Hakan Şükür, Sergen Yalçın (Arif Erdem 81), Abdullah Erçan. **Manager:** Mustafa Denizli.

8.45pm, 14 June 2000
Attendance: Stade Roi Baudouin II, Brussels
Attendance: 44,500
Referee: José María García Aranda (Spain)

ITALY 2 (Totti 6, Fiore 66)
BELGIUM 0

ITALY: Toldo, Zambrotta, Maldini (c), Nesta, Cannavaro, Iuliano, Albertini, Conte, Inzaghi (Marco Delvecchio 77), Totti (Del Piero 63), Fiore (Massimo Ambrosini 83).

BELGIUM: De Wilde, Deflandre, Van Kerckhoven (Marc Hendrikx 46), Staelens (c), Valgaeren, Vanderhaeghe, Goor, Verheyen (Mbo Mpenza 67), É. Mpenza, Wilmots, Strupar (Nilis 58).

Booked: Conte (44), Zambrotta (45+2), Wilmots (70).

8.45pm, 15 June 2000
Philips Stadion, Eindhoven
Attendance: 28,510
Referee: Dick Jol (Netherlands)

SWEDEN 0
TURKEY 0

SWEDEN: Hedman, Gary Sundgren, Lučić, Björklund, Mellberg, Mjällby (c), Alexandersson (Anders Andersson 63), Håkan Mild, K Andersson (Pettersson 46), Larsson (Magnus Svensson 78), Ljungberg.

TURKEY: Rüştü, Ümit (Tayfun 45), Ogün (c) (Tugay 59), Fatih, Alpay, Hakan Ünsal, Okan, Muzzy Izzet (Sergen 58), Hakan Ş, Arif, Suat Kaya.

Booked: Mjällby (68), Suat (5).

8.45pm, 19 June 2000
Philips Stadion, Eindhoven
Attendance: 29,500
Referee: Vítor Melo Pereira (Portugal)

ITALY 2 (Di Biagio 39, Del Piero 88)
SWEDEN 1 (Larsson 77)

ITALY: Toldo, Ciro Ferrara, Maldini (c) (Nesta 42), Iuliano (Cannavaro 46), Paolo Negro, Pessotto, Di Livio (Fiore 64), Ambrosini, Vincenzo Montella, Del Piero, Luigi Di Biagio.

SWEDEN: Hedman, Mellberg, P. Andersson (c), Björklund, Tomas Gustafsson (K. Andersson 75), Mjällby (D. Andersson 56), Svensson (Alexandersson 52), Mild, Osmanovski, Larsson, Ljungberg.

8.45pm, 19 June 2000
Stade Roi Baudouin II, Brussels
Attendance: 43,000
Referee: Kim Milton Nielsen (Denmark), replaced by Günter Benkö (Austria) in the 41st minute

TURKEY 2 (Hakan Ş 45+2, 70)
BELGIUM 0

TURKEY: Rüştü, Ogün (c), Fatih, Alpay, Tayfun, Suat, Abdullah, Tugay (Tayfur 37), Hakan Ş, Okan (Ergün 77), Arif (Osman Özköylü 87).

BELGIUM: De Wilde, Deflandre, Van Kerckhoven, Staelens (c), Valgaeren, Vanderhaeghe, Goor (Hendrikx 60), Verheyen (Strupar 63), É. Mpenza, Wilmots, Nilis (Gilles De Bilde 79).

Booked: Tayfun (50), Osman (88), Vanderhaeghe (44), É. Mpenza (63).
Sent off: De Wilde (84).

GROUP B	P	W	D	L	F	A	GD	Pts
ITALY	3	3	0	0	6	2	+4	9
TURKEY	3	1	1	1	3	2	+1	4
BELGIUM	3	1	0	2	2	5	−3	3
SWEDEN	3	0	1	2	2	4	−2	1

Italy and Turkey qualified.

GROUP C
Spain, Norway, Slovenia, Yugoslavia

With tiki-taka's gleaming geometrics still almost a decade away, Spain were far less than the sum of their photogenic, big-name parts. Against the crude Norwegians in Rotterdam, they predictably came unstuck.

Though Egil Olsen was long gone, his countrymen still revelled in being reviled. They had three good forwards in Ole Gunnar Solskjær, Tore André Flo and Steffen Iversen, but Nils Johan Semb's ugly long-ball tactics seemed designed to starve them of the ball. And yet, it worked. Pep Guardiola was permitted to weave pretty patterns in midfield, but his final pass always found a white shirt; and Deportívo La Coruña's Fran 'played so stiffly that at one point he appeared to hyperventilate', as one Spanish broadsheet put it.

Solskjær headed André Bergdølmo's cross on to the bar in the first half, but Norway hardly had another sniff until their grotesque 66th-minute winner. Goalkeeper Thomas Myhre thumped a monumental free kick upfield towards the Spanish box, and his opposite number José Molina yelled, 'It's mine, it's mine!' at defender Paco Jémez while charging out to punch. The tall Iversen got there ahead of him, sending a back-header looping into the unguarded goal.

Spain had averaged more than four goals per game in the qualifiers, but were now impotent against a strong defence, even though Norway had lost the magisterial Ronny Johnsen to injury. Myhre saved from Gaizka Mendieta at his near post and Raúl headed Guardiola's cross badly off target, but they were resorting to desperate high balls long before the end. 'A magnificent festival of football,' sniggered one Oslo paper's headline.

'Maybe I shouldn't have gone for that ball, but that's the way I play, and I'll die with it,' Molina babbled. 'Only God makes no mistakes. This has been a blow. I'm fucked, of course. All life has prepared me for this moment, and in the first game I'm in the shit.' He never played for Spain again.

———

Little was expected from Slovenia except the stereotypical small-nation virtues of courage and blanket defence. Yugoslavia knew them well, and not just because of geography: Vujadin Boškov had coached Slovenia's manager Srečko Katanec at Sampdoria a decade earlier. But the Yugoslavs were embarrassed for most of a jaw-dropping match in Charleroi.

Slovenia's kingpin, Zlatko Zahovič, enjoyed a strained relationship with Katanec, and would later undermine him so poisonously at the 2002 World Cup that Katanec sent him home before resigning in disgust. But he was at his best here, proving a constant menace to Yugoslavia's cumbersome defenders. His first goal arrived so suddenly that the TV coverage, busy showing a replay of a shirt-pull, missed him burying Aleš Čeh's cross with a downward header.

Slovenia reached half-time with their lead intact – and within seconds of Boškov bringing on another reinforcement, striker Savo Milošević, 1-0 became 2-0. Distracted by the substitution, Yugoslavia were caught ball-watching as Miran Pavlin outjumped Miroslav Đukić and nodded Zahovič's free kick into the bottom corner.

Yugoslavia's painfully slow libero Siniša Mihajlović now embarrassed himself in more ways than one. Shortly after being booked for punching Udovič, his moronic pass across his own box was intercepted by the delighted Zahovič, who shot past Kralj for Slovenia's third. Within minutes, Mihajlović was gone after shoving Udovič to the ground for a second booking. As Vítor Melo Pereira's red card came out, he laughed nihilistically in the referee's face.

Three goals and one man down, Yugoslavia looked doomed. But now the underdogs abruptly folded. First, after Đukić acrobatically kept the ball in from a corner, it dropped off the bar for Milošević to score easily. Then Drulović collected Predrag Mijatović's cross, took a touch and drilled the ball home. Almost immediately, the tiny Porto winger outpaced Čeh, got to the byline and pulled the ball back to give Milošević another tap-in. From 3-0 to 3-3 in six minutes.

Still, Slovenia should have won. Zahovič's last-minute set-piece caused chaos in the Yugoslav box, but Željko Milinovič's header was hacked away by Ivan Dudić with Kralj stranded. A mad match, emotionally exhausting for all concerned. 'There's nothing more a manager can do,' said Katanec. 'At 3-1, I wanted them to attack more.'

═══

Raúl would finish up on 44 goals for Spain, but only one of them was scored in the European Championship finals. At least it was a beauty. Early on against Slovenia in Amsterdam, when Míchel Salgado's shot deflected off two opponents outside the box, he reacted instantly to hit a screamer into the top corner.

Slovenia's winger Mladen Rudonja was something of an anti-Raúl, scoring only once in an eventual 65 caps. Still, he tried hard here, having a shot deflected just wide by Salgado's hand, shooting over from a narrow angle, and forcing Molina's replacement Santiago Cañizares to knee to safety. Early in the second half, his cross found Milan Osterc and Zahovič unmarked on the six-yard line. Both players kicked the ball simultaneously (Zahovič, the alpha male, claimed it), and it bobbled into the corner.

But yet again, Slovenia conceded instantly. The blond Mendieta was in the middle of two blistering seasons with Valencia that briefly established him as one of the world's best players. Here, he glided past four opponents on the left and teed up Joseba Etxeberría. The shot was too close to Dabanovič, but went in anyway.

Cañizares later saved well from Marinko Galič and Zahovič, and Spain were hanging on at the end. Afterwards, manager José Antonio Camacho blamed his team's lame performance on the heat. Comment is superfluous.

═══

That evening in Liège, Yugoslavia took eight minutes to do to Norway what Spain hadn't managed in 90, as Milošević tore himself away from Dan Eggen's clutches to nudge Drulović's set-piece past Myhre. That should have set things up nicely, with Norway having to come out and play, but what followed was desperately unsightly.

The Scandinavians created few opportunities: Kralj tipped Flo's shot around the post, and the impressive Erik Mykland set up Iversen for a header which Eirik Bakke unwittingly diverted over the bar. All the while, Yugoslavia ran down the clock with relentless hacking, diving and time-wasting. Slaviša Jokanović peevishly elbowed Solskjær and Bent Skammelsrud, Mykland was ludicrously booked for protesting Stojković's dive, and Kralj seemed capable of clearing the pitch of fit players: his mistimed punch broke Iversen's nose, and he accidentally kicked Slobodan Komljenović in the face.

Near the end, Yugoslavian substitute Mateja Kežman was sent off for inexplicably clattering Mykland moments after coming on. Later still, the mountainous John Carew should have rescued a point when Solskjær played him in, but his finish trickled wide. Not Euro 2000's poorest match, but certainly its sourest.

═══

As the crunch loomed, both Norway and Slovenia had every incentive to take risks. A win would put Norway through, and would be enough for Slovenia unless Spain-Yugoslavia ended in a high-scoring draw. But, mystifyingly, neither team tried to grasp the nettle in Arnhem.

Little Mykland created Norway's best chance, teeing up Iversen to volley beyond the far post; Carew, sliding in, just missed connecting with it. In the second half, Solskjær should have been sent off for violently fouling Čeh, and Bjørn Otto Bragstad headed Rudonja's cross over his own bar. But these were isolated incidents in a match which seemed to last for weeks. After the interminable stoppage time petered out, the Norwegians stood around in the centre circle waiting to hear the news from Brugge.

═══

Spain's showdown with Yugoslavia is the game everyone remembers from Euro 2000. Even in an eventful, exciting competition, it stood out as undiluted footballing psychedelia. So it's strange to note that the opening half-hour was undistinguished and frequently dirty, with both Goran Đorović and Fran limping off prematurely.

Nonetheless, Yugoslavia started brightly: Mihajlović blasted over, and Paco almost put Drulović's cross into his own net. Their opening goal was simplicity itself. When Salgado lost possession, Drulović swung over a good cross, and the three Spaniards around Milošević allowed him to head downwards past Cañizares.

The white-booted Alfonso soon found Spain's equaliser. Raúl forced his way into the box via a ricochet off Niša Saveljić, then left the loose ball to the Betis striker, who drove it left-footed into the corner.

At half-time, Camacho and Boškov threw on winger Pedro Munitis and holding midfielder Dejan Govedarica respectively. Within six minutes, both were on the scoresheet. First, Drulović glided past Sergi and squared to Govedarica, whose right-footer swished over Cañizares and in off the bar. Fifty-eight seconds later, Spain levelled in near-identical fashion. When Etxeberría pulled the ball back to Munitis, the winger controlled it with one touch before hitting a spectacular shot in off the post.

Yugoslavia's relentless fouling eventually came home to roost. When Jokanović got the dismissal he'd deserved against Norway, his actual offence (tripping Munitis) was innocuous, but referee Gilles Veissière had seen enough and showed him a second yellow. Moments later, an irate Yugoslav fan invaded the pitch and charged towards Veissière; Guardiola blocked him off before stewards removed him.

Camacho brought on big Ismael Urzaiz, meaning Spain now had three strikers and two wingers. But soon they fell behind again. Abelardo and Paco couldn't clear Mihajlović's set-piece, Govedarica lofted it across the goalmouth, and the unmarked Komljenović jabbed in from close range. For a side coached by a legendary full-back, Spain defended conspicuously badly.

Needing two goals to survive, they piled forward late on. In the 94th minute, Kralj saved Alfonso's header and Raúl just about kept the ball in play. As he crossed, Abelardo and Govedarica came together at the back post. The Spaniard theatrically tumbled and Veissière gave a penalty, endearing himself to Yugoslavia's fans that little bit more. Mendieta sent Kralj the wrong way.

But the stoppage time still wasn't over, thanks to that pitch invasion. With 96 minutes on the clock, Guardiola pumped a very un-Pep-like high ball into the box. Urzaiz outjumped two defenders to head it across, and it sat up nicely for the unmarked Alfonso, who drew back his left foot and tiredly drove it into the ground. It reared up off the turf and bounced past the helpless Kralj.

The entire Spanish bench sprinted on to the field in joy. Like Govedarica and Munitis, Alfonso never scored for his country again.

At the final whistle, not knowing the Norway-Slovenia result, the devastated Yugoslavs were under the impression they were out of the competition. Another member of their lunatic fringe, wrapped in the national flag, now attempted to attack poor Veissière, who was also pelted with coins, one of them cutting his cheek.

For this, and for their players' indiscipline, the Yugoslavian FA were fined £49,000 by UEFA. 'Remember this name – Gilles Veissière – for biased, dishonest calls,' seethed Yugoslavian TV commentator Duško Korać live on air. 'Everything began well, but the footballing magic was destroyed by a single French referee,' snarled Belgrade broadsheet *Politika Ekspres*. *Večernje Novosti* compared the referee to another Frenchman widely despised in Serbia, the UN's Kosovo envoy Bernard Kouchner.

So farewell, then, Norway, the brutalist matchstick-men of this picturesque tournament. As they had done at USA 94, they went out after foolishly playing for 0-0 in their third game. Manager Semb claimed that they had 'tried to play offensively throughout the tournament': he was right, but not in the way he imagined. But at least somebody did well out of it. Iversen revealed in his 2012 autobiography that he financed his post-tournament holiday in Miami by betting that each of Norway's matches would witness fewer than 2.5 goals.

6pm, 13 June 2000
De Kuip, Rotterdam
Attendance: 41,500
Referee: Gamal al-Ghandour (Egypt)

NORWAY 1 (Iversen 66)
SPAIN 0

NORWAY: Thomas Myhre, Vegård Heggem, Henning Berg (c) (Dan Eggen 59), Bjørn Otto Bragstad, André Bergdølmo, Eirik Bakke, Erik Mykland, Bent Skammelsrud, Steffen Iversen (Vidar Riseth 89), Tore André Flo (John Carew 71), Ole Gunnar Solskjær. **Manager:** Nils Johan Semb.

SPAIN: José Molina, Míchel Salgado, Francisco Jémez 'Paco', Pep Guardiola, Agustín Aranzábal, Fernando Hierro (c), Joseba Etxeberría (Gaizka Mendieta 72), Juan Carlos Valerón (Iván Helguera 80), Ismael Urzaiz, Raúl González, Francisco González 'Fran' (Alfonso Pérez 72). **Manager:** José Antonio Camacho.

Booked: Bergdølmo (32), Etxeberría (18) Salgado (70).

8.45pm, 13 June 2000
Stade du Pays de Charleroi, Charleroi
Attendance: 16,478
Referee: Vítor Melo Pereira (Portugal)

SLOVENIA 3 (Zahovič 23, 57, Pavlin 52)
YUGOSLAVIA 3 (Milošević 67, 73, Drulović 70)

SLOVENIA: Mladen Dabanovič, Željko Milinovič, Marinko Galič, Darko Milanič (c), Džoni Novak, Aleš Čeh, Miran Pavlin (Zoran Pavlović 74), Amir Karić (Milan Osterc 78), Mladen Rudonja, Zlatko Zahovič, Sašo Udovič (Milenko Ačimović 64). **Manager:** Srečko Katanec.

YUGOSLAVIA: Ivica Kralj, Ivan Dudić, Albert Nađ, Slaviša Jokanović, Miroslav Đukić, Siniša Mihajlović, Vladimir Jugović, Dejan Stanković (Dragan Stojković 36), Predrag Mijatović (c) (Mateja Kežman 82), Darko Kovačević (Savo Milošević 52), Ljubinko Drulović. **Manager:** Vujadin Boškov.

Booked: Milanič (32), Mihajlović (56).
Sent off: Mihajlović (60).

6pm, 18 June 2000
ArenA, Amsterdam
Attendance: 42,500
Referee: Markus Merk (Germany)

SPAIN 2 (Raúl 4, Etxeberría 60)
SLOVENIA 1 (Zahovič 59)

SPAIN: Santiago Cañizares, Salgado, Abelardo Fernández, Guardiola (Helguera 81), Aranzábal, Hierro (c), Etxeberría, Valerón (Vicente Engonga 89), Alfonso (Urzaiz 71), Raúl, Mendieta.

SLOVENIA: Dabanovič, Milinovič, Galič, Milanič (c) (Aleksander Knavs 68), Novak, Čeh, Pavlin (Ačimović 82), Karić, Rudonja, Zahovič, Udovič (Osterc 46).

Booked: Pavlin (11), Milanič (24), Novak (53), Karić (85), Aranzábal (62), Helguera (82).

8.45pm, 18 June 2000
Stade Maurice Dufrasne, Liège
Attendance: 27,250
Referee: Hugh Dallas (Scotland)

YUGOSLAVIA 1 (Milošević 8)
NORWAY 0

YUGOSLAVIA: Kralj, Slobodan Komljenović, Niša Saveljić, Goran Đorović, Đukić, Jokanović (Dejan Govedarica 89), Jugović, Stojković (c) (Nađ 84), Mijatović (Kežman 87), Milošević, Drulović.

NORWAY: Myhre, Heggem (Stig Inge Bjørnebye 35), Bragstad, Eggen, Bergdølmo, Bakke (Roar Strand 76), Mykland, Skammelsrud (c), Iversen (Carew 71), Flo, Solskjær.

Booked: Jokanović (28), Jugović (81), Drulović (81), Nađ (90+3), Mykland (31), Bakke (66).
Sent off: Kežman (88).

6pm, 21 June 2000
GelreDome, Arnhem
Attendance: 22,500
Referee: Graham Poll (England)

SLOVENIA 0
NORWAY 0

SLOVENIA: Dabanovič, Milinovič, Galič (Ačimovič 83), Knavs, Novak, Čeh (c), Pavlin, Karić, Rudonja, Zahovič, Ermin Šiljak (Osterc 86).

NORWAY: Myhre, Bergdølmo, Bjørnebye, Bragstad, Eggen, Ståle Solbakken (c), Mykland, Iversen, Carew (Bakke 61, Strand 83), Flo, Solskjær.

Booked: Pavlin (44), Mykland (24), Solskjær (59).

6pm, 21 June 2000
Jan Breydel Stadion, Brugge
Attendance: 24,000
Referee: Gilles Veissière (France)

SPAIN 4 (Alfonso 38, 90+6, Munitis 51, Mendieta 90+4 pen)
YUGOSLAVIA 3 (Milošević 30, Govedarica 50, Komljenović 75)

SPAIN: Cañizares, Salgado (Pedro Munitis 46), Sergi Barjuán, Paco (Urzaiz 64), Abelardo (c), Guardiola, Helguera, Fran (Etxeberría 22), Alfonso, Raúl, Mendieta.

YUGOSLAVIA: Kralj, Komljenović, Đorović (Jovan Stanković 12), Jokanović, Đukić, Mihajlović, Jugović (Govedarica 46), Stojković (c) (Saveljić 68), Mijatović, Milošević, Drulović.

Booked: Sergi (62), Komljenović (27), Jokanović (38), J. Stanković (45), Stojković (56), Saveljić (87).
Sent off: Jokanović (63).

GROUP C	P	W	D	L	F	A	GD	Pts
SPAIN	3	2	0	1	6	5	+1	6
YUGOSLAVIA	3	1	1	1	7	7	0	4
NORWAY	3	1	1	1	1	1	0	4
SLOVENIA	3	0	2	1	4	5	−1	2

Spain and Yugoslavia qualified.

GROUP D
Netherlands, Czech Republic, Denmark, France

At Euro 84, Euro 92 and France 98, the winner of France v Denmark had gone on to lift the trophy. This Danish team weren't a patch on the Big Mac Gang, let alone Sepp Piontek's swashbucklers, but they should have drawn first blood in Brugge. After 110 seconds, Marcel Desailly failed to intercept Ebbe Sand's simple ball, which put Jon Dahl Tomasson through on goal. A confidence-free zone at this stage of his career, Tomasson shot straight at Fabien Barthez.

France took the hint. Nicolas Anelka went around Peter Schmeichel before sliding the ball ineptly into the side-netting, and soon Laurent Blanc showed him how it was done. The veteran sweeper came up from the back and found Thierry Henry, who released Anelka again, and Schmeichel came out to save as the striker dived. While referee Günter Benkö was debating whether to give a penalty, Blanc scored easily.

'The Danes were snarling and sometimes violent,' Emmanuel Petit recalled. But that wasn't enough. First, Zidane's magnificent pass found Henry on the left, and he switched on the turbo to run half the length of the field before stroking the ball across Schmeichel. Sylvain Wiltord hoovered up the third goal in stoppage time, tapping home his future Arsenal team-mate Patrick Vieira's cross. Easy in the end, but France would need to be tighter than this against the better teams.

═══

The Netherlands went back to black against the Czech Republic in Amsterdam, lining out in dark shorts rather than the white of France 98. 'I felt that black emits more power,' said Frank Rijkaard. 'White: clean, neat and attractive football. Black: you throw yourself in front of the ball in the last minute and stop a goal.' Instinctive caution before facing a team as dangerous as the Czechs.

As host teams tend to, the Dutch began with their tails up. Pavel Srníček saved well from Dennis Bergkamp, Patrick Kluivert and Boudewijn Zenden in the opening stages, before Bergkamp turned Petr Gabriel inside out and fizzed a left-footer past the far post. But as the half wore on, the skilful Czechs quietened the crowd with some good football. The Netherlands lost their way badly enough to be booed off at half-time.

Straight from the restart, Pavel Nedvěd's superb cross was stubbed wide by Karel Poborský. And in the battle of the giants, Jaap Stam couldn't contain Jan Koller. Showing brilliant technique, the striker sent Nedvěd down the right, but when Nedvěd pulled it back to him, Edwin van der Sar beat away his close-range shot.

The woodwork now saved the Netherlands twice. First, Nedvěd outjumped Edgar Davids to head Jiří Němec's cross on to the post, before Van der Sar smothered it on the line. Rijkaard later said, 'We had a little angel sitting on our goal line.' Then Koller, the sky god, met Poborský's free kick with an even better header that hit the bar.

The Netherlands didn't deserve a draw, but walked away with a win, thanks to Pierluigi Collina. The Czechs had good reason to be wary of the referee, who had sent off Tomáš Řepka (twice) and Nedvěd in Serie A, all for dissent. Two minutes from time, he was their nemesis again. As Marc Overmars's cross came over, Ronald de Boer jumped with Němec and fell in a heap. Collina pointed to the spot as Nedvěd dropped to his knees in horror.

Replays showed Němec holding a handful of orange jersey but, crucially, also being obstructed himself. 'We're always the victims of this kind of *duikelingen*, so I thought I might as well do it myself,' admitted De Boer. His brother Frank flashed a superb penalty into the top corner.

Czech anger now bubbled over. While cautioning Giovanni van Bronckhorst for hacking Rosický, Collina suddenly ran over to the touchline and eyeballed the already-substituted Radek Látal. Whatever was said, out came the red card, making Látal the only man to be sent off in two Euros.

In the 94th minute, the Czechs almost got the equaliser that would've been the least they deserved, but Radek Bejbl scuffed Koller's knockdown wide in imitation of Poborský's earlier miss. The Dutch had enjoyed enough let-offs for several matches. 'Send the referee a bouquet of flowers, and be happy,' Johan Cruyff remarked on Dutch TV that evening.

In Brugge, French manager Roger Lemerre and 15 of his players were shunning media duties due to what they saw as personalised criticism, especially of captain Didier Deschamps. UEFA reminded Lemerre that, under tournament rules, he was legally obliged to speak to the media. 'Lemerre didn't have the same character as Aimé Jacquet,' Bixente Lizarazu recalled. 'He had a *foufou* [crazy] side sometimes.'

The Czechs pushed France hard in another fine match. After one minute, Nedvěd capped a flowing move with a powerful drive which Barthez fisted away. After five, Koller headed Němec's cross wastefully wide. And after seven, France took a farcical lead.

When Zidane closed down Gabriel, the Czech stopper's inept back-pass went straight to Henry, who stretched those long legs to run on and prod the ball under Srníček. Gabriel was only playing due to Jan Suchopárek's and Tomáš Votava's injuries, and this sledgehammer blow ended his international career. 'He hit the wrong notes unworthy of his name,' sniggered *L'Équipe*.

Chances kept coming. Henry stabbed across the face of the goal before angrily booting an advertising hoarding; and Poborský dribbled around Deschamps to find Němec, who walloped it miles over. A classic engine-room workhorse, Němec was famously so taciturn that his nickname was 'Němej' ('mute').

If the opening goal was a gift, so was the equaliser. After Petit lost the ball, Deschamps flattened Nedvěd a yard outside the box. Referee Graham Poll nonetheless gave a penalty, which Poborský thumped down the middle. But on the hour, the covering Karel Rada was caught out badly by Henry's lofted pass, and Youri Djorkaeff darted in to rattle home a low finish.

Zidane did his usual second-half disappearing act, while the sainted Lilian Thuram should have been sent off for his reducer on Řepka. But France saw out the game in relative comfort, apart from Koller rising above Desailly to head against the bar again. Czech manager Jozef Chovanec said his players' two performances had left 'a good business card for our football', and French paper *Libération* hailed them as one of the five best sides in the competition. But after just two matches, they were the first team out.

———

To stoke up Euro fever in Rotterdam, the Nationale-Nederlanden insurance company plastered the biggest graphic display in the world on to its 40-storey headquarters: a futuristic and expensive image of the begoggled Edgar Davids charging through the side of the building like a crazed cyborg. But he and his colleagues made a meal of seeing off Denmark at De Kuip.

Rijkaard's team couldn't stop giving the ball away, allowing the Danes to come at them. Morten Bisgaard's cross-shot was parried by Van der Sar before he thumped the rebound off Allan Nielsen's head, and Thomas Gravesen curled a shot on to the bar.

At the other end, Overmars blazed wide after Schmeichel couldn't hold Kluivert's shot, and Davids wasted a one-on-one. Finally, a goal came for the Dutch. Kluivert put Bergkamp through, and when Schmeichel came out to block, Kluivert coolly passed the loose ball through a crowd of players into the net.

The chunky Zenden, later a crowd whipping-boy at Liverpool, looked useful in this tournament. For the second goal, he chased a bouncing ball out to the left, turned Bisgaard and crossed to the back post, where Ronald de Boer walked it in.

The 36-year-old Schmeichel raged hard against the dying of the light, incessantly bollocking his weary defenders. He saved well from Kluivert and Zenden, but was powerless when Reiziger raced 60 yards upfield and shaped to shoot before squaring it for Zenden, who couldn't miss.

Even when handed a free swing near the end, Denmark spurned it. Van der Sar sprinted off his line to bundle Sand over, but Michael Schjønberg wafted the penalty wide and was instantly substituted. A far sterner test now awaited the Dutch, albeit against a B team.

———

There were three sharks in Group D, and one anchovy. It's sometimes said of the European Championship that it doesn't contain any Saudi Arabias or El Salvadors, but this Laudrup-less Danish team were as close as you got. Not that their supporters were ungrateful to manager Bo Johansson on his last night in charge. 'Tak for alt, Bosse,' read one banner at the Stade Maurice Dufrasne.

Eager to send him off well, Denmark played spiritedly against the Czechs, and Tomasson's overhead kick and header drew good saves from Srníček. But as soon as Šmicer fired Poborský's cross into the roof of the net on 64 minutes, the Danes wilted. Schmeichel was still moaning at his defenders about that one when Šmicer ran on to Koller's headed flick, lifted the ball over the big man and tapped into an open goal. The Czechs went home with as many points as England and fewer than Norway, but they were on a different footballing planet to those outfits.

=====

The meeting of the world champions and the co-hosts in Amsterdam might have been the match of the tournament had anything rested on it other than top spot. But though Lemerre rested his stars, it was all relative: his line-up included players from Real Madrid, Chelsea, Arsenal, Roma and PSG.

Under little pressure, both teams enjoyed themselves. Just after Phillip Cocu headed against Bernard Lama's tracksuited legs, France scored with a header of their own: Christophe Dugarry converted Johan Micoud's near-post corner as reserve goalkeeper Sander Westerveld barely got off the ground.

The Dutch soon hit back. Bergkamp's superb ball left the flat-footed Frank Lebœuf exposed, and Kluivert cut on to his right foot before belting a searing shot across Lama's bows and inside the far post. Ducking responsibility, Lebœuf gave it loads of 'not my fault' shoulder-shrugging towards Lemerre's dugout.

Play zipped from end to end. Bergkamp's shot bounced up over Lama to come back off the bar, and Johan Micoud, a cultured playmaker eternally in Zidane's shadow, chipped Westerveld from 50 yards before the back-pedalling keeper palmed it over the bar. From the corner, Stam headed out to Wiltord, whose shot was diverted in by David Trezeguet for 2-1.

Early in the second half, the profligate Dugarry ran on to Desailly's pass but smashed the ball at Westerveld, a miss France soon paid for. They were still organising their defensive wall for a free kick when Frank de Boer surprised them, spearing a shot into the top corner off the underside of the bar.

For the winner, Lebœuf was again culpable, missing his header when Westerveld's goal kick sailed downfield. Zenden latched on to the loose ball and neatly slotted it home as Christian Karembeu and Desailly arrived too late. Afterwards, Desailly went ballistic in the dressing room. 'When Marcel is angry, it's scary,' recalled Robert Pirès. 'When you're young, like I was, you say nothing back, you shut up. "Yes, yes, Marcel, you're right."'

But the damage was negligible: France would remain based in Genval and play their quarter-final in Brugge, where they had already won twice. 'Everything's going to plan,' said Lemerre. Defeat? What defeat? Gallic shrugs all round.

6pm, 11 June 2000
Jan Breydel Stadion, Brugge
Attendance: 28,100
Referee: Günter Benkö (Austria)

FRANCE 3 (Blanc 16, Henry 64, Wiltord 90+2)
DENMARK 0

FRANCE: Fabien Barthez, Lilian Thuram, Bixente Lizarazu, Emmanuel Petit, Laurent Blanc, Marcel Desailly, Didier Deschamps (c), Youri Djorkaeff (Patrick Vieira 58), Nicolas Anelka (Sylvain Wiltord 82), Zinedine Zidane, Thierry Henry. **Manager:** Roger Lemerre.

DENMARK: Peter Schmeichel (c), Søren Colding, René Henriksen, Michael Schjønberg, Jan Heintze, Stig Tøfting (Thomas Gravesen 72), Allan Nielsen, Morten Bisgaard (Martin Jørgensen 72), Jon Dahl Tomasson (Mikkel Beck 79), Ebbe Sand, Jesper Grønkjær. **Manager:** Bo Johansson.

Booked: Schjønberg (90).

8.45pm, 11 June 2000
ArenA, Amsterdam
Attendance: 50,833
Referee: Pierluigi Collina (Italy)

NETHERLANDS 1 (F. de Boer 89 pen)
CZECH REPUBLIC 0

NETHERLANDS: Edwin van der Sar, Michael Reiziger, Jaap Stam (Bert Konterman 75), Frank de Boer (c), Giovanni van Bronckhorst, Clarence Seedorf (Ronald de Boer 57), Phillip Cocu, Edgar Davids, Patrick Kluivert, Dennis Bergkamp, Boudewijn Zenden (Marc Overmars 78). **Manager:** Frank Rijkaard.

CZECH REPUBLIC: Pavel Srníček, Tomáš Řepka, Petr Gabriel, Karel Rada, Radek Látal (Radek Bejbl 70), Jiří Němec (c), Tomáš Rosický, Pavel Nedvěd (Vratislav Lokvenc 89), Jan Koller, Vladimír Šmicer (Pavel Kuka 83), Karel Poborský. **Manager:** Jozef Chovanec.

Booked: F. de Boer (36), Van Bronckhorst (89), Nedvěd (22), Poborský (48), Řepka (66).
Sent off: Látal (90), on the substitutes' bench.

6pm, 16 June 2000
Jan Breydel Stadion, Brugge
Attendance: 28,100
Referee: Graham Poll (England)

FRANCE 2 (Henry 7, Djorkaeff 60)
CZECH REPUBLIC 1 (Poborský 35 pen)

FRANCE: Barthez, Thuram, Vincent Candela, Petit (Djorkaeff 46), Blanc, Desailly, Deschamps (c), Vieira, Anelka (Christophe Dugarry 55), Zidane, Henry (Wiltord 89).

CZECH REPUBLIC: Srníček, Řepka, Gabriel (Milan Fukal 46), Rada, Bejbl (Lokvenc 49), Němec (c), Rosický (Marek Jankulovski 62), Nedvěd, Koller, Šmicer, Poborský.

Booked: Thuram (62), Gabriel (14), Němec (67), Jankulovski (69).

8.45pm, 16 June 2000
De Kuip, Rotterdam
Attendance: 51,117
Referee: Urs Meier (Switzerland)

NETHERLANDS 3 (Kluivert 57, R. de Boer 66, Zenden 77)
DENMARK 0

NETHERLANDS: Van der Sar (Sander Westerveld 89), Reiziger, Konterman, F. de Boer (c), Van Bronckhorst, Cocu, Davids, Overmars (R. de Boer 62), Kluivert, Bergkamp (Aron Winter 76), Zenden.

DENMARK: Schmeichel (c), Colding, Henriksen, Schjønberg (Thomas Helveg 82), Heintze, Gravesen (Brian Steen Nielsen 67), A. Nielsen (Tøfting 61), Bisgaard, Tomasson, Sand, Grønkjær.

Booked: Van Bronckhorst (4), Reiziger (10), Konterman (55), Van der Sar (80), A. Nielsen (50).

8.45pm, 21 June 2000
Stade Maurice Dufrasne, Liège
Attendance: 18,000
Referee: Gamal al-Ghandour (Egypt)

CZECH REPUBLIC 2 (Šmicer 64, 67)
DENMARK 0

CZECH REPUBLIC: Srníček, Řepka, Fukal, Rada, Bejbl (Jankulovski 62), Němec (c), Patrik Berger, Nedvěd, Koller (Kuka 74), Šmicer (Lokvenc 79), Poborský.

DENMARK: Schmeichel (c), Helveg, Henriksen, Schjønberg, Heintze (Colding 68), Tøfting, BS Nielsen, Bjarne Goldbæk, Tomasson, Beck (Miklos Molnar 74), Grønkjær.

Booked: Poborský (52), Fukal (62), Rada (69), Grønkjær (52), Tøfting (56), Molnar (85).

8.45pm, 21 June 2000
ArenA, Amsterdam
Attendance: 51,000

Referee: Anders Frisk (Sweden)

NETHERLANDS 3 (Kluivert 14, F. de Boer 51, Zenden 59)

FRANCE 2 (Dugarry 8, Trezeguet 31)

NETHERLANDS: Westerveld, Paul Bosvelt, Stam, F. de Boer (c), Arthur Numan, Cocu, Davids, Overmars (Peter van Vossen 90), Kluivert (Roy Makaay 60), Bergkamp (Winter 78), Zenden.

FRANCE: Bernard Lama, Christian Karembeu, Candela, Vieira (Deschamps 90), Frank Lebœuf, Desailly (c), Johan Micoud, Robert Pirès, Dugarry (Djorkaeff 67), David Trezeguet, Wiltord (Anelka 80).

Booked: Davids (81), Cocu (85), Dugarry (45), Desailly (75), Vieira (90).

GROUP D	P	W	D	L	F	A	GD	Pts
NETHERLANDS	3	3	0	0	7	2	+5	9
FRANCE	3	2	0	1	7	4	+3	6
CZECH REPUBLIC	3	1	0	2	3	3	0	3
DENMARK	3	0	0	3	0	8	−8	0

The Netherlands and France qualified.

QUARTER-FINALS
Portugal v Turkey
Italy v Romania
Spain v France
Netherlands v Yugoslavia

In a forgettable opening quarter-final, Portugal gobbled up the already-spent Turks. Under a closed roof in Amsterdam, Luís Figo looked every inch one of the world's best players, showing why the Portuguese press had coined the term *Figodependência* to evoke their team's reliance on him. Weeks later, Real Madrid would break the world transfer record to tempt him away from Barcelona for £37m.

With Portugal owning the ball, the last thing Turkey needed was to lose a man. But after half an hour, a clash between Couto and Alpay under a high ball ended with Couto on the deck clutching his face and Alpay staring at referee Dick Jol's red card. Replays showed Couto jumping into the back of Alpay, who then threw a very weak dig in his general direction. Still, them's the rules, and Alpay had given Couto exactly what he had wanted.

Near the end of a niggly first half, Figo sent a teasing cross in from the right, and Gomes eluded his marker Fatih before stooping to head home; Alpay might have stopped him, but Alpay wasn't there. Within moments, João Pinto committed a horrible miss, banging Rui Costa's cross wide from close range. All the drama was being crammed into an action-packed few minutes before half-time. Jol, who had failed to dismiss Johan Mjällby in Turkey's second game, now punished them again by failing to give Couto his second booking after he felled Arif in the box. And Arif tossed away the lifeline, putting his penalty too close to Baía.

Portugal soon had a two-goal cushion. Figo went the long way around Hakan Ünsal on the right, rolled the ball to the far post, and again Gomes couldn't miss. Somewhere in Madrid, Florentino Pérez was licking his lips. Easy for Portugal, with Jorge Costa, Gomes and Bento all going close before the end, but you wondered what might have happened if Jol had got his decisions right.

===

In another one-sided affair in Brussels, Italy had little trouble in despatching the patched-up Romanians. Francesco Totti was in sparkling form, adding some showbiz to this functional team and, for once, living up to his world-class billing. He opened the scoring by chesting down Fiore's cushioned pass and prodding past Bogdan Stelea.

The shaven-headed Hagi had returned to slow Romania down to strolling pace again. But he displayed a rare burst of speed just after Totti's goal, flying down the right with Mark Iuliano and Maldini exposed. As Toldo advanced, Hagi lobbed him, but the ball bounced against the post and came back out.

Hagi was then the victim of one of the worst fouls of the tournament, a scissors lunge by Demetrio Albertini which warranted a red but got a yellow. The sense that it wasn't Romania's day grew when Inzaghi, uncharacteristically onside, ran on to Albertini's through ball and shot through Stelea. A great pass, but Albertini shouldn't have been on the pitch.

Romania weren't coming back. Hagi, enraged, took revenge by proxy when he put Antonio Conte out of the competition with an equally outrageous challenge which, again, only got a yellow. 'I knew it was premeditated. He wanted to break my leg,' said Conte, who rejected Hagi's apology afterwards.

Minutes later, Hagi was gone for good. When Gianluca Zambrotta clipped his heels, Melo Pereira showed him a second yellow for diving, a humiliating yet hilarious conclusion to a 17-year international career. Days later, he cursed the Romanian media in an open letter: 'Newspapers and journalists from my country have made me mourn.' Meanwhile, Italy increasingly looked like a team to be avoided.

=====

In *De Telegraaf,* Johan Cruyff again dipped his poison pen in an inkwell of pus. 'Things aren't going as well as they look,' he wrote. 'Bergkamp is weak; Kluivert, regardless of his two goals, has done nothing; and Davids should talk less with the referee and opponents and play more.'

'If Cruyff wants to help,' Bergkamp retorted, 'instead of talking to the press, he should come and talk to us. Should we play better and lose? I don't know what to think any more.' Davids, never one to take a slagging lying down, said, 'There are lots of things Cruyff doesn't know. He's not out on the pitch. I'll never take him seriously again.' Even Johan Neeskens, Cruyff's old lieutenant and now Rijkaard's assistant, expressed his weariness of it all.

Yugoslavia had run their opponents close at France 98, with Predrag Mijatović missing a penalty at 1-1 and Bergkamp getting away with stamping viciously on Mihajlović. 'If the Dutch think they know our game, they're wrong,' Savo Milošević said, 'because I never know how Yugoslavia will play.' But their ludicrous tournament came to an end as they were drowned in the tub of De Kuip before an exultant home crowd.

Yugoslavia had no answer to the Netherlands' intelligent movement and staccato passing (and the cynicism of Davids, who gave away 11 free kicks without getting booked). First, Bergkamp's cross drifted over the stationary Mihajlović, and Kluivert got there before Kralj to poke home. Soon, 1-0 became 2-0 when Kluivert tapped in Davids's precise cross, with Mihajlović again exposed.

For their third goal, Dejan Govedarica erratically sliced into his own net while trying to put the ball out for a corner. It was initially credited to Kluivert, who soon claimed his actual hat-trick by cushioning Zenden's pass inside the far post. And after Cocu's long shot clipped the bar, Overmars wrapped up the rout with two consummate finishes. First, after flicking Bergkamp's pass into the air with his instep, he struck a coruscating volley into the top corner from 25 yards. His second, and the Netherlands' sixth, was tapped in after another Cocu rocket came back off the post to fall perfectly for him.

Incongruously, Yugoslavia had the last word. After Mijatović's splendid half-volley struck the bar, Milošević pounced to make himself Euro 2000's joint top scorer, then dolefully trudged away. But it wasn't enough to prevent this being the biggest slapping in the history of the finals. Belgrade newspaper *Glas Javnosti* called it 'a smack in the eye, a debacle, an utter fiasco', and the veteran Dragan Stojković accused Boškov of bullying him: 'The intolerance he showed was unbearable. He shoved me around so much. I should have packed it in and gone home.'

Meanwhile, Cruyff was temporarily placated. 'Awesome football,' he wrote in *De Telegraaf.* 'Forget what I said last week.'

———

Roger Lemerre, now friends again with the French media, compared the knife-edge nature of the quarter-final against Spain with the executions at Place de Grève in medieval Paris: 'The guillotine is installed. You have three steps to climb. You go up them. Sometimes, you have the chance to go down them.' The evening heat probably had some of the crowd wishing they could jump into one of Brugge's canals instead. But had they done so, they would have missed a thrilling match.

After Vieira and Dugarry missed early headed sitters, Spain stirred themselves, and Guardiola's angled free kick was curling inside the near post before Barthez punched clear. They then saw their callow superstar waste a fantastic opportunity. Sent through by wonderful combination play between Guardiola and Alfonso, Raúl panically snatched at his shot, which Barthez turned over the bar. It wouldn't be the low point of his night.

Guardiola, dismissed beforehand as an over-the-hill 'zombie' by one Madrid paper, performed superbly: another splendid pass released Munitis to cut inside Thuram and rifle just wide. The pace and trickery of the 5ft 5.5in winger unnerved Thuram, who recalled, 'I was never in more trouble than on this night. It's my worst memory. The guy never stopped dribbling past me.' Munitis soon signed for Real Madrid, to sit on the shelf as one of their many neglected baubles.

Minutes later, Agustín Aranzábal brought down Djorkaeff to end a French counter-attack. 'Well done,' Salgado told Aranzábal as he got up. Guardiola, overhearing, snapped, 'Well done? Look where the free kick is!' After Zidane's platinum right foot had whipped it over the wall and into the top corner, Guardiola sneered at Salgado, 'Well done, yeah?'

On 38 minutes, France's lead was rubbed out. Alfonso found Munitis in space on the left, where Thuram dived in and clipped his leg. Pierluigi Collina pointed to the spot. Mendieta placed the penalty down the middle as Barthez dived right.

But France's second goal owed everything to the energy of Vieira, who loped from the centre circle to the edge of the Spanish box, saw Djorkaeff on the right and picked him out with an inch-perfect ball. Djorkaeff took one touch before hitting a shot on the run which rocketed past Cañizares at the near post. He later called this goal the single best memory of his career: 'An act of pure football. Control and hit.'

The second half began as the first half had ended: with Thuram in trouble. Munitis got past him again and picked out Alfonso, but the striker miscontrolled it and Barthez saved bravely at his feet. Meanwhile, Paco brought down down Henry with a rugby tackle, but was spared a red card because Aranzábal was the last man.

Despite Camacho's extraordinary decision to withdraw the livewire Munitis, Spain had all the play in the final stages. In the 90th minute, they thought they had their equaliser too. Barthez foolishly tried to grab the ball through Abelardo's legs from behind, the big defender toppled, and Collina gave another penalty. Who would take it? Not Mendieta, long since subbed off after Lizarazu had dominated him. So the responsibility fell on Raúl to keep Spain in the competition – but he blew it, lifting a wild effort high into the crowd.

'I cried on the pitch, in the dressing room and in the hotel,' said the distraught young prince. 'I needed to vent. I was a long time waiting for this moment. Opportunities go by. There'll be more.' But Spain wouldn't win a trophy until he had left the stage. Madrid tabloid *Marca*'s verdict was pitiless 'Raúl made Spain cry. Tuesday is his 23rd birthday. It will be, without doubt, the saddest of his life.'

6pm, 24 June 2000
ArenA, Amsterdam
Attendance: 42,000
Referee: Dick Jol (Netherlands)

PORTUGAL 2 (Gomes 44, 56)
TURKEY 0

PORTUGAL: Baía (c), Jorge Costa, Couto, Dimas, Costinha (Sousa 46), Bento, Figo, Conceição, Gomes (Sá Pinto 75), Rui Costa (Capucho 87), João Pinto.

TURKEY: Rüştü, Tayfur, Hakan Ü, Ogün (c) (Sergen 84), Fatih, Alpay, Ergün, Tayfun, Hakan Ş, Arif (Oktay Derelioğlu 62), Okan (Suat 62).

Booked: João Pinto (29), Couto (37), Rui Costa (39), Costinha (41), Sousa (60), Okan (32), Hakan Ü (56), Ogün (82).

Sent off: Alpay (30).

8.45pm, 24 June 2000
Stade Roi Baudouin II, Brussels
Attendance: 42,000
Referee: Vítor Melo Pereira (Portugal)

ITALY 2 (Totti 33, Inzaghi 43)
ROMANIA 0

ITALY: Toldo, Zambrotta, Maldini (c) (Pessotto 46), Nesta, Cannavaro, Iuliano, Albertini, Conte (Di Biagio 55), Inzaghi, Totti (Del Piero 75), Fiore.

ROMANIA: Stelea, Filipescu, Chivu, Belodedici, Ciobotariu, Gâlcă (Lupescu 68), Petre, Munteanu, Moldovan (Ganea 54), Hagi (c), Mutu.

Booked: Albertini (38), Hagi (55).
Sent off: Hagi (59).

6pm, 25 June 2000
De Kuip, Rotterdam
Attendance: 51,504
Referee: José María García Aranda (Spain)

NETHERLANDS 6 (Kluivert 24, 38, 54, Govedarica 51 og, Overmars 78, 90+1)
YUGOSLAVIA 1 (Milošević 90+2)

NETHERLANDS: Van der Sar (Westerveld 65), Bosvelt, Stam, F. de Boer (c), Numan, Cocu, Davids, Overmars, Kluivert (Makaay 60), Bergkamp, Zenden (R. de Boer 86).

YUGOSLAVIA: Kralj, Komljenović, Saveljić (J. Stanković 56), Govedarica, Đukić, Mihajlović, Jugović, Stojković (c) (D. Stanković 52), Mijatović, Milošević, Drulović (Kovačević 70).

Booked: Bosvelt (48).

8.45pm, 25 June 2000
Jan Breydel Stadion, Brugge
Attendance: 30,000
Referee: Pierluigi Collina (Italy)

FRANCE 2 (Zidane 32, Djorkaeff 44)
SPAIN 1 (Mendieta 38 pen)

FRANCE: Barthez, Thuram, Lizarazu, Vieira, Blanc, Desailly, Deschamps (c), Djorkaeff, Dugarry, Zidane, Henry (Anelka 81).

SPAIN: Cañizares, Salgado, Aranzábal, Paco, Abelardo (c), Guardiola, Helguera (Gerard López 77), Mendieta (Urzaiz 57), Alfonso, Raúl, Munitis (Etxeberría 73).

Booked: Deschamps (60), Alfonso (55), Guardiola (61), Salgado (64), Paco (71).

SEMI-FINALS
France v Portugal
Netherlands v Italy

After shining against Spain, France came down to earth with a bump in Brussels, huffing and puffing for a semblance of fluency all night against an equally lacklustre Portugal. At least the violence at the end woke everyone up.

As was the case in Marseille in 1984, the opening goal came out of nothing after a dull opening period. Deschamps, seemingly asleep, got outmuscled by Sérgio Conceição 25 yards out; the ball broke to Nuno Gomes, who spun around to fire a half-volley past a surprised Barthez.

For a time, the French engine seized up. Vieira was kept occupied by Figo, Zidane contributed little except one great run past two men, and Desailly should have seen red for going over the ball on Rui Costa. Vieira: 'It was difficult until half-time. We talked a lot in the dressing room, and we thought it would be a shame to lose like this.'

Early in the second half, Anelka made his one useful contribution, holding off Vidigal and teeing up Henry, whose shot brushed Couto and found its way into the corner for 1-1. But with France remaining uninspired and Portugal going into their shell, the game worsened. Baía finger-tipped Petit's volley around the post; and early in extra time, João Pinto almost won it for Portugal on the golden goal, shooting just wide.

Penalties were six minutes away when Baía came out to block Trezeguet. The ball ran loose to Wiltord, almost on the byline. His shot from the proverbial impossible angle was halted by Abel Xavier's hand as the defender fell backwards at the near post, prompting referee Günter Benkö to blow for a penalty.

Portugal now lost their heads in an embarrassing outburst of emotional incontinence, surrounding Benkö and linesman Igor Šramka to scream in their faces, prompting manager Humberto Coelho to come on to the field and restrain them. Almost unnoticed in the pandemonium, Figo simply walked off the pitch and down the tunnel. After a four-minute delay, Zidane lifted the penalty high to Baía's right. Being a golden goal, it was the last kick, but Gomes was irrelevantly sent off anyway for thumping Benkö.

Several Portuguese received lengthy bans: nine months for Abel Xavier, eight for Gomes, and six for Bento, who had tried to take Benkö's red card from him. Figo's reaction was horribly graceless ('When I think that this official will go on to referee other games, it pains me'), and Baía baselessly alleged a UEFA conspiracy. The dignified Coelho resigned days later, appalled, you would like to think, by his players' unstinting childishness.

After the Netherlands annihilated Yugoslavia, Ruud Gullit said he would have preferred a 2-0 stroll, because the margin of victory might lead to overconfidence. But in Amsterdam, they initially picked up where they'd left off against Yugoslavia, their clever runs pulling Italy all over the pitch. Early on, Bergkamp's cushioned pass split the defence and sent through Cocu, who shot too high as Toldo charged out.

Every move flowed through Bergkamp, who almost broke the deadlock by crashing a shot off the far post. The play moved unremittingly in one direction, as though the ArenA pitch had been lifted up at one end and tilted towards the Italian goal. And on 34 minutes, they went down to ten men. Zenden dribbled past Zambrotta, the defender brought him down crudely, and Markus Merk showed him a second yellow card.

Soon, Italy were in a bigger hole. Nesta pulled Kluivert back as he was poised to shoot, for an obvious penalty – but Frank de Boer put it at the right height for Toldo, who turned it around the post.

Still, there seemed no reason for the Netherlands to panic. Kluivert's fine header brought another save from Toldo, and the same player then showed wonderful close control before shooting wide. As the Dutch walked off at half-time, they could reassure themselves that they had the extra man, the home advantage and the upper hand.

On the hour came another gift for the Netherlands. Davids twisted past Iuliano, the most cumbersome of Italy's defenders, and was brought down. Kluivert went for placement rather than power, but saw his soft little penalty hit the foot of the post. One of those days?

The Dutch hogged 70 per cent possession, but there was a frantic feel to their attacks now. And Merk's refereeing helped the team doing all the fouling. Iuliano should have had a second booking for flattening Davids, and Luigi Di Biagio got away with a bad tackle on Bergkamp. Comically, Italy almost snatched it in the 93rd minute. Frank de Boer was outmuscled by Marco Delvecchio with pathetic ease, but the substitute's soft shot went straight at Van der Sar.

In extra time, Italy kept repelling everything, and again the golden chance went to their lanky substitute. Totti punted another long ball downfield, and yet again De Boer looked bad, trailing in the wake of the less-than-speedy Delvecchio. Only Van der Sar's leg prevented a golden goal.

As the penalties got under way, the outcome felt predestined. De Boer put his kick down Toldo's throat, while Stam's effort was so wild it flew into the ArenA's upper tier. Totti followed it with a Panenka pastiche that the Italian press called 'il cucchiaio', the spoon. When Van der Sar saved from Maldini, the Netherlands had a glimmer of hope – but Toldo snuffed it out, stopping

Paul Bosvelt's weak effort with one hand. Italy were in the final. Rijkaard resigned immediately, saying, 'It's a law that once a thing like this happens, it's time for another man to take over.'

There was little point in condemning Italy's conservatism: with a few exceptions, the Netherlands were technically superior footballers to them. Still, they had needed extraordinary luck as well as resolve. A team can't be said to have defended flawlessly if they give away two penalties, have a man sent off for persistent fouling and cough up several great chances, not to mention the red card Iuliano should have got.

One Brussels newspaper described Italy's approach as having 'a charming ugliness': in an exquisite tournament full of colour and light, their counterpoint of shade and shadow was lending it more definition, more detail. Could they now go one step further and carry the day into night?

8.45pm, 28 June 2000
Stade Roi Baudouin II, Brussels
Attendance: 50,000
Referee: Günter Benkö (Austria)

FRANCE 2 (Henry 51, Zidane 117 pen)
PORTUGAL 1 (Gomes 19)
France won on the golden goal after extra time

FRANCE: Barthez, Thuram, Lizarazu, Vieira, Blanc, Desailly, Deschamps (c), Petit (Pirès 87), Anelka (Wiltord 72), Zidane, Henry (Trezeguet 105).

PORTUGAL: Baía (c), Abel Xavier, Dimas (Rui Jorge 91), Jorge Costa, Couto, Costinha, Figo, Vidigal (Bento 61), Gomes, Rui Costa (João Pinto 78), Conceição.

Booked: Vieira (23), Desailly (39), Vidigal (44), Figo (54), Jorge Costa (55), Dimas (62), João Pinto (107).

Sent off: Gomes (116).

6pm, 29 June 2000
ArenA, Amsterdam
Attendance: 51,300
Referee: Markus Merk (Germany)

ITALY 0
NETHERLANDS 0
Italy won 3-1 on penalties after extra time
Shoot-out: Di Biagio 1-0, F. de Boer saved, Pessotto 2-0, Stam shot over, Totti 3-0, Kluivert 3-1, Maldini saved, Bosvelt saved.

ITALY: Toldo, Zambrotta, Maldini (c), Nesta, Cannavaro, Iuliano, Albertini (Pessotto 78), Di Biagio, Inzaghi (Delvecchio 67), Del Piero, Fiore (Totti 83).

NETHERLANDS: Van der Sar, Bosvelt, Stam, F. de Boer (c), Van Bronckhorst, Cocu (Winter 95), Davids, Overmars, Kluivert, Bergkamp (Seedorf 87), Zenden (Van Vossen 77).

Booked: Zambrotta (15), Iuliano (17), Toldo (38), Maldini (45+2), Di Biagio (87), Zenden (28), Davids (50), Van Bronckhorst (75), Stam (93).
Sent off: Zambrotta (34).

FINAL
France v Italy

Before the semi-finals, *De Telegraaf* had carried out an opinion poll among the Dutch public, asking them who would win Euro 2000. Italy picked up a nice round number of votes: zero. So much for democracy.

In Rotterdam, Thierry Henry's instinctive half-volley surprised Toldo early on, bouncing off his near post. But little else was memorable about a cagey first half. Zidane, engulfed by relentless pressing, managed only a terrible free kick; as it flew over, Desailly nastily elbowed Cannavaro in the face. Cannavaro called Desailly 'a horse' afterwards, presumably not of the Istabraq variety.

Just after half-time, Zidane made his only real contribution, sending Henry away with a fine pass, but Cannavaro got back brilliantly to block the shot. Zoff then took the fateful decision to replace Fiore with Alessandro Del Piero. Two minutes later, his team went in front.

With Lizarazu clinging to him like a limpet, Totti managed a lovely back-heel that found the overlapping Pessotto. Blanc and Desailly failed to cut out the cross, and Delvecchio arrived at the right moment to score his first international goal, side-footing home from six yards.

Totti was at the heart of the move that should have wrapped up Italy's second European title. Darting into the French half, he found Del Piero on the left. Despite Thuram bearing down on him, the substitute had time to take two touches, but scuffed a woeful effort wide. The football gods hadn't finished with Del Piero yet. In the 84th minute, Massimo Ambrosini's pass gave him a near-identical opportunity, but he squandered this one too, tapping it against Barthez's foot.

Seconds of stoppage time remained when Barthez thumped a long, desperate free kick towards Italy's box. Trezeguet nodded it on, and Cannavaro couldn't stop it reaching Sylvain Wiltord on the left. He chested it down before hitting an unexceptional low shot which passed through Nesta's legs. It was still meat and drink for Toldo – but the goalkeeper was fatally slow to get down. Getting some of his glove on the ball, but not enough, he watched despairingly as it trickled into the far corner. The Italian subs, congregating on the touchline, instantly sank back down into the dugout – except for Conte, who leaned against it wearing the expression of a man watching his house burn to the ground.

Italy now had nothing left to give: the last-ditch manner of their capitulation had broken them. And when the exhausted Albertini miscontrolled Cannavaro's pass after 13 minutes of extra time, substitute Robert Pirès pounced on it. '[The Italians] were dead,' he said. 'I saw their faces. The right side of their defence was burned.'

He slipped past Albertini and Cannavaro, reached the byline and picked out another substitute, David Trezeguet. The striker drew back his left foot and slammed a half-volley into the top corner. 'It was a complete blackout,' Pirès reflected. 'On the ground, I saw Toldo collapsed, and the ball in the net. I felt like I was flying.'

Dino Zoff, who had come within 45 seconds of the prize, sensationally resigned next day after football expert Silvio Berlusconi accused him of being 'the last of the amateurs' for not setting anybody to mark Zidane (who hadn't influenced the game at all). 'I don't take lessons in dignity from Signor Berlusconi,' he retorted. 'I was offended as a man. Berlusconi doesn't have to tell me what to do.'

But what a finish to a marvellous competition. Euro 2000 was a huge shot in the arm for international football: three weeks of excellent teams carrying the fight to each other. The group stage alone witnessed more goals than the entirety of Euro 96, and the poorest sides went home as soon as possible. Many top-class players seized the moment; not just the obvious stars like Figo, Zidane, Kluivert, Nedvěd, Totti and Guardiola, but unexpected discoveries like Chivu, Conceição, Zahovič, Milošević and Toldo.

France now joined West Germany of 1972 and 1974 in holding the world and European titles simultaneously. And yet it couldn't have happened but for the tragic profligacy of a player whose stop-start international career never touched the heights of his club career. 'Money is important, because it helps you to live better,' Alessandro Del Piero told the press weeks earlier after his latest contract with Juventus made him the world's highest-paid footballer. 'But there are lots of things in life you simply can't buy.'

8pm, 2 July 2000
De Kuip, Rotterdam
Attendance: 48,200
Referee: Anders Frisk (Sweden)

FRANCE 2 (Wiltord 90+3, Trezeguet 103)
ITALY 1 (Delvecchio 55)
France won on the golden goal after extra time

FRANCE: Barthez, Thuram, Lizarazu (Pirès 86), Vieira, Blanc, Desailly, Deschamps (c), Djorkaeff (Trezeguet 76), Dugarry (Wiltord 58), Zidane, Henry.

ITALY: Toldo, Pessotto, Maldini (c), Nesta, Cannavaro, Iuliano, Albertini, Di Biagio (Ambrosini 66), Delvecchio (Montella 86), Totti, Fiore (Del Piero 53).

Booked: Thuram (58), Di Biagio (31), Cannavaro (42), Totti (90).

2004

LENNART JOHANSSON hesitated before opening the envelope at a conference centre in Aachen on 12 October 1999. For months, Spain had been the unbackable favourites to host Euro 2004. But another name was on the slip of paper: Portugal. Their bid, under the slogan 'We Love Football', saw them spend €250m on redeveloping five stadia and building five new ones, including a half-finished structure in the north-western city of Braga, of which more later.

In footballing terms, this tournament was coming too late for Portugal, who had slid downhill since 2000 and then appointed the extremely expensive Luiz Felipe Scolari, a World Cup winner with Brazil, as manager. A Gene Hackman lookalike, Scolari could call on several of Porto's Champions League winners, as well as Manchester United's coruscating winger Cristiano Ronaldo, still raw but clearly a superstar in the making.

France were defending their crown in a state of vulnerability. The glory of Rotterdam had been followed by a catastrophic 2002 World Cup in which they couldn't even score a goal. Manager Roger Lemerre got canned, and his successor Jacques Santini won all eight qualifiers against weak opposition. But the team looked old: Zinedine Zidane was 32, Fabien Barthez almost 33, Lilian Thuram 32, Bixente Lizarazu 34, Marcel Desailly pushing 35.

In Group B, the French would face England, whose Golden Generation (cough) were on their last chance until the next one. To add to his old firm of Beckham, Gerrard, Owen et al., Sven-Göran Eriksson now had the precocious 18-year-old Everton striker Wayne Rooney, whose unnerving directness had terrorised Premier League defences. But Eriksson self-defeatingly shoved Paul Scholes, his best midfielder, on to the left so that neither Gerrard nor Lampard had to ride the bench. And he had lost his best centre-back, Rio Ferdinand, to a ban for missing a drugs test.

Still, England looked in better shape than Germany. Rudi Völler had worked wonders to drag an undistinguished squad to the 2002 World Cup Final, but surely couldn't repeat the trick. Four months after that final in Yokohama, his team scraped a 2-1 win at home to the Faroe Islands. In the return game in Tórshavn, it was goalless with 88 minutes on the clock before Fredi Bobic and Miroslav Klose scored to avert a total humiliation.

After yet another poor result, a 0-0 draw in Reykjavik, Völler exploded in a live TV interview, angered by Günter Netzer's analysis in the studio. 'It's a load of crap,' he yelled. '[Netzer] spoke of a new low for Saturday night entertainment. After every match where we don't score, it's a new, even lower, low point. I can't listen to this shit any more!' By now, there was no disguising German ordinariness. A 5-1 friendly defeat by Romania moved Franz Beckenbauer to exclaim, 'Anyone looking at this result will think it's a printing error.'

Another German manager, Berti Vogts, never seemed a good fit for Scotland in the same group. After losing embarrassingly in Lithuania, they scraped into a play-off against the Netherlands, surprisingly won the first leg 1-0, then got battered 6-0 in Amsterdam. Wales won their first five games, including a rousing 2-1 victory over Italy, but their momentum petered out to hand them a play-off with Russia. The first leg in Moscow ended goalless, and the Welsh blew it with a gutless performance in Cardiff four days later, losing 1-0. Yegor Titov, Russia's best midfielder, tested positive afterwards for a stimulant; UEFA banned him for a year, but refused Wales's demands for a replay.

Ireland, too, flopped. With the air still polluted from Roy Keane's Saipan meltdown, the FAI sacked Mick McCarthy after defeats by Russia and Switzerland. Replacement Brian Kerr had performed miracles with underage Irish teams in the 1990s, but the only teams he beat here were Albania and Georgia before a no-show in Basel finished Ireland off. Still, they did better than their Northern neighbours, who failed to score at all in Group 6.

After the Netherlands' failure to qualify for the 2002 World Cup, the KNVB sacked Louis van Gaal and brought Dick Advocaat back. He had a small handful of exciting kids: the electric winger Arjen Robben, the mouthy playmaker Wesley Sneijder, the inventive Rafael van der Vaart. But the Czechs, a team they never enjoyed facing, were waiting for them again in Group D. So were surprise packet Latvia, who qualified after a string of minimalist away wins (one of them via a last-minute own goal by San Marino's Carlo Valentini) and a stirring comeback from 2-0 down in Istanbul. 'Germany and the Netherlands will take 11 stars to Portugal, but we'll take a very friendly family,' promised manager Aleksandrs Starkovs, who conducted all his football matters in Russian rather than Latvian.

Greece were back, for the first time since 1980. After defeats by Spain and Ukraine seemed to have killed them off instantly, they suddenly began to click as a unit under their Goethe-quoting manager Otto Rehhagel, a salty seadog whose career had ebbed and flowed for decades in the Bundesliga. His first game, a 5-1 defeat in Helsinki, saw one Greek headline ask, 'So you think you know everything, Mr Super Trainer?'

The turning point was a gutsy win over Spain in Zaragoza, in which Greece survived a second-half onslaught after Stelios Giannakopoulos scored from distance. Six wins in a row, without a goal conceded, saw them pip Spain to automatic qualification. 'For us, it started two years before the actual tournament itself,' said captain Theo Zagorakis. 'That was when we began to feel it.'

Spain still qualified easily by winning their play-off against Norway – who had emerged from a group that overflowed with last-ditch drama. On the penultimate night of action, in Copenhagen, Martin Laursen's 95th-minute equaliser kept Denmark alive and dashed qualification out of Romania's hands: the east Europeans were left to curse the wastefulness of Adrian Mutu, Florin Cernat and Florin Bratu, who between them missed four sitters in the closing stages when Romania were leading 2-1.

Simultaneously, in Sarajevo, Bosnia-Herzegovina couldn't find the winner against Denmark that would have taken them to the finals. Elvir Bolić's header missed by inches in the 86th minute, and Denmark hung on to win the group. Just two points separated them from fourth-placed Bosnia, with Norway and Romania in between.

The margins promised to be even closer in what looked like the most open European Championship in years. Days before the big kick-off, Rudi Völler remarked presciently, 'Little things will decide the matches.'

GROUP A
Portugal, Greece, Russia, Spain

The general attitude to Greece's prospects was summed up by a dismissive preview in *The Observer* which surmised that they 'lack the class to get out of the group; however, the heat could mean that they pick up a point against Russia'. But in Porto, they pooped Portugal's opening-day party with an unexpected and hilarious win.

The pre-match assumption that Greece would be happy to draw was dispelled in the opening seconds as Angelos Charisteas kicked fresh air in the box. Portugal soon paid for their looseness when Georgios Karagounis pounced on Paulo Ferreira's sloppy pass. Nobody challenged him as he bore down on goal, and his weak low shot bobbled inside the post, making goalkeeper Ricardo Pereira look bad.

Portugal tottered throughout the first half. The *geração de ouro*'s last survivors – Fernando Couto, Luís Figo and Rui Costa – were all awful, and Maniche and Costinha struggled without Deco, their 'brain' at Porto. Greece could have scored twice more early on, but Charisteas shot wide after Costinha's mistake, and Takis Fyffas thumped Zisis Vryzas's cross wildly over the bar.

Along with Deco, Cristiano Ronaldo came on at half-time, but the teenager's first contribution was best forgotten. Sprinting back in pursuit of Giourkas Seitaridis, he clipped the Greek's heels for a penalty which Angelos Basinas slotted into the top corner, leaving Portugal in disarray.

As time ebbed away, the outstanding Seitaridis deflected Ronaldo's shot past the post, and goalkeeper Antonis Nikopolidis turned Nuno Gomes's effort around the same upright. Stoppage time was almost up by the time Ronaldo headed home Figo's corner; the home fans barely cheered as it hit the net. Portugal already seemed holed beneath the waterline, sinking in *saudade* again.

═══

As usual, Spain were a stylish but flimsy outfit, over-endowed in some positions and impoverished in others. And their baseball-capped manager Iñaki Sáez, a long-time coach of their youth teams, couldn't dispel the perception that he was keeping the seat warm for a bigger name. But in Faro-Loulé, they sparkled sporadically in overcoming the disappointing Russians.

Raúl alone might have had a hat-trick. He shot across the face of the goal, put a header wide under no pressure, and blazed off target from a good position. But on the hour, Russia buckled. Substitute Juan Carlos Valerón (on the pitch for only 36 seconds) controlled Carles Puyol's cross with his first touch, steered it away from Aleksei Smertin with his second, and buried it with his third.

Russia's lack of belief reflected the defeatism of their manager Georgi Yartsev, who had whinged about drawing three Mediterranean/Aegean sides ('I wanted northern nations that would die in the heat like us'). With Viktor Onopko injured and Yegor Titov suspended, they created only one good opening, when Dmitri Alenichev skated around three defenders on the left before Iker Casillas blocked his shot.

Russian centre-back Roman Sharonov was sent off near the end, getting his second caution for tripping young Fernando Torres. Earlier, Rolan Gusev should have been off for a nasty lunge on Vicente, who tortured Yevseyev throughout.

Beforehand, playmaker Aleksandr Mostovoi had sourly denigrated Russia's chances, dismissing his team-mates' ability ('We lack spark: you look at Spain and you see things, but not with Russia') and hinting darkly that UEFA would look after Spain because of their big travelling support. Now he attacked Yartsev for overworking the team in training. 'We were totally shattered,' he said. 'I don't think Spain were worked as hard as we were before this tournament. I'm really angry about it. I don't think we'll qualify now.'

The RFU's powerful boss, Vyacheslav Koloskov, shot back that Mostovoi 'only pretended to give his all on the pitch' and, inevitably, he was sent home for insubordination. 'Bridges have been burned,' sighed a headline in Russian paper *Sport Express*, a pun on Mostovoi's surname, which translated as bridge.

═══

If Russia's tournament was already disintegrating, Greece's was scaling new heights. In sunny Porto, they had Spain's number once again, scrapping out a deserved draw. The Spanish had the youngest squad in the competition (average age 25.5); a more seasoned team might have seen the game out without wavering.

One Spanish newspaper described Greece as 'not the cavalry of Alexander, but as effective and functional as a Bauhaus building'. They were prepared to show their studs, as were Spain. The first half was littered with bad fouls: Kostas Katsouranis on Raúl, Carlos Marchena on Karagounis, Giannakopoulos on Puyol, Karagounis on Joseba Etxeberría, and Iván Helguera on Vryzas. All were deservedly booked, and all except Katsouranis protested indignantly.

But Spain's goal was exquisite. When Michalis Kapsis underhit a pass outside Greece's box, Raúl fooled Traianos Dellas by back-heeling it to Fernando Morientes, who stepped inside Katsouranis and cracked his shot into the far corner.

Instead of drawing encouragement from that, Raúl sank into a slough of despond (though UEFA idiotically named him man of the match). He ought to have made it 2-0 in the second half when Joaquín served him a perfect cross, but headed feebly over. That miss proved fatal minutes later. After Helguera failed to head away Vassilios Tsiartas's cross, Charisteas chested it down and shot straight at Casillas, the ball going in off the keeper's leg. TV cameras caught first Sáez, then King Juan Carlos in the VIP box, looking sick.

Helguera rounded off his miserable day when he put another header straight at Nikopolidis. Afterwards, Rehhagel complained about the colour of the nets: 'They should be white and cheerful, not black and depressing.' The 65-year-old was fast becoming one of the personalities of the tournament.

═══

Scolari reached for his axe before Portugal met Russia in Lisbon, dropping three defenders and replacing Rui Costa with Deco. 'Half-nil will be enough.

We have to win,' he said. FPF president Gilberto Madail was so stressed he felt unable to attend the game, but he needn't have worried.

An early goal set Portugal on their way: Deco's cross-shot arrived at Maniche's feet, and he reacted before Yevseyev to shoot deftly home. Russia were still in the game when they lost their goalkeeper. Dmitri Sennikov's suicidal back-pass put Pauleta through, and the ponytailed Sergei Ovchinnikov raced outside of his box to block with his chest. A great save – but referee Terje Hauge, notorious in Norwegian football as an inflexible stickler, mistook it for handball and off Ovchinnikov went.

Replacement goalkeeper Vyacheslav Malafeev finger-tipped Figo's shot on to a post after a succulent Portuguese move, before Figo was taken off to give Ronaldo more game-time. The teenager grabbed his chance, seeing his cross converted by Rui Costa near the end. At last, Scolari had found his best line-up.

=====

Before the eliminated Russians faced Greece, their camp received an undignified fax from Scolari begging them to do their best. Watched by the biggest travelling support they had ever taken to a tournament (many of whom were super-wealthy oligarchs domiciled in the area), they instantly gave him what he wanted.

Early on, Katsouranis fell over trying to clear. Dmitri Kirichenko, reacting instantly, burst between two defenders and toe-poked the ball past Nikopolidis with 67 seconds on the clock – the fastest goal ever scored in the European Championship finals.

The 6ft 4in Dmitri Bulykin soon doubled Russia's lead with a forceful diving header from Gusev's corner. As Greece reeled, 2-0 almost became 3-0: Basinas inadvertently cushioned another Gusev cross into the path of Andrei Karyaka, who shot horribly over. Like Raúl's header, this was a moment that had far-reaching consequences for the tournament. Meanwhile, another Bulykin header clipped a post.

Then came one of the pivotal moments of Euro 2004. Zisis Vryzas spent the tournament on the left wing, and would score only nine times in a 68-cap international career. But now he tucked away the most important goal of his life. Trapping the ball on his thigh, he turned past Sharonov and lifted his shot over Malofeev.

At this stage, Greece were still going out on goal difference, and Russia controlled the second half. Late on, Aleksei Bugaev's cross rolled past three team-mates in the goalmouth, and Kirichenko couldn't force it home. At the final whistle, the Greeks had to pray that Portugal and Spain hadn't played out a draw.

In the Iberian derby in Lisbon, two youthful pin-ups made their first starts of the tournament. Still very raw, Cristiano Ronaldo and Fernando Torres both missed first-half sitters, Torres nodding Xabi Alonso's corner wastefully over the bar and Ronaldo heading wide with Casillas stranded.

But with Spain unable to stop giving the ball away, Portugal's winner just before the hour was little surprise. Maniche's pass was flicked on by Figo to Nuno Gomes, who had replaced Pauleta at the break. Gomes twisted away from his marker Juanito and let fly, his shot whizzing through the defender's legs and past Casillas. Though hardly a top-class striker, Gomes tended to come up trumps in big matches.

Spain blew enough chances to win two games. Raúl's abysmal tournament cratered with his latest wasted header, Torres shot wide when Alonso sent him through, Ricardo Carvalho headed Albert Luque's lob off the line, and Juanito nodded the resulting corner on to the bar. With Sáez inexplicably unwilling to bring on Valerón, Portugal murdered Spain on the break in the closing stages. Raúl Bravo cleared off the line from Maniche, and Casillas smothered Gomes's shot.

Spain were out of time, and out full stop (they would have survived, at Greece's expense, if Kirichenko had converted that cross). Sáez resigned after losing only two of his 23 matches, but his waste of Valerón and refusal to use the brilliant young Xavi made that stat look irrelevant.

For the buoyant Portuguese, things suddenly looked much brighter. Sports paper *A Bola*'s untranslatable front-page headline read simply, 'Uff!!' As the nation celebrated, Lisbon's mobile phone network crashed under the weight of traffic. But Scolari's men had answered the call.

5pm, 12 June 2004
Estádio do Dragão, Porto
Attendance: 48,761
Referee: Pierluigi Collina (Italy)

GREECE 2 (Karagounis 6, Basinas 51 pen)
PORTUGAL 1 (Ronaldo 90+3)

GREECE: Antonis Nikopolidis, Giourkas Seitaridis, Traianos Dellas, Michalis Kapsis, Takis Fyssas, Theodoros Zagorakis (c), Angelos Basinas, Georgios Karagounis (Kostas Katsouranis 46), Angelos Charisteas (Vassilis Lakis 74), Zisis Vryzas, Stelios Giannakopoulos (Demis Nikolaidis 68). **Manager:** Otto Rehhagel.

PORTUGAL: Ricardo Pereira, Paulo Ferreira, Fernando Couto (c), Jorge Almeida de Andrade, Rui Jorge Dias, Francisco da Costa 'Costinha' (Nuno Soares 'Gomes' 66), Luís Figo, Nuno Ribeiro 'Maniche', Pedro Resendes 'Pauleta', Rui Manuel Costa (Anderson de Souza 'Deco' 46), Simão Sabrosa (Cristiano Ronaldo 46). **Manager:** Luiz Felipe Scolari.

Booked: Karagounis (39), Seitaridis (76), Costinha (21), Pauleta (57).

7.45pm, 12 June 2004
Estádio do Algarve, Faro-Loulé
Attendance: 28,182
Referee: Urs Meier (Switzerland)

SPAIN 1 (Valerón 60)
RUSSIA 0

SPAIN: Iker Casillas, Carles Puyol, Carlos Marchena, Iván Helguera, Raúl Bravo Sanfélix, David Albelda, Rubén Baraja (Xabi Alonso 59), Joseba Etxeberría, Fernando Morientes (Juan Carlos Valerón 59), Raúl González (c) (Fernando Torres 78), Vicente Rodríguez. **Manager:** Iñaki Sáez.

RUSSIA: Sergei Ovchinnikov, Vadim Yevseyev, Aleksei Smertin (c), Roman Sharonov, Dmitri Sennikov, Yevgeni Aldonin (Dmitri Sychyov 68), Rolan Gusev (Vladislav Radimov 46), Dmitri Alenichev, Dmitri Bulykin, Aleksandr Mostovoi, Marat Izmailov (Andrei Karyaka 74). **Manager:** Georgi Yartsev.

Booked: Baraja (43), Marchena (66), Albelda (85), Gusev (12), Sharonov (27), Smertin (29), Aldonin (32), Radimov (90).

Sent off: Sharonov (88).

5pm, 16 June 2004
Estádio do Bessa, Porto
Attendance: 25,444
Referee: Luboš Michel (Slovakia)

GREECE 1 (Charisteas 66)
SPAIN 1 (Morientes 28)

GREECE: Nikopolidis, Seitaridis, Dellas, Kapsis, Fyssas (Stelios Venetidis 86), Zagorakis (c), Katsouranis, Karagounis (Vassilios Tsiartas 53), Charisteas, Vryzas, Giannakopoulos (Nikolaidis 49).

SPAIN: Casillas, Puyol, Marchena, Helguera, Raúl Bravo, Albelda, Baraja, Etxeberría (Joaquín Sánchez 46), Morientes (Valerón 65), Raúl (c) (Torres 80), Vicente.

Booked: Katsouranis (7), Giannakopoulos (24), Karagounis (27), Zagorakis (61), Vryzas (90), Marchena (16), Helguera (37).

7.45pm, 16 June 2004
Estádio da Luz, Lisbon
Attendance: 59,273
Referee: Terje Hauge (Norway)

PORTUGAL 2 (Maniche 7, Rui Costa 89)
RUSSIA 0

PORTUGAL: Ricardo, Miguel Monteiro, Ricardo Carvalho, Andrade, Nuno Valente, Costinha, Figo (c) (Ronaldo 78), Maniche, Pauleta (Gomes 57), Deco, Simão (Rui Costa 63).

RUSSIA: Ovchinnikov, Yevseyev, Smertin (c), Aleksei Bugaev, Sennikov, Aldonin (Vyacheslav Malafeev 45+2), Dmitri Loskov, Alenichev, Aleksandr Kerzhakov, Karyaka (Bulykin 79), Izmailov (Vladimir Bystrov 72).

Booked: Carvalho (24), Deco (85), Smertin (16), Yevseyev (21), Alenichev (90+2).
Sent off: Ovchinnikov (45).

7.45pm, 20 June 2004
Estádio do Algarve, Faro-Loulé
Attendance: 24,347
Referee: Gilles Veissière (France)

RUSSIA 2 (Kirichenko 2, Bulykin 17)
GREECE 1 (Vryzas 43)

RUSSIA: Malafeev, Aleksei Anyukov, Sharonov (Sennikov 56), Bugaev, Yevseyev, Radimov, Gusev, Alenichev (c), Bulykin (Sychyov 46), Karyaka (Igor Semshov 46), Dmitri Kirichenko.

GREECE: Nikopolidis, Seitaridis, Dellas, Kapsis, Venetidis (Fyssas 89), Basinas (Tsiartas 42), Zagorakis (c), Katsouranis, Charisteas, Vryzas, Dimitris Papadopoulos (Nikolaidis 70).

Booked: Sharonov (15), Anyukov (28), Karyaka (39), Alenichev (65), Radimov (71), Malafeev (88), Vryzas (45), Dellas (86).

7.45pm, 20 June 2004
Estádio José Alvalade, Lisbon
Attendance: 47,491
Referee: Anders Frisk (Sweden)

PORTUGAL 1 (Gomes 57)
SPAIN 0

PORTUGAL: Ricardo, Miguel, Carvalho, Andrade, Valente, Costinha, Figo (c) (Armando Gonçalves 'Petit' 77), Maniche, Pauleta (Gomes 46), Deco, Ronaldo (Couto 84).

SPAIN: Casillas, Puyol, Juan Gutiérrez 'Juanito' (Morientes 79), Helguera, Raúl Bravo, Albelda (Baraja 65), Alonso, Joaquín (Albert Luque 71), Torres, Raúl (c), Vicente.

Booked: Pauleta (7), Gomes (65), Albelda (8), Juanito (68), Puyol (74).

GROUP A	P	W	D	L	F	A	GD	Pts
PORTUGAL	3	2	0	1	4	2	+2	6
GREECE	3	1	1	1	4	4	0	4
SPAIN	3	1	1	1	2	2	0	4
RUSSIA	3	1	0	2	2	4	− 2	3

Portugal and Greece qualified.

GROUP B
France, England, Croatia, Switzerland

It seemed certain that France would walk Group B, and probable that England would join them – an impression not dispelled by the error-strewn opener between Croatia and Switzerland in Leiria, where a gorgeous new stadium was overlooked by an even more beautiful 12th-century castle.

Time had been unkind to the Croats. Their septuagenarian coach Otto Barić, an unapologetic homophobe ('There's no place in my team for a gay') wearing a horribly obvious wig, had lost not only all the big-name veterans but also first-choice goalkeeper Stipe Pletikosa to a thigh injury. Pletikosa's replacement, the visibly nervous Tomislav Butina, would make an almighty meal of saving Benjamin Huggel's long shot in the second half.

Butina was ropey, but his opposite number looked worse. The 36-year-old Jörg Stiel's highlights reel included a booking for dissent, some dithering that gave Niko Kovač a free header, and a piece of slapstick when he and right-back Bernt Haas tried to kick the ball simultaneously after leaving it for each other.

Media reports had claimed Switzerland's Francophone and Germanic players couldn't understand each other in training. In one of the strangest moments of the tournament, their offside trap disintegrated before half-time when Dario Šimić floated a free kick into the box, leaving five Croats onside. Stiel pushed Josip Šimunić's header off the line, and Ivica Olić nodded the rebound on to the bar from almost under it.

Early in the second half, Johann Vogel received his second yellow card for moronically kicking the ball away, but the one-paced Croatians couldn't make their extra man count. A goalless draw was a bad result for both teams.

Miroslav Blažević, the old sage of 1998, afterwards dismissed Croatia as 'a bunch of amateurs, not real footballers' and said Barić was leading them 'like a blind man', forcing HNS president Vlatko Marković to broker a truce between him and Barić. 'Blažević should shut up,' said defender Robert Kovač. 'We're a little country. We don't have extraordinary players any more.'

———

Euro 2004 would witness the birth of the name-appeal midfield partnership that helped keep England stunted for nearly a decade, with Sven-Göran Eriksson meekly acceding to media demands that domestic superheroes Steven Gerrard and Frank Lampard both be picked. This box-office approach to team selection almost saw England home against France in Lisbon. But not quite.

Adidas's new silver-sheened ball, the Roteiro, seemed a little light for the occasion, with France hitting countless efforts off target in the first half and both teams overhitting passes. But seven minutes before the interval, England scored with their first real effort. David Beckham floated in one of his set-piece specials, and Lampard outjumped Mickaël Silvestre to head home the first goal France had conceded in a year.

France had two quick strikers, a good winger and the world's best creative attacker, but no urgency whatsoever. And on 73 minutes, England seemed poised to finish them off. Rooney's signature move at the time was to run thrillingly and directly at the opposition defence with the ball glued to his boot. Now he did it again, lobbing the ball over Lilian Thuram and charging deep into French territory. Silvestre backed off, then brought him down – but Beckham's feeble penalty was easy for Barthez.

As his team curled up into a big white ball, Eriksson withdrew Owen, Rooney and Scholes. But in stoppage time, as Claude Makélélé – France's least threatening outfield player – hovered outside the box, Emile Heskey senselessly bowled him over. Zidane's free kick whizzed over the wall and past David James to nestle inside the far post.

A stunning kick in the teeth for England, who didn't know what was coming next. A minute later, under no pressure, Gerrard unaccountably knocked a feeble back-pass toward James. Henry, suddenly coming to life, gobbled it up; James came steaming out and knocked him flying into the air. Penalty. After discreetly vomiting, Zidane fired it into the same corner as the free kick. There was barely any time left for England to restart.

'We thought we had the game won, and we should have won it,' Eriksson said, but he had blown it with those craven substitutions. After seeing what Croatia and Switzerland had offered, however, England must have known they would be fine.

———

The build-up to their meeting with Switzerland was boozy, boisterous and bloody. For two nights, Algarve's Montechoro Strip was the scene of incessant rioting by English fans, with several local bars trashed before riot police restored order. 'They go to the bars, drink all day, then someone says something which sparks it all off,' said local restaurateur José Malheiro.

For an hour in Coimbra, England were sloppy. Sol Campbell and Gerrard both glanced Swiss set-pieces just past their own goal, while John Terry blocked Alex Frei's shot. Meanwhile, Rooney was frenziedly putting himself about, getting a yellow card for clobbering Stiel.

But Switzerland had nothing to show for their pressure, and eventually England made them pay. On the left, Owen waited for Rooney's run into the six-yard box, then placed a cross on to his head. The goal briefly made Rooney the youngest scorer in European Championship history; he celebrated by booting the corner flag.

Soon, a gift landed in England's lap when Bernt Haas got two bookings for stupid fouls on Gerrard and Ashley Cole. As Switzerland faded away, Rooney's daisy-cutter hit the post and rebounded in off Stiel's head, before Gerrard made it 3-0, tapping home Gary Neville's cross. England were alive again, even if the scoreline flattered them. Meanwhile, Switzerland sent Frei home after TV footage showed him spitting on Gerrard. It wouldn't be the last European Championship that he would leave prematurely.

———

In Leiria, what looked to be a routine win for France over Croatia suddenly turned into something else entirely. Perhaps the sight of certain French stars showboating at 1-0 caused something to snap in Croatian minds. In a rousing second half, they carried the game to their supposed betters, playing some great football.

Initially, though, they again looked poor, and individual ineptitude handed France the opening goal. When Zidane swung a free kick into the box, Igor Tudor seemed in two minds whether to trap it or clear it, before his long leg pushed it past Butina.

Croatia kept standing off Zidane, seemingly content to admire him running the game. Just before half-time, he set up what would have been the best goal of the competition, outrageously back-flicking Henry's short corner into the goalmouth where William Gallas, arriving at speed, headed it wide.

The Croats showed a better attitude after half-time, roared on by their raucous fans, one of whose chants translated as, 'Play, you gays!' (perhaps Barić had been preaching to the choir). Before long, they drew level. Olivier Dacourt lost possession, Silvestre lunged in on Đovani Roso to give away another penalty, and Milan Rapaić put it away. Now we had a match.

More French laziness – a terrible David Trezeguet pass on halfway – was punished when Dado Pršo cut into the box from the right and glided past Silvestre. The veteran Marcel Desailly misjudged the bounce, allowing Pršo to thrash it high into the net. The French were so shaken that they went into an impromptu huddle, and their equaliser was a sickener for Croatia. Tudor, having a nightmare, underhit a back-pass to Butina, whose clearance was blocked by Trezeguet's arm with referee Kim Milton Nielsen unsighted. The striker rolled it into an empty goal as Croatia protested bitterly.

But France should still have lost. In stoppage time, Zidane (who had long since disappeared) gave the ball away and Olić pulled it back for the rugged Ivica Mornar, who brushed off Desailly before blazing over. 'Maybe the gods decided it was better that way,' Mornar mused, 'and my goal will come on Monday [against England].'

———

The French wrapped it up against Switzerland, as expected. But again they were complacent, not bothering to pick up the talented Hakan Yakin, who caused them trouble in the opening stages. Meanwhile, Henry missed a hat-trick of scoreable headers and got booked for a desperate dive.

Zidane showed him the way, nipping between Stiel and Christoph Spycher to glance home Pirès's corner. But Switzerland soon hit back. Yakin dummied Gygax's pass, and Johan Vonlanthen got in behind the wretched Silvestre and slid the ball past Barthez. It made him the youngest ever scorer in the finals at 18 years and 141 days, breaking Rooney's short-lived record.

Late on, Henry finally delivered. First, he held off Spycher before side-footing Louis Saha's cross home. Then he galloped down the left, cut inside Murat Yakin and prodded the ball past Stiel. But France's next opponents would be less accommodating than Switzerland.

——

After their heroics against France, Croatia were breathing fire. 'Every child born in Croatia has two rules,' Đovani Roso declared before they faced England in Lisbon. 'First, you go to church, and the second rule is football. God made us fighters. I'm warning England that we want victory more than them.'

At first, it looked like Roso's fighting words weren't just windy nonsense as England began disastrously. When Rapaić sent a free kick into the box, Ashley Cole's clearance flew towards his own goal. David James did well to save, but it bounced off Terry's knee and Niko Kovač jabbed it in.

At least England could now forget about trying to sit on a lead for the entire game again. A move involving six players saw Michael Owen burst into the box, and when Butina kept him out, Rooney headed across the goalmouth for Paul Scholes to nod home his first international goal since 2001.

By half-time, England were ahead. After good work by Owen and Scholes, Croatia stood back, allowing Rooney to unleash a magnificent shot which Butina scraped but couldn't save. A third English goal was likely long before it arrived: exchanging passes with Owen, Rooney charged through a square defensive line and kept his nerve with a cool finish.

Because England couldn't defend dead balls to save their lives, the game wasn't over. Ledley King failed to pick up Tudor, who headed Darjio Srna's free kick into the corner, prompting James to scream, 'Two fucking free kicks!' But if England's defending was unsteady, Croatia's was worse. Lampard strode up to the edge of the box unchallenged, dribbled past Šimunić and scored with a low shot for 4-2.

By now, Rooney's teenage rampage had taken on an unnerving momentum. Gibbering English journalists kept likening the man-child to various animals (gorilla, bull, baby elephant, rhino), while the starstruck Eriksson compared him to Pelé at the 1958 World Cup. 'I'm frightened because of the pressure it puts on him, but I can't stop it,' he said.

5pm, 13 June 2004
Estádio Dr Magalhães Pessoa, Leiria
Attendance: 24,090
Referee: Lucílio Cardoso Cortez Batista (Portugal)

CROATIA 0
SWITZERLAND 0

CROATIA: Tomislav Butina, Dario Šimić (Darijo Srna 61), Robert Kovač, Josip Šimunić, Borislav Živković (c), Niko Kovač, Nenad Bjelica (Đovani Roso 74), Ivica Mornar, Dado Pršo, Tomo Šokota, Ivica Olić (Milan Rapaić 46). **Manager:** Otto Barić.

SWITZERLAND: Jörg Stiel (c), Bernt Haas, Murat Yakin, Patrick Müller, Christoph Spycher, Johann Vogel, Benjamin Huggel, Raphaël Wicky (Stéphane Henchoz 83), Alex Frei, Hakan Yakin (Daniel Gygax 87), Stéphane Chapuisat (Fabio Celestini 55). **Manager:** Köbi Kuhn.

Booked: Pršo (13), Bjelica (30), Rapaić (48), Živković (51), Mornar (52), Vogel (4), Huggel (41), Stiel (73).
Sent off: Vogel (50).

7.45pm, 13 June 2004
Estádio da Luz, Lisbon
Attendance: 62,487
Referee: Markus Merk (Germany)

FRANCE 2 (Zidane 90+1, 90+3 pen)
ENGLAND 1 (Lampard 38)

FRANCE: Fabien Barthez, William Gallas, Bixente Lizarazu, Mikaël Silvestre (Willy Sagnol 79), Lilian Thuram, Patrick Vieira, Claude Makélélé (Olivier Dacourt 90+4), Robert Pirès (Sylvain Wiltord 76), David Trezeguet, Zinedine Zidane (c), Thierry Henry. **Manager:** Jacques Santini.

ENGLAND: David James, Gary Neville, Ashley Cole, Ledley King, Sol Campbell, Steven Gerrard, David Beckham (c), Frank Lampard, Wayne Rooney (Emile Heskey 76), Michael Owen (Darius Vassell 69), Paul Scholes (Owen Hargreaves 76). **Manager:** Sven-Göran Eriksson.

Booked: Pirès (49), Silvestre (72), Scholes (54), Lampard (71), James (90+2).

5pm, 17 June 2004
Estádio Cidade de Coimbra, Coimbra
Attendance: 28,214
Referee: Valentin Ivanov (Russia)

ENGLAND 3 (Rooney 23, Stiel 75 og, Gerrard 82)
SWITZERLAND 0

ENGLAND: James, G. Neville, Cole, John Terry, Campbell, Gerrard, Beckham (c), Scholes (Hargreaves 70), Rooney (Kieron Dyer 83), Owen (Vassell 72), Lampard.

SWITZERLAND: Stiel (c), Haas, M. Yakin, Müller, Spycher, Celestini (Ricardo Cabanas 54), Huggel, Wicky, Frei, H. Yakin (Johan Vonlanthen 84), Chapuisat (Gygax 46).

Booked: Rooney (18), Celestini (23), Haas (49).
Sent off: Haas (60).

7.45pm, 17 June 2004
Estádio Dr Magalhães Pessoa, Leiria
Attendance: 29,160
Referee: Kim Milton Nielsen (Denmark)

CROATIA 2 (Rapaić 48 pen, Pršo 52)
FRANCE 2 (Tudor 22 og, Trezeguet 64)

CROATIA: Butina, Šimić (c), Igor Tudor, R. Kovač, Šimunić, N. Kovač, Roso, Bjelica (Jerko Leko 68), Pršo, Šokota (Olić 73), Rapaić (Mornar 87).

FRANCE: Barthez, Gallas (Sagnol 81), Silvestre, Thuram, Desailly (c), Vieira, Dacourt (Benoît Pedretti 79), Wiltord (Pirès 70), Trezeguet, Zidane, Henry.

Booked: Tudor (39), Roso (61), R. Kovač (64), Leko (78), Vieira (32), Dacourt (60).

7.45pm, 21 June 2004
Estádio Cidade de Coimbra, Coimbra
Attendance: 28,111
Referee: Luboš Michel (Slovakia)

FRANCE 3 (Zidane 20, Henry 76, 84)
SWITZERLAND 1 (Vonlanthen 26)

FRANCE: Barthez, Sagnol (Gallas 46, Jean-Alain Boumsong 90+2), Lizarazu, Silvestre, Thuram, Vieira, Makélélé, Pirès, Trezeguet (Louis Saha 75), Zidane (c), Henry.

SWITZERLAND: Stiel (c), Henchoz (Ludovic Magnin 85), M. Yakin, Müller, Spycher, Vogel, Cabanas, Wicky, Vonlanthen, H. Yakin (Huggel 60), Gygax (Milaim Rama 85).

Booked: Henry (47), H. Yakin (43), Wicky (66), Huggel (75).

7.45pm, 21 June 2004
Estádio da Luz, Lisbon
Attendance: 57,047
Referee: Pierluigi Collina (Italy)

ENGLAND 4 (Scholes 40, Rooney 45+1, 68, Lampard 79)
CROATIA 2 (N. Kovač 5, Tudor 73)

ENGLAND: James, G. Neville, Cole, Terry, Campbell, Gerrard, Beckham (c), Scholes (King 70), Rooney (Vassell 72), Owen, Lampard (Phil Neville 84).

CROATIA: Butina, Šimić (Srna 67), Tudor, R. Kovač (Mornar 46), Šimunić, Živković (c), N. Kovač, Roso, Pršo, Šokota, Rapaić (Olić 55).

Booked: Šimić (63).

GROUP B	P	W	D	L	F	A	GD	Pts
FRANCE	3	2	1	0	7	4	+3	7
ENGLAND	3	2	0	1	8	4	+4	6
CROATIA	3	0	2	1	4	6	−2	2
SWITZERLAND	3	0	1	2	1	6	−5	1

France and England qualified.

GROUP C
Italy, Denmark, Sweden, Bulgaria

As Italy prepared to face Denmark, their morale was so low that Giovanni Trapattoni told captain Fabio Cannavaro to ask the press to stop criticising the team, in a transparent attempt to whip up an España 82-like siege mentality. A similar outcome seemed unlikely.

Some Danish fans trolled Italy by hanging a South Korea flag from the stadium gantry in Guimarães, but Trapattoni showed he had learned nothing from that debacle by selecting an insipid line-up. Francesco Totti, used as a playmaker rather than behind two strikers as he preferred, was dreadful, Alessandro Del Piero disappointed yet again, and Christian Vieri looked overweight and over the hill.

In contrast, Denmark showed you didn't need a team of Zidanes and Figos to play good attacking football. Gianluigi Buffon got both fists to Thomas Helveg's thunderbolt, Martin Laursen couldn't force home Jon Dahl Tomasson's flick-on, Tomasson was farcically booked for diving when Cannavaro floored him for an obvious penalty, and he later brought another excellent save from Buffon, who kicked Dennis Rommedahl's follow-up off the line.

Italy weren't completely supine: Thomas Sørensen had earlier made an outstanding double save from Del Piero and Totti. Still, 0-0 was generous to them. Afterwards, Trapattoni declared, 'There was absolutely nothing wrong with us, mentally or psychologically. We're not insane. We're trying to paint a painting with a new set of brushes. It will take time.'

At the final whistle, Totti (who had earlier elbowed Christian Poulsen in the stomach and stamped on René Henriksen's knee) childishly refused Helveg's handshake. Days later, UEFA banned him for three matches after Danish TV footage showed him spitting on Poulsen. 'Indifendibile!' screamed *La Repubblica*. An editorial in *Gazzetta dello Sport* demanded that he be sent home for 'shaming our flag'.

'I'm distraught,' Totti said. 'I don't recognise myself from the images. I give a full public apology. The true Francesco Totti is not the one on the video.' But his dastardly doppelgänger had just scuppered a big-money transfer to Real Madrid, and his tournament was now over unless Italy made the semis.

══

Sweden's clash with Bulgaria in Lisbon marked the return of their magisterial kingpin Henrik Larsson, tempted out of international retirement by a 110,000-signature petition back home. But the Bulgarians were the better team for an hour before the Barcelona-bound striker blew them away.

Swedish vulnerabilities at right-back were exposed by Martin Petrov, an inventive winger who kept coming at the out-of-position Teddy Lučić. Zoran Janković volleyed one of his crosses just off target, and Petrov himself went closer still from an improbable angle.

In the battle of the one-paced beanpoles, Zlatan Ibrahimović defeated Dimitar Berbatov on points. He created Sweden's opener, beating the offside trap on the right and crossing to give Freddie Ljungberg an open goal.

That goal was well against the run of play, and Bulgaria almost scored twice as the second half began, Janković wasting a free header and Petrov slashing a shot millimetres wide. Sweden then went 2-0 up with one of the great European Championship goals. When Erik Edman lashed over a cross from the left, Larsson launched himself to meet it with a stunning full-length diving header, a real time-capsule from the 1970s. With Bulgaria still dazed, he instantly scored again, finishing a move he had begun by steaming in at the far post to smash home Anders Svensson's cross.

Bulgaria's spirit now flooded away. When Vladimir Ivanov tripped Ljungberg (possibly outside the box), Ibrahimović selfishly hogged the penalty that would have given Larsson a hat-trick. Unruffled, Larsson created the fifth with a beautiful pass for substitute Marcus Allbäck to belt a high shot over goalkeeper Zdravko Zdravkov. One more goal would have given Sweden the biggest win in the history of the finals, in a match that hadn't felt like a thrashing at all.

=====

Carved out of a mountainside quarry, Braga's Estádio Municipal was one of the strangest stadia on the planet: two normal stands, a rugged cliff face behind one goal (you half-expected to spot a backpacker climbing it) and a grassy hillock behind the other. But enough ordnance survey, what about the football? Well, Denmark's win over the dispirited Bulgarians was untidy, unsightly and vaguely depressing, just like the plastic bags blowing around on the hill behind the goal.

Thomas Gravesen set the tone by clobbering Marian Hristov after ten seconds, which was unpunished by referee Lucílio Cortez Batista but avenged with several hard Bulgarian challenges. Denmark, unrecognisable from their first game, still had too much for Bulgaria, who were inept beyond belief. Ivanov kicked two shots off the line, Tomasson rounded Zdravkov to hit the side-netting, and eventually the Danes went in front as Martin Jørgensen squared for Tomasson to tap into a gaping net.

Cortez Batista lost control near the end. When Zdravko Lazarov was scythed down by Niclas Jensen, he ignored it, so Bulgarian captain Stiliyan Petrov exploded and received a second caution for dissent. Petrov's first booking, for a lunge on Gravesen, warranted a red itself, while Jensen should have got a second yellow for his own foul.

Not until stoppage time did Denmark finish the job. Winger Jesper Grønkjær, absent against Italy following the death of his mother, played a one-two with Tomasson and sent a neat finish into the corner. His frenzied celebration, screaming into a TV camera lens, was misinterpreted as a release from personal agony: 'Don't misunderstand me, you've always got emotion when you score a goal.' Ebbe Sand hit the bar with the last kick, but Denmark hadn't deserved a three-goal margin.

=====

'Sorry Denmark' gulped an Italian banner at the Dragão as they faced Sweden, referring to Totti's spitulence. Another one read 'No Baggio, no party'. It was proved correct, though only after a first half in which Italy played their best football since Euro 2000. Trap had bowed to media pressure to pick Andrea Pirlo, and his team immediately looked better – for a while.

Vieri, an extinct volcano, should have had three goals by the interval. He barged through to force Isaksson into a point-blank stop, and put two free headers over, both of which he would have once scored in his sleep. Just as Sweden were starting to think they could make it to half-time, Serie A's problem child gave Italy the lead. Antonio Cassano was by far the youngest player in their squad, a little malcontent forever fighting the world. He could play, too, and his glanced header from Panucci's cross gave Isaksson no chance.

Italy now sat on their lead for the whole second half, an approach which had cost them dearly in the 2002 World Cup against Croatia and South Korea. As Sweden tentatively came forward, Trapattoni's substitutions were so craven he might as well have waved a white flag from his dugout: two midfielders for two strikers, and a defender for a midfielder.

Left-winger Mattias Jonson now became a thorn in Italian flesh. Cannavaro inelegantly hacked his cross over the bar, Buffon fisted away his powerful shot, and he eluded Giuseppe Favalli to head Larsson's cross over. So Italy had been given fair warning long before Sweden's ludicrous late equaliser.

When a corner wasn't cleared, frantic head-tennis ensued before Buffon and Ibrahimović hurled themselves at the ball. The striker got there first, throwing out a leg to flick it over his shoulder with his back to goal. It looped under the bar in a high, freakish parabola, eluding Vieri's jump on the line. Ibrahimović, otherwise dire (as he so often was in big matches), called it 'a lucky goal, but also an incredible goal'. True on both counts.

To their impotent fury, Italy's fate now rested in Swedish hands. Or perhaps Danish ones. Confused? Amused? You will be. Unless you're Italian.

=====

First, Trapattoni's team had to get their own house in order against Bulgaria. But a 2-2 draw between Sweden and Denmark would eliminate them even if they beat the Bulgarians 20-0, due to UEFA's head-to-head tiebreaker (Italy had scored fewest goals in the matches between the three sides). The Italian press immediately predicted a Scandinavian stitch-up.

In foul weather in Guimarães, Bulgaria refused to play ball anyway, with Martin Petrov torturing Panucci and forcing Buffon into two impressive saves. Just before half-time, the mountain fell on Italy; or, rather, on Berbatov, clumsily flattened by Marco Materazzi. Petrov converted the penalty.

But Italy found a quick equaliser after half-time. When Cassano rifled Zambrotta's cross against the bar, it came down on the line – but Simone Perrotta made it academic, knocking it in from point-blank range.

Now it was all Italy. Substitute Vieri wasted three more free headers, and when Kiril Kotev tripped Cassano in the box, referee Valentin Ivanov waved play on. Finally, they broke through: Stefano Fiore dummied over Del Piero's cross, and Cassano swept it into the roof of the net. But as his ecstatic celebratory run took him down the touchline, his face cinematically collapsed into despair: he had seen his team-mates' expressions on the bench, and realised that the news coming in from Porto was bad. Fatally bad.

———

'We are honest people,' said Danish coach Morten Olsen. 'We're going out to win the game, and that's all.' His Swedish counterpart Tommy Söderberg added, 'We won't make a deal with Denmark.' The opening stages alone, full of hard tackles in the driving rain, vindicated both teams' integrity.

A draw would put Sweden through, but the maths were less favourable to Denmark, who quickly got on top, with Jon Dahl Tomasson their main man: Isaksson saved well from him before he teed up Grønkjær to shoot into the side-netting. Tomasson, who had flopped at Newcastle in 1997/98, now showed how far he had come since, taking Sand's lay-off in his stride and hitting an unstoppable 25-yarder that dipped into the top corner.

Falling behind woke Sweden up. Sørensen foiled Larsson and Ibrahimović with an agile double save, before Henriksen's leg diverted Mellberg's header on to the post. Denmark deserved their half-time lead, but within two minutes of the restart it was gone. Larsson was barged over by Sørensen as he chased a long pass, and picked himself up to put the penalty down the middle.

Denmark regained the lead when a corner was headed out to Kasper Bøgelund on the edge of the box. The defender's shot ricocheted off two Swedes, falling kindly for Tomasson to tuck it away stylishly. But as the hourglass's grains ran out, Sweden scraped a lucky equaliser. Christian Wilhelmsson skipped past the tired Helveg, Sørensen ineptly spilled his near-post cross, and Jonson pounced from six yards. The goalkeeper's mistake probably had him hastily removing the Amalfi coast from his list of holiday destinations, but why would he have wanted to look inept to help Sweden qualify?

Trapattoni took it stoically; others weren't as dignified. 'Someone should be ashamed, and it's not us,' whined Buffon. 'I hope the [Danish] players' children didn't watch the match, or they will have been corrupted.' Pirlo barefacedly claimed the result was 'programmed'. Milan vice-president Adriano Galliani saw it in eugenic terms: 'We got as many points as the players who are blond and beautiful. But we're dark and not as beautiful.' Some Italian media called the result a *biscotto* (biscuit), baked in advance. A false statistic that Sweden and Denmark had only drawn three times in 98 meetings was also circulated: the real figure was 15 in 96. In Rome, the Danish embassy was pelted with eggs.

In truth, Trapattoni's tactics hadn't kept pace with modern trends and his stars hadn't done their stuff. Easier to blame a stitch-up. But not everyone in Italy fell for it. 'A team gone to seed: don't look for excuses,' said *La Repubblica*. *Il Messaggero* growled, 'A single word is all that's needed – resignation.' And *Gazzetta dello Sport* pitilessly dismissed Trapattoni's record as 'four years of failure, from Japan to Portugal'. He resigned within weeks.

5pm, 14 June 2004
Estádio D. Afonso Henriques, Guimarães
Attendance: 29,595
Referee: Manuel Mejuto González (Spain)

DENMARK 0
ITALY 0

DENMARK: Thomas Sørensen, Thomas Helveg, René Henriksen (c), Martin Laursen, Niclas Jensen, Daniel Jensen, Christian Poulsen (Brian Priske 76), Dennis Rommedahl, Jon Dahl Tomasson, Ebbe Sand (Claus Jensen 69), Martin Jørgensen (Kenneth Perez 72). **Manager:** Morten Olsen.

ITALY: Gianluigi Buffon, Christian Panucci, Gianluca Zambrotta, Alessandro Nesta, Fabio Cannavaro (c), Cristiano Zanetti (Gennaro Gattuso 57), Simone Perrotta, Mauro Camoranesi (Stefano Fiore 68), Christian Vieri, Francesco Totti, Alessandro Del Piero (Antonio Cassano 64). **Manager:** Giovanni Trapattoni.

Booked: Tomasson (29), Helveg (67), Cannavaro (62), Cassano (70), Gattuso (81), Totti (90+3).

7.45pm, 14 June 2004
Estádio José Alvalade, Lisbon
Attendance: 31,652
Referee: Mike Riley (England)

SWEDEN 5 (Ljungberg 32, Larsson 57, 58, Ibrahimović 78 pen, Allbäck 90+1)
BULGARIA 0

SWEDEN: Andreas Isaksson, Teddy Lučić (Christian Wilhelmsson 41), Erik Edman, Andreas Jakobsson, Olof Mellberg (c), Tobias Linderoth, Mikael Nilsson, Anders Svensson (Kim Källström 77), Zlatan Ibrahimović (Marcus Allbäck 81), Henrik Larsson, Freddie Ljungberg. **Managers:** Tommy Söderberg and Lars Lagerbäck.

BULGARIA: Zdravko Zdravkov, Vladimir Ivanov, Rosen Kirilov, Ivaylo Petkov, Predrag Pažin, Georgi Peev, Marian Hristov, Stiliyan Petrov (c), Dimitar Berbatov (Vladimir Manchev 76), Zoran Janković (Velizar Dimitrov 62), Martin Petrov (Zdravko Lazarov 84). **Manager:** Plamen Markov.

Booked: Linderoth (52), Ibrahimović (65), I. Petkov (18), Kirilov (22), Janković (23), Ivanov (70).

5pm, 18 June 2004
Estádio Municipal, Braga
Attendance: 24,131
Referee: Lucílio Cardoso Cortez Batista (Portugal)

DENMARK 2 (Tomasson 44, Grønkjær 90+2)
BULGARIA 0

DENMARK: Sørensen, Helveg, Henriksen (c), Laursen, N. Jensen, D. Jensen, Thomas Gravesen, Rommedahl (Jesper Grønkjær 23), Tomasson, Sand, Jørgensen (C. Jensen 72).

BULGARIA: Zdravkov, Ivanov (Lazarov 51), Kirilov, I. Petkov (Zlatomir Zagorčić 40), Ilian Stoyanov, Peev, Hristov, S. Petrov (c), Berbatov, Janković (Milen Petkov 81), M. Petrov.

Booked: N. Jensen (10), Sand (58), Kirilov (4), Stoyanov (50), S. Petrov (77), Zagorčić (80), Hristov (83), M. Petrov (84).
Sent off: S. Petrov (83).

7.45pm, 18 June 2004
Estádio do Dragão, Porto
Attendance: 44,926
Referee: Urs Meier (Switzerland)

ITALY 1 (Cassano 37)
SWEDEN 1 (Ibrahimović 85)

ITALY: Buffon, Panucci, Zambrotta, Nesta, Cannavaro (c), Gattuso (Giuseppe Favalli 76), Perrotta, Andrea Pirlo, Vieri, Cassano (Fiore 70), Del Piero (Camoranesi 82).

SWEDEN: Isaksson, Nilsson, Edman (Allbäck 77), Jakobsson, Mellberg (c), Linderoth, Wilhelmsson (Mattias Jonson 67), Svensson (Källström 55), Ibrahimović, Larsson, Ljungberg.

Booked: Gattuso (39), Cannavaro (46), Zambrotta (58), Edman (54), Linderoth (75).

7.45pm, 22 June 2004
Estádio D. Afonso Henriques, Guimarães
Attendance: 16,002
Referee: Valentin Ivanov (Russia)

ITALY 2 (Perrotta 48, Cassano 90+4)
BULGARIA 1 (M. Petrov 45 pen)

ITALY: Buffon, Panucci, Zambrotta, Nesta, Marco Materazzi (Marco Di Vaio 83), Fiore, Perrotta (Massimo Oddo 68), Pirlo, Bernardo Corradi (Vieri 53), Cassano, Del Piero (c).

BULGARIA: Zdravkov (c), Daniel Borimirov, Pažin (Kiril Kotev 64), Zagorčić, Stoyanov, M. Petkov, Hristov (Dimitrov 79), Lazarov, Berbatov, Janković (Valeri Bozhinov 46), M. Petrov.

Booked: Materazzi (44), M. Petrov (45), Bozhinov (49), Stoyanov (66), Lazarov (80).

7.45pm, 22 June 2004
Estádio do Bessa, Porto
Attendance: 26,115
Referee: Markus Merk (Germany)

DENMARK 2 (Tomasson 28, 66)
SWEDEN 2 (Larsson 47 pen, Jonson 89)

DENMARK: Sørensen, Helveg, Henriksen (c), Laursen, N. Jensen (Kasper Bøgelund 46), D. Jensen (Poulsen 66), Gravesen, Grønkjær, Tomasson, Sand, Jørgensen (Rommedahl 57).

SWEDEN: Isaksson, Nilsson, Edman, Jakobsson, Mellberg (c), Andersson (Allbäck 81), Jonson, Källström (Wilhelmsson 72), Ibrahimović, Larsson, Ljungberg.

Booked: Edman (36), Källström (63).

GROUP C	P	W	D	L	F	A	GD	Pts
SWEDEN	3	1	2	0	8	3	+5	5
DENMARK	3	1	2	0	4	2	+2	5
ITALY	3	1	2	0	3	2	+1	5
BULGARIA	3	0	0	3	1	9	− 8	0

Sweden and Denmark qualified.

GROUP D
Germany, Netherlands, Latvia, Czech Republic

If you had taken a punt on which former Soviet republic (other than Russia) would be the first to qualify for a major tournament, Latvia would have been low on the list. Yet here they were. Prime minister Indulis Emsis even promised to dye his hair green if his compatriots got out of Group D.

The team they fielded against the Czech Republic in Aveiro had an average of 58 caps each. They would need all their wiles against talented opponents for whom Petr Čech was a superb goalkeeper, Pavel Nedvěd the reigning European Footballer of the Year, Karel Poborský still a livewire and Jan Koller a fearsome centre-forward.

In the first half, Marek Jankulovski, Tomáš Rosický and Poborský all went close for the Czechs. But Latvia's tall centre-back Igors Stepanovs, who had struggled at Arsenal for years, was superb throughout. And not just defensively: his exquisite 40-yard ball put Andrejs Prohorenkovs away down the left, and Māris Verpakovskis tapped in the low cross to give Latvia a surprise lead.

The Czechs staged a second-half barrage. Poborský shaved the post from long range, then set up a sitter for Milan Baroš, who stubbed it wide. The pressure eventually told. Poborský slung in another cross, goalkeeper Aleksandrs Koļinko botched his punch, and Baroš chested it down to rattle it in.

Tough on Latvia, and more pain awaited them near the end. Koļinko sliced a clearance across the goalmouth, where Zemļinskis miscued to the edge of the box. Substitute Marek Heinz, who had earlier clipped the bar from long range, drilled it into an unguarded net. 'Latvia were disciplined in an almost militaristic way,' said Czech manager Karel Brückner, who looked unnervingly like a much-aged Heinz. But they had fallen out of lockstep at just the wrong moment.

═══

In Porto, the poorest Dutch team in 20 years collided with the poorest German team in, erm, four years. 'They're star-studded, but they're not a group,' Hans van Breukelen, the Euro 88 goalkeeper, remarked of his countrymen. 'They're mainly individuals, luxury scorers. Almost none of them likes to do the dirty work.'

It soon became clear the Netherlands were in much worse shape than Germany. Lone striker Ruud van Nistelrooy was capable of battling two centre-backs by himself, but Dick Advocaat's long-ball tactics saw him live off up-and-unders. And with Michael Ballack dominating Edgar Davids (who was humiliatingly replaced at half-time by the 20-year-old Wesley Sneijder), Germany took a deserved if accidental lead when Torsten Frings's speculative free kick from the left drifted through a dozen players to bounce in off the far post.

Germany were so comfortable that Rudi Völler felt able to bring on two of his least experienced players, Fabian Ernst and the 20-year-old Bastian Schweinsteiger. But near the end, Ernst was robbed too easily by Andy van der Meijde, whose cross was hooked in by Van Nistelrooy while he held off Christian Wörns.

The Netherlands could even have won it: Oliver Kahn, mostly a bystander on his 35th birthday, did well to punch away Phillip Cocu's late header. Germany, far better than expected, felt as though they had lost. 'We had the Dutch where we wanted them,' lamented Didi Hamann. Kahn added, 'This group will remain open until the last minute.'

═══

The demoralised Germans looked like a different team four days later. Of all their shocking performances between 1998 and 2005, their humiliation against Latvia in Porto was as bad as it got.

The Latvians began violently: after 26 seconds, Andrejs Isakovs crashed through the back of Frings, earning himself a booking. But referee Mike Riley later made numerous bad calls, failing to spot Wörns's serial fouling, Philipp Lahm receiving a forearm smash, and an obvious penalty when Frank Baumann pulled down Verpakovskis early in the second half.

The 5ft 8in Verpakovskis, a yellow-pack Rooney, kept charging at defenders and daring them to foul him. Before half-time, he accelerated away from three Germans and sprinted half the length of the field, but his soft finish was easy for Kahn. Meanwhile, Ballack was a shadow of his usual thrusting self: his subsequent man of the match award from UEFA rivalled Raúl's against Greece for surreality.

At the death, aerial killer Miro Klose headed Lahm's cross wide, and Latvia had their point. 'This is an historic draw – I almost said win,' said Latvia's delighted manager Aleksandrs Starkovs. Verpakovskis was dismissive of Germany: 'We played much harder games than this in the qualifiers.' Ouch.

From the start, the meeting of the Czech Republic and the Netherlands in Aveiro felt like a classic for the ages. After 60 seconds, Tomáš Rosický's delicate chip set up Koller, who volleyed over the bar. Then Marek Jankulovski burst between three Dutchmen to shoot straight at Edwin van der Sar.

The third attack of the game brought a goal – but not for the Czechs. Arjen Robben flighted a free kick to the back post, where Poborský left Wilfred Bouma unmarked to score with a stooping header. 'That's the first time in three years we've given away a set-piece goal,' said Brückner afterwards, declining to name the culprit.

The Dutch went 2-0 up in controversial circumstances. As Van Nistelrooy walked back from an offside position, Davids's pass sent Robben away – suddenly putting Van Nistelrooy behind the ball, and onside. Instantly he turned around, sprinted back and tapped home the cross, despite Czech protests. Nobody ever exploited the offside laws more ruthlessly than this guy.

Instead of keeping it tight, the Dutch immediately conceded a preventable goal. Their captain Cocu passed straight to Baroš, who ran at big Jaap Stam and then twisted away from him. Cocu dashed back to cover, but Baroš got past him too and squared it for Koller, who took his time before slotting it home. 'I have to look in the mirror,' said the usually impeccable Cocu afterwards. 'Partly due to my error, our European Championship is hanging by a silk thread. We have one foot back in the Netherlands.'

Now both teams were shooting on sight. Čech tipped over Johnny Heitinga's 25-yarder, before clever work by Nedvěd and Poborský culminated in Koller's back-heel being deflected just wide. Davids concluded a marvellous first half by hitting the post.

'The Dutch played great, like we did,' Nedvěd said. 'People were having fun.' In the second half, he made the match his personal property. His raking pass played Poborský in to shoot against Van der Sar's legs, and Poborský returned the favour by setting him up for a volley which the goalkeeper saved well.

The match turned on Advocaat's introduction of 34-year-old Paul Bosvelt to replace Robben, his best attacking threat. The unfathomable substitution would forever be known as '*de wissel*', the switch, in Dutch football lore. It was met with mass booing by their fans. And as the Dutch tired in the evening heat, the game was increasingly played around their box. There was an inevitability about the equaliser. The irrepressible Nedvěd eluded Bosvelt and lofted over a cross for Koller, who used that massive barrel chest to divert it into Baroš's path. The half-volley rocketed into the top corner.

The sense that the match was slipping out of Dutch hands increased when Heitinga pushed Nedvěd over and received his second yellow card. From the free kick, Nedvěd's blast brought another flying save from Van der Sar, who then kept out David Rozehnal's follow-up. The Dutch simply couldn't contain Nedvěd, who now hammered an awesome 35-yarder against the bar.

With two minutes left, the Czechs won the game in style. Van der Sar went full-length to save Heinz's hard shot magnificently, but the rebound fell to Poborský, who shaped to smash it home – before pulling it back into the goalmouth for a visibly surprised Šmicer to tap in.

Still the drama wasn't over. Substitute Rafael van der Vaart threw himself at Bouma's long ball, but the ball skimmed off his boot to bounce narrowly wide. In the final seconds, Heinz's shot – the 57th goal attempt of the evening – whooshed across the face of the Dutch goal. In Prague, tens of thousands watching a big screen in the picturesque Old Town Square chanted, 'Karel to the castle!' in tribute to Brückner.

The Dutch queued up to knife Advocaat. Overmars: 'I don't know what his thought processes were.' Patrick Kluivert: 'Some of the substitutions weren't good. Robben played a very good match. That's not a change I would've made.' Assistant coach Wim van Hanegem, asked what would happen if his boss tried the same thing again, replied half-jokingly, 'I'll knock him down.'

Advocaat retorted, 'If they want to put everything down to the Robben change, they can do that. I'm used to the criticism.' Some travelling Dutch fans held a whip-round, spent it on a plane ticket to Amsterdam, and presented him with it via room service at the Netherlands' hotel in Albufeira. By now, he had imposed a media blackout. On himself.

—————

Needing help from his conquerors, Advocaat must have blanched when he saw the line-up Brückner fielded against Germany four nights later. But the Dutch had little trouble with their own task, making short work of Latvia in Braga.

First, Davids won a dodgy penalty when Vitālis Astafjevs tripped him outside the box. Van Nistelrooy tucked it away in front of the cliff face, and doubled the lead by diverting Cocu's header home, again offside when Clarence Seedorf's initial cross came in.

Although Van der Sar parried Andrejs Rubins's shot, Latvia were never in the game, and the tall Roy Makaay wrapped it up with a composed finish after Robben lured three Latvians into his web. Advocaat was sour afterwards, still smarting from the Czech debacle: 'Standards and values have been breached. I have difficulty with the way I've been treated by some people.'

It was the Netherlands' only win of the tournament, against brave minnows who'd battled hard. 'Together with our supporters, we've given a good impression of our country,' said the cheerful Starkovs. 'It's a pleasure to finish the tournament with some respect.'

===

In Lisbon, Germany initially lorded it over the Czechs' reserves. Ballack, back to his best after his Latvian horror show, was again a class apart, using the ball superbly. He scored a wonderful goal in the first half, crashing a half-volley into the top corner after good work by Bernd Schneider and Schweinsteiger.

Germany seemed well on their way. But the Czechs scored a lot of good goals in this competition, and on the half-hour they got another against the run of play, when the impressive Heinz curled in a 25-yard free kick from a tight angle.

In the second half, Ballack worked overtime. He had a header saved by goalkeeper Jaromír Blažek, thumped a vicious shot inches wide, and hit the post after turning Roman Týce inside out. Later, Schneider and Kevin Kurányi spurned free headers. Had Germany possessed one striker in even middling form, they would probably have made the semis. None of the five forwards Völler used in the tournament managed to score.

The turning point came when referee Terje Hauge turned down two very strong German penalty appeals. First, when Tomáš Hübschman cleared Wörns's header off the line, Blažek pulled Kurányi to the ground before blocking Lukas Podolski's follow-up. Hübschman then handled in the box, and, minutes later, the Czechs grabbed an undeserved but oddly inevitable winner. Baroš raced on to Poborský's pass, cut inside Jens Nowotny and held off Wörns; Kahn's leg blocked his first shot, but he converted the rebound easily.

The paralysed Germans created nothing in the time remaining. For the second Euros running, they had been dumped out by eager benchwarmers. But this was much more of a hard luck story than the shame of Rotterdam.

Völler resigned, despite the efforts of DFB boss Gerhard Mayer-Vorfelder to change his mind. 'Unlike 2000, this was not a humiliation, and we have some promising young players,' he said. 'But our attacking play is a real cause for concern. For the moment, we can't match the great footballing nations.' Perennially popular, he was spared personal criticism: everyone knew he wasn't working with prime cuts. To his successor, his old strike partner Jürgen Klinsmann, he bequeathed his young gems Lahm, Schweinsteiger and Podolski. And now German football began its long, slow climb back to the top.

5pm, 15 June 2004
Estádio Municipal, Aveiro
Attendance: 13,000
Referee: Gilles Veissière (France)

CZECH REPUBLIC 2 (Baroš 73, Heinz 85)
LATVIA 1 (Verpakovskis 45+1)

CZECH REPUBLIC: Petr Čech, Zdeněk Grygera (Marek Heinz 56), René Bolf, Tomáš Ujfaluši, Marek Jankulovski, Tomáš Galásek (Vladimír Šmicer 64), Tomáš Rosický, Pavel Nedvěd (c), Jan Koller, Milan Baroš (Martín Jiránek 87), Karel Poborský. **Manager:** Karel Brückner.

LATVIA: Aleksandrs Koļinko, Aleksandrs Isakovs, Igors Stepanovs, Mihails Zemļinskis, Oļegs Blagonadeždins, Vitālijs Astafjevs (c), Imants Bleidelis, Valentīns Lobaņovs (Vīts Rimkus 90), Māris Verpakovskis (Marians Pahars 81), Andrejs Prohorenkovs (Juris Laizāns 71), Andrejs Rubins. **Manager:** Aleksandrs Starkovs.

7.45pm, 15 June 2004
Estádio do Dragão, Porto
Attendance: 48,917
Referee: Anders Frisk (Sweden)

GERMANY 1 (Frings 30)
NETHERLANDS 1 (Van Nistelrooy 81)

GERMANY: Oliver Kahn (c), Arne Friedrich, Philipp Lahm, Christian Wörns, Jens Nowotny, Frank Baumann, Torsten Frings (Fabian Ernst 79), Dietmar Hamann, Kevin Kurányi (Fredi Bobic 85), Michael Ballack, Bernd Schneider (Bastian Schweinsteiger 68). **Manager:** Rudi Völler.

NETHERLANDS: Edwin van der Sar, Johnny Heitinga (Pierre van Hooijdonk 74), Jaap Stam, Wilfred Bouma, Giovanni van Bronckhorst, Phillip Cocu (c), Andy van der Meijde, Edgar Davids (Wesley Sneijder 46), Ruud van Nistelrooy, Rafael van der Vaart, Boudewijn Zenden (Marc Overmars 46). **Manager:** Dick Advocaat.

Booked: Kurányi (12), Ballack (90+1), Cocu (29), Stam (73).

5pm, 19 June 2004
Estádio do Bessa, Porto
Attendance: 22,344
Referee: Mike Riley (England)

LATVIA 0
GERMANY 0

LATVIA: Koļinko, Isakovs, Stepanovs, Zemļinskis, Blagonadeždins, Astafjevs (c), Bleidelis, Lobaņovs (Laizāns 70), Verpakovskis (Dzintars Zirnis 90+2), Prohorenkovs (Pahars 67), Rubins.

GERMANY: Kahn (c), Friedrich, Lahm, Wörns, Baumann, Frings, Hamann, Schneider (Schweinsteiger 46), Bobic (Miroslav Klose 67), Ballack, Kurányi (Thomas Brdaric 78).

Booked: Isakovs (1), Astafjevs (79), Friedrich (21), Hamann (42), Frings (53).

7.45pm, 19 June 2004
Estádio Municipal, Aveiro
Attendance: 29,935
Referee: Manuel Mejuto González (Spain)

CZECH REPUBLIC 3 (Koller 23, Baroš 71, Šmicer 88)
NETHERLANDS 2 (Bouma 4, Van Nistelrooy 19)

CZECH REPUBLIC: Čech, Grygera (Šmicer 25), Jiránek, Ujfaluši, Jankulovski, Galásek (Heinz 62), Rosický, Nedvěd (c), Koller (David Rozehnal 75), Baroš, Poborský.

NETHERLANDS: Van der Sar, Heitinga, Stam, Bouma, Van Bronckhorst, Cocu (c), Clarence Seedorf (Van der Vaart 86), Davids, Van Nistelrooy, Arjen Robben (Paul Bosvelt 58), Van der Meijde (Michael Reiziger 79).

Booked: Galásek (55), Seedorf (9), Heitinga (26).
Sent off: Heitinga (75).

7.45pm, 23 June 2004
Estádio Municipal, Braga
Attendance: 27,904
Referee: Kim Milton Nielsen (Denmark)

NETHERLANDS 3 (Van Nistelrooy 27 pen, 35, Makaay 84)
LATVIA 0

NETHERLANDS: Van der Sar, Reiziger, Stam, Frank de Boer (c), Van Bronckhorst, Cocu, Seedorf, Davids (Sneijder 77), Van Nistelrooy (Roy Makaay 70), Robben, Van der Meijde (Overmars 63).

LATVIA: Koļinko, Isakovs, Stepanovs, Zemļinskis, Blagonadeždins, Astafjevs (c), Bleidelis (Andrejs Štolcers 83), Lobaņovs, Verpakovskis (Pahars 62), Prohorenkovs (Laizāns 74), Rubins.

Booked: Lobaņovs (53).

7.45pm, 23 June 2004
Estádio José Alvalade, Lisbon
Attendance: 46,849
Referee: Terje Hauge (Norway)

CZECH REPUBLIC 2 (Heinz 30, Baroš 77)
GERMANY 1 (Ballack 21)

CZECH REPUBLIC: Jaromír Blažek, Jiránek, Bolf, Rozehnal, Pavel Mareš, Galásek (c) (Tomáš Hübschman 46), Roman Týce, Jaroslav Plašil (Poborský 70), Vratislav Lokvenc (Baroš 59), Heinz, Štěpán Vachoušek.

305

GERMANY: Kahn (c), Friedrich, Lahm, Wörns, Nowotny, Frings (Lukas Podolski 46), Hamann (Klose 79), Schneider, Kurányi, Ballack, Schweinsteiger (Jens Jeremies 86).

Booked: Týce (48), Nowotny (38), Lahm (74), Wörns (83).

GROUP D	P	W	D	L	F	A	GD	Pts
CZECH REPUBLIC	3	3	0	0	7	4	+3	9
NETHERLANDS	3	1	1	1	6	4	+2	4
GERMANY	3	0	2	1	2	3	−1	2
LATVIA	3	0	1	2	1	5	−4	1

The Czech Republic and the Netherlands qualified.

QUARTER-FINALS
Portugal v England
France v Greece
Sweden v Netherlands
Czech Republic v Denmark

Ahead of the first quarter-final in Lisbon, the prospective duel between future Manchester United team-mates Cristiano Ronaldo and Wayne Rooney dominated the headlines. There had been some bad feeling between the pair since Rooney brutally fouled the showboating Ronaldo at Old Trafford the previous December. 'I remember that tackle very well,' Ronaldo recalled. 'How could I forget it? But I don't want to get involved in personal fights.' In the event, he would largely disappoint and his nemesis wouldn't even make it to the half-hour mark.

As in Eindhoven in 2000, the technical gap between the teams yawned wide. But England had found some momentum by now. After 144 seconds, they also found a goal out of nothing. David James's monumental clearance floated deep into Portuguese territory, and Costinha's lazy backward header dropped perfectly for Michael Owen, who pirouetted 360 degrees before stabbing it over Ricardo.

Portugal proceeded to swarm all over England. Ronaldo was denied by Ashley Cole's good tackle and Sol Campbell's follow-up block, while Maniche, Gomes, Costinha and Miguel all went close to varying extents. But then, pivotally, England lost the talismanic Rooney to a broken metatarsal when Jorge Andrade stood on him. Replacement Darius Vassell battled hard, but simply wasn't an international striker.

In the second half, Portugal owned the ball but did little, while Eriksson showed he had learned nothing from the France defeat by replacing Scholes and Gerrard with Phil Neville and Owen Hargreaves. With 15 minutes left, Scolari brought off the untouchable Figo, who took it badly, stomping down the tunnel without glancing at his manager. 'I didn't see that. They only pay me to watch the match,' Scolari quipped. In the 83rd minute, all his lottery numbers came up as Figo's replacement Hélder Postiga sneaked between Terry and Campbell to shoulder Maniche's cross into the top corner.

With 30 seconds left, fate gave England another painful boot in the groin. Campbell headed the otherwise anonymous Beckham's free kick against the bar, and nodded in the rebound – but referee Urs Meier penalised John Terry for obstructing Ricardo with his arm.

The otherwise uneventful extra time exploded into life ten minutes from the end. After Cole cleared Simão's header off the line, Rui Costa set off on a long run, shook off Neville's stumbling challenge and cracked a magnificent shot in off the bar. But England wouldn't give up: Terry headed Beckham's corner back across the box, and Frank Lampard shot home on the turn from six yards.

Beckham began the penalty shoot-out by getting so far under the ball that it didn't even come close to hitting the bar. 'Even within the Camp of the Favoured, there is a hierarchy, and Beckham sits at its summit,' wrote David Walsh in the *Sunday Times*. 'How badly did he have to play to be substituted?'

Rui Costa's effort was every bit as bad, soaring high into the Lisbon night. The next six penalties all went in, and when Ricardo took off his gloves to save Vassell's hesitant effort, the game was up. Hilariously, Ricardo himself fired the final penalty past James. 'I just put it in the place where he couldn't reach, because he was a very big guy, the size of a building. I had a cold mind.'

England's manager, players and media enablers blamed the pitch, the heat, Meier – anything but their own failings. 'I went to see the referee after the game, but I will not tell you what was said,' said Eriksson, trying to have it both ways. And Meier made for a convenient short-term hate figure. *The Sun* published his personal details, exhorted readers to bombard him with e-mails, and sent two reporters to his home in Switzerland to plant a St George flag in his garden. 'These people have nothing to do with journalism,' he said. 'They're trying to destroy me.'

There were some voices of sanity. The inestimable Brian Glanville of the *Sunday Times* noted, 'It was crass and churlish of Eriksson to join the chorus, however mutedly, against Meier. Evasive of him to keep telling us how few official internationals he has lost, thus posing the central question, that he loses the ones that matter.' Eriksson would go on to make all the same mistakes at the 2006 World Cup in Germany.

═══

'Ancient Greece had 12 gods, modern Greece has 11,' read the slogan on the side of their team bus, although you wondered how their reserves felt about it. But surely this was the end of the road? Not against France's gang of sated multimillionaires. Afterwards, UEFA would fine the FFF €6,000 because France's players came out of their dressing room late for both halves, an indication of their commitment.

Santini had set up his team with a right-back (Thuram) at centre-back and vice versa (Gallas). Zidane yet again went missing, while Henry was marked into oblivion by Seitaridis. The industrious Greeks managed only five goal attempts – but all were on target. Fabien Barthez fumbled Katsouranis's shot against a post, and punched Fyssas's dipping volley over the bar.

Greece's second-half winner was well deserved. On the right, Zagorakis easily got past Lizarazu, who staggered into the advertising boards. When the cross came over, Charisteas's header into the corner was no less impressive for the fact that Thuram had run away from him.

France barely responded at all, and Henry blew their only chance by heading wide in stoppage time. 'This failure signifies the end of a whole generation, the dismal end of the reign,' thundered *Le Parisien*. Santini, already out the door, estimated his own culpability as 'anywhere between one per cent and 99 per cent', which won't surprise any Spurs fans reading this.

Was there even more to come from Greece? Surely not. 'The Greek team are spoilers but very able and well-coached,' Des Lynam wrote in his *Daily Telegraph* tournament diary. 'I can't see them going any further, though. The French were out of sorts.'

———

The Netherlands aren't renowned for winning ugly, but this 2004 vintage was one of their less stylish incarnations. Sweden were even harder on the eye, so it was a long evening in Faro-Loulé.

Young Robben unveiled what would become his signature move early, cutting inside Mikael Nilsson from the right to hit a hard left-footer that brought a great save from Isaksson. Later, he moved over to the left to torture Alexander Östlund. The Dutch looked the better side, but in a game as boring as this it was all relative.

In extra time, Isaksson spilled Robben's shot on to his own post, then made amends by saving Seedorf's free kick. In between, Van Nistelrooy whacked a great chance wide. Sweden replied by hitting the woodwork twice. Larsson showed brilliant close control before shooting against the bar, and Ljungberg's drive struck an upright.

All the Netherlands' penalties were good – except Cocu's, which brushed the post. But by then, Sweden had missed too, Ibrahimović capping his lame performance with a woeful effort. And when Olof Mellberg shot too close to Van der Sar, Robben held his nerve to send Advocaat's higgledy-piggledy team into the last four. 'Dick, does your wife understand you?' asked a large banner in the Dutch end.

==========

The Danes and Czechs were both on a roll, but the first half they contested in Porto was an insomnia cure. The Czechs looked tired, despite most of them having enjoyed a full week's rest, and should have gone down to ten men when Jankulovski stamped on Helveg.

'We performed fantastically in the first half,' Morten Olsen lied afterwards. Early in the second, his team fell behind after suicidally giving Euro 2000's tallest player a free header. Martin Laursen, jumping too early for Poborský's corner, was marooned as Koller's tungsten-plated forehead did the rest.

In the second half, the temporarily lethal Baroš wrapped everything up. First, Poborský's weighted pass, bent around two defenders, put him through to chip Sørensen. Two minutes later, Nedvěd set him up and he held off Laursen before walloping a shot into the roof of the net.

Brückner's only trophy in 31 years of management had been a Slovakian Cup with Inter Bratislava in 1995, won on penalties before a tiny crowd. But he now looked a good bet to add a bigger prize to his uncluttered sideboard.

7.45pm, 24 June 2004
Estádio da Luz, Lisbon
Attendance: 62,564
Referee: Urs Meier (Switzerland)

PORTUGAL 2 (Postiga 83, Rui Costa 110)
ENGLAND 2 (Owen 3, Lampard 115)
Portugal won 6-5 on penalties after extra time
Shoot-out: Beckham shot over, Deco 1-0, Owen 1-1, Simão 2-1, Lampard 2-2, Rui Costa shot over, Terry 2-3, Ronaldo 3-3, Hargreaves 3-4, Maniche 4-4, Cole 4-5, Postiga 5-5, Vassell saved, Ricardo 6-5.

PORTUGAL: Ricardo, Miguel (Rui Costa 79), Carvalho, Andrade, Valente, Costinha (Simão 63), Figo (c) (Postiga 75), Maniche, Gomes, Deco, Ronaldo.

ENGLAND: James, G. Neville, Cole, Terry, Campbell, Gerrard (Hargreaves 81), Beckham (c), Scholes (P. Neville 57), Rooney (Vassell 27), Owen, Lampard.

Booked: Costinha (56), Deco (85), Carvalho (119), Gerrard (37), G. Neville (45), P. Neville (92).

7.45pm, 25 June 2004
Estádio José Alvalade, Lisbon
Attendance: 45,390
Referee: Anders Frisk (Sweden)

GREECE 1 (Charisteas 64)
FRANCE 0
GREECE: Nikopolidis, Seitaridis, Dellas, Kapsis, Fyssas, Basinas (Tsiartas 85), Zagorakis (c), Katsouranis, Charisteas, Nikolaidis (Lakis 61), Karagounis.

FRANCE: Barthez, Gallas, Lizarazu, Silvestre, Thuram, Dacourt (Wiltord 72), Makélélé, Pirès (Jérôme Rothen 79), Trezeguet (Saha 72), Zidane (c), Henry.

Booked: Karagounis (6), Zagorakis (50), Zidane (44), Saha (86).

7.45pm, 26 June 2004
Estádio do Algarve, Faro-Loulé
Attendance: 27,762
Referee: Luboš Michel (Slovakia)

NETHERLANDS 0
SWEDEN 0
The Netherlands won 5-4 on penalties after extra time
Shoot-out: Källström 0-1, Van Nistelrooy 1-1, Larsson 1-2, Heitinga 2-2, Ibrahimović shot over, Reiziger 3-2, Ljungberg 3-3, Cocu hit post, Wilhelmsson 3-4, Makaay 4-4, Mellberg saved, Robben 4-5.

NETHERLANDS: Van der Sar, Reiziger, Stam, De Boer (c) (Bouma 35), van Bronckhorst, Cocu, Seedorf, Davids (Heitinga 61), Van Nistelrooy, Robben, Van der Meijde (Makaay 87).

SWEDEN: Isaksson, Alexander Östlund, Nilsson, Jakobsson, Mellberg (c), Jonson (Wilhelmsson 64), Linderoth, Svensson (Källström 81), Ibrahimović, Larsson, Ljungberg.

Booked: De Boer (30), Van der Meijde (48), Makaay (116), Ibrahimović (58), Östlund (88).

7.45pm, 27 June 2004
Estádio do Dragão, Porto
Attendance: 41,092
Referee: Valentin Ivanov (Russia)

CZECH REPUBLIC 3 (Koller 49, Baroš 63, 65)
DENMARK 0

CZECH REPUBLIC: Čech, Jiránek (Grygera 39), Bolf (Rozehnal 65), Ujfaluši, Jankulovski, Galásek, Rosický, Nedvěd (c), Koller, Baroš (Heinz 70), Poborský.

DENMARK: Sørensen, Helveg, Henriksen (c), Laursen, Bøgelund, Poulsen, Gravesen, Grønkjær (Rommedahl 77), Tomasson, Jørgensen (Peter Løvenkrands 85), C. Jensen (Peter Madsen 71).

Booked: Jankulovski (10), Ujfaluši (45), Nedvěd (61), Poulsen (51), Bøgelund (56), Gravesen (77).

SEMI-FINALS
Portugal v Netherlands
Czech Republic v Greece

The Netherlands were contesting their fourth semi-final in five European Championships with a team that wouldn't live long in the memory. They made little impression in Lisbon as Portugal called the tune.

Luís Figo, his earlier outburst forgiven by Scolari, gave his best performance of the competition. Early on, he served his youthful apprentice with two chances: Ronaldo put the first one millimetres off target and tapped the second straight at Van der Sar. It was third time lucky when he headed home Deco's corner while Van Bronckhorst stood uselessly behind him.

The Netherlands almost levelled instantly, Overmars shooting over the bar. But Portugal soon turned the heat back up as Van der Sar blocked Pauleta's close-range effort, both a great save and a glaring miss. Overmars was now a beaten docket after countless injuries, and escaped being sent off for a horrible foul on Nuno Valente. By then, Portugal should have been two up. Figo, destroying Van Bronckhorst, skipped past him to hammer a swerving shot against the post.

The nadir of Pauleta's tournament came after half-time. When Cocu failed to head away Ricardo's goal kick, he chased after it but blasted his shot into Van der Sar's midriff. He was surpassed for incompetence by the Portuguese TV directors minutes later. Busy replaying Stam heading the ball out of play, they missed Maniche receiving a short corner from Ronaldo and hitting a magnificent curler in off the far post.

The Dutch looked beaten, but Jorge Andrade let them back into it. Stretching to put Van Bronckhorst's cross out for a corner, he could only slice it over Ricardo's head and in. When Van Nistelrooy and Van Bronckhorst later converged on Cocu's cross, an equaliser seemed certain, but they both failed to connect. Close in the end, but 2-1 didn't convey Portugal's superiority.

The curtain now came down on the international careers of De Boer, Overmars, Stam and Michael Reiziger, with Davids soon to join them. Advocaat couldn't get away from Portugal fast enough to resign. 'We've not seen him,' said Reiziger as the Dutch waited at Faro airport to fly home. 'He's gone.'

———

At Euro 2000, Pierluigi Collina's strange refereeing decisions had sunk the Czech Republic against the Netherlands. In the second semi-final, in Porto, he was their nemesis again, helping to produce an outcome that was nothing short of a disaster for the tournament.

All night, Collina smilingly allowed Greece to foul the Czechs, while plenty of other transgressions occurred behind his back. The Greeks' performance was an orgy of shirt-pulling, ankle-tapping, nudging, arm-locking, injury-faking and several violent challenges. The foul count at the end was 24-15 to the Czechs, utterly absurd given what was actually happening on the field.

The gap in class saw the Czechs control the first half. Rosický's volley hit the bar, Nikopolidis parried Jankulovski's powerful shot, and when Koller's looping header dropped out of the sky, the Greek goalkeeper fumbled it. But the real turning point came on 33 minutes, when Pavel Nedvěd and Kostas Katsouranis converged on Rosický's cross. Both missed it, and Nedvěd fell in a heap as his knee gave way. Devastated, he howled with despair while being helped off the field.

The loss of their inspirational captain hit the Czechs hard. After the interval, Koller and Rosický both went close, but the first-half fluency had gone. Though Baroš dribbled past Kapsis and Fyssas to shoot wide near the end, the Czechs now looked like a jaded team.

So to extra time, whereupon Greece did something utterly unexpected: they mounted two attacks. Čech rashly charged out of his goal as Stelios Giannakopoulos headed past him, before René Bolf stopped Charisteas tapping into an open goal. Then the giant Dellas lost his marker Ujfaluši to get in a strong header which Čech saved.

The killing blow arrived at the very end of the first half of extra time. In his post-tournament diary for an Athens newspaper, Dellas wrote, 'We could see the Czechs were very tired. We got a corner. I looked up at the scoreboard. It read 14:36 – a now-or-never situation.' Tsiartas swung over the corner, and Dellas evaded Bolf at the near post to head his team into the final. Deserved glory for the best defender of the tournament, but horrifically harsh on the Czechs, for whom all was lost.

The silver goal – introduced because the golden one gave the conceding team no chance to respond – meant that if a team scored in extra time, they had to hold out until the end of the 15-minute half, rather than the full 30 minutes. But Dellas's silver header was effectively golden anyway, coming so near the end of the first period that the Czechs couldn't even kick off again. 'I believe we played very cleverly. We shut off all their avenues and their strong points,' said the scorer afterwards. But the constant fouling and simulation undermined any claims to true defensive excellence.

Of course, none of this mattered to Rehhagel and his players. But those who lamented the loss of a potentially classic Portugal-Czech Republic final would now have their worst fears confirmed.

7.45pm, 30 June 2004
Estádio José Alvalade, Lisbon
Attendance: 46,679
Referee: Anders Frisk (Sweden)

PORTUGAL 2 (Ronaldo 26, Maniche 58)
NETHERLANDS 1 (Andrade 63 og)

PORTUGAL: Ricardo, Miguel, Carvalho, Andrade, Valente, Costinha, Figo (c), Maniche (Couto 87), Pauleta (Gomes 75), Deco, Ronaldo (Petit 68).

NETHERLANDS: Van der Sar, Reiziger, Stam, Bouma (Van der Vaart 56), Van Bronckhorst, Cocu (c), Seedorf, Davids, Van Nistelrooy, Robben (Van Hooijdonk 81), Overmars (Makaay 46).

Booked: Valente (44), Figo (90), Ronaldo (27), Overmars (39), Robben (71).

7.45pm, 1 July 2004
Estádio do Dragão, Porto
Attendance: 42,449
Referee: Pierluigi Collina (Italy)

GREECE 1 (Dellas 105+1)
CZECH REPUBLIC 0
Greece won on the silver goal after extra time

GREECE: Nikopolidis, Seitaridis, Dellas, Kapsis, Fyssas, Basinas (Giannakopoulos 72), Zagorakis (c), Katsouranis, Charisteas, Vryzas (Tsiartas 91), Karagounis.

CZECH REPUBLIC: Čech, Grygera, Bolf, Ujfaluši, Jankulovski, Galásek, Rosický, Nedvěd (c) (Šmicer 40), Koller, Baroš, Poborský.

Booked: Seitaridis (23), Charisteas (70), Karagounis (87), Galásek (48), Šmicer (55), Baroš (102).

FINAL
Portugal v Greece

Two years on from Yokohama, another huge international final pitted Big Phil Scolari against a German adversary. But on a tedious night at the Estádio da Luz, the hosts simply didn't show up.

Portugal's impotence was extraordinary given their depth of talent: it took them quite some time to muster a meaningful attempt, Nikopolidis tipping Miguel's drive around the post. Two minutes later, Greece came closer. Vryzas and Katsouranis combined well to feed Charisteas, before Ricardo's knee cleared the danger.

After the interval, another long spell of nothingness ticked slowly by before Seitaridis won a corner off Ronaldo. If Portugal had watched DVDs of Greece's wins over France and the Czechs, they must have fallen asleep while doing so. For the third consecutive game, a cross from the right yielded Greece's only goal as Charisteas got above Carvalho, Costinha and Ricardo to head in Basinas's corner – their only attempt on target all night. Ricardo protested that Vryzas had impeded him, but referee Markus Merk didn't care.

Some of Portugal's stars choked more noisily than others. Last among equals was Deco, whose anaemic performance meant Ronaldo and Figo hardly saw the ball. When Portugal did finally contrive a chance, their wonderboy spurned it. Rui Costa's needle-worked pass got Ronaldo through Greece's offside trap, but his first touch was heavy and his second saw him shoot too high.

Figo managed one flourish in the final minute, turning brilliantly with three Greeks around him – but Fyssas's toe deflected his shot wide. Although Merk (bizarrely, Rehhagel's dentist in Germany for years!) blew up 30 seconds before the end of stoppage time, Portugal could probably have played for another month without scoring. Ronaldo wept like the child he still was, Eusébio handed out the runners-up medals wearing a face like a plateful of mortal sins, and Figo ripped his off his neck while walking away. But Scolari took his beating like a man: 'I don't think it's bad for football. Greece have a wonderful defence, and play on the mistakes of their opponents. It's up to us, the more offensive teams, to find a way past the system.'

If nobody could break Greece down, that was hardly their problem. 'I'd prefer to take the cup home and let football go a little bit backwards,' Giannakopoulos said. 'We were there to be beaten, but no one did it except Russia. For years, we played great football and nobody really noticed us. They have now.'

In Athens, pandemonium reigned. Graffiti reading 'Impossible is a fact' appeared around the city, and the Greek press went berserk. *Athliki*: 'National delirium – the masters of Europe.' *Protathlitis*: 'They have silenced the whole world.' *Espresso*: 'Super Greece! The planet is blue.' *Apogevmatini*: 'Greece on the throne of Europe.' Greece were wise to milk it. Within five years, the country had been economically beggared by brutal austerity imposed by the European Central Bank. One hoped that the Greek people's sublime memories of 2004 gave them some solace in the bad times.

French laziness, Czech misfortune and Portuguese cowardice meant Greece were pushing at an open door. This was part of a wider pattern across Euro 2004, a Twilight of the Nike/Adidas Gods in which big names – Henry, Totti, Zidane, Raúl, Gerrard, Beckham, Ibrahimović – failed dismally to justify their billing. It ought to require more than aerial ability, dogged defending and relentless fouling to win a European Championship. It usually does. But not this time. Rehhagel and his team got rudely turned over by neighbours Albania in their very next competitive match. They didn't qualify for the 2006 World Cup.

7.45pm, 4 July 2004
Estádio da Luz, Lisbon
Attendance: 62,865
Referee: Markus Merk (Germany)

GREECE 1 (Charisteas 57)
PORTUGAL 0

GREECE: Nikopolidis, Seitaridis, Dellas, Kapsis, Fyssas, Basinas, Zagorakis (c), Katsouranis, Charisteas, Vryzas (Papadopoulos 81), Giannakopoulos (Venetidis 76).
PORTUGAL: Ricardo, Miguel (Ferreira 43), Carvalho, Andrade, Valente, Costinha (Rui Costa 60), Figo (c), Maniche, Pauleta (Gomes 74), Deco, Ronaldo.

Booked: Basinas (45+2), Seitaridis (63), Fyssas (67), Papadopoulos (85), Costinha (12), Valente (90+3).

2008

WITH THE event now too gargantuan for any smallish European nation to stage it, there was some inevitability about it being co-hosted for the second time in three tournaments. Austria and Switzerland were awarded the finals in December 2002; Austria erected a new stadium in Klagenfurt and tidied up three others, while the Swiss rebuilt four existing grounds.

Switzerland looked far stronger than their neighbours, having come home undefeated from the 2006 World Cup in Germany without conceding a goal. In contrast, many Austrians feared an abject humiliation, with thousands signing an online petition demanding that the team withdraw from the competition.

For the first time since 1984, no British or Irish team made the cut. England's demise was the noisiest. After five years of decadent complacency, Sven-Göran Eriksson had wandered off into the sunset to count his millions. The press loudly demanded a native-born replacement, and Steve McClaren got the job on the strength of leading Middlesbrough to the UEFA Cup Final, where Sevilla had slaughtered them.

After a shambolic 0-0 draw against Macedonia at Old Trafford, things unravelled in Zagreb, where assistant coach Terry Venables's ill-advised use of 3-5-2 resulted in a drippy 2-0 defeat. But home wins over Israel and Russia steadied the ship. Even after England were overwhelmed in Moscow, Russia's subsequent defeat by Israel meant that on the final night, all McClaren's team needed was a point at home to the already-qualified Croats. Instead, giving one of the most catastrophic performances in their history, they sank to a stunning 3-2 defeat, with novice goalkeeper Scott Carson having a meltdown behind a wonky offside trap. McClaren, ridiculed for sheltering under an umbrella in the downpour, walked the plank the next morning.

Few gave Scotland a chance in a group containing World Cup finalists France and Italy. But two stirring wins over the French put them in the mix, and when Ukraine were beaten 3-1, qualification seemed on. Typically, they then lost in Tbilisi, which left them needing to beat Italy at Hampden Park. At 1-1 with seconds to go, Alan Hutton was fouled near his own corner flag by Giorgio Chiellini, but referee Manuel Mejuto González bizarrely gave Italy the free kick. Andrea Pirlo floated it over, Christian Panucci headed home, and the Scots were sunk.

The sole highlight of Wales's campaign, a 5-2 win in Trnava, merely mirrored an earlier 5-1 home defeat by Slovakia. In the same group, Ireland paid for the FAI's decision to appoint Steve Staunton as manager. After an unprecedentedly appalling rout in Nicosia, Ireland needed stoppage time goals to avoid losing at home to Cyprus and drawing in San Marino. Staunton, now a national laughing stock, didn't see out the campaign.

Northern Ireland missed out too, much more creditably. At Windsor Park, David Healy's hat-trick saw them sensationally defeat Spain 3-2, and fine wins over Sweden and Denmark followed. But the North's eccentric habit of beating good teams and losing to bad ones proved fatal. Iceland did the double over them, and another shocker in Riga finished them off.

Following their Belfast ordeal, Spain lost again in Stockholm, but manager Luis Aragonés rescued matters by winning eight of the nine remaining qualifiers. To his already enviable collection of artists, he had added Barcelona's young creator Andrés Iniesta and the slender Valencia winger David Silva. But question marks hung over the defence, where Carles Puyol lacked pace and Sergio Ramos redefined the phrase 'gaffe-prone'. Sweden followed Spain into the finals, thanks to UEFA handing Denmark a 3-0 defeat after a pitch invader attacked referee Herbert Fandel during their ding-dong 3-3 draw at home to the Swedes.

For Germany, the feelgood factor of the 2006 World Cup was still swirling around. Jürgen Klinsmann's vaguely aristocratic assistant Joachim Löw had succeeded him, the youngsters blooded at Euro 2004 were now seasoned operators, and Michael Ballack still ran the midfield stylishly. While Löw's central defenders didn't look up to it and goalkeeper Jens Lehmann was an unreliable hothead, Germany were clearly a good team again.

Few of the dark horses looked like a winner. Greece's sequel to 2004 was awaited with less than bated breath, although Otto Rehhagel and most of his old guard were still there. France, still adjusting to life after Zinedine Zidane, were in a downward spiral under the incompetent and blasé Raymond Domenech. The Netherlands, coached by Marco van Basten, were a work in progress. Portugal had scraped into the finals with a tense 0-0 draw against Roy Hodgson's Finland in Porto. And Russia's equally unimpressive qualification suggested little could be expected from them.

Meanwhile, the weather over the Alps was turning distinctly variable and high-precipitation as June 2008 began. Not great news for the well-heeled ski crowd, but ideal conditions for fast attacking football on wet pitches.

GROUP A
Switzerland, Czech Republic, Turkey, Portugal

For the opening ceremony at Basel's St-Jakob Park, UEFA served up a stereotypical parade of skiers, cows, snowy mountains and yodellers. The most interesting thing about the afternoon didn't come to light until nearly a decade later: FIFA president Sepp Blatter's nose was put badly out of joint by being seated eight places away from the centre of the VIP box. It proved a pivotal moment in the breakdown of personal relations between Blatter and UEFA president Michel Platini, ahead of both men's spectacular downfalls.

In a boring encounter under grey skies, neither Switzerland nor the Czechs offered much. The meaty-faced Alex Frei looked lively in the first half, forcing Petr Čech into two capable saves. But before the interval, his tournament collapsed as badly as it had in 2004, when he had been sent home for spitting at Steven Gerrard. Here, Zdeněk Grygera's foul tore his knee ligaments, and he wept tears of fury as he was helped off the field and out of the competition.

Cagey and cautious, the Czechs didn't deserve their 71st-minute winner. When Tomáš Galásek headed the ball toward Switzerland's box, their entire defence pushed up too late. Substitute Václav Svěrkoš stayed just onside as it came over the top, then shinned it across the wrong-footed goalkeeper Diego Benaglio and into the corner.

Switzerland's luck stayed rotten to the end. Referee Roberto Rosetti missed Tomáš Ujfaluši handling in the box, Čech saved superbly from Tranquillo Barnetta in the resulting scramble, and Johan Vonlanthen's close-range follow-up hit the underside of the bar.

'This is football,' Swiss manager Köbi Kuhn said fatalistically. 'It's not about justice.' He had more important things to worry about: his wife Alice was in a coma after a severe epileptic attack.

———

Had you been told at the end of Portugal v Turkey in Geneva that one of these teams would make the semis, you would have well believed it. The Portuguese were slick and quick throughout, the two-goal margin scarcely reflecting their superiority.

The 23-year-old Cristiano Ronaldo drifted around like a terrifying giant murder-hornet, seeing Turkish goalkeeper Volkan Demirel fingertip his free kick on to a post. Turkey's striker Nihat Kahveci recalled, 'We were shoulder

317

to shoulder. He wasn't going faster than me, so I said, "Wow, it's true that I'm fast." But I didn't know that Cristiano had a button to accelerate. And suddenly he pushed it. And in that moment, I understood I wasn't so fast.'

However, it fell to someone else to make the breakthrough. Two parts footballer to three parts nightclub bouncer, Pepe would later achieve notoriety for his serial brutishness in Real Madrid's colours. But somewhere in there, amid the histrionics and violence, was a good player struggling to get out. After an hour, he played a one-two with Nuno Gomes and lifted it over Volkan just before a Turk flattened him.

Turkey were a rabble at times. When Hakan Balta misjudged a bounce and hacked Simão Sabrosa just outside the box, referee Herbert Fandel missed it, so Gomes played to the whistle and struck the post. The same player later headed against the bar, and the second goal finally arrived when João Moutinho's 360-degree turn and pass set up the mohawked Raul Meireles for a simple finish. Already Portugal looked a cut above everyone else in the group.

———

After his team swatted the Czech Republic aside four days later, Scolari revealed that he had been pleasantly surprised by Karel Brückner's selection of Milan Baroš ahead of the half-fit Jan Koller. Baroš didn't play badly, but his 2004 form was long gone and Portugal handled him easily.

The Czechs couldn't say the same of Ronaldo. Early on, he played a one-two with Gomes before Čech saved at his feet; the ball ran loose to Deco, and though Čech again did well, the playmaker banged in the rebound.

But the Czechs soon made headway up their right, against makeshift left-back Paulo Ferreira, who was nowhere to be seen as Marek Jankulovski shot wide. Soon, Libor Sionko headed in Jaroslav Plašil's corner for the equaliser. The winger, who had flopped at Rangers in 2006/07, looked much brighter here.

In the second half, the double-marked Ronaldo eased his team ahead again with a crisp right-footer from outside the box. By now, the Czechs' 35-year-old anchorman Galásek simply couldn't keep up with Portugal's combination play. And Sionko missed the equaliser late on, heading Plašil's cross too close to goalkeeper Ricardo.

Deco was again involved as Portugal sealed the win, picking out Ronaldo in a near-empty Czech half. Ronaldo then showed untypical generosity, drawing Čech out to hand a tap-in to substitute Ricardo Quaresma, one of many Portuguese next big things who never fulfilled their promise. Less than an hour after the final whistle, Scolari was named as Chelsea's new manager. But Portugal's tournament had already peaked.

In a rain-spattered tournament, no fixture got a worse drenching than the meeting of Switzerland and Turkey in Basel, leaving everyone present as wet as speckled trout. In aquatic conditions, with the ball getting stuck on the sodden grass every few seconds, Switzerland kept shooting on sight. Barnetta went closest when Volkan palmed his effort around the post; at the other end, Arda Turan headed against the woodwork.

Turkey paid for that when Philippe Senderos's punt downfield sent Eren Derdiyok through on the right. He skipped around Volkan, then squared it across the goalmouth for the unmarked Hakin Yakin. Again the ball stopped dead on the saturated surface, but Yakin had enough time to jog over and tap it in, before 'celebrating' morosely (he was ethnically Turkish himself). Minutes later, Valon Behrami fed him an identical chance, but he sliced it ineptly wide from three yards.

'I prayed to God for the rain to stop,' said Turkey's manager Fatih Terim. Eventually it eased, just as substitute Semih Şentürk sneaked behind Ludovic Magnin and headed Nihat's cross through Benaglio's soaked gloves. The talented Yakin then screwed up a four-against-one break by shooting straight at Volkan, who bravely stopped Ricardo Cabanas converting the rebound.

All these Swiss misses came home to roost in stoppage time. Arda cut inside two defenders on the left, and his drive came off Patrick Müller's heel and floated over Benaglio's head. Rough on the hosts, for the second consecutive game, and now they were out. 'For five years, a whole country had been looking forward to this tournament. And lo and behold, for us it lasted just five days,' sighed Lausanne paper *Le Matin*. But Turkey were only getting started. 'Euro 2008 began for us tonight,' Terim declared. How right he was.

At last, there was some good news for Kuhn as his wife came out of her coma hours before Switzerland faced Portugal. His team, rising to the occasion, gave him a fine send-off in his 73rd and final game as manager.

With qualification secured, Scolari rested eight players, and the sight of Quaresma doing an early rabona suggested that Portugal were only half-interested. Still, their reserves dominated the first half and should have had a penalty when the clumsy Stephan Lichtsteiner took Nani's legs. Quaresma's free kick later came off goalkeeper Pascal Zuberbühler's hands to hit the bar, and after half-time, Nani hit the post when Lichtsteiner's miscue let him in.

But the Swiss were due a break. First, Derdiyok's flick fell into Yakin's path and he slotted it through Ricardo's legs. Then, near the end, Fernando Meira stuck out a leg, Barnetta tumbled, and Yakin's penalty sealed Switzerland's first European Championship win. Portugal topped the group regardless, but their momentum, a useful quality in a three-week tournament, was gone.

=====

With the Czechs and Turks level on every metric, UEFA announced that if their meeting in Geneva ended all square, a penalty shoot-out would take place after 90 minutes. But, like one or two other European Championship classics of the past, things only ignited after a grim opening half-hour. Jan Koller, fit again, did his salmon-on-stilts routine to meet Grygera's cross with a fierce header that crashed in off the underside of the bar.

Soon, Koller nearly doubled his money, heading over the bar as Servet Çetin tugged his shirt. On the hour, he broke through to shoot wide, but it didn't matter: a minute later, the Czechs went 2-0 up, Plašil stabbing home Sionko's cross at the back post.

It seemed we wouldn't be getting that penalty shoot-out after all. Turkey were then amazingly lucky not to go 3-0 down as Ján Polák shot against the post, then Emre Aşık sliced a clearance up in the air, and as Polák lunged for it, Emre kicked him in the head, drawing blood. Referee Peter Fröjdfeldt, who waved play on, would have given a foul anywhere else on the pitch.

That was the turning point. Minutes later, Hamit Altıntop's cross eluded everyone in the Czech box except Arda, whose shot crept in via Čech's gloves and the post. A bad one for the experienced goalkeeper, but not as bad as what came next.

The Turks poured forward, hunting the equaliser that would keep them alive. Now came the nadir of Čech's entire career. With three minutes left, he claimed another Altıntop cross but ineptly dropped it, leaving Nihat with an empty goal and a tap-in. Months earlier, he had blundered badly in the League Cup Final, gifting Tottenham's Jonathan Woodgate the winner. This was worse.

Penalties were looming, but Nihat settled matters with a stupendous goal. Taking Altıntop's pass in his stride, he stayed onside as the Czech defence stepped up too late, whirled full circle and lashed a wonderful dipping shot in off the bar for 3-2. 'All Turks remember where they were when I scored this goal,' he recalled. 'I was told a thousand stories about it: the people who threw things around at home, those who were thrown to the ground, those who hurt their heads while jumping.'

In the second minute of stoppage time, anarchy reigned in the Turkish box as Volkan and Servet collided under a high ball. While it bounced out of play, Volkan and Koller squared up. The goalkeeper shoved the striker in his wardrobe-sized chest, and though Koller's collapse was risible, Volkan had to go (no penalty, though, as the ball had gone dead). With all Turkey's subs used, striker Tunçay Şanlı went in goal, but the Czechs couldn't contrive a shot in the time remaining.

Not the best way for the ice-cool Brückner to sign off after seven years as Czech manager. 'I cannot explain it,' he said. 'It was a collapse.' Nobody was in the mood to kick poor Čech while he was down. 'Petr is deeply sorry,' said Jankulovski. 'He's saved us many times in the past.'

Meanwhile, Turkey's campaign was starting to take on a supernatural feel. 'I say to the people: get on the streets, celebrate this victory, profit from this moment,' roared Terim, whose cigars, open-buttoned shirts and exposed chest hair gave him the look of an ageing Aegean playboy living off a shipping-empire inheritance.

6pm, 7 June 2008
St Jakob-Park, Basel
Attendance: 39,730
Referee: Roberto Rosetti (Italy)

CZECH REPUBLIC 1 (Svěrkoš 71)
SWITZERLAND 0

CZECH REPUBLIC: Petr Čech, Zdeněk Grygera, Tomáš Ujfaluši (c), David Rozehnal, Marek Jankulovski, Tomáš Galásek, David Jarolím (Radoslav Kovač 87), Jan Polák, Jan Koller (Václav Svěrkoš 56), Libor Sionko (Stanislav Vlček 83), Jaroslav Plašil. **Manager:** Karel Brückner.

SWITZERLAND: Diego Benaglio, Stephan Lichtsteiner (Johan Vonlanthen 75), Ludovic Magnin, Philippe Senderos, Patrick Müller, Gökhan Inler, Gelson Fernandes, Valon Behrami (Eren Derdiyok 84), Marco Streller, Alex Frei (c) (Hakan Yakin 46), Tranquillo Barnetta. **Manager:** Köbi Kuhn.

Booked: Magnin (59), Vonlanthen (76), Barnetta (90+3).

8.45pm, 7 June 2008
Stade de Genève, Geneva
Attendance: 29,016
Referee: Herbert Fandel (Germany)

PORTUGAL 2 (Pepe 61, Meireles 90+3)
TURKEY 0

PORTUGAL: Ricardo Pereira, José Bosingwa, Képler Laveran 'Pepe', Ricardo Carvalho, Paulo Ferreira, Armando Gonçalves 'Petit', João Moutinho, Simão Sabrosa (Raul Meireles 83), Nuno Soares 'Gomes' (c) (Luís da Cunha 'Nani' 69), Cristiano Ronaldo, Anderson de Souza 'Deco' (Fernando Meira 90+2). **Manager:** Luiz Felipe Scolari.

TURKEY: Volkan Demirel, Hamit Altıntop (Semih Şentürk 76), Hakan Balta, Servet Çetin, Gökhan Zan (Emre Asık 55), Emre Belözoğlu (c), Mehmet Aurélio, Mevlüt Erdinç (Sabri Sarıoğlu 46), Nihat Kahveci, Tunçay Sanlı, Colin Kazim-Richards. **Manager:** Fatih Terim.

Booked: Kazim-Richards (4), Gökhan (51), Sabri (73).

6pm, June 11, 2008
Stade de Genève, Geneva
Attendance: 29,016
Referee: Kyros Vassaras (Greece)

PORTUGAL 3 (Deco 8, Ronaldo 63, Quaresma 90+1)
CZECH REPUBLIC 1 (Sionko 17)

PORTUGAL: Ricardo, Bosingwa, Pepe, Carvalho, Ferreira, Petit, Moutinho (Meira 75), Simão (Ricardo Quaresma 80), Gomes (c) (Hugo Almeida 79), Ronaldo, Deco.

CZECH REPUBLIC: Čech, Grygera, Ujfaluši (c), Rozehnal, Jankulovski, Galásek (Koller 73), Marek Matějovský (Vlček 68), Polák, Milan Baroš, Sionko, Plašil (Jarolím 84).

Booked: Bosingwa (31), Polák (22).

8.45pm, 11 June 2008
St Jakob-Park, Basel
Attendance: 39,730
Referee: Luboš Michel (Slovakia)

TURKEY 2 (Semih 57, Arda 90+2)
SWITZERLAND 1 (Yakin 32)

TURKEY: Volkan, Altıntop, Emre Aşık, Hakan, Servet, Gökdeniz Karadeniz (Mehmet Topal 46), Aurélio, Tümer Metin (Semih 46), Nihat (Kazim-Richards 85), Tunçay, Arda Turan.

SWITZERLAND: Benaglio, Lichtsteiner, Magnin (c), Senderos, Müller, Inler, Fernandes (Ricardo Cabanas 76), Behrami, Derdiyok, Yakin (Daniel Gygax 85), Barnetta (Vonlanthen 66).

Booked: Tuncay (31), Aurélio (41), Hakan (48), Derdiyok (55).

8.45pm, 15 June 2008
St Jakob-Park, Basel
Attendance: 39,730
Referee: Konrad Plautz (Austria)

SWITZERLAND 2 (Yakin 71, 83 pen)
PORTUGAL 0

SWITZERLAND: Pascal Zuberbühler, Lichtsteiner (Stéphane Grichting 83), Magnin (c), Senderos, Müller, Inler, Fernandes, Behrami, Derdiyok, Yakin (Cabanas 86), Vonlanthen (Barnetta 83).

PORTUGAL: Ricardo, Miguel Monteiro, Pepe, Bruno Alves, Carvalho, Ferreira (Jorge Ribeiro 41), Meira, Miguel Veloso (Moutinho 71), Meireles, Hélder Postiga (Almeida 74), Nani, Quaresma.

Booked: Yakin (27), Vonlanthen (37), Barnetta (81), Fernandes (90+2), Ferreira (30), Ribeiro (64), Meira (78), Miguel (81).

8.45pm, 15 June 2008
Stade de Genève, Geneva
Attendance: 29,016
Referee: Peter Fröjdfeldt (Sweden)

TURKEY 3 (Arda 75, Nihat 87, 89)
CZECH REPUBLIC 2 (Koller 34, Plašil 62)

TURKEY: Volkan, Altıntop, Hakan, Emre Gungör (Emre Aşık 63), Servet, Topal (Kazim-Richards 57), Aurélio, Semih (Sabri 46), Nihat, Tunçay, Arda.

CZECH REPUBLIC: Čech, Grygera, Ujfaluši (c), Rozehnal, Jankulovski, Galásek, Matějovský (Jarolím 39), Polák, Koller, Sionko (Vlček 85), Plašil (Michal Kadlec 80).

Booked: Topal (6), Aurélio (10), Arda (62), Emre Aşık (73), Galásek (80), Ujfaluši (90+4), Baroš (90+5, on substitutes' bench).
Sent off: Volkan (90+2).

GROUP A	P	W	D	L	F	A	GD	Pts
PORTUGAL	3	2	0	1	5	3	+2	6
TURKEY	3	2	0	1	5	5	0	6
CZECH REPUBLIC	3	1	0	2	4	6	− 2	3
SWITZERLAND	3	1	0	2	3	3	0	3

Portugal and Turkey qualified.

GROUP B
Austria, Croatia, Poland, Germany

After ten years of terrible results, Austria sat 93rd in FIFA's world rankings, sandwiched between Mozambique and Thailand. But what they lacked in finesse, they compensated for in enthusiasm. That nearly got them a draw against Croatia in Vienna.

'I'll never forget the hours before the Croatia game, with the huge crowd and the *rot-weiß-rot* flags. It was surreal,' manager Josef Hickersberger recalled in 2016. But though the atmosphere in a packed Ernst-Happel-Stadion was heady and heaving, Croatia quickly punctured it. The tireless Ivica Olić was bundled over by René Aufhauser in the box, and Luka Modrić ignored the mass whistling to stroke the penalty down the middle as Jürgen Macho dived right.

Instead of kicking on, Croatia wilted in the heat. The steadily improving Austrians, winning everything in the air, could have scored five. In the first half, Sebastian Prödl and Joachim Standfest sent free headers wide. In the second, Croatian goalkeeper Stipe Pletikosa fumbled another header from Martin Harnik and saved Ümit Korkmaz's shot. At the death, Roman Kienast nodded narrowly wide while Dario Knežević tried to strangle him with his own shirt. Most of the Croats slumped exhausted on the turf at the final whistle; Modrić's penalty had been their only shot on target.

═══

Before Germany faced Poland, a phoney war was in full swing. Warsaw tabloid *Super Express* ran a photoshop of Poland's manager Leo Beenhakker holding up Jogi Löw's and Michael Ballack's decapitated heads, under the headline 'Leo, daj nam ich głowy!' (Leo, give us their heads!). The mortified Beenhakker described it as 'an awful thing'. Another Polish paper, *Fakt*, exhorted the team to 'repeat Grunwald', when Polish and Lithuanian forces defeated the Teutonic Knights in July 1410.

Poland's midfielder Jacek Krzynówek, who played in the Bundesliga, noted that all this was 'part of the psychological war, and it didn't start yesterday or the day before, but a long time ago'. In Klagenfurt, he should have scored inside 40 seconds, but volleyed miles over an unguarded goal after Jens Lehmann botched a punch.

Germany quickly took control, and Miroslav Klose put an open goal on a plate for Mario Gómez, whose giant leg stabbed it inches wide. On the bench, one of Beenhakker's assistants reacted with bizarre joy, as if Poland had scored themselves. Later, Ballack's trickery set Klose free on the right, and again he provided another open goal, this time for Lukas Podolski, who buried it. The sad-faced scorer, born in Upper Silesia, said afterwards, 'This victory does not over-enthuse me. I didn't celebrate my goals because Poland is part of my heart.'

Artur Boruc later touched Ballack's thunderbolt over the bar, and Germany finally turned out the lights when Bastian Schweinsteiger robbed Paweł Golański and fed Klose, who miskicked into the air. Podolski waited for it to drop, then planted it in the top corner. The Poles would have to wait until October 2014 to get one over on their neighbours for the first time.

———

But Germany tripped at the very next hurdle, losing to the much-improved Croats in a match that got better as it went on. After 20 minutes of nothing whatsoever, a well-worked goal broke the torpor. Danijel Pranjić's teasing cross was too high for even the 6ft 6in Per Mertesacker, and when it landed, Darijo Srna reacted quicker than Marcell Jansen to score at the far post. A good player with an irritating penchant for simulation and belligerence, Srna dedicated this goal to his brother Igor, who had Down syndrome.

Germany offered little in attack as Croatia held possession well, with Niko Kranjčar twice going close. The outstanding Modrić, whom his manager Slaven Bilić called 'the alpha and omega of the team', saw his long-range shot slip through Lehmann's hands for a corner, and the goalkeeper then endured a much worse moment. Ivan Rakitić's cross hit Podolski, and Lehmann was deceived as it bounced against his post to fall kindly for Olić, who knocked it in.

Substitute Bastian Schweinsteiger began the move that threw Germany a lifeline. Philipp Lahm crossed from the left, Ballack's header caused confusion, and Podolski volleyed in the loose ball. But while two-goal comebacks are what German teams do best, this one was already out of reach. In stoppage time, Schweinsteiger was sent off for pushing over Jerko Leko after the Croat fouled him from behind. Modrić might have gone himself moments later, for a nasty lunge on Torsten Frings, who had kicked him several times in the first half. A bad day for Germany all round.

===

They were lucky that neither Poland nor Austria took three points from a messy match that evening in Vienna. The Poles were continuously carved open in a frantic and one-sided first half, as Austria tore holes in their flat-footed defence and hopeless offside trap. That they weren't several goals behind at the interval was solely down to their goalkeeper.

On three occasions between the 11th and 16th minutes, Boruc kept Poland in the tournament. First, Mariusz Jop's dithering saw Harnik race through, but Boruc made himself big and deflected the shot wide. Then Korkmaz's excellent play presented Harnik with a chance, only for the keeper to block with his legs. Finally, Andreas Ivanschitz's magnificent pass from inside his own half took out five Poles and put Christoph Leitgeb in, but again Boruc flew out to save.

Football being what it is, Poland then went 1-0 up in fraudulent circumstances. Marek Saganowski's shot brushed off Emanuel Pogatetz and Macho before reaching Roger Guerreiro, a Brazilian at Legia Warsaw who had been fast-tracked Polish citizenship months earlier. Standing at least a yard offside, he side-footed it in at the far post.

Austria seemed spent after that blow, and Poland controlled a much quieter second half, with Macho pulling off a superb double save from Jacek Bąk and Dariusz Dudka. But the hosts were still worth their controversial equaliser. Two minutes into stoppage time, a free kick was floated into the Polish box. Prödl tried to jump for it but was held down by Mariusz Lewandowski. Referee Howard Webb paused, then pointed to the spot as half a dozen Poles surrounded him with murder in their eyes.

There was no denying that Lewandowski had fouled Prödl. The bone of contention was why Webb had chosen that particular moment to suddenly punish one team for the offence, when it had been going on for the entire night (Golański, for instance, had done it equally blatantly to Ivanschitz just after half-time). In the bedlam, 38-year-old substitute Ivica Vastić kept his nerve and slammed the penalty past Boruc with his final kick in international football, becoming the oldest goalscorer in the history of the finals (and winning the group for his native Croatia in the process).

'It looks like I'm a specialist for late goals,' Vastić smiled afterwards, referring to his equally dramatic equaliser against Chile at France 98. 'It's not easy to concentrate in those conditions. But I was calm.'

Recriminations abounded as the Polish press turned Webb into a hate figure. Death threats filled the air, and Poland's prime minister Donald

Tusk made things worse by moronically remarking that he 'wanted to kill' Webb. Beenhakker said, 'I'm 43 years in this business, I think [I'm] always very correct with referees, never been suspended, but this is something I really cannot understand. [Webb] probably wants to show he is a big boy.' Hickersberger took a more philosophical view: 'If the referee decides, then it's as if God decides.'

======

Boruc's heroics had been in vain: only an outlandish combination of scorelines could save Poland now. 'I hope Bilić picks his mother-in-law,' Beenhakker joked. The Croatian manager rested nine players, but his team still cruised to victory.

After a bright Polish start which saw Dariusz Dudka squander a free header, Croatia Lite took command. Pranjić chipped wide when clean through; Hrvoje Vejić missed a header even easier than Dudka's; and Boruc's quick reactions kept out Rakitić, Pranjić and Ivan Klasnić. It seemed only a matter of time. And it was. Eight minutes after the interval, Klasnić was shoved over on the edge of the box. As referee Kyros Vassaras played advantage, Pranjić set up the striker to clip a fine finish across Boruc.

Late on, Ebi Smolarek's pass played in Tomasz Zahorski, but Croatia's ponytailed keeper Vedran Runje spread himself to block the hesitant shot. It was the story of Poland's tournament. Beenhakker was long gone by the time they hosted Euro 2012, at which they once again failed to win a match.

======

In Vienna, Austria were hoping for a rerun of Córdoba 1978, with or without a sequel to Hans Krankl's legendary *Wunder-Tor*. Before the game, Martin Harnik claimed the Germans were 'shitting their pants'. Hickersberger swiftly rebuked him for his 'low remarks [creating] useless animosity'.

Germany's players had staged a clear-the-air meeting following the Croatia defeat, with Löw not invited. Here, they still looked unimaginative and sluggish – but also tighter and better organised.

Almost 75,000 ticketless fans (many wearing T-shirts commemorating the 1978 result) packed the Viennese fanzone to watch a frenetic match which saw the prolonging of Mario Gómez's public death by a thousand sitters. Following good work by Klose, he somehow shanked the ball airborne in front of an open goal, then allowed the much shorter György Garics to beat him to the rebound and head it off the line.

As Austria called the tune, new boy Erwin Hoffer was prominent. He should have had a penalty when Metzelder barged him, miscontrolled a Martin Harnik cross before Lehmann flew out to save, and got booked for taking out Ballack. When Lehmann nervously spilled Aufhauser's shot for a corner, an upset felt possible.

Before half-time, referee Manuel Mejuto González sent off Löw and Hickersberger for verbally abusing his fourth official. The two managers, both wearing thunderous expressions, shook hands before trudging up into the stands, where Löw sat next to Chancellor Angela Merkel in the VIP box.

As it turned out, Germany had one gem stashed away in their locker. Early in the second half, Ivanschitz chopped down Lahm, and Ballack stepped up to strike a 75mph missile of a free kick into the top corner. The skipper had picked a good time to make his first real contribution to Euro 2008: that morning, one Austrian newspaper had derided him as a 'loser', while another mocked-up an image of him naked.

Austria flagged near the end. Aufhauser almost flicked a corner into his own net, Macho beat away Klose's shot, and substitute Oliver Neuville cocked up a three-on-two break by firing wide with the last kick of the match. Germany could breathe again, even if the aesthetics left much to be desired. 'The triumph of ugly football,' snorted the *Süddeutsche Zeitung*.

The Austrian press hailed a huge improvement after a decade of decay, and called for Hickersberger to stay on, though he resigned anyway. 'If we'd had [Marc] Janko in the form of 2009,' he said, referring to his injured striker, 'we'd have made the quarter-finals.' Austria bowed out with the worst record of any European Championship host since the group stage was introduced in 1980, but they were clearly better than that.

6pm, 8 June 2008
Ernst Happel Stadion, Vienna
Attendance: 51,428
Referee: Pieter Vink (Netherlands)

CROATIA 1 (Modrić 4 pen)
AUSTRIA 0

CROATIA: Stipe Pletikosa, Vedran Ćorluka, Josip Šimunić, Robert Kovač, Danijel Pranjić, Niko Kovač (c), Darijo Srna, Niko Kranjčar (Dario Knežević 61), Ivica Olić (Ognjen Vukojević 83), Luka Modrić, Mladen Petrić (Igor Budan 72). **Manager:** Slaven Bilić.

AUSTRIA: Jürgen Macho, Sebastian Prödl, Martin Stranzl, Emanuel Pogatetz, René Aufhauser, Joachim Standfest, Ronald Gërçaliu (Ümit Korkmaz 69), Jürgen Säumel (Ivica Vastić 61), Roland Linz (Roman Kienast 73), Andreas Ivanschitz (c), Martin Harnik. **Manager:** Josef Hickersberger.

Booked: R. Kovač (51), Pogatetz (3), Säumel (21), Prödl (68).

8.45pm, 8 June 2008
Wörthersee Stadion, Klagenfurt
Attendance: 30,461
Referee: Tom Henning Øvrebø (Norway)

GERMANY 2 (Podolski 20, 72)
POLAND 0

GERMANY: Jens Lehmann, Philipp Lahm, Marcell Jansen, Per Mertesacker, Christoph Metzelder, Clemens Fritz (Bastian Schweinsteiger 56), Torsten Frings, Michael Ballack (c), Mario Gómez (Thomas Hitzlsperger 75), Miroslav Klose (Kevin Kurányi 90+1), Lukas Podolski. **Manager:** Joachim 'Jogi' Löw.

POLAND: Artur Boruc, Marcin Wasilewski, Michał Żewłakow, Jacek Bąk, Paweł Golański (Marek Saganowski 75), Dariusz Dudka, Mariusz Lewandowski, Wojciech Łobodziński (Łukasz Piszczek 65), Maciej Żurawski (c) (Roger Guerreiro 46), Euzebiusz Smolarek, Jacek Krzynówek. **Manager:** Leo Beenhakker.

Booked: Schweinsteiger (64), Smolarek (40), Lewandowski (60).

6pm, 12 June 2008
Wörthersee Stadion, Klagenfurt
Attendance: 30,461
Referee: Frank De Bleeckere (Belgium)

CROATIA 2 (Srna 24, Olić 62)
GERMANY 1 (Podolski 79)

CROATIA: Pletikosa, Ćorluka, Šimunić, R. Kovač, Pranjić, N. Kovač (c), Srna (Jerko Leko 80), Ivan Rakitić, Olić (Petrić 72), Modrić, Kranjčar (Knežević 85).

GERMANY: Lehmann, Lahm, Jansen (David Odonkor 46), Mertesacker, Metzelder, Fritz (Kurányi 82), Frings, Ballack (c), Gómez (Schweinsteiger 66), Klose, Podolski.

Booked: Srna (27), Šimunić (45+2), Leko (90+2), Modrić (90+3), Ballack (75), Lehmann (90+2).
Sent off: Schweinsteiger (90+1).

8.45pm, 12 June 2008
Ernst Happel Stadion, Vienna
Attendance: 51,428
Referee: Howard Webb (England)

AUSTRIA 1 (Vastić 90+3 pen)
POLAND 1 (Guerreiro 30)

AUSTRIA: Macho, György Garics, Prödl, Stranzl, Pogatetz, Aufhauser (Säumel 74), Christoph Leitgeb, Ümit Korkmaz, Harnik, Ivanschitz (c) (Kienast 64), Linz (Vastić 64).

POLAND: Boruc, Wasilewski, Żewłakow, Bąk (c), Mariusz Jop (Golański 46), Dudka, Lewandowski, Guerreiro (Rafał Murawski 85), Saganowski (Łobodziński 83), Smolarek, Krzynówek.

Booked: Korkmaz (56), Prödl (72), Wasilewski (58), Krzynówek (61), Bąk (90+3).

8.45pm, 16 June 2008
Wörthersee Stadion, Klagenfurt
Attendance: 30,461
Referee: Kyros Vassaras (Greece)

CROATIA 1 (Klasnić 53)
POLAND 0

CROATIA: Vedran Runje, Dario Šimić (c), Hrvoje Vejić, Knežević (Ćorluka 27), Pranjić, Leko, Vukojević, Nikola Pokrivač, Ivan Klasnić (Nikola Kalinić 74), Rakitić, Petrić (Kranjčar 75).

POLAND: Boruc, Wasilewski, Żewłakow (c), Dudka, Jakub Wawrzyniak, Murawski, Lewandowski (Adam Kokoszka 46), Łobodziński (Smolarek 55), Guerreiro, Saganowski (Tomasz Zahorski 69), Krzynówek.

Booked: Vejić (45), Vukojević (85), Lewandowski (38), Zahorski (84).

8.45pm, 16 June 2008
Ernst Happel Stadion, Vienna
Attendance: 51,428
Referee: Manuel Mejuto González (Spain)

GERMANY 1 (Ballack 49)
AUSTRIA 0

GERMANY: Lehmann, Arne Friedrich, Lahm, Mertesacker, Metzelder, Fritz (Tim Borowski 90+3), Frings, Ballack (c), Gómez (Hitzlsperger 60), Klose, Podolski (Oliver Neuville 83).

AUSTRIA: Macho, Garics, Martin Hiden (Leitgeb 55), Stranzl, Pogatetz, Aufhauser (Säumel 63), Christian Fuchs, Korkmaz, Harnik (Kienast 67), Ivanschitz (c), Erwin Hoffer.

Booked: Stranzl (13), Hoffer (31), Ivanschitz (48).

GROUP B	P	W	D	L	F	A	GD	Pts
CROATIA	3	3	0	0	4	1	+3	9
GERMANY	3	2	0	1	4	2	+2	6
AUSTRIA	3	0	1	2	1	3	− 2	1
POLAND	3	0	1	2	1	4	− 3	1

Croatia and Germany qualified.

GROUP C
Netherlands, Italy, France, Romania

In Zürich, the tournament's most glamorous group opened with its dire match. The Romanian manager Victor Pițurcă's nickname was Satan, due to his fondness for dressing in black, but most neutral viewers might have been calling him something else by the end of this life-sapping 0-0 draw with a Thierry Henry-less France, who were little better.

The creative bankruptcy of both teams soon became apparent, and hardly anything happened all afternoon. Nicolas Anelka headed Franck Ribéry's bouncing cross over the bar, and later drove a shot into the side-netting. Meanwhile, Răzvan Cociş almost diverted another Ribéry cross into his own net, but goalkeeper Bogdan Lobonț managed to clutch it. Romania's tall centre-backs Gabriel Tamaş and Dorin Goian spent the afternoon heading away crosses in their sleep.

Early in the second half, the disappointing Florent Malouda came to life, jinking past two Romanians before shooting beyond the angle of post and bar. Another Ribéry run set up a chance for young Karim Benzema, which he passed straight into Lobonț's arms. But Romania hung on for their first clean sheet in the European Championship, at the 11th attempt.

Near the end, there was a lingering shot of Michel Platini on the Letzigrund's big screen, looking so zoned-out that he seemed to be in a trance of tedium. 'I would've liked to win the game 10-0,' France's manager Raymond Domenech drawled, 'but that didn't happen.'

======

Après France et Roumanie, le déluge. Even with Robin van Persie and Arjen Robben injured, the Netherlands took brutal revenge for 2000 on Italy, blitzing the World Cup winners in Bern with a display of freewheeling counter-attacking.

With his inspirational captain Fabio Cannavaro out of the tournament after tearing ankle ligaments six days earlier, Roberto Donadoni sent out the oldest starting line-up in European Championship finals history. Their average age was 30.8, with only two players in their 20s, Andrea Barzagli and Andrea Pirlo. The record would stand until 2016, when the Italians broke it once more.

Before long, their slow rearguard was being stretched by the darting Dutch attackers. First, Dirk Kuyt fed the rapacious Ruud van Nistelrooy to take the ball around Gianluigi Buffon, but the angle was too narrow and the chance was lost. Soon afterwards, Van Nistelrooy had his goal, in questionable circumstances. Buffon, coming to punch Rafael van der Vaart's free kick, accidentally laid out Christian Panucci, who fell in a dazed heap a yard off the field. While this was happening, Wesley Sneijder's shot was diverted in by Van Nistelrooy, standing a mile offside.

Except he wasn't. The mere fact of Panucci's presence (and while he had certainly been clobbered, he wasn't too hurt to look up and see what was happening) placed Van Nistelrooy onside, to Italy's amazement and anger. UEFA's spokesperson said afterwards, 'Even if a player is not on the field, he is in the game.' The rule had been introduced to stop defenders sneakily stepping over the goal line to put strikers offside, but in situations like this, its limitations were obvious.

Minutes later, Pirlo's inswinging corner was headed off the line by Giovanni van Bronckhorst. Showing extraordinary lung power, the left-back sprinted nearly 70 yards to receive the return ball from van der Vaart in the Italian half. He looked up and hit a cross-field pass to Kuyt, who headed it into the box, and Sneijder nipped in to hook a neat finish over Buffon.

With Pirlo shining, Italy were lively – Di Natale shooting too high, Gianluca Zambrotta firing wide from an angle, Alessandro Del Piero stinging Edwin van der Sar's hands. The pivotal moment came when Antonio Cassano's lofted ball left Luca Toni bearing down on Van der Sar, but the striker lifted his shot crudely into the stands.

There was immediately another scare for the Netherlands, Van der Sar beating away Pirlo's free kick. Again they capitalised fully. From the rebound, Van Bronckhorst again raced downfield and was fed by Sneijder. He put it on a plate for Kuyt to shoot at Buffon; but Kuyt retrieved the ball and crossed for Van Bronckhorst, whose header went straight at Zambrotta and squeezed over the line.

Thirty seconds after coming on, Ibrahim Afellay almost made it 4-0, skipping past Fabio Grosso and grazing the bar. Only then was Italy's torture finally over. It was their biggest hiding in the finals, even though they could have scored five or six themselves. 'I cannot name a single player on my team who played badly,' marvelled Marco van Basten. His old friend and golf partner Donadoni was castigated for leaving out Roma's Daniele De Rossi in order to keep the Milan midfield together. And what a difference two years made for Marco Materazzi: embarrassingly off the pace here, he got hauled off early in the second half and was never capped again.

'Give us back Lippi!' howled *Tuttosport*, while *Corriere dello Sport* ludicrously called it Italy's worst ever European Championship performance. The display was much better than the scoreline, but Buffon still felt moved to ask for 'a pardon from all Italians who care about sport'. Getting killed on the counter-attack, it seemed, was still *calcio*'s biggest mortal sin.

Italy now played their part in another crazy match in Zürich, against a Romanian team who showed more enterprise in the first 20 minutes than they had in 90 against France. Buffon saved well from Adrian Mutu and Tamaş, and Panucci unwittingly flicked Cristian Chivu's free kick against his own post.

Toni and the recalled Del Piero both squandered headers before half-time, and by the end of the game Toni's tally of missed chances stood at four. But he was unlucky in first-half stoppage time when he headed past Lobonţ, only to be wrongly flagged offside.

Romania went ahead on 55 minutes, in startlingly sudden fashion. After Grosso tripped Florentin Petre, the free kick was taken so swiftly that the TV director almost missed the sight of Mutu bursting through to lift his shot over Buffon. The replays were unflattering to Zambrotta, who had tried to head the ball back to his keeper and failed to spot Mutu lurking.

Italy took barely 100 seconds to equalise. The 35-year-old Panucci had received a 4/10 rating from *Gazzetta dello Sport* after the Netherlands game, the lowest of all their players. Now he clawed back some credit. When Chiellini headed a corner into the goalmouth and Tamaş failed to react, he stabbed it in from almost under the bar.

The next big chance fell to Romania, as Grosso blocked Petre's rasping shot with his back. Meanwhile, Toni's nightmare continued as he failed to stab home Del Piero's brilliant pass, then suffered another bad offside call when Cassano played him in. Even his third great assist of the day, via his massive chest, ended in failure when De Rossi's header was kept out by Lobonţ – who then saved coolly as Cosmin Contra was about to score an own goal.

Defeat would put Italy out, and they looked the hangman in the eye late on. As Mutu crossed, Panucci was caught throttling Daniel Niculae, and referee Tom Henning Øvrebø gave a penalty. The notoriously flaky Mutu took it – even Lobonţ would have been a safer bet. With painful predictability, his kick was kept out by Buffon. A terrific save, but also a huge failure of nerve from a player whose unreliability had cost Romania qualification for Euro 2004 in Copenhagen earlier in the decade. 'I chose to shoot down the centre, because Buffon knew me: we had played together at Juventus,' Mutu said in 2020. 'Many thought I had intentionally missed.' Like many other things in his wayward career, he would live to regret it.

===

Some 150,000 Dutch supporters – almost one per cent of the Netherlands' population – were estimated to be in Bern for their team's meeting with France. Almost all of them had to settle for watching it on the city fanzone's big screen. They were treated to a second consecutive three-goal win by their team, with the scoreline again concealing a multitude of sins.

Their first goal came from their least-heralded player. Dirk Kuyt was a finesse-free zone, but he had one of the best work ethics in the game, which he showed when winning a corner off William Gallas. From that corner, he rose above Malouda to head a fine goal.

But this dishevelled, demoralised French side still had enough ability to scare the Dutch. Sidney Govou, a serial non-scorer, saw his shot kept out by Van der Sar's knee, and wasted another chance after excellent interplay between Malouda, Ribéry and Patrice Evra.

France began the second half with a flurry, screaming for a penalty when Henry's close-range effort hit André Ooijer's arm, but Ooijer couldn't have hoped to get out of the way (and hadn't even been looking at the ball). Minutes later, Malouda's overhead kick put Henry through with only Van der Sar to beat, but he ineptly lobbed the chance miles over.

The Netherlands eventually left France in the dust with three great goals. First, Van Nistelrooy's clever flick gave the substitute Robben a clear run down the left, and his cross found another substitute, Robin van Persie. The shot flew straight at Grégory Coupet, but bobbled over the line for 2-0.

France didn't give up, with van der Sar fisting away Ribéry's shot and Bafétimbi Gomis shanking the rebound into the crowd. Soon the scoreline looked slightly more realistic. Willy Sagnol sent a tantalising cross into the Dutch goalmouth, and a just-offside Henry arrived ahead of Joris Mathijsen to guide it home with his left instep.

But straight from the kick-off, Sneijder was given a fatal amount of space, and his pinpoint ball got Robben to the byline. The angle looked too narrow for a shot, but Robben went for it anyway as Lilian Thuram closed him down, firing a real rocket over Coupet's head. Not an ideal way for Thuram, one of the greats, to sign off from international football.

Sneijder himself wrapped it up. Latching on to Van Persie's pass, he ran away from the tired Jérémy Toulalan and hit a dipping drive that struck the underside of the bar before hitting the top corner. Slightly harsh on France, but Henry did himself no credit at the end by grinningly embracing Van Persie. Afterwards, Evra and Patrick Vieira fought in the tunnel, and Vieira's miserable evening was compounded when Van Nistelrooy, an old adversary in the Premier League, waited outside the French dressing room to taunt him.

The Netherlands had shown none of this panache in a qualifying campaign which had seen them lose in places like Minsk and Constanţa. Suddenly, almost overnight, they looked like champions-in-waiting. Their prime minister Jan-Peter Balkenende helpfully announced that he was keeping his diary free for 29 June, the day of the final. Were they playing too well, too soon?

———

Like Scolari against Switzerland and Bilić against Poland, Van Basten rested most of his team with top spot assured. His benchwarmers knocked Romania out without breaking sweat.

Romania had to win unless France v Italy ended all square, and never looked like doing it. Other than Raţ creating a wonderful opportunity for Răzvan Cociş, who ballooned it sky-high, they hardly mounted a meaningful attack as the Dutch reserves tormented them, with Van Persie (twice), Khalid Boulahrouz and Robben all missing chances. Lobonţ brilliantly turned Van Persie's shot around the post early in the second half, but was powerless to prevent Klaas-Jan Huntelaar slotting in Afellay's cross.

The inevitable second goal arrived when Demy de Zeeuw picked out Van Persie, who finished powerfully into the roof of the net while holding off a

Romanian. Pițurcă, looking even grimmer than usual, was left to curse his decision not to try to beat France.

=====

Before France faced Italy at the Letzigrund, rumours swirled that Thuram and Sagnol had asked Domenech to leave them out. Whatever the truth, neither man played. Domenech, a bad manager, was also an unlucky one: in the opening minutes, Franck Ribéry injured his ankle while fouling Zambrotta and was stretchered off.

But France were a rabble anyway. The profligate Toni blew more opportunities, and Panucci's header from a corner was kept out by Coupet and Claude Makélélé on the line. When a simple ball over the top exposed Eric Abidal, he hacked Toni from behind in the box. A red card and a penalty, which Pirlo swept into the top corner. As Abidal walked off, the veteran Thuram took off his tracksuit and began warming up – but Domenech instead threw on the less celebrated Jean-Alain Boumsong, in the process sacrificing Ribéry's replacement Samir Nasri.

Coupet later tipped Grosso's free kick on to the post, but that just delayed the inevitable. When another free kick was touched short to Daniele De Rossi, Henry chose that exact moment to turn sideways and stick out a leg, diverting the shot past Coupet. Not quite an own goal, but not far off. Italy now shut the game down, and in stoppage time Toni capped his unforgettable performance by leathering his latest atrocity over the bar.

Interviewed on TV afterwards, Domenech made a show of himself by proposing to his girlfriend. His fate seemed sealed when FFF president Jean-Pierre Escalette bemoaned 'a ringing failure from a sporting standpoint, and perhaps worse, in terms of the French national team's degrading image'. But, amazingly, the FFF board's 18 wise men then extended his contract, with Escalette mumbling that 'the bravest solution is not to follow public opinion or the media's wishes'. David Trezeguet, left out of the squad, immediately retired from international football. Most French fans probably felt like joining him.

6pm, 9 June 2008
Letzigrund, Zürich
Attendance: 30,585
Referee: Manuel Mejuto González (Spain)

FRANCE 0
ROMANIA 0

FRANCE: Grégory Coupet, Willy Sagnol, William Gallas, Lilian Thuram (c), Éric Abidal, Claude Makélélé, Jérémy Toulalan, Franck Ribéry, Karim Benzema (Samir Nasri 78), Nicolas Anelka (Bafétimbi Gomis 72), Florent Malouda. **Manager:** Raymond Domenech.

ROMANIA: Bogdan Lobonț, Cosmin Contra, Razvan Raț, Gabriel Tamaş, Dorin Goian, Mirel Rădoi (Nicolae Dică 90+3), Razvan Cociş (Paul Codrea 64), Cristian Chivu (c), Daniel Niculae, Adrian Mutu (Marius Niculae 78), Bănel Nicoliță. **Manager:** Victor Pițurcă.

Booked: Sagnol (51), D. Niculae (27), Contra (40), Goian (43).

8.45pm, 9 June 2008
Stade de Suisse Wankdorf, Bern
Attendance: 30,777
Referee: Peter Fröjdfeldt (Sweden)

NETHERLANDS 3 (Van Nistelrooy 26, Sneijder 31, Van Bronckhorst 79)
ITALY 0

NETHERLANDS: Edwin van der Sar (c), André Ooijer, Joris Mathijsen, Khalid Boulahrouz (Johnny Heitinga 77), Giovanni van Bronckhorst, Orlando Engelaar, Nigel de Jong, Dirk Kuyt (Ibrahim Afellay 81), Ruud van Nistelrooy (Robin van Persie 70), Wesley Sneijder, Rafael Van der Vaart. **Manager:** Marco van Basten.

ITALY: Gianluigi Buffon (c), Christian Panucci, Gianluca Zambrotta, Andrea Barzagli, Marco Materazzi (Fabio Grosso 54), Gennaro Gattuso, Massimo Ambrosini, Andrea Pirlo, Luca Toni, Antonio Di Natale (Alessandro Del Piero 64), Mauro Camoranesi (Antonio Cassano 75). **Manager:** Roberto Donadoni.

Booked: De Jong (58), Toni (27), Zambrotta (35), Gattuso (51).

6pm, 13 June 2008
Letzigrund, Zürich
Attendance: 30,585
Referee: Tom Henning Øvrebø (Norway)

ROMANIA 1 (Mutu 55)
ITALY 1 (Panucci 56)

ROMANIA: Lobonț, Contra, Raț, Tamaş, Goian, Chivu (c), Rădoi (Dică 25), Florentin Petre (Nicoliță 60), D Niculae, Mutu (Cociş 88), Codrea.

ITALY: Buffon (c), Zambrotta, Grosso, Panucci, Giorgio Chiellini, Simone Perrotta (Cassano 57), Daniele De Rossi, Pirlo, Toni, Del Piero (c) (Fabio Quagliarella 77), Camoranesi (Ambrosini 85).

Booked: Mutu (43), Chivu (58), Goian (75), Pirlo (61), De Rossi (90+2).

8.45pm, 13 June 2008
Stade de Suisse Wankdorf, Bern
Attendance: 30,777
Referee: Herbert Fandel (Germany)

NETHERLANDS 4 (Kuyt 9, Van Persie 59, Robben 72, Sneijder 90+2)
FRANCE 1 (Henry 71)

NETHERLANDS: Van der Sar (c), Ooijer, Mathijsen, Boulahrouz, Van Bronckhorst, Engelaar (Robben 46), De Jong, Kuyt (Van Persie 55), van Nistelrooy, Sneijder, Van der Vaart (Wilfred Bouma 78).

FRANCE: Coupet, Sagnol, Patrice Evra, Gallas, Thuram (c), Makélélé, Toulalan, Ribéry, Sidney Govou (Anelka 75), Thierry Henry, Malouda (Bafétimbi Gomis 60).

Booked: Ooijer (51), Makélélé (32), Toulalan (82).

8.45pm, 17 June 2008
Stade de Suisse Wankdorf, Bern
Attendance: 30,777
Referee: Massimo Busacca (Switzerland)

NETHERLANDS 2 (Huntelaar 54, Van Persie 87)
ROMANIA 0

NETHERLANDS: Maarten Stekelenburg, Boulahrouz (Mario Melchiot 58), Bouma, Heitinga (c), Tim de Cler, Engelaar, Demy de Zeeuw, Afellay, Klaas-Jan Huntelaar (Jan Vennegoor of Hesselink 83), Van Persie, Robben (Kuyt 61).

ROMANIA: Lobonţ, Contra, Raţ, Tamaş, Sorin Ghionea, Chivu (c), Cociş, Codrea (Dică 72), M. Niculae (D. Niculae 59), Mutu, Nicoliţă (Petre 82).

Booked: Chivu (78).

8.45pm, 17 June 2008
Letzigrund, Zürich
Attendance: 30,585
Referee: Luboš Michel (Slovakia)

ITALY 2 (Pirlo 25 pen, De Rossi 62)
FRANCE 0

ITALY: Buffon (c), Zambrotta, Grosso, Panucci, Chiellini, Gattuso (Alberto Aquilani 82), Perrotta (Camoranesi 64), De Rossi, Toni, Pirlo (Ambrosini 55), Cassano.

FRANCE: Coupet, François Clerc, Evra, Abidal, Gallas, Makélélé, Toulalan, Ribéry (Samir Nasri 10, Jean-Alain Boumsong 26), Benzema, Henry (c), Govou (Anelka 66).

Booked: Pirlo (44), Chiellini (45+4), Gattuso (54), Evra (18), Govou (47), Boumsong (72), Henry (85).
Sent off: Abidal (24).

GROUP C	P	W	D	L	F	A	GD	Pts
NETHERLANDS	3	3	0	0	9	1	+8	9
ITALY	3	1	1	1	3	4	− 1	4
ROMANIA	3	0	2	1	1	3	− 2	2
FRANCE	3	0	1	2	1	6	− 5	1

The Netherlands and Italy qualified.

GROUP D
Greece, Sweden, Russia, Spain

In Innsbruck, one eventual semi-finalist tore another apart as thunder and lightning raged across the snow-capped skyline. Russia didn't deserve to lose 4-1, but Spain's rapid-fire passing overwhelmed them at times. Centre-backs Denis Kolodin and the out-of-position Roman Shirokov were annihilated by the electric pace and movement of Fernando Torres and David Villa.

The Russians were up against it before a ball was kicked: Andrei Arshavin, their gifted playmaker, was suspended after a red card against Andorra in the qualifiers. On 20 minutes, they fell behind as Shirokov surrendered possession to Joan Capdevila, then slowly jogged back while Kolodin was struggling to close off Torres. As goalkeeper Igor Akinfeev came out, Torres nudged the ball sideways to Villa in front of an open goal.

Russia responded with bright, attacking football, and Konstantin Zyryanov should have done better than hit the post from Aleksei Anyukov's cross. But their tackle-phobic midfield made it easy for Spain. Torres broke through to shoot wide, then saw another effort saved by Akinfeev, who also pushed Villa's shot around the post.

Three minutes before the break, Russia struck the woodwork again when Roman Pavlyuchenko twanged a shot off the bar. But Spain's second goal was even cheaper than the first. Zyryanov's inept corner left nearly the entire Russian team stranded in the Spanish box, Andrés Iniesta surged into the gap, and his glittering pass played Villa in to shoot through Akinfeev's legs.

In the second half, substitute Cesc Fàbregas created the third goal with a first-time pass to Villa, who shrugged off the feeble Shirokov to claim his hat-trick. 'I scored three,' he said afterwards, 'but today, the one who opened the can was Torres.'

The Russians promptly produced another spell of good play. Pavlyuchenko's powerful shot whistled past the post, and the same player scored with a header after Shirokov nodded on Zyryanov's corner. Luis Aragonés cautiously checked his watch after it went in, but needn't have worried. In stoppage time, Kolodin's casualness handed Xavi a shooting chance which Akinfeev saved well, but an offside Fàbregas nodded home the rebound.

Russia's illustrious Dutch manager Guus Hiddink complained that the scoreline flattered Spain, but acknowledged his team's frailties. 'For the second and fourth goals, you can't just blame the defence,' he said. 'The whole team failed. It's a matter of knowing when the fire starts, and knowing when to be firemen.'

———

Greece's element of surprise was gone, and with it pretty much everything else. Against Sweden in Salzburg, their craven 5-4-1 formation committed dozens of petty fouls – the first by 2004 hero Angelos Charisteas, who got booked after 63 seconds for clobbering Petter Hansson.

Sweden themselves weren't up to much. Their full-backs were two midfielders, and the once-mighty Henrik Larsson was now 36 and well past it. Even so, they dominated this drab encounter between two ageing teams: 12 of the 22 starters were over 30, with just one, Vasilis Torosidis, under 26.

Sweden's opening goal took an age to arrive, but was worth the wait. Tall, tempestuous and exceedingly fond of himself, Zlatan Ibrahimović had earned a reputation for failing to deliver against good sides: at almost 27, he still hadn't scored in the knockout stage of the Champions League. He only got one shot on target here, but what a shot it was; exchanging passes with Larsson outside the box, he walloped a magnificent rising drive into the top corner. Lagerbäck quickly substituted him to save him for Spain.

The killer goal was utterly hideous. Larsson, clean through, shot straight at goalkeeper Antonis Nikopolidis, Johan Elmander hacked the loose ball high into the air, and it dropped under the Greek crossbar. Jumping against Sotiris Kyrgiakos, Hansson inadvertently trapped the ball with his calf, then kneed it against Giourkas Seitaridis. The rebound hit his leg and bobbled in from one yard out as Nikopolidis haplessly hugged the post.

Greece already looked doomed. 'In 2004, a miracle happened, but a miracle happens once every 30 years, and that's why you call it a miracle,' their manager Otto Rehhagel mused. 'You can't have it every other week, then it wouldn't be a miracle.'

Although Villa had grabbed the glory against Russia, Torres was coming off the back of a 33-goal debut season for Liverpool and didn't take long to punish Sweden in Innsbruck. From a short corner, Silva chipped the ball into the goalmouth, and Torres got in front of Hansson to stick out a boot and divert it in.

But after the Captain Caveman lookalike Carles Puyol went off with a thigh strain, Spain coughed up a cheap equaliser. Sergio Ramos, pure milkshake running through his veins as usual, slipped on the soaked grass as Ibrahimović burst into the box. The striker got little power on the shot, but the wet ball squirted through Iker Casillas's gloves.

Ibrahimović's strained knee saw him retire at half-time, and Sweden's ambition went with him. When goalkeeper Andreas Isaksson spilled Silva's shot, Villa accidentally kneed him in the face, and Torres couldn't score into an open net as the keeper lay injured. And for all their intricacy, Spain's stoppage-time winner came from a huge hoof by Capdevila. The Swedes fatally allowed it to bounce through to Villa, who outpaced Hansson before finishing lethally in the corner. 'How did Villa do that?' a delighted Aragonés wondered.

In Salzburg, Greece's ordeal continued as they slid to defeat against Russia, thanks to one of the most bizarre goals of the tournament. Diniyar Bilyaletdinov's cross was bouncing out for a goal kick before Nikopolidis unaccountably chased after it. Sergei Semak beat him to the ball and acrobatically hooked it back into the goalmouth, where Zyryanov couldn't miss.

Greece had ditched 5-4-1 for 4-3-3, but the closest they came to scoring was a total accident: Angelos Basinas's long free kick saw Igor Semshov almost knock it into his own net. At the other end, Pavlyuchenko repeatedly worked his way into good positions only to let himself down with inadequate shooting.

Rehhagel raised some eyebrows when, before the end, he high-fived Russian fans behind his dugout and signed autographs. The result eliminated his team, whose defence of their crown had been pathetic. Russia, however, could now welcome back the man who made them tick.

═══

First, there was the small matter of the Spain-Greece dead rubber. Repeating what he had done against Saudi Arabia at the 2006 World Cup, Aragonés gave his second string a run-out. What ensued was deeply unmemorable.

Fàbregas nearly forced Basinas into an own goal, and Xabi Alonso frightened Nikopolidis with a shot from inside his own half which sailed wide. But Greece saved some face from a miserable tournament by taking the lead before half-time, when Georgios Karagounis dropped a free kick on to Charisteas's unmarked head.

In the end, class told. After Alonso powerfully rattled the post from long range, Rubén de la Red – a product of Real Madrid's underused *cantera* system – thumped Dani Güiza's knockdown in off the bar. With two minutes left, Güiza himself headed in Luis García's cross to send the reigning champions home whitewashed. 'We played like hypochondriacs,' said striker Ioannis Amanatidis of his team's efforts. 'Total fear football.'

═══

'He has a lack of game fitness, game rhythm,' Hiddink said of Russia's twinkle-toed talisman before the showdown with Sweden. But he picked Andrei Arshavin anyway. The slight, wide-eyed 27-year-old had been the master soloist in Zenit St Petersburg's UEFA Cup Final win a month earlier, his ornate passes pulling Rangers apart in Manchester. Russian tongues were hanging out en masse as they awaited his return from suspension. He didn't let them down.

Winning almost all the 50-50s, Russia had the whip hand long before they went in front. Arshavin headed Anyukov's cross just off target, stabbed wide after dazzling interplay down the right, and saw his vicious cross pushed over the bar by a back-pedalling Isaksson. From the corner, Zhirkov's piledriver just cleared the post.

Domination is useless if you don't make it count, so Hiddink must have sighed with relief when Russia scored a sumptuous goal. Semshov and Zyryanov combined on the right, and the latter fed Anyukov, who squared it for Pavlyuchenko to finish.

Larsson soon got above Kolodin to send a header against the bar but, unfazed, Russia resumed their onslaught. When Ibrahimović gave the ball away, Pavlyuchenko hit the woodwork after good play from Semak, whose header on the rebound was clawed behind by Isaksson.

The crimson tide drowned Sweden after 50 minutes. Semshov exchanged passes with Arshavin, then set Zhirkov racing down the left with a lovely weighted ball. Zhirkov pulled the ball across for Arshavin to reach it ahead of two defenders and steer it into the far corner. The move was so incisive that it made the excellent first goal look crude.

Sweden had no answer to this space-age football. When Zyryanov stormed through from midfield for the umpteenth time, his shot was deflected on to the post via Hansson's skull. Minutes later, Pavlyuchenko nodded another good chance into Isaksson's arms, and finally sent an abysmal finish trickling wide after Arshavin's sublime no-look pass set Ivan Saenko free.

Arshavin almost made it 3-0 at the end, streaking through before Isaksson's left hand denied him. But what a statement of intent he and Russia had made. 'Mr Hiddink, is there any chance you might consider coaching Sweden?' a journalist from a Stockholm paper asked plaintively at the post-match press conference.

6pm, 10 June 2008
Tivoli-Neu, Innsbruck
Attendance: 30,772
Referee: Konrad Plautz (Austria)

SPAIN 4 (Villa 20, 44, 75, Fàbregas 90+1)
RUSSIA 1 (Pavlyuchenko 86)

SPAIN: Iker Casillas (c), Sergio Ramos, Joan Capdevila, Carles Puyol, Carlos Marchena, Xavi Hernández, Marcos Senna, Andrés Iniesta (Santi Cazorla 63), Fernando Torres (Cesc Fàbregas 54), David Villa, David Silva (Xabi Alonso 77). **Manager:** Luis Aragonés.

RUSSIA: Igor Akinfeev, Aleksei Anyukov, Yuri Zhirkov, Denis Kolodin, Roman Shirokov, Sergei Semak (c), Konstantin Zyryanov, Igor Semshov (Dmitri Torbinskiy 58, Roman Adamov 70), Roman Pavlyuchenko, Dmitri Sychyov (Vladimir Bystrov 46), Diniyar Bilyaletdinov. **Manager:** Guus Hiddink.

8.45pm, 10 June 2008
EM Wals-Siezenheim Stadion, Salzburg
Attendance: 31,063
Referee: Massimo Busacca (Switzerland)

SWEDEN 2 (Ibrahimović 67, Hansson 72)
GREECE 0

SWEDEN: Andreas Isaksson, Niclas Alexandersson (Fredrik Stoor 74), Olof Mellberg, Petter Hansson, Mikael Nilsson, Anders Svensson, Christian Wilhelmsson (Markus Rosenberg 78), Freddie Ljungberg (c), Zlatan Ibrahimović (Johan Elmander 71), Henrik Larsson, Daniel Andersson. **Manager:** Lars Lagerbäck.

GREECE: Antonis Nikopolidis, Giourkas Seitaridis, Sotiris Kyrgiakos, Traianos Dellas (Ioannis Amanatidis 70), Paraskevas Antzas, Angelos Basinas (c), Kostas Katsouranis, Georgios Karagounis, Angelos Charisteas, Theofanis Gekas (Georgios Samaras 70), Vasilis Torosidis. **Manager:** Otto Rehhagel.

Booked: Charisteas (2), Seitaridis (51), Torosidis (61).

6pm, 14 June 2008
Tivoli-Neu, Innsbruck
Attendance: 30,772
Referee: Pieter Vink (Netherlands)

SPAIN 2 (Torres 15, Villa 90+2)
SWEDEN 1 (Ibrahimović 34)

SPAIN: Casillas (c), Ramos, Capdevila, Puyol (Raúl Albiol 24), Marchena, Xavi (Fàbregas 59), Senna, Iniesta (Cazorla 59), Torres, Villa, Silva.

SWEDEN: Isaksson, Stoor, Mellberg, Hansson, Nilsson, Svensson, Elmander (Seb Larsson 79), Andersson, Ljungberg (c), Larsson (Kim Källström 87), Ibrahimović (Rosenberg 46).

Booked: Marchena (53), Svensson (55).

8.45pm, 14 June 2008
EM Wals-Siezenheim Stadion, Salzburg
Attendance: 31,063
Referee: Roberto Rosetti (Italy)

RUSSIA 1 (Zyryanov 33)
GREECE 0

RUSSIA: Akinfeev, Anyukov, Zhirkov (Vasily Berezutsky 87), Kolodin, Sergei Ignashevich, Semak (c), Zyryanov, Semshov, Pavlyuchenko, Torbinskiy, Bilyaletdinov (Ivan Saenko 70).

GREECE: Nikopolidis, Seitaridis (Karagounis 40), Kyrgiakos, Dellas, Torosidis, Basinas (c), Katsouranis, Christos Patsatzoglou, Charisteas, Nikos Liberopoulos (Gekas 61), Amanatidis (Stelios Giannakopoulos 80).

Booked: Saenko (77), Torbinskiy (84), Karagounis (42), Liberopoulos (58).

8.45pm, 18 June 2008
EM Wals-Siezenheim Stadion, Salzburg
Attendance: 30,883
Referee: Howard Webb (England)

SPAIN 2 (De la Red 61, Güiza 88)
GREECE 1 (Charisteas 42)

SPAIN: Pepe Reina, Álvaro Arbeloa, Fernando Navarro, Juan Gutiérrez 'Juanito', Raúl Albiol, Alonso (c), Rubén de la Red, Iniesta (Cazorla 58), Dani Güiza, Fàbregas, Sergio García.

GREECE: Nikopolidis (c), Loukas Vyntra, Kyrgiakos (Antzas 62), Dellas, Nikos Spiropoulos, Basinas, Katsouranis, Karagounis (Alexandros Tziolis 74), Charisteas, Dimitris Salpingidis (Giannakopoulos 86), Amanatidis.

Booked: Güiza (41), Árbeloa (45), Karagounis (34), Basinas (72), Vyntra (90+1).

8.45pm, 18 June 2008
Tivoli-Neu, Innsbruck
Attendance: 30,772
Referee: Frank De Bleeckere (Belgium)

RUSSIA 2 (Pavlyuchenko 24, Arshavin 50)
SWEDEN 0

RUSSIA: Akinfeev, Anyukov, Zhirkov, Kolodin, Ignashevich, Semak (c), Zyryanov, Semshov, Pavlyuchenko (Bystrov 90), Andrei Arshavin, Bilyaletdinov (Saenko 66).

SWEDEN: Isaksson, Stoor, Mellberg, Hansson, Nilsson (Marcus Allbäck 79), Svensson, Elmander, Andersson (Källström 56), Ljungberg (c), Larsson, Ibrahimović.

Booked: Semak (57), Arshavin (65), Kolodin (76), Isaksson (10), Elmander (49).

GROUP D	P	W	D	L	F	A	GD	Pts
SPAIN	3	3	0	0	8	3	+5	9
RUSSIA	3	2	0	1	4	4	0	6
SWEDEN	3	1	0	2	3	4	− 1	3
GREECE	3	0	0	3	1	5	− 4	0

Spain and Russia qualified.

QUARTER-FINALS
Portugal v Germany
Croatia v Turkey
Netherlands v Russia
Spain v Italy

In the build-up to the first quarter-final in Basel, the German media accused Jogi Löw's team of regressing to the bad old days. 'The players have played a type of football totally at odds with the ideals of their manager,' sighed *FT Deutschland*. 'They've played in a wholly un-Löwian style. Not out of spite – they simply can't do any better.' Meanwhile, the *Frankfurter Rundschau* complained that 'this team was supposed to show genteel combination football, but now we're back to "closing down spaces", "doubling up", running, fighting, biting and scratching'.

The suspended Löw's replacement for the night was his assistant Hansi Flick, an unsung midfielder at Bayern Munich in the 1980s who would ultimately lift the Champions League as their manager in August 2020. But Germany chose a good time to play their best game in years, taking Portugal apart on the break with only one striker and a five-man midfield.

They went ahead with a wonderful goal. A move involving seven players mushroomed down the left wing as Lukas Podolski exchanged rapid-fire passes with Klose, then Ballack. The youngster beat two defenders to the byline, flashed over a low cross, and Schweinsteiger swooped at close range. The best team goal of the tournament.

Before long, the stunned Portuguese were on the canvas again, with Klose heading in Schweinsteiger's set-piece as Ronaldo forgot to pick him up. But Scolari's team hit back before the interval. Ronaldo accelerated past Mertesacker, and though his shot went straight at Lehmann, Nuno Gomes knocked in the rebound.

After half-time, Germany tightened their grip. Ronaldo, who had done little in the first half, now vanished without trace. Just after the hour, Portugal leaked another cheap goal: another Schweinsteiger set-piece, another free header, this time for Ballack, who clearly shoved Ferreira in the back as they jumped.

When Hélder Postiga nodded Nani's cross in from close range, it came too late to save Portugal. They had been shown up as a collection of talented wide players shoehorned into various positions, rather than a proper team. And Germany, as they so often do, had clicked at just the right time.

In Vienna, the most tumultuous climax that the European Championship ever witnessed was preceded by two hours of near-uninterrupted boredom. The initially electric atmosphere in the Ernst Happel Stadion, a red-and-white cauldron where the Croatian fans vastly outnumbered their Turkish counterparts, steadily leaked out of a match that crammed all its incident into its very last seconds.

Turkey's squad was close to falling apart. A barrage of injuries had left Fatih Terim with 15 outfield players, and Rüştü Reçber came in for his 117th cap to replace the suspended Volkan in goal. But the veteran had almost nothing to do.

In the first half, when Luka Modrić fluttered through the Turkish defence and sent over an inviting cross, Olić fired it against the bar and Kranjčar headed the loose ball wide. But that was it for the entire first half, other than a Mehmet Topal 35-yarder which whizzed wide. Terim had seen what Croatia's three playmakers had done to Germany, and his midfield crushed the breath out of them.

The second half was even drearier. Late on, Srna's curled free kick was heading for the top corner before Rüştü rolled back the years to keep it out. In the very last minute, the manically busy Olić showed again that his finishing didn't match his work rate when he poked another Modrić centre into the goalkeeper's hands.

In extra time, the Turks finally crept forward. Tunçay poked a chance wide, and Gökhan Zan headed a corner over the bar. But with barely a minute left, Croatia scored what was surely the winner. Modrić, doing brilliantly to keep the ball in play, found the strength to accelerate down the right and cut into the box. As Rüştü bore down on him, he crossed to Ivan Klasnić, who headed in from close range. Overjoyed, Slaven Bilić dashed on to the field to celebrate with his players.

With time effectively up, Turkey frantically kicked off. Rüştü thumped one last desperate up-and-under, Croatia's weary defenders didn't clear it properly, and substitute Semih Şentürk lashed the loose ball high to Pletikosa's right with unnerving suddenness. A stunning ending, surely the most dramatic in any knockout match in a big tournament. Turkey were so shattered that only one of them had enough energy to celebrate with Semih.

The Croatians seemed spooked in the penalty shoot-out. Modrić set the tone by shooting feebly wide. And when Rüştü threw himself to the left to save Mladen Petrić's kick at 3-1, Turkey's surreal comeback was complete. They had now played 414 minutes in Euro 2008, been in the lead for nine of them, and were in the semi-finals.

'My players cried like kids,' Bilić said. 'The pain of this defeat will stay with us forever.' He fulminated bitterly at two minutes of stoppage time being added on instead of one, but he had contributed to that by invading the pitch to hug Klasnić.

Somehow, Turkey were in the last four. 'I saw some players lying on the grass,' said Terim. 'I told them to pick themselves up. I wasn't about to give up. I never have, in all of my career.' Back home, the national daily *Aksam* trumpeted, 'We now pass Vienna and march on for the cup,' using a dodgy historical analogy drawn from the Ottomans' failed siege of the city in September 1683. Another paper, *Sabah*, blared, 'Miracles are our job', while *Takvim* declared that 'Terim's tigers work a miracle'. The Turks, it seemed, were the new Greeks.

=====

'I'd like to be named traitor of the year in the Netherlands,' Guus Hiddink laughed before he and Russia faced his homeland in Basel. He got his wish in a game that witnessed Andrei Arshavin ('the most intelligent player I have ever seen' according to Hiddink) give one of the great European Championship performances.

From the start, Arshavin was turning the screw, seeing Van der Sar save his side-footed drive brilliantly. When the corner was cleared to Denis Kolodin, the blond defender blasted a 35-yard drive which Van der Sar punched over the bar with both fists. From the subsequent corner, Kolodin tried again from even further out, almost in the centre circle: the shot screamed just beyond post and bar.

At the interval, Van Basten threw on Robin van Persie, who sliced badly wide within seconds of the restart. Minutes later, Russia had a deserved lead.

Again Arshavin was involved, putting the industrious Semak away on the left, and Pavlyuchenko got ahead of Mathijsen to convert the cross.

The Netherlands now had to force the play, leaving gaps, and Van der Sar needed every inch of his 6ft 5in frame to palm away Pavlyuchenko's lob. But near the end, they found an undeserved equaliser. Sneijder, who'd had a nightmare, curled a dangerous free kick into the Russian box, and Van Nistelrooy lost Sergei Ignashevich to score with a downward header at the far post.

Russia almost went into extra time with ten men, but referee Luboš Michel's linesman alerted him that the ball had gone dead just before Kolodin fouled Sneijder for a second booking. Pavlyuchenko now spectacularly hit the bar, Kolodin's latest ballistic missile flew millimetres wide, and Zhirkov was denied a blatant penalty when Johnny Heitinga barged him.

Arshavin finished off the Netherlands with two more delightful flourishes. First, he glided up the left and delivered a pinpoint cross to the far post which was diverted in by Torbinskiy. In the celebrations, so many Russians jumped on top of Torbinskiy that a camera captured his terrified face at the bottom of the pile, screaming at them to stop physically crushing him. Minutes later, Anyukov's quick throw caught the tired Dutch defence unawares. Arshavin chased it, accelerated, turned and swept a first-time shot through Van der Sar's legs from a sharp angle.

'I kept [Arshavin] on because I believed he could make the difference, and because he'd already had his holidays,' said Hiddink. The playmaker, having shown the continent his qualities, now basked in the glow of comparisons with Zidane, Cruyff and Laudrup which didn't feel unjustified at the time.

═══

Euro 2008's first blocks of empty seats were sighted in Vienna as the Mediterranean derby went the distance. Aragonés brought back all his big names, but Spain looked unrecognisable from the team that had destroyed Russia. With Pirlo suspended, Italy were even more one-dimensional.

In a match that made Croatia v Turkey look good, there was very little to report. Casillas's legs kept out Mauro Camoranesi, and when Torres had a shot blocked after beating two defenders, Silva curled the rebound wide. At the other end, Buffon got away with spilling Marcos Senna's shot against his post. Meanwhile, Villa received the daftest booking of the tournament, for diving, when he had clearly slipped.

In extra time, Casillas tipped Di Natale's header over the bar and Buffon saved Villa's angled shot, but penalties always seemed inevitable. De Rossi's kick was the right height for Casillas, and Di Natale's was feebler yet. Fàbregas lashed home the ninth kick to put Spain into their first semi-final since 1984. 'Italy were bad,' admitted Aragonés, 'but we were too, unfortunately.'

8.45pm, 19 June 2008
St Jakob-Park, Basel
Attendance: 39,374
Referee: Peter Fröjdfeldt (Sweden)

GERMANY 3 (Schweinsteiger 22, Klose 26, Ballack 61)
PORTUGAL 2 (Gomes 40, Postiga 87)

GERMANY: Lehmann, Friedrich, Lahm, Mertesacker, Metzelder, Hitzlsperger (Borowski 73), Simon Rolfes, Ballack (c), Klose (Jansen 89), Podolski, Schweinsteiger (Fritz 83). **Manager:** Hans-Dieter Flick.

PORTUGAL: Ricardo, Bosingwa, Pepe, Carvalho, Ferreira, Petit (Postiga 73), Moutinho (Meireles 31), Simão, Ronaldo, Deco, Gomes (c) (Nani 67).

Booked: Friedrich (48), Lahm (49), Petit (26), Pepe (60), Postiga (90).

8.45pm, 20 June 2008
Ernst Happel Stadion, Vienna
Attendance: 51,428
Referee: Roberto Rosetti (Italy)

TURKEY 1 (Semih 120+2)
CROATIA 1 (Klasnić 119)
Turkey won 3-1 on penalties after extra time
Shoot-out: Modrić wide, Arda 1-0, Srna 1-1, Semih 2-1, Rakitić wide, Altıntop 3-1, Petrić saved.

TURKEY: Rüştü Reçber, Altıntop, Hakan, Emre A., Gökhan, Sabri, Topal (Semih 76), Kazim-Richards (Uğur Boral 61), Nihat (c) (Gökdeniz 117), Tunçay, Arda.

CROATIA: Pletikosa, Ćorluka, Šimunić, R. Kovač, Pranjić, N. Kovač (c), Srna, Rakitić, Olić (Klasnić 97), Modrić, Kranjčar (Petrić 65).

Booked: Tunçay (27), Arda (49), Uğur (89), Emre A. (107).

8.45pm, 21 June 2008
St Jakob-Park, Basel
Attendance: 38,374
Referee: Luboš Michel (Slovakia)

RUSSIA 3 (Pavlyuchenko 56, Torbinskiy 112, Arshavin 116)
NETHERLANDS 1 (Van Nistelrooy 86)

After extra time

RUSSIA: Akinfeev, Anyukov, Zhirkov, Kolodin, Ignashevich, Semak (c), Zyryanov, Semshov (Bilyaletdinov 69), Pavlyuchenko (Sychyov 115), Arshavin, Saenko (Torbinskiy 81).

NETHERLANDS: Van der Sar (c), Boulahrouz (Heitinga 54), Ooijer, Mathijsen, Van Bronckhorst, Engelaar (Afellay 62), De Jong, Kuyt (Van Persie 46), Van Nistelrooy, Sneijder, Van der Vaart.

Booked: Kolodin (71), Zhirkov (103), Torbinskiy (111), Boulahrouz (50), Van Persie (55), Van der Vaart (60).

8.45pm, 22 June 2008
Ernst Happel Stadion, Vienna
Attendance: 48,000
Referee: Herbert Fandel (Germany)

SPAIN 0
ITALY 0
Spain won 4-2 on penalties after extra time
Shoot-out: Villa 1-0, Grosso 1-1, Cazorla 2-1, De Rossi saved, Senna 3-1, Camoranesi 3-2, Güiza saved, Di Natale saved, Fàbregas 4-2.

SPAIN: Casillas (c), Ramos, Capdevila, Puyol, Marchena, Xavi (Fàbregas 60), Senna, Iniesta (Cazorla 59), Torres (Güiza 85), Villa, Silva.

ITALY: Buffon (c), Zambrotta, Grosso, Panucci, Chiellini, Aquilani (Del Piero 108), Perrotta (Camoranesi 58), De Rossi, Toni, Cassano (Di Natale 75), Ambrosini.

Booked: Iniesta (11), Villa (72), Cazorla (113), Ambrosini (31).

SEMI-FINALS
Germany v Turkey
Spain v Russia

Walking out against Germany in Basel, Turkey could draw upon only five of the players who had started their first match 18 days earlier, with their half-deserted bench containing one goalkeeper and six outfielders. Terim publicly pondered using reserve keeper Tolga Zengin as an emergency substitute outfielder, while UEFA, learning its lesson from 1996, ruled out calling up new players.

In keeping with their overall tournament, the Turks took the lead with a weird goal. Philipp Lahm went to sleep at a throw-in, and Sabri slung in a low cross which was missed by Germany's other defenders – but not by Colin Kazim-Richards. The London-born striker's shot floated high over Lehmann and came back off the bar. Uğur Boral, following up, shot straight at Lehmann's legs but the ball squeezed in anyway.

But Turkey lost their lead within minutes, as Thomas Hitzlsperger's pass released Podolski down the left. The cross was low, dangerous and perfect for Schweinsteiger, who nipped in front of Topal at the near post to score with a neat flick.

Shortly after the interval, Sabri Sarıoğlu violently chopped down Lahm right on the line of the area – but referee Massimo Busacca didn't even award a free kick. With Ballack having a quiet evening, the Germans' second-half performance was an unsatisfying stick-or-twist. They were looking stuck for ideas until Klose intervened 11 minutes from the end. Rising to meet Lahm's cross, he jumped above two defenders and Rüştü to send his header looping into the unguarded net.

But few people outside the St Jakob Park saw it happen. Earlier, the TV feed from UEFA's international broadcast centre in Vienna had gone down, due to a massive thunderstorm causing a power cut. Now, across Europe, TV screens went black for seven minutes, causing almost everyone to miss Klose's goal. On German channel ZDF, commentator Béla Réthy had to deliver his commentary down a landline, while a station in Hong Kong was reduced to relaying information from a fan in the stadium on a mobile phone.

The visuals were restored in time for Turkey's latest fantasy-land comeback. Overlapping on the right, Sabri wriggled past Lahm, got to the byline and crossed to the near post. Semih, too quick for Mertesacker, poked it between Lehmann and the upright.

But it didn't come late enough to buy Turkey an extra half-hour. Lahm had been at fault for both Turkish goals but, with seconds left, now atoned in style. Out on the left, he exchanged passes with Hitzlsperger, who threaded a superb return ball between four Turks to present him with a shooting opportunity. Eyes down, he sealed a cracking game with an equally great goal, holding his nerve and blasting it high into the small gap that Rüştü left at the near post.

A fourth miraculous Turkish recovery was too much to ask. But what a crazy, convulsive spectacle Terim and his team had given us.

On the morning of the second semi-final in Vienna, a big transfer story broke across the European press. Ronaldinho was heading for the Camp Nou exit door after two seasons of decline, and Barcelona had reportedly decided that Andrei Arshavin was ripe to be prised away from Zenit St Petersburg.

'The transfer fee should be about €25m,' said Dennis Lachter, Arshavin's agent. 'This is a great opportunity for him.' To what degree the story interfered with his state of mind, on the day of the biggest match of his life, will never be known, but he performed unrecognisably from his Swedish and Dutch spectaculars, contributing nothing.

Playing in gold and black, Spain seemed hesitant during a boring first half under yet another thundery downpour. Akinfeev saved from Torres, then from Villa, whose tournament ended early when he injured his calf while taking a free kick. But with the imperious Marcos Senna stalking Arshavin's every move, Russia's only goal threat came from Pavlyuchenko, who missed their best opportunity when he stubbed Zyryanov's cross wide.

Early in the second half, Spain found a lead they would not relinquish. Xavi found Iniesta on the left, then continued his run into the box as Iniesta came inside and drew two defenders. Arriving at just the right time, he side-footed the return ball through the legs of a surprised Akinfeev.

Soon afterwards, Iniesta's magnificent pass forced Anyukov to head off the line as Torres was about to score. Torres himself was guilty of the worst miss of the night, kneeing Ramos's cross wide. But Russia were soon put out of their misery. The substitute Dani Güiza, an unexceptional striker best known for having a glamorous significant other, needed only four minutes to succeed where Torres had failed, chesting down Fàbregas's flick and lifting it over Akinfeev.

Silva's drilled finish to make it 3-0, following a move down the left involving Iniesta and Fàbregas, was an irrelevance. Güiza might have scored a fourth, but Akinfeev prevented it becoming a total hiding. 'You're the best there are,' Aragonés told his players afterwards. 'If we don't win the European Championship, it's because I did a shit job.'

'We were physically weaker than Spain,' Arshavin said. 'When you don't have the strength, it's hard to get through. You have to rely on tactics.' And he never did get that dream transfer, with the deal falling apart after Barcelona drew the line at a €15m fee. A year to the day after this game, he sacked Lachter as his agent. Still, he'd always have Basel.

8.45pm, 25 June 2008
St Jakob-Park, Basel
Attendance: 39,374
Referee: Massimo Busacca (Switzerland)

GERMANY 3 (Schweinsteiger 26, Klose 79, Lahm 90)
TURKEY 2 (Uğur 22, Semih 86)

GERMANY: Lehmann, Friedrich, Lahm, Mertesacker, Metzelder, Hitzlsperger, Rolfes (Frings 46), Ballack (c), Klose (Jansen 90+2), Podolski, Schweinsteiger.

TURKEY: Rüştü (c), Sabri, Topal, Hakan, Gökhan, Aurélio, Altıntop, Kazim-Richards (Metin 90+2), Semih, Ayhan Akman (Mevlüt 81), Uğur (Gökdeniz 84).

Booked: Semih (53), Sabri (90+4).

8.45pm, 26 June 2008
Ernst Happel Stadion, Vienna
Attendance: 51,428
Referee: Frank De Bleeckere (Belgium)

SPAIN 3 (Xavi 50, Güiza 73, Silva 82)
RUSSIA 0

SPAIN: Casillas (c), Ramos, Capdevila, Puyol, Marchena, Xavi (Alonso 69), Senna, Iniesta, Torres (Güiza 69), Villa (Fàbregas 34), Silva.

RUSSIA: Akinfeev, Anyukov, Zhirkov, V. Berezutsky, Ignashevich, Semak (c), Zyryanov, Semshov (Bilyaletdinov 56), Pavlyuchenko, Arshavin, Saenko (Sychyov 57).

Booked: Zhirkov (56), Bilyaletdinov (60).

FINAL
Spain v Germany

'I hope for an attractive finale with lots of goals, but I expect a game of patience,' Franz Beckenbauer wrote in his *Bild* column on the morning of the final in Vienna. His instincts were correct. As in 1984, a pleasing tournament didn't get the climax it deserved, but the right team won.

Though not without some early jitters. After just 80 seconds, Ramos's stupid no-look pass across his own box handed the ball to Miroslav Klose, but Puyol pressured the striker into running it out of play. That failed to wake Aragonés's team up, and they took a quarter of an hour to find their feet.

But after Silva moved over to Germany's left, pushing Philipp Lahm backwards, Spain immediately looked better. When Torres headed Ramos's centre against the foot of the post, Germany were only saved by nobody being there to bury the rebound. And on 33 minutes, the golden-haired boy's speed of thought and foot proved the difference.

Xavi's pass towards Torres seemed to pose no danger, with Lahm there to shepherd it back to Lehmann. But the impetuous goalkeeper dashed off his line anyway, and Lahm's efforts to hold off the on-running Torres were inadequate. As the two Germans momentarily hesitated, Torres darted between them and dinked it over Lehmann with an exquisite touch. Lahm, who made very few other glaring errors in a long international career, didn't reappear for the second half. 'He relaxed for a moment, and I took advantage,' said Torres.

With poor Hitzlsperger playing piggy-in-the-middle as Spain pinged the ball around, Germany's possession share dwindled after the interval. And Löw brought on perhaps the least inspiring trio of subs in any major tournament final: the journeyman defender Jansen, the second-rate striker Kuranyi, and the confidence-free Gómez. Their best chance came just before the hour, when Schweinsteiger chested the ball down for Ballack to hit a powerful shot that bounced narrowly off target. At the other end, Torsten Frings's knee blocked Iniesta's shot on the line.

Spain should have been down to ten men by that stage. Maybe even nine. Silva headbutted Podolski after the German confronted him over a rough challenge – but, amazingly, referee Roberto Rosetti didn't even book him. Earlier, Ballack had his temple split open by Senna, and Klose received a painful kick in the family jewels from Carlos Marchena.

Casillas lifted Spain's first trophy for 44 years in front of an underwhelming cloud of silver ticker-tape. Later, as Schweinsteiger stood in the mixed zone being interviewed, half the Spanish team bounced past him in a loud conga-line of celebration. If that had been an accident, the fact that they came back seconds later to do it again looked like a snide attempt to rub a beaten opponent's nose in it. Meanwhile, Ballack and 1996 hero Oliver Bierhoff, now working for the DFB, had to be separated after Bierhoff asked the tired, dejected captain to bring a large 'Danke!' banner over to Germany's fans.

Euro 2008 had been stirring and colourful, but it wasn't another 2000, let alone 1976 or 1984. Good defences were thin on the ground, and there weren't enough games where both teams played really well. Nor was there any real sense that Euromania had swept through both host countries. The huge fanzones were packed for some games, such as Switzerland v Turkey and Austria v Germany, but deserted for others. In Vienna, cultural institutions like the Kunsthistorisches Museum and the Wiener Staatsoper reported catastrophic drops in attendances (the regular clientele, it seemed, feared the idea of hooligans spilling out of the nearby fanzone).

But there had been plenty to remember on the field of play. Turkey's series of improbable escapes at two minutes to midnight. The quick-fire thrusts of the Dutch. Germany's succession of well-worked team goals. Russia suddenly looking like one of the best sides in the world, even if only for two matches. And, of course, Spain's spectacular metamorphosis from underachieving weaklings to the best team in Europe. They exuded flair, pace, a killer instinct – and a rough edge: no other team committed more fouls in the tournament. All that skill came with a sharp physical pay-off. But Podolski, Ballack and Klose could have told you that for free.

8.45pm, 29 June 2008
Ernst Happel Stadion, Vienna
Attendance: 51,428
Referee: Roberto Rosetti (Italy)

SPAIN 1 (Torres 33)
GERMANY 0

SPAIN: Casillas (c), Ramos, Capdevila, Puyol, Marchena, Xavi, Senna, Iniesta, Torres (Güiza 78), Fàbregas (Alonso 63), Silva (Cazorla 66).

GERMANY: Lehmann, Friedrich, Lahm (Jansen 46), Mertesacker, Metzelder, Frings, Hitzlsperger (Kurányi 58), Ballack (c), Klose (Gómez 79), Podolski, Schweinsteiger.

Booked: Casillas (43), Torres (74), Ballack (43), Kurányi (88).

2012

EVEN THOSE who harboured doubts about the ultimate destination of the 2012 finals had to admit that the less well-heeled half of the continent deserved a few weeks in the sun. Since 1976, eastern Europe had hosted no tournaments at all, and just one European Cup final (2008), so staging a huge showpiece was long overdue.

In April 2007, Poland and Ukraine's bid easily beat Italy 8-4 in UEFA's final run-off ballot. Italy's bid was done no favours by the repercussions of the depressing *calciopoli* scandal, though the Poles had been dealing with a match-fixing scandal of their own, something which didn't go unnoticed by the Italians.

Both halves of the project were plagued by bad press as the finals approached. Ukraine took so long to build its stadia that in late 2009, UEFA threatened to strip it of the tournament unless the pace of work increased. Kiev's Olimpiyskiy Natsionalnyi Sportivnyi Kompleks (which would host the final) and Lviv's Arena were both skeletal construction sites with a year to go. One host city, Dnipropetrovsk, couldn't get its act together and was replaced by Kharkiv (the same thing happened on the Polish side, Chorzów giving way for Poznań). Questions, too, were raised about the quality of Ukraine's hotels and airports, and Poland's roads and transport systems. Everything got done on time, but at a terrible price. BWI, the global construction union, revealed before the tournament that 20 stadium labourers lost their lives on-site, eight at the Olimpiyskiy alone.

As in 2008, it was doubtful whether the two hosts would have qualified for the finals if they had been required to. Poland's hopes rested on the Borussia Dortmund trio of full-back Łukasz Piszczek, winger Kuba Błaszczykowski and striker Robert Lewandowski, who had just won back-to-back Bundesliga titles. Ukraine had made the last eight of the 2006 World Cup in Germany, but most of that team were gone, and star man Andriy Shevchenko was pushing 36 and back in Ukraine's Premier Liha after a woeful stint with Chelsea.

After winning the 2010 World Cup in South Africa, Spain were almost unbackable as favourites. Their triumph was dull and anaemic (they won all four knockout games 1-0), but their status as kings of international football was now indisputable. Most of the 2008 side were still there, and the supporting cast would have walked into the line-up of most other national teams. The lethal David Villa had broken his leg, however, prompting manager Vicente Del Bosque to adopt an austere 4-6-0 formation that surely made things easier for deep-defending opponents.

The Spanish had overcome Germany in the World Cup semi-final. Jogi Löw's team now looked better than in 2008, with new faces including a beast of a goalkeeper in Manuel Neuer, clever playmakers Mesut Özil and Toni Kroos, and Thomas Müller, a lanky young forward who had an Ian Rush-like ability to sniff space in the box. But a ridiculous 5-3 defeat by Switzerland two weeks before the finals strongly suggested something wasn't right.

They were odds-on to win Group B, where Denmark would surely make up the numbers as Portugal (still over-dependent on Cristiano Ronaldo) and the Netherlands duked it out for second place. It was hard to know what to make of the Dutch, whose collective name was mud in the wake of their brutish behaviour in the World Cup Final in Johannesburg. They relied almost exclusively on the front three of Wesley Sneijder, Robin van Persie and Arjen Robben, the last of whom had just given a breathtakingly incompetent performance for Bayern Munich against Chelsea in the Champions League Final.

In Group C, few observers gave Ireland a hope. Giovanni Trapattoni's team had qualified chiefly on the strength of an extraordinary defensive performance by centre-back Richard Dunne in Moscow. A nervous home win over Armenia then handed them a play-off with Estonia, the softest touch left in the competition, and they romped to an easy win in Tallinn. But an earlier 3-2 home defeat by Russia had brutally exposed Ireland as a basic, one-paced side and Trapattoni seemed to learn nothing from the experience whatsoever.

In the same group, Italy were expected to pull up few trees. The suave Cesare Prandelli, who had replaced Marcello Lippi after a disastrous World Cup, had two world-class players: the near-impassable Gianluigi Buffon in goal, and the midfield puppeteer Andrea Pirlo. Otherwise, his team had no shortage of hard-bitten types like Roma's linchpin Daniele De Rossi and Juventus stoppers Giorgio Chiellini and Leonardo Bonucci, but it looked short of quality if Pirlo got closed down.

England tiptoed into the tournament with their lowest expectations in decades. Their 4-1 embarrassment by Germany in Bloemfontein had left lasting scars and when, to no one's regret, Fabio Capello resigned five weeks before the finals after falling out with the FA, the beetle-browed Roy Hodgson was named as his successor ahead of bookies' favourite Harry Redknapp. No big clear-out had ensued after the World Cup, and Hodgson would have stuck with the creaking Steven Gerrard/Frank Lampard axis but for Lampard's thigh injury. Adding to England's troubles, Wayne Rooney would miss the first two games after kicking Montenegro's Miodrag Džudović in a qualifier. At least the draw had been kind.

France were coming off the back of an even worse World Cup than England's or Italy's. After ridding themselves of Raymond Domenech's dead hand, they immediately fell to a mortifying 1-0 defeat at home to Belarus. Manager Laurent Blanc was later lucky to keep his job when recordings emerged of him saying the number of underage black and Arab players in French football academies should be capped. Ultimately, only Samir Nasri's late penalty at home to Bosnia spared France a play-off.

Many people were more concerned with what might happen off the pitch at Euro 2012 than on it. In a pre-tournament BBC documentary about Polish and Ukrainian hooliganism, former England defender Sol Campbell warned black fans to stay at home and watch on TV, or risk 'coming back home in a coffin'. Kindling was thrown on the fire by Ukraine's manager Oleh Blokhin, who smugly snorted that 'there's no racism in Ukrainian football'.

The prospects of serious hooliganism were slim, due to the huge security operation mounted by Polish and Ukrainian authorities. Concerns over Ukraine's political situation seemed more well-founded: the republic was mired in turbulence, and a long, drawn-out civil war between Ukrainian forces and pro-Russian separatists in the east of the country was only two years away. Had any of this even been hinted at in the mid-2000s, Chechnya would have had more chance of hosting the European Championship than Ukraine. But all that was still in the future. One way or another, Euro 2012 promised to be a little different.

GROUP A
Poland, Greece, Russia, Czech Republic

The opening match couldn't have begun better for the pumped-up Poles. Roared on by a noisy crowd in Warsaw, they were well worth their half-time lead against Greece. Kuba Błaszczykowski, released down the right by Ludovic Obraniak, crossed for his fellow Dortmunder Robert Lewandowski to put away an emphatic downward header.

Looking overawed and unfit, Greece then lost defender Sokratis Papastathopoulos to an outrageous second caution for mildly obstructing Rafał Murawski. Papastathopoulos's first booking was even more of a joke, received for contesting a header with Lewandowski. Referee Carlos Velasco Carballo, possibly under pressure from UEFA to show a strong hand, then missed Polish defender Damien Perquis handling in his own box.

But big twists were in store. 'It was 1-0 [at half-time], against weakened rivals,' Lewandowski said after the tournament. 'There was silence in the dressing room. I said we had to score the second goal to be sure of winning. The coach [Franciszek Smuda] instead said to play calmly and wait.'

With little to lose, Greece's manager Fernando Santos threw on Dimitris Salpingidis. The hard-working little striker soon capitalised on a calamitous error by Polish goalkeeper Wojciech Szczęsny, who came out for a low cross, missed it completely and watched the substitute knock it in from close range.

The confidence visibly drained out of Poland. As Greece began to realise they could win, Georgios Samaras sliced wide from close range. Minutes later, Kostas Fortounis put Salpingidis through, and Szczęsny rounded off his disastrous afternoon by tripping him. Even Velasco Carballo knew it was a penalty and red card. On came reserve keeper Przemysław Tytoń, who made himself an instant hero by saving Georgios Karagounis's soft spot-kick.

Poland were hanging on at the end, with Salpingidis having a goal disallowed for Fortounis's marginal offside and Samaras wasting another chance. 'I felt I had the weight of 40 million people on my shoulders,' Smuda said. 'We were under great pressure. Some of the players were paralysed. Most of them had never played in a tournament before. Some of them burned down.'

Russia had their own goalkeeping problems, with Igor Akinfeev out of the tournament due to knee trouble, but understudy Vyacheslav Malafeev had little to do in their enjoyable demolition of the Czech Republic in Wrocław. They were so dominant that the inept finishing of Aleksandr Kerzhakov, who put none of his seven shots on target, didn't matter.

Roman Shirokov, a disaster in Euro 2008 as a stop-gap centre-half, looked much better in midfield. He set up the first goal, crossing for Kerzhakov to head against the far post before Alan Dzagoev slotted the rebound under Petr Čech. And he scored the second himself, following some great work by the revitalised Andrei Arshavin, who laid on a string of chances for the forwards. Kerzhakov reacted too slowly to reach his fabulous pass – but Shirokov, who had kept running, dinked the ball over Čech's dive.

The Czechs were being overrun in midfield, where Igor Denisov walked all over Tomáš Rosický. But a dead-cat bounce fell into their lap in the second half. Jaroslav Plašil's pass found Václav Pilař, who rounded Malafeev and tucked away the chance from an angle. 'At that moment, I was happy,' said Pilař. 'But now, I'm not happy at all.'

Instead of wavering, Russia revved up through the gears. The anti-hero Kerzhakov spurned three more chances, prompting even Russia's fans to jeer him. When manager Dick Advocaat replaced him with Roman Pavlyuchenko, the goals flowed again. Dzagoev grabbed his second with a powerful effort after Pavlyuchenko teed him up, and Pavlyuchenko himself made it 4-1 with an even better goal, holding off Roman Hubník to slam the ball high past Čech.

Advocaat seemed reluctant to face reality. 'I'll pick Kerzhakov again,' he said. 'Today, he did a lot for the team. But he forgot to score.'

=====

Taciturn and cautious, Czech manager Michal Bílek was already unpopular with the fans, who booed and whistled him even before matches kicked off. But his battered team climbed from the canvas with an untidy win over Greece in Wrocław.

By the sixth minute, they were 2-0 up. The bearded, long-haired Petr Jiráček scored the first, planting a shot past goalkeeper Kostas Chalkias after Plašil set him up. Before Greece had time to think, they conceded again. Jiráček sent Theodor Gebre Selassie down the right, Chalkias let the cross slip through his hands, and Pilař bundled the ball in at the far post.

The 38-year-old Chalkias soon went off with a torn hamstring, ending his international career. At the other end, it took Greece 40 minutes to try a shot. But after the interval, bad goalkeeping again threw them a lifeline. Four years earlier in Geneva, Petr Čech's gaffe had killed his team against Turkey. Now he was culpable again, colliding with Tomáš Sivok while coming for a cross. Like Salpingidis against Poland, Fanis Gekas had an open goal and did the needful. TV footage captured Čech mouthing 'Okay, okay' to his defenders, though not their responses.

Unlike Poland, the Czechs declined to fall to bits thereafter, and they had an easy ride until the end. A commentator on Italian channel RAI was moved to describe Greece on air as 'shit': no manners, but what a critic.

=====

The previous December, at the finals draw in Kiev, gasps filled the auditorium when Poland and Russia came out of the hat together. For good measure, the fixture fell on Russia Day, 12 June. But it would have been loaded with historical baggage no matter what date it was played on.

A plane crash in Russian fog in April 2010 had killed Poland's president Lech Kaczyński and several other notable figures in Polish public life. The conspiracy theory of a mass assassination found favour with numerous Poles. On the day of the game, a section of Russia's support staged a provocative march along the route to the stadium. Despite the presence of 6,000 police in central Warsaw, Polish hooligans were waiting near the Poniatowski bridge on the Vistula river. The clashes put 24 in hospital and resulted in 184 mostly Polish arrests.

At the Stadion Narodowy, a huge banner weighing half a ton covered the away end. Depicting the Russian nationalist hero Dmitri Pozharsky holding a massive sword, it bore the words 'THIS IS RUSSIA', a reference to Warsaw being under Russian control from 1815 to 1915. None of this enhanced the reputation of Russia's fans, some of whom had racially abused the Ethiopian-descended Czech defender Gebre Selassie during their first game.

Early on, Malafeev saved Sebastian Boenisch's point-blank header with his feet, but Poland otherwise made no headway in a first half full of hard running and little else. Russia were neater in possession, but their final ball was invariably bad. Eight minutes before the break, however, they took the lead when Alan Dzagoev evaded Piszczek to head Arshavin's free kick into the far corner.

Basic national pride dictated that Poland couldn't give up without a fight. They came back strongly after half-time, and Malafeev saved twice from Lewandowski before a spectacular equaliser arrived. When Obraniak gave Błaszczykowski an opening on the right, the captain stepped between two Russians, cocked back his left foot and smacked a swerving drive into the top corner for one of the best goals of Euro 2012.

The match petered out after that, with both sides content not to lose face. A draw was about right, and probably for the best: as the match drew to a close, an unnervingly large number of riot police gathered in front of the Russian end. 'My dream was not to lose, and we didn't lose,' said Smuda, again displaying his gift for inspirational rhetoric.

Wrocław was 75 miles from the Czech border, so thousands of their fans turned up for the showdown with the co-hosts. The situation, though, seemed doable for Poland: win at home to a side thrashed by Russia. The enterprising Obraniak fed Błaszczykowski with a chance which Čech blocked with his legs, and Lewandowski – not yet the world-class scoring machine he would become – sliced badly wide after Murawski set him up.

But Smuda had sold the jerseys, picking three holding midfielders in a game his team had to win. Polish impetus soon faded away, and when half-time brought news of a goal in the Russia-Greece game, the Czechs shook themselves awake, knowing they would be out if everything stayed the same.

Lewandowski later claimed that as the game wore on, Poland's players were forced to abandon Smuda's cagey tactics and attack more. 'I understand that against an offensive Russia, we played more cautiously,' he said, 'but why did we go in against the Czechs with a 4-3-2-1 formation? We had to win.'

They paid dearly on 72 minutes. Tomáš Hübschman robbed Murawski and the ball came to the veteran Milan Baroš, who in turn found Jiráček. The midfielder, aided by Marcin Wasilewski slipping on the wet grass, saw his finish slither under Tytoń. Poland now threw everything at their opponents, and Michal Kadlec twisted gymnastically to clear Błaszczykowski's stoppage-time lob off the line. It wouldn't have sent the Poles through, but it would have put the Czechs out.

The result cost Smuda his job. He was Poland's tenth national coach in 16 years, an indication of deeper problems – which may have been on Błaszczykowski's mind when, afterwards, he bitterly attacked Polish FA president Grzegorz Lato for alleged broken promises. Lewandowski didn't hold back either: 'We definitely have better players than the results we have achieved. We're not worse than the Czechs. The coach had a lot of time to prepare us for the most important event of our lives. He didn't do it. We overdid it with the gym sessions. I would really like to say that we were well prepared. But we weren't.'

=====

Like the Poles, Russia had it in their own hands and blew it. Top of the table and needing only a draw, Advocaat's team were down in third by the final whistle. Greece, useless until now, found themselves in the quarter-finals almost by accident.

Either team might have scored early. First, Karagounis's corner was hooked goalward by Katsouranis, forcing Malafeev into a good one-handed save. Then Arshavin nipped in front of Vasilis Torosidis to prod the ball into Michalis Sifakis's arms. Russia would win the shot count 25-5, but hardly any were a danger to Greece's inexperienced keeper.

Kerzhakov at last got a shot on target, and scraped the post with another one, but he was otherwise horrendous and got subbed at the break. By then, Greece had scored with the last action of the half. A long throw down the right wing caught the veteran Sergei Ignashevich sleeping, and he headed it into the path of Karagounis, who burrowed into the box and hit a shot that seemed to pass through Malafeev too easily.

Russia's attempts to play their way through a massed defence repeatedly foundered, and the closest shaves came at the other end. Karagounis should have had a penalty when Ignashevich flattened him, Aleksei Anyukov side-footed over his own crossbar, and Georgios Tzavelas's free kick hit the post.

As in 2004, Greece were again the masters of minimalism: three games, five shots on target, three goals, four points, qualification. The result was rough on Arshavin, who had gamely rolled back the years, and on Dzagoev, one of the sharpest forwards in the competition – but hardly on the well-paid Advocaat, who had wasted his resources and now resigned. 'We should have won, but we didn't,' he said. 'I suppose in some way I will be blamed for that, but I'm not too interested in what people say about me.'

Plainly the better team had gone out, and the result sucked a lot of technical quality out of the competition. But if anyone felt sorry for Russia, all they had to do was think back to that banner in Warsaw.

6pm, 8 June 2012
Stadion Narodowy, Warsaw
Attendance: 56,070
Referee: Carlos Velasco Carballo (Spain)

POLAND 1 (Lewandowski 17)
GREECE 1 (Salpingidis 51)

POLAND: Wojciech Szczęsny, Łukasz Piszczek, Marcin Wasilewski, Damien Perquis, Sebastian Boenisch, Eugen Polanski, Rafał Murawski, Maciej Rybus (Przemysław Tytoń 70), Robert Lewandowski, Ludovic Obraniak, Jakub 'Kuba' Błaszczykowski (c). **Manager:** Franciszek Smuda.

GREECE: Kostas Chalkias, Vasilis Torosidis, José Holebas, Sokratis Papastathopoulos, Avraam Papadopoulos (Kyriakos Papadopoulos 37), Ioannis Maniatis, Kostas Katsouranis, Georgios Karagounis (c), Fanis Gekas (Kostas Fortounis 68), Georgios Samaras, Sotiris Ninis (Dimitris Salpingidis 46). **Manager:** Fernando Santos.

Booked: Papastathopoulos (35), Holebas (45+2), Karagounis (54).

Sent off: Papastathopoulos (44), Szczęsny (68).

8.45pm, 8 June 2012
Stadion Miejski, Wrocław
Attendance: 40,803
Referee: Howard Webb (England)

RUSSIA 4 (Dzagoev 15, 79, Shirokov 24, Pavlyuchenko 82)
CZECH REPUBLIC 1 (Pilař 52)

RUSSIA: Vyacheslav Malafeev, Aleksei Anyukov, Aleksei Berezutsky, Sergei Ignashevich, Yuri Zhirkov, Igor Denisov, Roman Shirokov, Konstantin Zyryanov, Aleksandr Kerzhakov (Roman Pavlyuchenko 73), Andrei Arshavin (c), Alan Dzagoev (Aleksandr Kokorin 84). **Manager:** Dick Advocaat.

CZECH REPUBLIC: Petr Čech, Theodor Gebre Selassie, Roman Hubník, Tomáš Sivok, Michal Kadlec, Jaroslav Plašil, Petr Jiráček (Milan Petržela 76), Václav Pilař, Milan Baroš (David Lafata 85), Jan Rezek (Tomáš Hübschman 46), Tomáš Rosický (c). **Manager:** Michal Bílek.

6pm, 12 June 2012
Stadion Miejski, Wrocław
Attendance: 41,105
Referee: Stéphane Lannoy (France)

CZECH REPUBLIC 2 (Jiráček 3, Pilař 6)
GREECE 1 (Gekas 53)

CZECH REPUBLIC: Čech, Gebre Selassie, Sivok, Kadlec, David Limberský, Hübschman, Plašil, Jiráček, Baroš (Tomáš Pekhart 64), Rosický (c) (Daniel Kolář 46, František Rajtoral 90), Pilař.

GREECE: Chalkias (Michalis Sifakis 23), Torosidis, Holebas, K. Papadopoulos, Katsouranis, Maniatis, Georgios Fotakis (Gekas 46), Karagounis (c), Samaras, Fortounis (Kostas Mitroglou 71), Salpingidis.

Booked: Rosický (27), Jiráček (36), Kolář (67), Torosidis (34), K. Papadopoulos (56), Salpingidis (57).

8.45pm, 12 June 2012
Stadion Narodowy, Warsaw
Attendance: 55,920
Referee: Wolfgang Stark (Germany)

POLAND 1 (Błaszczykowski 57)
RUSSIA 1 (Dzagoev 37)

POLAND: Tytoń, Piszczek, Wasilewski, Perquis, Boenisch, Polanski (Adam Matuszczyk 85), Murawski, Dariusz Dudka (Adrian Mierzejewski 73), Lewandowski, Obraniak (Paweł Brożek 90+3), Błaszczykowski (c).

RUSSIA: Malafeev, Anyukov, Berezutsky, Ignashevich, Zhirkov, Denisov, Shirokov, Zyryanov, Kerzhakov (Pavlyuchenko 70), Arshavin (c), Dzagoev (Marat Izmailov 79).

Booked: Lewandowski (60), Polanski (79), Denisov (60), Dzagoev (75).

8.45pm, 16 June 2012
Stadion Miejski, Wrocław
Attendance: 41,480
Referee: Craig Thomson (Scotland)

CZECH REPUBLIC 1 (Jiráček 72)
POLAND 0

CZECH REPUBLIC: Čech (c), Gebre Selassie, Limberský, Sivok, Kadlec, Hübschman, Plašil, Jiráček (Rajtoral 84), Baroš (Pekhart 90+1), Kolář, Pilař (Rezek 88).

POLAND: Tytoń, Piszczek, Wasilewski, Perquis, Boenisch, Polanski (Kamil Grosicki 56), Murawski (Mierzejewski 73), Dudka, Lewandowski, Obraniak (Brożek 73), Błaszczykowski (c).

Booked: Limberský (12), Plašil (87), Pekhart (90+4), Murawski (22), Polanski (47), Wasilewski (61), Błaszczykowski (87), Perquis (90).

8.45pm, 16 June 2012
Stadion Narodowy, Warsaw
Attendance: 55,920
Referee: Jonas Eriksson (Sweden)

GREECE 1 (Karagounis 45+2)
RUSSIA 0

GREECE: Sifakis, Torosidis, Georgios Tzavelas, Papastathopoulos, K. Papadopoulos, Katsouranis, Maniatis, Karagounis (c) (Grigoris Makos 67), Samaras, Gekas (Holebas 64), Salpingidis (Ninis 83).

RUSSIA: Malafeev, Anyukov (Izmailov 81), Berezutsky, Ignashevich, Zhirkov, Denisov, Shirokov, Denis Glushakov (Pavel Pogrebnyak 72), Kerzhakov (Pavlyuchenko 46), Arshavin (c), Dzagoev.

Booked: Karagounis (61), Holebas (90+4), Anyukov (61), Zhirkov (69), Dzagoev (70), Pogrebnyak (90+3).

GROUP A	P	W	D	L	F	A	GD	Pts
CZECH REPUBLIC	3	2	0	1	4	5	− 1	6
GREECE	3	1	1	1	3	3	0	4
RUSSIA	3	1	1	1	5	3	+2	4
POLAND	3	0	2	1	2	3	− 1	2

The Czech Republic and Greece qualified.

GROUP B
Netherlands, Denmark, Germany, Portugal

Denmark were widely seen as a tasty entrée for the Netherlands' big names to dine upon, but they turned that idea on its head in a half-empty Metalist Stadion in Kharkiv. Not quite a sensation, but certainly not a result most people saw coming, though Belgian website Sporza should have won some sort of award for its post-match headline of 'Egoland 0-1 Legoland'.

Bert van Marwijk made a rod for his own back by picking a player barely old enough to order a legal drink. With Erik Pieters injured, he turned to the PSV left-back's understudy, Jetro Willems, who had barely 20 Eredivisie appearances to his name. Aged 18 years and 71 days, Willems became the youngest player ever to appear in the European Championship, beating Enzo Scifo's record but looking nervous throughout.

Denmark's first-half winning goal came from a man who was something of a fifth columnist. Left-winger Michael Krohn-Dehli had toiled in Dutch football for six seasons, flopping at Ajax and Sparta Rotterdam. Here, though, when Simon Poulsen's cross broke to him outside the box, he shaped to shoot with his right foot, then skipped past the off-balance Johnny Heitinga and drilled it through Maarten Stekelenburg's legs.

Their pride stung, the Dutch poured forward. When Danish goalkeeper Stephan Andersen's terrible goal kick went straight to Arjen Robben, the winger struck the post. Ibrahim Afellay botched a free header, then slashed another effort over the bar. The Netherlands' main hope of goals, Robin van Persie, had a major off-day and squandered three decent opportunities, but his rival Klaas-Jan Huntelaar, wearing a face like thunder on the bench, did no better when he came on.

Surviving a late handball claim against Lars Jacobsen, Denmark clung on for a memorable victory. 'They only made half a chance and they scored,' Heitinga sniped. 'There's no way anyone can say Denmark deserved to win. You can't have played well when you give so many chances away.' But the Dutch goose was already cooked.

═════

'The European Championship is like an F1 race without the warm-up,' Jogi Löw mused after Germany laboured to beat Portugal in Lviv. 'You have to get off the grid as fast as you can.' His team moved at the speed of a combine harvester for most of the game, and Portugal were worse. Only José Mourinho, sitting in the VIP box with his mega-agent pal Jorge Mendes, might have found something to enjoy as two cagey teams cancelled each other out.

Paulo Bento's players had been sharply criticised in recent weeks for ostentatious shows of wealth when Portugal had an unemployment rate of 36 per cent among under-30s. Their habit of appearing at glitzy functions, often at sponsors' behest, drew savage criticism, as did the FPF's decision to base the squad at an ultra-expensive Polish spa hotel in Opalenica. Manuel José, Portugal's answer to Sam Allardyce, called the national setup 'a circus' and growled, 'Behind this team is a country where most people are not hopping from party to party. Looking at this squad is like watching *Big Brother*.'

During a shocking first half, the crowd were so bored that an avalanche of toilet paper was hurled on to the pitch, prompting the stadium announcer to warn that the match could be abandoned. At least the half ended in excitement. After Germany didn't clear a corner, Pepe's instant shot hit the underside of the bar and came down on the line, narrowly missing Philipp Lahm's hand.

But Germany's winner exposed Pepe's bad habit of switching off at dangerous moments. He allowed the powerfully built Mario Gómez to drift away from him as Sami Khedira's cross came over; and Gómez, who was about to be substituted, headed it inside the far post.

Portugal's performance deserved nothing, but they could have equalised three times near the end. Nani's booming cross dropped on to the bar, Manuel Neuer sprang off his line to deny Silvestre Varela, and finally, Holger Badstuber blocked Nani's goalbound effort. Why hadn't they played like this from the start?

At the end, Cristiano Ronaldo disgustedly ripped off his captain's armband, provoking more derision at home, with Benfica legend António

Simões calling him 'egocentric and irresponsible'. Things could only get better for Portugal. Couldn't they?

━━━

They could, and against Denmark in Lviv, they did. Initially, a hammering looked on the cards as Bento's team strolled into a two-goal lead. First, Pepe succeeded where he had failed against Germany, ramming home a near-post header from João Moutinho's corner while the Danes ball-watched. Then Hélder Postiga reacted quicker than Simon Kjær to get on the end of Nani's excellent pass and smash it into the roof of the net. The Portuguese were cruising – though their main man wasn't.

In a childish but amusing attempt to troll Ronaldo, some Danish fans began chanting Lionel Messi's name, and it seemed to work. In the first half, he dragged a good chance wide, hammered a free kick into the wall after a melodramatic warm-up routine, and was thwarted two yards out by Kjær's tackle.

Nicklas Bendtner, of all people, showed Ronaldo how it was done. The bulky Arsenal forward was a figure of fun in English football, praising himself at every opportunity despite his obvious inadequacies. But he always enjoyed himself against Portugal: his three goals in three internationals against them now became five in four. He could hardly miss the first one. Jakob Poulsen's cross to the far post was headed back across goal by Krohn-Dehli, and Bendtner nodded home from under the bar.

In the second half, Ronaldo wasted two one-on-ones, hitting the first against Andersen and putting the second miserably wide. Those misses looked even worse when Bendtner climbed above Pepe to head in Jacobsen's cross for 2-2, then pulled down his shorts to reveal bookmaker-sponsored underpants (UEFA fined him €80,000). With little time left, Portugal were fortunate to scrape a winner. The substitute Varela took a fresh-air swipe at Fábio Coentrão's cross, but recovered to bang in the loose ball.

Afterwards, Ronaldo did himself few favours in the mixed zone. 'You know where Messi was this time last year?' he asked a journalist who mentioned the chanting. 'He was being eliminated in the Copa América, in his own country. I think that's worse, no?' Oh dear.

━━━

Things were as mellow as ever in the Dutch camp, with Van Persie, Huntelaar and Nigel de Jong all refusing to talk to the media. Before the meeting with Germany, Wesley Sneijder appealed for everyone to get along. 'It's time we let go of these pathetic egos,' he said. 'We don't need a psychologist with the team. We're grown-up men. We have to stop living on little islands.'

In muggy heat in Kharkiv, the premier grudge match of European football had a restrained air to it. Van Persie's disappointing tournament continued when, early on, he tamely clipped the ball into Neuer's hands after outpacing Mats Hummels. Meanwhile, Mesut Özil volleyed against a post.

Almost all Germany's attacks were down the right, targeting the vulnerable young Willems. From one such move, they scored first. Özil cut inside to feed Bastian Schweinsteiger, who played a surgical ball to Gómez. The big man controlled it first time before spinning 180 degrees and finishing low past Stekelenburg.

Gómez, utterly appalling in the Champions League Final some weeks earlier, was suddenly looking like a proper striker. Soon, he scored another fine goal. He, Müller and Schweinsteiger played a neat triangle on the right; another inch-perfect Schweinsteiger ball created the opening and Gómez simply ignored Willems to stride on to it and wallop a magnificent shot across Stekelenburg. Dutch magazine *Voetbal International* called Gómez the 'killer van Oranje', adding, 'Gómez pulled the trigger as lethally as ever. Give the Bayern striker a cowboy hat and he can play Lucky Luke.'

Mark van Bommel's long, violent international career came to an end at half-time, while Van Marwijk threw on Huntelaar and put Van Persie on the left. The switch paid off when Van Persie picked the ball up in his new position, dashed forward and cracked a spectacular shot past Neuer. But in the final moments, Stekelenburg almost humiliated himself after trying to dribble around Miroslav Klose in his own goalmouth and, in truth, 3-1 would have been fairer than 2-2.

Huntelaar's petulant slap at Schweinsteiger summed up Dutch impotence, as did the sight of the substituted Robben ripping off his jersey and sullenly trudging around the perimeter of the pitch. Amazingly, they could still qualify despite losing two out of two, but surely the jig was up. 'Oh, oh, Oranje,' groaned *De Telegraaf*. Across the border, *Der Spiegel* went with, 'Das war super, Mario!'

In desperation, Robben made a shameless public appeal to Germany to 'fulfil their sporting duty' against Denmark. Löw sent out a strong side but they took their time putting the match to bed.

Denmark worked hard, with William Kvist sticking to Özil like a leech, but they couldn't get the ball off Germany – so it was no surprise when they fell behind, Lukas Podolski finishing well after Gómez miscontrolled Müller's cross. A curiosity of a player, 'Prinz Poldi' looked no great shakes at club level but scored bucketloads for his country.

Denmark, who certainly didn't lack spirit, quickly equalised. When Jacobsen's corner was headed back into the danger area by Bendtner, little

Krohn-Dehli, an unexpected minor star of this tournament, rose above the much taller Gómez to flick it home.

The Danes had one more big chance, but Jakob Poulsen shaved the post after Bendtner set him up. Our old friend Carlos Velasco Carballo screwed up again here, denying Bendtner a clear penalty after Badstuber pulled him back. And Germany's winner, when it came, felt like the banal punchline of a well-worn joke. A quick counter-attack ended with right-back Lars Bender darting in front of two defenders and stabbing Özil's pass beyond Andersen.

Denmark, who had over-achieved, might have done even better with a little more ambition. 'The Danes fell with honour,' noted Copenhagen newspaper *Børsen*. But Kvist was nearer the mark when he cursed the 'two stupid goals' that sent his team home.

=====

Cristiano Ronaldo seemed to be positively inviting brickbats by sporting two different hairstyles against the Netherlands in Kharkiv. But when he played this well, he could get away with anything. He singlehandedly propelled Portugal into the quarter-finals with his best performance in any major tournament.

Needing at least a two-goal win, the Dutch started brightly. Robben drew three defenders into his orbit, then squared it to Van der Vaart, whose streaking drive flew across Rui Patrício and just inside the far post. Another great Dutch goal to fig-leaf their otherwise woeful tournament.

Now Ronaldo's one-man show began as he ran away from Ron Vlaar and saw his shot smack the outside of the post. Right-back Gregory van der Wiel was nowhere to be seen, stranded up the other end; and the young defender's ordeal continued when his appalling back-pass went straight to Postiga, whose shot was pushed wide by Stekelenburg.

Portugal were playing their best football of the competition, and soon the equaliser arrived. After Willems gave the ball away, João Pereira slipped a wonderful pass through to Ronaldo, who again left Vlaar for dead and side-footed it past the goalkeeper.

Van Marwijk made no substitutions at the interval, and it was reported in the Dutch press afterwards that when he exhorted Robben to get back and help the defence, Robben threw yet another tantrum by yelling, 'Ik ben gebroken. Hou je bek, man!' (I am broken. Shut your mouth, man!) Blatant insubordination which also left Van der Wiel isolated against the best player in Europe.

In the second half, Ronaldo picked out Nani, who shot straight at Stekelenburg's midriff, both a good save and a bad finish. Eventually, Ronaldo closed the deal, stopping Nani's cross dead with his left foot as poor Van der Wiel hurtled past in the wrong direction, then pulling the trigger with his right.

He hit the woodwork with another long-range missile near the end; so did Van der Vaart, but the Netherlands were dead ducks by then. Having signed a new contract just before the tournament, Van Marwijk now stepped down.

The Dutch were the first top seeds ever to be whitewashed in a European Championship group. Robben: 'We all need to take a good look in the mirror. Everyone has failed. Some things have happened in the squad, but we have to keep them internal. There were just too many egos in the team.' Not least his own.

7pm, 9 June 2012
Stadion Metalist, Kharkiv
Attendance: 28,000
Referee: Damir Skomina (Slovenia)

DENMARK 1 (Krohn-Dehli 24)
NETHERLANDS 0

DENMARK: Stephan Andersen, Lars Jacobsen, Simon Kjær, Daniel Agger (c), Simon Poulsen, Niki Zimling, William Kvist, Christian Eriksen (Lasse Schöne 74), Nicklas Bendtner, Dennis Rommedahl (Tobias Mikkelsen 84), Michael Krohn-Dehli. **Manager:** Morten Olsen.

NETHERLANDS: Maarten Stekelenburg, Gregory van der Wiel (Dirk Kuyt 85), Johnny Heitinga, Ron Vlaar, Jetro Willems, Nigel de Jong (Rafael van der Vaart 71), Mark van Bommel (c), Wesley Sneijder, Robin van Persie, Arjen Robben, Ibrahim Afellay (Klaas-Jan Huntelaar 71). **Manager:** Bert van Marwijk.

Booked: Poulsen (78), Kvist (81), Van Bommel (67).

9.45pm, 9 June 2012
Arena Lviv, Lviv
Attendance: 32,990
Referee: Stéphane Lannoy (France)

GERMANY 1 (Gómez 72)

PORTUGAL 0

GERMANY: Manuel Neuer, Jérôme Boateng, Philipp Lahm (c), Holger Badstuber, Mats Hummels, Sami Khedira, Bastian Schweinsteiger, Thomas Müller (Lars Bender 90+4), Mario Gómez (Miroslav Klose 80), Mesut Özil (Toni Kroos 87), Lukas Podolski. **Manager:** Joachim 'Jogi' Löw.

PORTUGAL: Rui Patrício dos Santos, João Pereira da Silva, Bruno Alves, Képler Laveran 'Pepe', Fábio Coentrão, Raul Meireles (Silvestre Varela 80), Miguel Veloso, João Moutinho, Hélder Postiga (Nélson Oliveira 70), Cristiano Ronaldo (c), Luís da Cunha 'Nani'. **Manager:** Paulo Bento.

Booked: Badstuber (43), Boateng (69), Postiga (13), Coentrão (60).

7pm, 13 June 2012
Arena Lviv, Lviv
Attendance: 31,840
Referee: Craig Thomson (Scotland)

PORTUGAL 3 (Pepe 24, Postiga 36, Varela 87)
DENMARK 2 (Bendtner 41, 80)

PORTUGAL: Rui Patrício, João Pereira, Alves, Pepe, Coentrão, Meireles (Varela 84), Veloso, Moutinho, Postiga (Nélson 64), Ronaldo (c), Nani (Rolando Pires 89).

DENMARK: Andersen, Jacobsen, Kjær, Agger (c), S. Poulsen, Zimling (Jakob Poulsen 16), Kvist, Eriksen, Bendtner, Rommedahl (Mikkelsen 60), Krohn-Dehli (Schöne 90+2).

Booked: Meireles (29), Ronaldo (90+2), J. Poulsen (56), Jacobsen (81).

9.45pm, 13 June 2012
Stadion Metalist, Kharkiv
Attendance: 37,750
Referee: Jonas Eriksson (Sweden)

GERMANY 2 (Gómez 24, 38)
NETHERLANDS 1 (Van Persie 73)

GERMANY: Neuer, Boateng, Lahm (c), Badstuber, Hummels, Khedira, Schweinsteiger, Müller (Bender 90+2), Gómez (Klose 72), Özil (Kroos 81), Podolski.

NETHERLANDS: Stekelenburg, Van der Wiel, Heitinga, Joris Mathijsen, Willems, De Jong, Van Bommel (c) (Van der Vaart 46), Sneijder, Van Persie, Robben (Kuyt 83), Afellay (Huntelaar 46).

Booked: Boateng (87), De Jong (80), Willems (90).

9.45pm, 17 June 2012
Arena Lviv, Lviv
Attendance: 32,990
Referee: Carlos Velasco Carballo (Spain)

GERMANY 2 (Podolski 19, Bender 80)
DENMARK 1 (Krohn-Dehli 24)

GERMANY: Neuer, Bender, Lahm (c), Badstuber, Hummels, Khedira, Schweinsteiger, Müller (Kroos 84), Gómez (Klose 74), Özil, Podolski (André Schürrle 64).

DENMARK: Andersen, Jacobsen, Kjær, Agger (c), S. Poulsen, Zimling (Christian Poulsen 78), J. Poulsen (Mikkelsen 82), Kvist, Eriksen, Bendtner, Krohn-Dehli.

9.45pm, 17 June 2012
Stadion Metalist, Kharkiv
Attendance: 37,445
Referee: Nicola Rizzoli (Italy)

PORTUGAL 2 (Ronaldo 28, 74)
NETHERLANDS 1 (Van der Vaart 11)

PORTUGAL: Rui Patrício, João Pereira, Alves, Pepe, Coentrão, Meireles (Custódio Castro 72), Veloso, Moutinho, Postiga (Nélson 64), Ronaldo (c), Nani (Rolando 87).

NETHERLANDS: Stekelenburg, Van der Wiel, Mathijsen, Vlaar, Willems (Afellay 67), De Jong, Van der Vaart (c), Sneijder, Huntelaar, Van Persie, Robben.

Booked: João Pereira (90+2), Willems (51), Van Persie (69).

GROUP B	P	W	D	L	F	A	GD	Pts
GERMANY	3	3	0	0	5	2	+3	9
PORTUGAL	3	2	0	1	5	4	+1	6
DENMARK	3	1	0	2	4	5	−1	3
NETHERLANDS	3	0	0	3	2	5	−3	0

Germany and Portugal qualified.

GROUP C
Spain, Italy, Ireland, Croatia

David Villa's leg break had left Vicente Del Bosque with a stark choice: use an inferior replacement like Roberto Soldado or Fernando Llorente, or try something completely different. So, in Gdańsk, Spain lined up against Italy in a bizarre 4-6-0 with Cesc Fàbregas as a non-striker. The results were predictably constipated.

Like all Spain's opponents, Italy were crushed on the passing count (780-426), but they looked the better team otherwise. Andrea Pirlo, the very model of a modern midfield general, stole Xavi's thunder with a terrific performance. Early on, the reformed delinquent Antonio Cassano took his superb long pass, arrowed inside Álvaro Arbeloa and hit a shot which was parried unconvincingly by Iker Casillas. Within minutes, the goalkeeper just about held Claudio Marchisio's volley.

With Italy's wing-backs Christian Maggio and Emanuele Giaccherini flying forward, and Fàbregas not even trying to discommode their big centre-halves, the closest Spain came in the first half was an Andrés Iniesta lob which drifted too high. Seconds later, Italy should have scored, but Casillas made a fantastic stop from Thiago Motta's downward header.

After half-time, Spain got a let-off when their doziest player suffered his latest brain-fart. Mario Balotelli was offering little except petulance until Sergio Ramos's pickled thought processes handed him a great chance. When the defender botched a back-pass, Balotelli pounced and bore down on goal, but dithered and took so many touches that Ramos got back and nicked the ball off his toe. Prandelli immediately substituted him.

But with Pirlo on your side, there would always be another chance coming along soon. On 64 minutes, the maestro left Sergio Busquets for dead, accelerated past Xavi and played Balotelli's replacement, Antonio Di Natale, through to sweep the ball over Casillas. You just knew what Balotelli would have done in the same situation.

To their credit, Spain equalised instantly. After some spicy interplay between Xavi and Iniesta, David Silva poked a Pirlo-esque ball through for Fàbregas to slide it under Buffon. Undeterred, the Italian fans resumed their endless choruses of Seven Nation Army.

Substitute Fernando Torres, who had been a spent force since 2010, wasted Spain's two best chances. First, he tried to dribble around Buffon, who dispossessed him with boot rather than glove. Later, in a similar situation, he decided to shoot early but put it well over. With two minutes left, the ball got stuck between Marchisio's legs before he shot straight at Casillas.

And so ended the best match of the tournament. 'Why don't we innovate even further? In the second half, we could come out without a goalkeeper,' tweeted a Spanish journalist with sledgehammer sarcasm. Luis Aragonés, Del Bosque's predecessor, admitted that 'the inclusion of Cesc in place of any forwards surprised me', while José Mourinho said, 'The continuous touches between Xavi, Iniesta and Fàbregas are useless if you don't create any danger to Buffon.'

Spain's players blamed the dry surface. 'It's lamentable that we still have to play on pitches like that,' whinged Fàbregas. But it hadn't prevented Pirlo from looking like one of the gods of the modern game. 'It's the same for both teams,' he shot back.

Before Ireland took on Croatia in Poznań, Robbie Keane talked of how his team's presence at the finals was a balm to the spirits of a country battered by the financial crash. But while their fans were as raucous as ever, anyone who had seen Ireland in the qualifiers knew they would need all the luck they could get.

Instead, they crashed on take-off. After 150 seconds, Darijo Srna's cross hit Stephen Ward and fell to Mario Mandžukić. The header was soft, but the 36-year-old Shay Given dived ridiculously slowly as it bounced in off the post. Given later revealed that he received injections from German doctor Hans-Wilhelm Müller-Wohlfahrt in order to play. Looking at this performance, you wondered if Müller-Wohlfahrt had pumped him full of tranquillisers.

But Ireland equalised while their energy levels were still buzzing, as Sean St Ledger outjumped Vedran Ćorluka at the back post to head in Aiden McGeady's free kick. Thanks to some plank in the crowd blowing a loud whistle, most people in the stadium (and plenty of TV viewers) hesitated when the ball hit the net.

Given couldn't do much about the farcical episode which saw Croatia regain the lead before half-time. Again a corner wasn't dealt with, and when Luka Modrić's shot flew into a crowd of players, Ward's swipe sent the ball to the one place Ireland didn't want it to go: straight to Nikica Jelavić, who happily scooped it over Given.

Three minutes into the second half, it was all over including the shouting. In an inversion of Ireland's equaliser, Mandžukić got above St Ledger to head against the post, and it rebounded in off the back of Given's head for an unpreventable own goal. Keane was later denied a clear penalty when Gordon Schildenfeld clattered him, but the way he was playing, he would have missed it anyway. Ireland's 14-match unbeaten run and 18th place in FIFA's rankings now looked like tricks of the light.

=====

Croatia were a long-time bogey team for Italy, who hadn't beaten them since 1942 and couldn't do it in Poznań either. Prandelli kept faith in Balotelli up front, but he was again ineffectual, with the Croatian fans racially goading him throughout. For this, and some flares landing on the pitch, UEFA fined the HNS €80,000.

Claudio Marchisio had already brought a brilliant double save out of Stipe Pletikosa by the time Pirlo gave Italy a deserved lead, sending a delectable free kick over the wall and inside the near post for the only dead-ball goal scored in Euro 2012. When Croatia's equaliser did eventually arrive, it was entirely preventable. Giorgio Chiellini mistimed his jump as Ivan Strinić's cross sailed over his head; behind him, Mandžukić killed it with one touch and thrashed it in off the post.

Still the flares and chants filled the air, even though Balotelli had long since gone off. 'I don't want these people supporting us,' Croatia's manager Slaven Bilić said afterwards. With smoke enshrouding the Italian box, referee Howard Webb looked ready to halt the match. Croatia could even have won it when Buffon spilled Rakitić's long shot in the sixth minute of stoppage time.

Once again, Italy had paid a price for not finishing off vulnerable opponents. 'When you play like that, you just have to close the game,' said Prandelli. But they had an insurance policy: a game against the worst team in the competition.

=====

Against Spain in Gdańsk that evening, Ireland's tournament lurched from bad to farce. They controlled the game for 70 seconds, during which Iker Casillas went full-length to punch away Simon Cox's long shot. Then the reigning champions woke up, and so did their unloved number nine.

This Irish team could restore any striker's confidence – even Torres's. Early on, his run was halted by Richard Dunne, but he stole the ball back, ran around Ward and slammed it high into the net as Given fell on his knees like a supplicant.

Trapattoni's line-up and tactics were again hard to understand. The only new face was Cox, West Bromwich Albion's fourth-choice striker, who he used on the left wing. As rain cascaded down, Spain could have had two more goals quickly, Given saving Silva's low drive, Torres missing from close range. Aiden McGeady's idiotic dummy outside his own box then gave Silva another chance which Given blocked, and the goalkeeper ended the half by tipping an Iniesta thunderbolt over his bar.

After the interval, for the fourth half of football in a row, Ireland conceded inside four minutes. Again Given was at fault, punching Iniesta's shot out to Silva, whose hips sent St Ledger and Ward the wrong way before his shot passed through three pairs of Irish legs and into the bottom corner. Given partly redeemed himself with the finest save of the tournament, jack-knifing in mid-air to keep out Xavi's swerver.

For the third goal, the inadequate McGeady got robbed in midfield by Silva, whose quick pass allowed Torres to stroll through the debris of Ireland's defence and send a good finish over Given's shoulder. The substitute Fàbregas scored the fourth, receiving a short corner and rifling the ball in off the far post from an angle, past the punch-drunk Given. He didn't bother celebrating, either a sign of his displeasure at being dropped or a reflection on how useless Ireland were.

As the game petered out, the PGE Arena reverberated to the strains of Irish fans bellowing the maudlin ballad 'The Fields Of Athenry', prompting Arsène Wenger to tell his French TV co-commentator to stay quiet so they could listen to the singing. Back in ITV's studio in London, Roy Keane laid into his countrymen for what he regarded as ingrained defeatism. He wasn't asked what he would have preferred instead – mass booing, perhaps, or deathly silence.

Before Spain and Croatia met in Gdańsk, it was known that a 2-2 draw would save them at Italy's expense, in a rerun of Denmark v Sweden at Euro 2004. Bilić tried to dampen down Italian paranoia: 'The whole of Italy and Europe can calm down. [Fixing games] is a part of the brain we don't have. If the final score is 2-2, fine. That can happen. It's not going to be 7-7, which would be strange. To the Italians, I say: trust in us.'

Croatia should have had a penalty when the ever-reliable Ramos kicked Mandžukić, but with Spain's keep-ball sucking the life out of the game, chances were rare. Silva's sublime pass saw Iniesta stab too close to Pletikosa, and Torres was kept out by the goalkeeper's knee. But that was it for the first half.

In the second, Spain held the ball like a sulky child clutching a favourite toy. But Croatia had a big chance on the hour. Modrić's brilliant cross found Rakitić alone at the back post, but he planted his header straight at Casillas.

The rebound hit Busquets and came back to Rakitić, whose second header was hacked to safety by Xabi Alonso.

With 11 minutes left, Croatia again opened Spain up as Casillas moved sharply to save Perišić's volley. The east Europeans were then denied another clear penalty: Busquets crudely held Ćorluka down at a corner, but referee Wolfgang Stark missed it. They soon paid for his mistake. Fàbregas's chip found Iniesta as the Croats pushed up too late, and the playmaker squared it to Jesús Navas, who happily ran the ball into the open goal. Croatia claimed offside, but replays showed Navas level with Iniesta.

'I'll have sleepless nights thinking about that,' sighed Rakitić of his earlier miss. A relieved Del Bosque conceded that Spain lacked 'profundidad' (depth in their play), while Ramón Besa, writing in *El País*, likened the game to a tense Alfred Hitchcock thriller. Fine margins all round.

===

Confounding expectations, Ireland gave Italy a game in Poznań, helped by Andrea Pirlo turning in his worst performance in living memory. He began by letting a simple ball roll past him after just two seconds, allowing Kevin Doyle to charge through on goal: Buffon flew out to smother the danger.

Pirlo hardly improved thereafter, sending a glaring number of passes astray. But he still set up Italy's opener. Again Given looked poor: a hopeful long shot by Cassano bounced off his chest, and the Milan striker then met Pirlo's corner with a near-post header which sneaked over the line before Damien Duff could clear.

In the second half, Keith Andrews's piledriver made Buffon work, concentrating Italian minds. But it all turned sour for the West Brom midfielder late on when he picked up a second booking for pulling Pirlo's shirt. He angrily booted the ball into the stands, doubling his one-match ban. Balotelli, on as a substitute, wrapped up the win a minute later. As a corner sailed over, he backed into John O'Shea, buying himself the space to score with a hooked volley on the turn.

Ireland's fans were different class, moving Prandelli to remark, 'I've never been so emotional during a set of national anthems.' But Duff was their only player to do himself credit in the tournament, never giving up as he plugged countless gaps. Given could point to some great saves as well as the howlers, the wholehearted Andrews scraped a pass, and the others were out of their depth, managed by a man out of time in every sense. 'Despite a brave show from the players in Poznań, this experience has been a sobering lesson,' wrote Daniel McDonnell in the *Irish Independent*. 'The party's over.'

6pm, 10 June 2012
PGE Arena, Gdańsk
Attendance: 38,869
Referee: Viktor Kassai (Hungary)

SPAIN 1 (Fàbregas 64)
ITALY 1 (Di Natale 61)

SPAIN: Iker Casillas (c), Álvaro Arbeloa, Jordi Alba, Sergio Ramos, Gerard Piqué, Xavi Hernández, Sergio Busquets, Xabi Alonso, Cesc Fàbregas (Fernando Torres 74), Andrés Iniesta, David Silva (Jesús Navas 64). **Manager:** Vicente Del Bosque.

ITALY: Gianluigi Buffon (c), Emanuele Giaccherini, Giorgio Chiellini, Daniele De Rossi, Leonardo Bonucci, Christian Maggio, Thiago Motta (Antonio Nocerino 90), Claudio Marchisio, Mario Balotelli (Antonio Di Natale 56), Andrea Pirlo, Antonio Cassano (Sebastian Giovinco 65). **Manager:** Cesare Prandelli.

Booked: Alba (66), Arbeloa (84), Torres (84), Balotelli (37), Bonucci (66), Chiellini (79), Maggio (89).

8.45pm, 10 June 2012
Stadion Miejski, Poznań
Attendance: 39,550
Referee: Björn Kuipers (Netherlands)

CROATIA 3 (Mandžukić 3, Jelavić 43, Given 49 og)
IRELAND 1 (St Ledger 19)

CROATIA: Stipe Pletikosa, Darijo Srna (c), Ivan Strinić, Gordon Schildenfeld, Vedran Ćorluka, Ognjen Vukojević, Ivan Rakitić (Tomislav Dujmović 90+2), Luka Modrić, Nikica Jelavić (Niko Kranjčar 72), Mario Mandžukić, Ivan Perišić (Eduardo da Silva 89). **Manager:** Slaven Bilić.

IRELAND: Shay Given, John O'Shea, Stephen Ward, Sean St Ledger, Richard Dunne, Glenn Whelan, Aiden McGeady (Simon Cox 54), Keith Andrews, Kevin Doyle (Jonathan Walters 53), Robbie Keane (c) (Shane Long 75), Damien Duff. **Manager:** Giovanni Trapattoni.

Booked: Modrić (53), Kranjčar (84), Andrews (45+1).

6pm, 14 June 2012
Stadion Miejski, Poznań
Attendance: 37,096
Referee: Howard Webb (England)

CROATIA 1 (Mandžukić 72)
ITALY 1 (Pirlo 39)

CROATIA: Pletikosa, Srna (c), Strinić, Schildenfeld, Ćorluka, Vukojević, Rakitić, Modrić, Jelavić (Eduardo 83), Mandžukić (Kranjčar 90+4), Perišić (Danijel Pranjić 68).

ITALY: Buffon (c), Maggio, Chiellini, De Rossi, Bonucci, Giaccherini, Motta (Riccardo Montolivo 62), Marchisio, Balotelli (Di Natale 69), Pirlo, Cassano (Giovinco 83).

Booked: Schildenfeld (86), Motta (56), Montolivo (80).

8.45pm, 14 June 2012
PGE Arena, Gdańsk
Attendance: 38,869
Referee: Pedro Proença (Portugal)

SPAIN 4 (Torres 4, 70, Silva 49, Fàbregas 83)
IRELAND 0

SPAIN: Casillas (c), Arbeloa, Alba, Ramos, Piqué, Xavi, Busquets, Alonso (Javi Martínez 65), Torres (Fàbregas 74), Iniesta (Santi Cazorla 80), Silva.

IRELAND: Given, O'Shea, Ward, St Ledger, Dunne, Whelan (Paul Green 80), McGeady, Andrews, Cox (Walters 46), Keane (c), Duff (James McClean 76).

Booked: Alonso (54), Martínez (76), Keane (36), Whelan (45+1), St Ledger (84).

8.45pm, 18 June 2012
PGE Arena, Gdańsk
Attendance: 39,076
Referee: Wolfgang Stark (Germany)

SPAIN 1 (Navas 88)
CROATIA 0

SPAIN: Casillas (c), Arbeloa, Alba, Ramos, Piqué, Xavi (Álvaro Negredo 89), Busquets, Alonso, Torres (Navas 61), Iniesta, Silva (Fàbregas 73).

CROATIA: Pletikosa, Domagoj Vida (Jelavić 66), Strinić, Schildenfeld, Ćorluka, Vukojević (Eduardo 81), Srna (c), Rakitić, Mandžukić, Modrić, Pranjić (Perišić 66).

Booked: Ćorluka (27), Srna (44), Strinić (53), Mandžukić (90), Jelavić (90+1), Rakitić (90+3).

8.45pm, 18 June 2012
Stadion Miejski, Poznań
Attendance: 38,794
Referee: Cüneyt Çakır (Turkey)

ITALY 2 (Cassano 35, Balotelli 90)
IRELAND 0

ITALY: Buffon (c), Ignazio Abate, Chiellini (Bonucci 57), Andrea Barzagli, Federico Balzaretti, De Rossi, Motta, Marchisio, Di Natale (Balotelli 74), Pirlo, Cassano (Alessandro Diamanti 63).

IRELAND: Given, O'Shea, Ward, St Ledger, Dunne, Whelan, McGeady (Long 65), Andrews, Doyle (Walters 76), Keane (Cox 86), Duff (c).

Booked: Balzaretti (28), De Rossi (71), Buffon (73), Andrews (37), O'Shea (39), St Ledger (84).
Sent off: Andrews (89).

GROUP C	P	W	D	L	F	A	GD	Pts
SPAIN	3	2	1	0	6	1	+5	7
ITALY	3	1	2	0	4	2	+2	5
CROATIA	3	1	1	1	4	3	+1	4
IRELAND	3	0	0	3	1	9	−8	0

Spain and Italy qualified.

GROUP D
Ukraine, Sweden, France, England

By the summer of 2014, the gleaming €300m Donbass Arena would be lying abandoned and battle-scarred as Ukrainian and pro-Russian forces battled for control of the city of Donetsk. Here, it witnessed Group D get off to a soporific start as England and France played out a boring draw.

England should have gone ahead when Ashley Young sent James Milner through with a clever pass – but after rounding Hugo Lloris, he shot clumsily into the side-netting. Eventually, the deadlock was broken by a simple goal. Steven Gerrard swung over a free kick from the right, and Joleon Lescott's forehead did the rest.

Joe Hart, an uneven goalkeeper at the best of times, was culpable for France's equaliser as Samir Nasri's shot beat his sluggish dive at the near post. Nasri's celebration involved theatrical 'shush' gestures in the direction of the press box. 'That's between him and his detractors,' said manager Laurent Blanc. 'That's something personal.'

Both sides settled for a draw long before the end. 'I've only had three games,' Roy Hodgson protested. 'You don't become a really good team in three matches and ten training sessions.' But England wouldn't get much better over the next four years either.

—

UEFA's boffins worked out that Andriy Shevchenko had the ball for just 15 seconds during Ukraine's win over Sweden in Kiev. In this brief time, he scored twice. Not bad for a man pushing 36.

Zlatan Ibrahimović, almost as old, worked hard and saw his header brush the post from Seb Larsson's centre. Early in the second half, he was in the right place at the right time. Andriy Yarmolenko failed to head away Larsson's cross, Kim Källström returned it to the danger area, and there was Ibrahimović to side-foot it under goalkeeper Andriy Pyatov.

Ukraine's response was instant and energetic. Oleh Husyev galloped 50 yards up the right and found Yarmolenko, whose pinpoint cross was met with an equally accurate header by Shevchenko, showing that some of the old killer instinct remained. He then re-emphasised the point, getting in front of his marker Ibrahimović at the near post to stick away another fine header from Yevhen Konoplyanka's corner.

Sweden might have saved themselves, but Johan Elmander shot wide after Ibrahimović's back-heel set him up. 'I'm so happy,' Shevchenko beamed. 'Six months ago, I had loads of problems with my knee and back. I couldn't imagine I would play in the Euros. I feel ten years younger.'

—

But Ukraine now fell to earth with a dismal squelch against France. After four minutes of play, a thunderstorm lashed down on the Donbass Arena with frightening force, forcing referee Björn Kuipers to bring the teams back to the dressing rooms. Television schedules around Europe were briefly thrown into chaos; an hour passed before play resumed.

Left-winger Jérémy Ménez, who resembled Dani Alves's surlier younger brother, was France's danger man. In the first half, he saw a goal disallowed for offside, ballooned over the bar after robbing Serhiy Nazarenko, and shot against Pyatov's legs. After being booked for fouling Shevchenko, he ought to have been sent off for leaving a foot in on Yevhen Selin.

So he shouldn't have been on the pitch when he gave France the lead early in the second half. Karim Benzema fed him before he stepped inside his victim Selin and tucked away the shot. Within three minutes, the contest was over. Again Benzema was involved, his pass taking out two Ukrainians to find Yohan Cabaye, who shrugged off Husyev and beat Pyatov with another low drive. Soon afterwards, Cabaye twanged a half-volley off the post.

It was France's first win in a tournament since the 2006 World Cup semi-final against Portugal. 'I hope the next victory isn't another six years in coming, because I won't be here to speak to you,' quipped Blanc, 'as I will long since have been fired by then.'

In Kiev, Hodgson made a bold move, bringing in the much-maligned Andy Carroll up front. In January 2011, Kenny Dalglish and Liverpool had broken the transfer record for a British footballer to sign Carroll for £35m, to widespread hilarity. Against a Swedish team who were shaky under high balls, though, he proved a useful blunt instrument.

The rainstorm in Donetsk delayed the kick-off here by 15 minutes. England soon got their noses in front: Martin Olsson's hacked clearance came out to Steven Gerrard, who swung in a good cross for Carroll to happily gobble up. Of Sweden's last eight goals conceded, this was the seventh header.

But after the interval, England buckled. Ibrahimović fired a free kick into the wall, then volleyed the rebound into a packed goalmouth. It broke to the veteran Olof Mellberg, whose shot Hart half-saved. Glen Johnson, who had played everybody onside seconds earlier, sliced it into his own net.

Johnson, who had been signed by Chelsea and Liverpool for big money before flopping at both clubs, couldn't be relied on. His laziness put Sweden in front, as he left Mellberg alone to score with a downward header from Larsson's set-piece. Ibrahimović, emollient as always, shouted, 'Fuck you!' at Hart during the celebrations.

Hodgson now brought on the quick but often aimless Theo Walcott. And the move paid off immediately. Young's corner was headed out to the edge of the box, and Isaksson allowed Walcott's tame shot to curve over him for 2-2. The scorer's sheepish shrug said it all.

England won the game with an odd goal. Walcott burst between two Swedes to pull it back for Danny Welbeck, who back-heeled home from close range while falling over. You wanted to believe that Welbeck meant it, despite his chronic ineptitude in front of goal: at the time, he was in the middle of a run of five goals in 58 games for Manchester United.

The result put Sweden out. 'The operation was a success, but the patient died,' sighed manager Erik Hamrén. 'Hang me, not the team. I like Roy very much, so let England win the whole shit!'

———

France's meeting with Sweden in Kiev was preceded by a minute's silence for Thierry Roland, the legendary French commentator, who had died aged 74. But his countrymen did him no justice, showing a shameful lack of desire.

Sweden should have led long before they did. Ola Toivonen and Seb Larsson passed up free headers, and Toivonen then shot into the side-netting after Philippe Mexès's error let him go around Lloris. The goalkeeper later got both hands to Larsson's close-range effort, but could do nothing about Sweden's magnificent opener: Larsson sent over a high cross and Mexès failed to pick up Ibrahimović, who met it with a crunchy volley.

The only surprising thing about Sweden's second goal was that it took until stoppage time to arrive. Substitute Samuel Holmén volleyed Wilhelmsson's cross into the ground and off the bar, before Seb Larsson followed up to bury the loose ball. France's inexcusable languor had condemned them to a quarter-final against the reigning champions.

———

In Donetsk, a Shevchenko-less Ukraine swarmed all over England, with Yarmolenko, Marko Dević and Husyev all going close in a stirring opening period. Already it looked a tournament too far for Ashley Cole, who struggled against the speedy Yarmolenko. Meanwhile, Rooney was out of shape and slow, wasting a simple header. After the interval, he fared better with an even easier chance. Gerrard's cross deflected off Dević, and Pyatov inexcusably let it bounce under his hand; Rooney headed in from a yard out.

There was one more close shave for England to survive. With Johnson stranded miles upfield, Artem Milevskiy fed Dević for a shot which looped up off Hart and was dropping into the net until Terry scissor-kicked it to safety. Linesman István Vad failed to notice the ball crossing the line by a foot before Terry's intervention, although Milevskiy was offside in the build-up anyway.

At the press conference afterwards, Oleh Blokhin disagreeably challenged a reporter to come outside and have 'a man conversation' with him. If Ukraine had done themselves a modicum of justice, their manager hadn't.

7pm, 11 June 2012
Donbass Arena, Donetsk
Attendance: 47,400
Referee: Nicola Rizzoli (Italy)

ENGLAND 1 (Lescott 30)
FRANCE 1 (Nasri 39)

ENGLAND: Joe Hart, Glen Johnson, Ashley Cole, Joleon Lescott, John Terry, Steven Gerrard (c), Scott Parker (Jordan Henderson 78), James Milner, Danny Welbeck (Theo Walcott 90+1), Ashley Young, Alex Oxlade-Chamberlain (Jermain Defoe 77). **Manager:** Roy Hodgson.

FRANCE: Hugo Lloris (c), Mathieu Debuchy, Patrice Evra, Adil Rami, Philippe Mexès, Alou Diarra, Yohan Cabaye (Hatem Ben Arfa 84), Florent Malouda (Marvin Martin 85), Karim Benzema, Samir Nasri, Franck Ribéry. **Manager:** Laurent Blanc.

Booked: Oxlade-Chamberlain (34), Young (71).

9.45pm, 11 June 2012
Olimpiyskiy Natsionalnyi Sportivnyi Kompleks, Kiev
Attendance: 64,290
Referee: Cüneyt Çakır (Turkey)

UKRAINE 2 (Shevchenko 55, 62)
SWEDEN 1 (Ibrahimović 52)

UKRAINE: Andriy Pyatov, Oleh Husyev, Yevhen Selin, Yevhen Khacheridi, Taras Mykhalyk, Anatoliy Tymoshchuk, Andriy Yarmolenko, Serhiy Nazarenko, Andriy Voronin (Ruslan Rotan 85), Andriy Shevchenko (c) (Artem Milevskiy 81), Yevhen Konoplyanka (Marko Dević 90+3). **Manager:** Oleh Blokhin.

SWEDEN: Andreas Isaksson, Mikael Lustig, Olof Mellberg, Andreas Granqvist, Martin Olsson, Rasmus Elm, Kim Källström, Seb Larsson (Christian Wilhelmsson 68), Ola Toivonen (Anders Svensson 62), Zlatan Ibrahimović (c), Markus Rosenberg (Johan Elmander 71). **Manager:** Erik Hamrén.

Booked: Källström (11), Elm (83).

7pm, 15 June 2012
Donbass Arena, Donetsk
Attendance: 48,000
Referee: Björn Kuipers (Netherlands)

FRANCE 2 (Ménez 53, Cabaye 56)
UKRAINE 0

FRANCE: Lloris (c), Debuchy, Gaël Clichy, Rami, Mexès, Diarra, Cabaye (Yann M'Vila 68), Jérémy Ménez (Martin 73), Benzema (Olivier Giroud 76), Nasri, Ribéry.

UKRAINE: Pyatov, Husyev, Selin, Khacheridi, Mykhalyk, Tymoshchuk, Yarmolenko (Oleksandr Aliyev 68), Nazarenko (Milevskiy 60), Voronin (Dević 46), Shevchenko (c), Konoplyanka.

Booked: Ménez (40), Debuchy (79), Mexès (81), Selin (55), Tymoshchuk (87).

10pm, 15 June 2012
Olimpiyskiy Natsionalnyi Sportivnyi Kompleks, Kiev
Attendance: 64,640

Referee: Damir Skomina (Slovenia)

ENGLAND 3 (Carroll 23, Walcott 64, Welbeck 78)
SWEDEN 2 (Johnson 49 og, Mellberg 59)

ENGLAND: Hart, Johnson, Cole, Lescott, Terry, Gerrard (c), Parker, Milner (Walcott 61), Andy Carroll, Welbeck (Oxlade-Chamberlain 90), Young.

SWEDEN: Isaksson, Granqvist (Lustig 66), Jonas Olsson, Mellberg, M. Olsson, Källström, Larsson, Svensson, Ibrahimović (c), Elmander (Rosenberg 79), Elm (Wilhelmsson 81).

Booked: Milner (58), Mellberg (63), J. Olsson (72), Svensson (90+1).

9.45pm, 19 June 2012
Olimpiyskiy Natsionalnyi Sportivnyi Kompleks, Kiev
Attendance: 63,010
Referee: Pedro Proença (Portugal)

SWEDEN 2 (Ibrahimović 54, Larsson 90+1)
FRANCE 0

SWEDEN: Isaksson, Granqvist, Mellberg, J. Olsson, M. Olsson, Källström, Larsson, Svensson (Samuel Holmén 79), Ibrahimović (c), Emir Bajrami (Wilhelmsson 46), Toivonen (Pontus Wernbloom 78).

FRANCE: Lloris (c), Debuchy, Clichy, Rami, Mexès, Diarra, M'Vila (Giroud 83), Nasri (Ménez 77), Benzema, Ben Arfa (Malouda 59), Ribéry.

Booked: Svensson (70), Holmén (81), Mexès (68).

9.45pm, 19 June 2012
Donbass Arena, Donetsk
Attendance: 48,700
Referee: Viktor Kassai (Hungary)

ENGLAND 1 (Rooney 48)
UKRAINE 0

ENGLAND: Hart, Johnson, Cole, Lescott, Terry, Gerrard (c), Parker, Milner (Walcott 70), Wayne Rooney (Oxlade-Chamberlain 87), Welbeck (Carroll 82), Young.

UKRAINE: Pyatov, Husyev, Selin, Khacheridi, Yaroslav Rakytskiy, Tymoshchuk (c), Yarmolenko, Denys Harmash (Nazarenko 78), Dević (Shevchenko 70), Milevskiy (Bohdan Butko 77), Konoplyanka.

Booked: Gerrard (73), Cole (78), Tymoshchenko (63), Rakytskiy (74), Shevchenko (86).

GROUP D	P	W	D	L	F	A	GD	Pts
ENGLAND	3	2	1	0	5	3	+2	7
FRANCE	3	1	1	1	3	3	0	4
UKRAINE	3	1	0	2	2	4	− 2	3
SWEDEN	3	1	0	2	5	5	0	3

England and France qualified.

QUARTER-FINALS
Czech Republic v Portugal
Germany v Greece
Spain v France
England v Italy

If Portugal weren't quite pushing at an open door in Warsaw, they were allowed to walk right up to the threshold by the unambitious Czechs, who didn't have a single shot on target all night. The point of this negativity was to suffocate Ronaldo, but it didn't even work.

In the first half alone, he forced Petr Čech into a good save, saw an overhead kick sail wide, and shot against the near post. After the interval, he hit the woodwork for the fourth time in the tournament, with a free kick. It wasn't all Ronaldo, but it was all Portugal: Hugo Almeida headed waywardly wide, and Čech repelled good shots from Nani and Moutinho.

Just as it seemed a repeat of the Euro 96 sucker-punch might be on the cards, quality told. Moutinho, excellent throughout, sent over a great cross and Ronaldo darted in front of Gebre Selassie to bury a diving header. 'We knew we weren't on [Portugal's] level when it comes to football,' said Michal Bílek ruefully.

═══

The gags doing the rounds before Germany's meeting with Greece in Warsaw centred on how many goals Angela Merkel would tell the Greek defence to concede. *Bild*, Germany's biggest tabloid, appealed to its readership's worst instincts with a front page of 'Bye bye Greeks, we can't rescue you today'. Apart from the 1964 final, it's hard to think of another European Championship game that took place in a more delicate political context.

In the whole first half, Greece didn't touch the ball in the German box once. Michalis Sifakis, his gloves seemingly coated in goose-grease, failed to hold efforts by Khedira (twice) and Özil early on, and young Marco Reus missed four reasonable chances before the break.

If Greece could just somehow survive to half-time – but no. Instead, Philipp Lahm took a pass from Özil 25 yards out and turned on to his favoured right foot to hit a zipping, dipping shot beyond Sifakis, evoking memories of his even sexier strike against Costa Rica in the 2006 World Cup. Up in the VIP box, sitting well away from any Greek politicians, Merkel clapped wildly.

But on 55 minutes, Greece delayed the inevitable by doing something very out of character: they counter-attacked. Salpingidis flew down the right and crossed, Jérôme Boateng hesitated and missed it, and Samaras side-footed home off Neuer's hand.

The backlash came quickly as Germany scored three in 13 minutes. First, Boateng's cross was too high for Miro Klose but dropped perfectly for Khedira, who banged it in. Klose, who wore a conflicted expression of pained satisfaction as the ball hit the net, didn't have to wait for long before outjumping Avraam Papadopoulos to head home a set-piece.

Klose was involved in the fourth, too, as Sifakis saved at his feet: Reus finished the job by striding on to the loose ball and leathering it in off the bar. It wasn't hard to see why Germany were coming to be viewed as the great entertainers of Europe, a mantle they hadn't often donned since 1972.

Referee Damir Skomina gave the Greeks a cheap penalty near the end when Torosidis's cross hit Boateng's arm. Salpingidis put it away, then blew a kiss to the fans behind the goal. Greece had been well beaten – but, crucially in this context, not humiliated.

———

France had never lost competitively to Spain before, but the outcome in Donetsk felt predestined. Laurent Blanc predicted that his team would have no more than 33 per cent possession; in the event, they got 45 per cent. In sweltering evening heat, with Spain playing endless intricate triangles around impotent opponents, the game was the sporting equivalent of a disturbed child pulling limbs off an insect until it died.

Blanc picked two right-backs (Mathieu Debuchy and Anthony Réveillère), aiming to neutralise Andrés Iniesta and Jordi Alba on that side. It worked like a dream for 18 minutes. Then Debuchy fatally stumbled, falling in a heap as Alba crossed for Xabi Alonso to score with a downward header. Blanc called it an 'infuriating' goal afterwards.

The rest of the game was painfully bad. The atmosphere, already flat, dwindled to near-stillness. A Mexican wave broke out after half an hour and rippled around the stadium for five minutes. Gerard Piqué headed over the bar, and near the end Lloris flew off his line to deny Fàbregas. Otherwise, it was an interminable exercise in keep-ball, reminiscent of Bob Paisley's Liverpool beating some part-time Scandinavians in their sleep in the early 1980s. France had just one shot, a Cabaye free kick which Casillas turned over the bar.

Alonso (who had earlier tried to score from inside his own half) converted a penalty in stoppage time after Réveillère flattened Pedro, but most people had nodded off by then. Samir Nasri castigated a French journalist afterwards, 'You're looking for shit. You're looking for trouble. Fuck you. There, now you'll be able to say that I've been badly brought up.' The FFF handed him a three-match ban.

Blanc, too, resigned as his team went home 'with their heads bowed' (*Le Monde*) after 'an inglorious defeat' (*France Football*). Jean-Michel Larqué, the midfield heartbeat of the great 1970s Saint-Étienne side, remarked, 'The levels of intellect and talent in this team are catastrophic. Les Bleus are rubbish and stupid.'

———

Gazzetta dello Sport's front page ahead of Italy-England was a mock-up of Daniele De Rossi as James Bond, above the headline '007: Operazione Gerrard', whom De Rossi would be shadowing. In Kiev, the redoubtable Roma midfielder took little time to get involved, hitting a swerving 30-yarder that smacked the inside of the post. England's riposte was immediate: Milner's low cross found Glen Johnson, who scooped it upwards for Buffon to instinctively push it away.

But after that, all Italy, for two long hours. The magisterial Pirlo ran through his full repertoire – threaded 40-yard mega-passes, delicate cushioned lay-offs, wickedly inswinging set-pieces – all while dropping so deep that he sometimes ended up in his own box. Rooney and Welbeck half-heartedly followed him around for a while, then gave up.

One of Pirlo's gems put Balotelli clean through, but the striker took a bad second touch, allowing John Terry to block. Minutes later, Riccardo Montolivo's no-look pass exposed Terry and Balotelli smashed the chance down Hart's throat. Later, Hart pushed away Cassano's venomous shot on the turn, and Lescott's lunge stopped Balotelli scoring under the bar.

In the second half, England kept giving Pirlo time to thread his needlework. When Marchisio's header caught their defence asleep, it fell perfectly for De Rossi to smack a volley wide before burying his head in his hands; and Hart's fine double save from Cassano and Balotelli was followed by Montolivo blootering the rebound too high.

For the final 20 minutes, England simply curled up into a big white ball on the edge of their box. As stoppage time ran out, they eventually had another shot. Carroll headed Cole's cross into the goalmouth, where Rooney was loitering unmarked – but, toppling backwards, he bicycle-kicked miles over.

In extra time, substitute Alessandro Diamanti's cross-shot bounced off the far post with Hart beaten and, late on, Antonio Nocerino's header was disallowed for offside. During the penalty shoot-out, Hart kept jumping around on his line while screaming and pulling crazed faces, but England's charmed life was almost over. Hart didn't get near any of Italy's kicks; even Montolivo's miss was pulled well wide.

Pirlo remarked, 'I saw the goalkeeper was really fired up, and I thought about doing [something different].' He topped off his wonderful performance by gently floating a Panenka down the middle as Hart jumped to the right. It messed with English minds, especially those of the two

Ashleys: Young's kick cannoned off the bar, and Buffon easily saved Cole's scared little shot.

At 12.24am local time, Diamanti (a penalty king at West Ham in 2010/11) stepped up. Again Hart went through his daft bogeyman routine, this time sticking his tongue out. Much good it did him. England were out, their inadequacy summed up by the stat that Hart touched the ball more times than any of their outfielders.

Prandelli and his assistant Demetrio Albertini now walked through the night to visit a monastery near their training ground in Wieliczka: they had agreed to celebrate each Italian win with pilgrimages to religious sites. On this evidence, there might be more to come.

8.45pm, 21 June 2012
Stadion Narodowy, Warsaw
Attendance: 55,590
Referee: Howard Webb (England)

PORTUGAL 1 (Ronaldo 79)
CZECH REPUBLIC 0

PORTUGAL: Rui Patrício, João Pereira, Alves, Pepe, Coentrão, Meireles (Rolando 88), Veloso, Moutinho, Postiga (Hugo Almeida 40), Ronaldo (c), Nani (Custódio 84).

CZECH REPUBLIC: Čech (c), Gebre Selassie, Limberský, Sivok, Kadlec, Hübschman (Pekhart 86), Plašil, Jiráček, Baroš, Vladimír Darida (Rezek 61), Pilař.

Booked: Nani (26), Veloso (27), Limberský (90).

8.45pm, 22 June 2012
PGE Arena, Gdańsk
Attendance: 38,751
Referee: Damir Skomina (Slovenia)

GERMANY 4 (Lahm 39, Khedira 61, Klose 68, Reus 74)
GREECE 2 (Samaras 55, Salpingidis 89 pen)

GERMANY: Neuer, Boateng, Lahm (c), Badstuber, Hummels, Khedira, Schweinsteiger, Marco Reus (Mario Götze 80), Schürrle (Müller 67), Özil, Klose (Gómez 80).

GREECE: Sifakis, Torosidis, Tzavelas (Fotakis 46), Papastathopoulos, K. Papadopoulos, Katsouranis (c), Maniatis, Makos (Nikos Lyberopoulos 72), Samaras, Salpingidis, Ninis (Gekas 46).

Booked: Samaras (14), Papastathopoulos (75).

9.45pm, 23 June 2012
Donbass Arena, Donetsk
Attendance: 47,000
Referee: Nicola Rizzoli (Italy)

SPAIN 2 (Alonso 19, 90+1 pen)
FRANCE 0

SPAIN: Casillas (c), Arbeloa, Alba, Ramos, Piqué, Xavi, Busquets, Alonso, Silva (Pedro Rodríguez 65), Iniesta (Cazorla 84), Fàbregas (Torres 67).

FRANCE: Lloris (c), Anthony Réveillère, Clichy, Rami, Laurent Koscielny, M'Vila (Giroud 79), Cabaye, Malouda (Nasri 65), Benzema, Ribéry, Debuchy (Ménez 64).

Booked: Ramos (31), Cabaye (42), Ménez (76).

9.45pm, 24 June 2012
Olimpiyskiy Natsionalnyi Sportivnyi Kompleks, Kiev
Attendance: 64,340
Referee: Pedro Proença (Portugal)

ITALY 0
ENGLAND 0
Italy won 4-2 on penalties after extra time
Shoot-out: Balotelli 1-0, Gerrard 1-1, Montolivo shot wide, Rooney 2-1, Pirlo 2-2, Young hit bar, Nocerino 3-2, Cole saved, Diamanti 4-2.

ITALY: Buffon (c), Abate (Maggio 90+1), Bonucci, Barzagli, Balzaretti, De Rossi (Nocerino 80), Montolivo, Marchisio, Balotelli, Pirlo, Cassano (Diamanti 78).

ENGLAND: Hart, Johnson, Cole, Lescott, Terry, Gerrard (c), Parker (Henderson 94), Milner (Walcott 61), Welbeck (Carroll 60), Rooney, Young.

Booked: Barzagli (82), Maggio (93).

SEMI-FINALS
Spain v Portugal
Germany v Italy

The Donbass Arena was dotted with unfilled seats for the first semi-final, another gruesome match involving Spain. In two hours, Rui Patrício and Iker Casillas would make just four meaningful saves between them.

João Moutinho was again outstanding, but Portugal hardly went forward. Spain, stuck in their infinite passing loop, tried two shots in the entire first half, one from Arbeloa and another from Iniesta, both of which went over. Ronaldo did the same at the other end, then drilled another into the side-netting. Hot stuff.

Not until the last minute was there some excitement. Portugal broke upfield, four on two, but when Raul Meireles put the chance on a plate for Ronaldo, he clubbed it too high.

Portugal's big chance had gone; Spain's arrived in extra time. Alba burst into the box and crossed to find Iniesta, six yards out. The playmaker swung a tired right leg at it and saw Rui Patrício fall on it.

The penalties were a relief. Rui Patrício parried Alonso's opening kick, but Moutinho then hit his penalty straight at Casillas. Meanwhile, Ramos, of all people, scored with another Panenka homage. Del Bosque, admitted, 'I had no idea he was going to do that.'

Portugal's stony-faced stopper Bruno Alves had enjoyed a fine tournament, so of course he was the one to miss, nearly breaking the crossbar. The cameras now focused on an anguished-looking Ronaldo, who was down for Portugal's fifth kick. But if Spain scored their next one, Portugal wouldn't get to take another. So it proved, as Fàbregas shot in off the post.

Not for the first time, Ronaldo's glory-hunter tendencies had blown up in his face. But who's to say he would have scored anyway? Weeks earlier, in the Champions League semi-final, he had missed for Real Madrid against Bayern Munich. Small consolation that Portugal had shown Spain could be hustled out of their seamless stride.

Down all Germany's decades of success, there's one thing they have never managed to do: defeat Italy in a competitive match. They would fail to do it again in Warsaw, with paralysis gripping them when the chips were down.

The game is remembered for Mario Balotelli's double KO in the first half, by some distance the highlight of his career. What's forgotten is that Germany might have been three up before he scored. First, Kroos's corner landed on Hummels's knee and was going in before Pirlo's thigh (or arm, suggested one camera angle) knocked it off the line.

Germany kept pressing. When Boateng's cross created confusion in Italy's goalmouth, Buffon pushed it against Andera Barzagli's legs and was relieved to see it bobble behind. Kroos then let fly from 25 yards, and the goalkeeper needed both hands to repel it.

Italy reeled under the pressure, but suddenly hit Germany with a sucker-punch. Pirlo's raking pass began the move, and Cassano wriggled away from Hummels too easily before crossing. In the middle, Balotelli rose above the sluggish Badstuber and headed it past Neuer.

Hummels, a fine technician but not always a commanding defender, was soon shown up again. As he ambled 40 yards away from where he should have been, Montolivo's long ball over the top caught him and Lahm exposed. Balotelli raced away, bore down on goal, then lashed a shot into the top corner as Neuer fell helplessly on one knee. His Greek-statue celebration, tearing off his shirt, cost him a booking.

In the second half, Germany left so much space behind them that they might have been thrashed. Balotelli almost claimed a hat-trick when shooting across the goal, Marchisio wasted two opportunities to kill the game off, and Di Natale put another golden chance into the side-netting after running through a near-deserted German half.

In stoppage time, the Germans got a lucky penalty when Federico Balzaretti chested the ball on to his own arm while Klose was pulling his shirt. The otherwise invisible Özil tucked away the kick, but it was too late.

'This young man is called Italy,' Maurizio Crosetti wrote of Balotelli in *La Repubblica* the next morning, 'because Italy is now also a black man.' Given how his career panned out, it's hard to believe now that he was once seen as a shining young star of the European game – chiefly on the strength of this match, the only time he truly justified the hype.

For Germany, there were recriminations after another bloodless semi-final defeat. 'Can we still believe in Jogi?' *Bild am Sonntag* asked. But the DFB stood by their man. Like Franz Beckenbauer after Euro 88, Löw learned a few things from this one, and led Germany to their fourth World Cup in Rio two years later.

9.45pm, 27 June 2012
Donbass Arena, Donetsk
Attendance: 48,000
Referee: Cüneyt Çakır (Turkey)

SPAIN 0
PORTUGAL 0
Spain won 4-2 on penalties after extra time
Shoot-out: Alonso saved, Moutinho saved, Iniesta 1-0, Pepe 1-1, Piqué 2-1, Nani 2-2, Ramos 3-2, Alves hit bar, Fàbregas 4-2.

SPAIN: Casillas (c), Arbeloa, Alba, Ramos, Piqué, Xavi (Pedro 87), Busquets, Alonso, Negredo (Fàbregas 54), Iniesta, Silva (Navas 60).

PORTUGAL: Rui Patrício, João Pereira, Alves, Pepe, Coentrão, Meireles (Varela 113), Veloso (Custódio 106), Moutinho, Almeida (Nélson 81), Ronaldo (c), Nani.

Booked: Ramos (40), Busquets (60), Árbeloa (84), Alonso (113), Coentrão (45), Pepe (61), João Pereira (64), Alves (86), Veloso (90+3).

8.45pm, 28 June 2012
Stadion Narodowy, Warsaw
Attendance: 55,540
Referee: Stéphane Lannoy (France)

ITALY 2 (Balotelli 20, 36)
GERMANY 1 (Özil 90+2 pen)

ITALY: Buffon (c), Balzaretti, Chiellini, Bonucci, Barzagli, De Rossi, Montolivo (Motta 64), Marchisio, Balotelli (Di Natale 70), Pirlo, Cassano (Diamanti 58).

GERMANY: Neuer, Boateng (Müller 71), Lahm (c), Badstuber, Hummels, Khedira, Schweinsteiger, Kroos, Gómez (Klose 46), Özil, Podolski (Reus 46).

Booked: Balotelli (37), Bonucci (61), De Rossi (84), Motta (89), Hummels (90+4).

FINAL
Spain v Italy

Hours before the final in Kiev, Arsène Wenger wrote in his column for Eurosport.com that Spain had 'betrayed their philosophy and turned it into something more negative: [their possession game] now seems to be first and foremost a way not to lose'. But a surprise was in store.

Creatively clogged up until now, Spain sprang for Italy's throat like a mongoose, strangling Pirlo so ruthlessly that he lost possession a staggering 18 times. A sumptuous move created their opening goal. Iniesta split Italy's defence with a scalpelled ball to Fàbregas, who beat Chiellini to the byline and saw his cross headed in by the Mowgli-like David Silva.

Italy got stuck in a cycle of losing the ball, waiting ages to get it back, then surrendering it again. They soon lost Chiellini to a thigh injury, and while the top-knotted Balzaretti was a quality replacement, it meant Prandelli used up a substitute at a very early stage – which would have consequences later on.

Italy briefly got a foothold in the match as Casillas saved two shots from Cassano, but Spain promptly stepped on the gas again. Alba played a one-two with Xavi and ran on to a fabulous return pass which took out three Italians. Alba didn't give Buffon the chance to close him down, clipping his shot early and low around the goalkeeper.

In the opening minute of the second half, substitute Di Natale almost had Italy back in it, guiding his header too high from Abate's cross. Within minutes, he wasted their second and final big chance, served up by Montolivo. Ramos let him get away and Piqué was nowhere to be seen, but he drove his shot at Casillas and could only poke the rebound at the goalkeeper.

As his team wilted, Prandelli brought on his final sub. But Thiago Motta tore his hamstring almost immediately, forcing Italy to see out the match with ten men. In what was now effectively a training session, they held out until the 84th minute, when substitute Fernando Torres latched on to Xavi's magnificent pass and slid the ball under Buffon for 3-0.

And now it really was all over: Italy had never managed to score three in a European Championship finals match, and weren't going to do it now. With two minutes left, as Buffon dived at Torres's feet, he slipped it to yet another sub, Juan Mata, who knocked it into a gaping net to surpass West Germany's record final-winning margin in 1972.

Spain were the first team to retain the trophy. But how good were they? At the time, they seemed untouchable. Xavi and Iniesta were among the true greats, Alonso, Busquets and Silva excellent lieutenants, Alba a star in the making. In fact, they had already peaked: their humiliations at Dutch and Chilean hands in the 2014 World Cup revised plenty of opinions, and Italy would take painful revenge on them at Euro 2016. Still, nobody could get ahead of them for now. Their waves of passing (nearly 700 per match) were awesome yet distinctly sterile. Aesthetes saw them as lifting football to a new plane of perfection; others denounced them as purveyors of soulless, technical tedium. The truth was somewhere in between.

Overall, eastern Europe's first international tournament since 1976 had been a middling mixed bag. Not one game was a dead rubber, the smooth organisation had made light of all the scare stories, the fears of widespread racism staining the event hadn't been realised, and the refereeing was largely sensible, give or take the occasional Velasco Carballo. But uniformity was the order of the day, with well-drilled sides neutralising each other (only Ireland had looked out of place). And we hadn't seen a single great game.

That said, with eight more teams and 20 extra matches on the way in four years' time, many suspected 2012 might be the last half-decent European Championship for a while. If it ain't broke, break it.

9.45pm, 1 July 2012
Olimpiyskiy Natsionalnyi Sportivnyi Kompleks, Kiev
Attendance: 63,170
Referee: Pedro Proença (Portugal)

SPAIN 4 (Silva 14, Alba 41, Torres 84, Mata 88)
ITALY 0

SPAIN: Casillas (c), Arbeloa, Alba, Ramos, Piqué, Xavi, Busquets, Alonso, Fàbregas (Torres 75), Iniesta (Juan Mata 87), Silva (Pedro 59).

ITALY: Buffon (c), Abate, Bonucci, Barzagli, Chiellini (Balzaretti 21), De Rossi, Montolivo (Motta 57), Marchisio, Balotelli, Pirlo, Cassano (Di Natale 46).

Booked: Piqué (25), Barzagli (44).

2016

OUT ON his ear as UEFA president by the time it kicked off, Michel Platini's fingerprints were nonetheless all over the hollow edifice of Euro 2016. The tournament mushroomed to 24 teams, and the first 36 matches would shave off just eight of them, using the dreaded 'four best third-placed teams' format of Italia 90. But *Platoche*, brought down by the FIFA corruption scandal in October 2015, would be absent from the party in his homeland. Distraught in the wake of his career being destroyed, yet reluctant to provoke further conflict with UEFA, he tearfully struck himself off the guest list of the event he lovingly called 'my baby'.

France's own chances of emulating Platini's 1984 vintage looked unclear: too many good attackers to accommodate, not enough quality defenders. And Didier Deschamps, winner of this tournament as captain in 2000, didn't seem a natural fit as manager, especially after a disappointing 2014 World Cup in which his team bloodlessly succumbed to Germany in the quarter-finals.

Defending champions Spain entered the fray looking weaker than they had done in a decade, after a feeble defence of their world title in Brazil, but Vicente Del Bosque had enough credit in the bank to stay on as manager. Excepting Xavi and David Villa, all the legends were still around, with the untouchable Andrés Iniesta first among equals. Still, Spain looked vulnerable if you could get in behind their slow defence.

Like Spain, England endured a rotten World Cup – but with no plausible alternative available, Roy Hodgson stayed on. All the false gods of the past decade were either gone or out of gas. After a series of experiments involving Jordan Henderson, Jack Wilshere, Michael Carrick, James Milner, Ross Barkley and Jonjo Shelvey, the old firm of Steven Gerrard and Frank Lampard were ultimately replaced by Dele Alli and Eric Dier, who had played 25 minutes between them in the qualifiers.

Germany's defeats in Dublin and Warsaw suggested that some of their players had yet to stagger out of the VIP lounge after winning the World Cup in Rio. But despite losing the imperious Philipp Lahm and goal machine Miroslav Klose, Jogi Löw still presided over vast resources: superstars like Toni Kroos, Mesut Özil and Thomas Müller, the exciting attacker Julian Draxler, and a seemingly ready-made replacement for Lahm in Joshua Kimmich. With good ball-players in every position, Germany looked the team to beat.

The same couldn't be said for Italy, who turned up with an even thinner-looking squad than in 2012. Manager Antonio Conte all but admitted they were a poor side. 'This isn't a good moment for our football,' he told the Italian public. 'Please stay close to the team. It's important for the players to feel your trust in them.' Italy looked like sitting ducks in their opening game against a Belgian team which had so much quality (Eden Hazard, Jan Vertonghen, Kevin De Bruyne, Thibaut Courtois) that they looked certainties for at least the semis, even if Marc Wilmots was an unconvincing manager.

The tournament's expansion threw up some Cinderella stories. Wales and Northern Ireland both made their Euro debuts, meaning that Gareth Bale and, erm, Kyle Lafferty would get to play in a major tournament at last. Albania qualified with the aid of a bizarre 3-0 walkover away to Serbia, in a match interrupted by a drone wrapped in an Albanian flag. And the debut of Iceland, who were reaping the rewards of huge investment in coaching and facilities, put everything else in the shade. Their population of 335,000 made them the smallest country ever to qualify for a major tournament. Among their victims in the qualifiers were the Netherlands, who crashed and burned barely 15 months after almost reaching the 2014 World Cup Final.

But all this was an irrelevance next to the threat posed to Euro 2016 by some of the most dangerous people on earth. On 13 November 2015, while France played Germany in a friendly in Saint-Denis, three suicide bombings by Islamic State took place outside the Stade de France, mercifully claiming only one other life. Elsewhere in Paris, gunmen were massacring 89 people at a rock concert and dozens more at various nightspots.

Four months later, more suicide attacks killed 34 people in Brussels. UEFA vice-president Giancarlo Abete speculated gloomily that the tournament might be played behind closed doors: 'Euro 2016 is the kind of event we can't delay or postpone.' It didn't happen, but the fact that the idea had been aired at all spoke volumes.

GROUP A
France, Romania, Albania, Switzerland

Its thumb on the pulse as usual, UEFA decreed that 'This One's for You', a blast of anodyne Eurotrance by David Guetta, would be the sound of Euro 2016. It blared out before and after every match, whether anyone wanted to hear it or not, and got its first airing during a florid opening ceremony before the hosts and Romania opened the ball at the Stade de France.

Romania were seen as cardboard cut-outs for the hosts to rip apart, with a squad based either at home or in backwaters like Israel, Qatar and La Liga 2. But they should have scored the first goal of Euro 2016 after four minutes. When Florin Andone flicked on Nicolae Stanciu's corner, Bogdan Stancu met it at the far post, blasting the ball into goalkeeper Hugo Lloris's midriff.

Thereafter, France's stars were a no-show. Antoine Griezmann vanished after heading against the post, and the heavily hyped Paul Pogba (who had the FFF logo shaved into the side of his head) kept giving the ball away. Romania began the second half with Stancu wasting another great chance, chesting down Stanciu's chip before wafting a soft shot wide.

Before the hour, they paid for his wastefulness when Olivier Giroud got his head to Dimitri Payet's looping cross before goalkeeper Ciprian Tătărușanu, glancing it home. But Romania deservedly drew level when Stanciu was tripped by Patrice Evra's lazy leg. Stancu, shrugging off the burden of his earlier misses, calmly converted the penalty.

France lost their way badly in the final stages, and there was barely a minute of normal time left when Payet suddenly stepped away from Hoban, ignored four more Romanians around him and belted a jewel of a shot into the top corner to win the match. Didier Deschamps breathed out, then immediately substituted the weeping Payet. Harsh on Romania, but they looked good enough to escape this group.

The meeting of Switzerland and Albania in Lens resembled the social media meme where two identical Spider-Men point accusingly at each other. Five of the Swiss line-up had Albanian or Kosovan ancestry, while nearly half Albania's team were born or raised in Switzerland. There was even a Xhaka brother on either side: Granit for Switzerland and Taulant for Albania.

On their tournament debut, the Albanians got off to the most demoralising of starts. Xherdan Shaqiri floated over a corner, goalkeeper Etrit Berisha came out waving to his mother, and Fabian Schär nodded home a simple header. Berisha commendably shrugged it off, making four fine saves from Haris Seferović alone: two one-on-ones, a near-post block and a good one-handed stop. But by half-time, Albania had lost their captain.

Lorik Cana slipped, then handled the ball on the ground, and out came a second yellow card.

Though Blerim Džemaili's free kick later hit the post, Switzerland looked ordinary. And Albania had little luck. Just before Cana's red card, Swiss left-back Ricardo Rodríguez stamped on Elseid Hysaj, warranting a straight red from referee Carlos Velasco Carballo, who didn't even show a yellow. Later, he missed Stephan Lichtsteiner pole-axeing Ermir Lenjani in the box.

Justice was almost done near the end. Amir Abrashi's pass put substitute Shkëlzen Gashi through, but he hesitated and Swiss goalkeeper Yann Sommer pushed his shot over the bar. A let-off for Switzerland, especially Shaqiri, who had seemed to let the Albanian fans' relentless booing get to him.

= = =

Surprisingly, Iordănescu made four changes for Romania's meeting with Switzerland in Paris. Dropping the impressive Stanciu seemed particularly ill-advised, and again a lack of a cutting edge let them down.

Seferović, profligate again, missed two chances before Romania went ahead with another penalty. Lichtsteiner, a serial offender, was caught yellow-handed holding Alexandru Chipciu's shirt. Stancu slipped as he hit the spot-kick, but it went in.

In beautiful sunshine, Romania couldn't build on their lead. Chipciu cut inside Lichtsteiner before shooting wide, Săpunaru's shot nicked a defender and grazed the post, Hoban had a close-range shot blocked, and Johan Djourou almost knocked Gabriel Torje's cross into his own net.

Switzerland made the most of these let-offs. When Romania didn't deal with a corner, the ball dropped for Admir Mehmedi, whose left foot leathered it in. Manager Vladimir Petković missed the goal because he had his back turned organising the instantly aborted substitution of Mehmedi. 'I'm told it was excellent,' he said.

Iordănescu later bollocked a Romanian journalist ('You're just lying, it's misinformation') over a report that striker Denis Alibec had smoked a cigarette before coming on as a sub against France. The Romanian press weren't finished with Alibec yet.

= = =

Everything was set up for France to annihilate Albania, but they suffered more big-night jitters in Marseille. Although Deschamps dropped Pogba and Griezmann, replacements Anthony Martial and Kingsley Coman were no better, and his team were turgid and tentative on a pitch that cut up badly.

'You're playing in a Euros, not a friendly. You have to give more,' Deschamps exhorted his players at the break. But early in the second half, Albania almost overturned the table when Ledian Memushaj nudged the ball on to a post. It's tempting to wonder how nervous hosts struggling for fluency would have reacted to falling behind.

When Giroud headed against the woodwork, French president François Hollande visibly winced in the VIP box; with two minutes left, Pogba slipped at the crucial moment after N'Golo Kanté played him in. But soon afterwards, the tiring Albanians allowed Rami to cross from the right, and nobody picked up the substitute Griezmann as he headed home. A real sickener.

It was France's first attempt on target. They scored with their second, too. Deep into stoppage time, André-Pierre Gignac's lay-off found Payet, who stepped inside Taulant Xhaka and swept a fine shot low into the corner. 'Génie ou chanceux, Didier Deschamps?' asked one French newspaper headline. Genius or lucky?

———

That left a simple task for Romania: beat Albania. But in Lyon, they turned in one of their worst ever performances, again not helped by weak refereeing. When Albanian defender Migjen Basha lived up to his surname by karate-kicking Hoban's shoulder, Pavel Královec merely booked him.

Regardless, Romania were always second best and deserved to lose to Albania's first goal in a tournament. When Andi Lila crossed, Armando Sadiku gave Vlad Chiricheş the slip and nodded it back across Tătăruşanu and in. A moment in a million for a tiny country who had never been here before.

The 36-year-old Lucian Sânmărteăn, Romania's most talented player, came on but vanished in the face of relentless tackling. Though Andone's long shot clipped the bar, Albania deservedly saw it out. Thanks to Euro 2016's stupid format, they had to wait for several days to find out they were gone, but they could look back at this maiden voyage with considerable pride.

Afterwards, Iordănescu castigated a reporter who hyperbolically accused him of presiding over 'the shame of the century', replying, 'I'm not sure you've done anything constructive in your life. Let the Romanian press judge me.' Judge him they did, not least the legendary László Bölöni, who also tore into Alibec: 'He's a disgrace. He's fat, slow and stinks of laziness.' Let's hope that cigarette was worth it.

———

Simultaneously, in Lille, an eventful opening almost saw Paul Pogba score four times against Switzerland – three at the right end. After almost scoring an own goal before Johan Djourou helpfully fell in the way, he tested Yann Sommer twice with strong shots, then hit an even harder one which rattled the bar. Schär later cleared Laurent Koscielny's header off the line; but with the game dying of self-inflicted asphyxia, the second half was an informal détente pact, enlivened only by the ball bursting when Valon Behrami tackled Griezmann, and by Payet crashing a volley off the bar.

Embarrassingly for Switzerland's kitmakers Puma, the shirts of Xhaka (twice), Mehmedi and Embolo all tore like toilet paper during the game, prompting Shaqiri to joke that he hoped they didn't make condoms. Meanwhile, France had worn a new kit designed overnight by Nike, because their away strip's blue/red shoulders contravened UEFA's regulations. Four torn shirts, one kit change, one burst ball – and no goals.

9pm, 10 June 2016
Stade de France, Saint-Denis
Attendance: 75,113
Referee: Viktor Kassai (Hungary)

FRANCE 2 (Giroud 57, Payet 89)
ROMANIA 1 (Stancu 65 pen)

FRANCE: Hugo Lloris (c), Bacary Sagna, Patrice Evra, Adil Rami, Laurent Koscielny, N'Golo Kanté, Blaise Matuidi, Paul Pogba (Anthony Martial 77), Olivier Giroud, Antoine Griezmann (Kingsley Coman 66), Dimitri Payet (Moussa Sissoko 90+2). **Manager:** Didier Deschamps.

ROMANIA: Ciprian Tătărușanu, Cristian Săpunaru, Răzvan Raț, Dragoș Grigore, Vlad Chicheș (c), Ovidiu Hoban, Mihai Pintilii, Adrian Popa (Gabriel Torje 82), Bogdan Stancu, Nicolae Stanciu (Alexandru Chipciu 72), Florin Andone (Denis Alibec 61). **Manager:** Anghel Iordănescu.

Booked: Giroud (69), Chicheș (32), Raț (45), Popa (78).

3pm, 11 June 2016
Stade Bollaert-Delelis, Lens
Attendance: 33,805
Referee: Carlos Velasco Carballo (Spain)

SWITZERLAND 1 (Schär 5)
ALBANIA 0

SWITZERLAND: Yann Sommer, Stephan Lichtsteiner (c), Johan Djourou, Fabian Schär, Ricardo Rodríguez, Granit Xhaka, Valon Behrami, Blerim Džemaili (Fabian Frei 75), Haris Seferović, Xherdan Shaqiri (Gelson Fernandes 88), Admir Mehmedi (Breel Embolo 62). **Manager:** Vladimir Petković.

ALBANIA: Etrit Berisha, Elseid Hysaj, Ansi Agolli, Mërgim Mavraj, Lorik Cana (c), Burim Kukeli, Amir Abrashi, Odise Roshi (Sokol Çikalleshi 74), Armando Sadiku (Shkëlzen Gashi 82), Taulant Xhaka (Ergys Kaçe 62), Ermir Lenjani. **Manager:** Gianni De Biasi.

Booked: Schär (14), Behrami (67), Cana (23), Kaçe (63), Kukeli (89), Mavraj (90+2). Sent off: Cana (36).

6pm, 15 June 2016
Parc des Princes, Paris
Attendance: 43,576
Referee: Sergei Karasev (Russia)

ROMANIA 1 (Stancu 18 pen)
SWITZERLAND 1 (Mehmedi 57)

ROMANIA: Tătărușanu, Săpunaru, Raţ (Steliano Filip 62), Grigore, Chiricheş (c), Andrei Prepeliţă, Torje, Pintilii (Hoban 46), Stancu (Andone 84), Chipciu, Claudiu Keşerü.

SWITZERLAND: Sommer, Lichtsteiner (c), Djourou, Schär, Rodríguez, Xhaka, Behrami, Džemaili (Michael Lang 83), Seferović (Embolo 63), Shaqiri (Shani Tarashaj 90+1), Mehmedi.

Booked: Prepeliţă (22), Chipciu (24), Keşerü (37), Grigore (76), Xhaka (51), Embolo (90+4).

9pm, 15 June 2016
Stade Vélodrome, Marseille
Attendance: 63,670
Referee: Willie Collum (Scotland)

FRANCE 2 (Griezmann 90, Payet 90+6)
ALBANIA 0

FRANCE: Lloris (c), Sagna, Evra, Rami, Koscielny, Kanté, Matuidi, Martial (Pogba 46), Giroud (André-Pierre Gignac 77), Coman (Griezmann 68), Payet.

ALBANIA: Berisha, Hysaj, Agolli (c), Mavraj, Arlind Ajeti (Frédéric Veseli 85), Kukeli (Xhaka 74), Andi Lila (Roshi 71), Abrashi, Sadiku, Ledian Memushaj, Lenjani.

Booked: Kanté (88), Kukeli (55), Abrashi (81).

9pm, 19 June 2016
Parc Olympique Lyonnais, Lyon
Attendance: 49,752
Referee: Pavel Královec (Czech Republic)

ALBANIA 1 (Sadiku 43)
ROMANIA 0

ALBANIA: Berisha, Hysaj, Agolli (c), Mavraj, Ajeti, Migjen Basha (Cana 83), Lila, Abrashi, Sadiku (Bekim Balaj 59), Memushaj, Lenjani (Roshi 77).

ROMANIA: Tătărușanu, Săpunaru, Alexandru Măţel, Grigore, Chiricheş (c), Prepeliţă (Lucian Sânmarteăn 46), Hoban, Popa (Andone 68), Stancu, Stanciu, Alibec (Torje 57).

Booked: Basha (6), Memushaj (85), Hysaj (90+4), Măţel (54), Săpunaru (85), Torje (90+3).

9pm, 19 June 2016
Stade Pierre-Mauroy, Lille
Attendance: 45,616
Referee: Damir Skomina (Slovenia)

FRANCE 0
SWITZERLAND 0

FRANCE: Lloris (c), Sagna, Evra, Rami, Koscielny, Yohan Cabaye, Sissoko, Pogba, Gignac, Griezmann (Matuidi 77), Coman (Payet 63).

SWITZERLAND: Sommer, Lichtsteiner (c), Djourou, Schär, Rodríguez, Xhaka, Behrami, Džemaili, Embolo (Seferović 74), Shaqiri (Fernandes 79), Mehmedi (Lang 86).

Booked: Rami (25), Koscielny (83).

GROUP A	P	W	D	L	F	A	GD	Pts
FRANCE	3	2	1	0	4	1	+3	7
SWITZERLAND	3	1	2	0	2	1	+1	5
ALBANIA	3	1	0	2	1	3	− 2	3
ROMANIA	3	0	1	2	2	4	− 2	1

France and Switzerland qualified.

GROUP B
England, Russia, Wales, Slovakia

In Bordeaux, the media hyped Wales's clash with Slovakia as a duel between a man-bun and a mohawk. Slovakia's manager Jan Kozák talked up the talents of Marek Hamšík, then tried some mind games on Gareth Bale: 'He'll be tough to play against. I should know, I'm a Real Madrid fan. But I won't be asking for his autograph.'

Hamšík landed the first blow, helped by Bale dawdling in possession out wide. He robbed the Real Madrid man, slalomed around four more Welshmen and shot past goalkeeper Danny Ward before Ben Davies booted it off the line.

Brilliant defending, which soon looked even better. As Bale bent a free kick over Slovakia's wall, goalkeeper Matúš Kozáčik stepped sideways, leaving a fatal gap for the ball to drift over the line. Wales's remarkable tournament was on its way.

The match should have been ten-a-side by half-time. Neil Taylor went in studs-up on Hamšík, yet referee Svein Oddvar Moen waved play on; Martin Škrtel thuggishly elbowed Jonny Williams in the head for a clear penalty and red card, but escaped sanction.

Slovakia improved after the break, equalising when Robert Mak fed substitute Ondrej Duda, who had come on 50 seconds earlier: the new man dummied, evaded Ashley Williams and shot into the corner. Wales were wobbling, but their fans' misty-eyed choruses of 'Land of My Fathers' gave them a second wind, and substitute Hal Robson-Kanu shinned the ball in for a messy winner after Ramsey glided past Škrtel.

Wales clung on, surviving Adam Nemec's late diving header against the post, for their first tournament win since 1958. Kozák mused, 'I don't think they were better. They had more luck.' Close, but no autographs.

=====

Eighteen years on from France 98, England's lunatic fringe again made their presence felt in Marseille in the days before their opener against Russia, lobbing bottles at riot police at the Vieux Port. Then, hours before the match, hundreds of Russians – wearing ski masks, gumshields and Premier League jerseys as disguises – laid into anyone in their path with baseball bats and telescopic truncheons, in a preview of later events at the Vélodrome.

Roy Hodgson used the fading Wayne Rooney in midfield, but his resources were plentiful compared to his Russian counterpart. Leonid Slutsky, who looked like a salty old seadog propping up a bar in Vladivostok, was being paid expenses only by the Russian FA. After cleaning up Fabio Capello's mess in the qualifiers, his plans were destroyed when his midfield kingpins Igor Denisov and Alan Dzagoev got injured before the tournament, hugely weakening an already thin squad.

England should have buried them, but the best chances fell to the less than ruthless Adam Lallana, who saw a shot parried by the impressive Igor Akinfeev and another go wide. Rooney, playing surprisingly well in midfield, brought two more fine saves from the goalkeeper with powerfully struck shots.

Eventually, England broke through: Georgi Shchennikov fouled Dele Alli outside the box, and Eric Dier thumped the free kick into the top corner. They should have kicked on, but Hodgson's ill-judged substitutions killed their momentum. And in stoppage time, Russia suddenly found a equaliser: Shchennikov crossed, and Vasily Berezutsky outjumped Danny Rose and Alli to score with a looping header as Joe Hart stood and watched.

At the final whistle, balaclava-wearing Russians charged into an English-occupied section to wreak havoc. On TV, Hart was seen telling fans behind his goal to 'be safe'; most fled for the exits. Down on the pitch, Vitaly Mutko, the Russian sports minister, saluted his marauding countrymen with a clenched fist. Russia got off lightly, receiving a €150,000 fine and a threat of expulsion if more violence occurred.

––––

Four days later, there were more unappealing scenes as Russian and Slovakian fans fought on the streets of Lille. Rainy weather saw the Stade Pierre-Mauroy's roof closed with the floodlights on for a 3pm kick-off.

The running battle between two huge men, Russia's striker Artyom Dzyuba and Slovakia's defensive pillar Jan Ďurica, lent a compelling subplot to an otherwise awful match. Eventually, Hamšík injected some class with an excellent ball down the left to Vladimír Weiss, who fooled Berezutsky and Igor Smolnikov before belting a shot into the far corner.

Hamšík then scored a splendid second, taking the ball at a short corner, beating Oleg Shatov and thrashing a heatseeker in off the far post. Once again, though, Russia shook themselves awake late on, as substitute Denis Glushakov spectacularly headed home Shatov's cross. Near the end, Glushakov blasted just wide, and Dzyuba looked certain to score before Tomáš

Hubočan intervened. Slovakia grimly ran down the clock and celebrated with obvious relief.

=====

By the time England faced Wales in Lens, Joe Hart was cock of the walk again. ITV's cameras captured him in the tunnel before kick-off, shouting, 'Come on, boys. Pride! Get that ball! Move that fucking ball.' Pride, as usual, came before a fall.

Wales survived an early scare when Raheem Sterling ineptly shot over from close range. But now Hart's tournament lurched from embarrassing to disastrous. After Rooney fouled Robson-Kanu almost 40 yards out, Bale shooting from there seemed pointless, but he had a go anyway. Hart got a hand on the ball but it squirted pitifully over the line. The kind of clanger that derails entire careers.

At the interval, Hodgson rejigged his strike pairing, replacing Kane and Sterling with Jamie Vardy and Daniel Sturridge. His boldness quickly paid off. Sturridge crossed, Ashley Williams botched a defensive header and the ball came to Vardy, who gobbled up the equaliser.

England went for Wales's throat. Ben Davies got away with a handball in the box, Rooney and Gary Cahill had shots blocked, and Sturridge miscued a good chance. Finally, in stoppage time, young Marcus Rashford flicked the ball to Sturridge, who poked it in off goalkeeper Wayne Hennessey's leg. Wales felt sorry for themselves, but they had conceded two bad goals and played too deep.

=====

Against Slovakia in Saint-Étienne, Hodgson made six changes, but England remained lumpy. New right-back Nathaniel Clyne overlapped well, but his good work was wasted as Vardy, Sturridge and Lallana all missed chances.

The narrowest squeak came on the hour, Škrtel clearing Dele Alli's half-volley off the line. England themselves survived a fright when Chris Smalling weakly chested the ball back to Hart and Róbert Mak almost nipped in to score, but Slovakia didn't really deserve 0-0, let alone a win.

'Sooner or later, we'll get the reward for our play,' Hodgson growled. 'Someone might find themselves on the end of a tough result. Soon we'll make someone pay.' Meanwhile, Hart brought a social media scalding upon himself when he waffled, 'Nobody will want to play us. I haven't had anything to do in the whole tournament, to be honest.'

=====

Thirteen years after Wales were deprived of a place at Euro 2004 by Russia in sour circumstances, they took delicious revenge in Toulouse against the worst team in the competition. First, Joe Allen hit a simple pass down the middle, Sam Vokes dummied, and Ramsey ran through the ruins of Russia's defence to lift it over Akinfeev.

Wales's second goal was even cheaper. Bale, running into Russian territory, drew six white shirts into his orbit. Shirokov kicked the ball off his toe, but it went straight to Neil Taylor, who blasted the chance at Akinfeev before converting the rebound.

With Wales rampant, Akinfeev saved with his legs from Vokes after Bale beat three men, and Bale himself put an easy header over the bar. At half-time, Vasily Berezutsky was replaced by his twin Aleksei (on their 34th birthday), but Wales finished Russia off when Ramsey found Bale, whose shot hit Akinfeev before sailing in. 'Geographically, we're small,' said manager Chris Coleman, 'but if you're judging us on passion, we could be described as a continent tonight.'

Slutsky resigned, but the criticism back home was directed at his useless players. 'These weren't our footballers. You can buy that uniform in any store,' read one Twitter meme, referencing Vladimir Putin's denial that the soldiers who occupied Crimea in 2014 were Red Army troops. Politician Gennady Zyuganov called for 'a Stalinist mobilisation' to replace the '11 millionaires running around the field with half-bent legs'.

Given the post-tournament antics of striker Aleksandr Kokorin and midfielder Pavel Mamaev, perhaps Zyuganov had a point. Days after this game, smartphone footage captured them partying in a Monte Carlo nightspot, where they spent €250,000 on champagne. Their choice of soundtrack – the Russian anthem – provoked more anger than the conspicuous consumption. One Russian politician tweeted, 'Others must have been pouring the champagne. These two would've missed the glasses.'

6pm, 11 June 2016
Nouveau Stade de Bordeaux, Bordeaux
Attendance: 37,831
Referee: Svein Oddvar Moen (Norway)

WALES 2 (Bale 10, Robson-Kanu 81)
SLOVAKIA 1 (Duda 61)

WALES: Danny Ward, Chris Gunter, Neil Taylor, Ben Davies, James Chester, Ashley Williams (c), David Edwards (Joe Ledley 69), Joe Allen, Jonny Williams (Hal Robson-Kanu 71), Gareth Bale, Aaron Ramsey (Jazz Richards 88). **Manager:** Chris Coleman.

SLOVAKIA: Matúš Kozáčik, Peter Pekarík, Dušan Švento, Ján Ďurica, Martín Škrtel (c), Patrik Hrošovský (Ondrej Duda 60), Juraj Kucka, Róbert Mak, Michal Ďuriš (Adam Nemec 59), Marek Hamšík, Vladimír Weiss (Miroslav Stoch 83). **Manager:** Ján Kozák.

Booked: Hrošovský (31), Mak (78), Weiss (80), Kucka (83), Škrtel (90+2).

9pm, 11 June 2016
Stade Vélodrome, Marseille
Attendance: 62,343
Referee: Nicola Rizzoli (Italy)

ENGLAND 1 (Dier 73)
RUSSIA 1 (V. Berezutsky 90+2)

ENGLAND: Joe Hart, Kyle Walker, Danny Rose, Chris Smalling, Gary Cahill, Eric Dier, Dele Alli, Adam Lallana, Harry Kane, Wayne Rooney (c) (Jack Wilshere 78), Raheem Sterling (James Milner 87). **Manager:** Roy Hodgson.

RUSSIA: Igor Akinfeev, Igor Smolnikov, Georgi Shchennikov, Sergei Ignashevich, Vasily Berezutsky (c), Aleksandr Golovin (Roman Shirokov 77), Roman Neustädter (Denis Glushakov 80), Oleg Shatov, Artyom Dzyuba, Aleksandr Kokorin, Fyodor Smolov (Pavel Mamaev 85). **Manager:** Leonid Slutsky.

Booked: Cahill (62), Shchennikov (72).

3pm, 15 June 2016
Stade Pierre-Mauroy, Lille
Attendance: 38,989
Referee: Damir Skomina (Slovenia)

SLOVAKIA 2 (Weiss 32, Hamšík 45)
RUSSIA 1 (Glushakov 80)

SLOVAKIA: Kozáčik, Pekarík, Tomáš Hubočan, Ďurica, Škrtel (c), Viktor Pečovský, Kucka, Mak (Ďuriš 80), Duda (Nemec 67), Hamšík, Weiss (Švento 72).

RUSSIA: Akinfeev, Smolnikov, Shchennikov, Ignashevich, V. Berezutsky (c), Golovin (Mamaev 46), Neustädter (Glushakov 46), Shatov, Dzyuba, Kokorin (Shirokov 75), Smolov.

Booked: Ďurica (46).

3pm, 16 June 2016
Stade Bollaert-Delelis, Lens
Attendance: 34,033
Referee: Felix Brych (Germany)

ENGLAND 2 (Vardy 56, Sturridge 90+2)
WALES 1 (Bale 42)

ENGLAND: Hart, Walker, Rose, Smalling, Cahill, Dier, Alli, Lallana (Marcus Rashford 73), Kane (Jamie Vardy 46), Rooney (c), Sterling (Daniel Sturridge 46).

WALES: Wayne Hennessey, Gunter, Taylor, Davies, Chester, A. Williams (c), Ledley (Edwards 67), Allen, Robson-Kanu (J. Williams 72), Bale, Ramsey.

Booked: Davies (62).

9pm, 20 June 2016
Stade Geoffroy Guichard, Saint-Étienne
Attendance: 39,051
Referee: Carlos Velasco Carballo (Spain)

ENGLAND 0
SLOVAKIA 0

ENGLAND: Hart, Nathaniel Clyne, Ryan Bertrand, Smalling, Cahill (c), Dier, Jordan Henderson, Lallana (Alli 61), Vardy, Wilshere (Rooney 56), Sturridge (Kane 76).

SLOVAKIA: Kozáčik, Pekarík, Hubočan, Ďurica, Škrtel (c), Pečovský (Norbert Gyömbér 67), Kucka, Mak, Duda (Švento 57), Hamšík, Weiss (Milan Škriniar 78).

Booked: Bertrand (52), Pečovský (24).

9pm, 20 June 2016
Stadium Municipal, Toulouse
Attendance: 28,840
Referee: Jonas Eriksson (Sweden)

WALES 3 (Ramsey 11, Taylor 20, Bale 67)
RUSSIA 0

WALES: Hennessey, Gunter, Taylor, Davies, Chester, A. Williams (c), Ledley (Andy King 76), Allen (Edwards 74), Sam Vokes, Bale (Simon Church 83), Ramsey.

RUSSIA: Akinfeev, Smolnikov, Dmitri Kombarov, Ignashevich, V. Berezutsky (Aleksei Berezutsky 46), Mamaev, Glushakov, Shirokov (c) (Golovin 52), Dzyuba, Kokorin, Smolov (Aleksandr Samedov 70).

Booked: Vokes (16), Mamaev (64).

GROUP B	P	W	D	L	F	A	GD	Pts
WALES	3	2	0	1	6	3	+3	6
ENGLAND	3	1	2	0	3	2	+1	5
SLOVAKIA	3	1	1	1	3	3	0	4
RUSSIA	3	0	1	2	2	6	− 4	1

Wales, England and Slovakia qualified.

GROUP C
Germany, Ukraine, Poland, Northern Ireland

After a long dry season, Northern Ireland were tasting their first tournament in 30 years. They were the homeliest team seen at the finals since Denmark in 1964: a goalkeeper just released by Hamilton Academicals, a right-back from Fleetwood Town, a left-winger from Millwall, and various other players from the English Championship.

They looked weak on paper, and were little better on grass against Poland in Nice. The Poles dominated, but struggled to break down a nine-man defence, with superstar striker Robert Lewandowski double-marked throughout.

Lewandowski's partner Arkadiusz Milik looked inept and missed several chances, at one point blazing into the stands from six yards. Meanwhile, a schoolyard-like goalmouth melée ended with Michał Pazdan shooting into the side-netting. But early in the second half, the North's walls crumbled. Piszczek's cross was met by Milik, whose weak shot went through Craig Cathcart's legs and past the unsighted Michael McGovern.

Kyle Lafferty, who had scored freely in the qualifiers but hardly touched the ball here, said, 'The whole performance wasn't a Northern Ireland performance. We didn't turn up today. I think on Thursday we'll put it right, and go into the final game against Germany fighting for something.'

=====

Ukraine should have held few fears for Germany, but gave them a surprisingly strong test in Lille. Up against fast wingers in Andriy Yarmolenko and Yevhen Konoplyanka, German full-backs Jonas Hector and Benedikt Höwedes looked vulnerable. Early on, Manuel Neuer turned Konoplyanka's shot over the bar, then saved Yevhen Khacheridi's strong header.

Later, after Konoplyanka shot past Neuer, Jérôme Boateng almost ran the ball over the line before scrambling it away. But by then, Germany were ahead. Shkodran Mustafi, later a fan favourite at Arsenal, gave Serhiy Sydorchuk the slip to head home Toni Kroos's free kick.

The masterful Kroos later clipped the bar and Sami Khedira missed a one-on-one against goalkeeper Andriy Pyatov, but Jogi Löw's team never seemed fully in command. Moments after Mesut Özil blew another one-on-one, Mustafi almost headed an own goal past a stranded Neuer; as it bounced wide, Neuer flattened Yevhen Seleznyov, but referee Martin Atkinson missed it. Not until stoppage time could Germany relax. Özil flew down the left and picked out Bastian Schweinsteiger, who'd come on seconds earlier and crashed the cross past Pyatov.

The other talking point, a bizarre one, was TV footage of Löw reaching down his trousers during the game, then sniffing his fingers. 'Sometimes you do things subconsciously,' he apologised. 'It happened and I'm sorry. It was adrenalin and concentration. I'll try to behave differently in the future.' The veteran Lukas Podolski defended him, telling the press, 'About 80 per cent of you here have at some point scratched your balls.'

=====

With a war going on back home, Ukraine's was a divided camp. Tensions were evident between the Dynamo Kiev and Shakhtar Donetsk contingents, and manager Mykhaylo Fomenko was criticised for picking players with connections to Russia, such as Seleznyov, who had just joined Kuban Krasnodar 'to feed my family'.

Defender Yaroslav Rakytskyi, a Donetsk native, refused to sing the national anthem before matches. Midfielder Taras Stepanenko raised eyebrows by revealing that he had holidayed in Russian-occupied Crimea. And when German tabloid *Bild* claimed that cigarette butts and beer cans had littered Ukraine's dressing room after the Germany match, defender Artem Fedetskyi replied, 'We have no players who drink beer. Maybe someone wants to provoke us. We behave in a civilised way. You can check the DNA from the cigarettes.'

Northern Ireland knew it was now or never. Manager Michael O'Neill obtained extra video footage of the Poland game from UEFA, realised he needed strength in midfield and speed out wide – and dropped five players, including Lafferty. His gamble came off as his team gave the performance of their lives in Lyon.

Konoplyanka was smothered by veteran Aaron Hughes, while Jamie Ward gave the 37-year-old Vyacheslav Shevchuk a hard time on the same flank. As the North dominated, Pyatov kept out Stuart Dallas and Steven Davis, while Corry Evans was crowded out in a goalmouth scramble.

Early in the second half, Northern Ireland claimed their first European Championship goal. Oliver Norwood whipped a free kick to the far post, and centre-half Gareth McAuley – almost as old as Shevchuk – shook off Khacheridi to head it in.

The suspension of play for five minutes just before the hour, due to hailstones, came at a good time for Northern Ireland. And the long period of stoppage time yielded their second goal. Substitute Josh Magennis slipped the ball to Dallas, Pyatov spilled his shot and another sub, Niall McGinn, buried the rebound. 'When you get a performance of passion, commitment and pure heart like that, there's nothing more you can ask for as a manager,' O'Neill beamed. As Van Morrison put it: wouldn't it be great if it was like this all the time?

━━━

Every so often, the football gods treat us to that rarest of things, a fantastic goalless draw (Italy's strangling of the Netherlands at Euro 2000 comes to mind). Germany's clash with Poland at the Stade de France failed to fall into this category.

Using a weird formation that saw Mario Götze swallowed up by Poland's huge defenders, Germany were pedestrian beyond belief. Kroos again impressed but, in what was becoming a recurring theme of Euro 2016, neither team got a shot on target in an awful first half. At the beginning of the second, with Germany asleep, the unmarked Milik somehow failed to convert Kamil Grosicki's cross from three yards, getting vague facial contact on the ball before it went wide.

Mass booing greeted the end of a shocking match. Boateng criticised his strikers afterwards: 'It's all good until we reach the final third, but we're not dangerous.' Özil retorted, 'That's his opinion. He certainly knows how to play attacking football.' Miaow!

━━━

There was more trouble in Marseille before the Galician derby between Poland and Ukraine, most of it internecine warfare between gangs from

Polish Ekstraklasa clubs. Once the football began, Ukraine looked decent in patches but, as against Germany, came away with nothing.

Poland had the best chances, with the unimpressive Milik shooting at Pyatov and Lewandowski shovelling a sitter over the bar. It was left to Lewy's former Borussia Dortmund team-mate (although not his actual mate; they didn't get on) Kuba Błaszczykowski to settle things. The midfielder, a dead ringer for *Game of Thrones* villain Ramsay Bolton, came on at half-time and soon scored the only goal, swerving past Ruslan Rotan and finishing deftly with his strong left foot.

With Kamil Glik winning everything in the air, Ukraine couldn't trouble Poland before the end. This was their fifth consecutive Euro finals game without scoring, creating an all-time record. Fomenko resigned days later.

Meanwhile, in Paris, Germany won the group by dismembering Northern Ireland in all but goals. O'Neill's team were again so unambitious that they resembled a San Marino or Andorra trying to keep it semi-respectable by curling up into a ball.

Only the incredible performance of goalkeeper Michael McGovern – clubless after being released by Hamilton Academicals – prevented a rout. In the first 15 minutes alone, he kept out Müller when one on one, stopped Özil with his legs, clutched Mats Hummels's header and made another point-blank save from Götze. Müller then headed against the woodwork, and several more German efforts (Özil, Kimmich, Müller again) flew narrowly off target.

Northern Ireland's charmed life soon ended. Müller drew out McGovern and two defenders before pulling it back to Mario Gómez, whose finish hit McAuley's boot on its way in. The scorer and creator chest-bumped like two cavemen celebrating a hippo kill.

The onslaught continued. Müller hit the bar from Götze's cut-back, Khedira smashed another effort into Conor Washington's face, and a bad bobble saw Gómez shoot against his own leg. In the second half, the disappointing Götze chested down Kimmich's pass but blasted it at McGovern, then pushed another chance wide before Löw took him off. The indefatigable McGovern flew to his right to keep out Khedira's drive, and Gómez nodded the rebound wide as the goal gaped. And although Germany then eased off, Gómez's header brought one last fine save from McGovern.

'We're a very small nation, and we were playing the world champions, so you have to be realistic,' said O'Neill, but this performance compared unflatteringly to what Iceland were achieving elsewhere in Euro 2016 with barely a quarter of the population. Despite losing two out of three, the North knew they would survive as third-placers if results went their way in Group

D, and so it proved. Great news for their fans, less so for those who wanted to watch good contests.

6pm, 12 June 2016
Allianz Riviera, Nice
Attendance: 33,742
Referee: Ovidiu Haţegan (Romania)

POLAND 1 (Milik 51)
NORTHERN IRELAND 0

POLAND: Wojciech Szczęsny, Łukasz Piszczek, Artur Jędrzejczyk, Kamil Glik, Michał Pazdan, Grzegorz Krychowiak, Jakub 'Kuba' Błaszczykowski (Kamil Grosicki 80), Krzysztof Mączyński (Tomasz Jodłowiec 78), Robert Lewandowski (c), Arkadiusz Milik, Bartosz Kapustka (Sławomir Peszko 88). **Manager:** Adam Nawałka.

NORTHERN IRELAND: Michael McGovern, Conor McLaughlin, Craig Cathcart, Jonny Evans, Gareth McAuley, Paddy McNair (Stuart Dallas 46), Oliver Norwood, Shane Ferguson (Conor Washington 66), Kyle Lafferty, Steven Davis (c), Chris Baird (Jamie Ward 76). **Manager:** Michael O'Neill.

Booked: Kapustka (65), Piszczek (89), Cathcart (69).

9pm, 12 June 2016
Stade Pierre-Mauroy, Lille
Attendance: 43,035
Referee: Martin Atkinson (England)

GERMANY 2 (Mustafi 19, Schweinsteiger 90+2)
UKRAINE 0

GERMANY: Manuel Neuer (c), Benedikt Höwedes, Jérôme Boateng, Shkodran Mustafi, Jonas Hector, Sami Khedira, Toni Kroos, Mesut Özil, Thomas Müller, Mario Götze (Bastian Schweinsteiger 90), Julian Draxler (André Schürrle 78). **Manager:** Joachim 'Jogi' Löw.

UKRAINE: Andriy Pyatov, Artem Fedetskyi, Yevhen Khacheridi, Yaroslav Rakytskyi, Vyacheslav Shevchuk (c), Taras Stepanenko, Serhiy Sydorchuk, Viktor Kovalenko (Oleksandr Zinchenko 73), Roman Zozulya (Yevhen Seleznyov 66), Yevhen Konoplyanka, Andriy Yarmolenko. **Manager:** Mykhaylo Fomenko.

Booked: Konoplyanka (68).

6pm, 16 June 2016
Parc Olympique Lyonnais, Lyon
Attendance: 43,000
Referee: Pavel Královec (Czech Republic)

NORTHERN IRELAND 2 (McAuley 49, McGinn 90+6)
UKRAINE 0

NORTHERN IRELAND: McGovern, Aaron Hughes, Cathcart, J. Evans, McAuley, Dallas, Norwood, Corry Evans (McNair 90+3), Washington (Josh Magennis 84), Davis (c), Ward (Niall McGinn 69).

UKRAINE: Pyatov, Fedetskyi, Khacheridi, Rakytskyi, Shevchuk (c), Stepanenko, Sydorchuk (Denys Harmash 76), Kovalenko (Zinchenko 83), Seleznyov (Zozulya 71), Konoplyanka, Yarmolenko.

Booked: Ward (63), Dallas (86), J. Evans (90+4), Seleznyov (40), Sydorchuk (67).

9pm, 16 June 2016
Stade de France, Saint-Denis
Attendance: 73,648
Referee: Björn Kuipers (Netherlands)

GERMANY 0
POLAND 0

GERMANY: Neuer (c), Höwedes, Boateng, Mats Hummels, Hector, Khedira, Kroos, Özil, Müller, Götze (Schürrle 66), Draxler (Mario Gómez 71).

POLAND: Łukasz Fabiański, Piszczek, Jędrzejczyk, Glik, Pazdan, Krychowiak, Błaszczykowski (Kapustka 80), Mączyński (Jodłowiec 76), Lewandowski (c), Milik, Grosicki (Peszko 87).

Booked: Khedira (3), Özil (34), Boateng (67), Mączyński (45), Grosicki (55), Peszko (90+3).

6pm, 21 June 2016
Stade Vélodrome, Marseille
Attendance: 58,874
Referee: Svein Oddvar Moen (Norway)

POLAND 1 (Błaszczykowski 54)
UKRAINE 0

POLAND: Fabiański, Thiago Cionek, Jędrzejczyk, Glik, Pazdan, Krychowiak, Piotr Zieliński (Błaszczykowski 46), Jodłowiec, Lewandowski (c), Milik (Filip Starzyński 90+3), Kapustka (Grosicki 71).

UKRAINE: Pyatov, Fedetskyi, Bohdan Butko, Khacheridi, Oleksandr Kucher, Ruslan Rotan (c), Stepanenko, Zinchenko (Kovalenko 73), Zozulya (Anatoliy Tymoshchuk 90+2), Konoplyanka, Yarmolenko.

Booked: Kapustka (60), Rotan (25), Kucher (38).

6pm, 21 June 2016
Parc des Princes, Paris
Attendance: 44,125
Referee: Clément Turpin (France)

GERMANY 1 (Gómez 29)
NORTHERN IRELAND 0

GERMANY: Neuer (c), Joshua Kimmich, Boateng (Höwedes 76), Hummels, Hector, Khedira (Schweinsteiger 69), Kroos, Özil, Müller, Götze (Schürrle 55), Gómez.

NORTHERN IRELAND: McGovern, Hughes, Cathcart, J. Evans, McAuley, Dallas, Norwood, C. Evans (McGinn 84), Washington (Lafferty 59), Davis (c), Ward (Magennis 70).

GROUP C	P	W	D	L	F	A	GD	Pts
GERMANY	3	2	1	0	3	0	+3	7
POLAND	3	2	1	0	2	0	+2	7
NORTHERN IRELAND	3	1	0	2	2	2	0	3
UKRAINE	3	0	0	3	0	5	−5	0

Germany, Poland and Northern Ireland qualified.

GROUP D
Spain, Czech Republic, Turkey, Croatia

At their fifth European Championship, Croatia again wore the bridle of dark horses, prompting the question of how heavily a dark horse can be backed before it ceases being one. They were too strong for Turkey in Paris, even if the Turks should have scored first, Ozan Tufan heading Gökhan Gönül's cross straight at goalkeeper Danijel Subašić.

Luka Modrić soon punished them, showing fantastic technique to meet Selçuk İnan's clearance with a dipping volley into the bottom corner. Croatia should have won handsomely, with Darijo Srna's free kick and Ivan Perišić's header both hitting Turkish timber. They almost blew it in the 93rd minute – but when Hakan Balta met Burak Yılmaz's knockdown, the bloodied Vedran Ćorluka blocked the shot.

So Croatia had three points, but plenty of bruises. Referee Jonas Eriksson bottled out of booking Oğuzhan Özyakup for hacking Modrić, and awarded only a free kick when Volkan Şen raked Srna's knee. A sign of things to come in the tournament.

———

In Toulouse, the Czech Republic battened down the hatches against Spain and almost lived to tell the tale. For a long time, the reigning champions were held at bay by a 32-year-old on Bursaspor's books in Turkey. Tomáš Sivok gave one of the great unsung defensive performances in international history, putting in innumerable blocks, headers and interceptions. 'For us, the match wasn't physically demanding, rather psychological,' he said afterwards. 'You have to be lucky, because Spain are almost always a step ahead.'

Spain dominated but created few chances, and when Cesc Fàbregas hacked off the line before Pavel Kadeřábek could pounce, it concentrated Spanish minds. Alba miscontrolled with only Petr Čech to beat, substitute Aritz Aduriz glanced Sergio Ramos's cross wide, and another sub, Thiago Alcântara, was denied when Ladislav Krejčí nicked the ball off his toe.

But just as the Czechs thought they had done enough, Tomáš Rosický's weary clearance allowed Andrés Iniesta to cross from the left, and Gerard Piqué nipped between Sivok and Roman Hubník to head past Čech. 'We had the game completely under control, and that's the most important thing,' lied a relieved Vicente Del Bosque.

———

After flying home for his father's funeral, Croatian captain Darijo Srna returned to face the Czechs in Saint-Étienne, shedding tears during Croatia's anthem. He gave an understandably muted performance in a boring first half, during which Croatia struggled to break down a packed defence.

Eventually, Jaroslav Plašil got robbed by Milan Badelj, who sent Perišić up the left. As the winger executed a stepover, Sivok shielded the near post – so Perišić shot inside the far one. A terrific goal from a player whose histrionics at Borussia Dortmund had compelled Jürgen Klopp to discard him.

At the break, Czech manager Pavel Vrba castigated his men for 'playing hide and seek', but Marcelo Brozović soon sent Rakitić through to chip Čech for 2-0, seemingly sealing the Czechs' fate. Then, out of the blue, Modrić injured his groin and went off – and everything changed.

When substitute Milan Škoda pulled one back with a header, it initially seemed an irrelevance. But Croatia were blown off course mentally when their fans began hurling missiles on to the pitch behind Čech's goal, forcing referee Mark Clattenburg to halt the game. As a PA announcement was made in Croatian ('Leave the stadium, don't embarrass our country'), one firework exploded in a steward's face.

With no Modrić to control the tempo, Croatia were a rabble when the match restarted. In total, Clattenburg added on ten minutes. After two, Vida handled in the box. Penalty. Another Czech substitute, Tomáš Necid, smashed it in for 2-2. As the Czechs forced a succession of corners, threatening to win a game they'd hardly been in, Croatia's manager Ante Čačić threw on two more defenders before the end.

'The problem is that our country doesn't want to mess with these sporting terrorists,' Čačić said, a reference to the power wielded by ultras groups in Croatian football. Srna called it 'the hardest match of my career', and Zagreb broadsheet *Jutarnji List* lamented, 'Scandal at the Euros … Everybody talks of shame… Is there a danger of us dropping out of the championship?'

Vrba twisted the knife, pointedly praising the Czech fans. 'They pushed us to the draw. They were not only the 12th and 13th man, but also the 14th. A huge thank you to them.'

———

Turkey's white away kit faded downwards into light blue like a J cloth, so it was apposite that Spain wiped the floor with them in Nice. Sergio Ramos was booked after 50 seconds for clattering Burak Yılmaz, but Turkey lacked the wherewithal to tempt him into adding to his 21 career red cards – or to do anything else.

Álvaro Morata had already pressured Hakan Balta into knocking the ball against the post by the time he put Spain ahead, nodding home Nolito's cross. Soon, Turkey authored their own demise. Mehmet Topal's clumsy header inadvertently teed up Nolito, who slipped as his shot crept in.

After half-time, a 20-pass Spanish move crescendoed when the offside Jordi Alba gave Morata a tap-in for 3-0. Meanwhile, Turkish playmaker Arda

Turan was so poor that Turkey's fans jeered him. 'They made my mother cry,' he said afterwards.

'The first half-hour was fine. But then there were two mistakes, one of them unbelievable,' manager Fatih Terim growled. 'Our team threw in the towel. I didn't like it. I'll never accept it.'

===

Spain's showdown with Croatia would be a personal nightmare for Ramos, whose athleticism and macho leadership never quite compensated for his bucking-bronco tendencies. Nonetheless, his team drew first blood in Bordeaux. David Silva's pass slashed Croatia's defence open, Fàbregas stroked it past Subašić, and Morata made sure under the bar.

But now Spain wobbled. Nikola Kalinić robbed David De Gea in his own box and the ball fell to Rakitić, whose chip hit the bar to land on the line. Realising this lot weren't invincible any more, Croatia equalised in first-half stoppage time as Ramos sleepily allowed Kalinić to flick home Perišić's cross.

De Gea, usually so good, had a nightmare here. In the second half, his weak punch gave Tin Jedvaj a chance that he blocked with his thigh; the ball broke to Marko Pjaca, whose overhead kick sailed wide. Ramos then spurned a free header. Another goal was coming, but for whom? For Spain, it seemed, when Silva collapsed under Šime Vrsaljko's soft contact and referee Björn Kuipers gave a penalty. Srna physically jostled Kuipers and might have been sent off – but Ramos, no penalty king, saw Subašić save his kick.

When Croatia sealed an exhilarating victory late on, De Gea again looked poor. As Perišić galloped down the left, he seemed to have the shot covered – but let it fly inside his near post. Vrsaljko took revenge on Silva by kicking his shot off the line in stoppage time, and Croatia had won the group.

The result meant Spain would probably face Italy, then Germany, then France. Croatia's own route – likely Portugal, Switzerland and the badly coached Belgians – looked mouthwateringly clear. 'Čudo u Bordeauxu!' roared one Croatian paper, citing 'a miracle in Bordeaux'. But with Ramos helping you, who needed divine intervention?

===

Turkey, almost out of time, finally pulled out a performance against the Czechs in Lens. Their teenage winger Emre Mor needed little time to show why Borussia Dortmund had just signed him, cantering down the right and crossing for Burak to half-volley home.

In response, Sivok headed against the woodwork and Kadeřábek broke through to shoot at Volkan. Kadeřábek's next sortie was ended by İsmail

Köybası's forearm smash, which drew blood and a booking. That one was tame next to David Pavelka's horrendous challenge on Selçuk, for which he somehow escaped a red card.

Sivok and Gökhan's clash of heads caused a long second-half stoppage, but Turkey's concentration didn't waver like Croatia's. They put the game to bed when the offside Mehmet Topal set up Ozan, who wellied the chance in.

The Czechs had fallen a long way from 2008, let alone 2004; there wasn't a Sionko in this mundane team, never mind a Nedvěd or a Poborský. Vrba resigned, stung by Czech journalists contrasting Terim's blooding of Emre with his own reluctance to use Václav Černý and Patrik Schick.

Like Albania, Turkey now sat on their suitcases before learning their fate. Because they hadn't won by four, their efforts inadvertently pushed Northern Ireland into the last 16. A farce.

3pm, 12 June 2016
Parc des Princes, Paris
Attendance: 43,842
Referee: Jonas Eriksson (Sweden)

CROATIA 1 (Modrić 41)
TURKEY 0

CROATIA: Danijel Subašić, Darijo Srna (c), Domagoj Vida, Vedran Ćorluka, Ivan Strinić, Milan Badelj, Marcelo Brozović, Ivan Rakitić (Gordon Schildenfeld 90), Mario Mandžukić (Marko Pjaca 90+3), Luka Modrić, Ivan Perišić (Andrej Kramarić 87). **Manager:** Ante Čačić.

TURKEY: Volkan Babacan, Gökhan Gönül, Hakan Balta, Mehmet Topal, Caner Erkin, Ozan Tufan, Selçuk İnan, Oğuzhan Özyakup (Volkan Şen 46), Cenk Tosun (Emre Mor 69), Arda Turan (c) (Burak Yılmaz 65), Hakan Çalhanoğlu. **Manager:** Fatih Terim.

Booked: Strinić (80), Cenk (31), Hakan Balta (48), Volkan Şen (90+1).

3pm, 13 June 2016
Stadium Municipal, Toulouse
Attendance: 29,400
Referee: Szymon Marciniak (Poland)

SPAIN 1 (Piqué 87)
CZECH REPUBLIC 0

SPAIN: David De Gea, Juan Francisco Torres 'Juanfran', Gerard Piqué, Sergio Ramos (c), Jordi Alba, Sergio Busquets, Andrés Iniesta, David Silva, Álvaro Morata (Aritz Aduriz 62), Cesc Fàbregas (Thiago Alcântara 70), Manuel Agudo 'Nolito' (Pedro Rodríguez 82). **Manager:** Vicente Del Bosque.

CZECH REPUBLIC: Petr Čech, Pavel Kadeřábek, Tomáš Sivok, Roman Hubník, David Limberský, Jaroslav Plašil, Theodor Gebre Selassie (Josef Šural 86), Vladimír Darida, Tomáš Necid (David Lafata 75), Tomáš Rosický (c) (David Pavelka 88), Ladislav Krejčí. **Manager:** Pavel Vrba.

Booked: Limberský (61).

6pm, 17 June 2016
Stade Geoffroy Guichard, Saint-Étienne
Attendance: 38,376
Referee: Mark Clattenburg (England)

CROATIA 2 (Perišić 37, Rakitić 59)
CZECH REPUBLIC 2 (Škoda 76, Necid 90+4 pen)

CROATIA: Subašić, Srna (c), Vida, Ćorluka, Strinić (Šime Vrsaljko 90+8), Badelj, Brozović, Rakitić (Schildenfeld 90+7), Mandžukić, Modrić (Mateo Kovačić 62), Perišić.

CZECH REPUBLIC: Čech, Kadeřábek, Sivok, Hubník, Limberský, Plašil (Necid 86), Jiří Skalák (Šural 67), Darida, Lafata (Milan Škoda 67), Rosický (c), Krejčí.

Booked: Badelj (14), Brozović (74), Vida (90+3), Sivok (72).

9pm, 17 June 2016
Allianz Riviera, Nice
Attendance: 33,409
Referee: Milorad Mažić (Serbia)

SPAIN 3 (Morata 34, 48, Nolito 37)
TURKEY 0

SPAIN: De Gea, Juanfran, Piqué, Ramos (c), Alba (César Azpilicueta 81), Busquets, Iniesta, Silva (Bruno Soriano 64), Morata, Fàbregas (Jorge Resurrección 'Koke' 71), Nolito.

TURKEY: Volkan B., Gökhan, Hakan B., Mehmet, Caner, Ozan, Selçuk (Yunus Mallı 70), Oğuzhan (Olcay Şahan 62), Burak, Arda (c), Hakan Ç. (Nuri Şahin 46).

Booked: Ramos (1), Burak (9), Ozan (41).

9pm, 21 June 2016
Nouveau Stade de Bordeaux, Bordeaux
Attendance: 37,245
Referee: Björn Kuipers (Netherlands)

CROATIA 2 (Kalinić 45, Perišić 87)
SPAIN 1 (Morata 7)

CROATIA: Subašić, Srna (c), Tin Jedvaj, Ćorluka, Vrsaljko, Badelj, Marko Rog (Kovačić 82), Rakitić, Nikola Kalinić, Pjaca (Duje Čop 90+2), Perišić (Kramarić 90+4).

SPAIN: De Gea, Juanfran, Piqué, Ramos (c), Alba, Busquets, Iniesta, Silva, Morata (Aduriz 67), Fàbregas (Thiago 84), Nolito (Bruno 60).

Booked: Rog (29), Srna (70), Vrsaljko (70), Perišić (88).

9pm, 21 June 2016
Stade Bollaert-Delelis, Lens
Attendance: 32,836
Referee: Willie Collum (Scotland)

TURKEY 2 (Burak 10, Ozan 65)
CZECH REPUBLIC 0

TURKEY: Volkan B., Gökhan, Hakan B., Mehmet, İsmail Köybası, Ozan, Selçuk, Emre (Olcay 69), Burak (Cenk 90), Arda (c), Volkan Ş. (Oğuzhan 61).

CZECH REPUBLIC: Čech (c), Kadeřábek, Sivok, Hubník, Daniel Pudil, Darida, Plašil (Daniel Kolář 90), Bořek Dočkal (Šural 71), Necid, Pavelka (Škoda 57), Krejčí.

Booked: İsmail (35), Hakan B. (50), Plašil (36), Pavelka (39), Šural (87).

GROUP D	P	W	D	L	F	A	GD	Pts
CROATIA	3	2	1	0	5	3	+2	7
SPAIN	3	2	0	1	5	2	+3	6
TURKEY	3	1	0	2	2	4	− 2	3
CZECH REPUBLIC	3	0	1	2	2	5	− 3	1

Croatia and Spain qualified.

GROUP E
Belgium, Italy, Ireland, Sweden

In a formidable group, Ireland were once again cast as makeweights. But they had it so easy against Sweden at the Stade de France that Jeff Hendrick, their flaxen-haired midfielder, had time to tuck his fringe behind his ear before playing a pass. Soon afterwards, he hit the crossbar with a well-struck drive.

As confidence pulsed through Irish veins, John O'Shea just failed to connect for a tap-in and Robbie Brady fizzed another long-range rocket narrowly over. Unrecognisable from Giovanni Trapattoni's 2012 palookas, Ireland were well worth the lead that came their way early in the second half as Seamus Coleman's cross fell for Wes Hoolahan to half-volley it into the far corner. The clever Norwich playmaker had been roundly ignored for years by Trapattoni, who seemed to view him as some sort of existential threat to the team.

Going behind jolted Sweden awake, and they began exposing Ciaran Clark, a surprise selection ahead of Richard Keogh. First, he wildly hacked Forsberg's cross into the air, and then from the corner his second miscue brought a fantastic save from goalkeeper Darren Randolph. His lack of nous finally told when he headed the otherwise anonymous Zlatan Ibrahimović's cross into his own net.

The game petered out after that, although Andreas Granqvist disgraced himself by stamping on Aiden McGeady's ankle. 'We lack quality,' Ibrahimović said. But shouldn't he have provided it?

===

Italy, it seemed, were easy pickings for Belgium in Lyon. Antonio Conte had lost three good midfielders in Claudio Marchisio, Riccardo Montolivo and Marco Verratti, and had so few quality forwards that Southampton's Graziano Pellè was the main striker. Their line-up (average age just under 31 and a half) was the oldest in Euros history.

Belgium had their own problems. Star man Eden Hazard had been wretched all season for Chelsea, and after the game, it emerged that manager Marc Wilmots had arranged a practice match days earlier between his first XI and reserves, lining up the latter in Italy's 3-5-2 formation. The subs won 4-0.

Enthusiastic from the start, Italy took a deserved lead when Toby Alderweireld ball-watched Leonardo Bonucci's long pass: the perennially underrated Emanuele Giaccherini controlled it, then bent his shot around Thibaut Courtois. Conte had once remarked, 'If Giaccherini was called Giaccherinho, you'd constantly be saying how skilful he was.'

Belgium's danger men were suffocated by the BBC, Juventus's praetorian guard of Bonucci, Andrea Barzagli and Giorgio Chiellini. Eden Hazard simply disappeared, while Kevin De Bruyne was a fish out of water on the right. In the second half, Courtois prevented it being a hammering, going full-length to stop Pellè's header and then keeping out a venomous shot by Ciro Immobile.

Late on, Italy sealed an outstanding team performance when Immobile teed up Antonio Candreva, who unselfishly picked out the unmarked Pellè for a close-range volley. Conte, often caricatured as a screaming sergeant-major, suddenly looked like a serious tactician. But his opposite number sounded delusional: 'Italy just played on the counter-attack. They didn't play real football. They were pretty much there on the sofa, they were pretty relaxed.' For all Wilmots's bluster, he was making tin out of gold.

In Toulouse four days later, however, Italy were ludicrously cagey against a Swedish side that Ireland had exposed as ordinary. A terrible match witnessed some breathtaking incompetence: Victor Lindelöf hitting a cross miles out under no pressure, Chiellini failing to control a simple pass, Marco Parolo running the ball out of play in a promising situation. On 72 minutes, however, there was some comedy to enjoy. Ibrahimović, lurking offside at the far post, somehow shot over the bar from two yards – then exhorted the linesman to flag him offside and spare his blushes.

Eventually, Italy stirred into life. Parolo's header clipped the bar, and with two minutes left, the Brazilian-born Éder darted between three defenders and steered a superb shot beyond goalkeeper Andreas Isaksson. A goal out of keeping with such a bad match, but it put Italy through.

As recriminations engulfed Belgium's camp, Courtois publicly lambasted Wilmots ('We were tactically outclassed'), then rowed with him on the squad's flight to Bordeaux. The goalkeeper only kept his place because the alternative was the gaffe-prone Simon Mignolet.

But against Ireland, Belgium had things easy. Hazard blasted a great chance too high, Yannick Carrasco's goal was disallowed for offside, and Hoolahan nodded Alderweireld's header off the line. Ireland, playing for 0-0, weren't defensively strong enough to achieve it. And Martin O'Neill's lone-striker stratagem was a disaster. Living on long-ball starvation rations, Shane Long took a physical battering. At one point, referee Cüneyt Çakır penalised him for standing still as three opponents jumped beside him.

An even worse decision sealed Ireland's fate after half-time. As Belgium defended a corner, the airborne Alderweireld kicked Long in the head. A penalty and a red card, surely? Not with this ref. De Bruyne instantly flew up the right, where James McCarthy dived in on halfway, making it easy for him. He rolled the ball to the edge of the box, and Lukaku put it away. Ireland should have had a spot-kick and an extra man; instead, they were trailing.

Out of his depth at Euro 2012, Stephen Ward now saw all three Belgian goals come down his side. For the second, Thomas Meunier crossed for Axel Witsel to convert a downward header. And the third was a replica of the first. Hazard, fancying it today, scampered up the flank, Clark did the same thing as McCarthy, and the winger squared it to Lukaku, who knocked it into the same corner. Belgium were alive again.

═══

Before Sweden's last-chance meeting with Belgium in Nice, Ibrahimović announced that if they lost, his international career was over. He fought hard to keep them alive, and had a second-half goal disallowed for unclear reasons. But a Belgian win always felt more likely. Meunier and Lukaku both went close, and Dries Mertens showed excellent footwork before Isaksson turned his drive around the post.

With six minutes left, De Bruyne blocked Granqvist's header under the bar, Hazard immediately sprinted up the left and pulled the ball back Nainggolan to crash home a spectacular curving shot from 25 yards. Belgium were through without living up to their billing.

The Swedes now prepared for life without their arrogant alpha male. Ibrahimović had gone to two World Cups and four Euros without imposing himself on any of them: he clocked out on 62 international goals, but while many were stunners, few had gone in when it really mattered.

═══

The bad news for Ireland was that they had to beat Italy in Lille to survive. The good news was that, with qualification assured, Conte rested nine men.

Ireland began positively, having little choice. Hendrick's long-range effort flew inches too high, while big Daryl Murphy and Shane Duffy went close with headers. But before half-time, another refereeing blunder was flung in Ireland's face like a custard pie. Federico Bernardeschi barged James McClean from behind for an obvious penalty, but referee Ovidiu Haţegan shook his head.

The decision took the wind out of Irish sails, and they didn't create another chance for a long time. As time ebbed away, Martin O'Neill finally sent on Hoolahan but, within seconds, another substitute – the lively Lorenzo Insigne – rattled the post. The warning jolted Ireland alive. Near the end, McGeady dispossessed Bonucci outside Italy's box. The ball ran to Hoolahan, who had enough time to take six touches – but he put his shot in the worst possible place, down goalkeeper Salvatore Sirigu's throat.

It typified Hoolahan that, rather than hide in a hole after screwing up the biggest moment of his career, he immediately looked for the ball again. Moments later, he swept a looping cross towards Italy's goalmouth, where Robbie Brady was racing in behind Bonucci. The Norwich man got there ahead of Sirigu to nudge a corkscrew header into the unguarded net. Ireland had done it at five minutes to midnight.

Afterwards, Brady embraced his weeping brother in the stands, one of the images of the tournament. 'Remaining in Europe,' gloated the *Irish Times*'s headline, a nod to Brexit across the water. In Italy, *Gazzetta dello Sport* opened its match report with, 'Che cuore, Irlanda' (what heart, Ireland). It continued, 'The Irish were flying, they went beyond their obvious technical limitations. We don't dare to think what would have happened had Barzagli stayed on the bench. Actually, we do: we would've been swamped.'

6pm, 13 June 2016
Stade de France, Saint-Denis
Attendance: 73,419
Referee: Milorad Mažić (Serbia)

IRELAND 1 (Hoolahan 48)
SWEDEN 1 (Clark 71 og)

IRELAND: Darren Randolph, Seamus Coleman, Ciaran Clark, John O'Shea (c), Robbie Brady, Glenn Whelan, Jeff Hendrick, James McCarthy (Aiden McGeady 85), Shane Long, Wes Hoolahan (Robbie Keane 78), Jonathan Walters (James McClean 63). **Manager:** Martin O'Neill.

SWEDEN: Andreas Isaksson, Mikael Lustig (Erik Johansson 45), Victor Lindelöf, Andreas Granqvist, Martin Olsson, Seb Larsson, Kim Källström, Oscar Lewicki (Albin Ekdal 86), Marcus Berg (John Guidetti 59), Zlatan Ibrahimović (c), Emil Forsberg. **Manager:** Erik Hamrén.

Booked: McCarthy (43), Whelan (77), Lindelöf (61).

9pm, 13 June 2016
Parc Olympique Lyonnais, Lyon
Attendance: 55,408
Referee: Mark Clattenburg (England)

ITALY 2 (Giaccherini 32, Pellè 90+2)
BELGIUM 0

ITALY: Gianluigi Buffon (c), Matteo Darmian (Mattia De Sciglio 59), Andrea Barzagli, Giorgio Chiellini, Leonardo Bonucci, Antonio Candreva, Daniele De Rossi (Thiago Motta 78), Marco Parolo, Graziano Pellè, Éder Citadin (Ciro Immobile 75), Emanuele Giaccherini. **Manager:** Antonio Conte.

BELGIUM: Thibaut Courtois, Laurent Ciman (Yannick Carrasco 75), Jan Vertonghen, Thomas Vermaelen, Toby Alderweireld, Marouane Fellaini, Radja Nainggolan (Dries Mertens 62), Axel Witsel, Romelu Lukaku (Divock Origi 73), Kevin De Bruyne, Eden Hazard (c). **Manager:** Marc Wilmots.

Booked: Chiellini (65), Éder (75), Bonucci (78), Motta (84), Vertonghen (90+1).

3pm, 17 June 2016
Stadium Municipal, Toulouse
Attendance: 29,600
Referee: Viktor Kassai (Hungary)

ITALY 1 (Éder 88)
SWEDEN 0

ITALY: Buffon (c), Alessandro Florenzi (Stefano Sturaro 85), Barzagli, Chiellini, Bonucci, Candreva, De Rossi (Motta 74), Parolo, Pellè (Simone Zaza 60), Éder, Giaccherini.

SWEDEN: Isaksson, Lindelöf, Johansson, Granqvist, Olsson, Larsson, Källström, Ekdal (Lewicki 79), Guidetti (Berg 85), Ibrahimović (c), Forsberg (Jimmy Durmaz 79).

Booked: De Rossi (69), Buffon (90+3), Olsson (90).

3pm, 18 June 2016
Nouveau Stade de Bordeaux, Bordeaux
Attendance: 39,493
Referee: Cüneyt Çakır (Turkey)

BELGIUM 3 (R. Lukaku 48, 70, Witsel 61)
IRELAND 0

BELGIUM: Courtois, Thomas Meunier, Alderweireld, Vertonghen, Vermaelen, Mousa Dembélé (Nainggolan 57), Witsel, Carrasco (Mertens 64), R. Lukaku (Christian Benteke 83), De Bruyne, Hazard (c).

IRELAND: Randolph, Coleman, Clark, O'Shea (c), Stephen Ward, Whelan, Hendrick, McCarthy (McClean 62), Long (Keane 79), Hoolahan (McGeady 71), Brady.

Booked: Vermaelen (49), Hendrick (42).

9pm, 22 June 2016
Allianz Riviera, Nice
Attendance: 34,011
Referee: Felix Brych (Germany)

BELGIUM 1 (Nainggolan 84)
SWEDEN 0

BELGIUM: Courtois, Meunier, Alderweireld, Vertonghen, Vermaelen, Nainggolan, Witsel, Carrasco (Mertens 71), R. Lukaku (Benteke 87), De Bruyne, Hazard (c) (Origi 90+3).

SWEDEN: Isaksson, Lindelöf, Johansson, Granqvist, Olsson, Larsson (Durmaz 70), Källström, Ekdal, Berg (Guidetti 63), Ibrahimović (c), Forsberg (Erkan Zengin 82).

Booked: Meunier (30), Witsel (45+1), Ekdal (33), Johansson (36).

9pm, 22 June 2016
Stade Pierre-Mauroy, Lille
Attendance: 44,268
Referee: Ovidiu Haţegan (Romania)

IRELAND 1 (Brady 85)
ITALY 0

IRELAND: Randolph, Coleman (c), Shane Duffy, Richard Keogh, Ward, McClean, Hendrick, McCarthy (Hoolahan 77), Daryl Murphy (McGeady 70), Long (Stephen Quinn 90), Brady.

ITALY: Salvatore Sirigu, Federico Bernardeschi (Darmian 60), Bonucci (c), Barzagli, Angelo Ogbonna, Motta, Sturaro, Florenzi, Immobile (Lorenzo Insigne 74), Zaza, De Sciglio (Stephan El Shaarawy 81).

Booked: Long (39), Ward (73), Sirigu (39), Barzagli (78), Zaza (87), Insigne (90+1).

GROUP E	P	W	D	L	F	A	GD	Pts
ITALY	3	2	0	1	3	1	+2	6
BELGIUM	3	2	0	1	4	2	+2	6
IRELAND	3	1	1	1	2	4	− 2	4
SWEDEN	3	0	1	2	1	3	− 2	1

Italy, Belgium and Ireland qualified.

GROUP F
Portugal, Iceland, Austria, Hungary

After qualifying effortlessly, Austria were touted as contenders to make the semis. In the Mitteleuropa derby in Bordeaux, they almost decked Hungary inside 30 seconds when their superstar, Bayern Munich's David Alaba, hit the post from long range. It would have been the fastest goal ever scored in the finals.

Hungary were no spring chickens. Goalkeeper Gábor Király, aged 40, was making history as the oldest man to play in a European Championship, while midfielder Zoltán Gera was Euro 2016's oldest outfield player at 37. But they looked sprightlier than Austria in a match marred by relentless diving.

Hungarian striker Ádám Szalai was among the prime culprits. He had somehow gone 18 months without scoring for club or country, but broke that appalling duck on 62 minutes, combining with László Kleinheisler before sliding the return ball beneath goalkeeper Robert Almer.

When Martin Hinteregger slammed home an equaliser, Austrian joy instantly turned to ashes in their mouths. Not only was it disallowed, but referee Clément Turpin sent off Aleksandar Dragović for hacking Tamás Kádár just before Hinteregger scored (Christian Fuchs and Ádám Nagy should have gone too for their assaults on Attila Fiola and Marcel Sabitzer).

Hungary sealed it in style: Tamás Priskin's fabulous pass released baby-faced substitute Zoltán Stieber, who ran on to lift the ball over Almer. A first European Championship win for them since 1964, and a crushing blow for their neighbours.

———

Roughly 2.6 per cent of Iceland's population were in Saint-Étienne to see them wrestle a draw off Portugal, whose biggest name cut a sour figure throughout. Instructed by manager Fernando Santos to lead the line, Cristiano Ronaldo soon drifted out to the wing.

Iceland had been under pressure for some time before Nani put Portugal ahead, tucking away André Gomes's near-post cross. But their equaliser, early in the second half, was near-identical: the headbanded Birkir Bjarnason volleyed home Jóhann Berg Guðmundsson's centre from close range as Pepe inexplicably ran away from him.

Portugal won the shot count 27-4, but couldn't score again. Halldórsson saved from André Gomes and Quaresma, then emerged victorious from some goalmouth pinball; Nani headed inches wide and afterwards Ronaldo embarrassed himself by savaging Iceland. 'They celebrated like they'd won the Euro cup. That's a small mentality,' he fumed. 'That's why they'll do nothing. They only tried to defend.' His tournament, and Portugal's, would get worse before it got better.

———

Four days later, Marseille's magnificent Vélodrome witnessed more disorder. Not from the Icelanders, but from the blackshirt fringe of Hungary's otherwise well-behaved support, dozens of whom fought stewards before kick-off.

The tracksuit-bottomed Király had already saved from Guðmundsson by the time he dropped Hungary in it (literally), spilling a corner. His defenders hesitated, expecting a whistle, while Ragnar Sigurðsson fell over him and Kádar threw a leg at Aron Gunnarsson. Referee Sergei Karasev, perhaps deciding the two things added up to an infringement, gave a penalty which Gylfi Sigurðsson converted.

Hungary managed no shots on target all day: even their late equaliser came when Birkir Már Sævarsson clumsily bundled Nemanja Nikolić's cross into his own net (Ádám Pintér, behind him, would have scored anyway). Still, Iceland almost stole it with the last kick. Sigurðsson's free kick rebounded off the wall to the veteran Eiður Guðjohnsen, whose shot cannoned off Richárd Guzmics and flew just wide. Hungary were through; Iceland would have to wait.

Ronaldo's attack on Iceland, the tournament's sweethearts, made him the pantomime villain of Euro 2016 overnight. Against Austria in Paris, winning a record 128th Portuguese cap, he threatened constantly but simply couldn't score.

The overworked Almer prevailed in a one-on-one with Nani, and parried Vieirinha's venomous follow-up behind. Later, when Nani headed against the post, João Moutinho thumped the rebound over. But things stubbornly refused to happen for Ronaldo until, late on, Hinteregger pulled him down in the area. Referee Nicola Rizzoli (who had earlier allowed Julian Baumgartlinger to foul Moutinho viciously twice) gave a penalty, but Ronaldo sealed his excruciating evening by hitting the post.

Portugal had now scored once from 50 attempts in two games, leaving them in serious danger. Days later, Ronaldo's stock fell further. Buttonholed by a Portuguese TV reporter while out walking, he reacted by grabbing the hack's microphone and tossing it into a nearby lake. When would things start going right for him?

Within four days, it transpired. On an exhilarating afternoon in Lyon, Hungary led Portugal three times and still didn't win. José Mourinho would have come out in hives watching it.

Clad in garish green, Portugal dominated initially, then suddenly went behind. An uncleared corner was returned with interest from 25 yards by Zoltán Gera, whose sweetly struck half-volley whizzed through a spearmint-coloured forest of defenders. It didn't quite deserve UEFA's Goal of the Tournament award: it wasn't even the best goal in this match.

When the double-marked Ronaldo dropped deeper to turn creator, his magnificent pass created Portugal's first equaliser. It took out four Hungarians and found Nani, who outpaced Guzmics and finished neatly.

The madcap second half was a minute old when Hungary won a free kick 25 yards out. Balázs Dzsudzsák, seemingly willing to shoot from anywhere, tried to curl it around the wall; it clipped André Gomes and wrong-footed Rui Patrício. Dzsudzsák injured his neck in the celebrations as his team-mates piled on.

Portugal were still reeling when Gergő Lovrencsics raced through to hit the side-netting. Going 3-1 down might have finished them off; instead, they pulled level again with the most exquisite goal of Euro 2016. As João Mário galloped down the right, Hungary's novice left-back Mihály Korhut stood off. The cross was delivered behind Ronaldo but, elegantly extending his right leg, he somehow back-heeled it behind himself and into the far corner.

The match sped into overdrive as Portugal fell behind again to another deflected Dzsudzsák free kick. After crashing it into the wall, his follow-up shot nicked Nani's boot, and Rui Patrício was again stranded. Dzsudzsák instantly injured himself again, hurting his hip while vaulting the advertising hoardings; referee Martin Atkinson booked him for leaving the pitch.

Santos now threw on the mercurial Ricardo Quaresma, and was rewarded as Quaresma created Portugal's third equaliser within moments, delivering a fantastic cross to Ronaldo, who rose above Roland Juhász to bullet home a superb header. But Hungary nearly sneaked it at the end, Szalai hitting the post from Dzsudzsák's cross. Afterwards, Ronaldo petulantly refused to shake any Hungarian hands. At least his team were through as runners-up to face England.

═══

Or were they? In Saint-Denis, Iceland and Austria were still playing, deadlocked at 1-1, with Iceland third in the table and Austria bottom.

In the 94th minute, the Austrians mounted one last heave. But their long ball into Iceland's box was repelled and then thumped downfield, allowing Theódór Elmar Bjarnason to run unimpeded half the length of the pitch. He calmly found Arnór Ingvi Traustason at the far post: the substitute shot straight at Almer, but the ball squeezed in. Iceland would still have qualified had Traustason missed, but the goal pushed Portugal down to third – and a date with Croatia, not England.

Iceland had deserved their win. Early on, Guðmundsson's piledriver hit the angle of post and bar, and they went ahead when Gunnarsson's hefty throw was flicked on by Kari Árnason and stabbed home by Böðvarsson.

A lifeline came Austria's way when Ari Freyr Skúlason pulled Alaba in the box. Referee Szymon Marciniak's penalty award looked generous in real time, but correct on the replays; Aleksandar Dragović took it, but sealed his awful tournament by hitting the post. Austria did draw level when substitute Alessandro Schöpf linked well with Alaba, swerved past Árnason and coolly shot past Halldórsson. But then came Traustason's late show – and Iceland, against all odds, were through.

Ronaldo looked foolish, and he wasn't alone. Roy Hodgson and his assistant Ray Lewington were in Paris on the day, but instead of scrutinising potential opponents in a stadium 30 minutes from their hotel, they enjoyed a boat cruise down the Seine. Hodgson, rejecting suggestions he was taking Iceland lightly, said, 'We sent five people to Paris to watch Iceland-Austria.' One of them, Gary Neville, was captured on TV punching the air in delight as Traustason scored.

6pm, 14 June 2016
Nouveau Stade de Bordeaux, Bordeaux
Attendance: 34,424
Referee: Clément Turpin (France)

HUNGARY 2 (Szalai 62, Stieber 87)
AUSTRIA 0

HUNGARY: Gábor Király, Attila Fiola, Richárd Guzmics, Ádám Lang, Tamás Kádár, Zoltán Gera, Krisztián Németh (Ádám Pintér 89), Ádám Nagy, Ádám Szalai (Tamás Priskin 69), Balázs Dzsudzsák (c), László Kleinheisler (Zoltán Stieber 79). **Manager:** Bernd Storck.

AUSTRIA: Robert Almer, Florian Klein, Aleksandar Dragović, Martin Hinteregger, Christian Fuchs (c), Julian Baumgartlinger, Martin Harnik (Alessandro Schöpf 78), Zlatko Junuzović (Marcel Sabitzer 59), Marc Janko (Rubin Okotie 65), David Alaba, Marko Arnautović. **Manager:** Marcel Koller.

Booked: Németh (80), Dragović (33).
Sent off: Dragović (66).

9pm, 14 June 2016
Stade Geoffroy Guichard, Saint-Étienne
Attendance: 38,742
Referee: Cüneyt Çakır (Turkey)

PORTUGAL 1 (Nani 31)
ICELAND 1 (B. Bjarnason 50)

PORTUGAL: Rui dos Santos Patrício, Adelino Vieira 'Vieirinha', Raphaël Guerreiro, Képler Laveran 'Pepe', Ricardo Carvalho, Danilo Pereira, André Tavares Gomes (Éderzito Macedo 'Éder' 84), João Moutinho (Renato Sanches 71), Cristiano Ronaldo (c), João Mário Naval (Ricardo Quaresma 76), Luís da Cunha 'Nani'. **Manager:** Fernando Santos.

ICELAND: Hannes Þór Halldórsson, Birkir Már Sævarsson, Ari Freyr Skúlason, Ragnar Sigurðsson, Kári Árnason, Aron Gunnarsson (c), Jóhann Berg Guðmundsson (Theódór Elmar Bjarnason 90), Gylfi Sigurðsson, Kolbeinn Sigþórsson (Alfreð Finnbogason 81), Jón Daði Böðvarsson, Birkir Bjarnason. **Managers:** Lars Lagerbäck and Heimir Hallgrímsson.

Booked: Bjarnason (55), Finnbogason (90+4).

6pm, 18 June 2016
Stade Vélodrome, Marseille
Attendance: 60,842
Referee: Sergei Karasev (Russia)

ICELAND 1 (G. Sigurðsson 39 pen)
HUNGARY 1 (Sævarsson 88 og)

ICELAND: Halldórsson, Sævarsson, Skúlason, R. Sigurðsson, Árnason, Gunnarsson (c) (Emil Hallfreðsson 66), Guðmundsson, G. Sigurðsson, Sigþórsson (Eiður Guðjohnsen 84), Böðvarsson (Finnbogason 69), B. Bjarnason.

HUNGARY: Király, Roland Juhász (Szalai 84), Guzmics, Lang, Kádár, Gera, Nagy, Dzsudzsák (c), Priskin (Dániel Böde 66), Kleinheisler, Stieber (Nemanja Nikolić 66).

Booked: Guðmundsson (42), Finnbogason (75), Sævarsson (77), Kádár (81), Kleinheisler (83), Nagy (90+1).

9pm, 18 June 2016
Parc des Princes, Paris
Attendance: 44,291
Referee: Nicola Rizzoli (Italy)

PORTUGAL 0
AUSTRIA 0

PORTUGAL: Rui Patrício, Vieirinha, Raphaël, Pepe, Carvalho, William Carvalho, André Gomes (Éder 83), Moutinho, Ronaldo (c), Quaresma (João Mário 71), Nani (Rafa Silva 89).

AUSTRIA: Almer, Klein, Sebastian Prödl, Hinteregger, Fuchs (c), Baumgartlinger, Harnik, Stefan Ilsanker (Kevin Wimmer 87), Sabitzer (Lukas Hinterseer 85), Alaba (Schöpf 65), Arnautović.

Booked: Quaresma (31), Pepe (40), Harnik (47), Fuchs (60), Hinteregger (78), Schöpf (86).

6pm, 22 June 2016
Parc Olympique Lyonnais, Lyon
Attendance: 55,514
Referee: Martin Atkinson (England)

PORTUGAL 3 (Nani 42, Ronaldo 50, 62)
HUNGARY 3 (Gera 19, Dzsudzsák 47, 55)

PORTUGAL: Rui Patrício, Vieirinha, Eliseu Pereira, Pepe, Carvalho, William, André Gomes (Quaresma 61), Moutinho (Sanches 46), Ronaldo (c), João Mário, Nani (Danilo 81).

HUNGARY: Király, Lang, Juhász, Guzmics, Mihály Korhut, Gera (Barnabás Bese 46), Pintér, Dzsudzsák (c), Szalai (Németh 71), Ákos Elek, Gergő Lovrencsics (Stieber 83).

Booked: Guzmics (13), Juhász (28), Gera (34), Dzsudzsák (56).

6pm, 22 June 2016
Stade de France, Saint-Denis
Attendance: 68,714
Referee: Szymon Marciniak (Poland)

ICELAND 2 (Böðvarsson 18, Traustason 90+4)
AUSTRIA 1 (Schöpf 60)

ICELAND: Halldórsson, Sævarsson, Skúlason, R. Sigurðsson, Árnason, Gunnarsson (c), Guðmundsson (Sverrir Ingi Ingason 86), G. Sigurðsson, Sigþórsson (Arnór Ingvi Traustason 80), Böðvarsson (T.E. Bjarnason 71), B. Bjarnason.

AUSTRIA: Almer, Dragović, Prödl (Janko 46), Hinteregger, Fuchs (c), Baumgartlinger, Klein, Ilsanker (Schöpf 46), Sabitzer (Jakob Jantscher 78), Alaba, Arnautović.

Booked: Skúlason (36), Sigþórsson (51), Árnason (78), Halldórsson (82), Janko (70).

GROUP F	P	W	D	L	F	A	GD	Pts
HUNGARY	3	1	2	0	6	4	+2	5
ICELAND	3	1	2	0	4	3	+1	5
PORTUGAL	3	0	3	0	4	4	0	3
AUSTRIA	3	0	1	2	1	4	-3	1

Hungary, Iceland and Portugal qualified.

SECOND ROUND
Switzerland v Poland
Wales v Northern Ireland
Croatia v Portugal
France v Ireland
Germany v Slovakia
Hungary v Belgium
Italy v Spain
England v Iceland

The knockout stages began not with a bang, but with a droning snore. Saturday, 25 June witnessed three games, four goals, maybe ten shots on target, and too many unforced errors to count. The first of those games was by far the best.

In Saint-Étienne, Poland ran the first half against a Swiss team who seemed weirdly reluctant to attack. After just 20 seconds, Johan Djourou's terrible back-pass saw Lewandowski catch goalkeeper Yann Sommer in possession, but the ever-reliable Milik spooned it over an open goal.

Milik would waste several more chances, but Poland's pocket rocket again made the difference before half-time. Lewandowski dummied Grosicki's flighted pass, and the unmarked Błaszczykowski slotted it through Sommer's legs.

In the second half, Schär escaped a red card for clattering Lewandowski, but by then the tide had turned. Fabiański finger-tipped away Rodríguez's free kick, Seferović hit the bar, and finally the meatball-like Shaqiri came alive to score one of the great European Championship goals, twisting in mid-air to meet Lichtsteiner's cross with a spectacular bicycle kick in off the post.

Extra time brought two close calls, one for each team. Fabiański acrobatically kept out Derdiyok's header, and Piszczek miscontrolled Grzegorz Krychowiak's superb pass before being crowded out. Poland, visibly weary, seemed likely to lose the penalties, but all their kicks were perfect – especially Krychowiak's clincher, blasted into the top corner – and Xhaka's wild shot wide was the only miss of the shoot-out. They then embarrassed themselves by goading Swiss fans behind the goal, getting pelted with missiles in return. Their excuse – that they had been booed earlier for going down injured – sounded hollow.

=====

Nobody anticipated sexy football from the first British derby in a tournament knockout match, and all expectations were lived down to. The most recent meeting of Wales and Northern Ireland, in a 2011 friendly in Dublin, had attracted 529 punters. There were 84 times as many people in the Parc des Princes, but they saw little for their money.

Northern Ireland had the first real shot, Stuart Dallas forcing Wayne Hennessey to save at his far post. After that, hardly anything: Aaron Ramsey's close-range goal was disallowed for offside; Jamie Ward, the North's best player, saw a 20-yarder touched over the bar by Hennessey; and early in the second half, Sam Vokes ineptly headed wide from a great position, paying for it as Coleman instantly substituted him.

After his German heroics, Michael McGovern was sorely underworked here. But he couldn't prevent Wales's undeserved winner, when Gareth McAuley poked Bale's low centre into his own net under pressure from Robson-Kanu – though the real blame lay with Aaron Hughes, who had given Bale ample space. Michael O'Neill had shown impressive nous in spreading around the tiny sliver of butter on his knife, but his team hadn't done enough for their departure to be lamented.

======

Saturday, 25 June, the longest day, had one more mouldy morsel on the plate. And we had been warned. 'If you could win the European Championship with only draws,' Fernando Santos mused before Portugal met Croatia in Lens, 'I'd sign on the dotted line right now.'

Neither Ronaldo nor Modrić, both unfit, could influence a staring contest that was the first fixture in Euros finals history not to witness a shot on target by either side in 90 minutes. After half an hour, José Fonte stamped on Rakitić's leg but escaped a red card. In the second half, Brozović fired over while the TV director was showing a replay of something more important. Later, Vida headed Srna's cross wide, to the frustration of its target Mandžukić.

The final whistle condemned the crowd and the dwindling TV audience to another half-hour of tedium. But neither team seemed to fancy penalties, because extra time's final five minutes saw more action than the previous 115. When Perišić headed Marko Pjaca's cross on to the post, Portugal broke upfield and Sanches fed Nani, whose diagonal ball picked out Ronaldo. Now came the night's first attempt on target – immediately followed by its second. Danijel Subašić kept Ronaldo out at close range, but Quaresma nodded the rebound into an open goal.

Enough time remained for Pjaca to beat four Portuguese and reach the byline, but Raphaël shoved him from behind and he couldn't get the cross in. At the death, Vida hooked a dropping ball agonisingly wide, and that was that. Modrić wept; millions of viewers across Europe were probably busy snoring.

Portuguese austerity felt incongruous for a football nation accustomed to being the tortured artists of many a tournament. 'We'd like to play nice football, but that's not always a way to win big competitions,' said Santos. Perhaps Portugal were finally growing tired of catching the bride's bouquet.

———

In Lyon the following afternoon, astonishingly, France were put on the canvas inside two minutes. When Pogba took Shane Long's legs in the box, it was third time lucky for Ireland after getting screwed against Belgium and Italy. Robbie Brady, fast becoming the emblem of his country's campaign, put the penalty in off the post – and suddenly the unthinkable seemed on.

Ireland might have added to their lead through Murphy's opportunistic volley and Duffy's free header. Deschamps said afterwards that, at half-time, 'there was a need for calm, and a need to shake the coconut tree'. He brought on winger Kingsley Coman, and France began to click. The equaliser arrived when Ward stood off Bacary Sagna, who crossed for Griezmann to lose James McCarthy and score with a wonderful header.

France then went in front using a tactic Ireland normally coped well with. Duffy and Keogh collided under Rami's high ball, Giroud headed it down for Griezmann, and the striker finished precisely into the corner. A catastrophic spell for Ireland was completed when Duffy tripped Griezmann as he streaked through on goal; referee Nicola Rizzoli whipped out the red card.

Ireland, out on their feet (they'd had three days of rest to France's six – *bon travail*, UEFA), did well to keep it to 2-1. Substitute André-Pierre Gignac might have grabbed four goals in 17 minutes: he shot straight at Randolph, struck a swerver against the bar, and scuffed Blaise Matuidi's and Coman's crosses wide. Deschamps claimed the comeback 'made the supporters fall in love with these players', which was pushing it, but France were clearly improving. 'Le doublé de Griezmann sauve la maison,' trumpeted *Le Parisien*; the two goals of Griezmann save the house.

Realistically, this was an ideal ending for Ireland: a gallant exit against a side nobody expected them to beat. 'This isn't something we want to rest on,' said Martin O'Neill. But 17 months on, his suicidal substitutions granted Christian Eriksen the freedom of Dublin in a horrifying 5-1 home defeat by Denmark in a World Cup play-off, and a year later he was gone. Ireland's good showing in France had been the end of something, not the beginning.

———

There was another early goal when Germany met Slovakia in Lille later that day. Instead of setting the match up nicely, it killed it off. Jérôme Boateng's volley into the bottom corner, from a half-cleared corner after Matúš Kozáčik had tipped over Sami Khedira's header, was the cue for Germany to shake the rust out of their shooting boots.

When the clumsy Škrtel pushed Mario Gómez in the box, Özil's powderpuff penalty was easy for Kozáčik. No matter. With Kroos scattering his calibrated passes around, the ball hardly left Slovakia's half. Özil, Müller (twice) and Draxler (also twice) all spurned opportunities before Gómez finally buried Draxler's cut-back.

With Hamšík blotted out, Slovakia had nothing. The impressive Draxler made it three after Mats Hummels nodded on Kroos's corner: nice technique, shame about the marking. 'They're very strong, and it's difficult to play against teams like that sometimes,' said Jan Kozák. 'We had a little bit of fear, and they showed so much quality it was difficult to do anything.'

———

Belgium, moving through the gears, were rarely in danger against Hungary in Toulouse. Gábor Király had already saved from Lukaku and De Bruyne by the time Toby Alderweireld headed in De Bruyne's floated free kick.

For a while, Hungary made a game of it. Dzsudzsák, again their best player, shaved a post and Lovrencsics missed the woodwork by inches. But Belgium soon tightened their grip: Király hurt his hand while touching another De Bruyne free kick on to the bar, and kept out a strong shot from Dries Mertens.

After flickering in the first half, Eden Hazard ran amok in the second. The winger, heavily criticised for the collapse at Chelsea which saw José Mourinho sacked, had gone almost a year without scoring a league goal. But when he was in the mood, he was uncontainable. In the final stages, he singlehandedly obliterated Hungary.

First, showing extraordinary pace, he centred for Michy Batshuayi to tap in. Scarcely 90 seconds later, he cut in from the left like Arjen Robben in reverse, eluded Lang, then darted between Guzmics and Nagy before clubbing a right-foot hammer past Király. He had no role in the fourth goal in stoppage time: another substitute, Yannick Carrasco, ran on to Nainggolan's pass to shoot under Király.

'We saw the difference on the pitch,' said Hungary's German manager Bernd Storck. 'We've never played against a team like that.' And the renaissance was already over; by October 2017, after embarrassing results against the Faroe Islands and Andorra, Storck was gone. Nice while it lasted, though.

———

The meeting of Italy and Spain began under a downpour at the Stade de France. As Del Bosque sheltered in his dugout, the baseball-capped Conte hopped about on the touchline getting drenched, an indication of their respective stomachs for the fight.

Conte had done his homework, packing the midfield. Marco Parolo pursued Spain's stars like the taxman, forcing them to use the flanks, where they weren't strong. Soon David De Gea was working overtime, turning Pellè's header behind, then palming Giaccherini's overhead kick on to the post before our old friend Cüneyt Çakır ludicrously whistled for high feet.

But Italy's opener exposed De Gea again. After spilling Eder's free kick, he grabbed the onrushing Giaccherini by the legs. Before Çakır could give a penalty, Giorgio Chiellini tapped home.

There was no respite for De Gea after the interval: he saved from Éder after Pellè's sublime back-heel, and later fumbled Mattia De Sciglio's cross before Giaccherini missed the gaping net. Not until the 89th minute did Spain have a chance, when the ball dropped invitingly for Piqué to shoot weakly at Buffon. In stoppage time, Italy knocked the crown out of their tired hands. The effervescent Insigne found Matteo Darmian, whose cross came off Ramos before Pellè smashed it in for a replica of his goal against Belgium.

Spain had crashed hard. Del Bosque, seeing the writing on the wall, retired after eight years. *El Mundo Deportívo* mocked La Roja as 'La Floja' (the weak), while *Marca* reflected, 'We are no longer the best. 2008–2016.' And by 2018, when Russia put them out of the World Cup on penalties, Spain were just another team.

═══

Four days before England faced Iceland in Nice, in one of those moments on which entire centuries turn, the great British public voted to terminate the country's 43-year membership of the European Union – forcing prime minister David Cameron to resign. Britain, it appeared, was hell-bent on economic suicide. Now England's footballers roared in unison, 'Hold our real ale!'

It's forgotten now that they got off to a dream start. Sterling ran on to Sturridge's pass, collided with goalkeeper Halldórsson, and Rooney stroked home the penalty. But within 80 seconds, they conceded a ridiculous equaliser. Long throws hadn't been in vogue in English football since Rory Delap's mortar-bombs for Stoke City, but Iceland never got the memo. Gunnarsson hurled one into the English box, Árnason flicked it on, and the ball dropped for Ragnar Sigurðsson to volley home while Kyle Walker stared at him. Iceland had done exactly the same thing to Austria five days earlier, but how could England have been expected to know that?

Now came the final humiliation of Joe Hart's tournament from hell. Böðvarsson helped the ball on to Kolbeinn SigÞórsson, whom Walker fatally allowed to take two touches. The shot was weak but, in his current form, Hart could let in almost any shot on target, however soft or poorly aimed. The ball squirted under his left hand and trickled over the line at snail's pace.

The second half was one of the worst in England's history, a morass of awful passing, tactical paralysis and overhit shooting. When Hodgson appeared on screen, one Belgian TV commentator exclaimed, 'He's watching the game like a cow watching a train pass by. He has no idea what is happening!' Meanwhile, Harry Kane jabbed the worst free kick of the tournament several yards wide.

With 20 minutes left, Vardy's pace opened the door, but Ragnar Sigurðsson stopped him with one of the tackles of the tournament. Iceland then almost put the match to bed: Gunnarsson held off Jack Wilshere before Hart blocked his shot for a corner.

Near the end, Kane miserably ballooned another free kick out of play, triggering mass booing from England's fans. In the final seconds, the colossus Árnason glanced Walker's cross behind as Vardy was poised to head home. At the end, England's players sank to the grass, seemingly too embarrassed to let the viewing public see their faces.

Hodgson resigned within minutes. At a farcical press conference in Chantilly the next day, he seemed aggrieved at having to be present at all. 'I don't really know what I'm doing here,' he told the media. Write your own punchline.

3pm, 25 June 2016
Stade Geoffroy Guichard, Saint-Étienne
Attendance: 38,842
Referee: Mark Clattenburg (England)

POLAND 1 (Błaszczykowski 39)
SWITZERLAND 1 (Shaqiri 82)
Poland won 5-4 on penalties after extra time
Shoot-out: Lichtsteiner 0-1, Lewandowski 1-1, Xhaka wide, Milik 2-1, Shaqiri 2-2, Glik 3-2, Schär 3-3, Błaszczykowski 4-3, Rodríguez 4-4, Krychowiak 5-4.

POLAND: Fabiański, Piszczek, Jędrzejczyk, Glik, Pazdan, Krychowiak, Błaszczykowski, Mączyński (Jodłowiec 101), Lewandowski (c), Milik, Grosicki (Peszko 104).

SWITZERLAND: Sommer, Lichtsteiner (c), Djourou, Schär, Rodríguez, Xhaka, Behrami (Fernandes 77), Džemaili (Embolo 58), Seferović, Shaqiri, Mehmedi (Eren Derdiyok 70).

Booked: Jędrzejczyk (58), Pazdan (111), Schär (55), Djourou (117).

6pm, 25 June 2016
Parc des Princes, Paris
Attendance: 44,342
Referee: Martin Atkinson (England)

WALES 1 (McAuley 75 og)
NORTHERN IRELAND 0

WALES: Hennessey, Gunter, Taylor, Davies, Chester, A. Williams (c), Ledley (J. Williams 63), Allen, Vokes (Robson-Kanu 55), Bale, Ramsey.

NORTHERN IRELAND: McGovern, Hughes, Cathcart, J. Evans, McAuley (Magennis 84), Dallas, Norwood (McGinn 79), C. Evans, Lafferty, Davis (c), Ward (Washington 69).

Booked: Taylor (58), Ramsey (90+4), Dallas (44), Davis (67).

9pm, 22 June 2016
Stade Bollært-Delelis, Lens
Attendance: 33,523
Referee: Carlos Velasco Carballo (Spain)

PORTUGAL 1 (Quaresma 117)
CROATIA 0
After extra time

PORTUGAL: Rui Patrício, Cédric Soares, Pepe, José Fonte, Raphaël, William, André Gomes (Sanches 50), Adrien Silva (Danilo 108), Ronaldo (c), João Mário (Quaresma 87), Nani.

CROATIA: Subašić, Srna (c), Vida, Ćorluka (Kramarić 120), Strinić, Badelj, Brozović, Rakitić (Pjaca 110), Mandžukić (Kalinić 88), Modrić, Perišić.

Booked: William (78).

3pm, 26 June 2016
Parc Olympique Lyonnais, Lyon
Attendance: 56,279
Referee: Nicola Rizzoli (Italy)

FRANCE 2 (Griezmann 58, 61)
IRELAND 1 (Brady 2 pen)

FRANCE: Lloris (c), Sagna, Evra, Rami, Koscielny, Kanté (Coman 46, Sissoko 90+3), Matuidi, Pogba, Giroud (Gignac 73), Griezmann, Payet.

IRELAND: Randolph, Coleman (c), Duffy, Keogh, Ward, McClean (O'Shea 68), Hendrick, McCarthy (Hoolahan 71), Murphy (Walters 65), Long, Brady.

Booked: Kanté (27), Rami (44), Coleman (25), Hendrick (41), Long (72).
Sent off: Duffy (66).

6pm, 26 June 2016
Stade Pierre-Mauroy, Lille
Attendance: 44,312
Referee: Szymon Marciniak (Poland)

GERMANY 3 (Boateng 8, Gómez 43, Draxler 63)
SLOVAKIA 0

GERMANY: Neuer (c), Kimmich, Boateng (Höwedes 72), Hummels, Hector, Khedira (Schweinsteiger 76), Kroos, Müller, Gómez, Özil, Draxler (Lukas Podolski 72).

SLOVAKIA: Kozáčik, Pekarík, Gyömbér (Kornel Saláta 84), Ďurica, Škrtel (c), Hrošovský, Kucka, Škriniar, Ďuriš (Stanislav Šesták 64), Hamšík, Weiss (Ján Greguš 46).

Booked: Kimmich (46), Hummels (67), Škrtel (13), Kucka (90+1).

9pm, 26 June 2016
Stadium Municipal, Toulouse
Attendance: 28,921
Referee: Milorad Mažić (Serbia)

BELGIUM 4 (Alderweireld 10, Batshuayi 78, Hazard 80, Carrasco 90+1)
HUNGARY 0

BELGIUM: Courtois, Meunier, Alderweireld, Vertonghen, Vermaelen, Nainggolan, Witsel, Mertens (Carrasco 70), R. Lukaku (Michy Batshuayi 76), De Bruyne, Hazard (c) (Fellaini 81).

HUNGARY: Király, Lang, Juhász (Böde 79), Guzmics, Kádár, Gera (Elek 46), Pintér (Nikolić 75), Nagy, Szalai, Dzsudzsák (c), Lovrencsics.

Booked: Vermaelen (67), Batshuayi (89), Fellaini (90+2), Kádár (34), Lang (47), Elek (61), Szalai (90+2).

6pm, 27 June 2016
Stade de France, Saint-Denis
Attendance: 76,165
Referee: Cüneyt Çakır (Turkey)

ITALY 2 (Chiellini 33, Pellè 90+1)
SPAIN 0

ITALY: Buffon (c), Florenzi (Darmian 84), Barzagli, Bonucci, Chiellini, De Sciglio, De Rossi (Motta 54), Parolo, Pellè, Éder (Insigne 82), Giaccherini.

SPAIN: De Gea, Juanfran, Piqué, Ramos (c), Alba, Busquets, Iniesta, Silva, Morata (Lucas Vázquez 70), Fàbregas, Nolito (Aduriz 46, Pedro 82).

Booked: De Sciglio (24), Pellè (54), Motta (89), Nolito (41), Alba (89), Busquets (89), Silva (90+4).

9pm, 27 June 2016
Allianz Riviera, Nice
Attendance: 33,901
Referee: Damir Skomina (Slovenia)

ICELAND 2 (R. Sigurðsson 6, Sigþórsson 18)
ENGLAND 1 (Rooney 4 pen)

ICELAND: Halldórsson, Sævarsson, Skúlason, R. Sigurðsson, Árnason, Gunnarsson (c), Guðmundsson, G. Sigurðsson, Sigþórsson (T.E. Bjarnason 77), Böðvarsson (Traustason 89), B. Bjarnason.

ENGLAND: Hart, Walker, Rose, Smalling, Cahill, Dier (Wilshere 46), Alli, Sterling (Vardy 60), Kane, Rooney (c) (Rashford 86), Sturridge.

Booked: G. Sigurðsson (38), Gunnarsson (65), Sturridge (47).

QUARTER-FINALS
Poland v Portugal
Belgium v Wales
Germany v Italy
France v Iceland

Poland's minimalist progress had seen Robert Lewandowski take five hours of football to get a shot on target, suggesting their defensive approach was emasculating one of Europe's best strikers. Against Portugal in Marseille, however, he took barely 90 seconds to blow away the cobwebs, banging in Kamil Grosicki's fine cross after William Carvalho didn't track his run.

Referee Felix Brych later failed to spot a clear penalty when Michał Pazdan flattened Ronaldo, but Portugal equalised within minutes anyway. Renato Sanches played a give-and-go with Nani, raced on to the return pass and smacked a succulent left-footer past Fabiański.

The second half was like a different match – an infinitely worse one. Ronaldo, having another bad night, miscued wide instead of feeding João Mário, then sclaffed another chance before Pazdan blocked Adrien Silva's follow-up. In the closing stages, Krychowiak wrestled Pepe to the ground, no mean feat physically but also another cast-iron penalty. Again Brych failed to see it.

By the end of the abysmal extra time, Ronaldo had taken 36 shots in the competition, as many as Italy's whole team. Learning his lesson from the Spain debacle in 2012, he made sure to take the first penalty, and scored. The next seven kicks went in too. And when Błaszczykowski, visibly tense, hit his kick at the perfect height for Rui Patrício, Quaresma held his nerve to put Poland out. Spanish paper *Marca* noted that 'Portugal sigue en el tiempo de Quaresma' (Portugal are still observing Lent), a play on words conflating the winger's surname with *cuaresma*, the Spanish word for the religious festival – and also a dig at this team's tendency to do the bare minimum.

═══

Marc Wilmots remained as popular with the Belgian press as an over-zealous expenses checker, but his team had won their last three games by a combined score of 8-0 and you couldn't say fairer than that. In an end-to-end contest in Lille, they initially looked certain to do to Wales what they had done to Ireland and Hungary.

With Vertonghen injured and Vermaelen suspended, Wilmots picked 21-year-old defenders Jason Denayer and Jordan Lukaku. Both looked nervous, but Wales were shaky too: in the seventh minute, Belgium might have scored four times. Yannick Carrasco shot straight at Hennessey, the rebound saw Thomas Meunier's volley cleared off the line by Taylor and Williams, Hazard's follow-up hit Taylor to float over the bar, and Romelu Lukaku just missed connecting with the corner.

Soon afterwards, Wales fell behind as Radja Nainggolan, who physically resembled Neymar's tougher older brother, served up a sequel to his wonder-strike against Sweden. Struck with force from 30 yards, the ball kept rising all the way as it flashed under the bar. If Nainggolan's heavy smoking irritated his paymasters at Roma, it hadn't done his right foot any harm.

But Belgium's rookies soon caved in. From Ramsey's corner, Williams eluded Denayer to score with a downward header – helped by De Bruyne drifting away from guarding the post.

Wales upped the pace, with Bale, Ramsey and Williams all spurning chances. And early in the second half, after a spell of Belgian pressure, the least-heralded player on the pitch suddenly scored the goal of his life.

Turning into Johan Cruyff for one unforgettable second, Robson-Kanu collected Ramsey's pass near the penalty spot, turned 180 degrees to control it, fooled Meunier and Marouane Fellaini by dragging the ball behind himself, pivoted on his heel, then steadied himself and side-footed past Courtois for a stupendous goal. After scoring twice for Wales in six years, he had doubled his money in this tournament.

Belgium's situation was hardly irretrievable. But Wilmots left the uninspiring Axel Witsel on the pitch, waited too long to bring on Mertens, and effectively removed Hazard and De Bruyne from proceedings by humping high balls up to Fellaini. Late on, Nainggolan was denied a penalty after Williams trod on his foot: his Willem-Dafoe-in-*Platoon* reaction probably put referee Damir Skomina off. And Wales immediately clinched the match. Chris Gunter raced down the right, and Vokes shrugged off Meunier to meet his cross with a near-post bullet header, very like Bryan Robson against France in Bilbao in 1982.

Buoyant and irrepressible, Wales had broken their illustrious opponents over their knee. 'You dream about nights like this,' said Coleman. 'It's indescribable.' But Welsh courage was only half the story: Belgium had totally blown it.

Courtois castigated Wilmots so angrily that he was removed from the dressing room. 'I've lost a Champions League final before, but this feels worse,' he said. 'I gave [Wilmots] my opinion. I pointed the finger where it had to go.' Wilmots retorted, 'I'm a coach, not a magician. We lost 50 per cent of our backline. You can't simply replace experience.' Two weeks later, he was fired.

The meatiest quarter-final on paper, Italy's clash with Germany in Bordeaux never ignited. The Germans and their new three-man backline looked stilted against unadventurous opponents, resulting in a poor match which took forever to get going.

Eventually, early in the second half, Germany scored a well-worked goal. It originated from some fabulous play by Mario Gómez, belying his tree-trunk reputation. Out on the left, his slide-rule pass took out three Italians, and Jonas Hector's cross fell for Özil to score at close range.

Buffon later saved marvellously from Gómez's 180-degree back-heel, and Italy were looking goosed when Boateng idiotically jumped with both arms raised to handle Chiellini's flick-on: not Germany's last stupid handball of Euro 2016. Bonucci fired the penalty into the corner.

Extra time's only highlight came when Insigne wriggled past the vulnerable Boateng to shoot straight at Neuer. The farcical penalties lasted for an age. Zaza, seemingly tap-dancing during his run-up, ballooned over; Özil hit the post, Pellè's pathetic effort dribbled wide, and Schweinsteiger lifted a shot into the stands. Well into sudden-death, Matteo Darmian put Italy's ninth penalty at Neuer, leaving Hector to administer the *coup de grâce* with a kick that crept under Buffon's hand.

Conte resigned, claiming he hadn't felt enough love from his bosses. 'Only the president [Carlo Tavecchio] was close to me,' he said. 'I leave a small war machine behind me. This team can grow.' But he could scarcely have imagined how quickly it would all burn down. The FIGC's brains trust replaced him with Gian Piero Ventura, an uncharismatic insider with a thin CV and, 16 months later, Italy missed the World Cup for the first time since 1958 – just as Conte was crashing and burning at Chelsea.

Knowing they would occupy a permanent place in French football's Chamber of Horrors if they screwed this one up, Didier Deschamps's big names wasted little time in blowing Iceland away in Saint-Denis. 'It was a mental thing,' sighed Iceland's co-manager Lars Lagerbäck afterwards. 'We just didn't use our brains or play our normal way.'

Olivier Giroud, a yellow-pack Ibrahimović who always fared well against defenders less physically imposing than himself, rammed the first dagger through the minnows' breastplate. Matuidi's pass gave him a clear run on goal (although he was marginally offside), and his shot passed through the spreadeagled Halldórsson.

Pogba then went through Böðvarsson for a short cut to score the second with a thumping header from Griezmann's corner. The match was already finished as a contest when Sissoko teed up Payet, whose left foot did the rest, and Griezmann, put through by Matuidi, scooped the ball over Halldórsson for 4-0.

Early in the second half, Iceland recovered some dignity with a well-worked goal, Sigþórsson stabbing Gylfi Sigurðsson's cross inside the near post. But France instantly scored a fraudulent fifth. Birkir Bjarnason got the ball with a clean tackle, only for Giroud to dive for a free kick (to the anger of Bjarnason, who got booked). Payet floated it into the box, and Giroud photocopied his goal against Romania by rising above Halldórsson.

But Iceland had the final word, Bjarnason getting his head to Skúlason's looping cross, and only Eliaquim Mangala's clearance under the French bar stopped it ending 5-3. At the end, Gunnarsson led his players over to their fans for one final valedictory lash of their synchronised 'clap of war' – only for the Stade de France's PA system to drown them out with Coldplay. You want symbolism?

9pm, 30 June 2016
Stade Vélodrome, Marseille
Attendance: 62,940
Referee: Felix Brych (Germany)

PORTUGAL 1 (Sanches 33)
POLAND 1 (Lewandowski 2)
Portugal won 5-3 on penalties after extra time
Shoot-out: Ronaldo 1-0, Lewandowski 1-1, Sanches 2-1, Milik 2-2, Moutinho 3-2, Glik 3-3, Nani 4-3, Błaszczykowski saved, Quaresma 5-3.

PORTUGAL: Rui Patrício, Cédric, Pepe, Fonte, Eliseu, William (Danilo 96), Sanches, Adrien (Moutinho 74), Ronaldo (c), João Mário (Quaresma 80), Nani.

POLAND: Fabiański, Piszczek, Jędrzejczyk, Glik, Pazdan, Krychowiak, Błaszczykowski, Mączyński (Jodłowiec 98), Lewandowski (c), Milik, Grosicki (Kapustka 82).

Booked: Adrien (70), William (90+2), Jędrzejczyk (42), Glik (66), Kapustka (89).

9pm, 1 July 2016
Stade Pierre-Mauroy, Lille
Attendance: 45,936
Referee: Damir Skomina (Slovenia)

WALES 3 (A. Williams 31, Robson-Kanu 55, Vokes 86)
BELGIUM 1 (Nainggolan 13)

WALES: Hennessey, Gunter, Taylor, Davies, Chester, A. Williams (c), Ledley (King 78), Allen, Robson-Kanu (Vokes 80), Bale, Ramsey (James Collins 90).

BELGIUM: Courtois, Meunier, Jason Denayer, Alderweireld, Jordan Lukaku (Mertens 75), Nainggolan, Witsel, Carrasco (Fellaini 46), R. Lukaku (Batshuayi 83), De Bruyne, Hazard (c).

Booked: Davies (5), Chester (16), Gunter (24), Ramsey (75), Fellaini (59), Alderweireld (85).

9pm, 2 July 2016
Nouveau Stade de Bordeaux, Bordeaux
Attendance: 38,764
Referee: Viktor Kassai (Hungary)

GERMANY 1 (Özil 65)
ITALY 1 (Bonucci 78 pen)
Germany won 6-5 on penalties after extra time
Shoot-out: Insigne 0-1, Kroos 1-1, Zaza over, Müller saved, Barzagli 1-2, Özil hit post, Pellè wide, Draxler 2-2, Bonucci saved, Schweinsteiger over, Giaccherini 2-3, Hummels 3-3, Parolo 3-4, Kimmich 4-4, De Sciglio 4-5, Boateng 5-5, Darmian saved, Hector 6-5.

GERMANY: Neuer (c), Höwedes, Boateng, Hummels, Hector, Khedira (Schweinsteiger 16), Kimmich, Kroos, Gómez (Draxler 72), Özil, Müller.

ITALY: Buffon (c), Florenzi (Darmian 86), Barzagli, Bonucci, Chiellini (Zaza 120+1), De Sciglio, Sturaro, Parolo, Pellè, Éder (Insigne 108), Giaccherini.

Booked: Hummels (90), Schweinsteiger (112), Sturaro (56), De Sciglio (57), Parolo (59), Pellè (91), Giaccherini (103).

9pm, 3 July 2016
Stade de France, Saint-Denis
Attendance: 76,833
Referee: Björn Kuipers (Netherlands)

FRANCE 5 (Giroud 12, 59, Pogba 20, Payet 43, Griezmann 45)
ICELAND 2 (Sigþórsson 56, B. Bjarnason 84)

FRANCE: Lloris (c), Sagna, Evra, Samuel Umtiti, Koscielny (Eliaquim Mangala 72), Sissoko, Matuidi, Pogba, Giroud (Gignac 60), Griezmann, Payet (Coman 80).

ICELAND: Halldórsson, Sævarsson, Skúlason, R. Sigurðsson, Árnason (Ingason 46), Gunnarsson (c), Guðmundsson, G. Sigurðsson, Sigþórsson (Guðjohnsen 83), Böðvarsson (Finnbogason 46), B. Bjarnason.

Booked: Umtiti (75), B. Bjarnason (58).

SEMI-FINALS
Wales v Portugal
Germany v France

After the party, the comedown. Wales were spent, and Portugal sensed it in Lyon. 'Hora de ganhar,' time to win, exhorted *A Bola*'s front page on the morning of the game. Santos's team took it to heart.

Not for the first time in the tournament, Gareth Bale simply didn't show, with two appalling first-half shots his only contributions. By then, Portugal should have had a penalty: as James Collins put Ronaldo in a headlock, referee Jonas Eriksson was ball-watching.

Both teams were booed off at the break, but Portugal soon came alive. João Mário rolled a short corner to Raphaël, and Ronaldo somehow hung in the air above James Chester as the cross came over: his header was so powerful that the ball rebounded 15 yards out of the net. Before Wales had time to think, Portugal whacked them again. Ashley Williams stepped out as Ronaldo's scuffed shot came in, but Nani opportunistically stuck out a leg to divert it past Hennessey.

Wales might have lost by many more. Ronaldo slashed a dead-ball heatseeker just over, Nani's shot bounced off Hennessey before João Mário thumped the rebound wide, and the goalkeeper did well to grasp Fonte's header. Contrariwise, when Fonte rugby-tackled Vokes in the box, Eriksson again failed to act.

By the closing stages, the dragon was breathing fumes and Portugal were doing measure-your-heights in their own half, casually lobbing the ball over the heads of exasperated Welshmen. Ronaldo dribbled around Hennessey to shoot into the side-netting, and Bale took out his frustrations by kicking Cédric in the face.

'We've now sampled tournament football,' Coleman said. 'We want some more. There was a psychological barrier we needed to go through for the first one, given it had been so long. We'll give the World Cup campaign a hell of a crack.' But Ireland soon harried his team out of a place at Russia 2018, and within months he was overseeing Sunderland's slide into League One.

At the final whistle, a journalist suggested to Santos that this was his career's greatest moment. 'Congratulate me after the final,' he replied.

═══

'Of course he's a great coach,' Toni Kroos said of Jogi Löw before Germany met France in Marseille. 'He's the coach of the world champions, so he must be good.' Others dismissed Löw as a *gärtner* (gardener), doing little more than watering a verdant lawn of superstars. But as the first half unfolded, his team played their best football of the competition.

Germany's failure to pull the trigger seemed a temporary hold-up. Müller slid in to scoop Emre Can's cross beyond the far post, Can himself hit a half-volley which Hugo Lloris palmed away, the goalkeeper then tipped Schweinsteiger's curler over the bar, and young Samuel Umtiti cleared as Müller looked certain to score.

France would have taken 0-0 at the break. Instead, they went in leading. When Schweinsteiger and Patrice Evra jumped for a corner, the German unaccountably handled. Griezmann, who had missed from the spot for Atlético Madrid in the Champions League Final weeks earlier, waited two minutes to take the penalty but still scored.

In the second half, France turned the screw. Griezmann's shot flicked off Boateng to loop just over, and Germany were floundering long before the second goal arrived. Manchester United would soon sign Paul Pogba for a world record £89m, ignoring his many defects (no pace, a bad first touch, few goals). But here, he came up trumps for Deschamps.

Höwedes played Kimmich into trouble, and the right-back's leaden first touch allowed Pogba to steal possession. Faced with Shkodran Mustafi at the byline, he bamboozled the defender with stepovers, then pinged over a delicate cross. Neuer's feeble punch landed at the feet of Griezmann, who prodded it through a thicket of players for his sixth goal of the tournament.

Past masters at clawing back two-goal deficits, Germany never looked like doing it here. Kimmich, desperate to atone, crashed a shot against the woodwork, and his header (deflected off Müller) forced Lloris into a wonderful save in injury time – but it was France's night. Never the nation's favourite as player or manager, Deschamps deserved to savour this win after getting everything right. 'This was a very tough game, against a team who made us suffer,' he said. 'But we suffered together. I'm proud of them all.'

A third semi-final exit in four tournaments suggested a lack of killer instinct on Germany's part. 'We were clearly territorially superior,' Löw said. 'We played a great game. We just didn't have any luck. I can't blame anyone.'

The reaction back home was considered but critical. 'Löw is admired as a Bundes-Buddha,' mused *Der Spiegel*. 'He practically single-handedly sent the [stereotype of] ugly Germans away. He advertises Nivea and wears Hugo Boss. He looks just as good in Slim Fit shirts as in the Commerzbank hoodie, as good on a rental bike as in a Porsche. In the heat of Marseille, did he fall into the trap of believing too much in himself? Quite possibly.'

9pm, 6 July 2016
Parc Olympique Lyonnais, Lyon
Attendance: 55,679
Referee: Jonas Eriksson (Sweden)

PORTUGAL 2 (Ronaldo 50, Nani 53)
WALES 0

PORTUGAL: Rui Patrício, Cédric, Bruno Alves, Fonte, Raphaël, Danilo, Sanches (André Gomes 74), Adrien (Moutinho 79), Ronaldo (c), João Mário, Nani (Quaresma 87).

WALES: Hennessey, Gunter, Taylor, Collins (J. Williams 66), Chester, A. Williams (c), Ledley (Vokes 58), Allen, Robson-Kanu (Church 63), Bale, King.

Booked: Alves (71), Ronaldo (72), Allen (8), Chester (62), Bale (88).

9pm, 7 July 2016
Stade Vélodrome, Marseille
Attendance: 64,078
Referee: Nicola Rizzoli (Italy)

FRANCE 2 (Griezmann 45+2, 72)
GERMANY 0

FRANCE: Lloris (c), Sagna, Evra, Umtiti, Koscielny, Sissoko, Matuidi, Pogba, Giroud (Gignac 78), Griezmann (Cabaye 90+2), Payet (Kanté 71).

GERMANY: Neuer, Kimmich, Höwedes, Boateng (Mustafi 61), Hector, Emre Can (Götze 67), Schweinsteiger (c) (Leroy Sané 79), Kroos, Müller, Özil, Draxler.

Booked: Evra (43), Kanté (75), Can (36), Schweinsteiger (45+1), Özil (45+1), Draxler (50).

FINAL
Portugal v France

He always looked as though he should have been lurking in the back room of a New Jersey funeral parlour in *The Sopranos*, but Fernando Santos's impassive countenance masked a nice line in self-deprecation. The day before the final, he was asked about the criticism Portugal had received during the competition. 'I want it to continue!' he exclaimed. 'Tomorrow, I want us to win without deserving it!'

Making their entrance, the French and Portuguese players could have been forgiven for thinking they were walking on to the set of a 1970s disaster movie, with thousands of tiny insects filling the air. The Stade de France had fallen victim to a moth infestation after its floodlights were left on overnight for security reasons.

Portugal botched three simple passes in the opening moments: early butterflies to add to the moths. Then came the incident that seemed to have decided the final. When Ronaldo collected a short pass from Cédric, Payet slammed into his standing leg, warranting an instant yellow, maybe a red. Inexcusably, referee Mark Clattenburg didn't even give a free kick.

In the following minutes, Ronaldo lay down on the pitch, tears filling his eyes, a moth landing on his face. He hobbled off, then came back on, moving gingerly with his left knee strapped. In the 25th minute, he fell again, couldn't continue, and got stretchered off to a standing ovation. Eighteen years after the World Cup Final on the same pitch, the Stade de France was again a graveyard for a superstar named Ronaldo. Ricardo Quaresma came on, but Portugal were surely done for.

When the hosts did eventually start playing, they were powered by an unlikely source. Moussa Sissoko, fresh from a woeful season with relegated Newcastle, ran through to have a shot which Rui Patrício tipped over, then turned away from Adrien before the goalkeeper beat away his fierce effort with both hands. All through the first half, clearly not fancying a season in the Championship, he turned in the sort of display that Pogba had been pre-billed to give.

France began the second half well, a long spell of pressure climaxing with the otherwise anonymous Pogba volleying miles over – but by now, Portugal had survived long enough to know they could pull this off. That sense grew on 66 minutes. Coman beat Cédric on the left and placed a cross on a plate for Griezmann, who headed ineptly over the bar when it really was easier to score.

Portugal continued to hold firm, and in the second minute of stoppage time, Euro 2016 had its Rob Rensenbrink moment. Pepe, otherwise impeccable, got turned by substitute André-Pierre Gignac, whose mishit shot gently bounced off the post. The near-miss slashed France's confidence like a machete.

Portugal should have gone ahead in extra time when their tall substitute Éder met Quaresma's corner with a header that Lloris pushed away. And with 12 minutes left, everything was turned upside down. Clattenburg's eyesight again failed him as he booked Koscielny for a handball committed by Éder. Raphaël twanged the free kick off the bar, and France breathed again – but not for long. João Moutinho fed Éder, who brushed Koscielny aside and hit the shot of his life. It bounced twice as it skidded past Lloris's hand into the bottom corner. It was only Éder's fourth goal for Portugal in 29 caps.

Stunned and paralysed, France created nothing before time ran out. At Clattenburg's final whistle, Ronaldo wept again. 'We've missed a unique opportunity to win a Euros in our own country,' Deschamps said. 'There are no words. The disappointment is huge. It'll take time to digest it.' He would have his moment, lifting the World Cup in Moscow two years later.

'We were as simple as doves, and as wise as serpents,' Santos remarked. His team felt like apposite winners of such a flat tournament. Euro 2016 was cheapened by its own giganticism, stuffed with boring games where teams circled and shadowboxed each other. The figure of 2.12 goals per match was the lowest since 1996 (astonishingly, 12 per cent of them were scored in two matches, Portugal v Hungary and France v Iceland). Just three red cards were shown in 51 matches, with referees clearly under orders to minimise stoppages.

Throughout the tournament, countless column inches and pixels in the French media were spent on how the team's wins were unifying a shaken nation still reeling from the horrific events of 2015. But the trouble under the Eiffel Tower during the final, when a car was set ablaze and police tear-gassed a crowd trying to enter an already packed fanzone, showed that nobody could relax. Four days later, just as the French authorities were breathing a sigh of relief after a terrorism-free tournament, a militant drove a lorry into a Bastille Day crowd in Nice, killing 84.

In 1980, the European Championship had almost yawned itself into oblivion in front of tiny crowds, prompting fears for its viability. Michel Platini, more than any other individual, was the event's saviour. Now, three decades on from that beautiful, sun-drenched summer of 1984, the wheel turned full circle as he and UEFA bloated and diminished the competition to an undisguisable degree.

Platini himself was reportedly so depressed by his downfall that he watched almost none of Euro 2016 on TV. Two months later, he was formally replaced as UEFA president by his spiritual opposite, an unknown Slovenian lawyer named Aleksander Čeferin. And another of his awful *idées fixes* – the far-flung, identity-free Euro 2020 – was still to come. Or was it?

9pm, 10 July 2016
Stade de France, Saint-Denis
Attendance: 75,868
Referee: Mark Clattenburg (England)

PORTUGAL 1 (Éder 109)
FRANCE 0
After extra time

PORTUGAL: Rui Patrício, Cédric, Pepe, Fonte, Raphaël, William, Adrien (Moutinho 66), Sanches (Éder 79), Nani, Ronaldo (c) (Quaresma 25), João Mário.

FRANCE: Lloris (c), Sagna, Evra, Umtiti, Koscielny, Sissoko (Martial 110), Matuidi, Pogba, Giroud (Gignac 78), Griezmann, Payet (Coman 58).

Booked: Cédric (34), João Mário (62), Raphaël (95), William (98), Fonte (119), Rui Patrício (120+3), Umtiti (80), Matuidi (97), Koscielny (107), Pogba (115).

BIBLIOGRAPHY

11 Freunde

20Minutes.fr

ABC Sevilla

A Bola

ActualDeCluj.ro

Addicted by Tony Adams and Ian Ridley, Willow Books

adevarul.ro

Algemeen Dageblad

Al Jazeera

A Matter of Life and Death – A History of Football In 100 Quotations by Jim
   White, Head Of Zeus

AS

Associated Press

The Athletic

bancada.pt

BBC One

Berliner Zeitung

Berlingske

The Blizzard

Born to Manage by Terry Venables, Simon & Schuster

Børsen

Brilliant Orange by David Winner, Bloomsbury

BWINT.org

ceskatelevize.cz

Champions Magazine

Correio da Manhã

Daily Mail

Daily Mirror

Daily Record

Daily Star

Daily Telegraph

Danish Dynamite by Rob Smyth, Lars Eriksen and Mike Gibbons, Bloomsbury

Das Reboot by Raphael Honigstein, Yellow Jersey Press

Delfi.lv

denik.cz

Der Spiegel

Der Standard

Der Tagesspiegel

De Telegraaf

De Volkskrant

DFB.de

Les Diables Rouges by Christian Hubert, Gamma Sport

Die Presse

Die Mannschaft by Ludger Schulze, Copress

Die Welt

DutchSoccerSite.org

EcoDiario.es

El Mundo

El País

EnfantsDuServette.ch

England Managers by Brian Glanville, Headline Books

ESPN

euro2000.org

europe1.fr

Eurosport

Evening Herald

Evening Standard

express.de

fanatik.ro

Football and National Identities in Spain by Alejandro Quiroga, Palgrave Books

FootballWriters.co.uk

footboom.com

FootyMatters.com

FourFourTwo

France Football

fyens.dk

GameOfThePeople.com

Gazet van Antwerpen

Gazzetta dello Sport

gol.hr

Governance, Citizenship and the New European Football Championships by Georg Spitaker and Wolfram Manzenreiter, Routledge Books

The Guardian

Idnes

IlSole24Ore.com

The Independent

International Herald Tribune

Irish Independent

Irish Times

irozhlas.cz

ITV

Izvestiya

Jutarnji List

Kaiser

Kicker

kurier.at

La Chevauchée Fantastique de Georges Grün by Georges Grün and Jean-Louis Donnay, Gamma Sport

La Nouvelle Gazette

La Repubblica

laola1.at

LaVozDeGalicia.es

Le Monde

LePoint.fr

L'Équipe

Le Parisien

Les Bleus à l'Euro by Alexandre Seban, De Boeck Supérieur

Le Soir

L'Express

Libération

Libertad Digital

Making Fairness In Turkish Football by Yağmur Nuhrat, Brown University Press

Marca

Match

Metri Nieuws XL

Mitteldeutsche Zeitung

Mladá Fronta DNES

Moscow Times

mujfotbal.cz

My Life In Football by Kevin Keegan, Macmillan

nadlanu.com

NaTemat.pl

Nemzeti Sport

Newsweek

New York Times

NRC Handelsblad

observador.pt

The Observer

Og Det Var Denmark, SF Studios

Pickles Magazine

PolskaTimes.pl

Press Association

Przeglad Sportowy

Público

Record

Reuters

RTE 2

RTP Notícias

RTP.pt

RusCrimea.org

Russian Winters by Andrei Kanchelskis, De Coubertin Books

Sabado

samlib.ru

Scotland's Game, BBC Scotland

The Scotsman

se.pl

Shoot!

Sky Sports

Soccer Empire by Laurent Dubois, University of California Press

So Foot

Soviet Sport

Sommeren '92, directed by Kasper Barfoed

Spain by Graham Hunter, BackPage Press

SpartakWorld.ru

sport.cz

sport.orf.at

sport.pl

Sport Express

Sport-Express.ua

Sportivnye Vykhodnye

sports.fr

Sports Illustrated

sport.TN.Nova.cz

sporza.be

SPTFM.ro

Stern

Storie di Calcio

the42.ie

The Story of the World Cup by Brian Glanville, Faber Books

The Sunday Business Post

Studio Sport, NOS

Süddeutsche Zeitung

Sunday Times

Sydney Morning Herald

TheAntiqueFootball.com

The Times

TheWorldGame.SBS.com

Tor! by Uli Hesse-Lichtenberger, When Saturday Comes Books

tportal.hr

Tuttosport

Twelve Yards by Ben Lyttleton, Bantam Press

tyden.cz

UEFA: 60 Years at the Heart Of Football by André Vieli, UEFA Books

UEFA – 60 Years of History, UEFA.com

UEFA Euro 2012 Technical Report

UEFA Euro Story DVD box set

utro.ru

Vesti

VG.no

VitoshaNews.com

Voetbal International

Vorarlberg Online
WalesOnline.co.uk
When Football Came Home by Mike Gibbons, Pitch Publishing
When Saturday Comes
wiadomości.wp.pl
Wiener-Zeitung
World Football Insider
The World Through Soccer by Tamir Bar-On, Rowman & Littlefield
World Soccer
Wprost
WP Sportowe Fakty
Ziarul de Iaşi

Also available at all good book stores

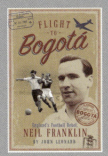

9781785316548

9781785316869

9781785316463

9781785316531

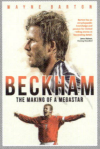

9781785316760

9781785316708

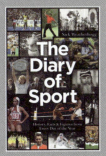

9781785316289

9781785315381

9781785316487